Practical Oracle8i™

Building Efficient Databases

Practical Oracle8i™

Building Efficient Databases

Jonathan Lewis

ADDISON–WESLEY

Boston • San Francisco • New York • Toronto • Montreal
London • Munich • Paris • Madrid
Capetown • Sydney • Tokyo • Singapore • Mexico City

The publisher offers discounts on this book when ordered in quantity for special sales. For more information, please contact

Pearson Education Corporate Sales Division
One Lake Street
Upper Saddle River, NJ 07458
(800) 382-3419
corpsales@pearsontechgroup.com

Visit AW on the Web: www.awl.com/cseng/

Library of Congress Cataloging-in-Publication Data

Lewis, Jonathan.
      Practical Oracle8i : building efficient databases / Lewis, Jonathan.
            p.   cm.
      ISBN 0-201-71584-8
      1. Oracle (Computer file)   2. Relational databases.   I. Title.
QA76.9.D3 L475 2000
005.75'85—dc21   00–045389

Text printed on recycled and acid-free paper.
ISBN 0201715848
2 3 4 5 6 7 CRS 04 03 02 01
2nd Printing   April 2001

Contents

Preface

Why Another Book?

Since there are so many books about Oracle already on the market, why have I bothered to sit down and add to the pile? In the age of Internet news groups and Web sites, it isn't for the fame. And given the specialized nature and likely circulation of such a tome, it probably isn't for the fortune.

Every now and again, usually while I've been rattling on enthusiastically about some obscure and esoteric feature of the way in which Oracle works, I've been asked, Why don't you write a book about Oracle since you know so much about it? My answer has always been the same: If you write a technical book about Oracle, it will be out of date by the time you've finished writing it, and within a year of publication it will be 20% misleading, inappropriate, or just plain wrong.

I have, however, finally given in to temptation because I've spent too long traveling around the world helping people to get the best out of their databases, and discovering time and again that the single biggest aid to success is to start well by picking the most appropriate features for the job.

This book is my attempt to tell you about some of the more useful things I have discovered while designing or fixing a few of the more thought-provoking databases that I have come across. I'm writing it partly for the challenge, and partly because I enjoy making Oracle work well and want to pass on some of the interesting and entertaining insights I have had. I hope you enjoy reading it and, more important, I hope you get a better feeling for what the Oracle database can do for you.

Who Is It For?

There are four stages to doing a job well:

1. Knowing what can be done
2. Knowing whether it should be done
3. Being able to do it in theory
4. Being able to do it in practice

Many of the books about Oracle currently on the market seem to focus on the finer points of the third and fourth steps. My aim is to help you with the first two, although this entails including practical observations relevant to the third and fourth steps.

This book does not exist to thrill the hard-core specialists by supplying subtle secrets and technical tweaks that will allow them to squeeze an extra half of a percent from their database. This book is here to help everyone get to a stage where they can put together a system that gives response times that are reasonable, considering the investment made in hardware, software, and human effort. Whether you are a manager, designer, database administrator, or programmer, there is something in this book for you. For the manager it gives a wide-ranging view of what Oracle is capable of and what you can expect your team to achieve. For the designer it outlines the possibilities offered by the many features of the relational database management system. For the database administrator it describes how using the right features correctly can make managing the database much easier. For the programmer (who is always keen to know how things really work) it makes it possible to connect the code that he writes to the features he is using, so that he can structure his code in the most appropriate way.

Which Version of Oracle?

A couple of years ago, a collection of information technology directors in the United Kingdom were asked what they perceived to be the biggest problems they had in managing their departments. Somewhere in the top ten was this response: the rate at which Oracle Corporation produces new versions and upgrades of their products. If Oracle keeps moving that fast, how do you pick a target when writing a book about it?

My strategy for tackling problems is the same regardless of the version of Oracle with which I'm working, so when you read this book you don't really have to worry about which version of Oracle you are using. However, I am going to focus as much as I can on Oracle 8.1.5—for the simple reason that it is the latest version (at least it was when I started writing).

It is also worth noting that Oracle 8.1.5 is the first "proper" release for some years to introduce many new features aimed at increasing the range of tasks that the database can handle efficiently and cost-effectively, which means, unfortunately, that it also introduces even more ways of allowing you to mix and match the wrong features.

Inevitably, between the time I started writing and the time this book was published, Oracle 8.1.6 went on general release. In that release, Oracle introduced features that it refers to as the *analytic functions*. The scope for reducing the programming effort and runtime workload on heavy-duty queries is so dramatic that I have felt compelled to include some details of analytic functions in Chapter 23.

What's in This Book?

Most of the books relating to Oracle seem to fall into one of three groups: the tuning guide, the enhanced manual, and the guide to relational database design. This book falls, I hope, outside all three groups. It works outward from the database engine itself and gives you some good ideas on how to use that engine to implement your application.

This book encourages you to consider just two important principles— how to think when designing an Oracle-based application, and how to ensure that you pick the most appropriate features of Oracle when implementing your system.

Whatever else it may be, though, this book is not a technical book. Or at least it's not a *very* technical book. I am not planning to go into any great and intricate detail about the internal workings of Oracle. (After all, I don't want the book to be out of date before it's published.) I do, however, take a little time to describe a couple of the central architectural features in some detail. I explain, in a simple way, the very small number of critical mechanisms that are key to the way in which the Oracle database engine works, and then I describe the ways in which these mechanisms can have a significant impact on how you have to design your application.

If you get to the end of this book feeling that it has made sense, then you are on track to avoid most of the traps that cause so many projects to end up overpriced, too complex, and poor performers.

What's *Not* in This Book?

There are a number of "value-added" modules that come with the Oracle relational database management system. In Oracle 8.1.5 these modules, such as *interMedia,* appear as embedded applications using the new "extensible framework" to add functionality for handling text, spatial data, time-based data and visual data. These add-ons are excluded from this book.

I have also ignored the "Web-enabling" features of Oracle 8.1.5, namely the PL/SQL packages that can be called to pass data from Oracle tables to Web pages, the inclusion of Java as an internalized database language, and the Web application server itself. The Web interface is, after all, simply another way to use the database, and Java is just another programming language that can be used to address the database.

The last major omissions are advanced queuing and replication, partly because they are too wide ranging to be covered in a single chapter, and partly because they too fall into the area of the more exotic add-ons that are likely to be of less benefit to the general user.

Looking back at the last three paragraphs, I think they really sum up my approach to application design: The database is much more important than the language or tool that may be talking to it. And that, of course, is precisely why it is necessary for the designers and programmers to understand how the database works. It doesn't matter how wonderful the application is, or how high-tech the language is, or how user-friendly the interface is. If you try to make the database behave in an unsuitable fashion, then you are unlikely to come to the end of the project feeling like a winner.

The Framework of the Book

The book is designed as a series of self-contained essays. Each essay pulls together a number of threads that might otherwise be scattered across several of the Oracle manuals, and presents an entire topic in a fashion that helps you to identify the risks and rewards of using a particular feature of the software.

This means that there is a degree of repetition from time to time. For example, the chapter on partitioning mentions some details of parallel query, and the chapter on parallel query comments on its particular application to partitioned tables.

You may also find that there are apparent contradictions in some of the comments I make and advice that I give. At one point (Chapter 8) I describe the benefits of wasting space to reduce the administrative burden, but at another point (Chapter 13) I make several comments about rebuilding data objects to pack the data and save space. Sometimes such points are not as contradictory as they may at first seem. Sometimes it is simply the case that different demands on resources call for completely different strategies.

You may find that a number of technical issues are addressed in a rather more informal fashion than you might hope. My intention is to give the flavor of how Oracle works without worrying too much about the exact detail of the internal operations. If you are already a highly skilled operative fully conversant with the way Oracle works, please be patient. Many of the omissions and vagaries in the early stages of this book are deliberate.

The book is divided into three main parts:

1. Part 1 (Chapters 1 through 4) is a very high-level view of the Oracle engine, how it should be approached, and why so many projects using Oracle fail to achieve their objectives.

2. Part 2 (Chapters 5 through 18) approaches Oracle from the "static" viewpoint of how the data can be stored, packed, and made visible within the database.

3. Part 3 (Chapters 19 through 24) is biased toward the "processing" side of Oracle, focusing more on the dynamic side of moving data in and around the database.

There are also four appendices:

1. Appendix A is a brief summary of some of the more interesting features of Oracle 8.1.5. It contains a mixed collection of features that I think are useful. In some cases I have made a big fuss about a little feature; in other cases you may decide I have completely ignored a big feature. Just because I don't mention some new features doesn't mean they aren't of any use—it may simply mean that I haven't come across, or imagined, an environment in which they would have a significant impact on the quality, clarity, or performance of a project.

2. Appendix B contains a brief description of the limited number of tuning tasks that should be adequate for most reasonably designed systems.

3. Appendix C provides a few hints on techniques for testing the relevance of features.

4. Appendix D contains a description of the main space management features of an Oracle database.

Conventions Used in the Book

> *Text in italics surrounded by a box highlights a special thought that you should always have at the back of your mind when using Oracle.*

A Cautionary Tale

A few years ago I had great success in designing a data warehouse for a large retail organization. The pivotal feature of the design was the appropriate use of partitioned views, initially using Oracle 7.2.3 but ultimately moving to Oracle 7.3.2. During the course of the implementation I built up a document that described in some detail two dozen problems, bugs, and workarounds we had had to face to make the system work.

A few weeks after the system went live, I was contacted by another large retail organization that was in the closing stages of implementing a data warehouse using Oracle. The purpose and scale of the project were identical to the one I had just completed. It too used partitioned views as the pivotal implementation mechanism, but the designer and database administrator had listed a couple of dozen problems that were causing them some grief, and they were looking for a few quick answers.

Armed with my list of solutions I strolled through their door confident in my ability to address all their problems. I discovered that their system, although ostensibly identical to the one I had just completed, was designed and implemented using a completely different set of strategies. We both had a list of two dozen bugs and problems—we overlapped on just one of them.

There are several morals to the tale:

- You know only what you've discovered so far.
- What worked last time might not work next time.
- Different isn't necessarily wrong.

Part I

Overview

CHAPTER 1

What Is Oracle?

When faced with Oracle for the first time, where is the novice supposed to start? If you add up the pages in the manuals for Oracle version 8.1.5, the total comes to something like 20,000 pages. Even if you restrict yourself to a fairly basic set, the total still runs to more than 9,000 pages. The error messages manual *alone* totals 1,700 pages.

Given this huge volume of information it is not surprising that many developments start with an application interface, a default database, and some simple tables—in the forlorn hope that the database will look after itself. Unfortunately this is completely the wrong approach. Oracle is not just a bucket into which you can throw your data.

If you wish to design an application that works well with an Oracle database you must understand something of how the Oracle database works. The application (and by this I mean the end-user interaction rather than the business requirement) cannot be allowed to dictate the database approach. There has to be a high level of cooperation and agreement between the application and the database. This may mean that certain aspects of the application interface may be constrained by the database, and some parts of the database may be inefficient to suit the needs of the application. In either case, there has to be a deliberate decision to make compromises.

So what is it about the Oracle relational database management system (RDBMS) that makes it something more than just a place for dumping data? This chapter describes the basic mechanics underpinning the key features of Oracle. They include the following:

- The system is a high-concurrency multiuser system. Readers do not block writers, and writers do not block readers.

- The system allows for a high degree of read consistency. If you start a long-running query, you do not see changes that other users have slipped in while your query was running.

- The system protects you from phantom data changes. If you execute a transaction to debit one account and credit another, it is not possible for anyone else to see the job half done under any circumstances.

■ The system has a high degree of recoverability. If you pull the plug on the computer while Oracle is running (and the hardware survives the shock), Oracle will then start up and recover itself automatically to the moment you switched off. Any incomplete transactions will subsequently be cleared up, so some data may seem to have disappeared.

You may recognize in this list the fundamental *ACID test* for databases: They should exhibit Atomicity, Consistency, Isolation, and Durability. Oracle offers all these with a high degree of concurrency.

If you stop to think about it for a minute you will appreciate that these features are pretty astounding, especially when you consider that Oracle Corporation has published details of a benchmark emulating 10,000 concurrent users (and I have heard mention of one benchmark hitting 50,000 concurrent users).

It should be obvious that the work Oracle does under the covers to enable these features is going to cost quite a lot in computer resources and is likely to have a number of interesting side effects. Inserting a single row into an Oracle table is a much more complex operation than adding a line to a file, and uses up a lot more of your computer's resources, in terms of central processing unit (CPU) time, memory, and sometimes input/output (I/O).

Although I said in the Preface that this was not going to be a highly technical book, the rest of this chapter describes the single most important technical feature underpinning the entire architecture of the Oracle database engine. An appreciation of the cunning and subtlety of this architecture will give you some insight into the amazing juggling act that the database engine manages to perform, and the cost in CPU time and other resources that this juggling act can take. To keep things as simple as possible, I have restricted my description to basics and ignored some of the minor details that are relevant to special cases, anomalies, and boundary conditions.

Data, Undo, and Redo

A complete Oracle database consists of four physical components:

1. A plain text parameter file, often referred to as the *init.ora file,* that basically lists the resources Oracle attempts to acquire as it starts up

2. A "control" file, usually mirrored, that Oracle uses to hold data about the other files in the database

3. A set of random-access data files that contain the actual data

4. A set of sequentially written log files that records all the changes made to the data

Internally the data files are split into blocks of the same size, typically 4K or 8K, although 2K, 16K, and 32K may be used depending on the operating system. This blocking arrangement makes it easier for Oracle to combine a random-access mechanism with a sophisticated and efficient buffering mechanism, but introduces the potential for wasted space at the boundaries of each block.

The block size has to be set at the time the database is created and cannot be changed thereafter, and one of the most common arguments about performance is the choice of the most appropriate block size for the system. The size of the buffer that Oracle uses to handle database blocks can, however, be adjusted each time the database starts up.

Once you have selected a data block size for the database, you cannot change it without rebuilding the entire database from scratch (see Chapter 10).

The data files are used for several classes of data: Some of it is the "real" end-user data, some of it is internal data or meta-data that describes the database itself, some is indexing information, some is scratch pad, and some is reserved as a special work area called the **undo** or **rollback** *area*. (Internally, Oracle tends to use the term **undo**, whereas most users seem to use the term **rollback**. From now on I shall stick with the more common usage.) The **rollback** area is used internally by Oracle every time it makes a change to data and records the steps needed to reverse that change. Despite this rather special usage, blocks in the **rollback** area are treated in exactly the same way as all the other blocks in the database. There are usually several such areas (known specifically as *rollback segments*) in the database. One of the tasks of the database administrator (DBA) is to decide how many rollback segments there should be and how large they should be—and as with all things related to Oracle, there is no one correct answer. Smaller is better, but it introduces the risk of a nonlethal but annoying side effect.

> *Try to keep the rollback segments small (see Chapter 8). This may make long-running queries fail with Oracle error ORA-01555, but it will reduce the I/O in general.*

The log files are handled completely differently from the data files. The log files list, in sequential order, every single change made to the database. Because of the sequential nature of this task, the log-writing process does not have to write a fixed amount of data, although the write size is usually padded to the nearest 1K or 512 bytes, nor does it have to write to random locations in the log files. Furthermore, the log writer never rereads what it has written. Because of this, the buffer allocated for log file usage is a *circular buffer* rather than a random-access buffer. (The log files actually fall into two classes— online and archived—and this means that a log file is read once in its life-time, but I'll pursue this topic in Chapter 24.)

Data Change

With this sketch of the data files and log files in mind, let's walk through all the steps involved in a simple data update.

Imagine that you have located in database block X a row that you want to change. The row is the fourth row in the block, and you want to change column A from the value 100 to the value 200. This requires two steps: First you issue a command to make the change (an ***update*** statement) and then you issue a command to "publish" the change (the ***commit*** statement) so that other users can see the changed data.

What happens as the first of these two steps takes place? A simplified list of actions (Figure 1-1), actually listed in nearly the reverse order to make the description intuitively clearer, looks like this:

1. Oracle reads the block into a data buffer and changes the value in the block.

2. Before it makes the change, Oracle looks in one of the rollback segments for a free block that it can use to write details of how to reverse this change. In other words, Oracle writes instructions into a rollback block that describe how to change column A of the fourth row of block X from 200 back to 100.

3. Before it can use this rollback block, Oracle has to put an entry into a special list (called the *transaction table*) in the first block (called the

segment header block) of the rollback segment to identify the transaction and to reserve the rollback space. Before Oracle can overwrite one of the entries in the transaction table, it has to make a copy of the entry to another location in the rollback segment in case it has to reverse this change.

4. To protect the *data change,* Oracle writes into the redo log (buffer) that the value has changed from 100 to 200. To protect the *rollback changes,* Oracle records them in the redo log (buffer) as well, and it does this before it makes the change to the data block.

Because every process that updates the data has to modify a rollback segment header block, rollback segment headers can easily become a bottleneck in update-intensive databases if there are too few rollback segments.

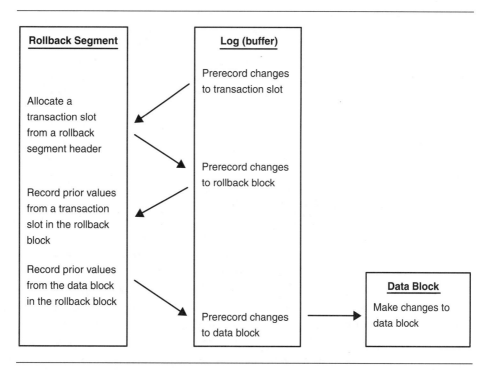

Figure 1-1. Order of actions in an uncommitted update.

Of course, part of the work that Oracle does in changing the original block includes attaching the address of the associated rollback block to the row, so Oracle goes flying back and forth between the data block and the rollback block as this simple update progresses.

As the memory image of each data block or rollback block is changed, it has to be "pinned" very briefly to stop other processes from trying to write into it at the same time and producing an irreconcilable mess. Also, while information is written into the redo log, Oracle has to operate a series of latching (or semaphore) mechanisms to ensure that no two processes try to modify the same bit of redo log at the same time. These two memory protection systems are completely different because the data buffer operates as a random-access buffer of discrete units of memory whereas the log buffer is used serially and in nonuniform chunks.

At this point, Oracle will, almost certainly, not write anything from either the data buffer or the redo log buffer back to the disk unless there is a lot of concurrent activity occurring elsewhere in the database.

I will come to the *commit* step in a moment, but first you have to ask yourself why Oracle does so much complicated work for a simple data change, and why this work helps Oracle offer the features of nonblocking multiuse, read consistency, transaction safety, and recoverability.

> *Oracle has to do far more work than you might expect to handle even a simple update.*

Uncommitted Data

If you go back to my list of the "basic mechanics," the first three points—no blocking, read consistency, and avoiding phantoms—are really covered by the existence of the rollback blocks. I may have just changed a row but I haven't yet committed that change. I may actually decide that it was a mistake and back it out (by issuing a *rollback* command instead of a *commit* command).

There are some database management systems that would view this degree of uncertainty as a serious threat. Should other processes see the old value or the new value if they try to read that block? What if they report the old value to another user and I commit my change? What if they report the new value and I roll back the change? To avoid the risk of producing a misleading report, some database management systems simply stop any other process from reading the block and wait for me to make my decision—a situation summed up by the phrase *writers block readers*. Some database systems will simply go straight ahead and read whatever appears to be in the block at that time—an operation described as a *dirty read*.

With Oracle, however, if a second process tries to read the row I have just changed, it will note that the row has changed recently and will identify the location of the relevant rollback information. It can then determine that the change has not yet been committed and therefore shouldn't be visible to the user, so it will copy the data block and use the rollback information to rebuild the previous version of the row before reporting it (Figure 1-2). With Oracle, writers do not block readers.

> *Because of the requirement for handling rollback issues, a simple read may do much more work than you would expect in an Oracle database.*

The argument about readers not blocking writers is similar: Some other database management systems stop one process from changing any data in a block because another process is going to want to read the data "sometime soon."

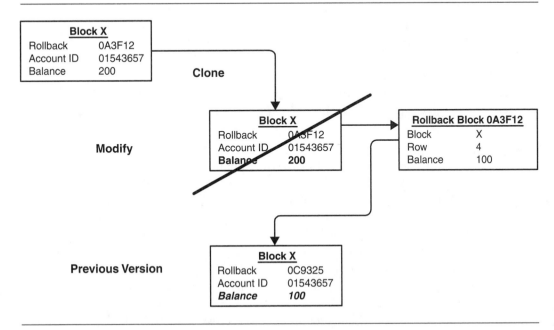

Figure 1-2. Rolling back.

Oracle doesn't care about this. As we have just seen, a reader process can reverse a change made by a writer. Thus a reader process does not have to keep writer processes away from data that it is about to use. Readers do not block writers.

For the same reason, our uncommitted change is not a threat to read consistency because Oracle can always find the rollback information that allows it to copy the current version of the data, and work backward to the earlier version it needs to see.

Exactly the same argument applies for phantom data: I won't see any of your changes until you publish them with a *commit* command, so I can't see dirty data halfway through a complex transaction.

The fourth point, recoverability, is a more significant issue. If you pull the plug at this point and then restart the database, the original data appears, and our failed attempt to change the data simply disappears. How does this happen?

There are two scenarios to consider. The first is that none of the data block changes and none of the log file entries was ever written to disk. In this case Oracle can simply take the view that if it never got written, it never happened.

With the second, more subtle, scenario either some log file entries or some of the data blocks and the log file entries were written to disk. One of the cunning features of Oracle's architecture is that it never does any work that it can avoid. However, it does make sure that a block from a data file is never written to disk before the most recent log entries about that block have also been written.

> *Before it writes a changed block to disk,* Oracle *always makes sure that it has first written the log file entry that describes the changes.*

As the database starts, it detects (through various time stamps known as *system change numbers* [SCNs] scattered around the control and data files) that it is restarting after a crash and begins crash recovery. This SCN is actually a meaningless, globally visible sequencing number. SCNs play a very large part in the read consistency and recovery functionality of Oracle. Every time a process issues a *commit* command, the SCN is incremented. On a periodic basis, the current SCN is written to various locations in the data files and the control files so that Oracle knows that a file is up to date to a particular point in time.

Crash recovery entails reading the changes recorded in the log files and applying them in turn to the data files so that, shortly after the database restarts, a recovery process acquires the data block, changes the critical value from 100 to 200, acquires the correct rollback block, builds the previously created rollback entries, and then continues to look through the log file for additional changes, including the rest of the transaction.

Eventually the process reads the highest numbered entry in the log file and decides that there is no more information about the transaction. The process will then deduce that the transaction was never committed, and will use the rebuilt rollback segment to reverse the transaction. Hey, presto! Our database is clean again.

Committed Data

Now we come to *commit*. How does this affect things?

When a process issues a *commit*, Oracle does several things. It puts a marker on the entry in the rollback segment header to mark the transaction as committed and, because this is a change to a data file block, the change is first written to the log file buffer. The log buffer up to that point is then flushed out to disk. If the data block is still in memory, the process *may* tidy it up a little bit, most significantly marking the transaction entry on the data block as *fast committed* by stamping it with the latest SCN. If the data block is no longer in memory, Oracle will *not* attempt to reread it and mark it.

> *The commit is a busy moment. The rollback segment header block and many, if not all, of the in-memory data blocks changed by the transaction are revisited and modified, and part of the log buffer has to be written.*

You may wonder why Oracle appears to be so casual about marking changed blocks as committed. The reason is evolution. Historically, pre-7.3, Oracle didn't mark *any* of the changed data blocks. It simply marked the transaction entry in the rollback segment and wrote the redo log to disk. Any subsequent process that needed to read the changed block would track through the rollback segment to check whether the change was committed, would write the commit SCN on the block, and would tidy it up. This was the process known as *delayed block cleanout*, and as a strategy it worked quite well when databases were small and users were few.

As databases got bigger, and the numbers of concurrent users increased, the impact of this mechanism on rollback segments, particularly header contention, increased. The mechanism also resulted in a *pinging* issue with Parallel Server (see Chapter 22), so Oracle introduced the *fast commit*, coupled with *delayed-logging block cleanout*. When the **commit** takes place, a "small" number of changed blocks are marked with the SCN, but the change is not logged. In most cases, the small number of blocks is sufficient to cover *all* the blocks affected by the transaction. In some cases, though, too many blocks have been changed, or some have been written back to disk. When such blocks exist, the older delayed block cleanout takes place.

You may note that I have not said anything about the data and the rollback blocks being written when the **commit** takes place. Other systems may write blocks to disk to "protect" the changes and to ensure that they do not get lost. Oracle does not need to do this because the log file is a guaranteed source of information about all the changes made to the database, in the order they were made.

In fact, Oracle never writes a data or rollback block to disk unless it really has to. Its philosophy, which is a great aid to performance, seems to be: Never do today what you can do tomorrow, because with a little luck you won't have to do it tomorrow either. (With the database engine this philosophy works well, although it may be inappropriate for other parts of the project life cycle.)

> *Oracle does not write data (or rollback) blocks if it can possibly avoid doing so. It is the redo log file that is critical to the continued survival of the database, and this gets streamed out continuously.*

How does a committed transaction affect the requirements for concurrency, consistency, avoiding phantoms, and recoverability?

Again, the first three requirements fall into the same area of argument, although with a couple of added refinements. Because the transaction is committed, there will now be a time stamp (SCN) associated with the changed row (unless the block was one of those not marked with a fast commit, in which case the process has to visit the relevant rollback blocks to determine whether the transaction has been committed and to ascertain its SCN). The process doing the reading also has an associated time stamp: the SCN value at the time the read request started.

If the reader's SCN matches or is higher than the SCN for the row (in other words, the row was changed before the read request started), then the reader can use the latest value of the row. If the reader's SCN is lower than the SCN for the row, then the system knows that the row was changed after the read request started, and it looks up the relevant rollback block, takes a copy of the data block in which the row is located, and uses the copy to reverse the change as before.

There is one very important difference though: Once a transaction has committed, the rollback blocks that it has used can be released for other transactions to use. Also, the transaction slot in the rollback header segment can be overwritten by another transaction. Oracle has an algorithm for using rollback that aims at avoiding overwriting rollback blocks and the transaction table entries in the rollback segment header for as long as possible. Eventually, however, the rollback block holding our reverse-engineering instruction to "change the fourth row of block X from 200 to 100," and the information that allows Oracle to rebuild "our" version of the entry in the transaction slot, disappears. If a read request that started a long time ago finally reaches our data block after this has happened, and tries to find the relevant rollback, it fails in one of two ways.

If the transaction table entry cannot be rebuilt, Oracle must assume that the data committed at some unknown time in the past, but won't be able to decide whether this was before or after our report started. At this point Oracle invokes error ORA-01555, "Snapshot too old." (In case you are wondering, Oracle does have a valid algorithm for working out the latest time at which the transaction could have committed—*an upper bound commit*—and it stamps the block with this value.)

It is possible, however, that the transaction table entry can be rebuilt but directs Oracle to modify the data block using a rollback block that has been overwritten. Again we get Oracle error ORA-01555, "Snapshot too old."

There is very little you can do about this error other than ensure you have plenty of rollback segments to reduce the rate at which the slots in the segment header transaction tables are recycled, and then make the rollback segments themselves large to reduce the rate at which rollback information is overwritten. This is the main reason that it is often impossible to stick to the aim of keeping rollback segments small.

Oracle's multiversion mechanisms stop readers and writers from blocking each other, permit read consistency, and avoid the problems of phantom data. However, the price of this power (apart from the extra work done to achieve it) is the occasional failure when rollback information has been overwritten.

> *If your database is busy with a high degree of update activity, then a long-running report may fail unexpectedly and randomly with error "ORA-01555: Snapshot too old."*

The recoverability of committed transactions is even simpler than the handling of uncommitted transactions. As before, a recovery process starts reading its way through the log file, copying changes into blocks as necessary. Eventually it hits the *commit* marker for our transaction and commits, and no further processing is needed for that transaction.

Side Effects of Rollback

In this simplified description of rollback and redo, we have considered only the interference of two processes. In a busy database system there may be many processes updating, deleting, and reading a common core of data.

It is not unreasonable to assume that sometimes the same data block can be updated several times in rapid succession by many different processes. At the same time there may be several more processes all busy running reports that eventually need an out-of-date version of this block. Let's review what happens to a very busy, or "hot," block in these circumstances.

Assume that the system SCN has just reached 999, and a report process started running when the SCN was at 900. The process reaches the hot block and discovers it to be at SCN 983, so it tracks down the relevant rollback blocks, copies the current version of the data block, and rolls that copy backward.

There is a problem: The rolled back copy is at SCN 975. We haven't rolled back far enough. This is okay because the rolled back block looks exactly as it did at SCN 975, which means it holds a pointer to the rollback block that describes how to reverse the change that took it to SCN 975, so the reader process can hunt down another bit of rollback and apply it to its copy of the data block to roll it back even further—perhaps to SCN 956, which is still not good enough (Figure 1-3). And so it goes, on and on, until several steps later the SCN on the copy drops from 902 to 889—the first time it has dropped below the SCN at which the reader process is running—and the block can finally be used by the report.

At the same time another report that started at SCN 923 hits the block, creates its personal copy of the block, and starts rolling that back to a suitably old version, and another report hits the block and starts to roll its copy backward to yet another SCN. Of course, not only are these processes rolling back copies of the data blocks in which they are interested; they may also be rolling back copies of rollback segment header blocks to sort out details of transaction slots from the past.

Apart from the cost in CPU time, this type of activity can lead to two I/O performance problems. First, you can end up with many different, out-of-date

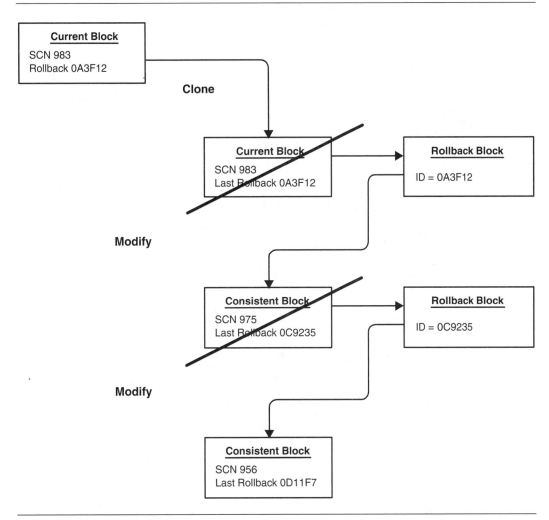

Figure 1-3.   Read consistency.

"consistent read" copies of the same block. These copies are stored in memory in the database block buffer and never get written to disk, so they do not present a direct I/O issue. Nevertheless, they are using up buffer slots and pushing out other blocks that may have to be reread, so they are posing an indirect I/O problem.

The second performance problem, which can become severe, arises from the excessive use of rollback blocks. Given the need to travel back far enough in time, Oracle starts to reread rollback blocks from disk. Any redundant I/O is bad news. Moreover, some of the internal mechanisms for managing rollback become stressed by the need to keep rebuilding backward, and this affects the performance of new changes as well.

> *Unless you have considered the nature and timing of the application tasks carefully, incorrectly specified rollback segments can become one of the most resource-intensive parts of your database.*

One of the common problems experienced by the novice is failing to understand rollback segments. If they are too small or too few, reports can crash unexpectedly; too big, and you get more I/O than you need; too few, and you get collisions between processes contending for slots in the transaction table in the rollback segment header. Rollback considerations can even force you to consider rescheduling parts of your batch processing.

Locating the Data

So far we have looked at the work Oracle does to change a single item of data once the correct block has been acquired. But how much work does Oracle have to do to find that block? Presumably the process started with a statement like

```
update account_balances
set balance = 200
where account_id = '01543657';
```

To handle this statement, Oracle first has to answer a lot of questions:

- What sort of thing is "account_balances"? (To keep it easy, we'll assume it's a table.)
- Does the user have the privilege to see and update account_balances?
- Does account_balances have columns BALANCE and ACCOUNT_ID?
- Are these columns of a suitable type and/or size?
- Are there any indexes on account_balances?
- Do any of these indexes start with the column ACCOUNT_ID?
- Are there any base-level statistics stored for the ACCOUNT_ID column?

- Is there a data distribution histogram for the ACCOUNT_ID column?
- Are there any constraints on the table that are going to affect the update?
- Are there any triggers on the table to be executed before or after the update?

The answers to these questions are stored in the database itself, in a set of tables known as the *data dictionary* (also known as the *system catalog*). So to start work on our update statement, Oracle may have to execute several Structured Query Language (SQL) statements of its own, such as

```
select … from obj$ where name = 'ACCOUNT_BALANCES';
        -- Is there an object called 'account_balances'?
select … from col$ where obj# = 3245;
        -- What are the columns in the object (now identified by id)
select … from cons$ where obj# = 3245;
        -- Are there any constraints on this object
```

Thus our simple update statement can kick off a huge amount of database activity before Oracle even begins to search for the correct block. Because this activity is really nothing more than normal reading from a few tables in the database, Oracle has to go through all the standard read-consistency work that we have already described.

Fortunately, Oracle maintains a buffer, called the *dictionary cache* or *row cache,* that tries to keep this type of meta-data information in memory for as long as possible after the initial read. However it is possible to flush or over-stress the cache, with the result that Oracle spends a lot of time accessing the database for dictionary information instead of executing code.

The dictionary cache exists to reduce the cost of using the data dictionary tables, but it can get stressed

Even after we have acquired huge amounts of information about the item we are accessing, we still haven't worked out how to get to the relevant block. At this point the optimizer cuts in to work out the best route to the data.

Oracle actually runs two optimizers, the Rule-Based Optimizer (RBO) and the Cost-Based Optimizer (CBO). Oracle Corporation keeps promising to drop the RBO, and indeed no one should be developing in 8.1.5 using the RBO because it has not been coded to deal with some of the more interesting features of 8.1.5 (development of the RBO stopped with Oracle 7). This book deals exclusively with the CBO.

There are actually two strategies available to the CBO: FIRST_ROWS and ALL_ROWS. With FIRST_ROWS optimization, Oracle aims to minimize the time it takes to start answering the question, to give the impression of best possible response time to an on-screen user, for example. With ALL_ROWS optimization, Oracle aims to minimize overall resource consumption to evaluate a complete solution—an approach that is more appropriate for a batch processing environment. It is possible to change the optimization strategy in midprogram, but not in midstatement.

> *New developments should use the CBO, but remember that the application can select two different strategies on the fly—online transaction processing (FIRST_ROWS) or batch (ALL_ROWS).*

To address our update, we can probably assume that there is a unique index on the ACCOUNT_ID column of the ACCOUNT_BALANCES table. The CBO has to decide whether to use this index or whether it should simply read through every block of the table, checking account_id on every single row. The choice is dictated largely by the estimated number of disk read requests that Oracle has to execute in each case.

This estimate is affected by a number of the entries listed in the parameter file (init.ora) that I mentioned earlier. The init.ora file supplies figures such as the following: the number of blocks that may be read with a single read request, the fraction of an index that is likely to be stored in memory, and the amount of memory that can be used for sorting before you start paging to disk. The estimate is also affected by the statistics you have gathered and written to the database, such as the number of rows in a table and the number of distinct keys in an index.

In our case, after running through just a couple of possible access paths, Oracle will almost certainly choose to use the unique index on account_id to get to the required row. In more complex cases, Oracle may have to examine hundreds of possible access paths to determine a best estimate. In complex cases this procedure may take seconds; in really extreme cases there have been reports of the optimizer spending many minutes working through tens of thousands of paths. By default, Oracle limits itself to 80,000 permutations for optimizing a single query block, but only examines all permutations of the table order when there are five or less tables in the block.

> *The cost of optimization can be quite significant. In extreme cases, anything you can do to reduce the amount of work done by the optimizer, such as* hinting, *is a good thing.*

We are finally closing in on our data block (Figure 1-4). Having decided to use the index, Oracle then takes the following steps (Add one [or in extremely large cases, add two] branch look-ups for larger tables and indexes):

1. Get the address of the segment header block for the index from the dictionary cache.
2. Check whether the segment header block is currently in the data block buffer. Read from disk if it is not.
3. Read the segment header block of the index to find the address of the root block of the index.
4. Check whether the index root block is currently in the data block buffer. Read from disk if it is not.
5. Reconstruct the index root block to the correct point in time if necessary.
6. Scan the index root block. Get the address of the branch block needed.
7. Check whether the branch block is currently in the data block buffer. Read from disk if it is not.
8. Reconstruct the branch block to the correct point in time if necessary.
9. Search the branch block. Get the address of the leaf block needed.
10. Check whether the leaf block is currently in the data block buffer. Read from disk if it is not.
11. Reconstruct the leaf block to the correct point in time if necessary.
12. Search the leaf block. Get the address of the table block needed.
13. Check whether the table block is currently in the data block buffer. Read from disk if it is not.

Finally, we are down to the data block and can worry about the work we need to do to make the change. What a lot of effort went into getting here!

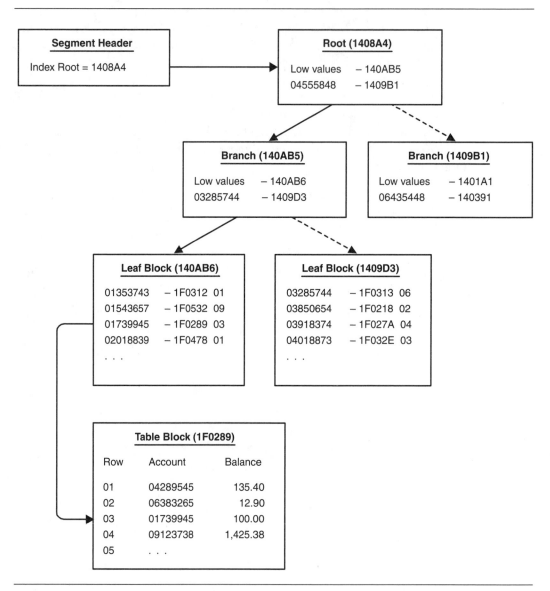

Figure 1-4. Finding a row.

Conclusion

As you can see from the informal descriptions and summary notes in this chapter, Oracle does a lot more work than is outwardly visible. Some of the undercover work is there to cope with the demands of multiple users at maximum concurrency, some is there to deal with recoverability, and a lot of it is there so that users can write simple SQL statements without having to know complicated file access routes to get at the data.

If you do not make allowances for the amount of undercover work that Oracle needs to do, and do not cater to the volume and side effects of that work, you are going to run into big performance problems regardless of how good the logical design of your application may appear.

CHAPTER 2

Why Do Projects Fail?

There is one extremely important principle to learn from Oracle database systems: *Ignorance is not bliss.* The more people you involve who do *not* have some understanding of how Oracle works, the higher your chances of rolling out a failure.

This chapter describes the most common forms of ignorance that usually contribute to the downfall of Oracle-based projects.

Ignoring the Technology

This principle alone is sufficient to ensure that your system is overpriced, ineffective, and underused. The Oracle database engine is not a simple product. As I indicated earlier, the manuals for Oracle 8.1.5 cover some 20,000 pages, and that doesn't include any of the design, reporting, or form generator tools, it's *just* the database engine. Clearly, there's plenty of scope for ignorance.

Given the massive amount of documentation, how can you possibly identify the little bit that is most appropriate to what you are trying to achieve? Many of the manuals describe the technical features of Oracle, features with exciting names and capabilities such as partitioned tables, index-organized tables, bitmap indexes, bitmap star transformations, symmetric replication, blobs, objects, and much, much more. Some of these features can do amazing things for your project, and some of them will be totally inappropriate and potentially disastrous.

Forget the exciting features though. We have already seen how much goes into the underlying architecture just to handle a simple change to a single data item. If you don't consider the implications and side effects of that architecture before you start grabbing for all the goodies, you haven't a hope of producing an effective application.

An easy way to wreck the project is to get a bit of process design on paper, pick a couple of exciting features, create a few tables, and start writing code.

There's a fair chance you'll get 90% of the code written before you discover that your model isn't going to work.

Avoiding the Arithmetic

Assume you have worked out that Oracle tables should not be treated exactly like flat files, and you've realized that Oracle has introduced something of an overhead to getting a bit of data with its read consistency and recoverability features.

You've highlighted various "sticky" points in what you are trying to achieve, and you've accommodated them in your design. You've decided on the Oracle features that you think are going to be appropriate for your requirement. What next?

The next step is to calculate whether Oracle will do the job, how long it will take, and how much hardware you will need. It is actually fairly easy to get a reasonable approximation for the most important parts of the system, provided you have a rough idea of the business activity that the system has to support.

Inevitably you may feel the need to apply a little guesswork, intuition, and imagination to the specification to predict how the system might be used three months or two years down the line. However, the point comes when you have to do some arithmetic.

> *Predicting performance is not an art. It is a science based on simple arithmetic. Getting a handle on the meaning of the business requirements is the art.*

As we have seen, Oracle really does only four things:

1. Locates and (optionally) changes data.
2. Generates rollback (a list of steps for reversing a change).
3. Locates and uses rollback to recreate read-consistent versions of the data.
4. Generates redo to log all changes made to the database.

It is relatively easy to work out the typical cost in logical I/O of locating and/or changing a single row of data. Your estimates have to be based on things like volume of data, data distribution, probable access methods, frequency of access, frequency of change, and so forth. Of course, it is somewhat time-consuming and tedious if you do it for every table in the database.

There are no simple rules to tell you how to work out what's going to happen, and often you don't find out in time about the odd "little" tasks that can add a massive workload that you didn't predict. Thus you may find the following ideas to be of some help. Each tip is accompanied by a warning that explains why it may not be entirely suitable for your system.

As a simple starting point, I tend to assume that acquiring a single row takes four logical I/Os (three steps down the layers of the index, and then one step for the table). For extremely large tables I allow five logical I/Os; for very small reference tables I allow three logical I/Os. The trouble with stating figures like this is that it doesn't allow for extra logical I/O caused by the side effects of read consistency, so you have to consider the other ways in which the table might be used in real life.

> *Getting one row from a table via a perfect index typically takes four logical I/Os. Typical systems can operate at approximately 10,000 logical I/Os per 100 MHz of CPU.*

I then try to work out roughly how frequently the rows will be required from a particular table. This is obviously totally dependent on the nature of the application. One point at which this estimation task often fails is when the nominal use of the table is described as *get a row from the table and . . .*, but the actual use of the table, whether it be for business reasons or mechanical implementation reasons, is more like *get 100 rows from the table, discard 99 of them, and with the remaining row. . . .*

Don't forget to count the little reference tables when sorting out logical I/O. Getting a row from the CLIENT table probably means you have to get a row from three or four other references tables at the same time. Unless you carefully count the activity on reference tables separately, the four logical I/Os you have just allowed to get one row probably need to be increased by a factor of three or four to allow for reference data.

You also have to account for inserts, updates, and deletes, which are more complex than simple selects. Again, I have a few approximations that I use to get a rough idea of the volume of logical I/O needed.

When you insert a row into a table, you may as well assume that every index on a table has to have an entry inserted at the same time. But this means Oracle has to find out where the index entry goes and write a rollback entry for each index: Call it 4 + 1 = 5 logical I/Os for each index, and 3 + 2 = 5 I/Os to handle the table. Don't forget that the redo log has to be generated for every change: Call it two entries per index (the index itself and the rollback) at a minimum of a couple of hundred bytes per redo entry and then add the typical size of an inserted row and a couple of hundred bytes of overhead.

Deletes are actually worse than inserts. With an insert, the rollback entries are small because the only reversal needed is to clear a directory entry in a block, although the redo log has to hold a copy of the incoming entries. With a delete, the rollback has to take a copy of the material deleted, which means the redo log has to record a larger change in the rollback, so the generated redo tends to be larger. However, because this is only a rough approximation, I allow the same logical I/O and redo estimates as for inserts.

I typically approximate updates as a select, followed by a small change that updates one index. That's four logical I/Os to find the row plus two for choosing the rollback, a couple of redo entries for the update and its rollback, four logical I/Os to find the index entry that has to be changed, and another four to find out where the changed entry should go, and one more I/O for writing to the rollback.

These figures are only very rough indications, and many systems will have a couple of objects or a couple of actions that are likely to be handled in an extreme way and therefore need special consideration. Nevertheless, jotting down a few figures (Table 2-1) is a good starting point for working out the viability of the system.

Do the arithmetic for the largest or most heavily used tables and then factor in the volume of access to derive total CPU cost, and the likely volume of

Table 2-1. Estimates for Predicting Performance

Operation	Object	No. of Logical I/Os	Redo
Select a row.	Small REF table	3	—
	Typical fact table	4	—
	Large fact table	5	—
Insert/delete a row.	Any table	3	400 bytes + row length
	Index (each)	4	200 bytes
	Rollback segment	2 + 1 per index	—
Update a row.	Any table	4	400
	Index	3 + 3	300
	Rollback segment	2 + 1	—

disk I/O needed to handle the redo log. Then double it all round to allow for "miscellaneous" work that never got into the specification.

Knowing the data distribution for these critical tables also allows you to estimate the likely fraction of logical I/O that will turn into physical I/O, and therefore allows you to estimate the number of disks needed to support the system.

Again, some typical approximations I adopt and massage to suit the system are as follows: Reference tables have indexes and table blocks in memory, so no physical I/O debt is incurred. Large tables may have the most frequently used indexes in memory, so take one physical I/O for each table row accessed. Special cases include the types of systems that accumulate data over time. Recent history may be nearly 100% cached; ancient history may require lots of physical I/O on the index.

Extremely large tables with an extra layer of branch blocks in the index may result in physical I/Os on the index leaf layer—say, one time in five as well as the physical I/O on the table.

Inserts, updates, and deletes are a bigger problem when it comes to physical I/O. Obviously there is a quantity of physical I/O as a result of acquiring the data to be changed, but eventually every changed data file block is written to disk. However, because Oracle avoids writing if possible, and then uses a background writing process to do the writing, the number of blocks written may have little to do with the number of blocks changed, and the timing of those writes may be completely out of sync with the timing of the data changes.

The only rule of thumb I apply for writes applies to very large tables only. I tend to assume that one row inserted or deleted equates, eventually, to one physical block write *per index*. Every other estimate I make is totally dependent on the details of the system.

> *Logical I/O can be relatively straightforward to calculate. The resulting physical I/O is much more subject to the specific nature of the system.*

This estimation method sounds reasonably straightforward, but there are plenty of ways to go wrong. Think, for instance, of how long the system may exist. What will be the effect of storing five years of data rather than two years? It is possible that you can simply add extra disks without affecting the data-processing cost; on the other hand, system life span may make a dramatic difference in the fraction of logical I/O that turns into physical I/O.

What about the longer lifetime of the database? Your calculations may be correct for a two-year-old database on its second birthday, but what might the database look like on its fourth birthday, when the volume of data it is holding is still only two years' worth, but the previous two years have been removed from the database? What might this do to the efficiency of any indexes? Did you remember to consider methods, costs, and a timetable for removing older data?

Getting an idea of the total logical and physical I/O you may need is a good step forward in identifying the scale of the problem. Don't forget, though, that you need to factor in the time element to get the I/O rates per second, so you also need to know the expected pattern of usage of the system. With this knowledge you can convert peak logical I/Os per second to a quantity of CPUs. A greater number of slower CPUs is often better than fewer but faster CPUs. And you can convert peak physical I/Os per second to number of disks. More, smaller disks are better than fewer, larger disks. I tend to assume, sometimes pessimistically, that a disk will handle no more than 30 I/Os per second, regardless of the manufacturer's rating.

Having worked it all out, adding a comfortable margin of error, and having passed it on to the acquisition group, you can now sit back confidently in anticipation of the fact that you are going to get an appropriate quantity of hardware for the job.

> *In all cases, aim to buy lots of small disks. In most cases, assume that more, slower CPUs are better than fewer, faster CPUs.*

Of course, the buyers may decide they can get a really good deal by buying 4 35GB disks instead of the 16 9GB disks you requested (after all, this change cuts down on I/O boards as well), and maybe 4 600-MHz CPUs would be cheaper than the 12 220-MHz CPUs you wanted. It is important to make sure that everyone understands why certain types of configurations are appropriate for specific types of jobs.

Fudging the Prototype

So you've got the basic design sorted out; decided on the general approach, the features to use, and how to use them; and you've specified the scale of the system and volume of hardware. At this point you should be proving that the system may be viable by building some sort of simplified model that proves your calculations are reasonable.

This isn't the same thing as a full-scale stress test or volume test. In fact, this is more of a "negative" test than anything else. Without spending too much effort, at this stage you should be trying to find ways of breaking things and proving your assumptions wrong.

A successful prototype does not guarantee a successful result, but at least it eliminates many of the potential pitfalls before you spend too much effort building the real thing. I recall one system that took nine months to develop, but the fundamental construction concept wasn't tested until two weeks before the system was due to go live, despite the fact that a quarter of a terabyte of data had been loaded. Not only was it obvious that the idea wasn't going to work in theory; it should have taken only two days and a couple of gigabytes to discover that it wasn't going to work in practice.

This may sound pretty hard to believe, but it is not all that rare. I have been called to five different sites in the last couple of years to sort out problems with partitioning. In all five cases the partitioning was being used to get performance benefits from partition elimination (see Chapter 12). In all five cases the implementation guaranteed that partition elimination would never occur.

If you are going to depend on a technological feature of Oracle, you need to make sure that you have tried to break it, in half a dozen ways, before you use it in production.

> *Before implementing a new Oracle feature, try to find out what will break it.*

There are some very obvious ways of getting the prototype wrong. It could simply be too small. What is the point of building a 100MB database to test the design of a 2TB database? Will a partitioned table with 3,650 partitions introduce some side effects that your test case of three partitions did not exhibit?

How many of the potential problems of a 1,000-user system will become visible if you never have more than three users testing it? I once had the task of restructuring an application that had been very carefully tested by the project manager, and very carefully tested for acceptance by one of the end users. It wasn't until 24 hours before the go-live date that the project manager discovered that he had achieved the near-impossible task of turning an Oracle database application into a single-user system.

On a more subtle level, it is fairly easy to produce a prototype that looks quite reasonable but responds uncharacteristically because the data sample used is completely unrealistic. A common error of this type is to generate random values to represent data that is far from random in real life. Quite often in real life you find that the special cases are the cases that appear most frequently.

The Pareto rule is quite well known in the form, "90% of the revenue comes from 10% of the customers." This rule also applies to databases in the form, "90% of the problems come from 10% of the data." Any skewed data is going to be a problem, and because it is skewed, the problem it presents will tend to appear with uncharacteristic frequency.

I recall a system that used the soundex() function on input names to identify people. In lab tests this seemed to work well, but the first trial run was in a part of Wales where it seemed that 10% of the population was named John Jones, and another 10% was named Evan Evans. Naturally some queries ran much more slowly than others, and equally naturally the slowest queries were the ones that had to be run most frequently, because 20% of the queries were for an Evans or a Jones.

Even building a database from a sample download of an existing system is fraught with risk. The very act of processing the data for download might be enough to invalidate it. The obvious risk is sorting: If you are testing an insurance claims system, the events for a single policy tend to be scattered over a long period of time. If, for the purposes of test data, you decide to dump 10,000 policies, might the data get loaded in policy order rather than time order, and might this affect the behavior of the system? Of course it will. Even if you avoid the sorting trap, how will a test system work when the 50 rows you want to query are normally spaced 10,000 rows apart, but happen to be spaced 100 rows apart on the test system?

Of course, even if you design a good model and populate it with real-istic data, you could still manage to abuse the scaling factors you apply to the prototype. Assume your live database will hold 200GB of data and will run on a machine with 2GB of memory. Would a prototype of 2GB of data be a reasonable model? Quite possibly. Would it be a reasonable test to run it on a machine with 2GB of memory? Probably not, unless you restrict Oracle's in-memory work area and the operating system buffer.

Remember, too, that a small model may work efficiently *because* it is a small model. A larger model may have to take different data access paths to be efficient, and those data access paths may be too slow when running on the production system. A very efficient hash join on a small system may turn into a very slow nested loop join when the data hits a critical size. To prove a proto-type, you need to examine not just the timed results of the tests but also the actual detailed access paths that Oracle takes to acquire your data, and you must confirm that they are the paths you would expect given the strategy you have chosen.

Confusing the Responsibilities

As we get closer to building the real system, we start to run into areas of responsibility. An easy way to push the project onto the downward slope to destruction is to be sloppy about assigning responsibilities.

By now you have a design strategy that includes some dos and don'ts, you have the arithmetic to demonstrate that the system is viable, and you have the proof of concept that demonstrates the expected access paths and response times, and validates the technical approach. How do you ensure that the development follows the strategy, that the access paths don't start to change without anyone noticing, and that completely different arithmetical results don't start to show up?

Obviously there are some roles that have to be handed out to keep the project alive. At this stage, as you start to build the application, the number of bodies involved in the project increases, as does the risk of failure.

There are two very easy ways to foul things up: Don't nominate an individual to do quality assurance (QA) testing on the code that is being written, and don't tell the developers anything about how Oracle works. In particular, don't give them a clue about the need to check the data access paths used by the code.

No matter how many times I see it, I still can't believe it when I meet programmers who are busy working away at an application but haven't been given any instruction in how Oracle works, and who don't have anyone dropping in from time to time to help them out until the DBA finally sees the code in the final stages of testing and sends it back for a rewrite.

Of course, the subject of DBAs is always hotly contested. What is a DBA for? Technically the answer is that a DBA should administer the database, which means keep it tidy and chugging along. In many ways DBAs are redundant, and there really shouldn't be a lot for a DBA to do. However, most DBAs seem to spend an awful lot of their time fighting fires for the information technology department because they are typically the one source of Oracle expertise. So do you need a DBA, and where should that DBA be kept?

Amazingly there are many sites where developers, production support, and DBAs are kept in three totally separate groups. This means that developers who haven't been taught how to use Oracle write inappropriate and inefficient code that is then patched up by production support personnel who are usually equally poorly trained, and the DBAs alternate between complaining about the code quality and griping about the amount of work they have to do to keep the system staggering along.

We seem to be back to "ignoring the technology," but a critical step in producing a successful application is to ensure that the programmers know how a database works and know how to test their code properly. The best way to do this is to keep all your programmers together with your Oracle expert (call her a DBA if you like, but she's actually much more than that these days). Then make sure your strategy documents are understood and followed, and that you have QA, training, and peer-group review sessions.

Sharing the Database

So you've got a good development project going. The team is well informed and well trained. The database structure is clean and sound. The whole system is coming together nicely and everything is working efficiently. Don't worry. It is still possible to snatch defeat from the jaws of victory with a little bit of scope creep or the dreaded parallel project.

Scope creep is in some ways the more obvious danger. Because you have designed an elegant and well-balanced system, and you have the strategy document with the arithmetic that describes what you are doing and why it works, you are fairly well protected. It should be fairly easy to demonstrate that cramming a little extra functionality into a small hole left in the specification could unbalance the whole thing and result in a surprisingly large impact on the viability of the system.

The *parallel project* can be much more insidious. You have a database, and others have an independent need for that data. They don't want to change it; they just want to look at it. Surely there's no harm in that. There is no need to change any of the functionality, no need for them to modify the data with an attendant risk of damage, it's just the occasional read now and then.

If you can't hand them the strategy document, and perform QA testing of their code to ensure that they stick to the strategy laid down by the documentation, then you may be allowing a massive overload on your system. The most extreme example of this problem that I have seen was on a parallel server system running half a dozen instances against a single database. The design was superb and the data partitioning was perfect. Throughput was measured in millions of complex operations *per hour*. Then another department decided to write a little Visual Basic application that needed to handle no more than 1,500 rows *per day*. The throughput of the main application dropped by a staggering 20%. Accessing data through the correct instance is critical to the optimal operation of the Oracle Parallel Server (see Chapter 22). The performance of the system in question depended critically on every bit of data going to the right instance every time. Unfortunately no one had mentioned this to the Visual Basic programmers, so every time they wanted a row they would hit any old instance, with the result that one of the other nodes would have to write a couple of hundred megabytes of data to disk. Although it was obvious from the symptoms what was happening, it was a little harder to find out who or what was making it happen. It actually took the company more than two weeks to identify the culprits, and only four hours to fix it.

Under all circumstances, the "extra little bit" added to a well-crafted database needs to be analyzed just as thoroughly as the initial design, and it should be created by people who understand why (not how) the system works.

Conclusion

The five section headings in this chapter are convenient handles for identifying key areas of development, but the message in all cases is the same. If you don't know enough about what you have to do, you can't do it well.

- Ignoring the technology means not knowing what can be done.
- Avoiding the arithmetic means not knowing enough about how much work has to be done by the database.
- Fudging the prototype means not knowing where and how the design needs to be tested, and tested to destruction.
- Confusing the responsibilities means everyone is allowed to be ignorant.
- Sharing the database means someone else has to know all you've learned.

If the knowledge is not available, the project cannot succeed. You must have a reasonable understanding of how the Oracle database management system works, and this knowledge must be available to everyone working on the project. If there are important reasons for choosing specific features of Oracle, then everyone involved has to know what they are and why they are relevant.

CHAPTER 3

How the Engine Works

If you take the most simplistic view of a database, what have you got? You insert data, massage data, delete data, report data, and eventually throw away the data. You need the data to be available on time, every time, and you need it to be correct, consistent, and you probably don't want intruders snooping through your data.

Of course, when your system also requires end-user input, the style and ease of use of the front end become highly significant. And when multinational companies are involved, demands for physical ownership and distributed databases start intruding. Nevertheless, whatever the peripheral arguments, there are only four key criteria used to judge the database itself: performance, resilience, integrity, and security. The most visible criterion, subject to the most severe judgment, is always performance.

> *Performance, resilience, integrity, and security are key to successful database design. Of these, performance is judged most frequently.*

A database costs money. The hardware on which it runs can be quite expensive. The license costs can be high, especially if the license fee is related to the CPU power of the machine. More significantly, the time of the people who design and build the system costs money, the time of the people who provide the data costs money, the time of the people who fix it when it isn't working properly costs money, and the time of the people who sit drumming their fingers waiting for answers costs money. Worst of all, the wrong decisions based on the wrong data cost a lot of money. Getting it right saves money in all sorts of ways.

There are numerous books available to tell you about producing a logical design for a database. Although I don't plan to say anything about this stage of the process, it is important to remember that there is a very sound basis for doing the job properly, and the process of describing your business requirement in the form of a "normalized" data model is very important.

One of the most important purposes of normalization is to eliminate the risk of *update anomalies*. Any one item of data should appear precisely once in the database. If a change in a single fact requires you to make multiple changes in the database (for instance, recording a person's name against both his address and his insurance policies), then something is wrong with the *logical* design. Furthermore, proper normalization makes it easier to identify questions that need to be asked to fill gaps in your understanding, and it makes it a lot easier to put realistic numbers (or at least to discover the complete absence of realistic numbers) against the things with which you are dealing.

The cornerstone of my personal approach to the physical database, however, is this: Once you know how to do it "right," you are allowed to do it "wrong." In other words, once you have completed a proper logical design, your physical design can be warped as much as necessary to meet the realistic constraints of the system.

The key word is *realistic*. Ideally it would be nice to turn the logical model straight into the physical model. In some cases this works perfectly well, but usually there are a number of reasons why it doesn't happen. In fact, there is usually only one real reason why the logical design is rarely mapped directly to the physical, and it is the proliferation of tables that a fully normalized model usually produces, although there are many variations of this argument:

- "The end users couldn't cope with joining lots of tables for their reports."
- "It takes a lot of administration in the end-user reporting tools to hide so many tables."
- "It takes a lot of administration to use database views to hide relationships between lots of tables."
- "Using views, especially with lots of tables in them, can result in very inefficient performance."
- "The optimizer isn't always very good at deciding how to join lots of tables."
- "The optimization step is sometimes very CPU intensive when lots of tables are involved."
- "It is very difficult to produce efficient code when it involves lots of tables."
- "It is very difficult to document code that operates complex joins across lots of tables."

In an ideal world, in which everyone knows exactly how Oracle works, and perfect information is available about the database and data distribution, it would be easy to pick holes in any of these arguments. In the real world, it is much easier to be sympathetic. So in the end, it is often necessary to butcher the logical design in a three-way trade-off between performance, clarity of code, and accessibility to end users. Fortunately, this is becoming less of a problem with OLTP systems, especially with the use of object-oriented and multitier styles of programming, which try to take the complexity of data processing away from the front end and push it back to a more central point.

> *Always design for efficiency, but avoid complexity. Never forget that success depends on performance, resilience, integrity, and security.*

With this thought in mind, the best approach to building a successful database can be summed up by answering four questions:

1. What are the most important few tasks that the system has to execute really efficiently?
2. How do I rig the database physically to address those tasks?
3. What implementation strategies will keep the code clean and simple?
4. What demands for resilience, integrity, and security are going to stop this design from being viable?

Although it is possible to create a few problems with network traffic, excess CPU usage, and process contention, ultimately the only significant threat to a database system is physical I/O. Disks operate hundreds if not thousands of times more slowly than the other parts of a computer system. The primary objective in designing the database is always going to be to minimize or reschedule the need for physical I/O. It is almost inevitable that this will also lead to minimized logical I/O, and hence less CPU usage, but it also increases the risk of contention between processes. To be successful in your objective, you need to understand how the database functions, and which activity is likely to generate which types of problem.

You could argue that this emphasis on performance ignores the need for integrity, security, and resilience. However, remember question 4 above: Which of these three features is going to make your design fail? To a large degree all strategies aimed at improving integrity, security, and resilience increase the amount of work that has to be done. The strategies themselves are usually simple in concept, but expensive in execution, and it is often the need for these three critical features that makes the required level of performance so hard to achieve.

For example, a simple strategy for improving resilience is to mirror all disks. Naturally this doubles the write activity, even though it may reduce average disk read times. Standard strategies for integrity consist of checking new data against existing data to ensure internal consistency, but such checks require work to be done (sometimes twice) and can incur significant maintenance overhead. Standard strategies for security involve runtime checking of the requested data against the identity of the requester. Again, this is a check that requires work to be done, and it can have enormous side effects on efficiency.

The I/O Trap

What causes I/O in Oracle databases? Let's look at the basic requirements for data processing. There are really only two options to consider, so this shouldn't take too long:

1. You want to read the content of an existing data block.
2. You want to change the content of an existing data block.

Reading Data

To read an existing data block, Oracle must first determine how to access the block, which it does by referring to the data dictionary. We know, however, that the data dictionary is just another part of the database, so Oracle may have to read some data dictionary blocks before it even gets around to thinking about accessing the block we want. Fortunately there is a cache (the dictionary cache, also known as the *row cache*) that usually ends up holding most of the dictionary. So, after an initial start-up period, dictionary access tends not to cause physical I/O.

The dictionary tells Oracle the options that exist for getting to the data block efficiently. The most commonly used quick-access method is the *B-tree index*, but other methods include bitmap indexes, hash clusters, and partitioning. These methods are discussed later, and a review of their costs and benefits, and suggestions for when, and when *not*, to use them is provided.

Let's review the work that Oracle does by the traditional analogy of looking up a name, Obadiah Smith, in the local telephone directory. Your first step might be to open the directory at the middle, which will usually put you in the M section. Take the right-hand section of the directory and halve it again. This will probably put you near the start of the S section. Repeat the process and you end up somewhere in the Smiths. At this point you start turning pages, checking each page heading until you reach "Smith, O," and then you start the laborious job of scanning each entry to find the one you want.

A B-tree index is the computer model of this search approach (Figure 3-1). Although a person might restrict their search of the telephone directory to first half/second half all the time (a *binary chop*) the computer could perhaps use first fiftieth/second fiftieth in its processing. In either case, the method of breaking down the search into smaller and smaller chunks is the same.

In Figure 3-1, we start at the root block and find the entry for Philips. Because the next entry overshoots our target, we jump to the branch block identified by Philips. In the branch block we find an entry for Smith N. Because the next entry overshoots, we jump to the leaf block identified by Smith N. Scanning through this we find Obadiah Smith. We use the pointer we find there to jump to the right table block and row.

Assuming that we have a relevant B-tree index, (see Figure 3-1), it takes only a few blocks near the top of the tree to cover a very wide range of data. Often, the root and branch blocks of an index are approximately 2% of the total space taken by the index. If this index is used frequently, then it is quite possible that these layers will very soon end up virtually pinned in Oracle's data buffer. We may have to do a physical I/O to get the correct leaf block from the bottom layer of the index, and then do a second physical I/O to get to the table.

Remember, though, that each search may require us to collect several blocks of data from the table. In our example, there may be several Obadiah Smiths. Perhaps we want them all, perhaps we want the Obadiah Smith who lives in a specific postal district but can't pin that one down until we go to the table and check the zip code of each one in turn.

In our example, it is possible that a single leaf block in the index may contain enough entries to point to every single Obadiah Smith in the table, but each Obadiah Smith is actually stored in a different data block. Consequently, our query response time is likely to be rather slow—on the order of 20 msec per existing Obadiah Smith. Depending on our use of the data, we may need to make a trade between including the zip code in the index hence using more space to allow us to find an individual person faster, or saving space but taking a longer time to find individuals with popular names.

Always aim for a combination of precision and relevance in data access.

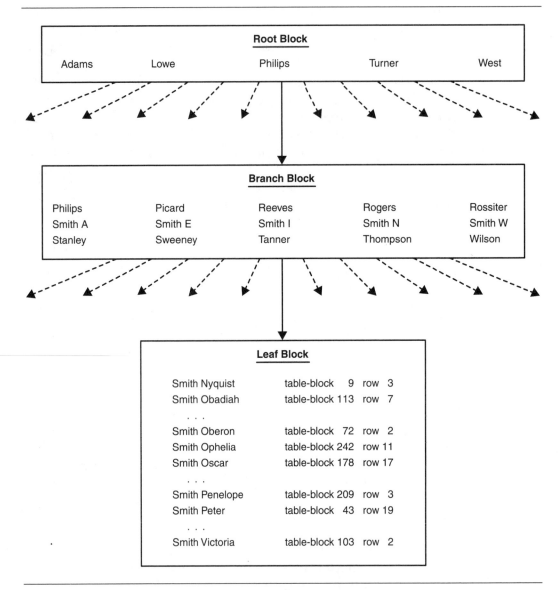

Figure 3-1.   The telephone directory B-tree approach.

To design an Oracle database for reading, you need to supply methods that allow for high-precision access to the required data. But even good indexing strategies may not be good enough. Think about a credit card account. Every day you use your credit card once or twice, and at the end of the month you get a statement with 45 items on it. Now imagine that the credit card company allows you to access its database through the World Wide Web to see your previous month's transactions:

```
select   details
from     transactions
where    card_id = 4921072573469734
and      transaction_date between '25-nov-1999' and '24-dec-1999';
```

Even with a perfect indexing strategy Oracle is going to have to find 45 different items that are scattered widely across a table, consisting of millions of rows per day, unless the credit card company has used some cunning design feature to ensure that all the data about your transactions ends up in a tight little clump as it arrives.

As an aside, if you buy a disk rated at 100 I/Os per second, how long will it take to respond to a single I/O request from your program? On a reasonably well used system, the answer is *not* one hundredth of a second. Why not? Because you are not going to be the only person using that disk, so your request is likely to queue up at various points in the system, waiting for earlier requests to complete. As a rough guideline, at a reasonable level of use in a multiuser environment, the total time for the request to complete is likely to be 2 to 2.5 times longer than you may expect, given the nominal speed of the disk.

Changing Data

We have already seen that a small change to a single item of data requires Oracle to do much more work than we would expect. The rollback data has to be generated and the log information has to be written. On the plus side, it is only the log file that actually has to be written to disk as you commit your changes to the data. The data blocks themselves eventually dribble out to disk as part of an ongoing background task. Nevertheless, the amount of rollback generated can be so large that a steady stream of rollback blocks is also written to disk, interfering with all the other I/O. This topic is considered in Chapter 8.

As far as log writing is concerned, one of the features of the recovery mechanism used by the Oracle database system is that it restricts itself to a limited number of log files. However, to achieve unlimited recovery, you need an unlimited number of log files. Because of this, you have the option of running the database in ARCHIVELOG mode, which means that Oracle copies (archives) each log file as it is filled. This can become one of the most significant I/O costs in a busy system.

Instead of a write-only log area, your system will write one log file and read another at the same time to create a copy of it. Moreover, the redo log is a preexisting file that Oracle keeps reusing, but the copy is a whole new file. And creating a new file is usually a more I/O-intensive operation than reusing an existing file.

Typically you will find that switching from NOARCHIVELOG mode to ARCHIVELOG mode probably doubles and could even come close to trebling the total volume of I/O your system has to handle. This topic is considered in Chapter 10.

There are many other factors that can slow down the task of writing. Obviously you cannot change a data item until you have managed to find the right block, so you need all those fast-access mechanisms that we discussed in the previous section on reading data. However, if you have a fast-access mechanism for getting at the data, you then need to maintain that mechanism (for example, to keep the index up to date) as you change the data, which leads to more block changes, which leads to more rollback records, which leads to even more redo log being generated.

It is an unfortunate side effect of changing data that the packing of that data tends to degrade. This is particularly true of indexes, in which a single extra entry into a leaf block may be enough to force a block to be split and its contents to be shared between two blocks. The I/O cost of using indexes (and other rapid-access methods) can increase significantly over time as more and more data is inserted or updated.

The view INDEX_STATS tells us about the packing of an index (see Chapter 6). The package DBMS_SPACE tells us something about the effective space use in other objects (see Appendix D).

There are times when you simply have to factor in the time to schedule rebuilding some (hopefully a very few) objects in your system to repack them to a reasonable degree of efficiency. Of course it is a sad fact of life that even though you are rebuilding one object to improve efficiency, the resulting I/O is bound to have a negative performance impact on the rest of the system.

Finally, despite my comment that I/O is ultimately the primary performance problem on Oracle databases, it is worth noting that there are other surmountable performance issues that start to appear most frequently in write-intensive systems. For example, if two separate processes both want to change data in the same block (and this can occur particularly in indexes), there will be a brief interval when one process has to have exclusive ownership of the block and the other process has to wait.

There are other examples of contention between concurrent processes, but in general they can be minimized. It is very important to anticipate this risk before the application is built, rather than discover it too late.

> *If your problem is more subtle than I/O, the dynamic performance view V$SYSTEM_EVENT can tell you where your system is losing time (see Appendix B).*

Side Effects

We have already noted some of the side effects of read consistency. If a reader process needs to see the data as it was at some previous time, it has to find rollback data and build a private copy of a block, applying the rollback as it goes. This could introduce extra physical I/Os if Oracle has to go back to disk for very old rollback blocks. Furthermore, we are reducing the effectiveness of the data block buffer, first by filling it with "spare," out-of-date copies of existing blocks, and second by filling it with old rollback blocks.

An additional, strange side effect is that readers can cause writes to take place. In Chapter 1, we looked at the steps involved in executing a ***commit*** command. In particular, if a changed data block is still in the data buffer at the moment of ***commit***, then Oracle sets a marker in the block to show that the change has been committed. However, if there are changed blocks that are no longer buffered, then Oracle does not go hunting for them because this requires some physical I/O. In fact, Oracle does not mark all the changed blocks that are still in the buffer if the number is too high. Instead, blocks that have not been marked are brought fully up to date the next time another process happens to read the block into memory. When the changed block is next accessed, Oracle notes the transaction ID in the data block and jumps to the transaction table in the relevant rollback segment header to find the SCN of that transaction. However, the original entry in the transaction table may have been overwritten, so Oracle may have to start tracking back through the transaction table rollback, trying to rebuild an old copy of the transaction table. If the transaction table can be rolled back far enough, then Oracle has the correct SCN and uses it to mark the data block. If not, Oracle may use the oldest SCN it has generated as a reasonable approximation (known as the *upper bound commit*) for the real SCN.

> *Processes that should be read-only processes can result in writes. This usually happens as a consequence of large data changes being made during a single prior transaction.*

In either case, this *delayed block cleanout* has done two things. First it has made Oracle read a number of rollback blocks. Second, it has actually changed a block that we merely wanted to read, which means that some redo has to be written to file, and the block itself is now considered to be "dirty" and will eventually have to be written to disk.

Delayed block cleanout tends to occur after a single transaction has made a large change to the database, typically affecting more than 10% of the buffer. The types of job that do this are large batch jobs or imports. There is no workaround for the problem itself because the delayed block cleanout *must* happen. However, it is fairly common practice to control the timing of the cleanout by forcing it to happen as the last step of the job. Serialized table scans and index scans are sufficient to make Oracle read and clean every block.

Conclusion

To a very large degree, the success of an implementation depends on the efficiency of reading and writing data. Although Oracle's underlying algorithm ensures that readers do not block writers and writers do not block readers, it is still the case that readers and writers interfere with each other, and the mechanisms that Oracle uses to bypass complete blocking introduce a number of performance-related side effects.

The performance of reads and writes ultimately depends on minimizing the total amount of physical I/O performed. The amount of I/O depends on the access techniques used, the precision with which data is requested, and the physical proximity of related items of data. Unfortunately, techniques for reducing I/O at read time tend to conflict with techniques for reducing I/O at write time.

CHAPTER 4

Classifying Your Target

When designing the physical database, you will usually find that there are just a few business-critical activities that the system has to support very well. In this context the phrase "very well" tends to mean "quickly."

Loosely speaking, there are really only four main classes of operation that you need to recognize and handle. Obviously the boundaries from one class to the next are fluid, and you are quite free to argue that my classifications are fairly arbitrary; however, they help to focus on the main issues you are likely to face when designing a system. Each of the following sections outlines the thoughts that go through my mind when I have to start planning how to tackle each of the different classes.

Manual Transaction Processing

I classify this type of system as one with a relatively low number of users performing a small number of complex transactions that require turnaround times appropriate to human response times. A good example is an insurance telemarketing business in which a phone operator converses with a customer while entering new data into the system, retrieving reference information, and possibly performing nontrivial calculations.

The critical feature is that during the course of a single transaction, the back end of the system has to react many times at human-dialog speeds to variations in inputs from the front end. Also, the front end of the system has a human being attached to it doing a nontrivial task, and a human being is fallible, makes mistakes, has to be checked, and appreciates proactive assistance.

Typically the system would be a classic client/server arrangement. The two key features of an input screen are the following:

1. **Instant validation on a field-by-field basis**—When you enter a client account number, you expect to see some meaningful client information such as name, zip code, and mother's maiden name bounced

back from the database as confirmation that the account number is correct. This has to be accomplished quickly because the user often expects to move on to ask for the next piece of raw data immediately.

2. **Drop-down lists**—When you have to enter a product, you may want to select from a list of product codes rather than having to type in a product code and validate it. Better yet, you may want to see a list of readable product names. At an even more extreme level of user-friendliness, you may like to have "automatic prediction à la Microsoft Excel" as you type in a product name, where each letter typed gives you a shrinking list of the possible ways you could complete the entry.

Features of this type can result in a lot of traffic between the front end and the back end. An important point to consider with network traffic when Oracle is involved is that a high bandwidth is *not* necessarily the limiting factor. Oracle tends to send small packets that require acknowledgment, so the turnaround time for each dialog between the front end and the back end can be the most significant problem. A system I investigated recently was losing "only" one tenth of a second on each trip because of some esoteric configuration problem with a dynamic link library (DLL). However, because it took 40 round-trips to accomplish one particular task, it spent nearly four seconds on a fairly trivial operation, which made the system unusable.

The second problem with friendly front ends is the effect of drop-down lists. It isn't uncommon for systems to generate completely unusable drop-down lists of several thousand items each time specific fields are hit. There are three separate overheads here: the time taken by Oracle to extract and sort the data, the time needed to pass it across the network in small packets, and (by far the longest) the time needed to unpack the data and copy it into the presentation layer.

The biggest issue about friendly front ends is that you have to pay for them somewhere. It seems to be axiomatic that if you take the easy option of building the front end using all the handy little developer widgets that allow for rapid development, you end up with a system that is heavy on traffic and database access. On the other hand, when you try to protect the network and database, you end up having to produce complex code and paying the cost of extra development time, higher risk of coding errors, and more difficulty with maintenance.

> *When coding user-friendly front ends with programmer-friendly tools, take care to check how much traffic goes back and forth to the database.*

When the moment of data entry ultimately occurs, it is likely to be a complex dataset that has to be applied to the database, with a strict set of integrity checks that has to take place. This means that the optimal strategy is probably one of passing a set of values to a database procedure and letting the complicated work take place close to the data. Of course this leaves you with the problem of having to choose between coding all validation twice (once for the front end and once for the database procedure) or coding it once in the database and increasing the traffic back and forth to the database.

Of course, particularly with the current flavor of the month being *customer relationship management,* we have to recognize that systems of this type may be treated like decision support systems (DSS). Thus we also need to be aware of the potential need for the database to survive heavy-duty, long-lasting queries. Fortunately, the relatively low volume of data input means that collisions between reads and writes are likely to be fairly painless.

Automatic Transaction Processing

At some point we move from relatively small numbers of users performing complex tasks to large numbers of users doing things that are extremely simple. An example of this is a real-time credit card system, in which every credit card transaction hits the system as it happens.

The biggest difference between this type of system and the previous one is that complex human interaction is almost factored out. At the point of sale, the human interaction may simply be to type a code and an amount, and then swipe the card through a reader. These actions form a fully self-contained unit before the card reader starts its dialog with the database. There is no need for the database to validate data entry and send human-readable information back to the card reader as the transaction progresses.

The upshot of this fact is that the transaction that actually takes place is a machine/machine dialog, with a very short, tight requirement. The traffic back and forth from front end to back end is minimal, and the need for validation at the back end is tiny: Does the card exist? Is it valid? What's the current balance? If there is a validation problem, the database just sends a "reject" message to the card reader.

Another example is the increase in on-line shopping over the Web. The most common design pattern to date seems to be that the front end calls for a display page, either static or more likely generated dynamically by a database procedure, and the user selects an object to add to the shopping basket. During a relatively short period of time, the user may go through several independent and trivial pseudo transactions, picking one item at a time, before committing to purchasing the entire basket with the last transaction— the credit card transmission. During that same time period, a number of other brief connections and disconnections have to be made to generate new screen displays.

The problems with both of these systems usually revolve quite simply around the number and rate at which connections to the database are made and broken, and the frequency with which tiny transactions arrive and are committed.

With large numbers of concurrent users popping in and out of the system continually, we are likely to increase the risk of contention between different processes. Apart from the simple problem of the machine trying to share its processing time over increasing numbers of processes, we also have the issue of very large numbers of SQL statements being fired at the system, and lots of little bits of data arriving at the same time and being packed into the same small number of data blocks. The former problem can usually be addressed by having a number of application server machines between the end users and the database that maintain permanent connections to the database. The latter problem requires you to understand why the application may cause internal data collisions, and how to reduce the effect of these collisions on the database.

In addition, we need to recognize that databases generated by automatic or semiautomatic processes are able to gather a lot more information much more quickly than databases generated by traditional manual processes, so the sheer scale of the database may introduce more problems. The volume and randomness of requests may require an ability to maintain (or work around) a very high level of I/O at all times.

Of course the issue of DSS-type queries is still there, but it is emphasized by the increase in the size of the database and the increased frequency of transactions. The cost of read consistency (see Chapter 1), as readers access changing data, can become very high. In addition, the Web-based systems often have an overhead of dealing with "lost customers," in which the final transaction is never made and the shopping basket has to be cleared by a regular batch process that hunts down "aged" but incomplete data and deletes it.

The costs of read consistency for DSS reports can become significant in systems involving large numbers of small transactions generated by highly concurrent users.

High Batch Throughput

Mobile phones provide an excellent example of this type of system. The volume of data generated by a single network in a single day is vast. A single phone call may result in literally dozens of electronic records being generated by the various black boxes between the two ends of the link. And all this data has to be collected and processed extremely quickly by the companies that control the mobile network. The scale of the operation is so vast that any attempt to handle one call at a time is doomed to fail. The standard mechanism is to collect a few dozen or a few hundred calls at a time and throw them at the database as a batch job.

Even then there is a need for all sorts of processing to be done step by laborious step. Does the phone number exist? To which account should it be billed? Is the call to be charged at peak, standard, weekend, or any other special rate? Is there a special discount for the destination number? Is the user still within her free-minutes quota? Isn't it a little odd that this user has made two hours of international calls today when she usually totals three minutes of local calls per day? And so on. The sheer volume of processing is the biggest threat here. Consider the following:

- How much of the work can you take out of the database? Rate look-up is a suitable target perhaps. A C routine for cross-referencing would be quicker than a standard database look-up.

- How much of the I/O can you keep in memory? Let's try to buffer every customer account, preferably in Oracle's buffer rather than the operating system buffers, so that the look-up wastes no time on real disk reads.

- How much work can be avoided by twisting the structure of the database and increasing the complexity of the logic? Let's keep the running total of minutes for the day and the period on the customer row so that we don't have to do any I/O for fraud checks. We'll copy the figures for each account out to history and reset the running totals each day the first time that the account is used. But what if the account is not used for a couple of days? Fast solutions easily become complex solutions.

- How do we avoid contention on inserts, with hundreds of rows going in to just the last few blocks on the CALLS table and indexes? Using multiple free lists may help. If this is not sufficient, perhaps hash partitioning on number, or range partitioning on the last digit of the number may solve the problem.

■ How do you cope with generating 2.5GB of redo log per hour at peak rates, and a redo allocation latch holding up the system? Restructure the system to use Oracle's Parallel Server, but watch out for the side effects of the method you have chosen to handle your partitioning.

■ How can you get data into the system and generate management reports at the same time, without the need for read consistency causing massive overheads? An obvious strategy is to use partitioning (see Chapter 12) and put some limits on the timing of management reports.

And so it goes. The volume of work that has to be done is so large that you spend your time moving from bottleneck to bottleneck, asking why you have a bottleneck, and determining the solution and its side effects.

> *When you have very high throughput, you need to predict where the bottlenecks and collisions are going to be, then design to minimize them.*

Data Warehouse

I'm sure that there will be many people who will disagree with me, but I always get the impression that the database aspect of data warehouses is relatively easy. The database tends to be just a very big heap that gets another bucketful of data thrown in every day, of which approximately 99% represents the previous day's accumulated addition to the warehouse and 1% constitutes corrections to data from the recent past.

It is true that there is often a lot of research needed beforehand to find out where the data originates, what it means, how it should be massaged to homogenize it, and so on. It is not unusual to find that it takes several weeks for people to decide what is supposed to happen, several more weeks to find out where the data originates and how to clean it up, then just a few days to implement an effective mechanism for manipulating the data, and then a few more weeks to write some "bulletproof" loader code that, alas, usually breaks a couple of months later.

Oracle is *very* good at crunching large volumes of data very quickly, and when the time scales for the data crunching are somewhat relaxed (as they tend to be with data warehouses), and when there is no real-time change taking place as you crunch the data (which tends to be the case with data warehouses), it is very easy to put together strategies that allow you to use the heavy-duty features of Oracle to their best effect.

The most important aspects of implementing data warehouses in Oracle are to decide the most appropriate partitioning strategy, and then to decide how many different summary levels you are going to precalculate, how often you are going to recalculate them, and how far into the past you are going to recalculate. It's very easy to get lost trying to be too clever with such summaries. Your aim at all times should be to keep things as simple as possible because simple means flexible, and the nature of data warehouses is such that good data warehouses encourage change, and very good data warehouses are flexible enough to respond to the change that they encourage.

> *For data warehouses, partitioning is a must. It lets you load data quickly, tidy up data quickly, and discard old data quickly.*

With most Oracle systems, I tend to say that you shouldn't try to fix a problem by throwing hardware at it. Problems are best fixed by identifying the design or implementation issues that caused them. In the case of data warehouses, though, sometimes the best solution is simply to throw in more hardware, because there are always "just a couple more" summary tables that would be a big help to someone.

The Internet Changes Everything

Given Oracle Corporation's current enthusiasm for Internet computing, I felt that I had to include a couple of comments on one of the current slogans. The Internet may change your lifestyle, the size of your database, and your options for shutdown. However, it's not going to make any fundamental difference in the way you think about making your database work.

If your database exists as the back end to an Internet application, it probably falls in the gray area between manual transaction processing and automatic transaction processing. The number of concurrent users may be large, and the number of sessions connecting and disconnecting could be large. The transaction dialog between the database and the front end will be small, because if it isn't you won't keep your customers for very long.

Is there any particularly special way you need to design your database to cover the Internet application? The pundits tell us that if your Web application can't respond in two seconds then you've lost a customer, which suggests you have to have a fantastically fast database to back up your operation. However, a great many of the sites I visit seem happy to waste 20 seconds of my time dumping a picture of the manager, the store front, today's special offer, and a fully pictorial menu on the screen before letting me get at the application, so I'm not convinced that it's going to make much difference to sales if the database activity (when it's finally allowed to happen) isn't as efficient as it could be.

I have yet to see, or have described to me, an Internet application that matches in the slightest degree the complexity of a typical client/server application. (I am sure that that statement alone will net me huge quantities of email putting me right.) Realistically it doesn't even seem possible to build a simple posting screen to post a journal that balances a few accounts as a true Internet application, although it is viable when the network is actually a high-speed in-house network and the cost of passing a rather chubby "thin client" down the line is negligible.

All the Internet applications I have examined to date have been extremely lightweight applications, and this seems largely to be dictated by two features of Internet computing: First, the turnaround time (and to some extent the bandwidth) across a typical Internet connection does not allow for the frequent and fluid dialog that can take place on a dedicated client/server link. And second, the target of an Internet application is to grab a very large number of customers. It is the second feature that is currently the limiting factor in the complexity of Internet applications. You would like to have thousands of customers using your system all the time, but the nature of Internet links is that connections from the customer to the server are continually making and breaking, with no guarantee that the customer will come back from one second to the next. Internet connections to your database do not open a session for a customer and keep that session open until the customer has done all he wants. A single customer "transaction" may consist of a dozen or more completely independent connections to the database, related only by the fact that the application sends in a cookie saying, Hey, this is still me and I was here a few seconds ago.

This is why so many people ask the question, How do I get the next 20 rows? If a customer puts a query to the database that has a 1,000-row answer, you can't pass 1,000 rows back in one shot because of the bandwidth/response time problem, so you have to pass back a few rows at a time. But how can you do this if your session terminates after you've passed back the first 20 rows? Using client/server with a permanent Oracle session dedicated to the dialog, there are all sorts of efficiencies built into the system that make this a non-problem—fetching the next set of rows is a natural SQL-type thing to do.

With an Internet connection though, the customer comes back to the system and asks, Remember me? I was here a little while ago and asked for some data. Can I have the next bit please? And Oracle says, No, you terminated the session so I closed the cursor. I can't fetch the next set of rows.

So what's the solution in the Internet environment? Option 1 is for the front end to know how many rows it has received so far and to keep repeating the query, possibly changing it slightly each time. For instance, on the first call it says, Get me the first 20 rows. The second time it says, Get me the first 40 rows and discard the first 20 rows. The third time it says, Get me the first 60 rows and discard the first 40, and so on. (In fact, the PL/SQL code generated by Oracle Designer for the Web application server uses a variant of this technique.) Option 2 is to write all the results into a permanent table on the first call, and add a spurious line number and a meaningless ID (passed back as a cookie perhaps) to each row written, then the second call will say, Get the stored result lines 21 to 40 for cookie code XXX. The third call will call for lines 41 to 60, and so on.

There are pros and cons to both approaches, but they both suffer from one important defect. They both make the database do a lot more work than a traditional client/server application does to get the results to the end user.

Current Internet applications may make your database work much harder than a simple client/server application by repeatedly requesting the same information. Consider using PL/SQL mechanisms (see Chapter 19) for limiting the size of such requests.

Even if the Internet allows you to come up with all sorts of new and exciting opportunities for doing business by collecting and disseminating information, it is not going to make any fundamental difference to the way you think about making your database work. The same old mechanical problems are still there, but the database is going to have to work harder and you are going to have to think more carefully about where things are going to break.

Conclusion

Different types of systems pose different threats. If you can identify the critical system activity that is likely to break the system, you are a long way toward identifying the features of Oracle that you must use to implement a successful system, and the amount of hardware you need to get the required level of performance.

At one end of the spectrum you have systems that need to cope with very large numbers of very small tasks, with a threat of process and network contention. At the other end of the spectrum you have a small number of processes that need to crunch a large volume of data in a small amount of time. Oracle has features to handle both extremes, but you have to recognize the need and match it to the feature before you start building the system.

Part II

Data Storage

CHAPTER 5

Making the Most of Tables

Because tables are the basis of everything in an RDBMS, it seems only right to start this part of the book with a chapter about tables.

Oracle 8.0 and 8.1 have introduced so many new features for tables that I have had to write several chapters devoted exclusively to the more exotic variations. We have partitioned tables (Chapters 12 and 13), index-organized tables (Chapter 14), object and nested tables (Chapters 15 and 16), large objects (LOBs) in tables (Chapter 17), temporary tables (Chapter 9), and materialized views, which are really tables (Chapter 23).

In fact, if you want to get a flavor of how complex and wide ranging the issue of table handling has become, you need only run a query such as

```
select view_name
from all_views
where view_name like 'ALL%TAB%';
```

Omitting some of the irrelevant views will give you the information listed in Table 5-1.

Given all the tempting things offered by all these options, what on earth could there be left to say about plain, simple, old-fashioned tables?

In fact, lurking in the 85 or so pages about creating and altering tables in the SQL reference manual, there are several little features of tables that are new to Oracle 8.1, and some previously existing features that are worth revisiting in light of the changes introduced by Oracle 8.1.

Table 5-1. Dictionary Entries about Tables

View	Purpose
ALL_ALL_TABLES	All the tables, regardless of type
ALL_NESTED_TABLES	Just the nested tables
ALL_OBJECT_TABLES	Just the object tables
ALL_PARTIAL_DROP_TABLES	Tables in the middle of drop column processing
ALL_PART_TABLES	The table-level details of partitioned tables
ALL_QUEUE_TABLES	Tables used by the advanced queuing option
ALL_SUMMARY_DETAIL_TABLES	Tables describing materialized views
ALL_TABLES	Just the plain old-fashioned relational tables
ALL_TAB_COLUMNS	Descriptions of each table's columns
ALL_TAB_COL_STATISTICS	Simple statistics about each table's columns
ALL_TAB_HISTOGRAMS	Data distribution histograms for all fully analyzed columns of tables, with minimum and maximum values for columns not fully analyzed
ALL_TAB_MODIFICATIONS	Approximate number of recent changes to tables
ALL_TAB_PARTITIONS	Details about the partitions of partitioned tables
ALL_TAB_SUBPARTITIONS	Details about the subpartitions of composite partitioned tables
ALL_UNUSED_COL_TABS	Details of tables with ready-to-drop unused columns

Rebuilding the Data

From time to time the typical DBA discovers that she needs to rebuild a table. It may be that the table was just sized very badly originally, perhaps new columns have been added that have caused serious migration problems, or perhaps large amounts of very old data have been removed by deleting lots of randomly scattered rows that have left holes everywhere.

The most common problem of this nature comes from first-in-first-out (FIFO) or "posting" tables—holding tables into which data dribbles gradually during the day, is processed, and then deleted over time. Because Oracle maintains a "high water mark" for a table, such tables are always considered to be as large as the largest size they have ever been. This often causes problems when a process stops for a while or an overnight batch introduces a large volume of data. Suddenly, the table becomes very large, and although it is subsequently emptied out, Oracle continues to treat it as a very large table with a surprising processing overhead. The worst example of this that I have seen was in a system in which rows passed through a FIFO table at a rate of approximately 100 per hour, but the overnight batch sent in 120,000 rows in one shot. Every two minutes during the day Oracle was executing a 16MB table scan across an almost empty table to find the odd couple of rows that had appeared recently.

In the past, all the options for rebuilding a table suffered from a degree of unpleasantness caused, not by the table itself, but by its dependencies. To rebuild a table you had, at some point, to drop the table. But dropping the table also resulted in all the privileges on the object disappearing at the same time. Moreover, you couldn't drop the table until you had disabled any foreign keys relating to the table, then you had to reenable all those foreign key constraints after re-creating the new copy of the table, and then you had to re-create all the indexes one by one, which might have caused locking problems if the table had gone into use in the interim. Finally you had to recompile any objects (views, procedures, and so on) made invalid by dropping the original table.

The problem of privileges and indexes could be handled (to a reasonable degree) by using the export/import method to re-create the table, but an import is a relatively slow way of getting data into the system because it cannot run in NOLOGGING mode (yet). You could get better speed by doing a "create table as select" (CTAS), but then you have to find a method for re-creating the privileges and indexes.

With Oracle 8.1, the issue is much less of a nuisance. You can now rebuild a table as part of standard SQL. A command such as the following rebuilds a table with a new storage clause, even changing the initial extent size of the table and putting it into a different tablespace. You can even use as many parallel execution slaves as you wish, without changing the parallelism of the table, to get the job done as quickly as possible.

```
alter table tab1 move
storage (initial 1m next 1m pctincrease 0)
pctfree 2
parallel 2
tablespace new_ts;
```

You still have to restrict end-user access to the table while using this command. The *move* command needs to take an exclusive lock on the table, so users won't be able to do any inserts, updates, or deletes while it is happening. In principle they can still run queries against the table while the move is actually taking place, but the moment the move is completed, any query running against the table may fail with the not unreasonable Oracle error "ORA-08103 object no longer exists."

Despite this restriction, the *move* command, when used properly, is likely to be a much more robust option than anything that went before. The *move* command doesn't lose privileges, it doesn't cause dependent objects to become invalid, and it doesn't lose index definitions.

An important thing to remember is that even though any indexes on the moved table will still keep their column definitions and storage clauses, they will have become unusable and will have to be rebuilt using the *alter index rebuild* command (see Chapter 6). While the indexes are unusable you will not be able to make any changes to the table that would affect an unusable index (such as inserts or deletes), and any *select* statements that want to access an unusable index will fail. In all cases you need to trap the Oracle error "ORA-01502 index is in an unusable state."

> *If you have to rebuild a table, always consider the **move** command first. Availability can be reduced, but the benefit to administrative safety and convenience is huge. There are no windows of opportunity for data to go missing.*

A funny little trap to watch out for is whether the move is logged. You can make the *move* command explicitly a NOLOGGING operation ("alter table X move nologging"), but even if you don't do this and the table is defined as a NOLOGGING table, either explicitly or by being created in a NOLOGGING tablespace, then the move does not generate any redo above a small amount for updates to the data dictionary. On the other hand, if the table is a LOGGING table, the behavior of the command depends on whether your database is running in ARCHIVELOG mode. If the database is archiving its redo logs, then the *move* command generates redo by default; if the database is *not* archiving the redo logs, then the *move* command does not generate redo under *any* circumstances (apart from the little bits for the data dictionary activity of course). You may test the procedure on a development system running without archiving and then move it to a production system running with archiving, and you may be surprised by the change in performance that this can make.

If you are already taking advantage of the more exotic new features of tables, you will have discovered that there are a few limitations, or omissions, in the *move* command. It would be nice, for example, to be able to change a heap-organized table to an index-organized table. It would be nice to be able to rebuild a LOB segment of a table without having to rebuild the table itself. But this is just the old complaint: Whatever Oracle gives us, we want more.

There is, by the way, an odd little bug associated with the *move* command. If the table in question has a security policy attached to it (see Chapter 21), then you may find that your session crashes when you try to move the table.

The invalidation of indexes also has an unexpected and potentially very unpleasant side effect. Again, I assume that this is a bug. Take a pair of tables with a primary key/foreign key referential integrity constraint, indexed (per normal performance requirements, see Chapter 6) at both ends of the relationship. Move the child table so that, as we have just seen, the index representing the foreign key relationship becomes unusable. If you now set a session to SKIP_UNUSABLE_INDEXES (see Chapter 6), then you can get into serious problems with referential integrity. For example, it is possible to run the following illegal sequence of statements, leaving a child row without a parent:

```
alter session set skip_unusable_indexes=true;
create table parent(id number primary key);
create table child (id_par number references parent);
create index ch_i on child(id_par);

insert into parent (id) values (1);
insert into child (id_par) values (1);

alter table child move;
    -- The index ch_i is now unusable
```

```
insert into parent(id) values(2);
insert into child (id_par) values (2);
delete from parent where id = 2;
    -- what, no error message!

commit;
```

> *Moving a table at the child end of a referential integrity constraint can result in the integrity being breached.*

So you do need to be careful about what tables you move, and what is going on around them as you move them. You should also make sure that you rebuild all associated indexes as quickly as possible. Of course, if you haven't named the primary key and unique key constraints, or associated them with named indexes, you may have to waste a bit of time hunting through the data dictionary to find out which indexes have to be rebuilt.

In case you are wondering how I discovered this defect, it wasn't entirely by accident. I was following a procedure known as, *What is this new feature going to break?,* when I came across the option for moving tables and noted that there was an option to bypass its side effect of making indexes unusable by setting the SKIP_UNUSABLE_INDEXES parameter. I immediately wondered what would happen to primary key/foreign key relationships.

I was actually trying to test a hypothesis that if the child index became unusable, then the old problem of child table locking would occur, and this is when I discovered that things were actually much worse than that. It seems that one of the requirements for successful Oracle implementations is that you have to be devious, cunning, cynical, patient, knowledgeable about the internal workings, and a bit lucky. (This particular defect is still present in Oracle 8.1.6 and 8.1.7, by the way.)

Packing the Data

Talking about rebuilding tables brings us to the issue of packing data into the table as effectively as possible. In the introductory section of this book I described my enthusiasm for minimizing I/O. One of the obvious methods for doing this is to ensure that data is packed in your tables as tightly as possible.

Since the early days of Oracle, the PCTFREE and PCTUSED parameters in the **create table** statement have existed to determine how much free space should be left in a block for future updates, and how low the block usage should drop before freed space can be reused.

Unfortunately, the effect of these parameters is rarely considered, and most databases run with every table left at the defaults of PCTFREE = 10 and PCTUSED = 40. Although in many cases this won't make much difference to the overall performance of the system, it is always worth considering adjusting the values for at least a few critical tables.

> *Always think about getting some benefit from PCTUSED and PCTFREE. Try to keep the data well packed, but watch out for too much free list activity (see Appendix D).*

There is an irritating issue with trying to keep your data well packed. In the days before partitioning, the standard way of eliminating very old data from a system was simply to delete it. This usually had the unfortunate effect of leaving lots of blocks partly filled but too far from the PCTUSED figure to go back on the free list. The result of this was a reduction in the total amount of data stored without any sign of the anticipated performance benefit or expected reclamation of space from the notional reduced storage requirement. So, if you had the luxury of acceptable downtime, the next step was to rebuild the table to repack the data, but this could cause a nasty problem.

Imagine you have some sort of order processing system in which each order goes through three main stages: "new," "in progress," and "completed." A new row requires 50 bytes of storage, an in-progress row takes up 100 bytes, and a completed row reaches its full maturity at 150 bytes (Figure 5-1). The canny DBA quickly works out that PCTFREE should be set to 65% to allow new rows to grow to full size without migrating (which also means setting PCTUSED to 35% or less, because the total of PCTUSED and PCTFREE has to be no more than 100).

Every month, most orders that were completed at least 12 months earlier are deleted from the system, but some are retained for various reasons. Over a period of time, the table becomes a little ragged because of this incomplete clearing process, so the DBA decides the time has come to rebuild the table and regain some space and efficiency.

Ask yourselves this question: What should the value of PCTFREE be (at least temporarily) as the table is being rebuilt? Assume 95% of the rows in the table are complete, 4% are in progress, and 1% are new. For the benefit of the completed rows, the best value for PCTFREE would be zero because the bulk of the data will never be updated again, but this would be disastrous for

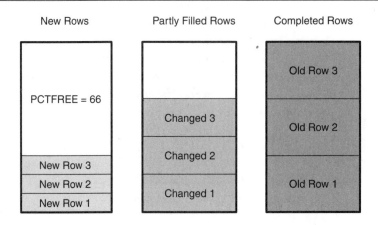

| New Rows | Partly Filled Rows | Completed Rows |

Figure 5-1. Row sizes change over time.

the more recent 5% of the data that needs plenty of room to grow. Conversely, if you set PCTFREE to 65% to accommodate the new data, or even 35% to compromise between the new data and the in-progress data, you waste a huge amount of space in the blocks that contain only completed data (Figure 5-2).

Of course you could get your spreadsheet going and decide on 2% as a reasonable weighted average—(95% ∘ 0 + 4% ∘ 35 + 1% ∘ 65)/100—and hope for the best. You could start playing complicated games with partial unloads and reloads, changing PCTFREE as you go. There are several tedious variations of making the best of an awkward situation.

> *Be careful when rebuilding a table in which the rows have dramatically different lengths at different stages of their life cycle. You may have to compromise between wasting huge amounts of space or allowing lots of future rows to migrate.*

With Oracle 8.1 there is an interesting (and probably accidental) solution to this problem in the command

```
alter table tabX minimize records_per_block;
```

(I've been saying to classes for years that "files have records, tables have rows," and then Oracle Corporation came up with this!)

Possible Rebuild at PCTFREE = 0

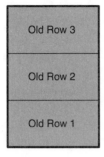
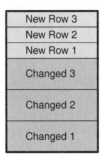

Possible Rebuild at PCTFREE = 33

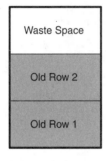
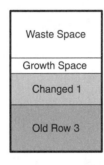
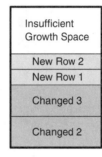

Figure 5-2.   Effects of rebuilding.

The effect of this command is to make Oracle scan the table to find the block with the largest number of rows, and record this limit in the data dictionary. Currently the value is not exposed in any of the xxx_TABLES views, but a representation of the value is kept in the SPARE1 column of the SYS.TAB$ table. The value stored in SPARE1 is "maximum number of rows per block" plus either 32,767 or 32,768—more on that later. Once this limit is set, Oracle will not store more than that number of rows in any block in that table. According to the manuals, the command exists to enable Oracle to reduce the storage required for bitmap indexes, and for this reason you cannot issue the command or the converse **nominimize** against a table that already has bitmap indexes in place (see Chapters 6 and 7).

If Oracle created this option to accommodate bitmap indexes, how does it affect our strategy on our three-size table? Ask yourself how many rows will fit in a 4K block, say, if each completed row takes 150 bytes. Allowing for the overhead, the answer is approximately 26 rows. Before the system goes live, create the table, insert 26 rows, then run the ***minimize*** command against the table, then set PCTFREE to zero, and delete the 26 rows.

From this point onward, you never have to worry about the side effects of rebuilding the table, Oracle will *never* allow more than 26 rows in a block. When you rebuild the table, each block will have just enough space left in it to allow exactly 26 rows to grow to completion, regardless of whether the rows are new, in progress, or complete (Figure 5-3). If the table is already in use before you get a chance to apply this strategy, then you may be able to get away with simply trying the ***minimize*** command to find out what happens. Unless the table has already been rebuilt a couple of times, you may find that the correct result drops out anyway.

> *When creating the application schema, consider applying the **minimize** command to a few critical tables before any data gets into the system.*

This is a wonderful idea. There is still one bug in it though. It looks as if the ***move*** command reads the SPARE1 column as 32,768 + max rows, whereas the normal ***insert*** command reads it as 32,767 plus max rows. Consequently, when you rebuild the table, the number of rows per block is one less than you would expect, although subsequent inserts then use the correct limit. The same bug seems to appear with direct mode inserting (in other words, using the /°+ APPEND °/ hint with a NOLOGGING table).

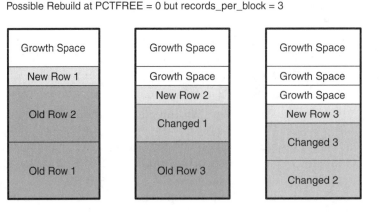

Possible Rebuild at PCTFREE = 0 but records_per_block = 3

Figure 5-3.   Effects of using ***records_per_block***.

However, because you should rarely have to resort to such a catastrophic task as a full table rebuild—a process that is going to take the data away from the users for quite some time—you can always apply a short-term workaround. Issue the *nominimize* command against the table and create some fake data in the table to ensure that one block has N + 1 rows in it. Once you have managed to engineer such a block, issue the *minimize* command so that Oracle sets the table's limit to N + 1 rows per block. Now delete the fake rows and rebuild the table. Because of the bug, the table will be built with N rows per block as required, at which point you can do a *nominimize/minimize* to set the maximum number of records per block to the correct value.

Bear in mind, though, that the *minimize* command requires Oracle to check every single block in the table to find the maximum number of rows recorded in any block. Thus, each *minimize* command results in a full table scan while locking the table exclusively. There is also the important little detail that the check is made against each block's row directory, *not* against the current number of rows in the table, so you may not get the result you expect if the table has suffered severe DBA abuse in the past.

More Packing

Following the theme of packing the data, rather than simply squeezing in all the data as tightly as possible, you could consider shuffling the data around so that the rows relevant to a query are as closely packed to each other as possible. This doesn't reduce the amount of space needed to store the data directly, but it does mean that the appropriate queries have to read fewer physical blocks to get their result.

One obvious strategy for doing this is to use an index-organized table (see Chapter 14), but there are overheads to this, and in a data warehouse environment you may not want to take this approach.

A feature that many users have been asking about for years offers an alternative. In Oracle 8.1, the ORDER BY clause can be used in views and in some CTAS (create table as select) statements. For slow-moving applications, such as data marts, a command like the following can make a dramatic difference to overall system performance if the most common and most time-critical queries use predicates involving TEST_COLUMNS:

```
create table sorted_data
nologging
parallel degree 4
pctfree 0
```

```
as
select * from unsorted_data
order by test_columns;
```

For very large tables it is difficult to find time to do this sort of rebuild, especially when you have to sort out privileges and rebuild indexes immediately afterward. But it becomes much more viable when applied to individual partitions of a partitioned table (see Chapters 12 and 13).

I must point out that rearranging the data like this wouldn't directly reduce the storage needed, but of course DBAs everywhere have often found that a side effect of rebuilding a table is improved efficiency because odd little spaces from updates and deletes in both the table and its indexes are eliminated, and there is some actual reduction in space needed.

If you are still using Oracle 7, this ordering feature has accidentally slipped backward into a patch release of 7.3.4, bypassing 8.0 to do so. In other versions it is possible to create sorted tables by using an /*+ INDEX () */ hint to make Oracle read the data through an index, but this can be very slow.

Dropping Columns

Another feature requested by users for years is the ability to drop columns from tables. Again, you never need to do this *in theory,* but from time to time a column may become redundant or you may have made a small error in the data model.

The cost of getting rid of a column from a table is significant, and the exercise should never be undertaken lightly. In general I advise people to replace the table with a view of the table that excludes the column, rather than wasting the time and effort of rebuilding the table.

Sometimes, though, both for space reasons and for performance reasons, you might actually decide to get rid of the column data entirely. There are a number of different ways in which you can use the drop-column commands in Oracle 8.1, but the best strategies probably take three steps.

Strategy 1

First you should mark the column as unused so that it disappears from sight. The space is still taken up, and the data is still stored in the data blocks, but for all practical purposes the column ceases to exist:

```
alter table ABC set unused column XYZ;
alter table ABC set unused (XYZ, PQR);
```

In general, this will be a fast process. However, if the column is used in an index, then the index will have to be dropped at the same time, and this could slow things down a little bit. You also need to be aware that any dependent objects will become invalid, so you may want to recompile packages and so forth immediately after you have set the column unused.

> *Don't forget to check dependencies and side effects before dropping a column (or anything else, for that matter).*

There are restrictions on what you can do. If the column you wish to drop is a primary key column, then you have to confirm your intentions by including a CASCADE CONSTRAINTS option, which has the effect of dropping the primary key constraint, the index on which it relies, and any associated foreign key constraints. Similarly, if the column is involved in a multicolumn constraint and you don't set all those columns unused simultaneously, then you have to include the CASCADE CONSTRAINTS option. It should go without saying that you can't drop a column that is in the primary key index of an index-organized table (see Chapter 14) or in the partition key of a partitioned table (see Chapter 12).

At this point, the data dictionary entry for the column has been changed so that the name is of the form SYS_Cnnnnn_{timestamp}$, and its property is "hidden, unused, data still in row." You could actually add a new column to the table with the same name as the column you have just marked. To identify tables with columns marked as unused, look at the view family xxx_UNUSED_COL_TABS.

If you exported the table at this point, the unused but not yet dropped column would not be exported, so you could use an export/import cycle to finish off the process. A more appropriate second step is to drop the column using the following command to clear the data from the rows. You should note that this command clears *all* columns that have been set unused:

```
alter table ABC
drop unused columns
checkpoint 999;
```

This is the command that takes the time, keeps the end users off the system, and flogs the database to death. Oracle does a table scan of the entire table, rewriting each block to remove the dropped column. This generates a very large amount of rollback, a very large amount of redo log, and Oracle needs to hold an exclusive lock on the table while this is happening, which is one reason why users need to be off the system. Given that the changed blocks (both table and rollback) are written back to disk through the data block buffer in the normal fashion, you may appreciate that dropping a column is a heavy-duty exercise. As a very rough guide for simple columns, the rollback generated for each row will be roughly 100 bytes plus the average column size being dropped; the redo will be approximately 250 bytes plus the average column size, even when the table is a NOLOGGING table.

> *Dropping columns results in a very heavy load on both rollback and redo.*

In addition, any query against the table that starts after the alter table command will wait for a "library cache lock"; in effect it waits for the dictionary definition of the table to stabilize so that the parse can complete properly. In principle, users can carry on using the system while the cleanup is taking place; in practice, they may not want to wait for responses.

There are six points to consider when issuing the drop column command:

1. If you omit the CHECKPOINT option then you will need a very large rollback segment and you can't "set transaction" to select a rollback segment in advance.

2. If you include the CHECKPOINT {integer} option, then Oracle commits every {integer} rows, although these commits won't actually appear in the session statistics as "user commits."

3. If you include the CHECKPOINT option but exclude the integer, Oracle commits every 512 rows.

4. If you use the CHECKPOINT option in a ***drop column*** statement while running large reports, you increase the risk of getting "ORA-01555: snapshot too old" errors from the reports. This is just a special case of the standard problem of long-running reports conflicting with numerous small transactions.

5. If you don't "checkpoint," or your checkpoint is large, you are likely to write a very large number of dirty blocks to disk that will require a delayed block cleanout the next time they are read. Thus you may want to do a serial table scan of the table after the drop is complete to force this cleanout to take place immediately. (Remember, although later versions of Oracle 7 introduced a FAST COMMIT mechanism and a

feature known as *delayed-logging block-cleanout,* that feature is relevant only to short transactions, affecting a small number of blocks.)

6. If the ***drop column*** command crashes, there is a special option to make it resume—ALTER TABLE DROP COLUMNS CONTINUE CHECKPOINT {integer}—and any other attempt to access the table will result in error "ORA-12986: columns in partially dropped state." To identify tables that crashed in middrop, look at the view family xxx_PARTIAL_DROP_TABS.

The most important thing to remember about the ***drop column*** command is that, despite comments to the contrary in all the manuals, *it usually does not free up space.* Why do I say this? In many cases a single column is likely to be a fairly small fraction of a row, so when you drop the column you are likely to free up a relatively small fraction of a block. So unless you have a particularly high setting for PCTUSED, the block is unlikely to go onto the free list. In other words, you may have created quite a lot of empty space, but not *usable* free space.

> *Dropping columns does not, in general, free up space that can be reused. Extra processing may be required for the space to become usable.*

Of course there will be cases when dropping the column releases enough space to put the block on the free list, but this could be nearly as bad because every single block is on a free list. There are two possible side effects. First, this could have a dramatic impact on performance if you were depending on new data being packed in the order it arrived. Instead of the next 20 rows being packed in the same block, you may find the next 20 rows being scattered one row per block over 20 different blocks. Second, if you have multiple free lists but issue the ***drop*** command without specifying a checkpoint, *all* the blocks will be attached to just one of the free lists. Consequently, you could have lots of free space in a table that could only be used for one of *N* transactions, where *N* is the number of free lists (see Appendix D).

These problems lead us to the third step of the strategy. Having dropped your unused columns you may want to use the ***alter table move*** command to rebuild and repack the table. This command reclaims the free space and repacks the rows pretty much as they were. The downside, as described earlier, is that you have to wait for another table scan, you have to rebuild all the indexes to accommodate the row movement, and you have to worry about the side effects of mixing old, full-size rows with new, short rows that still need space to grow. Nevertheless, this does suggest an interesting alternative strategy.

Strategy 2

When a column is set to unused, the ***alter table move*** command does not copy the content of the column when it copies the table. Instead, it populates the column in the new table with NULLs, saving nearly all the space that was previously held by the column. This tends to be much quicker than dropping the UNUSED column, largely because the ***move*** command generates virtually no rollback and can also be set to avoid generating redo log. The relative performance of the ***move*** command is also enhanced by the fact that the reading and writing is all direct and not through the data block buffer. Thus, other processes do not suffer from losing their buffered data while the move takes place. Furthermore, there are three beneficial side effects: First, all the blocks are generated as clean blocks and no subsequent reader has to perform a delayed block cleanout. Second, because the move does not generate rollback, neither of the rollback threats (running out of space or snapshot too old) can occur. And third, users can still query, but not change, the table while the move is in progress.

The order of events for strategy 2 then is simply

```
alter table ABC set unused column XYZ;
alter table ABC move;                         -- with options.
alter index ABC_PK rebuild online nologging;  -- etc.
```

As usual, you have to decide on the most appropriate compromise for the specific task. With this strategy you are still wasting 1 byte per unused column in each row. The unused column is still taking up one of the 1,000 columns you are allowed to have in the table. The main overhead, of course, is that you do have to rebuild all the indexes, so the time saving in moving the table may be lost in the index rebuild, and your code has to handle the occasional "ORA-08103: object does not exist," error or "ORA-01502: index is unusable" error gracefully.

There is one circumstance in which using this strategy and never actually dropping the column may be highly desirable. If you want to drop a column from a very large partitioned table, then the option to move a single partition at a time and rebuild its local indexes may be vastly more efficient than using the "proper" route of dropping the column. Using this approach you can even move multiple partitions concurrently, or spread the move over several days, whereas the standard *drop column* command has to run serially (in other words, one partition at a time) and has to run to completion before that table becomes available for reuse.

There is one important limitation to this option: If the column you are dropping is a LOB column, a varray stored as a LOB, or a nested table column, then the data and index segments associated with the external storage of that column are not dropped until you actually use the *drop* command. Even then it seems that a move followed by a drop can be much quicker than a drop followed by a move.

Up-to-Date Statistics (Nearly)

Another frequent request from DBAs has been for an easy way of finding out how many rows there are in a table without having to do a count(∘) or reanalyze the table. In Oracle 8.1 there is now a feature that comes close to answering this need. This is the MONITORING option, which can be used with *create table* and *alter table* commands. For example,

```
create table t1 (
    n1   number,
    v1   varchar2(30),
    t1   nest_type
)
monitoring
nested table t1 store as t_nest (monitoring);
```

Once a table is set in the monitoring state, an approximate count of inserts, updates, and deletes is kept in the SGA for the table, its partitions, and its subpartitions, although not its nested tables (see Chapter 16) unless they are monitored explicitly, as in the example. It is important to remember that this is only an approximation—not an exact count. One quirk, for instance, is that the statistics are updated to show the effects of a change even if you subsequently *roll back that transaction*.

Every 3 hours, or whenever the database is shut down cleanly, this running total of changes is written into the data dictionary by the system monitor (SMON) process and can be seen in the view family xxx_TAB_ MODIFICATIONS. These views also report the date and time at which the totals were updated, and whether the base table has been truncated since the last *analyze table* occurred. When a table is analyzed, its entry is deleted from xxx_TAB_MODIFICATIONS.

To check the number of rows in a table in Oracle 8.1, you need to look at NUM_ROWS in xxx_TABLES, then add the inserts and subtract the deletes from the matching xxx_TAB_MODIFICATIONS row. However, if in xxx_TAB_MODIFICATIONS the TRUNCATE column is set to YES, the number of rows in the table is (in principle) just Inserts − Deletes.

Apart from giving the DBA an idea of how far out the statistics stored in xxx_TABLES may be, the xxx_TAB_MODIFICATIONS has a more significant purpose. It is used by the DBMS_STATS package to determine the staleness of an object's statistics. This allows two of the options in the package DBMS_STATS (see Chapter 19) to restrict themselves to gathering statistics only for those tables with statistics that are sufficiently out of date to need new statistics.

There is a little bug in this feature. If a table is truncated, the TIMESTAMP and TRUNCATED columns are updated in xxx_TAB_MODIFICATIONS, but the treatment of the number of inserts, updates, and deletes is not consistent. The numbers in the table, and in the SGA, do not appear to be reset. If a table has been truncated since it was last analyzed, you should not, currently, trust the figures in xxx_TAB_MODIFICATIONS.

Wide Tables

I have already mentioned in passing that under Oracle 8.1 it is possible for a table to have 1,000 columns. I wasn't planning to say anything more about this, other than to comment that it is a feature that should be used only for extremely strange cases, such as holding the results of a multiple-choice questionnaire perhaps. However, Dave Ensor of BMC (dave_ensor@compuserve.com) pointed out in one of his highly entertaining and informative presentations that Oracle has to record a 1,000-column row as four separate, chained, row-pieces. As a follow-up, I decided to do a few experiments to determine whether there were any undesirable side effects. There were.

A row of 1,000 columns will be stored as three sections of 255 columns and one section of 235 columns, and Oracle uses its standard CONTINUED ROW FETCH mechanism to build the entire row. This means that the dynamic performance view V$SYSSTAT will show a large value for "continued rows" if you start using more than 255 columns in a table.

On the other hand, if you *analyze* a table that uses 1,000 columns, it will report zero chained rows unless some of the rows have actually been split across blocks. So you could easily end up wasting time trying to figure out from where your "continued row fetches" are coming.

In a similar vein, V$SYSSTAT throws up other problems. If you access a row made up of four row-pieces, then Oracle has to do four logical reads to build it—even if all four row-pieces are in the same block. If you use the "buffer hit ratio" (in other words, one of the formulas relating logical reads and physical reads) as an indicator of the database performance, then you will be deceived by the excess logical reads generated by this internal row chaining.

Of course, because 1,000-column rows are automatically treated as four separate row-pieces, you may hope that Oracle will be generous in its use of free space in the block, and pack these long rows on a piece-by-piece basis. It won't. If you typically have 12K rows made of four pieces of 3K and 16K blocks, you may hope that Oracle will put one row in the first block, and one piece from the next row in the same block before using the next block. Unfortunately, the whole of the next row will go into the next block, and 4K in the first block will be wasted.

Another quirk of long rows appears when you use the *minimize* command. Despite the fact that the *analyze* command reports no chained rows, and treats the row pieces as one row per block, the *minimize* command counts every row-piece. This is actually pretty insignificant in terms of the bitmap index issues for which the command should be used. On the other hand, it leaves me with a feeling of unease that perhaps a mix of 1,000-column tables with bitmaps (a fairly likely scenario if your table represents a questionnaire) may be a combination with a few other bugs waiting to be discovered.

Problems and Quirks

Oracle 8.1 (and in fact Oracle 8.0) introduced all sorts of hidden structures and columns in the data dictionary to support new features. If you depend on a reverse-engineering tool to generate code to rebuild bits of the database, check very carefully that it does a proper job and doesn't try to create tables with real columns named SYSNC0000400005$$.

The *alter table xxx move* command will crash your session in almost all cases if there is a security predicate on the table—even a predicate like 1 = 1, which allows you to see all the rows.

If you use the *minimize records_per_block* command, the *move* command interprets the value incorrectly and rebuilds the table with one row less per block than it should, which can waste a lot of space. The direct-mode insert (insert /*+ APPEND */ into tabX select . . . from tabY) has the same problem.

There is some evidence that the SPARE1 column has a secondary use. Most new tables have the value 178 in this column, and event 10058 is described as "use table scan cost in tab$.spare1." Be a little cautious of surprise side effects when using this feature.

I have mentioned the /*+ APPEND */ hint a couple of times in this chapter as a way of inserting data into a NOLOGGING table without generating redo log (see also Chapter 22). Be warned. If you have a prerow insert trigger on the table, the insert will be a normal, logged insert. If you have any indexes on the table, then changes to the indexes are logged regardless of whether the index is declared as NOLOGGING.

You cannot drop a column from a table owned by SYS. On the other hand, you shouldn't have any tables other than the data dictionary owned by SYS, so this shouldn't really affect you.

Although xxx_TAB_MODIFICATIONS records the number of inserts, updates, and deletes since the last time a table was analyzed, the values may be misleading after the table has been truncated.

Although it is possible to create tables with as many as 1,000 columns, it is generally not a good idea, and Oracle's implementation has a few interesting side effects of which you need to be aware.

Strategy Notes

Oracle Corporation has added a number of low-key, but very powerful, features to the basic handling of tables. These are largely aimed at reducing the burden and risk of administration.

It is much easier to rebuild tables and to drop columns than it used to be, but don't let this encourage you to make the decision to do so too casually. Rebuilding large tables is still rather expensive, even though it is much safer. Dropping columns, although possible and feasible, is essentially expensive if you also want to reclaim the freed space.

If you use tables as FIFOs or "posting" tables, then you should look at options for using the **move** command to rebuild the table at regular intervals to avoid the commonly occurring problem of the resources being wasted by the table growing to an extreme size and never shrinking again.

If you do decide to rebuild tables or to drop columns, make sure you consider carefully appropriate values of PCTFREE and PCTUSED, and the life cycle of the rows in the table. If the length of a row changes significantly over the lifetime of the row, you can take advantage of the MINIMIZE_RECORDS_PER_BLOCK feature (allowing for its little bug) to make sure that the table is filled as efficiently as possible when the rebuild is over, so that it won't be susceptible to serious row migration problems as time passes.

The option CREATE TABLE AS SELECT . . . ORDER BY is much more efficient at building a packed table than the old trick of creating a table by selecting through an index, particularly because it can be executed as a parallel create/select. It is much more reasonable now to repack tables in data marts on a regular basis to optimize critical queries, particularly if you have partitioned the tables into relatively small chunks.

It is now possible to monitor the rate of data change on a table. Use this feature only on carefully selected tables. Although the overhead appears to be small, and although SMON only updates the relevant data dictionary table every three hours, the cost of handling large numbers of tables could become significant.

CHAPTER 6

Basic Indexing

A key concept of relational databases is that items of information are "connected" purely on the basis of comparison. There are no pointers from one item to another. If you have ever loaded the scott/tiger demo tables you will know that a row in the infamous EMP table "belongs" to a row in the DEPT table only if Oracle can compare the department ID in the EMP table with the department ID in the DEPT table and find that they match.

A value-matching process like this gets very expensive if there are no shortcuts to avoid comparing every row with every other row, so Oracle (along with every other RDBMS vendor) has always provided indexing mechanisms to make this task cheaper. In fact, before the advent of partitioning, indexing was the only generally viable mechanism that existed in Oracle to reduce the cost of locating specific sets of data. (I am leaving hashing and clustering outside the scope of the book, in part because of the very small number of occasions when they are truly effective strategies for Oracle databases.)

> *Indexes exist to reduce the cost of data retrieval. Choose them carefully, treat them carefully, and make sure that Oracle has adequate statistics describing them.*

I have already made clear my belief that the most important aspect of getting the design right is to design for minimal I/O costs. In many cases this can be translated into making optimal use of indexes; however, unsuitable use of indexes can reduce physical I/O while ramping up logical I/O, which means CPU usage, to extraordinary levels. Getting the best out of indexes is so important to the success of a system that I intend to use this chapter to describe a few basics and technical details before moving on to enhancements and new features of indexing under Oracle 8.1.

B-Tree Indexing

Let us start with a quick review of a B-tree index, and an outline of how Oracle implements it.

Let's create a table (a clone of the view ALL_OBJECTS, say), pick a couple of columns that you may frequently use when querying the data (OBJECT_NAME and OBJECT_TYPE, say), and create an index on this pair of columns. We'll duplicate the rows to add a bit of bulk:

```
create table object_clone
nologging
as
select  object_name, object_type, owner, object_id
from    all_objects
;

insert /*+ append */ into object_clone
select * from object_clone;
commit;

create index obj_nt_idx on object_clone obc(
    obc.object_name, obc.object_type
)
nologging
pctfree 80;
```

The rather large value for PCTFREE is to make sure that we generate a lot of leaf blocks, and so we need at least a handful of branch blocks. This is not a value you would often choose in real life. Note, also, the /*+ APPEND */ hint. Because object_clone has been defined as a NOLOGGING table, this hint ensures that the inserts do not generate any redo log for the table changes, although there will still be redo generated for the index changes. I have also used an alias for the table in the ***create index*** command. In most cases this is redundant, but when creating indexes on object tables, or relational tables with object columns (see Chapter 15), you need to prefix the attribute names with this alias.

To create this index, Oracle reads object_name and object_type from every row in the table, then generates and appends the rowid to produce a three-column list. (The rowid is the absolute address of a row in a table. In a normal table it consists of the relative file number identifying the file within the tablespace, the relative block number identifying the block within the file, and the directory entry identifying the row within the block.) Oracle then sorts this list and writes it into consecutive blocks in a new index segment, leaving the specified PCTFREE of 80% empty space in each block to produce the *leaf* layer for the index.

Each leaf block contains a pointer to the next and previous leaf blocks in the chain so that when Oracle does an index range scan it can move from leaf block to leaf block without having to climb up and down the index to find out where to go next.

While it produces the leaf layer, Oracle builds *branch* layers for the index at the same time. The exact details of how this is done are a little messy because of all the special cases (first block of entire index, first branch block as first leaf of entire index is filled, and so on), so I'm going to ignore the special boundary cases and simplify the description.

Essentially, if the index is larger than a single block, Oracle collects the first entry and the block address (relative file number and block number within the file) of each leaf block, and writes them into an extra block known as a *first-level branch block*. The PCTFREE value is ignored for branch blocks, so they are very well packed.

If the number of leaf blocks is so large that the first branch block is filled, Oracle starts a new first-level branch block to record details of the next set of leaf blocks, and *also* creates a second-level branch block to record the first entry and block address of all the first-level branch blocks.

If the index is extremely large, so that the second-level branch is filled, then the process repeats recursively. Oracle allocates another second-level branch block and a new block to act as a third-level branch block, and so on. Eventually all the leaf blocks are complete, and the top-level singleton branch block is referred to as the *root block* (Figure 6-1).

I mentioned that the branch blocks ignore the PCTFREE figure to pack in data as tightly as possible. I've ignored this in Figure 6-1 to make the progression of values appear a little more clearly. In fact, the index had far more entries in the branch blocks than shown. There are a couple of other space-saving details in the branch blocks that make them different from leaf blocks.

In the first case, there are no forward and backward pointers from branch to branch. (They are not needed at the branch level because branch blocks do not participate in range scans.)

Second, to save just a few bytes more, the key entry for the very first entry in the branch block is omitted. Its value is implicitly less than the value of the second entry. (And just to confuse matters, you will find if you do various block dumps that the first entry is referred to as the −1st entry, the second entry as the 0th entry, and the third entry as the 1st entry!)

Finally, and most significantly, the values in the branch layer are trimmed back as much as possible so that the value stored is just enough to allow Oracle

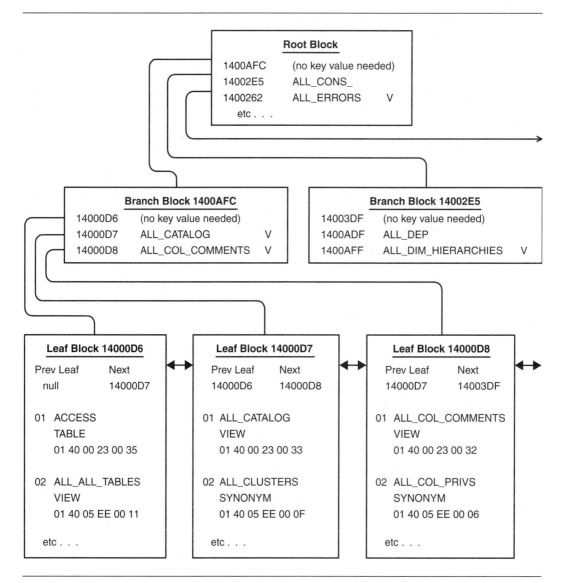

Figure 6-1.   Structure of Oracle B-tree index (nonunique).

to determine where its child block starts and the previous child block ends. For example, if the last entry in one leaf block is

```
(ALL_DEF_AUDIT_OPTS, VIEW, 01 40 08 7B 00 27)
```

and the first entry in the next leaf block is

```
(ALL_DEPENDENCIES, SYNONYM, 01 40 00 29 00 25)
```

then the entry in the branch block that points to the second leaf would be trimmed back to just ALL_DEP. This is just enough to let Oracle know that if it is searching for the (actually nonexistent) ALL_DEF_BLOCK_ACTIONS, it should be looking in the earlier of the two leaf blocks.

A point that Figure 6-1 and the notes here may have brought to your attention is the following: In a nonunique index, the rowid is actually added at the end of the list of index columns, and appears as part of the index for the purposes of Oracle's internal workings. This can mean that certain types of nonunique indexes (typically ones with low cardinality) can suffer from rather poor compression rates in the branch blocks, and can be a few percentage points larger than you might otherwise expect.

If you want to pursue the details of how indexes are created and stored, you can dump an index hierarchy to a trace file by finding its object ID from the view family xxx_OBJECTS and using one of the "event" calls to dump a trace file as follows:

```
select object_id
from user_objects
where object_name = 'OBJ_NT_IDX'
;

alter session set events 'immediate trace name treedump level NNN';
```

where NNN is the object_id returned from the *select* statement. This requires every block in the index to be read, so it should not be undertaken lightly. It will, however, show you the order in which blocks are allocated.

The output will be dumped into the current session's trace file, and will start something like the following:

```
----- begin tree dump
branch: 0x14000d5 20971733 (0: nrow: 5, level: 2)
    branch: 0x1400afc 20974332 (-1: nrow: 118, level: 1)
        leaf: 0x14000d6 20971734 (-1: nrow: 102 rrow: 102)
        leaf: 0x14000d7 20971735 (0: nrow: 103 rrow: 103)
        leaf: 0x14000d8 20971736 (1: nrow: 112 rrow: 112)
```

The important detail is probably the leaf entry, where the number of rows in the block is reported. The reason for two separate values, NROW and RROW, is that NROW is the total number of slots in the block directory currently in use, whereas RROW appears to be the number that would be in use after all current transactions have committed and the block has been cleaned.

You may notice the −1, 0, and 1 as the first entries in the leaf block lines. These tell you which entry in the branch block is the one that points to the leaf block. Remember my comment about the strange way that Oracle counts from −1? This is where it shows.

This dump tells you on a block-by-block basis how well used every leaf block is at present. It is worth doing it occasionally for just a few important indexes to check whether there is any skew in the way in which leaf blocks are used. After all, an index that is 75% used according to the ***analyze*** command may consist of 100 blocks that are half empty and 100 blocks that are completely packed, or it may contain 200 blocks that are all near 75% full. If you know the details, you can make a better choice about the need to rebuild the index. The former probably needs it; the latter probably doesn't.

You can also manipulate the HEX or decimal addresses of the blocks (for example, 0x14000d5 and 20971733 in the first line of the previous example) to supply file and block addresses to the dump command if you want to peer further inside the actual block structures:

```
alter system dump datafile NNN block MMM;
alter system dump datafile 5 block 213;
```

To do this properly, you really ought to use the DBMS_UTILITY. DATA_BLOCK_ADDRESS_BLOCK and DATA_BLOCK_ADDRESS_FILE procedures to convert from the decimal block number to the file and block numbers:

```
begin
    dbms_output.put_line(
        dbms_utility.data_block_address_file(
                dba => 20971733
        )
    );
    dbms_output.put_line(
        dbms_utility.data_block_address_block(
                dba => 20971733
        )
    );
end;
/
```

```
5
213
alter system dump datafile 5 block 213;
```

On most UNIX platforms (with the exception of AIX, I believe) you can get away with a bit of quick arithmetic on the HEX address. For example, the root block in the previous example is at 0x14000d5. Knock off the last five digits and convert them from "hex" to decimal to get the block number. Convert the top few digits from HEX to decimal and divide by four to get the file number. This is a lazy hangover from Oracle 6 days and only works with systems with less than 64 files.

Updates to the Index

There are many tales told about the effect of inserts, updates, and deletes on indexes. Most of them are untrue, although perhaps a kinder comment would be that they are inaccurate, incomplete, or out of date. Key features of how the content of an index block changes include the following:

1. An index entry is *never* changed. It is (marked as) deleted and then reinserted, even if the new value keeps it in the same leaf block. (Of course, it is generally considered bad practice to update columns that appear in indexes, and it is pretty inefficient. Unfortunately, it is sometimes the best thing to do.)

2. Space made available by a deletion cannot be reused, even by the same session, until the transaction has committed.

3. When a new insertion to an index block won't fit, the block splits. The location of the split depends to a fair degree on the actual value to be inserted. It is not always a simple 50/50 split.

4. When adjacent blocks become *nearly* empty, B-tree theory says they should be merged, but in practice Oracle does *not* merge blocks automatically.

5. When a block is *completely* empty it is put on the index's free list. However, even when it is on a free list, an empty index block keeps its place in the index tree structure until it is actually reused.

The first two points tell us that a B-tree index is subject to harder work than a table. It is very easy for B-tree indexes on busy tables, with lots of updates of indexed columns, to become significantly larger than you might expect. In particular, if you update a key in a full index block to a value that leaves it in the same index block, then the delete/insert rule means that the block will split.

The third point attacks the commonly held belief that basing an index on a column generated by a sequence leads to a sparsely populated index. If the sequence used for inserting rows is an ascending index, then the index is packed to 100%. Unfortunately, if the sequence is a *descending* sequence, the old story is true: The index operates at 50% efficiency. There are also sundry problems with using sequences to generate indexes under parallel server systems. Apart from the contention problems, space management issues have to be tested carefully too. Another issue to consider is the amount of free space to leave in an index when you create it. It is sometimes possible to estimate how many new entries will be added to index blocks after creation, and to leave an appropriate amount of free space so that index blocks become nearly full but never split.

> *Indexes based on an ascending sequence are 100% packed unless the packing is affected by updates, deletes, or parallel server activity.*

The fourth point explains why certain classes of activity result in very large, inefficient indexes existing to cover very small sets of data. The problem typically arises when a table is used as a FIFO, or queue, with a time stamp or sequence number used to list the correct order of rows. Assume a process exists to read the oldest row and to process it, deleting the row for successful processing and flagging it for unsuccessful processing. Unless you have 100% deletions on your processing, a small trail of old, unsuccessful rows gradually builds up, but each row requires one entry in an index leaf block—and leaf blocks are never merged. It takes just a very low failure rate in such a FIFO to end up with an index of 100 leaf blocks in which 99 blocks hold just one row, and one block holds all the "current" rows. At this point you find that FIFO processing seems to be much less efficient than you hoped.

> *Some types of activity have a disastrous side effect on the efficiency of indexes. In particular, data arriving in descending key order, and indexes used as FIFOs, can waste lots of space.*

The fifth point is included for completeness and as a warning to those who try to use the INDEX_STATS view as a way of measuring the effectiveness of an index. It is fairly common practice to compare the DEL_LF_ROWS and LF_ROWS values from this view as a measure of the efficiency of the index. However, index blocks can be both "in the tree," according to the various pointers in the index structure, *and* on the free list. It is possible for an index to have a very large number of DEL_LF_ROWS while still working very efficiently, because no query ever causes the empty part of the index to be traversed. Of course, even though such an index is *operating* efficiently, you might still choose to rebuild it to reclaim wasted space.

Low-Level Processing

Essentially there is very little difference between a block that holds table data and a block that holds index data. At the index leaf level, however, there is an important difference in the processing.

When you insert a row into a table, Oracle simply writes the row data into the top of the free space section of the block, shuffling up the other rows to eliminate holes if necessary, and uses one of the entries in the block directory to point to the row, creating a new entry at the end of the directory only if necessary.

When an item is inserted into an index, Oracle writes the index value into the top of the free space section of the block as before, but then rearranges the block's row directory to open up a slot for the new entry so that the directory lists the pointers in the order that returns the index key values in sorted order (Figure 6-2).

In the same way, a delete for a table entry simply clears the directory entry. But a delete for an index entry (when it is cleaned out), shuffles the end of the directory upward to close up the gap.

The upshot of this is that index access can be very efficient even when the block size is large. Because the entries in a block's row directory are arranged to point to the entries in order, the work required to find a specific entry can be done through a binary chop on the directory entries—an important CPU savings when a 32K block could, in theory, hold more than 2,000 entries. Then, to operate a range scan, Oracle simply has to step through the directory entries in a block to return the subsequent rows in the correct order. This is a good example of how Oracle trades a little extra work at one point in its processing to save a lot of work at another point.

Another important difference between table processing and index processing appears when you realize that an entry into an index has to go into the

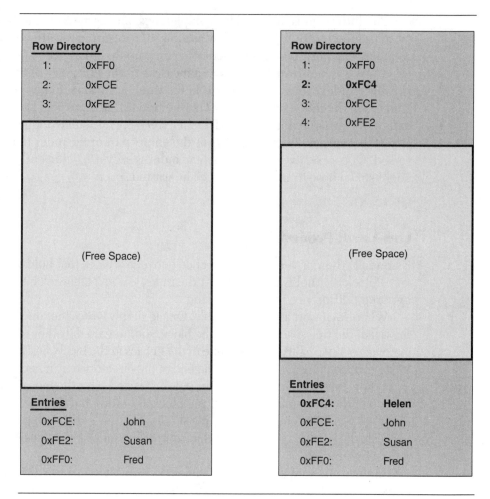

Figure 6-2.   Before and after inserting a new index entry.

"right" block. When you insert a row into a table, it is inserted into the first block on the list of blocks with some free space. When you insert an entry into an index, Oracle traverses the index to find the block where the first entry is just lower than the incoming value.

Imagine that you need to insert the value B into an index, and the index currently has its first leaf block full of As and its second leaf block empty except for a single C. Ideally, you could slip the new entry into the second block just in front of the C, but Oracle has to find the *highest block just lower than the incoming value,* so it *has* to insert the B value into the block full of

As. And because the block is full, it splits (probably somewhere near the top). Circumstances like this can lead to indexes that degrade rather more rapidly than you might expect.

One little question that pops up from time to time: If you update the columns of an index so that the entry does not change, what actually happens in the index block? The answer is, nothing. Oracle does not generate a duplicate "new" entry; in fact, it doesn't even lock the existing entry, even though it locks the row in the table.

Using the Index

To decide whether it is appropriate to use a specific B-tree index in a query, Oracle has only three criteria to test. First (and once upon a time the most important test), does the query supply a value for the leading column in the index definition? The values may appear as literal values, as bind variables, as column values from previously accessed tables, or through "transitivity" (which is slightly limited in Oracle's case to the inference that if col1 = col2 and col2 = {constant} then col1 = {constant}).

Second, are the predicates specified for the columns in that index likely to return a reasonably small number of rows? This will be inferred from the distinct key, number of rows, and number of nulls counts, combined with the low value, high value, and any histogram information stored in the data dictionary.

Take, for example, an index column on a table with no nulls, 1,000,000 rows, and 2,000 distinct values ranging from 0 to 1,000. What happens if you put in a query with a predicate of

```
where colX between 600 and 700
```

Because you are not targeting a single value, or list of values, Oracle uses the range supplied to estimate that you are after 10% of the table (the range of values requested is 100 compared with the difference between the minimum and maximum values, which is 1,000). In this case, the index is probably not going to be used. However, if you create a 20-bar histogram on the column, which happens to display the following results,

```
  1st 50,000 rows -   colX goes up to 0
      . . .
 19th 50,000 rows -   colX goes up to 0
 20th 50,000 rows -   colX goes up to 1000
```

then Oracle (and you) will recognize that the column is usually zero, with a smattering of nonzero values. Based on this information Oracle will infer that your requested range of 600 to 700 is probably one tenth of the last 50,000 rows that are in the twentieth bucket rather than the previous guess of one tenth of the whole table. In other words, the query may return only 5,000 rows instead of the previously estimated 100,000, and the chance of Oracle using the index increases.

Of course if you had analyzed the column to the maximum of 75 buckets, it may have shown that the only nonzero entries were in the seventy-fifth bucket, and things would look better still for the index. In cases like this, Oracle does not actually store all the repetitive buckets. (Why do more work than you have to?) It would only store the nineteenth and twentieth buckets, and infer that the previous 18 buckets had to be the same as the nineteenth. Nevertheless, histograms can take up a lot of space in the data dictionary and row cache, and should be used judiciously.

There is a bit of a problem with getting good results at this stage of the calculation when using multicolumn indexes because Oracle does not keep statistics about the data distribution of groups of columns. If you have an excellent index on "colA, colB, colC," but issue a query on just colA and colB, then Oracle can't necessarily get the right answer when trying to work out how effective the three-column index is for this case.

Another rather more serious issue at this point is the appearance of bind variables:

```
where colX between :b1 and :b2
```

Oracle cannot use histogram information to calculate the volume of data likely to be returned if the critical columns are supplied as bind variables. Unfortunately, bind variables are a good thing for large high-usage OLTP systems to get maximal concurrency. This leaves you with a no-win situation: If you include hints in your code to use the index, then the index will no doubt be used in the worst scenarios from time to time. If you don't include hints in the code, then the index may not be used even for the best scenarios. In many cases this means that the application program either has to supply the column as a literal value (stressing the library cache and reducing scalability if there are lots of different possible values), or the application program has to know more about the data than it should, and send one of a short list of suitably hinted queries to the database so that the value can be passed as a bind variable.

> *Histograms cease to be of any use for optimizing queries that use bind variables instead of literal values in their WHERE clauses. This poses a dilemma because the use of bind variables is desirable to reduce parsing costs and library cache contention.*

As the third stage of deciding whether to use an index, Oracle considers the CLUSTERING_FACTOR for the index to estimate how widely scattered across the table the expected collection of rows will be, and therefore how many physical I/Os are needed to collect them.

Two queries designed to return only 100 rows can perform dramatically differently. A banking application that calls for a bank statement for a customer will almost certainly have to find 100 rows scattered over a huge section of the table, resulting in 100 physical table reads with a turnaround time of two or three seconds. On the other hand, a refinery monitoring system asking for the state of the primary flow meters at 12:30 P.M. on May 14 would perhaps find that a similar number of data items for that point in time was stored in a couple of adjacent blocks, resulting in just three physical reads and a turnaround time of one thirtieth of a second.

Inevitably, there are always special cases that are exceptions to the simplified rules. For example, and contrary to common belief, it is possible for Oracle to use an index even when the leading column is not included in the query. Oracle 8.1 can choose to do a fast full scan or an index full scan on an index, instead of scanning a table. Oracle 8.1 can choose to use an index to avoid a sort, even when there are no conditions in the query that could make use of the index.

The bottom line, for *most* queries, is that you must use the leading columns of the index, and expect to return a low number of rows. When the returned rows are grouped tightly in the table, you may get away with a higher number of rows.

Bitmap Indexing

In later versions of Oracle 7+, and in response to the demand for data warehouse features, Oracle Corporation introduced bitmap indexes. These are indexes designed for use in large, slow-moving systems with a very low risk of concurrent updates. Bitmap indexes exist to answer random-content queries like

```
Tell me about the customer base
living in the London suburbs,
```

```
who own 2 cars,
have 3 children,
live in a 4-bedroom house
and the husband is a solicitor
```

Any single condition in this search would return a very large number of
rows, so there is no point in creating B-tree indexes on any one of the columns.
Nor is there likely to be any point in generating B-tree indexes on any specific
combination of columns because (1) the resulting B-tree would be very large,
(2) the next query may omit the critical "leading column" of any index you
choose to create (thus making it unlikely that Oracle will use the index), and
(3) a complete, covering set of indexes to meet all queries would be an enormous overhead on the system (in terms of both storage and maintenance).

To solve this type of problem we build bitmaps to describe the data.
Imagine we have just 10 rows in our dataset, with the values shown in Table
6-1 for cars, children, and bedrooms.

A bitmap representation of the CARS column is presented in Table 6-2.

Table 6-1.   Raw Data

ID	Cars	Children	Bedrooms
A	2	2	4
B	1	0	2
C	1	2	3
D	2	3	4
E	1	1	2
F	2	0	4
G	1	0	1
H	2	3	3
J	1	3	4
K	0	1	3

Table 6-2. A Bitmap for Cars

	A	B	C	D	E	F	G	H	J	K
0 Cars	0	0	0	0	0	0	0	0	0	1
1 Car	0	1	1	0	1	0	1	0	1	0
2 Cars	1	0	0	1	0	1	0	1	0	0

Each column of the bitmap in Table 6-2 corresponds to a row in the original dataset, and each row in the bitmap corresponds to one of the known values in the CARS column of the original dataset. The 1-bit in cell (0 cars,K) tells us that row K in the original dataset has a zero value in the CARS column.

Once we have built similar bitmaps for the BEDROOMS and CHILDREN columns, we can start combining bitmaps using Boolean algebra. Consider a search for rows containing two cars, three children, and four bedrooms. We pick just one string from each of the bitmaps and use "logical-AND" to combine them.

We lay out the bit strings one under the other (Table 6-3), then scan from top to bottom of each column looking for columns in which every cell is a 1, and rapidly discover that the D column is the only one that meets the requirement.

The options for tests are much more comprehensive than simple AND-ing, though. How about a search for people with three children who do not have four bedrooms? This will actually operate (in the index manipulation part, that is) just as rapidly as a simple AND. We simply have to remember that the

Table 6-3. Bitwise "AND"

	A	B	C	D	E	F	G	H	J	K
2 Cars	1	0	0	1	0	1	0	1	0	0
3 Children	0	0	0	1	0	0	0	1	1	0
4 Bedrooms	1	0	0	1	0	1	0	0	1	0
AND				1						

result of NOT(test) is achieved by changing ones to zeroes and vice versa (Tables 6-4 and 6-5).

In fact, this type of bitwise processing is so effective that Oracle has even made it possible (since version 7.3.4) to use it in the complete absence of bitmap indexes by setting the parameter B_TREE_BITMAP_PLANS to TRUE. If you do this, Oracle can use multiple B-tree indexes to acquire sets of rowids, then do some arithmetic to turn those rowids into bitmaps; do the AND-ing , OR-ing, and NOT-ing as required; and turn the resulting bitmap back into a list of rowids before fetching the rows from the table.

A few points to note about bitmap indexes. They tend to be very small. The size of a bitmap index before compression is roughly the number of different values in the column multiplied by the number of rows in the table divided by eight, if the table is well packed. Putting it another way: Before compression, the size of a bitmap index is 1 byte per row of the table for every eight values the column is allowed to hold. This suggests that a column is a candidate for a bitmap only if the number of different values that the column can hold is *relatively* small.

So far, I have not allowed for Oracle's compression algorithms. An interesting feature of bitmap indexes is that it is rather hard to predict how large the index segment will be. The size of a B-tree index is based very closely on

Table 6-4.   Bitwise "NOT"

	A	B	C	D	E	F	G	H	J	K
4 Bedrooms	1	0	0	1	0	1	0	0	1	0
Not 4 bedrooms	0	1	1	0	1	0	1	1	0	1

Table 6-5.   Three Children and Not Four Bedrooms

	A	B	C	D	E	F	G	H	J	K
3 Children	0	0	0	1	0	0	0	1	1	0
Not 4 bedrooms	0	1	1	0	1	0	1	1	0	1
AND								1		

the number of rows and the typical size of the entries in the index column. The size of a bitmap index is dictated by a fairly small number of bit strings, which may have been compressed to some degree, depending on the number of consecutive ones and zeros.

To pick an extreme example, imagine a table of 1,000,000 rows that has one column that may contain one of eight values (say, A to H) that has been generated in one of the following two extreme patterns:

1. All the rows for a given value appear together, so scanning down the table we get 125,000 rows with A, followed by 125,000 rows of B, and so on.

2. The rows cycle through the values in turn, so scanning down the table we get A, B . . . H repeated 125,000 times.

What will the bitmap indexes look like in these two cases?

For the first example, the basic map for the A value will be 125,000 one bits, followed by 875,000 zero bits, which will be trimmed off. Splitting the 125,000 bits into bytes, and adding the necessary overhead of approximately 12%, we get an entry for the A rows of 18K. A similar argument applies to each of the values B to H, so we get a total index size of roughly 8 × 18K, giving 156K.

For the second example, the basic map for the A value will be a one followed by seven zeros, repeated 125,000 times. There is no chance of compression here, so the A entry will start at 125,000 bytes. Adding the overhead, this goes up to 140K, and by repeating the argument for the values B to H, we get a total index of 1.12MB.

This wild variation in size looks like a threat, but to put this into perspective, a standard B-tree index on this column would run to approximately 12MB irrespective of the pattern of the data. It would probably take about ten times as long to build as well.

As we can see, the size of a bitmap index can be affected dramatically by the packing of the column on which it depends as well as the number of different possible values the column can hold and the number of rows in the table. The compression that is applied before the index is stored, and the amazing variation in the resulting index, does mean that the number of different values allowed in the column can be much larger than you might first expect. In fact, it is often better to think of bitmap indexes in terms of how many occurrences of each value there are, rather than in terms of how many different values exist. Viewing the issue from this direction, a bitmap is often better than a B-tree when each value occurs more than a few hundred times in the table.

If in doubt about the suitability of a bitmap index, just build it and see what happens. Remember that they can be created extremely quickly, mainly because Oracle has to do far less sorting to build them. In the past I have generated bitmaps at a rate of approximately ten seconds per million rows.

Finally, as you can see even from the very small sample dataset presented earlier, a single bitmap index is not likely to be much use on its own. Every individual part of our query identified 30% or more of the data. The power of bitmap indexes comes from combining several of them to produce a very small target set of rows in the table.

> *A single bitmap index is typically fairly useless. Any one value from one bitmap will return a large number of rows. Bitmaps work well only when several indexes are combined.*

There are four benefits of bitmap indexes:

1. You can have a large number of bitmap indexes that are individually very small, so a lot of information can be acquired from them with just a few I/Os.

2. A query on any random collection of indexed columns can be addressed by combining an arbitrary number of bitmap indexes.

3. By combining bitmaps in memory you identify the very small number of rows you really need.

4. Because you can identify exactly the right set of rows in the table, you don't make any redundant trips to the table.

A warning though: Bitmap indexes tend to be very dense objects. A single entry in a bitmap index often corresponds to a large number of rows in a table. The number may vary from a few hundred to a couple of thousand. If you lock an entry in a bitmap index (by inserting a row into the rowid range that it covers, say), you are holding a lock that can affect hundreds or thousands of other rows. Any process attempting to modify (insert, update, or delete) any other row to or from that value in that rowid range will have to wait until your transaction commits or rolls back. In fact I have found that under certain circumstances, Oracle can lock an extra, unrelated entry in the bitmap index, making the contention even worse, and somewhat unpredictable.

The important point to remember is that bitmap indexes are not appropriate for tables that are subject to any degree of concurrent modification, unless you are prepared to put up with an enormous amount of contention.

> *Bitmap indexes and OLTP systems do* not *mix.*

Oracle has introduced a special optimization strategy for maintaining bitmap indexes that involves postponing all the index updates from a SQL statement to the end of the statement and then handling the entire row-set as a single index update. (As opposed to the synchronized process that takes place with B-tree indexes in which the indexes are maintained as each row is affected.)

Despite this, and even in the complete absence of concurrent activity, updates to bitmap indexes are undesirable because a quirk in the implementation of updates tends to introduce fragmentation effects that result in large numbers of small "adjacent" bitmaps that result in extra space wasted and lengthier processing.

It is a cardinal rule of relational database systems that content is everything, and physical location such as the order in which rows are stored in a table is not significant to the end user. To create and use bitmap indexes, Oracle breaks this rule several times over.

The extents that make up a table are ordered and numbered by Oracle. The blocks within each extent are adjacent to each other, and there is a strict maximum to the number of rows that a data block can hold for a table. The absolute limit on the number of rows per block is roughly db_block_size/12, but Oracle does some calculations based on the number of NOT NULL columns in the table to determine whether it can get away with a smaller number, because this allows the bitmap index to be smaller, and therefore even more efficient. (This strategy may have had something to do with a reported bug in which bitmap indexes on tables with migrated rows used to result in queries returning incorrect results.)

To keep the arithmetic easy in the following example, let's imagine that Oracle has determined that a particular table can have an absolute maximum of 256 rows per block, so that each bitmap takes 32 bytes per block before compression. Based on this assumption, Oracle can take an arbitrary number and convert it to an absolute row location within a table. For example, given the number 5,964 and a table with the following three extents

- Extent 1 is in file 6 starting at block 42; size, 10 blocks
- Extent 2 is in file 6 starting at block 102; size, 10 blocks
- Extent 3 is in file 9 starting at block 1312; size, 10 blocks

we can calculate the nominal location of the 5,964th row as

5964 ÷ 256 = 23.296875   The row is in the 24th data block.
0.296875 × 256 = 76   The row is the 76th in that block.

Allowing for the segment header block in the first extent, and ignoring the possibility of *free list group blocks* and *unlimited extent blocks*, which may confuse the issue, the row is the 76th row in block 1316 of file 9.

Conversely, the third row of block 103 in file 6 (the second block of the second extent) will be at bit number: $256 \times (9 + 1) + 3 = 2{,}563$.

Given a mapping that allows Oracle to convert between a row address and a meaningless number, we can then generate bitmaps to describe the content of a column in the table.

Based on our 30-block table and a column definition that we need for our sample demographic query, we can build a bitmap that identifies the number of cars a household owns as follows:

1. Take a string of 7,424 bits (29 blocks × 256 rows) and set them to zero.
2. For each row in the table in which the number of cars is zero, calculate its location in the string and set the bit at that location to one.
3. Compress the string to save space (for example, eliminate the hundred or so zeros from the tail end of each block and eliminate sections where consecutive blocks have completely zero bitmaps).
4. Break up the string into reasonably sized chunks (up to approximately half an Oracle block).

This will leave you with a list of the form

```
(0, start rowid, end rowid, {section of bit string for rowid range})
(0, start rowid, end rowid, {section of bit string for rowid range))
```

Repeat the process for the rows in which the number of cars is one, to get a list of

```
(1, start rowid, end rowid, {section of bit string for rowid range})
```

and so on for each of the values for "number of cars" that currently exists in the table. When the entire list for all values is built, store it in a modified B-tree index in which the bitmap string is carried as a data column and the (value, rowid, rowid) is the key (Figure 6-3).

Index entry #0

41	Key value = 'A'
01 40 05 EE 00 00	Start Rowid
01 40 05 EE 00 77	End Rowid
00 5C 0C	Bitmap

Index entry #1

42	Key value = 'B'
01 40 05 EE 00 00	Start Rowid
01 40 05 EE 00 **67**	End Rowid
CF FE FF FF FF FF FF FF FF CC FF FF FF FF 0F	Bitmap

Index entry #2

43	Key value = 'C'
01 40 05 EE 00 **60**	Start Rowid
01 40 05 EE 00 77	End Rowid
CA E0 FF 0F	Bitmap

Figure 6-3.   Data stored in a bitmap leaf block. The table holds 100 rows.

By storing the start and end rowids as part of the key, Oracle optimizes the process of merging several sections of a single bitmap index or several different bitmap indexes. At any point in the process Oracle knows the current minimum and maximum rowids bounding the data, so Oracle need only merge that part of the next index that fits within the current range.

When you look at the schematic about how the bitmap is stored internally, two interesting thoughts may occur to you:

1. A bitmap entry is   (key, 6 byte rowid, 6 byte rowid, bitmap)
2. A B-tree entry is   (key, 6 byte rowid)

Imagine indexing a table in which every item occurred approximately five times, and the occurrences were always in little clusters. How would the two sets of entries for a bitmap index and a B-tree index compare? It is quite possible that the section of bitmap covering any one key value may be just 4 bytes long, so that the entire bitmap index entry for each key value would be something like

```
key-value + rowid   + rowid   + 4 bytes =
key-value + 6 bytes + 6 bytes + 4 bytes = 16 bytes + key-length
```

On the other hand the B-tree index would have to hold an entry for every single row in the cluster, so you would have

```
5 x key-value + 5 * rowid =
5 x key-value + 5 * 6 bytes = 30 bytes + 5 * key-length.
```

Even if you decided to create a compressed index for the B-tree (see Chapter 7), the B-tree entries would total something like

```
1 x key-value + 5 * rowid =
1 x key-value + 5 * 6 bytes = 30 bytes + key-length.
```

In other words, *for very special cases of data,* a bitmap index could be smaller than the equivalent B-tree index (and faster to build) even when the number of different values for the column is very high.

You might like to try the following experiment with three different variations of "bitmap" and "compress" in the index:

```
create table bit_test(bit_flag  not null)
nologging
as
select lpad(trunc(rownum/5),20)
from all_objects;

create /* bitmap */ index bti on bit_test(bit_flag)
/* compress */
nologging;

validate index bti;
select * from index_stats;
```

With approximately 2,800 rows in this table, which is typical for a default install of Oracle on UNIX, the uncompressed B-tree index came to approximately 90K, but the compressed B-tree came down to roughly 30K. However, the bitmap index was still 20% smaller at less than 24K. Given that the table had 560 different values, each occurring five times, this is not really in agreement with the normal directive that bitmap indexes are appropriate for columns with low cardinality.

If you want to do more experiments with bitmap indexes, the trunc() function and the mod() function are very useful. Selecting trunc(rownum/N) produces clusters of size N for consecutive values to test the effects of clustering, and mod(rownum,N) produces cycles of length N to test the effects of worst-case scattering of data.

Administration

B-tree indexes tend to degrade over time. The standard theory indicates that they settle into a steady state at 75% storage efficiency. Unfortunately, Oracle does not obey the rule about coalescing adjacent blocks when they are nearly empty, so indexes can become very inefficient. To help identify this problem you can use the ***analyze index validate structure*** command or the ***validate index*** command to populate the views INDEX_STATS and INDEX_HISTOGRAM, or the ***analyze index compute/estimate statistics*** commands to populate the various statistics columns in the family view xxx_INDEXES:

```
analyze index ABC_IND validate structure;
validate index ABC_IND;

analyze index ABC_IND compute statistics;
analyze index ABC_IND estimate statistics sample 1 percent;
```

The first two options give us some very detailed information about the quality of the index. Unfortunately, they take out a mode 4 (shared) lock on the table, which is rather restrictive in a live system because it stops all other processes from doing inserts, updates, or deletes. The information from view INDEX_STATS is included in Table 6-6.

There are a couple of other columns in the view INDEX_STATS that are relatively new, but I will leave those for the next chapter. If you find that most_repeated_key is hugely different from rows_per_key, then the view INDEX_HISTOGRAM may give you some more detailed information. For example, on a recent case in which rows_per_key was 5 and most_repeated_key was 588, the histogram results were those presented in Table 6-7.

Table 6-7 tells us that there are 1,377 keys with less than 64 rows each in the table, 3 keys with somewhere between 64 and 127 rows each, 5 keys with somewhere between 128 and 191 rows each, and so on, with the worst key value having somewhere between 576 and 639 occurrences.

Table 6-6. The INDEX_STATS View

Column	Description
HEIGHT	Number of steps from root to leaf inclusive. This rarely exceeds four and is often only three even for very large tables.
LF_BLKS	Number of leaf blocks in the index, some of which may be on free lists
BR_BLKS	Number of branch blocks in the index, some of which may be on free lists
LF_ROWS	Number of current rows in the index (excluding deleted rows)
BR_ROWS	Number of branch rows; usually similar to leaf blocks
BR_ROWS_LEN	Total space requirement in bytes for branch rows
LF_ROWS_LEN	Total space requirement in bytes for leaf rows (excluding deleted rows)
DEL_LF_ROWS	Number of deleted rows not yet cleaned out of blocks
DEL_LF_ROWS_LEN	Total space requirement in bytes for deleted leaf rows
BTREE_SPACE	Total usable space in bytes of allocated branch blocks and leaf blocks
USED_SPACE	Total space in bytes used by all leaf rows and all branch rows (excluding deleted leaf rows). If you were to rebuild the index with PCTFREE 0, this is roughly the size it would be.
PCT_USED	USED_SPACE/BTREE_SPACE expressed as a percentage. If it is significantly less than 75%, you should consider whether you need to rebuild the index (but see Chapter 7).
DISTINCT_KEYS	Number of different key values in the index; ignores deleted rows

(continued)

Table 6-6. (continued)

Column	Description
ROWS_PER_KEY	Average number of leaf rows per key value; ignores deleted rows. The smaller this number, the more precise the index when all columns are used in a ***where*** clause.
MOST_REPEATED_KEY	The number of occurrences of the most commonly used key. If this is dramatically different from the average rows per key, look at INDEX_HISTOGRAM, which describes a histogram of 16 bars showing how key frequencies are distributed.
BLKS_GETS_PER_ACCESS	An indication of how much work will have to be done to get a single specific row from the table using this index. This is the result of the calculation: HEIGHT + (ROWS_PER_KEY + 1)/2. This isn't really a useful measure, and I prefer to use AVG_DATA_BLOCKS_PER_ KEY from the family view xxx_INDEXES as the most significant estimate of work to be done in fetching data for a

The INDEX_HISTOGRAM view always holds 16 rows, and the REPEAT_COUNT column is always a power of two multiplied by each of the values from 0 to 15. In the example, we go from 0 × 64 to 15 × 64. This power-of-two approach does mean that the quality of information in the histogram can be spoiled by just a single extreme key, but in this example we can make a reasonable assumption that we have a significant number of good keys values, and then a small but highly undesirable set of keys ranging from unpleasant to extremely nasty. Clearly this is a really awkward index for which we should use the ***analyze index . . . for columns . . .*** command to generate some column histograms for the optimizer to use, because it looks as if we will want to use the index for some query values, and apply a table scan for others.

The statistical data that comes back from the view family xxx_INDEXES after estimating or computing statistics is presented in Table 6-8.

There are a couple of interesting numbers here (which is nice because they are acquired much more cheaply than the figures in the view INDEX_ STATS), but they only really tell you whether the index is notionally a good index or a bad index. They do not tell you anything about how much empty

Table 6-7. The INDEX_HISTOGRAM View

Repeat Count	Keys with Repeat Count
0	1377
64	3
128	5
192	1
256	2
320	0
384	3
448	0
512	1
576	1
640	0
. . .	. . .
960	0

space has appeared inside the index as a result of deletes, updates, and unlucky sequences of inserts.

If you want to get better information about the state of the index but want to avoid the locking problem of the VALIDATE options, then you need to supplement the figures by using the DBMS_SPACE package (see Chapter 19) to find out where the high water mark is on the index segment, and how many blocks are on the free list. Then you have to estimate the typical size of an index entry (pencil-and-paper job) and work out how effectively the rest of the space is used.

The other administrative problem that dogs indexes is whether they should exist at all. How do you prove that an index is actually useful, and used?

Table 6-8. Statistics from View Family xxx_INDEXES

Column	Description
BLEVEL	B-tree level, which is irritatingly one less than the height reported in the INDEX_STATS view
LEAF_BLOCKS	Same as LF_BLKS
DISTINCT_KEYS	Same as DISTINCT_KEYS
NUM_ROWS	Same as LF_ROWS, except for a bug that makes it very misleading
AVG_LEAF_BLOCKS_PER_KEY	The typical number of leaf blocks needed to hold all the entries for a single key value. This will often be just one, but should always be a small number (five or less as a guide). If it isn't, then the index is probably not a very useful index.
AVG_DATA_BLOCKS_PER_KEY	The typical number of table blocks needed to hold all the rows for a single key value. The smaller the better, because this is likely to be about the number of physical I/Os needed to get all the rows for a given key, and therefore is a good measure of how expensive it will be to use the index.
CLUSTERING_FACTOR	A measure of how rows with the same index key are scattered across the table. If the rows are widely scattered (bad), this value will be similar to the number of rows in the table. If the rows are tightly clustered (good), this number will be similar to the number of blocks in the table.

Unfortunately, although Oracle allows you to audit the access of a table, it does not allow you to audit accesses to a specific index. There are four near solutions to this problem:

1. Drop the index and see what happens. This is effective, but risky. You have to be really confident in your assessment of the utility of the index.

2. Test the query *indexed columns = {constant}*. If the index is not used for that, it won't be used for anything but very special queries, which

use tricks like JOIN INDEX optimization, fast full scans, or other index-only paths. So follow this with a code walkthrough to identify whether there are any such code paths that may appear.

3. Find out the object number of the suspect indexes and fire a (not too) regular query against the system view V$BH to count the number of blocks in the buffer belonging to that object. If the number is regularly more than a handful, then the index is probably used for querying. This assumes that the insert/delete rate on the table is low compared with the query rate, because any inserts and updates to the table have to read the index to find the right location for new entries.

4. Rebuild suspect indexes in their own tablespaces and leave them there for a few weeks, checking V$FILESTAT (see Appendix B) regularly. If the tablespaces appear to experience a high proportion of writes (more than approximately 30%) then there is a chance that the index is not used for data access. On the other hand, it is possible that the index is used so frequently that it is read and permanently buffered, so you have to know the application well enough to know whether this is likely to be the case (and you can confirm it with the query against V$BH).

Whatever else, though, there is also the problem of the index existing to satisfy just the year-end run, which happens outside the time window of your investigation, so you may drop an index with no side effects appearing until a disastrous batch runs several months later. (Of course in this case, the index should probably be built as part of the run and subsequently dropped anyway, but that's a completely different issue.)

Problems and Quirks

Index statistics from VALIDATE and COMPUTE/ESTIMATE STATISTICS are only relevant for B-tree indexes. The figures you get on bitmap indexes are meaningless.

Indexes on high-activity tables tend to degrade over time. It is important to recognize when this is a threat and when it does not matter. In many cases such indexes reach a steady state at roughly 75% efficiency. Provided this is a balanced 75%, you should probably live with this.

The cost of determining *in detail* the quality of an index is quite high—full index scans, possibly combined with shared locks on tables—so you cannot make frequent use of the best techniques.

Strategy Notes

A B-tree index can be as many as 32 columns wide, and a bitmap index can be as much as 30 columns wide (the two "missing" columns are taken up by the start and end rowids stored as part of the index key). However, you have to be under extreme stress to create an index with anything like this number of columns.

I haven't yet come across a system that needed to use two-column bitmap indexes, let alone 30-column bitmap indexes. Conversely, I often come across systems that have several single-column B-tree indexes in place when they ought to get rid of some of them and introduce a few multicolumn indexes.

The size of a bitmap index can change dramatically according to the way the rows are packed (a characteristic not displayed by B-tree indexes). If you have data that is most frequently accessed through a specific bitmap index, it may be worth rebuilding the data to produce a very small, highly desirable index. (Of course, packing the data will also reduce the number of different data blocks that have to be visited as well. The bitmap packing is just an added bonus.)

When you define a primary key/foreign key relationship between tables using constraints, it is often necessary to create an index on the foreign key columns to avoid locking problems. Specifically, when rows are deleted from the parent table, or the key of the parent table is updated, Oracle takes out a share lock on the child table if the foreign key is not indexed in some way. This often results in an excessive number of single-column indexes. Remember that if the parent is never going to be modified in this way then the child indexes do not need to exist, and the child indexes do not need to be an exact match for the parent key; they only need to start with the parent key columns. In this way, you can create a useful multicolumn index and cover a foreign key requirement at the same time.

> *Indexes to avoid lock contention on foreign keys are required only if you plan to update the parent key or delete parent rows. Indexes created for foreign keys only need to start with the foreign key columns. They can have more columns added to them.*

In OLTP systems, it is extremely important to be able to get to the correct data very efficiently. In other words, the correct set of high-precision (B-tree) indexes is critical. Naturally there is a trade-off to worry about. The more indexes you have on a table, the higher the overhead on inserts, deletes, and updates. However, any set of columns that is frequently used for data selection or table joining should be viewed as a candidate for indexing. The key questions when choosing indexes are

- Will a single key value return a small number of rows, thus improving query times?
- Will the index columns be updated with extreme regularity, degrading data load times?
- Will the index become inefficient over time, requiring maintenance windows for rebuilds?

You need to know enough about the data to be able to predict the way in which an index degrades over time. For example, although it is nice to have a 100% efficient index, it is an enormous waste of time and introduces an unnecessary risk of down-time to keep rebuilding an index that has a "natural" efficiency level of 75%. It is also deceptive to think that an index with an average efficiency of 90% is actually efficient at the point where it is being used most heavily. The opposite is also true. An index that has an average efficiency of only 10% may actually be very well packed in exactly the area where it is most used.

CHAPTER 7

Enhanced Indexing

As described in the last chapter, Oracle supports balanced B-tree indexes and bitmap indexes, and the implementation of indexing has changed only slowly over the last few years. Oracle 8.1 takes a dramatic leap forward both in features and effectiveness.

Oracle 8.1 introduces

- Compression on leading index columns to reduce the size of the index
- An option for storing values in descending order in the index
- An option for reducing the wasted space in bitmap indexes
- Indexes based on functions rather than pure data
- New optimizer capabilities for taking advantage of indexes
- Options for avoiding the impact of gross index administration

Oracle 8.1 also introduces user-defined operators and index types so that you can invent and code your own rapid-access paths into your own data, and include these access paths and costs in otherwise standard SQL statements. The SPATIAL DATA option and CONTEXT option are both implemented using this new extensibility feature; however, the need for extensibility is sufficiently exotic that I have excluded any comments on it from the scope of this book.

Compressed B-Trees

I have often found that some of the low-key, new features introduced by Oracle are much more useful than those that hit the headlines. Index compression is just such a feature.

Database performance depends so much on avoiding I/O that almost any mechanism for reducing I/O is bound to be beneficial. In the case of compressed indexes, the benefits are actually twofold: Not only does the index take up less space by holding more rowids per leaf block, but the resulting improvement in the index statistics increases the probability that the CBO will make use of the index.

An example of the command to create a compressed index is

```
create unique index prt_stk_val_idx on portfolio_holdings (
    portfolio_code,
    valuation_date,
    stock_code
)
compress 2
;
```

This statement creates a unique index on the three columns specified, but eliminates duplicate copies of the first two columns from each leaf block of the index by holding them in a special "prefix" area of the block. For a nonunique index you can compress all columns, for a unique index the maximum number of columns you can compress is one less than the number of columns in the index, but for bitmap indexes you can't use compression (there wouldn't be any benefit anyway). Figure 7-1 shows how a leaf block might look in this index.

The PORTFOLIO_HOLDINGS table in the example above may give you a hint about when compression may be especially useful. The table lists for

Actual Key Values			Representation when compressed		
			Prefix #0:	PFL1,26-Jun-1999	6 rows
			Prefix #1:	PFL1,27-Jun-1999	6 rows
PFL1,	26-Jun-1999,	AMZN	Entry #0:	AMZN	prefix #0
PFL1,	26-Jun-1999,	GLXO.L	Entry #1:	GLXO.L	prefix #0
PFL1,	26-Jun-1999,	IBM	Entry #2:	IBM	prefix #0
PFL1,	26-Jun-1999,	MSFT	Entry #3:	MSFT	prefix #0
PFL1,	26-Jun-1999,	ORCL	Entry #4:	ORCL	prefix #0
PFL1,	26-Jun-1999,	VOD.L	Entry #5:	VOD.L	prefix #0
PFL1,	27-Jun-1999,	AMZN	Entry #6:	AMZN	prefix #1
PFL1,	27-Jun-1999,	GLXO.L	Entry #7:	GLXO.L	prefix #1
PFL1,	27-Jun-1999,	IBM	Entry #8:	IBM	prefix #1
PFL1,	27-Jun-1999,	MSFT	Entry #9:	MSFT	prefix #1
PFL1,	27-Jun-1999,	ORCL	Entry #10:	ORCL	prefix #1
PFL1,	27-Jun-1999,	VOD.L	Entry #11:	VOD.L	prefix #1

Figure 7-1. Benefits of compressed leaf blocks in an index.

each portfolio, for each date, a list of the stocks in the portfolio with quantity and other details. This example is an approximation of a situation in a broker's back-office system designed for a broker with a select number of very wealthy clients. There are only a couple of hundred portfolios, each portfolio holds a couple of hundred stocks, many of the most commonly traded stocks appear in all the portfolios, and the data is kept for a couple of years only.

None of the columns in the table produces a particularly useful index by itself, and the multicolumn index above which was the optimum solution to address the most common user queries was rather large. The CBO tended to avoid using it even though the data clustering factor was very good. (In fact, the nature of the table was such that three single-column bitmap indexes would have been the best idea, but the table was subject to fairly frequent insertions and deletions, so bitmap indexes were not viable.)

By compressing the first two columns, each value for (portfolio_code, valuation_date) appeared only once per leaf block. The impact was dramatic. The size of the index was halved, and the change was sufficient to ensure that the CBO used it without needing any hints in the code.

> *Every nonunique index should be examined, and every multicolumn unique index should be checked for possible storage benefits from compression.*

Index compression leads to an interesting change in indexing strategy. In earlier versions of Oracle it was taken as gospel that a multicolumn index should start with the most selective column. (This directive was actually a bit misleading because it is obviously more important to start the index with a column that will be used in the query. The most selective column may be a column that is used only occasionally.)

I believe the standard argument in favor of this directive was that Oracle would be able to find the target row more efficiently if the first column tested was highly selective. This may have been true in Oracle version 5, which used an interesting index compression mechanism, but I doubt if there was actually much benefit in any version between Oracle 6.0 and Oracle 8.0.6. The space required for the leaf blocks of an index is independent of the ordering of the columns in the index definition. The number of steps that a binary chop needs to locate an index entry in a block is also independent of the ordering of the columns in the index.

In Oracle versions 6 to 8.0.6, the only thing affected by the ordering of the columns is the degree to which the branch-level entries can be trimmed. If the columns are ordered with the most selective first, then the size of each branch entry can be trimmed to the absolute minimum. Thus, fewer branch blocks would be needed in the index and very occasionally this could result in one branch layer less. Because branch blocks usually form a very small fraction of the total block count in an index, I would be surprised if this side effect of column ordering ever made much difference.

In Oracle 8.1, the situation is completely reversed. The space savings from compressing an index with a low-selectivity leading edge can be huge. Given the usual proviso that the leading columns of an index should be the ones that are used most frequently in queries, I am inclined to believe that a multicolumn index should be created with the least selective columns at the front to pack the leaf blocks into minimal space.

A particularly useful case for compressing indexes is in the primary key/foreign key trap (see Chapter 6). Given the nature of Oracle's enqueuing mechanism for locks, even very occasional updates to a parent table can result in a lot of time wasted on enqueues if the foreign key columns in the child table are not indexed. On the other hand, an index created on a child table purely for primary key/foreign key contention reasons is often a completely useless index for query purposes, and a huge waste of space. If you find that you *do* have to create a useless index to represent a foreign key, make sure that you compress it. The saved space is likely to be significant.

To identify compressed indexes, there are two columns in the view family xxx_INDEXES. The column called COMPRESSION is set to ENABLED if the index is compressed, and the column called PREFIX_LENGTH tells you how many columns have been defined as prefix columns.

The view INDEX_STATS (see Chapter 6) also has some new columns in it to deal with compression. There are PRE_ROWS and PRE_ROWS_LEN, which tell you about the number and storage requirement of prefixes that appear in your index. Comparing these values with LF_ROWS and LF_ROWS_LEN gives you an idea of the effectiveness of using compression. For example, with the figures

LF_ROWS = 6,803	LF_ROWS_LEN = 74,883
PRE_ROWS = 538	PRE_ROWS_LEN = 5,378

you can estimate that each prefix is approximately 5,378/538 = 10 bytes, and you have eliminated 6,803 − 538 = 6,265 duplicates of this prefix (in other words, 62,650 bytes in index leaf space has been saved by using compression, which is large compared with the 74,883 bytes needed for the rest of the leaf entries). As a rough guideline, it takes only a small prefix repeated a small number of times to make compression worthwhile, especially if the average index entry size is quite small anyway. In the example we have a 10-byte prefix repeated approximately 13 times each on an index entry that averages roughly 21 bytes, which is why the figures look so very good.

The INDEX_STATS view is not quite up to date with handling prefixes. Two of the columns produce slightly spurious numbers. In the first case, ROWS_PER_KEY can fall slightly below one. More significantly, PCT_USED does not accommodate the fact that some space in leaf blocks is used by prefixes, so you need to calculate your own PCT_USED as (LF_ROWS_LEN + BR_ROWS_LEN + PRE_ROWS_LEN)/BTREE_SPACE.

As with all new features, there are side effects to worry about when using compression. In the first place, there is a slight increase in CPU usage because Oracle has to scan through the list of prefixes to find the required prefix and the starting position of the first leaf entry for that prefix. Perhaps more important is the fact that the more leaf entries you pack into a block, the higher the probability that two transactions will need to change the same block at the same time. If you change a mission-critical index from uncompressed to compressed, it is worth checking that you do not experience an increase in "buffer busy waits" or "enqueue waits." There is little you can do about the former, other than reducing the compression on the index, but you might be able to address the latter by increasing INITRANS on the index.

There is also a trap to watch out for with partitioned tables (see Chapter 12). You can compress the indexes on a partitioned table, but all partitions have to have the same degree of compression. Unfortunately, it is possible to exchange a partition with a table that has the wrong degree of compression on its local indexes. Nothing goes wrong until the next time you hit the index, at which point the session crashes with an ORA-00600 error. I think we can assume that at some future date Oracle will produce a suitable warning when you try the exchange.

Minimize Records per Block

In the same vein as index compression, Oracle has supplied an option to reduce the size of bitmap indexes. In our previous discussion of bitmap indexes (see Chapter 6), I put forward the conjecture that Oracle assumes that every block in the table is capable of holding roughly (block_size/12) rows as the basis for a bitmap index. This introduces an overhead that gets quite significant if the number of rows in the block is actually very small. To address this situation, Oracle allows you to specify the maximum number of rows that should ever appear in a single block. The command has to be used after the table has been populated but before any bitmap indexes have been built. The syntax is

```
alter table XXX minimize records_per_block;
```

Oracle scans the table to determine the current maximum (yes, I know it says minimize in the command) number of rows, or more specifically the size of the largest row directory, that has ever appeared in a block for that table and records the result in the data dictionary so that it can ensure that no subsequent inserts break this limit. The bitmap indexes are then built to match this number of bits per block rounded up to the nearest multiple of eight. The effect of this is to eliminate a number of bytes that would otherwise be in the bitmap to represent large chains of zeros and redundant check summing.

The following samples show an entry in a bitmap index for the same rowid range before and after minimize. The index is on a six-block table with 16 rows in each block. The key value to which this entry in the index applies follows a pattern of three "hits" followed by nine "misses" eight times in a row. The three consecutive hits show up quite clearly in the 0x07 and 0x70 patterns; the rest of the string is compression information and some form of "checksumming" every 8 bytes. As you can see, the difference is quite significant:

```
Without Minimize - 19 bytes to represent 96 rows
    c9 07 70 f8 10 07 f8 0f 70 f9 10 07 70 f8 10 07 f8 0f 70

Minimize - 12 bytes to represent 96 rows.
    cf 07 70 00 07 70 00 07 70 d1 07 70
```

As with index compression, you could argue that this puts us into the situation in which a much larger number of table rows are covered by a much smaller number of index blocks. Consequently, there is a higher probability of two processes trying to update rows that are represented in the same index block. In practice, of course, you should not be creating bitmap indexes on tables that are subject to concurrent inserts/deletes anyway, so the issue is somewhat spurious.

Descending Indexes

It has been possible in the past to include the reserved word DESC (for descending) in the command to create indexes. Prior to Oracle 8.1 this was included to allow compatibility with DB2 syntax, but was completely ignored.

However you can now choose whether each column in an index should be stored in ascending or descending order:

```
create index desc_demo_i on desc_demo (owner, object_name desc);
```

This command creates an index with the OWNER column sorted in ascending order (the default) but the OBJECT_NAME sorted by descending order within OWNER. Oracle achieves this with a funny little fix-up to the data. The value for OBJECT_NAME is converted to something like its "ones complement," which is then stored in ascending order. The nature of the conversion ensures that the ordering is equivalent to storing the actual value in descending order. As an example, the value DUAL would normally be stored as the set of four bytes

```
0x44, 0x55, 0x41, 0x4C,
```

but this is converted to the five bytes

```
0xBB, 0xAA, 0xBE, 0xB3, 0xFF
```

Note especially the apparently redundant 0xFF at the end. Indexes with descending columns are slightly larger than the ascending equivalent. To explain the extra 0xFF, consider the value DUALITY, which in a descending index should be stored physically before the value DUAL (Table 7-1).

Table 7-1. Why the Extra Byte?

Value	Bytes	One's Complement
DUAL	44, 55, 41, 4C	BB, AA, BE, B3
DUALITY	44, 55, 41, 4C, 49, 54, 59	BB, AA, BE, B3, B6, AB, A6

As you can see, the pure byte-by-byte one's complement for DUAL still sorts numerically above the value for DUALITY, until you attach FF to the end of it, which allows you to compare FF with B6 in the corresponding position of the value for DUALITY.

If you examine the view families xxx_INDEXES, xxx_IND_COLUMNS, and xxx_IND_EXPRESSIONS, you will find that the index type is function based. The indexed column has a name like SYS_NCnnnnn$ and is identified as a DESC column; the expression for the column is the column name. However, you do not need to use the special system or session parameters normally required to take advantage of function-based indexes. You do need to ensure that the CBO is invoked for queries against this table, as the RBO is not able to handle descending indexes; consequently you may need to use the *analyze* command to generate statistics on the table and index.

Why might you want to have descending indexes, or descending columns in indexes? Primarily to avoid sorting. Sorting can be expensive, in both CPU use and I/O. The optimizer is increasingly able to recognize options for avoiding sorting, and one of the more obvious examples of this is the simple ORDER BY clause. With the index (owner, object_name desc) defined earlier, we could write a query of the following form and would find that Oracle would use the index to achieve a NOSORT order by

```
select * from desc_demo
where owner = 'SYS'
order by object_name desc
;
```

In earlier versions of Oracle we could not have avoided the sort. In fact, even with an ascending ORDER BY and an ascending index, the optimizer would not have been able to spot the option for ordering the rows without sorting unless we had included both index columns in the ORDER BY clause. In other words, we would have needed to write

```
select * from asc_demo
where owner = 'SYS'
order by owner, object_name
;
```

You may think that queries such as

```
select    max(object_name)
from      desc_demo2
where     owner = 'ORDPLUGINS';
```

would also benefit from a descending index, especially in the correlated subquery form so often used to find "the most recent occurrence of":

```
select * from data_table
where {main conditions}
```

```
and date_relevent = (
            select max(date_relevant)
            from data_table
            where {main conditions repeated}
    );
```

Unfortunately, this is not (yet) the case. Oracle 8.1 has a new optimization method for finding the minimum/maximum values in some cases of this form (the conditions in the subquery must allow for an index-only solution), which does not work if the critical column is indexed in descending order. The key feature of the execution path appears as

```
INDEX (RANGE SCAN (MIN/MAX))OF . . .
```

This new optimization method can in some cases eliminate the need for the INDEX_DESC hint combined with rownum = 1 and a carefully crafted index that otherwise had to be used to make this type of query efficient:

```
select * from data_table
where {main conditions}
and date_relevent = (
            select /*+ index_desc(dt dti) */
                    date_relevant
            from data_table dt
            where {main conditions repeated}
            and rownum = 1
    );
```

Thus you have the usual problem of deciding which of two benefits you want to take—the NO SORT ORDER BY, if you do use descending indexes, or the no-hints max() you can now get through the new optimizer method if you don't use a descending index. Personally I feel very uncomfortable using the INDEX_DESC hint because it requires exactly the right index to exist with exactly the right name. There is no easy dependency tracking method that ensures that one day someone won't decide to rename, or restructure, the index with the terrible consequence that everything still works but produces the wrong answers.

I have already discussed the way in which attempting to insert a new index entry in a full block will not necessarily split the block in the middle (see Chapter 6). In particular I pointed out that an entry at the top end of an index, caused perhaps by an ascending sequence, will not split the block at all whereas an entry at the bottom end of the index, caused perhaps by a descending sequence, will split the block in the middle. In the best case, an index populated by an ascending sequence will be 100% efficient whereas an index populated by a descending sequence will be 50% efficient. This introduces a curious quirk of descending indexes: If you have a system that, for whatever reason, happens to generate data in a naturally descending order, you could consider indexing it with a *descending* index, on the basis that the index would actually be built on ascending values and therefore would pack at 100% efficiency.

A couple of other points to bear in mind with descending indexes. You cannot create descending indexes that are reversed or bitmapped, not that there would be much point in doing so anyway. Also, you may not see much effect from using them anyway in small to medium-size datasets unless you have FIRST_ROWS optimization as your goal. Several of the special index-based optimization mechanisms tend to get bypassed in favor of table scans and sorts if you are running with ALL_ROWS optimization.

Reverse Key Indexes

I have heard a suggestion that reverse key indexes were introduced by Oracle Corporation to reduce a contention problem caused by the Oracle Parallel Server (OPS) (see Chapter 22) when an application used a meaningless sequential key and multiple nodes were involved in concurrent inserts.

Imagine that you have four different nodes trying to insert four new rows into a table with an existing 1,000,000 rows. The latest key values acquired from the four sequence caches on the four different nodes are 1000021, 1000041, 100061, and 100081. By setting up multiple free lists you can ensure that the four rows are inserted into four separate table blocks, but it seems inevitable that all four index entries will go into the same index leaf block so, apart from "buffer busy wait" contention, the four insert processes will experience a massive delay as the single block is "pinged" from node to node, at a couple of hundredths of a second per ping.

Why is a reverse key supposed to help? Look at the internal dumps of the values in Table 7-2. (If you want to view other values, you can select the expression at the head of each column from DUAL. The reverse() function is an undocumented function that has been around since at least version 7.3.)

It seems obvious that reverse key indexes will make a big difference to collisions on the index leaf. All four entries in the center, unreversed column are close to identical and therefore are likely to end up in the same index leaf block, whereas the entries in the right-hand, reversed column start with completely different values.

Table 7-2.   Reversing Sequences

Value	Dump(value,16)	Dump(reverse(value),16)
1000021	C4,2,1,1,16	16,1,1,2,C4
1000041	C4,2,1,1,2A	2A,1,1,2,C4
1000062	C4,2,1,1,3E	3E,1,1,2,C4
1000081	C4,2,1,1,52	52,1,1,2,C4

Looks can, of course, be deceiving. Without reversal, these particular key values are indeed likely to end up in the same block, and there is likely to be a collision of close keys indefinitely. However, although the reversed keys may not collide currently, what happens if there are more nodes in the system? Add another two nodes and you'll find that node 6 is inserting rows with values from 10000121, which reverses to 16,2,1,2,C4 and you are back in collision territory again.

Of course reversal does seem to reduce the amount of contention. With six nodes involved we have only one or two areas of contention instead of all six colliding with each other nonstop. But this is dictated to a large degree by the fact that the sequence cache size is 20. A different cache size results in a different pattern of contention, and changes in rates of insertion on different nodes can result in patterns of contention appearing and disappearing fairly randomly. (Actually you wouldn't use a cache size of 20 on an OPS system anyway, otherwise the SYS.SEQ$ table would be a severe point of pinging. It is surprising how many "performance" problems are actually caused by using default values when creating objects.)

What alternatives are there? How about setting the sequence cache size to 1,000,000? The four nodes would then be inserting values such as those presented in Table 7-3.

Although there would be a set of collisions on the first hundred or so inserts, very rapidly the different nodes would be inserting leaf entries into different leaves in the index, with a guarantee of virtually no contention ever appearing again! The "problem" of sequence-based primary keys causing pinging on OPS systems is one of understanding how sequences and indexes work, and is not an inherent issue.

Unfortunately, the contention problem is not the only one to consider. What about efficiency of storage? I mentioned in Chapter 6 that an ascending

Table 7-3. Sequences with a Large CACHE Value

Value	Dump(value)
1000001 .. 1000002	C4, 2, 1, 1, 2 .. C4, 2, 1, 1, 3
2000001 .. 2000002	C4, 3, 1, 1, 2 .. C4, 3, 1, 1, 3
3000001 .. 3000002	C4, 4, 1, 1, 2 .. C4, 4, 1, 1, 3
4000001 .. 4000002	C5, 5, 1, 1, 2 .. C4, 5, 1, 1, 3

sequence as a key would result in a packed index except under Oracle Parallel Server. The reason why the index is not packed under OPS is that the entries are *not* inserted in ascending order because each node has a local cache with its own section of the sequence. The upshot of this is that the index behaves in an undesirable fashion.

Emulating the simple sequence with a default cache of 20 across four nodes from the previous example, the index efficiency for a reversed key runs at roughly 66% after an insert of 40,000 rows, and on a nonreversed key it runs at approximately 69%. Bumping the cache size up to 1,000,000 drops the efficiency to 57% and 61% respectively.

In summary, using sequences or any other monotonically increasing value as a key under OPS is a bad thing. You either get caught by pinging on the leading leaf blocks or you get caught by enormous amounts of wasted space in the index. It isn't necessary to reverse the key to avoid the pinging, and doing so makes the storage problem worse anyway.

On nonparallel systems with multiple, concurrent processes inserting at high rates, the argument is slightly less clearcut. If you don't reverse the key you get a very well packed index and the possibility of "buffer busy waits" on the leading leaf block; if you reverse the key you avoid the "buffer busy waits" but waste a lot of space. There is, however, a potential solution to this conundrum, offered by hash and composite partitioning, which I discuss in Chapter 12. This solution offers the option of well-packed indexes and no contention.

Personally, I wouldn't bother to reverse the index until I could prove that "buffer busy waits" were a real problem (see Appendix B for notes on checking X$KCBFWAIT to identify the file in which they are occurring, and V$SYSTEM_EVENT for lost time).

Apart from my inclination to avoid doing something new unless I can put a number to the benefit, one reason for avoiding reverse keys for sequences is that it introduces an I/O overhead if you are interested in data that is clustered by time. Rows that were created at a similar time are, in the absence of deletions, usually physically close to each other in the table, but by reversing the index we use to get to the data we run the risk of scattering the relevant index blocks—an interesting reversal of the more common arrangement in which table entries are scattered but their index entries are colocated!

There are a couple of real drawbacks to using reversed indexes. Perhaps the one to be most careful of is that you cannot use them for SQL involving single-column ranges (for example, *colX between 99 and 101*). I suspect that this is probably not going to be a big issue, however, because the reason for using reverse keys is to sort out a potential performance issue with sequences as meaningless keys, and who wants to do a range scan on a meaningless key? Be warned though that you definitely do *not* want to reverse a key that is an extended time stamp, otherwise you lose the option for efficient queries like "what happened just after 5:30 P.M.?"

It is important to note that Oracle will still be able to use RANGE SCAN optimization on reversed indexes when you specify suitable conditions on the leading columns of a *multicolumn* index. This is because each column of the index is reversed separately, so the two-column entry (27th Dec 1999, 354) becomes

```
'77, C7, 0C, 1B, 01, 01, 01'   'C2, 04, 37'
```

which reverses to

```
'01, 01, 01, 1B, 0C, C7, 77'   '37, 04, C2'
```

and not

```
'37, 04,C2, 01, 01, 01, 1B, 0C, C7, 77'
```

Consequently, a query of the form date_col = to_date('27-dec-1999','dd-mon-yyyy') can use an index range scan to find all the relevant rows colocated in the index.

If you need to identify reversed indexes, their INDEX_TYPE in the view family xxx_INDEXES will be reported as NORMAL/REV.

Function-Based Indexes

Of course, the biggest fanfare on indexing came with the introduction of function-based indexes. Until version 8.1, an index could be created only on data of one or more columns exactly as it was stored in the database. In version 8.1, you can create an index on a "virtual column," which may be derived from other data.

Built-in Functions

As a starting point, let's examine that most common of indexing problems: How do I handle case-insensitive queries in Oracle? Consider a table with a column (NAME VARCHAR2(30)), which can be entered in mixed case but is often queried in uppercase. How do you make all queries efficient?

The snappy answer, of course, is that you've got a design error in the system and the users should be trained properly and pay the penalty if they get it wrong. The realistic answer, however, is that special cases do occur in data. People are fallible, and typing iMstakes mistakes are easy to make. Consequently, you sometimes need to have a "canonical" form of the entered data for query purposes, even though you use the entered form for reporting.

There used to be four basic solutions to the problem:

1. Put a check constraint on the column so users can't enter mixed-case data.
2. Create insert and update triggers on the table to change the column to uppercase.
3. Create insert and update triggers on the table to convert the column to uppercase and store it in an extra column on the table. Index the extra column and make sure that all queries use this secondary column.
4. Live with slow, table-scanning queries of the form "where upper(name) = FRED."

With Oracle 8.1, you now take the last option, but make it go faster by creating an index on upper(name):

```
create index peo_uppername_idx on person peo(upper(peo.name));
```

When you issue the command, Oracle creates a hidden column in the table definition (in SYS.COL$) with a name like SYS_NC0004$, and gives that column a default value—in this case, UPPER("NAME"). For regular users, this information can be seen through the view family xxx_IND_EXPRESSSIONS, and the index will be marked as index_type FUNCTION-BASED NORMAL in the view family xxx_INDEXES.

Before you can create function-based indexes, you must have the system privilege QUERY REWRITE, or if you plan to create this type of index against tables in other schemas, GLOBAL QUERY REWRITE.

To be able to make use of this index, you need to set the init.ora parameter QUERY_REWRITE_ENABLED to TRUE either at the session level or at the system level, and you need to ensure that the CBO is going to be invoked; hence you may need to analyze the table to generate statistics.

Once this is done, the expression upper(name) behaves almost identically to an ordinary column as far as optimization is concerned. Queries such as

```
select * from person where upper(name) = 'FRED';
select * from person where upper(name) like 'SM%';
```

use the index to access the data as rapidly as possible. Of course, it is possible that the optimizer will decide that the query for 'SM%' will return far too many rows and will ignore the index, particularly if you have built a histogram on the index with the *analyze table estimate statistics for all indexed columns* command. Bear in mind, of course, that the index won't be used for the simpler query

```
select * from person where name = 'FRED JONES';
```

If you "apply a function" to the expression (for example, substr(upper (name,1,20)), Oracle cannot (usually) take advantage of the index. Of course if you regularly need to apply this function to the expression, perhaps you have picked the wrong expression for indexing. It is perfectly legal to index complex expressions.

You can also index using arithmetic expressions such as colX × colY + sqrt(5). (Mathematicians will be pleased to note that Oracle will recognize in a subsequent query that this is actually the same as sqrt(5) + colY × colX; however, the usual rules apply in that Oracle is not quite clever enough to note that the following two predicates are the same. The first will be able to use the index; the second won't:

```
where   colX + colY + sqrt(5) = 77
where   colX + colY = 77-sqrt(5)
```

Another convenience of function-based indexes based on built-in functions is that SQL*Loader understands them and maintains them properly, even using direct load—and that's a benefit that you can't get from using triggers with a real derived column.

There are discrepancies and odd little problems, however, and you should not assume that anything you can do with a normal index will also work *currently* with a simple function-based index. You should always test very carefully any assumption you make about how a function-based index may work. These discrepancies are basically optimizer options that exist for normal indexes but have not yet been coded for function-based indexes. Consider, for example, the queries

```
select state, count(*) from person group by state;
select upper(name), count(*) from person group by upper(name);
```

The first query can use an INDEX ONLY mechanism if "state" is indexed, producing a "sort group by (nosort)" execution path. But even though we have created an index on upper(name), for the second query Oracle will use a table scan and will evaluate the expression for every row before sorting and aggregating. Similarly, there are examples in which a query based on a normal index will be able to use an "index (fast full scan)" to acquire the results most efficiently, whereas the equivalent query on a function-based index will fall back to a normal "index (range scan)." Finally, as we have already seen in the section on descending indexes, the special MIN/MAX() optimization will not work with function-based indexes.

> *There are several optimization options missing from the current implementation of function-based indexes. However, just because an expected feature does not appear in this release won't stop it from appearing in the next.*

One little trap to watch out for, which is very simple but very easy to overlook, is the following: Consider the example in which you create an index on upper(name). Remember that a predicate

```
where   name = 'FRED'
```

will not be able to use the index. To get the correct result and an efficient indexed access path, you have to use a degree of redundancy, like

```
where   upper(name) = 'FRED'
and     name = 'FRED'
```

User-Defined Functions

A function-based index is not restricted to simple expressions and Oracle built-ins. You can write your own functions in PL/SQL (or Java or C callouts) and create indexes based on them. For example, if you had an accounting package and needed to query data based on "future value," you might create a package containing a PL/SQL function called FV with input parameters of RATE, PERIODS, and PAYMENTS.

If you then had a table INVESTMENTS, with columns including (. . . RATES, PERIODS, PAYMENTS, . . .), you could create an index on "investments (fv(rates, periods, payments))" and write queries like

```
select
        investment_name,
        acquisition_date,
        fv(rates, period, payments) forward_value
from    investments
where   fv(rates, period, payments) > 100000
order by
        fv(rates, period, payments) desc
;
```

In this case, the optimizer would be able to use the function-based index to access the data very quickly, and despite the function apparently being called three times per row (WHERE clause, SELECT clause, and ORDER BY clause), Oracle may never call the function at all.

Function-based indexes based on user-defined functions behave just like function-based indexes on built-in functions, but there are a few problems with administration, which are largely to do with the privileges needed to see them and use them.

As with built-ins, you need the privilege (GLOBAL) QUERY REWRITE to be allowed to create a function-based index, and you need the init.ora parameter QUERY_REWRITE_ENABLED to be set to TRUE for the optimizer to be able to use the function-based index in queries, although any inserts, updates, and deletes you do will maintain the index properly even if this parameter is not set to TRUE.

You also need to have another parameter set properly to be able use the index—the QUERY_REWRITE_INTEGRITY parameter, which has to be set to the value TRUSTED. This, unfortunately, could become a bit of a problem because the same parameter is also highly significant to materialized views (see Chapter 23), and you might want to set it to

STALE_TOLERATED or ENFORCED for the purpose of using materialized views.

The next thing you have to do is ensure that the function you create is
defined as *deterministic*. Essentially Oracle has to believe that if it calls the
function again and again with the same input parameters, it will always get the
same answer. Oracle makes no attempt to check that you are telling the truth
when you use this key word. Once you've claimed that the function is deterministic, you can do what you like inside it. An example of an extremely non-
deterministic function is

```
create or replace function fv (
    i_rate      in      number,
    i_periods   in      number,
    i_payment   in      number
)
return number deterministic - this is the key word
as
begin
    -- how untrue can you get
    return to_number(to_char(sysdate,'yyyymmddhh24miss'));
end;
/
```

Once you can create and use the function-based index in your own
schema, you need to ensure that other users can do so as well. To do this you
may choose to grant EXECUTE on the function, and possibly create a synonym for the function (or package if it is packaged). One of the little features
of function-based indexes is that the function could be a method of an object
type (see Chapter 15), in which case anyone who can execute the type can
execute the function. If the function is a stand-alone function, though, there is
a better way of exposing it, and one that is safer anyway: Create a view on top
of the table that adds an extra column definition and is structured to make the
correct call to the function. From our previous example we could generate

```
create or replace view investments_v
as
select
        investment_name, rates, period, payments,
        acquisition_date,
        fv(rates, period, payments) forward_value
from    investments
;
```

There are three good reasons for doing this when using user-defined, function-based indexes. First, it removes the need to worry about making the function visible and granting the execute privilege. Second, it ensures that the function is always "called correctly" by the user. After all, the user only needs to type in a column name and doesn't have to remember function_name(parameter, . . .). Third, there is a nasty little trap with functions returning character types that this approach eliminates.

If a PL/SQL function returns a string, the string is always implicitly 4,000 bytes. So if you try to create an index on a PL/SQL function that returns a string, you are likely to hit Oracle error "ORA-01450: maximum key length (nnn) exceeded" unless you are using at least a 16K block size. Consequently, if you want an index on a string function, you actually need to build it on something like "substr(plsql_string_function,1,40)." The probability of users remembering to query on the right substring size is vanishingly small (and one day you might want to change it anyway).

> *Strings returned by PL/SQL functions are always 4,000 bytes long. You must substr() them if you want to use them in indexes.*

There is, unfortunately, a psychological drawback to hiding the function inside a view. Compare the following two SQL fragments:

```
where     pl_sql_function(colX) like '%xy%';
where     view_column like '%xy%';
```

In the first case, the visibility of the function is a warning that the code will have to do a table scan and call a function for each row. In the second case, the overhead appears to be "just" a table scan. It is possible to make things look too easy, and pay a massive performance penalty as a result.

So you've got everything sorted out, permissions are correct, the indexed virtual column is visible through a view, and everything works, although the usual restrictions about function-based indexes not doing everything that normal indexes do still hold. What can go wrong?

There's always the possibility of the function becoming temporarily invalid—for example, the specification of the package that contains the function may be recompiled. In this case the index is immediately disabled (check column FUNCIDX_STATUS in view family xxx_INDEXES). Any attempt to insert or delete data, or update index-related columns will fail with error "ORA-30554: function-based index XXX is disabled," unless the session parameter SKIP_UNUSABLE_INDEXES has been set to TRUE, and select statements that try to use the index will fail.

To recover from this, you need to issue the command to reenable the index. If the index is still valid (in particular, this means that no one has been inserting unindexed data by taking advantage of the SKIP_UNUSABLE_INDEXES parameter), and the function has not changed too much (essentially the input and output parameters have to be the same types in the same order), then the index can be marked as enabled with the following command, and normal processing can continue with minimum disruption:

```
alter index func_idx enable;
```

However, you may find that it is not possible simply to reenable the index, in which case you may need to drop the index and re-create it. This means that Oracle may start using the view to call the function directly, once per row, using a table scan, until you can rebuild the index. The index rebuild itself is a problem because it is an operation that locks the table until it completes, because function-based indexes cannot yet be built on-line.

> *A function-based index can be a wonderful aid to performance, but if it becomes "broken" the overheads while re-creating it are enormous.*

Administration

DBAs tend to spend quite a lot of time, and justifiably so, worrying about the efficiency of their indexing. In the past, it was often difficult to find suitable moments when you could do something about an inefficient index. Apart from the major new structural features available in indexes, Oracle 8.1 also introduces a number of administrative options aimed at reducing the burden of ensuring that indexes operate at a reasonable degree of efficiency.

Rebuild

The most obviously eye-catching of the new administrative aids is the option to rebuild an index while the table it references is still subject to all normal activity—including inserts, updates, and deletes. The basic syntax is

```
alter index XXX rebuild online;
```

While doing the rebuild you can choose to change various physical attributes such as storage parameters and tablespace. To save time and redo writes, the rebuild can also be specified as NOLOGGING:

```
alter index ZZZ rebuild online
tablespace users
nologging
pctfree 0
parallel 2
;
```

There are a few restrictions on this—some documented and some not. You cannot do an on-line rebuild of bitmap indexes, reversed indexes, LOB indexes, the secondary indexes on an index-organized table (see Chapter 14), or on function-based indexes (which includes indexes with descending columns). Despite indications in the "tram tracks" to the contrary, you cannot specify a degree of compression for an index while rebuilding it on-line, although you can remove the compression with the NOCOMPRESS command.

The other thing to bear in mind is that an on-line index rebuild requires two moments when there are no active transactions on the table: One moment is needed to start the rebuild and another is needed to end the rebuild. These moments could be quite hard to find on (say) a database of the automatic OLTP type with very large numbers of transactions. Unfortunately it is currently not possible to see what the process is waiting for, so the usual step of checking V$LOCK when a process appears to be hanging doesn't help, although V$SESSION_WAIT does at least show a wait for a null event.

There is also the problem that an on-line index rebuild requires three sets of storage space to be in existence at a time: the original index, the rebuilt index, and a logging segment (actually an index-organized table with a name like SYS_JOURNAL_nnnnn stored in the tablespace into which the rebuild is going) that is needed to allow DML on the base table to continue while the index is rebuilt. This could mean *a lot* of extra space that has to be made available temporarily.

To check whether an index is in the process of being rebuilt, check the view family xxx_INDEXES to see if the STATUS column reads INPROGRS. This status flag allows SMON to cut in and clean up the mess if an instance failure occurs in the middle of rebuild.

Coalesce

An alternative to rebuilding an index is to coalesce the index. In Chapter 6 I pointed out how indexes could become very inefficient because Oracle does not automatically merge adjacent leaf blocks that are nearly empty. In version 8.1, this issue is addressed through the *coalesce* command:

```
alter index XXX coalesce;
```

Unlike the *rebuild* command, *coalesce* does not demand extra space to maintain two copies of the index, nor is there any problem of locking tables and shutting out users. The *coalesce* command works by stepping through the index leaf blocks one at a time, and merging adjacent blocks if their total space usage is (roughly) inside the limit prescribed by the original PCTREE setting of the index.

This is done in a series of separate, recursive, but otherwise fairly ordinary transactions of relatively small size. This means that (1) the process tends to complete, (2) the process does not lock out other processing for any significant length of time but the process generates a lot of rollback and redo log, and (3) the process reads every leaf block in the index one at a time. To avoid waiting for other transactions, Oracle skips over any blocks that register uncommitted transactions.

The upshot of this is that the process can be quite expensive, although the expense can be spread over a long period of time, and it is noninvasive. There does seem to be an odd bug in the code, however, that causes Oracle to leave the job incomplete. I have seen coalesces clean and rewrite every block in the index, but only coalesce the first few blocks. Although this doesn't appear to do any damage, and is self-correcting if you repeat the coalesce, it does waste time, redo, and rollback.

One of the nicest things about the *coalesce* command is that it works in numerous cases when an on-line rebuild is not possible—for example, with reversed indexes and descending indexes. Whenever you find you cannot do an on-line rebuild, check whether *coalesce* is a viable option.

Statistics

One nice touch added to the *rebuild* command (whether on-line or off-line) is to compute statistics at the same time, so you no longer have to endure a two-stage, time-consuming process. Unfortunately, this breaks down on index-organized tables (see Chapter 14) and their secondary indexes even when done off-line.

The option to compute statistics is also available as part of the *create index* command, and again it fails for index-organized tables.

Rename

Another cute little addition to the *alter index* command is the option to change the name of the index. I have to admit that I've only just discovered this feature, even though it slipped in at Oracle 8.0:

```
alter index badly_named_index rename to brt_pk;
```

I like indexes to have names I can understand. So many of the object support indexes that Oracle needs end up with meaningless names, thus this command is extremely useful. Unfortunately there are some system-generated indexes that cannot be altered in any way (for example, LOB INDEX segments), so you have to find some other way of remembering what indexes with names like SYS_IL0000016847C00005$$ represent (in this case the LOB index for the LOB defined as column 5 of object 16847), or remember to give them meaningful names in the *create* statements that let you do so.

Optimization

One of the most common complaints about the CBO is that it frequently seems to choose table scans with merge joins or hash joins when the user knows, and can prove, that a nested loop join with an index would be much more efficient.

This is often the result of administrative issues rather than any significant fault with the optimizer. Typically these are issues such as the following:

- The optimizer mode has been set to CHOOSE, which is effectively equivalent to ALL_ROWS, which happens to favor table scans and hash/merge joins.
- Various init.ora parameters are unsuitable (for example, SORT_AREA_SIZE_SIZE or DB_FILE_MULTIBLOCK_READ_COUNT are unrealistically high), making the optimizer value the cost of table-scans and hash/merge joins too cheaply.
- The statistics on tables or indexes are out of date, particularly those indicating low or high values for columns, or those indicating the size of the object.

■ There are columns involved that have highly skewed data distributions, and the columns have not had histograms generated to allow Oracle to identify the skew.

■ Columns that need histograms are being targeted by SQL that uses bind variables, which make the histograms unusable.

However, when all other options have been rejected, there is one fundamental pattern of behavior that makes the CBO overestimate the cost of using indexes: the optimizer doesn't assume that data loaded in the early stages of a query may still be buffered during the later stages of the query. Consequently, it will produce an estimate of how many data blocks will have to be loaded into the buffer without allowing for the fact that some of the block loads will actually be "reuse" and will not require a real, expensive, physical read to take place.

The easiest way to see this is with a simple example of a carefully crafted nested loops join. I start with an indexed table with widely, but uniformly, scattered data and execute three queries against it:

```
select    pad1
from      s_data
where     n1 = 100;

select    pad1
from      s_data
where     n1 in (100, 200, 300, 400, 500, 600);

select    pad1
from      driver, s_data
where     s_data.n1 = driver.n1
and       driver.n1 between 50 and 650;
```

The table S_DATA and the first query have been designed to return five rows from five different locations in the table. The second query effectively does the same thing six times. The third query emulates the second query because I have rigged the data in the DRIVER table suitably (but Oracle doesn't necessarily know that this is the case).

Let us examine the execution plans and costs derived by Oracle:

```
Query 1-indexed access by single constant
SELECT STATEMENT Optimizer=CHOOSE (Cost=8 Card=5 Bytes=100)
  TABLE ACCESS (BY INDEX ROWID) OF S_DATA (Cost=8 Card=5 Bytes=100)
    INDEX (RANGE SCAN) OF SD_I (NON-UNIQUE) (Cost=3 Card=5)
```

There are three cost figures shown here:

1. The cost of the index access is 3, which I am inclined to relate to the fact that all the index entries for the given value are in the same leaf block, so Oracle has to read the root, one branch, and one leaf to get them. (You might also note that Oracle did get the cardinality right at 5.)

2. The cost for getting the table data is given as 8, which I assume is the three for the index plus another five for the five different blocks across which the five different rows are scattered.

3. The cost of the final select statement is given as 8, which is the cost of the table access with no further action.

Moving to query 2, a list of literal values, Oracle can be quite clever, and can examine the values to determine how much of the index it will have to hit. Note, by the way, the INLIST ITERATOR method, which in previous versions of Oracle would either switch to a table scan to handle the supplied list of values, or turn the query into a *concatenation* of six separately parsed queries. Oracle 8.1 is smart enough to recognize that it can simply execute the same simple query six times, which usually executes faster than the TABLE SCAN option, and parses faster than the CONCATENATION option:

Query 2–indexed access by list of constants
```
SELECT STATEMENT Optimizer=CHOOSE (Cost=33 Card=30 Bytes=600)
  INLIST ITERATOR
    TABLE ACCESS (BY INDEX ROWID) OF S_DATA (Cost=33 Card=30 Bytes=600)
      INDEX (RANGE SCAN) OF SD_I (NON-UNIQUE) (Cost=3 Card=30)
```

Let's look at the three costs associated with this query:

1. The cost of the index access is again 3. Oracle has estimated from the literal values that it need only do a total of three physical accesses to get all the necessary leaf data into memory (in fact, it needed to do a couple more).

3. The cost for getting the table data has gone up to 33, which happens to match perfectly with the fact that there are six literal values, each returns five rows, and each row is likely to be in its own block: $6 \times 5 + 3$ (from the index) = 33.

3. Finally, the cost of the select statement is, again, the cost of the table access.

```
Query 3—Nested loop table join.
SELECT STATEMENT Optimizer=CHOOSE (Cost=65 Card=35 Bytes=910)
  NESTED LOOPS (Cost=65 Card=35 Bytes=910)
    TABLE ACCESS (FULL) OF DRIVER (Cost=1 Card=8 Bytes=48)
    TABLE ACCESS (BY INDEX ROWID) OF S_DATA (Cost=8 Card=10640 Bytes=
    212800)
      INDEX (RANGE SCAN) OF SD_I (NON-UNIQUE) (Cost=3 Card=10640)
```

Query 3 is the query that highlights the problem: The total query cost is 65. Given that it should be doing exactly the same as the previous query, why has the estimated cost doubled? The short answer is that Oracle does *not* acquire any information that lets it assume that there are any efficiencies of scale to be gained. Look at the five costs in detail:

1. The cost of the index access is 3, exactly as for the single-value query at the start of the exercise, which seems to be reasonable. Don't ask why the cardinality is more than 10,000; there are a number of funny little bugs in the numbers generated by the CBO.

2. The cost for getting the table data is 8, which again matches the single-value query.

3. We have to remember, though, that the index access happens once for every row returned by the scan on the driving table. The cost of this scan is given as 1, with an estimated eight rows returned (CARD=8), which is slightly over the top for the actual data.

4. The cost of getting all the data should then be the cost of the driving scan itself plus the cost of an indexed access executed eight separate times. And indeed we get a total cost of $8 \times 8 + 1 = 65$.

5. Finally, the cost of the query is the cost of the nested loop—65.

The biggest problem with the CBO, at least from the average DBA's point of view, lies in step 4. Oracle has calculated the cost of a single access into the S_DATA table based on an input constant, and then multiplied that cost by its estimate of the number of times it will have to do that single access. Apart from the fact that the estimate of the rows returned from the driving table may be too high, the fact that the very first indexed access might load up enough of the data (particularly index blocks) to reduce the physical cost of all the subsequent accesses is not taken into account at all. In many cases this is highly unrealistic. In fact, in many critical cases the entire set of branch blocks and all of the relevant index blocks may be permanently cached in the database block buffer.

Oracle 8.1 introduces a pair of init.ora parameters to combat this effect:

- OPTIMIZER_INDEX_CACHING = integer   default value 0
- OPTIMIZER_INDEX_COST_ADJ = integer   default value 100

The OPTIMIZER_INDEX_CACHING parameter tells Oracle to include in its optimization calculations "for nested_loop joins" the assumption that a percentage of the index blocks in its execution path will be in the buffer rather than on disk. The default value of zero emulates the current practice of assuming that all index block hits will always be on disk. A suitable setting for this parameter is probably highly system dependent, but I would be inclined to set it to a value of 50% as a typical starting point for experimental purposes, and would be perfectly happy to run it right up to 100% if I thought that the behavior of the system justified it (for example, when a critical index has been allocated to the KEEP buffer; see Appendix D). With this parameter set to 100%, either in the init.ora or at the session level, the costing for the sample join changes to the following:

Query 3b–Nested loop table join–cached index calculation.
```
SELECT STATEMENT Optimizer=CHOOSE (Cost=41 Card=35 Bytes=910)
  NESTED LOOPS (Cost=41 Card=35 Bytes=910)
    TABLE ACCESS (FULL) OF DRIVER (Cost=1 Card=8 Bytes=48)
    TABLE ACCESS (BY INDEX ROWID) OF S_DATA (Cost=5 Card=10640Bytes=
    212800)
      INDEX (RANGE SCAN) OF 'SD_I' (NON-UNIQUE)
```

Notice how the cost for the index access has disappeared completely, reducing the cost of the S_DATA table access from 8 to 5. Consequently, the cost for the nested loop is now down from 65 to 41 = 8 (cardinality of DRIVER) × 5 (cost of table access) + 1—a result that improves the bias to using the index quite considerably.

The COST_ADJ parameter is similar but potentially even more aggressive at changing the cost of indexed access. The description in the Oracle 8.1 Reference Manual states: "The value of *integer* is a percentage indicating the importance the optimizer attaches to the index path compared with 'normal.' The value can be set to any value between 1 and 10,000, which means it can decrease or increase the estimate of the cost. The baseline value is 100, and, within rounding limits, any change to this value results in the table access cost being scaled by the current value divided by 100." Using the same example, resetting the OPTIMIZER_INDEX_CACHE parameter and setting the OPTIMIZER_INDEX_COST_ADJ parameter to 50, we see the following:

```
Query 3c-Nested loop table join-index cost halved.
SELECT STATEMENT Optimizer=CHOOSE (Cost=33 Card=35 Bytes=910)
  NESTED LOOPS (Cost=33 Card=35 Bytes=910)
    TABLE ACCESS (FULL) OF DRIVER (Cost=1 Card=8 Bytes=48)
    TABLE ACCESS (BY INDEX ROWID) OF S_DATA (Cost=4 Card=10640 Bytes=
    212800)
      INDEX (RANGE SCAN) OF SD_I (NON-UNIQUE) (Cost=3 Card=10640)
```

As you can see, the actual cost on the index has not been changed, but the cost on the table access has been halved (50/100) from the original 8 down to 4. The effect of this is that the cost of the nested loop is now 33 = 8 (cardinality of DRIVER) × 4 (halved cost of table access) + 1.

In effect, the parameter OPTIMIZER_INDEX_COST_ADJ behaves as if it were dictating to the optimizer the degree to which it can expect the table to be cached, whereas the parameter OPTIMIZER_INDEX_CACHING tells the optimizer the degree to which it can expect the index to be cached.

You may feel that this section has been a little heavy on the technical and mathematical side for a book that claimed that it was going to try to avoid being too deep in its interrogation into the inner workings of Oracle. The idea that I want to put across, however, even if some of the details may have to be changed with the next point release of Oracle, is that the CBO is a purely mathematical animal, and it is important to recognize that it is possible to understand the calculations that it is doing. Not only that, it is important to consider the way in which your physical data distribution controls the numbers with which Oracle works to produce its executions paths.

Index Joins

I have pointed out that Oracle 8.1 introduces a number of new optimization strategies. As an example of what one of the minor changes in Oracle 8.1 can do, it is worth looking at INDEX_JOIN. This is an example of one of the new optimization methods that may make your application run faster simply because you upgrade from 8.0 to 8.1. There is nothing particularly cunning or special about it, and nothing requires careful design consideration; it just happens to be the case that Oracle 8.1 can take advantage of existing, commonly occurring data structures in new, more efficient ways.

Consider the following slightly artificial example:

```
create table join1 (
    n1 number,
    n2 number,
```

```
    n3 number,
    p1 varchar2(800)
);

create unique index ji1 on join1(n1,n2);
create unique index ji2 on join1(n2,n3);

select  count(*)
from    join1
where   n1 = 17
and     n3 = 45
;
```

The traditional path for this query would be for Oracle to use the index (n1, n2) to access the table and check the value of column N3 for each row returned. However, I have created the P1 column as a rather large column to allow me to make the table rows rather large so that Oracle may have to do a lot of I/O to find all the rows for N1 = 17. You may note, therefore, that both the indexes JI1 and JI2 are likely to be rather small, and that by combining data from the two indexes Oracle could, in theory, derive the required result without visiting the table at all.

I had assumed that when an index join occurred, Oracle would scan the JI1 index for N1 = 17, then use the N2 value in each index entry to index into JI2. Perhaps with suitable datasets something of this sort could occur. In fact, when coerced with the hint /*+ INDEX_JOIN (JOIN1) */, my sample *select* statement actually chose the following alternative path:

```
SORT (AGGREGATE)
  VIEW OF 'index$_join$_001' (Cost=153 Card=1 Bytes=26)
    HASH JOIN
      INDEX (RANGE SCAN) OF 'JI1' (UNIQUE)
      INDEX (FAST FULL SCAN) OF 'JI2' (UNIQUE)
```

This entails using two indexes to generate two sets of rowids independently, and then hashing them together to find the common rows. As you can see from the cost, it was not a very efficient option for the dataset I generated. Perhaps this is the only way in which an index join currently works, and it is only beneficial in very special cases, or perhaps I was just unable to invent a suitable dataset to reveal the alternatives. However, it is worth keeping an eye on your applications for batch jobs that access large tables through small indexes. It is possible that an occasional INDEX_JOIN hint may make a difference.

Star Transformations

As I have said, many of the new optimization methods are relatively minor and don't really have much impact on how you might design your database. One new optimization feature, though, stands out as allowing a significant change to data warehouse design. This is the *bitmapped star transformation,* which is used to handle queries against a star schema. A *star schema* essentially consists of a single very large "fact" table surrounded by a number of parent "dimension" tables that are typically used to identify and add value to "meaningless ID" columns in the fact table.

Referring to Figure 7-2, assume you need to get some data from the fact table in the middle of the star. The rows to be selected are defined by some tests to be made against a few of the dimension tables around the outside of the star. For example, you might want to report

```
For all manufacturers in France
For all distributors in Germany
For all drugs of an analgesic nature
With a packaging type of 'capsules'
The total sales and returns over January 2000
```

In early versions of Oracle there were only one or two routes for this type of query:

```
scan the Sales table and for each row
    join to the effect table, eliminate all but analgesics
    join to the manufacturer table, eliminate those not from France
    join to the distributor table, eliminate those not from Germany
    join to the packaging table, eliminate all but capsules
sum the rows not eliminated.
```

An alternative might have been to start by scanning one of the four outlying tables, then joining to the SALES table before proceeding with the outward join to the other three tables.

Later versions of Oracle introduced the idea of a *star join* (not to be confused with the star transformation), which in the previous example requires you to build a fairly massive four-part B-tree index on the SALES table (PACKAGING_ID, EFFECT_ID, DISTRIBUTOR_ID, MANUFACTURER_ID), and the path would then be

```
scan the four outlying tables for relevant rows
produce the Cartesian product (N x M x P x Q rows)
```

```
for each element in the product
    index into the table to see if a Sales row exists
sum the rows returned.
```

There are three problems with this strategy:

1. The index is enormous.
2. It doesn't work if (in this example) you don't include the packaging in the query.
3. Cartesian products get very big very quickly (imagine 52 packages × 273 drugs × 12 manufacturers in France × 8 distributors in Germany, for a total of 1,360,000 combinations to check).

With suitable data distributions, mainly ones with small Cartesian products, in which there are usually some data to acquire at the end of each indexed access, this could be extremely effective in terms of performance, but the space requirement and the time needed to build a suitable set of B-tree indexes are generally prohibitive. In cases with large Cartesian joins and sparsely populated fact tables, the overhead is enormous.

There were two common solutions to such problems. One approach was to denormalize the data dramatically, copying values like the packaging type, manufacturer country, and so on, to the main fact table. The amount of wasted space was high, and the threat of massive maintenance (in some cases) was also high, but at least this allowed simple, direct bitmap indexing

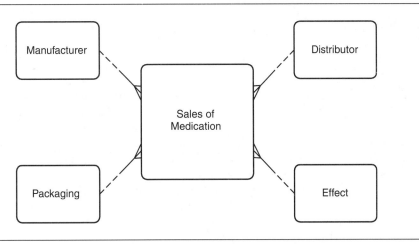

Figure 7-2. Simple star schema.

on the fact table to produce rapid results. Another solution was to prepare large numbers of precalculated summary results, trying to find a good compromise set that meant that users could get quick results most of the time and only have to make use of the large table occasionally (see Chapter 23).

The solution made available in Oracle 8—the star transformation—introduced a whole new optimization path unlike anything previously seen in Oracle. The surprise feature of this path is that it doubles back on itself. It starts at the outer tables, works into the center to produce the correct raw answer set, then revisits the outer tables to enhance the data in that subset.

There are three steps involved. First, set the init.ora parameter STAR_TRANSFORMATION_ENABLED to TRUE. Second, make sure that there are primary key indexes available on the dimension tables. Third, create bitmap indexes on the foreign key columns in the central fact table.

To perform the star transformation, Oracle visits each of the outlying tables in turn to collect the primary key values that match the query conditions. Once each set of primary keys has been identified, Oracle accesses the relevant bitmap indexes on the fact table, combines them to produce a bitmap identifying the (very specific) set of rows required, and then joins back to each of the outer tables using its primary key to add such things as textual descriptions and so forth.

A shortened form of the execution path when using only three of the outlying tables to drive the query might look something like the following (I have numbered each line to show the order in which Oracle acquires data):

```
nested loops
    nested loops
    nested loops
        table SALES by rowid                                  9
            bitmap conversion to rowids                       8
                bitmap AND                                            7
                    bitmap index fk_man merge of multiple keys    2
                        table scan of manufacturers               1
                    bitmap index fk_dis merge of multiple keys    4
                        table scan of distributors                3
                    bitmap merge index fk_eff of multiple keys    6
                        table scan of effects                     5
        table manufacturer by rowid              11
            index manufacturer_pk                10
    table distributor by rowid            13
        index distributor_pk              12
table effects by rowid            15
    index effects_pk              14
```

The highlighted section happens first and shows three of the outer tables being scanned to find suitable primary keys. The bitmaps for each of the sets of primary keys are acquired from the indexes on the central fact table, and the three resulting bitmaps are AND-ed together. Oracle then converts the final bitmap to a list of rowids, fetches the SALES rows, and for each row uses the primary key back to each of the surrounding dimension tables.

The upshot of this is that the plan is executed by scanning some (usually) small dimension tables, scanning some small bitmap indexes at a relatively low CPU cost, targeting very precisely the exact set of rows needed from the large table at a minimal I/O cost, and then finally taking a very efficient route back ___ excess supporting information from the dimension tables. In ___ nple join query and rewrites it as a query with an in- ___ stpone as much of the work as possible. If you had to ___ uld probably write something like

```
                                 ales

                 d_man in (select id from manufacturers where . . .)
                 id_dist in (select id from distributors where . . .)
                 id_effects in (select id from effects where . . .)
                            sal,
                        r   man,
                            dst,
        effects             eff
where
            man.id = sal.id_man
    and     dst.id = sal.id_dist
    and     eff.id = sal.id_eff
    ;
```

In fact, the star transformation is capable of slightly more subtle behavior; it can also handle the *snowflake schema* (Figure 7-3), a refinement of the star schema that allows more parent tables to be attached to the dimension tables shown.

The resolution method is essentially unchanged: The first step is to identify the minimum list of relevant primary keys of the directly attached dimension tables using any conditions on those tables and the outer tables before

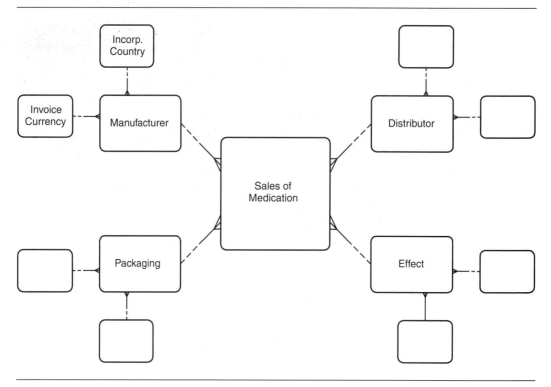

Figure 7-3.   Simple snowflake schema.

moving to the fact table, through the bitmaps, and out again through the primary key indexes.

Problems and Quirks

There are all sorts of new features to indexes in Oracle 8.1, and some of them may have funny little side effects that are easy to miss. If you depend on reverse-engineering tools for generating DDL to rebuild objects, watch out for simple problems like descending indexes: The index column is a hidden column with a name like SYS_NCxxxx$. Will your tool still work with Oracle 8.1?

Be very careful when using compressed indexes with partitioned tables. It is safe to do so, but if you write code to build scratch tables and then exchange them into the partition, it is possible you'll end up with index partitions that do not match the global degree of compression for the index. This results in an unexpected session crash the next time the partition is accessed.

Although MINIMIZE RECORDS_PER_BLOCK is a very effective way to save space on bitmap indexes, be very careful if you need to rebuild the table, or you may waste a huge amount of space in the table (see Chapter 5).

There are access paths that are not yet available to function-based indexes, so there may still be cases when it is better to create an actual column (populated by triggers) and index it, rather than creating an index on a virtual column (notwithstanding my repeated exhortation to save space at all times).

Function-based indexes based on user-defined functions can become disabled by a variety of accidents. This can lead to SQL queries and updates failing or massive performance problems until the index can be reenabled or rebuilt. And function-based indexes (whether based on built-in functions or user-defined functions) cannot be rebuilt on-line.

User-defined function-based indexes work only if QUERY_REWRITE_INTEGRITY is TRUSTED. This may collide with your requirements for materialized views, which may demand STALE_ALLOWED or ENFORCED.

Online index rebuilding (including index-organized tables) requires two quiet moments when there are no uncommitted transactions on the underlying table. Consequently, the actual start and completion time of a rebuild might not occur according to schedule.

The *coalesce* command sometimes does not coalesce the whole index, and acts as a long series of short, logged transactions. This could temporarily have a serious impact on performance and could certainly increase the chances of Oracle error "ORA-01555: snapshot too old."

Strategy Notes

Always consider compressing indexes, and rethink the column ordering of indexes to gain the maximum benefit from compression. In particular, compress any index that exists simply to avoid lock contention because of primary key/foreign key relationships.

If you think that Oracle is overestimating the cost of using index-based access paths and using table scan/merge/hash mechanisms too frequently—particularly if your understanding of the application allows you to recognize that there is a very good buffer hit rate on critical indexes and tables—you should adjust the two parameters OPTIMIZER_INDEX_CACHING and OPTIMIZER_INDEX_COST_ADJ to reflect the expected level of caching of the most critical indexes and tables respectively.

For data warehouse systems, always consider rigging a suitable value for "records per block," by doctoring an empty table if necessary before loading the data. The space savings on bitmap indexes are likely to be significant in systems with a fairly small number of rows per block.

Unless you can prove that you have a significant problem with "buffer busy waits" at the trailing edge of an index, don't bother reversing any of the columns. If you do reverse an index, check that the I/O overhead caused by the resulting inefficiency does not become more of a problem than the original "buffer busy waits."

When using function-based indexes on user-defined functions, it is best to create a view that makes the virtual index column visible. This reduces the amount of administration needed to handle privileges, makes subsequent SQL queries against the index easier to read and write, and eliminates an irritating little problem with string functions as indexes.

Always package the functions you use for user-defined function-based indexes. This allows you to rebuild the implementation of the function without disabling the index, which can lead to irritated users and a lot of wasted time.

The option to rebuild indexes on-line is a great benefit but should not be used casually. In the event of a crash during an index rebuild, SMON comes in to tidy up the mess and finish off the rebuild. Thus, it is not sensible to run more than one rebuild at a time.

The COALESCE feature is extremely useful, particularly for indexes that are associated with FIFO processing, which can very easily leave highly inefficient "trailing edges." If you have any indexes of this type, it is worth scheduling a coalesce on each of them very regularly, even once per day. Because of the bug that leaves the coalesce incomplete, I would start by making two consecutive calls to coalesce, and review the state of the critical indexes using the *treedump* command from time to time. Remember that COALESCE is an on-line option that works in many cases when an on-line rebuild is not permitted.

Bitmapped star transformations can work extremely well (even when combined with partitioned tables; see Chapter 13). Although there are some limitations on using bitmapped indexes (specifically, the potential for conflict in systems with multiple concurrent updates), they are very small, can be built very quickly, and work extremely effectively. Always consider the options for a star transformation strategy if you are handling very large datasets in a batch environment.

CHAPTER 8

Leveraging Tablespaces

The tablespace is the largest unit of the logical structure and can be made up from many physical files. There are several reasons for breaking up the database into discrete logical units, most relating to administration, a few relating to performance.

Oracle 8.1 introduces several new features at the tablespace level. Most are designed to make life easier for the administrator, but some of them may have a dramatic impact on the amount of time it takes to handle large volumes of data.

The most significant features are locally managed tablespaces that take the stress off the data dictionary, temporary tablespaces (see Chapter 9), and transportable tablespaces.

Tablespace Strategies

We have already seen that the active components of a database consist of the control files, the redo log files, and the data files. These three components have different types of I/O requirements, and some comments about these differences appear in Chapter 10.

However, there are several ways to categorize data file activity, and thus several different arguments to consider when splitting up your database into logical units. The most important point, of course, is that if any section of the data exhibits some degree of individualism in the way it is used, then it should be isolated so that you can see if the actual usage corresponds to the predicted use. Because Oracle records I/O costs only at the file level, not the object level, you need to use files (which in effect means tablespaces) as an indirect method of monitoring the actual I/O costs of critical objects in the database.

Rollback Tablespaces

The most obvious class of special object is the rollback segment, used internally by Oracle to record instructions on how to reverse recent changes to the database. The behavior pattern of rollback segments is sufficiently idiosyncratic compared with anything else that goes on in the database that rollback segments should not share a tablespace with any other object.

Ignoring for the moment some of the esoteric features of extending and shrinking, the body of a rollback segment is used in a cyclical fashion: As data is changed randomly throughout the rest of the database, Oracle writes steadily from the beginning of a rollback segment through to the end, and then comes back and overwrites the beginning, and so on in an endless loop. While this is going on, the header block of the rollback segment is being continuously updated as each transaction starts and finishes. From time to time processes may need to hop backward through recently used rollback blocks to rebuild a read-consistent image of the data they want to see.

There are some extremes, therefore, in how rollback segments affect I/O. In the best possible case you will be able to have very small rollback segments in a large buffer, and cycle round and round them so fast that they stay "hot" and can be reused before they are written to disk, and only get written to disk when a checkpoint occurs. In the worst possible case you may be forced to have very large rollback segments to accommodate repeated changes to a relatively small volume of data, and in this case the oldest rollback blocks may be written to disk long before you get a chance to reuse them. In fact, in some systems the rollback segments are the single largest cause of real physical I/O. Of course this I/O generally occurs in the background; nevertheless, it is likely to add a persistent baseline to the overall I/O load of the system.

Whatever the case, you need to be able to see the I/O on the rollback segments, so you need to keep rollback segments in tablespaces that hold nothing but rollback segments. Use any other approach and you will never know, for example, whether a sudden massive read load on a tablespace is the result of some data-related activity or of some anomaly in which rollback segments in the tablespace have been heavily used and are now being reacquired for read-consistency reasons.

There are a couple of special strategic points to consider with rollback segments. As I implied earlier, small is good—and rollback segments are unique in Oracle in that they can be defined to shrink automatically. When you create rollback segments, one of the parameters that defines them is their optimal size. You should aim to make this as small as possible. This means you have to monitor the V$ROLLSTAT view to see how frequently your rollback segments are growing and shrinking, and how far above the optimal size they get. Ideally, there should be only occasional growth (one or two per day perhaps) of a few extents at a time. When creating a tablespace for rollback segments, I tend to set things up so that when all the rollback segments are at their optimal size, approximately 50% of the tablespace is in use. This leaves far more room than is really needed for the occasional growth spurt, but tends to ensure that the odd rogue process won't crash with error "ORA-01650: unable to extend rollback segment."

> *When a rollback segment shrinks, any of the discarded blocks that are currently buffered are first written back to disk. Similarly, when rollback segments are taken off-line, any buffered blocks must first be written to disk. Finding the point of minimum I/O impact is not an easy exercise.*

Given enough time, and without an OPTIMAL setting, all end-user rollback segments in the database will become the same size. (There is one special SYSTEM rollback segment in the SYSTEM tablespace that falls outside this rule.) Thus you should generally create all rollback segments the same size. However, many applications have large batch processes from time to time, typically overnight or weekend processes, that need very large rollback segments to run to completion. If this is the case then you should consider setting up two completely independent tablespaces for rollback segments, one for the "normal" processing with a number of small rollback segments in it, and one for the "batch" processing with a smaller number of large rollback segments in it. Ideally you should take the small rollback segments off-line while the batch processes are running. If this is not possible, you should ensure that each batch process is attached to one of the large rollback segments as it starts by invoking the command

```
set transaction use rollback segment XXX;
```

Remember, when different activities have different characteristic behavior, you want to separate the activities as much as possible so that you can see that they are behaving as expected. You do not want the I/O statistics of heavy overnight processing concealing any anomalies in the I/O statistics generated by normal daily processing.

Temporary Tablespaces

In a similar vein, Oracle needs some space somewhere when a sort process won't fit in memory (or when the sort phase is complete and the resultant dataset has to be dumped somewhere temporarily). To make visible the amount of I/O resulting from such activity, some dedicated tablespaces should be set aside for this purpose. In fact in Oracle 8.1 we now have the ability to create a special kind of tablespace for exactly this purpose. I have written a whole chapter about temporary tablespaces (see Chapter 9), so I won't say anything further here, other than to point out that different users may handle vastly different volumes of data, so you may want to create two or three temporary tablespaces and allocate different users to them so that you can get an early warning when one user starts doing an uncharacteristic volume of sorting.

Classification

Apart from the tablespaces dedicated to rollback and temporary space, there are at least seven different reasons for categorizing tablespaces:

1. **Business relevance**—In a financial management system, for example, it probably makes sense to separate invoicing data from general ledger data largely for visual convenience. I won't say anything more on this particular aspect of tablespace management because it has very little to do with the mechanics of the database. However, if you are a software house supplying a modular package, you should appreciate the importance of being able to associate one module with one group of tablespaces as far as possible.

2. **Size of objects**—For reasons of administration, every single object in a tablespace should be made up of extents that are all exactly the same size. This can be effected with a minimal waste of space simply by grouping objects of roughly the same size (to within an order of magnitude) in the same tablespace.

3. **Type of activity**—The way in which indexes are used tends to be very different from the way in which tables are physically used. Similarly, some tables are necessarily subject to table scans whereas others should only be accessed by index paths. Some objects are frequently rebuilt, whereas most others are totally static. Some objects are created once and permanently fixed, and could be kept in read-only tablespaces. Some objects are able to be discarded, so they could be created without the need for redo log generation in NOLOGGING tablespaces.

4. **Volume of activity**—Objects that are low-activity objects, or objects that should get into the buffer and stay there, are worth special treatment. High-use objects that generate a lot of disk activity need to be isolated so that they can be proactively managed if load balancing becomes an issue.

5. **Backup**—The smallest logical unit of a database that can be backed up and independently recovered (using operating system methods rather than an Oracle export) is the tablespace. You may have reasons for allowing different parts of the database to be recovered to different points in time, and you may need to use tablespace allocation to allow this to happen.

6. **Transportability**—One of the new features of Oracle 8.1 is the ability to clone an entire tablespace from one database to another. For ease of administration, objects that are to be passed between databases should be grouped in a small set of tablespaces.

7. **Time-based changes in activity**—Particularly in data warehouse environments, very recent data may be accessed and changed much more heavily than very old data. By separating data according to age, you introduce options for read-only tablespaces, reduced size of backup, ease of discarding ancient data, and load balancing.

You can get a tremendous administrative advantage by using tablespaces sensibly to break up the database into manageable units.

Looking through this list, you can see that the bias is almost invariably toward using tablespaces for management reasons. There are a couple of side effects relating to performance: being able to see, for instance, that the right sort of activity is taking place just by looking at the I/O statistics of a tablespace; and always ensuring that scratch tables and indexes are built in NOLOGGING tablespaces. However, the most important feature of tablespace management is that it breaks down the tablespace from a vast collection of wildly varying little bits into a number of small, self-consistent groups.

Of course, given seven reasons for breaking up the database into different tablespaces, you could go overboard and end up with dozens of tablespaces even for a very small database. Be careful. Too much of anything is a pain; there's always room for compromise.

Locally Managed Tablespaces

Let's start by reviewing one of the oldest myths, and biggest wastes of DBA time, in the Oracle book of legends. Someone once said, "You get better performance if each object is stored in a single extent." It must be well over 10 years ago that Oracle published a white paper exploding this myth, and yet the claim lingers on.

Many DBAs still try to work out exactly how big a table will be, and allocate it in one extent (or one extent per file for load-balancing reasons). Many DBAs spend late nights exporting tables that have grown to multiple extents with the COMPRESS = Y option set so that they can reimport them as a single extent. Many DBAs find that they have tablespaces with all sorts of strange-size holes in them that cannot be used because they have done so many exports and imports to try to compress extents. Consequently, they spend entire weekends exporting and rebuilding entire tablespaces in search of the Grail of "one object/one extent." And it's all a huge waste of time and effort.

Oracle operates on data blocks (but see Chapter 15 for one special case), and apart from redo log generation tends to operate through random I/O. A small percentage of the work that Oracle does is sequential tablescans or sequential index scans that operate as a multiblock call to the operating system. The typical multiblock read call is 64K, although some platforms can beneficially perform reads up to 256K (and some can actually perform 1MB reads against raw devices). So, really, the only time when you are likely to take a performance hit from an object being split into multiple extents is when a table scan or index scan has to jump all over the place to find just 64K (or perhaps 256K). In other words, the only time when you probably ought to try to keep an object down to a single extent is when the object is (1) likely to be scanned frequently and (2) less than 256K.

> *Once an object is larger than 256K, there is no benefit in trying to ensure that it fits into a single extent.*

Having said that the cry of "one object/one extent" is a pointless call to arms, I must point out that this isn't a license to go for the opposite extreme and simply allow an object to add extents ad infinitum, even though Oracle now allows for unlimited extents as an option even on rollback segments. There are some side effects of having extreme numbers of extents in a single object, and I usually aim to design for 50 extents as a soft limit, and then worry about rebuilding an object if it exceeds 100 extents. The side effects relate to SMON and its cleanup procedures, which I describe later, and to parallel queries (see Chapter 22).

If one object/one extent is *not* a good strategy, what is? Once you realize the performance question is a nonissue, you have to ask yourself what benefit you can get from any sizing strategy. The obvious questions to ask are things like, What if I size an object too small and it needs to grow? What if I size an object too big and need to rebuild it? How much trouble am I going to have finding space if I need to rebuild an index that has become inefficient? What if I make a tablespace far too big and find myself wasting time backing up loads of empty space every night?

> *Every single extent in a tablespace should be the same size. If you follow this rule, any holes created will be reusable, and any object looking for space will always find holes of the right size.*

The bottom line on handling tablespaces is that you need to know that space will be available *and usable* if needed. The easiest way to ensure that this is the case is to insist that every object in a tablespace is made up of extents that are all exactly the same size. For example, pick a dozen medium/large tables that you think can share a tablespace. On one site medium/large may mean a fairly wide range—5 to 250MB. On another site it may mean a much tighter range—100MB to 1GB. Let's assume the former, and pick a good extent size. In this case I'd probably go for something between 10 and 20MB. Define the tablespace so that every extent *has* to be 10MB (I'll describe how in a moment), then create all objects with the TABLESPACE DEFAULT STORAGE clause.

After a few weeks or months of running, I'll have some tables that are still using only a couple of megabytes from the 10MB I've allocated to them, but I don't mind wasting a little empty space for the administrative convenience, and the only performance impact is a few extra seconds during backup to back up empty space. I'll also have a few tables that are up to a couple dozen extents, but this isn't a problem; reasonable numbers of extents don't cause any problems. If for some reason I have to rebuild one of the tables, it leaves a 10MB hole in the middle of the tablespace. But never mind, the next time I have to rebuild another table that hole will get refilled.

If I want to monitor the way that space is being used, I need only list two numbers:

1. "Size of tablespace" divided by "specified extent size," which gives me the total number of extents I will be able to allocate in that tablespace

2. Total number of extents allocated in the tablespace

It's not going to be very difficult to see how rapidly my space is being used, and to predict roughly when I need to "grow" the tablespace (or shrink the tablespace and save a bit of backup time). If I want to be a little more precise in my monitoring, I can enhance it to keep track of the number of extents per table. The beauty of setting an extent size that accommodates the larger objects getting to a few dozen extents means that I can watch them grow and see if my sizing predictions are close to reality. Another beneficial side effect of relatively small extents is that if I allocate several files to the tablespace (for load-balancing purposes perhaps), then the extents are allocated in a round-robin fashion across all those files.

Of course I may find fairly early on in my monitoring that one table is growing *much* faster than I had predicted. Perhaps it will be 1.5GB and 150 extents within a few months, rather than the 250MB and 25 extents that I had predicted. In this case I might well choose to create a separate tablespace for it (allocated in units of 50MB perhaps) and rebuild the object. At the same time I might reduce the size of the previous tablespace by resizing the file. After all, because I am allowing objects to grow 10MB at a time, there is bound to be a reasonable amount of empty space at the end of the file in the early life of the database.

The question, then, is how to ensure that every extent in a tablespace is the same size? Before Oracle 8.1, the best you could do was to define the default storage on the tablespace as something like the following:

```
create tablespace uni_old
datafile '/u01/oradata/prod/uni_old_01.dbf' size 251M
default storage (
    initial 5M
    next 5M
    pctincrease 0
)
minimum extent 5M
;
```

Initial, next, and pctincrease would ensure that any object created without an explicit storage clause would follow the 5MB pattern. The MINIMUM EXTENT clause would ensure that even if someone tried to create an object with an explicit storage clause, then Oracle would round the given sizing (and any subsequent calculated "next" sizing) to a multiple of 5MB, which is not perfect, but at least provides some reasonably good damage control. (If you're wondering whether there is any significance in the 1 of 251MB for the file size, there is: I can't be bothered with fiddly, hard-to-understand numbers, so having worked out a sensible size for a file I add 1MB to it to accommodate any odd overhead that Oracle may introduce.)

In Oracle 8.1, we have the locally managed tablespace, but more specifically we have the UNIFORM variant of the locally managed tablespace:

```
create tablespace uni_new
datafile '/u01/oradata/prod/uni_new_01.dbf' size 251M
extent management local
uniform size 5M
;
```

With this definition for a tablespace, it is *not possible* to create an extent of any size other than 5MB. If a user tries to create a table with an initial extent of 16MB, say, the resulting table will actually be created with four extents of 5MB each (in other words, the extents are fixed at 5MB but multiple extents are allocated to meet the total space demand).

There are actually many more benefits to locally managed tablespaces than just the total enforcement of extent sizing. Locally managed tablespaces are managed through a 64K bitmap in the file header, and each bit in this map corresponds to one extent in the file. This is very different from traditional tablespaces (now known as *dictionary-managed tablespaces*) in which the space is managed through two dictionary tables SYS.FET$ (free extents) and SYS.UET$ (used extents).

The biggest difference is, perhaps, in what happens when objects are dropped and created. In a dictionary-managed tablespace if you create an object, Oracle has to find space by hunting through the free extent table (FET$) for a large enough free extent, then allocate the space by deleting or changing the FET$ row and inserting a row into the used extent table (UET$) to indicate that space has been used. Conversely, dropping an object requires Oracle to delete rows from UET$, and insert rows into FET$. In both cases, these operations are protected by rollback and redo log generation. In a locally managed tablespace, creating an object requires Oracle to find space by running through the bitmap to find the first free bit and setting it; dropping an object requires Oracle to reset the corresponding bits.

This has two side effects. First, it is a little faster (though not a lot faster because of all the other tasks of dictionary management such as defining columns, dropping triggers, and so forth). Second, the action always tends to happen near the start of the data file. If you keep rebuilding objects in a locally managed tablespace, the objects tend to migrate to the start of the file, leaving the tail end of the file empty and available for resizing. This does not usually happen with dictionary-managed tablespaces because of the way Oracle tables (and SYS.FET$ is just another Oracle table) are used. If you repeatedly drop and rebuild an object in a dictionary-managed tablespace, it tends to go back and forth between its old and new positions, rather than migrating to the head of the file. This makes it much harder to tidy up and shrink a dictionary-managed tablespace.

There is another variant on the locally managed tablespace. Instead of UNIFORM SIZE, you can specify that a tablespace should be locally managed, but with the AUTOALLOCATE option. If you do this, Oracle will apply the same bitmap technology to handling the space for the tablespace, but each bit in the header will correspond to a 64K chunk of the file. However, when you create an object, Oracle will automatically vary the size of the extents it allocates, giving you the potential for an extent consisting of several bitmapped chunks. In the simplest case, the first 16 extents will be 64K chunks, each represented by a single bit; the next 16 extents will be 1MB chunks, each represented by 16 consecutive bits; and all further extents will be 8MB chunks represented by 128 consecutive bits. This pattern does get messed up a bit as the tablespace develops little holes and Oracle attempts to soak them up, and it is also affected by attempts to create objects with large initial extents. If you create an object with an initial extent of 20MB, Oracle probably won't start by giving you 16 extents of 64K each. It might jump straight to 20 extents of 1MB each or two of 8MB and four of 1MB or some other combination that happens to fit the currently free bits in the bitmap.

Frankly, I have to say that I haven't yet thought of any good reason for using tablespaces of the AUTOALLOCATE type. There is a note in the manuals that even the SYSTEM tablespace can be locally managed, but if so it has to be defined as AUTOALLOCATE, and all tablespaces holding rollback segments have to be the same. However, this is an error in the documentation (currently) and the SYSTEM tablespace still has to be system managed. It would be rather nice, though, if Oracle Corporation finally got around to sorting out some of the irritants in the space management of the SYSTEM tablespace.

If you want to find out what types of tablespace your system has, you can examine the view family xxx_TABLESPACES. The column ALLOCATION_ TYPE will be set to USER, UNIFORM, or SYSTEM, depending on whether the tablespace is dictionary-managed, locally managed with uniform allocation, or locally managed with autoallocation.

There are, inevitably, a couple of little traps to watch out for with locally managed tablespaces. Locally managed tablespaces are created with a default

MAXEXTENTS of UNLIMITED, and this cannot be changed. I don't like this, but with locally managed tablespaces it is much less of a threat than with dictionary-managed tablespaces because it doesn't really stress the system if you have too many bitmapped extents in an object, unlike the stress you get from a dictionary-managed object with thousands of extents.

The second trap is what happens if you extend the file. You may get into a position in which the 64K bitmap at the file header is too small and Oracle has to add an extra bitmap in the middle of the file, which may lead to a small performance overhead in space management. Again, I don't see this as much of a threat: The 64K header can map approximately 27,000 to 30,000 bits, and at 64K extents (which is definitely the absolute minimum you should use) this equates to a 2GB file. Because I prefer to avoid large files (see Chapter 10), this is good enough for me. In fact, I would view a 64K extent size on a 1.8GB file as a mistake. It suggests either that you have a lot of small objects, which means you should spread them across more tablespaces and smaller files, or that you have some large objects that are going to be made up of lots of extents.

Finally, there is an irritating feature that a file in a locally managed tablespace *always* has to be big enough to hold at least the bitmap plus one extent. In dictionary-managed tablespaces you could always "hide" a file that you accidentally added to a tablespace by sizing it down to one Oracle block. Oracle knew it was there, but never tried to use it because it was guaranteed to be too small. Consequently, you could effectively get rid of it without having to rebuild the tablespace. You can't do this same trick with locally managed tablespaces because Oracle forces you to make the file big enough for it to use. So if you add a file to a locally managed tablespace by accident, you're stuck with it until you drop and re-create the entire tablespace.

General Tablespace Management

Apart from the sizing aspect of managing tablespaces, I also listed the type of activity, the volume of activity, and aspects of backup as additional reasons for actively deciding how to split the database into tablespaces.

As far as activity on tablespaces is concerned, we can look at the dynamic performance view V$FILESTAT to tell us about read/write activity on the files. With a little SQL manipulation, we can sum this to activity at the tablespace level.

One of the oldest monitoring strategies for tablespaces is to split data across tablespaces so that tables and indexes never share tablespaces. Indexes are "always" read a single block at a time, tables may be read by table scans, but in general we hope that they will be read a single block at a time. Of course, these are generalizations that belong in the past: Newer versions of Oracle are able to do multiblock fast full scans of indexes, and table scans are no longer necessarily a bad thing. Nevertheless, splitting indexes from tables can still give us some indication of surprising activity. Consider the following example. The files whose names start with DFD hold tables; those starting with DFI hold indexes:

Fno	Reads	Blocks	Writes	Blocks	File
4	320,656	320,656	123,069	123,069	DFI_SL.DBF
22	1,251,490	1,418,522	28,377	28,377	DFD_SL.DBF
23	624,932	2,220,787	1,254	1,254	DFD_CL.DBF
26	26,719	27,177	97,782	99,606	DFI_SI.DBF

File 4, DFI_SI.DBF, appears to be behaving very properly for an index-only tablespace. Every read is a single-block read, and every write is a single-block write.

File 22, DFD_SL.DBF, is just a little suspect. A very large number of its read requests are single-block reads (by doing a little arithmetic we may infer that possibly 20,000 of the read requests were eight-block multiblock read requests, and 1,230,000 were single block). It is interesting to note that the tables in this file appear to have generated a lot less writing than the indexes in the correspondingly named indexes file, DIF_SL.DBF. On the other hand, this is not too strange. Quite possibly the tables have many indexes each and are subject to lots of sequential, well-packed, inserts.

File 23, DFD_CL.DBF, is clearly a complete disaster. On average, every read request has resulted in a multiblock read of three to four blocks. Given the volume of reads, something is clearly going wrong in a system that otherwise seems to be an OLTP system.

File 26, DFI_SI.DBF, is interesting. Despite being an index-based tablespace it has experienced multiblock reads and, more significantly, multiblock writes. The first thing to check is if any tables have been created by accident in this tablespace. If this is not the case, then quite possibly someone has been rebuilding indexes in the tablespace. Given that this is a production system, this probably should not have been happening, and should be investigated further.

As you can see, a simple report of activity on the files can very easily highlight anomalies in behavior—sometimes performance related, sometimes (as with DFI_SI.DBF) relating to database abuse.

But it is not just the type of activity on different objects that matters. The volume is significant too, from two different angles. Look at file 22 again. It has experienced 1,200,000 read requests—more than all the other files put together. It seems likely that this is a good target for review for load-balancing reasons. Some (if not all) of the tables in this tablespace seem to be subject to very heavy reads. Perhaps the tablespace should be split into two so that the busiest tables can be separated more easily across physical devices, or at least monitored in more detail. From a different perspective, look at files 4 and 26, where the number of blocks written to these files is quite large: What impact will this have on our backup strategy? It is a feature of hot backups that the volume of redo log generated can increase dramatically when you back up a tablespace that is subject to a large number of write requests. Do we need to consider moving some of the indexes out of these two tablespaces to reduce the performance impact of excessive redo log generation as we back them up?

Another aspect of classifying activity, and what to do about backups, comes from front-end DSS tools. Many of these work by building intermediate tables in the database before producing a final report and dropping the scratch tables. Perhaps you should ensure that any ID that does this has as its default a tablespace that has been defined as a NOLOGGING tablespace. After all, you won't need to rebuild the scratch tables if the database crashes, and perhaps you could even modify your backup procedure to ignore such tablespaces completely.

> *If you run a front-end tool that uses scratch tables to hold intermediate results, look at your options for taking advantage of NOLOGGING tablespaces.*

When a tablespace has been defined as NOLOGGING, any object created in it is, by default, a NOLOGGING object, which means that for some operations it does not generate redo log. The operations that are NOLOGGING are restricted to CREATE TABLE AS SELECT, CREATE INDEX, and INSERT AS SELECT with the /*+ APPEND */ hint included, although when you do the INSERT /*+ APPEND */, the updates to any existing indexes are still logged. These limitations reduce the benefit that you can get from NOLOGGING tablespaces, but it is worth checking.

Of course, when it comes to backups, one of the most significant benefits you can introduce is *not* to back up at all. It takes some time to back up a 500GB database, even with a rack of digital linear tape (DLT) drives. So if you can find a way of not doing the backup but still be safe, then that's got to be a big bonus. Again, tablespace management can help. There are only two things that you ever do to a tablespace: read it or write it. But if you can arrange your data so that you never have to write to a tablespace ever again, you need to back it up only once, and it's safe forever (as long as Oracle knows that you are never going to write to it again). It has been possible for many years now to declare a tablespace as a read-only tablespace. Typically this can be applied only to data warehouse solutions with a strong time element to the data. Today's data may be updated and corrected for a couple of weeks, but after two months it is guaranteed to be stable, and we can tell Oracle to make it read-only. Quite often a very large database will turn out to be a small, hot database with an old, cold, read-only archive attached. I have been to sites with databases measuring in the hundreds of gigabytes that needed only a couple of dozen gigabytes backed up each night.

> *To reduce the time needed for backup, always look for options for splitting out datasets that can be made read-only.*

Of course, when you do a backup, or at least a "hot" backup with the database still running, the tablespace is the unit of backup. While the tablespace is being backed up, it is possibly causing excessive amounts of data to be written to the on-line redo log. Because of this, and also because I don't like the idea of any one bit of a backup set being excessively large, I try to avoid defining enormous tablespaces. Sometimes it is unavoidable, but basically I like to keep tablespaces in the 1GB to 4GB range so that, in principle, I could dump an entire tablespace onto a small digital audiotape (DAT) drive or a couple of removable disk drives. Anything larger, and it becomes awkward to identify and transport the smallest bit of a backup that needs to be recovered. There have been extremes that break my rule of thumb. On one very large database, the "small unit" of backup turned out to be rather large, so we restricted each tablespace to 35GB and a single DLT tape.

Of course if you are using Oracle's *rman* program to manage the backup, the mechanism is different and the extra redo generation does not occur. However, many sites have reported that backing up with *rman* is currently slower than backing up with traditional "pre- *rman*" methods, so you may want to stick with tradition. Either way, I still like the idea of viewing the tablespace as the logical unit of backup and making sure that it can't get too big.

I have mentioned the idea of resizing files a couple of times as part of tablespace management simply to reduce the size of the backup. I don't approve of using Oracle features for resizing files as a casual solution to space management, and I particularly loathe the AUTOEXTEND feature. However, I am actually quite keen, in these days of ridiculously huge disks, to leave plenty of spare space in tablespaces for several weeks at a time to accommodate unforeseen events and errors in calculations. This strategy is especially appropriate to data warehouses using partitioned tables with a strong time element to them: Create space for this month's data, with a 100% safety margin, then in two months' time trim back the space. This has no impact on general performance of course. Unallocated blocks in tablespaces are a waste of space but not a waste of operational resources. Only unused blocks below the high water mark and unused bytes within blocks waste resources. However, over-size files do have to be backed up, and the empty space does affect the time, and tape, needed for the backup, so the time comes when the empty space should be reclaimed. To do this, you need to find the high water mark on each file in each tablespace, which can be done with something like the following:

```
select
    df.name,
    ceil(hwm.mb)                    hwm,
    20 * ceil((hwm.mb-1)/20)+1      target,
    round(df.bytes/1048576,0)       curr
from
    v$datafile      df,
    (
        select
            file_id,
            max((bytes/blocks)*(block_id+blocks-1))/1048576     MB
        from
            dba_extents
        group by
            file_id
    )                   hwm
where
    hwm.file_id = df.file#
and 20 * ceil((hwm.mb-1)/20)+1 < ceil(df.bytes/1048576)
order by
    df.ts#,
    df.name
;
```

This script has been adjusted to suit a system in which tables exist in tablespaces allocating 10MB per extent, and indexes exist in tablespaces allocating 5MB per extent. The nature of the code is to find the current high water mark in the tablespace (rounded up to the nearest megabyte) and then work out a suitable new size for the file based on leaving a little headroom. In this case I chose to make every file a multiple of 20MB with 1MB to spare:

File name	HWM	Target	Current
/dbs03/oradata/dwP/PDATA_200001_02.dbf	451	461	541
/dbs04/oradata/dwP/PDATA_200001_03.dbf	451	461	541
/dbs05/oradata/dwP/PDATA_200001_04.dbf	411	421	541
/dbs02/oradata/dwP/PINDX_200001_01.dbf	211	221	401
/dbs03/oradata/dwP/PINDX_200001_02.dbf	166	181	401
/dbs04/oradata/dwP/PINDX_200001_03.dbf	151	161	401
/dbs05/oradata/dwP/PINDX_200001_04.dbf	146	161	401

A minor variation in the script can then be used to generate a series of ***alter database datafile xxx resize*** commands.

You may be able to guess from the filenames that this particular database is a fairly large data warehouse using partitioning, and partitioning data by period (200001 is January 2000). What doesn't show up immediately is that the database is currently breaking one of my rules about tablespace naming. Avoid naming tablespaces according to time periods. This is particularly relevant to large, time-based data warehouses for which very old data is ultimately dropped off the back end of the database.

There is an unfortunate quirk to tablespace naming: Oracle never forgets a tablespace. In other words, Oracle never deletes it from the data dictionary table TS$. (I think this is some sort of hangover from Trusted Oracle, in which tablespaces have security labels associated with them.) Unfortunately, one of the permanently running Oracle processes called *SMON* scans this list of tablespaces every five minutes looking for tablespaces that might have some free space to coalesce. The size and cost of this scan grows indefinitely unless you adopt a strategy of recycling tablespace names. It is actually surprising how many databases experience a massive I/O load on the SYSTEM tablespace because of SMON.

The problem is reduced somewhat by the introduction of locally managed tablespaces, because the scanning problem is actually exacerbated by the number of free extents that get generated in poorly managed systems in a way that can't happen with locally managed tablespaces. Nevertheless, you need to make sure that the list of tablespace names does not get out of hand.

Transportable Tablespaces

Changing tack somewhat, imagine you have a data warehouse, and each week you generate a 30,000,000-row summary table that you want to copy to four other data marts scattered around the company. What is the most efficient way of moving the data? Prior to Oracle 8.1 you had two options:

1. Use a database link from each data mart in turn and issue:

```
Create data_mart_table
nologging
as
select * from data_warehouse_table@dw;
```

2. Export the table from the data warehouse, copy the file across the network, and import to each data mart. In this case the imports can be concurrent rather than serial.

Both solutions are quite resource intensive. One option keeps the work done by Oracle to a minimum, but floods the network; the other solution is cheap on network resources, but makes Oracle work very hard to load the data.

With Oracle 8.1 you have a new, cheap option, provided you stick within strict limits. In theory you can simply copy a set of tablespaces from the data warehouse machine to the data mart machine, then tell the Oracle instance running the data mart that it has a whole new tablespace to plug in.

The restrictions on this trick are just a little limiting. For a start, the two databases have to be running on the same platform from the same hardware vendor, and probably have to be running with extremely close versions of the operating system and Oracle. The two databases then have to have the same block size, character set, and national character set. At the data level there are additional restrictions relating to the data that may be in the tablespaces you want to transport. First and foremost, the tablespaces you are passing must contain a fully self-consistent dataset; for example, you cannot transport an index if you have not transported the table to which it belongs, and you cannot transport a child table if you do not transport the corresponding parent table, although strangely you can pass a table containing REFs without passing the objects to which the REFs refer. You cannot use transportable tablespaces to pass individual partitions of a partitioned table from one database to another; you have to exchange the partitions out of the table, then transport the tablespace and exchange them back in or pass the entire partitioned table. Apart from this, there are a couple of odd unimplemented features that add extra restrictions to what you can transport, and make it just a little bit harder to plan object distribution across tablespaces. The tablespace cannot include object tables (even though it can include nested tables), scoped REFs, function-based indexes, domain indexes (which crosses spatial data and context data off the list), various features of snapshot and replication data, tables with that have been set unused, or tables with long columns that have subsequently had extra columns added.

> *There are many limits on what can go into a transportable tablespace. During the early design phase, check that the Oracle data structures you want to transport are acceptable.*

The steps to transport a tablespace or group of tablespaces are quite simple. First, the tablespace must be made read-only with the command

```
alter tablespace TS_XXX read only;
```

You then need to export the tablespace's meta-data by passing a special set of parameters to the *exp* command. For the previous tablespace, an export parameter file like the following would be sufficient, and could be called with the command line "exp parfile=tt.par":

```
userid=sys/change_on_install
transport_tablespace=y
tablespaces=(ts_xxx)
file=metadata.dmp
```

You also have the option of exporting triggers, grants, and constraints. These may not, of course, be appropriate or workable in the target database.

This export is rather slow, which may be the result of a known bug that has been fixed in 8.1.6. The export contains information describing the objects, the owners of the objects, and the states of the data files in the listed tablespace so that the target data dictionary can be patched up with descriptions of the incoming tablespace. If you want to check that the set of tablespaces is going to be transportable (or at least that it is self-consistent), you can use the DBMS_TTS package to test the tablespace and then check the TRANSPORT_SET_VIOLATIONS view to list any problems:

```
execute dbms_tts.transport_set_check('ts_xxx',true)
select * from transport_set_violations;

VIOLATIONS
-------------------------------------------
TABLE DEMO.T3 in tablespace TS_XXX not allowed in transportable set
TABLE DEMO.TAB2 in tablespace TS_XXX not allowed in transportable set
```

In this case, both these tables were object tables that had to be dropped or moved out of the tablespace.

Once you have copied the data files and the dump file to the target system, you need to run the *imp* utility on the target database with a new parameter file like the following:

```
userid=sys/change_on_install
transport_tablespace=y
file=metadata.dmp
datafiles=('/u01/oradata/prod/df_xxx_01.dbf')
tablespaces=(ts_xxx)
tts_owners=(jpl1, demo)
fromuser=jpl1
touser=jpl2
```

The first four lines in the file are mandatory, but the list of tablespaces and object owners (tts_owners) will be read from the meta-data file. However, if you do include tts_owners=() and tablespaces=(), this information will be compared with the meta-data, and the import will fail if it does not match. datafiles=() does *not* have to match the set of names of the files that existed on the source database, so you do not have to rebuild an exactly matching directory structure on the target machine to copy the files to it.

Apart from changing the names of the data files on the fly, you can also use fromuser=() and touser=() to change the ownership of objects as the import takes place. The list of "from" users must be in the tts_owners list, and each "from" user must be matched by a "to" user who exists in the target database. For example, I could modify the previous parameter file to show

```
fromuser=(jpl1,demo)
touser=(scott,scott)
```

Technically, this option of merging users into the target database is legal, but be very careful that the two "from" users do not both own an object of the same type with the same name, or the import will fail.

Once the files have been copied, the import is surprisingly quick, after which you can finish up by converting the tablespace (on both the source and target databases) back to READ/WRITE mode with the command

```
alter tablespace TS_XXX read write;
```

It is rather unfortunate that partitions cannot be passed around in this way, because I can easily envisage this mechanism being used to transfer the latest week's (or latest day's) summaries from a data warehouse to a data mart, and it seems very likely that "the latest data" will tend to translate into "the latest partition." Of course this is just an irritant, not a showstopper, because you can work around the problem by exchanging partitions with tables before exporting the tablespaces. Nevertheless, it is another bit of infrastructure that has to be worked out and made bulletproof.

An important point to remember when transporting tablespaces is that the target tablespace must *not* exist on the target database before you try to import it. This gives you two options: you either keep replacing a tablespace by dropping it (including its contents), which can be rather time-consuming (especially if you haven't used locally managed tablespaces), or you keep adding new tablespaces, which leads you into the performance issue noted earlier about tablespace names never being deleted and the workload on SMON increasing with the number of tablespaces created. Think carefully about the strategy you are going to adopt when you start passing around tablespaces.

> *It is easy to export a transportable tablespace. The awkward and time-consuming part may be making a hole for it to fit in the receiving database.*

Tablespace Point-in-Time Recovery

In a similar vein to transportable tablespaces, Oracle 8.1 offers a very flexible path to *tablespace point-in-time recovery*. This allows you to keep your database running while restoring an older copy of a given tablespace in the database, and rolling it forward in time but leaving it out of sync with the rest of the database. (You might, for instance, need to do this because a batch run was executed twice on a critical dataset and has messed it up completely. Thus you need to take the dataset back into the past and try again, without denying the users access to the rest of the database.)

Part of your strategy, then, for splitting the database into tablespaces can be aimed at recognizing where serious errors could occur that could be addressed by tablespace point-in-time recovery (hereafter referred to as TSPITR). Ideally, the number of objects in any such tablespace or group of tablespaces should be as small as possible to minimize the potential side effects of referential integrity being put into disarray by different parts of the database operating at different points in time.

Traditionally, if you experienced a major problem that required you to revert some of your data to an earlier point in time, it was necessary to build (somewhere) a backup copy of your database, recover to a suitable point in time, then export the objects that you wanted to recover. These objects could then be dropped from the production database and imported from the backup database, or re-created through a database link using the *create table as select* command.

TSPITR reduces recovery time by using mechanisms similar to the transportable tablespace mechanism. In the safer version of the strategy, you build a minimal backup database on another machine and recover it to the best possible point in time. You then use the *exp* utility on the backup copy to create a meta-data file describing the recovered tablespaces, copy them to the primary database, and use the *imp* utility to reload the meta-data into the primary database.

In the dangerous version of the strategy, which you should use only if you don't have the machine resources to use the safe version, you put the tablespace to be recovered "off-line for recovery," then overwrite the files in the tablespace with the backup copies, find space for a minimal set of backup files (SYSTEM tablespace, and so on), and mount a "clone" database using a secondary, low-resource instance. The reason for mounting the clone database is that this cues Oracle to take special precautions to avoid damaging the primary database. Once the clone database has been recovered to the correct point in time, you follow the same procedure of using the *exp* utility to generate the meta-data file for the recovered tablespace. You then shut down the clone and use the *imp* utility to load the meta-data file describing the recovered tablespace into the primary database.

There are restrictions on how you can use TSPITR. They are largely to do with irrecoverable actions such as dropping tablespaces or creating new tablespaces or data files with the same name as previously existing tablespaces/data files. There are also special considerations for handling partitioned tables, especially because some partitions may need recovery and others may not. Again, there may be effectively irrecoverable actions, such as splitting partitions, that have taken place between the backup and the recovery target. Finally, there are a number of different types of objects that cannot be recovered with TSPITR:

- Any object that has been subject to NOLOGGING updates
- Objects owned by SYS (which includes rollback segments, of course)

- Tables with VARRAY columns
- Tables with nested tables
- Tables with external files
- Replicated master tables
- Snapshot logs
- Snapshot tables

It is worth noting that Oracle recommends that the "safest" way of performing a TSPITR is by using *rman* with a recovery catalog, and in conjunction with Oracle support. That should be sufficient to warn off most DBAs!

To me, the bottom line with TSPITR, especially the dangerous version, is that I'm sure it would work, but I'd hate to have to do it for real. If I did, I'd take a full backup first and then read the manual three times before starting. Perhaps the last word on TSPITR should come from the recovery manual itself:

> *"You should not perform TSPITR for the first time on a production system, or during circumstances where there is a time constraint."*

Problems and Quirks

Tablespace names are never removed from the data dictionary (cluster SYS.C_TS# table TS$), and by default, each tablespace entry occupies a minimum of one block in this cluster, even if it is a locally managed tablespace rather than a dictionary-managed tablespace. Because SMON scans TS$ every five minutes, you need to avoid letting the cluster get too large. Your options are (1) hack the SQL.BSQ script that creates the data dictionary to reduce the cluster size in the C_TS# cluster, but make sure you get official approval from Oracle Support first; or (2) recycle tablespace names as much as possible and avoid using time-related tablespace names, especially if you are taking advantage of transportable tablespaces.

Queries against the view families xxx_FREE_SPACE and xxx_EXTENTS are reputed to be much slower on systems with locally managed tablespaces because of the need to scan the 64K bitmap headers on files and segment headers. I'm not sure that this is entirely fair because the view families xxx_EXTENTS and xxx_SEGMENTS are now based on a much more complex union than they used to be (the nine-part SYS_OBJECTS view), which will have some impact even in the absence of locally managed tablespaces. In addition, the overhead on xxx_FREE_SPACE is likely to be a single read per file, which isn't really likely to be much more expensive than the overhead of scanning the C_TS$ cluster, which currently takes place.

There are some potentially irritating restrictions on transportable tablespaces, but the more common data-related ones can be worked around quite easily. Given the enormous improvement over the previous workload needed to move data from one database to another, it would not be gracious to complain too much about such details.

Strategy Notes

Do think carefully about how the different objects in your database have different handling characteristics, purposes, and sizes. Allocate them to different tablespaces accordingly so that you can monitor them more easily to check that actual use matches predicted use.

It is a very good idea to ensure that all the extents in a given tablespace are the same size. The easiest way to achieve this in Oracle 8.1 is to use locally managed tablespaces with the UNIFORM allocation option. You should not set the uniform size to anything less than 64K, and at this size you should not use a file larger than a few hundred megabytes.

I believe that modern disks are too big to be used efficiently. A total of 9GB of *active* data per device is probably a good top limit for an Oracle database. However, don't let this stop you from creating tablespaces that allow for plenty of spare room for "unused extents." You will experience an overhead during backup, but the extra space makes it easier to deal with rebuilding objects when necessary. When you feel that the tablespace is stable, you can shrink it down manually to a more appropriate size.

Transportable tablespaces are a great way of moving summary tables (for example) from a massive data warehouse to a small data mart very quickly. There are a few restrictions, though, on what can be done, especially with partitioned tables, so you need to think through the infrastructure very carefully.

Using TSPITR, you can recover an older, "hot" backup version of a tablespace into a live database while the database is running, but it is much safer to make sure you have sufficient spare capacity to do a partial recovery on a separate machine and then use a modified form of transportable tablespaces to move the recovered tablespace into production.

When working on development databases, do try to use tablespaces in a realistic way. It is very common to see development tablespaces with just one huge USERS tablespace (or even worse a huge SYSTEM tablespace and no USERS tablespaces). Keeping control of a database requires sensible use of tablespaces. You need to prove, with your development database, that you can place all your data objects where you want them before you start moving code to production.

CHAPTER 9

Temporary Space

Before the appearance of Oracle 8.1 there were two big issues about "temporary" storage in Oracle. The first was the need for DBAs to manage space required for "internal" purposes, and the second was the problem of how developers could safely and efficiently keep "scratch pad" workings in the database.

I have put these two issues together in a single chapter because the best answer to the developer problem includes using the feature aimed at DBAs.

Temporary Tablespaces

Whenever Oracle has to do any large-scale sorting (such as creating an index on a very large table or producing a summary from a large amount of data), there is a chance that the volume of data to be sorted is so large that the sort cannot be handled completely in memory, and one of the tablespaces has to hold intermediate sort runs.

> *The init.ora parameter SORT_AREA_SIZE allows you to specify the limit on the memory used by a single sort operation. There is often some benefit in increasing it from its default of 64K. A value of 1MB would not be unusual, but raising it above a few megabytes rarely helps.*

Oracle allows you to specify for each user the tablespace he should use for large sorts that need to write out intermediate results. In fact, most sites tend to have a single tablespace dedicated to this purpose, with all users configured to use it. In Oracle 7.3 it became possible to declare that a tablespace should be restricted to having a special content type of TEMPORARY for handling just this type of work. This had two important consequences.

First, it became illegal to create any permanent objects in such a tablespace. This ensured that DBAs monitoring the I/O activity on such tablespaces wouldn't be fooled by misleading results from activity resulting from permanent objects being muddled with sorting activity.

Second, instead of users' shadow processes creating a sort segment and adding extents every time they started sorting, and then dropping everything when the sort was complete, the instance itself would allocate a single sort segment in the tablespace. The instance would then add and drop extents only when really necessary, and would manage all the users' requests for sort space by keeping an in-memory map of who was using which extents. This reduced the impact on the data dictionary tables relating to space management (FET$, UET$, SEG$, and TS$), especially in a busy Parallel Query environment, and most particularly in a Parallel Server environment (see Chapter 22). Only as the instance was shut down would the single segment be released, to be cleaned up the next time the database started up.

> *If your "temporary tablespace" is always full, don't worry. This is normal behavior if the tablespace has been declared to have contents of type TEMPORARY. Check the view family XXX_TABLESPACES.*

There was still an irritating problem, though. Even though the tablespace was nothing more than a huge scribble pad with nothing but extremely transient rubbish in it, it was still a standard tablespace subject to all the rules of availability, backup, and recovery.

If you did a database backup, you had to back up the tablespace. If you had to do a full database recovery, you had to restore the tablespace. One site at which I worked recently had a 300GB database, of which 40GB was the tablespace they used for sorting, so every night they were backing up 40GB of empty space.

Of course it wasn't strictly necessary to back up and recover this tablespace. It is possible, as you recover a database, to tell Oracle that some tablespaces have gone missing and should be discarded, and this type of temporary tablespace is the obvious candidate for such cavalier treatment. You would have to be a fairly confident DBA to do this, though. I have occasionally suggested it as an option, and the idea has always been turned down, even though in principle it is perfectly safe (and in practice has been demonstrated to work).

As we shall see later, there is actually a valid argument against taking this approach with earlier versions of Oracle anyway—related to the trade-off between the time required for backups and the time limit imposed for recovery.

It is worth clarifying at this point how SORT_AREA_SIZE and SORT_AREA_RETAINED_SIZE affect sorting. The use of the former is quite well understood: When you sort, you sort in memory if you are allowed to allocate enough memory. The memory limit for a single sort operation is SORT_AREA_SIZE.

The use of the latter parameter is less well understood. The more recent descriptions in the manuals say something like "the SORT_AREA _RETAINED_SIZE is the amount of memory retained when a sort completes and the results are being returned." But what does this actually mean?

There is a bit of a problem answering this question, because the answer changes with the configuration of your database. Let's start with the traditional approach. Execute a statement that requires you to sort a reasonably large amount of data, but set SORT_AREA_SIZE to something large to accommodate it (for example, 8MB) and set SORT_AREA_RETAINED_SIZE to something small (say, 64K). A statement like the following (needing at least 500K for the result set, given the size of the rows) should be a good test. reverse() is included simply to avoid complications of the optimizer confusing the issue by deciding to do cunning indexed access paths to avoid sorting:

```
select reverse(objname), padding from
(
    select
            reverse(object_name)        objname,
            rpad('x',500)               padding
    from
            all_objects
    where
            rownum <= 1000
)
order by
        reverse(objname)
;
```

After running this statement you should get the following apparently contradictory results when you look at the dynamic performance views (see Appendix B):

- V$SYSSTAT—There have been no sorts to disk.
- V$FILESTAT—The files for the temporary tablespace have been written to and read from. In this case, approximately 670K of data was written and read.

Why the contradiction? In fact, both sets of statistics are true. None of the *sorting* went to disk because the volume of sort required was less than the sort area size. Checking the memory used in the program global area (PGA; one of the memory areas in an Oracle process), we would see an increase of 1.5MB, most of which would be memory required for sorting. However, the moment the sort was complete, and the SQL*Plus session was due to receive results, the sorted data was dumped into a temporary segment and an area matching SORT_AREA_RETAINED_SIZE was used in the user global area (UGA; another of the memory areas in an Oracle process) as a pipeline to pass the data from disk to the front end.

If we bump SORT_AREA_RETAINED_SIZE up to 2MB and repeat the test, nothing gets dumped to disk. Instead we see that the UGA has expanded by approximately 750K, and the PGA has expanded by roughly 800K. This gives us the total 1.5MB I had before, but now the memory allocated in the UGA is sufficient to hold the full result set without dumping it to disk.

The moral of the story is that you should always set SORT_AREA_RETAINED_SIZE to a reasonable fraction of SORT_AREA_SIZE (I tend to start at approximately 50% in most cases) to avoid unnecessary writes to disk after sorts are complete.

> *A reasonable rule of thumb for SORT_AREA_RETAINED_SIZE:*
> *Set it to half SORT_AREA_SIZE, then adjust gradually according to*
> *application requirements.*

There is a trap in this, though. The sample code I provided was for a very simple operation. It is very easy to write SQL code that requires more than one sort to take place at the same time. For example,

```
select
        b1.name, b2,name
from
        big_table_1 b1,
        big_table_2 b2
```

```
where
        b1.id = b2.id
order by
        b1.name
;
```

If the execution path for this query is a sort-merge join, then Oracle needs to perform three sorts, and keep three memory blocks open for intermediate results simultaneously.

First, big_table_1 has to be sorted by ID using a memory allocation up to SORT_AREA_SIZE. A window of SIZE SORT_AREA_RETAINED_SIZE is then kept on the sorted result, the rest of the result set (if there is any) is dumped to disk, and the memory used for the actual sort operation is (notionally) released.

Second, big_table_2 is sorted by ID in exactly the same way, resulting in two concurrent memory allocations of SORT_AREA_RETAINED_SIZE being open.

In the next step, the two windows are used to read the datasets, in order, back to the MERGE operation, which forwards the merged stream to a third SORT operation, resulting in the SORT_AREA_SIZE memory being (re)opened and a third SORT_AREA_RETAINED_SIZE being allocated. Consequently, your biggest memory demand is three lots of SORT_AREA_RETAINED_SIZE and one lot of SORT_AREA_SIZE.

If you expect to execute a large number of operations that open multiple concurrent sorts, then you need to allow for this by scaling back SORT_AREA_RETAINED_SIZE.

> *Complex SQL statements use at most one memory segment of size SORT_AREA_SIZE, but may use several memory segments of size SORT_AREA_RETAINED_SIZE concurrently.*

If you need to find out how often your application uses SQL that is complex enough to cause multiple allocations of SORT_AREA_RETAINED_SIZE, and want to estimate the scale of the resulting SORT operations, a good starting point is to look in V$SQL, which has a column labeled SORTS. Don't get too alarmed by high (more than two) numbers of sorts in a single statement. First, they may not be concurrent, and, second, the last couple of sorts in a query may not have many rows left to sort.

So What's New in 8.1?

In Oracle 8.1, the idea of disposable tablespaces, or at least tablespaces with disposable files, is now official: There are bits of the database that you don't have to back up or recover. In fact you *can't* recover them, as we shall see later.

You can create a "proper" temporary tablespace with the following SQL statement:

```
create temporary tablespace temp_proper
tempfile '/u01/data/oracle/D815/temp_p_01.dbf'
size 500064K
uniform size 500K;
```

This statement creates a tablespace that is NOLOGGING, LOCALLY MANAGED (see Chapter 8), and of content type TEMPORARY. Any real object created in this tablespace will generally "try" to avoid generating redo log. Extent management is through a bitmap at the start of each file in the tablespace, and thus has little effect on the data dictionary, and space can be allocated only for sorting and the new "scratch pad" types of table (discussed later).

The UNIFORM SIZE 500K clause means that every bit in the tablespace's bitmaps will correspond to exactly 500K, and every extent that gets created will be exactly 500K. If you omit this clause, then the default is 1MB. The smallest legal value is two Oracle blocks.

There is one important difference between temporary tablespaces and other locally managed tablespaces: they cannot be specified as AUTOALLOCATE. In other words, they cannot be system managed. I assume this is because system-managed tablespaces can allocate extents of different sizes, but Oracle's internal algorithms for handling a sort segment expect all the extents to be the same size.

You may have spotted the strange sizing of the data file. The odd 64K (which you need to add to every file in the temporary tablespace) is there to accommodate the file's header and the space-management bitmap, and the file will probably be larger by one more Oracle block when you look at it through the operating system.

You may want to be a little careful with sizing your files. Because temporary tablespaces are automatically uniform sizing, every extent is the same size, and the total available space is "file size – 64K." If you pick a very large extent size and forget to allow for that 64K, then you will end up wasting a large chunk of space at the end of the file. Actually, I usually tend to keep the numbers small and simple by sizing in megabytes, and then throwing away one extra megabyte, so I often end up with file sizes like 501MB or 1001MB.

There are some variations possible on the file header. Most of it is taken up by the bitmap that lists the extents in that file and whether they are used. Depending on your choice of database block size, there is room for 27,000 to 30,000 bits in the 64K header section. The "bitmap" is actually a lot closer to 2 bytes per extent, which would allow for roughly 1.8GB in a single file if you set the extent size at 64K.

If you choose to have very large files with very small extent sizes, which is not a very good idea, you will find that the header section of the file can be a multiple of 64K. If, on the other hand, you allow a file to start small and then extend it so much that it needs more bitmap space, then extra odd-size fragments of bitmaps will be created and scattered throughout the file.

You may have noticed the word *tempfile* appearing in the tablespace definition where you might normally expect to see the word *datafile*. Temporary tablespaces are created from very special temporary files, and there is a set of dynamic performance views relating to temporary files that correspond to those for normal data files (Table 9-1).

For tracking purposes, there are three other views associated with temporary tablespaces: V$TEMP_SPACE_HEADER, V$TEMP_EXTENT_POOL, and V$TEMP_EXTENT_MAP. Be careful of V$TEMP_EXTENT_MAP because it holds one row for every potential extent in every one of your temporary tablespaces. Thus it can be very large and it requires Oracle to read the bitmap blocks of each file in the buffer to interpret them. The view V$TEMP_EXTENT_POOL is possibly the most useful of these views because it tells you how many extents in each temporary tablespace are currently in use, either for sorting (which will also be reflected in V$SORT_SEGMENT) or as temporary tables.

Table 9-1. Datafile Views and Tempfile Views

Data Files	Temp Files	Purpose
V$DATAFILE	V$TEMPFILE	List of files (available even when database is shut down)
V$FILESTAT	V$TEMPSTAT	I/O activity and times
V$FILE_PING	V$TEMP_PING	Parallel Server pings per file
DBA_DATA_FILES	DBA_TEMP_FILES	List of files (available only when the database is open)

Temporary Files

If you decide to create very large files for your temporary tablespace, you may notice that the operation completes very quickly. When adding a 900MB file to a temporary tablespace with the following command, I found that the time to complete was just less than one second, compared with a couple of minutes for adding a similar-size file to a normal tablespace:

```
alter tablespace temp_proper
add tempfile '/u01/data/oracle/D815/temp_p_02.dbf'
size 900M;
```

Clearly, Oracle was formatting only the first 64K of the file, and not going to the trouble of zeroing out all the data in the rest of the file, as it does with ordinary data files. The reason for this is simple: Anything in the temporary tablespace is junk and can be thrown away at any time. If the database crashes, no one is going to worry about the data that was in the temporary tablespace.

Because of the dramatic difference in the speed of creating the temporary files, it becomes possible to make a backup of the database without making a backup of the temporary tablespaces. The recovery strategy is simply to recover the rest of the database, and then rebuild the temporary tablespace by re-creating its files afterward.

As I said earlier, this type of strategy has always been available for the brave of heart, but the downside of doing it before the invention of the "proper" temporary tablespace was that it took a lot of time to create and format a data file.

Typically, you may expect to spend a minute or two per gigabyte when creating a normal data file. This translates to approximately one hour for a 40GB tablespace of the normal kind. With this sort of target time, you could find that it was quicker to rebuild the tablespace by streaming it in from a tape backup. As so often happens with Oracle, you had to make a choice between two undesirable options—waste time (and tape) every day on backing up the temporary tablespace to get a faster recovery time, or save time on the backup but make the recovery time longer on the rare occasion when it was necessary to rebuild the tablespace. Using proper temporary tablespaces, you no longer have to face this dilemma.

If you have ever used the ***backup controlfile to trace*** command, you will be familiar with the ***create controlfile*** command that this generates. Do it with a temporary tablespace on-line and you will discover two new features. First, the tempfiles are not listed in the ***create controlfile*** command; second, there will be extra lines of code near the bottom of the file that look like

```
# Commands to add tempfiles to temporary tablespaces.
# Online tempfiles have complete space information.
# Other tempfiles may require adjustment.
ALTER TABLESPACE TEMP_PROPER ADD TEMPFILE
'/u01/data/oracle/D815/temp_p_01.dbf' REUSE;
# End of tempfile additions.
```

I pointed out earlier that the views V$DATAFILE and DBA_DATA_
FILES don't hold entries for temporary files. You may view this as a nuisance,
but there are a number of backup and recovery tools that use V$DATAFILE
or DBA_DATA_FILES as the source of filenames to be handled. By introducing two new views, Oracle has ensured that existing tools will avoid backing up
the unnecessary temporary files. Basically, your backup strategy can now safely
ignore all proper temporary tablespaces and you can re-create files for them
on the fly as needed.

One of the more interesting ways in which Oracle takes advantage of
the special tempfile facility is with *standby databases* (see Chapter 24). The
standby database is a "hot backup" of the production database running in permanent recovery mode, but with Oracle 8.1 you can suspend the recovery, open the
database in read-only mode, use it for reporting, and then switch it back to recovery mode. If you have a temporary tablespace predefined in the production database, you can add extra tempfiles to it when you start the standby database in
read-only mode—a great convenience if you want to use your standby for massive number-crunching reports that you never want to run on production.

Temporary Tables

In line with the introduction of proper temporary tablespaces, Oracle has also
produced proper temporary tables—in other words, tables that "cease to exist"
as soon as a transaction is committed or as soon as a session terminates. The
application code doesn't have to handle dropping the table.

The reason for writing about temporary tables in the same chapter as
Oracle's new-look temporary tablespaces is simply that the obvious place
(from Oracle's perspective) to put a temporary table is in a proper temporary
tablespace. A sample of the syntax is

```
create global temporary table t_temp1 (
    n1    number(4),
    v1    varchar2(32),
    constraint tt_pk primary key (n1)
)
on commit preserve rows;
```

There are a couple of points to notice about this statement. There are no storage clauses: Any such clause (for example, TABLESPACE, PCTFREE, STORAGE, and so on) results in error "ORA-14451: unsupported feature." This command does not allocate any space in the database; it simply puts the logical definition into the data dictionary.

The ON COMMIT clause is specific to temporary tables. The default option (ON COMMIT DELETE ROWS) is for the table to become spontaneously empty whenever you commit (or roll back) a transaction. However, with the PRESERVE ROWS option shown here, rows continue to exist for the duration of your session, but the table content (not the table definition) spontaneously ceases to exist when your session ends.

The key words *global temporary* identify this as an object that (1) only has to be declared once (as part of the application build perhaps) to have its definition available for use by all suitably privileged users but (2) never has any permanent physical existence.

The most immediate benefit of this is that there is only one definition of the table structure in the data dictionary. With previous versions of Oracle, if an application created a table to use temporarily as a scratch pad, Oracle would have to do a staggering amount of work putting entries into dictionary tables such as OBJ$ (objects), TAB$ (tables), IND$ (indexes), COL$ (columns), ICOL$ (index columns), CON$ (constraints), and CDEF$ (constraint definitions) to name the most common.

> You issue the **create global temporary table** command only once, to make the definition permanently available. If the same user ID issues the command again, the normal error "ORA-00955: name is already used" is raised.

You may note that it is possible to create indexes on temporary tables. The indexes are equally temporary. In the example, I use a primary key constraint to generate an index definition (again, no space is actually allocated at this point). I could equally have used a **create index** command against the table to produce the same effect. So what happens when you try to use this nonexistent object? For example,

```
insert into t_temp1 values (1,'one');
```

As soon as you insert any data into the table, extents are allocated to store the data *from your currently nominated temporary tablespace* (the one that

Oracle uses on your behalf for handling large sorts). In our example, two extents are allocated; one for the table data and one for the index data. If your current temporary tablespace is an ordinary tablespace, these extents show up in V$SORT_SEGMENT. If it is a "proper" temporary tablespace, they register in V$TEMP_EXTENT_POOL as well.

The beauty of this arrangement is that if another user also decides to insert data into T_TEMP1, they too will have a pair of extents allocated to them, and these extents will be completely independent from your extents. Effectively, every single user of this temporary table will have completely localized copies of the table all sharing the same structural definition. In fact, the different versions of the table could be in completely different tablespaces, if the users have been configured with different temporary tablespaces.

Unless you have used the ON COMMIT PRESERVE ROWS clause, the data you insert into the table simply disappears and the extents are deallocated every time you issue a *commit* command. If you have used ON COMMIT PRESERVE ROWS, the data and the extents disappear only as the session terminates. You can check the life span of data in a temporary table from the DURATION column of the view family xxx_TABLES. The value is either NULL (for an ordinary table), SYS$TRANSACTION, or SYS$SESSION.

From this point onward, T_TEMP1 behaves in almost all respects like a perfectly ordinary table. You can insert, update, or delete data, as well as commit, roll back, or truncate (which will drop the extents of a transaction-based temporary table). You can include it in complex joins and permanent views. There are, however, some restrictions on temporary tables.

You can't create index-organized temporary tables, and you can't partition them, which is not unreasonable because you probably shouldn't be planning to use temporary tables to store large amounts of data needing any subtle, high-performance processing.

Similarly, you cannot rebuild the index on a temporary table. But then again, temporary tables should really be quite small, and index rebuilds are usually worth doing only on very large objects.

You cannot create foreign key constraints on temporary tables, although you can create triggers that could be used to enforce a required check against a parent table.

You cannot enable parallel queries or parallel DML on temporary tables, although there is a small anomaly in error reporting that suggests you can. And you can't involve temporary tables in distributed transactions.

You cannot include nested tables or varrays in temporary tables, although simple user-defined object types and LOBs can be used as the columns of a temporary table.

You cannot create an index on a temporary table if any session is currently "bound" to the table—in other words, if any session has got data in its local version of the table. In fact, any attempt to change any aspect of the table definition, such as adding a column, while the definition is in use leads to the slightly misleading error "ORA-14452: attempt to create, alter or drop an index on temporary table already in use."

One particular consequence of this is that you cannot speed up creating temporary data with the usual trick of "insert data then create index." Once any session has any data in a temporary table, then that table cannot have an index definition added to it, even if your session is the only session with current data.

Given the half-public/half-private nature of global temporary tables, this is not too surprising. It suggests a feature aimed at embedded code in OLTP types of applications rather than completely ad hoc "cheap scratch pad" use. Perhaps in a later version of Oracle we will see "local" temporary tables with extra features aimed at eliminating even more of the work normally associated with "scratch pad" manipulation.

Perhaps the most important restriction on temporary tables at present is that the *analyze* command does not collect statistics. Where, after all, could you put the statistics if you collected them? Table statistics are usually stored in the table definition (in SYS.TAB$), and there is only one entry in the data dictionary for a global temporary table, regardless of how many users may have created their own local copies based on that definition.

The command *appears* to work insofar as no error message is produced, but in fact only user-defined statistical methods (also known as *domain indexes*, a somewhat esoteric option of little interest to most of us) can be applied to temporary tables.

> *You cannot supply statistics to the optimizer describing the data you have stored in a temporary table. The **analyze** command has no effect.*

The critical side effect of being unable to analyze temporary tables is that unhinted SQL code referencing nothing but temporary tables will use the RBO to determine the access path if your optimizer goal is set to CHOOSE. This isn't necessarily too much of a problem, although it makes some access paths unavailable. You might like to try this test:

```
create global temporary table t_temp1 (
    n1    number(4),
    v1    varchar2(32),
    constraint tt_pk primary key (n1)
)
on commit preserve rows;

insert into t_temp1
select rownum, object_name from all_objects;
commit;
analyze table t_temp1 compute statistics;
        -- The command will return VERY quickly.
        -- without raising an error.


set autotrace on explain

alter session set optimizer_mode = choose;
select count(*) from t_temp1;

alter session set optimizer_mode = all_rows;
select count(*) from t_temp1;
```

You should find that under CHOOSE optimization, Oracle has to do a table scan of T_TEMP1. Under ALL_ROWS optimization, Oracle can use an index-only scan (in this case, a fast full scan). The latter is an execution path that is not available to the RBO. If you repeat the experiment with a normal table instead of the temporary table, the statistics will be gathered and the query will choose the index scan both times.

Although things can go a little wrong when using a temporary table in isolation, the biggest performance problems can appear when you start to join temporary tables to permanent tables. It is possible, especially when the temporary tables are rather large, for Oracle to produce extremely bad access paths. For example, Oracle may decide to use a nested loop to step through a temporary table and then do a full table scan of a permanent table for each row it finds, when the "sensible" path (if you could analyze the temporary table) would be a hash join.

If you create views that include temporary tables, or write code that joins temporary tables to permanent tables, you probably need to include hints in your code.

There is, however, an interesting approach to dealing with this problem, invented and passed to the Usenet comp.databases.oracle.server news group by Thomas Kyte of Oracle Corporation (Tkyte@us.oracle.com). If you are

confident that a given global temporary table will always be used in exactly
the same way by everyone who uses it, then you can add "representative" statistics to the table definition with the DBMS_STATS package. For example,
if we knew that everyone who ever used the T_TEMP1 table always put
approximately 1,000 rows of roughly 25 bytes each into it, and assuming that
the Oracle block size was 4K, we could execute the following command
immediately after creating the table definition:

```
begin
    dbms_stats.set_table_stats(
        ownname =>  'JPL1',
        tabname =>  'T_TEMP1',
        numrows =>  1000,
        numblks =>  7
end;
/
```

Similarly, we could use the SET_INDEX_STATS and even the rather
more complex PREPARE_COLUMN_VALUES/SET_COLUMN_STATS
procedures to supply representative statistics about the indexes and columns
in the table.

Be careful, though, that you do not allow one user to insert 10 rows, and
another to insert 1,000,000 rows into the temporary table. The side effects of
unsuitable statistics may be even worse than having no statistics at all. For this
reason, you may choose to have multiple copies of each temporary table, one
each for small, medium, and large volumes of data.

> *You can "fake" representative statistics in a temporary table definition*
> *using the DBMS_STATS package. If you do this, every actual use of*
> *the temporary table has to be constrained to match the expected statis-*
> *tics within reason.*

So why would you use temporary tables anyway? Clearly, the noninter-
ference is a nice feature. Several sessions can use the same table definition
to access completely independent sets of data. This is likely to be much
more efficient than requiring several sessions to share the same data segment by identifying their individual data with some sort of tag. It also eliminates the perennial problem of a working table exploding to an enormous
size during the course of one batch run, say, and then appearing to be a

very large object thereafter even when it contains virtually no data. Because different sessions aren't actually creating their own tables all the time, the stress on the data dictionary is reduced. Also, because statements like ***select * from global_temp_table*** are considered to be the same statement irrespective of the user using it to refer to their local version of the table, using global temporary tables can reduce parse times and stress on the library latching mechanisms.

An obvious example of use is in the perennial problem of "get the next 20 rows of a query." If you have an environment in which a user's session stays live, then the problem of returning rows a page at a time could be addressed by truncating, then populating, a temporary table with the full result set and a meaningless row number on the first call, and then using the meaningless row number to return the next batch of rows thereafter. This is obviously more efficient than using a permanent table, as some applications do. Depending on the nature of the application, it may be much more efficient than the common strategy of rerunning the entire query on each call, counting and discarding rows as you go. It's also safer than this second strategy, which may find a changed set of data or different order of rows on each call.

More significantly, with regard to performance, a temporary table generates less redo than a normal table because Oracle does not generate any redo to protect the actual data (or index) blocks when you do inserts, updates, or deletes on a temporary table. However, because Oracle still has to generate rollback (undo) for any changes you make to the temporary table, in case you want to issue a rollback or rollback to savepoint command, and because rollback always has to be protected by redo (at present), you will find that there is still some redo generated when you use temporary tables. You may think that a temporary table defined with the ON COMMIT DELETE ROWS option would not need to generate rollback information, because any rollback implicitly discards the table. Bear in mind, though, that (1) you can still roll back to save points, which does not discard the table, and (2) you could start using serialized sessions and autonomous transactions, which might require your session to use rollback for internal reasons to hide some of its temporary table data from itself.

Fortunately this rollback and its corresponding redo can be eliminated too, at least from the table if not from the indexes. If your temporary tablespace is a "proper" temporary tablespace (or has been created with the NOLOGGING option), then you can use the /*+ APPEND */ hint with inserts to temporary tables to do "direct-load" inserts. For example,

```
insert /*+ append */ into t1
select rownum, object_name from all_objects;
```

Because you have to commit before you can read the data after such an insert, you have to define your temporary table with the ON COMMIT PRESERVE ROWS option. If you don't commit, you get the somewhat misleading error "ORA-12838: cannot read/modify an object after modifying it in parallel."

If you have indexes defined on the global temporary table when this direct insert takes place, the same mechanism is used for index maintenance as occurs with SQL∗Load in direct mode. The maintenance is postponed until all the data has been inserted into the table, and a new index is built by creating a temporary index on the new data and merging it with the existing index. (Interestingly, this doesn't seem to happen with normal tables. The indexes are maintained in real time, and they generate redo log in the normal fashion.)

When you have finished with the contents of the temporary table, there is another performance benefit when you clear them out. When you truncate or drop a *normal* table, any dirty blocks in the buffer that belong to that table are written to disk before the table is cleared. So if you frequently use tables to hold transient results, this can result in an excessive amount of writing. However, with global temporary tables in a proper temporary tablespace, this flush to disk does not take place. It seems as if Oracle is using the memory management algorithms on temporary tables that it uses on sorts—in other words, creating the tables in PGA memory up to SORT_AREA_SIZE, and only really writing the data into tablespace blocks when the temporary table finally exceeds the SORT_AREA_SIZE limit.

The overall savings you get from using temporary tables in this way can be significant. Clearly, any application that creates and drops small, transient tables very frequently should consider switching to global temporary tables to cut down the stress on the data dictionary. However, at the opposite extreme, an application that depends on large data loads may also be able to take advantage of temporary tables. A fairly common design strategy for data loads is to load a holding table (using SQL∗Load in direct mode), and, once the data is in the database, applying some form of SQL or PL/SQL processing to the data to clean it and enhance it. In many cases this includes selecting rows from the load table and inserting them into another intermediate table before moving them to the final production tables.

Inserts, updates, and deletes on temporary tables generate less redo than the same actions on a normal table. So if you create all your intermediate tables as global temporary tables, you may cut your total I/O cost by as much as 50%.

Even if you don't currently use an intermediate table in this way, but update the table you have loaded through SQL∗Load, you may reduce your total I/O by making an apparently redundant copy of the loaded data simply to get it into a global temporary table:

```
insert /*+ append */ into global_temporary_table
select * from sql_loaded_table;
```

Through this combined use of a temporary table and the direct-load mechanism, you get virtually no rollback and redo generated at this point unless you have indexes on the global temporary table, and even then the amount of rollback (and redo associated with rollback) is approximately half what you might expect.

Of course it would be nice to make the target of your SQL*Load a global temporary table. But SQL*Load is running its own session, so the moment the load completes, the session terminates and all the data ceases to exist!

Temporary LOBs

Another new feature in Oracle 8.1 is the *temporary LOB* (see Chapter 17). Before the introduction of temporary LOBs, you could only manipulate a LOB if you had a valid LOB locator, and the only way to get a valid LOB locator was to insert a LOB (initially perhaps an empty_clob() or empty_blob()) into a table, then select the LOB column for update. This meant that you were then manipulating real data in the database, which might necessarily be subject to rollback and redo log generation and other overhead.

In Oracle 8.1, you can simply invoke createtemporarylob() to create a LOB locator. This call grabs some space from your current temporary tablespace and creates a LOB locator to point to it:

```
dbms_lob.createtemporarylob(
        lob_loc => m_temp_lob,
        cache   => false,
        dur     => dbms_lob.session
)
;
```

The sort of thing you may want this for is to build a LOB, step-by-step, *in memory* before writing it out to a table. Perhaps you have a PL/SQL process that generates a report that traditionally you would have written to a flat file (using DBMS_OUTPUT or UTL_FILE) and "emailed" around the company. Now you can build the "flat file" line by line as a temporary LOB, then store it in a table and allow end users to call it up through a Web interface. If you tried to do this with a permanent LOB, the rollback and redo overhead would be significant.

As with temporary tables, a temporary LOB can be defined with two different durations: the session or the call. (In this context, a call represents the round-trip between a client and a server.) Because LOBs are supposed to be large objects, you may find that an application that takes advantage of temporary LOBs uses a lot of your temporary tablespace very quickly—another conflict of interest.

Problems and Quirks

Although Oracle's latest offering in the temporary storage arena is a great improvement over the past, it still suffers from one serious defect: conflict of interest. As I pointed out earlier, the space used by global temporary tables is always allocated in the user's temporary tablespace, and it is not possible to name an explicit alternative location. But the user's temporary tablespace is also where Oracle does any sorting on behalf of that user (for instance, when creating an index, doing a merge join of two datasets, or working out an aggregate query). Furthermore, temporary LOBs are also created in the temporary tablespace.

It is extremely likely that these three different types of operations will have very different behavior. If a sort goes to disk, it will inevitably be streaming large serial I/Os to and from the disk whereas an application that makes use of a temporary table is more likely to be doing relatively small, scattered I/Os. The use to which you might put a temporary LOB is bounded only by your imagination. Forcing all three activities to the same tablespace could cause the different types of operations to interfere with each other; more significantly (at least according to my philosophy), it makes it harder to decide what is going on. Appendix B points out my enthusiasm for the V$FILESTAT and V$TEMP-STAT views as two of the few things worth monitoring. If heavy serial sorts; multiple, light, random I/Os; and high-volume LOB access are all going to the same place, the quality of information in these views is seriously degraded.

Another defect with this one-tablespace-fits-all strategy comes in when you start to consider sizing. Efficient sorting tends to demand large extents, but if you are running a system with a large number of users all of whom want to use a couple of temporary tables with an index, you may need to allow for a very large number of extents being used concurrently for the temporary tables. Thus you want to use small extents to avoid wasting huge amounts of space. It would be nice to be able to address this problem by using an AUTOALLOCATE tablespace, which starts off allocating small extents then "grows" them very rapidly when a segment needs lots of space. However, as I mentioned earlier, this option cannot be used with temporary tablespaces.

I look forward to the time when Oracle allows three separate tablespaces to be associated with a user—the default, the sort, and the temporary tablespace. (And it doesn't take much effort to come up with demands for a couple more, such as splitting the default into the default for tables and the default for indexes, and splitting the temporary into one space for global temporary tables, another for their indexes, and a third for temporary LOBs.)

There are some inappropriate error messages associated with temporary tables. Mainly these appear to be examples of reusing an existing error message when a new, more precise one should have been created.

Finally, a fussy little detail—when you create *global temporary* tables and *temporary* tablespaces, the syntax to drop these objects is simply "drop table" and "drop tablespace." Personally, for reasons of consistency and aesthetics, I would prefer the ***drop*** commands to be similar to the ***create*** commands, in much the same way that ***create public rollback segment*** and ***create public synonym*** have to be balanced by ***drop public rollback segment*** and ***drop public synonym.***

Strategy Notes

Proper temporary tablespaces can be created very quickly if the space is available, and they have the immediate advantage that they are locally managed rather than dictionary managed, so there is potentially much less overhead and contention from using them. The surprise of Oracle 8.1 is that the default database created by the Oracle installation uses a traditional tablespace as the temporary tablespace. Always use proper temporary tablespaces.

Make sure that you are not backing up the files that make up temporary tablespaces. This would be a huge waste of time and tape. Temporary tablespaces can be rebuilt amazingly quickly.

Given that a user's temporary tablespace is used both for sorting and for her version of temporary tables, it is a good idea to separate "big sorters" from "little scribblers"; in other words, separate users who need to do large sorts from those who need to use small temporary tables. Create several temporary tablespaces, possibly with different uniform sizes, and allocate different users to them.

> *Pre-8.1 it was always a good idea to have at least two temporary tablespaces in any production system and to maintain scripts that could reallocate all users from one to the other very quickly. This allowed a rapid fix to be applied if one of the temporary tablespaces got damaged and went off-line.*

Think carefully before you decide you need to introduce a temporary table into an application. Even though the allocation and deallocation of space is much more efficient than it would be for normal tables, there is still room for contention between processes as extents are allocated and freed, especially for tables with ON COMMIT DELETE ROWS. An alternative option for efficient handling of small amounts of transient data can be found in PL/SQL tables of objects (see Chapter 16).

Be very careful about mixing temporary tables and permanent tables in time-critical code. Because the temporary tables have no statistics, the access paths chosen by Oracle in this type of situation could be inappropriate. This is not likely to be a problem if the temporary tables are very small, but if you do this type of thing with large temporary tables, you should probably include hints in the SQL that uses them.

It is possible to use the DBMS_STATS package to precreate "representative" statistics for temporary tables. If you do this, make sure that the actual use of those temporary tables does not put in "nonrepresentative" quantities of data.

Check your values for SORT_AREA_SIZE and SORT_AREA_RETAINED_SIZE. As a very rough rule of thumb, it is probably sensible to have SORT_AREA_RETAINED_SIZE set to a figure between 50% and 75% of SORT_AREA_SIZE. If you expect to execute lots of SQL that causes multiple, large, concurrent sorts, you may need to revise this figure downward to avoid excessive memory demand.

CHAPTER 10

Files, Raw, and RAID

Tablespaces and files make up the large-scale structure of an Oracle database. The tablespace is the largest unit of the logical structure, and the files that make up a tablespace are the largest unit of the physical structure.

There are a few other files involved in the day-to-day activity of the database of course—the control file(s), the redo log files (on-line and archived)—and these can have a significant impact.

In this chapter we shall see how important it is to have some understanding of how the file-level implementation of your database can make a big difference to performance and to ease of administration.

Files or Raw

One of the most heated discussions that ever goes on between DBAs is whether it is better to use file systems or raw (logical) volumes for their Oracle databases. The arguments tend to polarize to the following: Raw devices go faster versus raw devices are harder to manage.

In fact, it often seems that the most heated arguments occur because it is so hard to keep up with how technology changes. Some of the details of the arguments for and against raw devices relate to the way things were ten years ago (or even one year ago) and no longer apply.

The Management Issues

Once upon a time you could partition a hard disk in one of several ways dictated to you by the hardware supplier: A "massive" 512MB disk could perhaps be split into 128MB + 384MB, or into 96MB + 96MB + 320MB, or into a single 512MB unit, and then each partition had to be addressed through a specific device driver with names like /dev/rdsk/rd3c0s7, as supplied by the hardware supplier.

Configuration was through the UNIX command line, and then you had to create Oracle files that matched the available partition sizes. Too bad if you had configured 128MB + 384MB and your data grew too fast and you actually needed 150MB instead of 128MB.

Safety was another issue. Unless you kept strict paper controls and ensured that everyone with UNIX know-how was kept informed, you could easily find that someone had managed to overwrite your 128MB partition by superimposing the 512MB partition and writing into it.

But what is the real world like today? I have a graphical interface to the logical volume manager. With a few clicks I can see that I have six disks not yet in use on the system. I can attach them as three pairs of mirrors. (I am warned as I do so that there is a volume group defined on one of them already, but I knew that, and it was garbage I was deliberately discarding.)

A few more clicks and I have created two volume groups—one striped at 64K chunks across the three mirrored pairs and using 25% of the space, the other striped at 256K and using another 50% of the space, leaving me with 25% of the disk space free if I need to enlarge either of the volume groups. Just to make things clear to other administrators, I tag the volume groups for raw access only, and name them vg_oraProd_01 and vg_oraProd_02 to show that they are being used for Oracle data files on the production system.

It then takes just a few more clicks to specify a couple of logical volumes in each volume group (leaving some free space in each volume group for expansion), mark them for use as raw devices only, put an entry into the volume manager catalog to show that they are there for an Oracle database, and give them names that are appropriate for Oracle data files.

Raw devices—or at least their modern counterpart, raw logical volumes—don't really offer any big management problem.

The argument that raw devices are harder to manage than file systems is largely based on old technology. Logical volume managers make it easy to handle raw volumes.

Having said that, there is one feature for which using file systems is easier than using raw logical volumes (and consequently introduces a potential threat). In recent versions of Oracle, a facility has been introduced to allow Oracle to extend a data file if it runs out of space. You can give Oracle the option to do this automatically with commands like

```
alter database
datafile '/u00/oradata/demo/bad_news.dbf'
autoextend on
next 20m
maxsize unlimited
;
```

But if you are using raw logical volumes, you can't extend the file from Oracle's perspective until you have extended the volume by using the logical volume manager. Arguably this is a drawback to using raw volumes. This is even more marked when you consider the option for shrinking files. As you will have seen from my discussion on tablespace management (Chapter 8), there is sometimes a good case for being extravagant when sizing tablespaces on the basis that you plan to shrink them later. With file systems, such space can be easily reused in other files. It is sometimes a little more awkward to reuse the space when running on raw volumes. (In fact, some volume managers make both growing and shrinking impractical by demanding complete contiguity in their raw volumes.)

On the other hand using "autoextend" is basically dangerous, and the example I have given shows why. I have, of course, highlighted the worst possible case with my example, because not only is the data file allowed to grow unsupervised, but there is no limit set on the size it is allowed to reach. Consequently, a runaway process could grow the file to fill the file system before crashing. It could even attempt to grow the file to a size that Oracle (or the file system) can't handle properly, and effectively make the entire content of the file unavailable.

You may argue that this wouldn't really happen. You would put in an explicit limit using the maxsize command, and you would monitor the internal space usage of the file. But then, if you are monitoring properly anyway, you won't need to use autoextend; you would use a manual *resize* command at the appropriate time.

Another management issue targeted at raw devices is the limited support for backup. It is often seen as an issue (on UNIX systems at least) that there are several comforting ways to copy a file-system file, but only one way to copy a raw volume—the dd command. Personally, I was never too clear why one of the following lines was considered less acceptable than the other:

```
dd if=/u00/oradata/demo/system_01.dbf of=/dev/rmt0
tar cvf /dev/rmt0 /u00/oradata/demo/system_01.dbf
```

Both seem to be pretty incomprehensible, and I always got the database to write the scripts that did the backups anyway, so I had to be given the syntax of a backup command only once, and then I could forget it.

But, again, things have moved on. Not only do new file systems come with a new array of backup commands and mechanisms, but the backup technology itself comes complete with "Oracle personality modules" these days. You don't need to worry which operating system command is being used to handle the actual backup, you need only point the backup tool at the database instance.

The Performance Issue

Is there a performance benefit of raw devices over file systems? Yes and no.

The traditional UNIX file system with its block-based allocation can usually be shown to be several percent slower than typical logical volume management; on the other hand, newer extent-based file systems such as Veritas make the difference virtually insignificant. There are, of course, several things you can do badly with a file system to make it significantly slower than using raw volumes. There are features of logical raw volumes that can expose bad applications in a way that file systems may not. There are bits of technology that make the question more or less irrelevant.

There are two key features to consider when worrying about file-system performance. The first is the potential for incompatible block sizes, and the second is the difference between rewriting an existing file compared with creating a new file.

I mentioned earlier the importance of picking the correct Oracle block size when creating a database. There are several performance issues to consider when doing this: some of them are related to the way the database will be used, some to the availability of resources, and some to the way that the most important data is handled (see Appendix D). But moving away from database configurations, there is a need to check whether your file system is going to favor the Oracle block size you would like to use.

> *It is possible to choose an Oracle block size that is inappropriate for your file-system configuration, and has a significant impact on performance.*

Just as Oracle uses its block size as the smallest unit of internal storage, so the file system has a block size that it uses as its unit of reading and writing (and the disk subsystem has another, and the memory handling system has yet another). The file-system block size can have a critical impact on the performance of your database. Imagine that you have created a database with a 4K Oracle block size but the file system has been built with an 8K file-system block size. What happens when the database writer (DBWR) decides to write a block?

1. DBWR passes the Oracle block to the file system.
2. The file system calculates where to write it, but can't write just 4K.
3. The file system therefore reads the surrounding 8K file-system block from disk.
4. Once the file-system block is in memory, the 4K from Oracle is copied into it.
5. The file system then writes the updated 8K block to disk—whoops! The disk has moved on while the memory update was taking place.
6. The file system has to wait for (at least) another rotation to complete.

On average, a write to the file system that works the first time has to wait for half a rotation for the right bit of disk to come under the write heads. If the Oracle block is smaller than the file-system block, a write to the file system has to work in two passes and has to wait an average of 1.5 rotations. Table 10-1 gives some sample figures for mixing 2K, 4K, and 8K Oracle block sizes on a small HP9000. The figures show the time required to do 1,000 random writes to a file when the file-system block size is 8K. The point to notice is that when the size of the write matches the file-system block size, the time to write drops

Table 10-1. Performance Impact of Block Size Mismatch

No. of Writes	8K File System	Raw Device
1,000 writes of 2K	26.63 sec	11.39 sec
1,000 writes of 4K	25.70 sec	11.45 sec
1,000 writes of 8K	15.61 sec	12.05 sec

dramatically. You will also notice that the raw device doesn't suffer from the same problem, which is why some people "discover" that raw devices are much faster than file systems. Fortunately there are all sorts of cunning algorithms built into file systems for minimizing write time, so the nominal tripling of write time doesn't materialize. However, it is fairly easy to demonstrate that a block size mismatch like this can more or less double the average write time.

If you want to discover whether a particular block size is good or bad for your system, the easiest thing to do is write a little program to emulate a busy DBWR writing to a large file (1GB is totally adequate). A simple C program has little more to do than

```
iFileDes = open(szFilename, O_RDWR | O_DSYNC);

for (iLoopCt = 0 ; iLoopCt < 1000; iLoopCt++ ) {
    whereami = lseek(iFileDes,(rand()) * 4096, SEEK_SET);
    nbytes = write (iFileDes, (void *)mybuf, 4096);
}
```

This opens the file in the same DATA SYNC mode that Oracle opens data files for writing, then jumps to random locations on 4K boundaries writing 4K blocks. Change the 4096 to represent different Oracle block sizes and see which value gives you the best performance.

This type of writing covers the data files (and control files) quite nicely. However, an important part of the Oracle system is the REDO mechanism. Oracle streams data change details to the redo log files all the time, and the log writer (LWGR) process will write anything that is in the buffer whenever a user issues a ***commit*** command. This means that LGWR may be forced to write chunks of data that are smaller than the file-system block size. Depending on the type of application, this may not be much of a problem. A very busy OLTP application with lots of very small data changes will be writing very small chunks almost continuously and will experience block size incompatibility. A DSS-type system that does massive updates and inserts will tend to write very large chunks of redo at each commit, and will not notice the occasional delay resulting from block size incompatibility.

Of course there are two "improved technology" features of modern systems that can make this issue disappear, or hard to find. Some file systems allow for direct I/O. In other words, they ignore the file-system block size and write the exact amount of data (rounded up to the device block size) on request. NT has such a feature, as does the Advanced Veritas file system. The second technology feature is the battery-backed disk cache, which returns a "write confirmed" as soon as the data is in the cache. My little test on a 1GB file is unlikely to prove anything if you have a 4GB disk cache stuck in front of a 1TB black box. In this case you would need to run multiple copies of the process against lots of different files to find out if there is any real difference resulting from block size problems.

> *The redo log files are most likely to suffer from being on file systems because LGWR can be forced to write very small chunks of data very frequently. It is beneficial to put the redo logs on raw devices or on file systems that can implement direct I/O.*

There is one feature of file systems, and file system buffers especially, that doesn't appear in raw systems. Readers block writers and writers block readers. The file system keeps some critical information about each file in a data structure known as the *inode*, and every time a process wants to read or write to the file it has to lock the inode. Readers are allowed to share "read locks" on the inode, but each writer has to hold an exclusive lock on the inode for the duration of the write; this is largely to ensure that a reader does not manage to read a block in midchange. This means that a writer has to wait for all reads on a given file to complete, and a reader has to wait for a writer to complete.

In the past, Oracle used to have only one writer process, DBWR, so this was not a significant issue, but recent versions of Oracle allow for multiple database writer processes (dbwr_io_slaves or db_writer_processes) and also allow other processes to do "direct writes" to the database. It is possible for contention at the file-system level to have a noticeable impact on performance. For this reason, it is a good idea to aim for larger numbers of smaller files, rather than a small number of very large files, so that the potential for inode contention is reduced. It is also the case that modern, journaled file systems tend to be more efficient in the way they use the inode, so the lock periods tend to be shorter and the contention rate lower.

Archiving

I *did* say that there were two key issues to worry about when considering performance. The first was simply the block size; the second was the difference between overwriting an existing file and creating a new file.

It is often overlooked that Oracle spends most of its time operating on preexisting files, but has one job that must create new files on the fly, and this makes a big difference to file-system performance. Archived redo log files are created by copying filled on-line redo logs into a nominated subdirectory, but each archived redo log file has to be created from scratch.

As a file is created and extended, the file system has to go through four different steps. It has to find space for the growing file, it has to register with the file system that the space has been allocated and is no longer available for other files, it has to register in the file's internal "catalog" that the newly acquired space belongs to it, and it has to write the actual file contents. In a block-based file system (lots of very small chunks), this can take a lot of time. In an extent-based file system (in which space allocation can be handled in much larger chunks), the overhead is much smaller. Oracle has gone through several strategies to cope with the fact that archived redo logs have to be created from scratch (for example, allowing multiple archive writers [or archive slaves], allowing large buffers for archive copying, and so on).

> *Archived redo logs must be written to a file system, and they are created on the fly. This is the single slowest I/O operation that Oracle has to execute.*

Ultimately, therefore, the speed of the database may be limited by the speed with which you can create archived logs, and the question of whether raw systems are faster than file systems then becomes fairly irrelevant.

The fragment of C program I included earlier can be modified to approximate the behavior of the archive writer (ARCH) on your database system by removing the random *seek* command, adding the CREATE FILE option, and writing in chunks of 64K:

```
iFileDes = open(szFilename, O_RDWR | O_CREAT | O_DSYNC);
for (iLoopCt = 0 ; iLoopCt < 1000; iLoopCt++ ) {
        nbytes = write (iFileDes, (void *)mybuf, 65536);
}
```

If you try a test like this against the traditional UNIX file system, and a modern journaled file system, you will find the difference to be quite extraordinary. Table 10-2 is a sample of results from a small HP9000 system using the JxFS variant of Veritas as the journaled file system. The times are for creating and writing a file of 128MB using sequential writes of 32K. For comparative purposes, the time for overwriting a raw volume is included, even though you can't use raw volumes for archived redo logs.

Table 10-2. Overwriting Files versus Creating Files

Task	UNIX File System	Journaled File System	Raw Device
Create new file	7 min 25 sec	1 min 43 sec	Not applicable
Reuse existing file	3 min 33 sec	38 sec	31 sec

The interesting thing to note is that even on fast extent-based file systems it looks as if Oracle can fill an on-line redo log approximately three times as fast as it can archive it. The figures are, however, a little deceptive because LGWR could be writing much less than 32K, whereas ARCH could be writing 64K and running a couple concurrent slaves. This does suggest, though, that on very busy systems you need to isolate the archived redo logs as much as possible to allow ARCH to keep up with LGWR.

If you are running with a standby database (see Chapter 24), Oracle has moved the goalposts yet again. You are probably archiving at least one copy of your redo logs by sending them across SQL*Net to a remote machine, and the network turnaround time may become even more significant than the actual file-write times.

Conclusion

There is really no great distinction between raw systems and file systems as far as manageability and performance are concerned. Except for really extreme cases you may as well do what your operations team feels most comfortable with. There's a lot to be said for being on familiar territory when trouble arrives.

Redo log files in OLTP systems in particular may be kept very busy with LGWR writing chunks of data that are smaller than the file-system block size. This leads to delays resulting from a read-update-write cycle of disk activity. Unless the file system can do direct I/O and bypass the block size limitation, it is a good idea to put your redo logs on raw devices.

The fact that archived redo logs have to be on a file system, have to be created from scratch and not reused, and may be sent to a remote machine via SQL*Net may be the most important I/O issue to address anyway, which could make the choice between raw volumes and file systems pretty irrelevant.

Modern technology has introduced the battery-backed disk cache. Although this often offers little benefit to read performance (because of the extreme randomness of the reads that database activity tends to generate), it can hide any differences between raw volume and file system write performance.

There is a potential for inode contention on file systems, in which reader processes lock out writer processes, and writer processes lock out reader processes. Since there are usually very few writer processes in an Oracle system, this is not usually a problem. When a tablespace may be subject to multiple, concurrent, writes (typically the temporary tablespace, but also tablespaces where objects are frequently rebuilt by parallel query action), the issue can usually be minimized by creating the tablespace as several small files rather than a single very large file.

It takes little more than a single page of C to produce a program that can emulate all aspects of Oracle I/O so that you can test the actual performance of your own hardware configuration. Theoretical and generalized arguments may give you some clues about what to test, but can give you no concrete answers. Test your own system.

RAID Levels

I have noticed during recent months an increase in the number of black box solutions installed by small to medium-size offices. In particular, the *hardware RAID device* of 40GB to 160GB, which basically tends to mean five disks, a controller, and a few empty slots, seems to be increasingly popular as the platform for Oracle.

Forget any worries about whether you are going to use file systems or logical raw volumes. What's the best configuration for such a device? Even if you are in the realm of larger, hand-picked collections of hardware, what sort of strategies do you use when looking for resilience and recoverability of disk drives?

The solution in most cases these days is a RAID (originally meaning a *redundant array of inexpensive disks*) configuration, and in this section I hope to drop a few hints to help you get the best out of whatever pack of disks you have.

RAID comes in several flavors. The most common are

- RAID 0—striped
- RAID 1—mirrored
- RAID 0/1—striped and mirrored
- RAID 1/0—mirrored and striped
- RAID 5—rotating block parity

RAID 0

A good, general-purpose guideline for Oracle data files is to have as many spindles as possible, and to spread the I/O as widely and as finely as possible over them. Naturally, nothing about Oracle is simple, and you need to reserve a small number of disks exclusively for redo logs and archived redo logs.

But what if you have only a handful of disks? Simple striping across everything in sight at about 64K or 128K per disk is probably the best way of minimizing I/O contention (Figure 10-1). However, if one disk goes, then the entire database is gone, as are the on-line redo logs and the archived redo logs, and your only recovery option is to restore the last backup and roll forward to the most recently taped archive redo log file.

RAID 0 is a pretty good solution for avoiding I/O problems but the level of risk, or at least of lost time, resulting from data recovery is high. It may be appropriate for a small data mart, say, which is updated once per day by the application of a transportable tablespace (see Chapter 8), but for an OLTP system the risk of data loss is probably too high for most sites to take.

RAID 1

If the level of risk, lost time, and lost data offered by RAID 0 is too high, then you can go to the opposite extreme with RAID 1, which simply takes pairs or disks and keeps them as synchronized copies of each other (Figure 10-2).

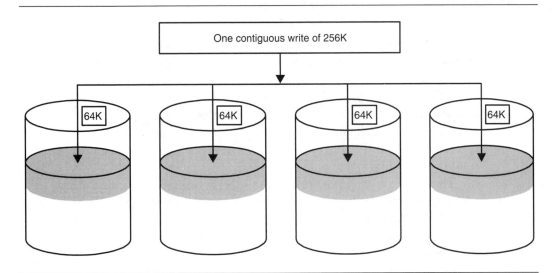

Figure 10-1.   Simple striping (RAID 0).

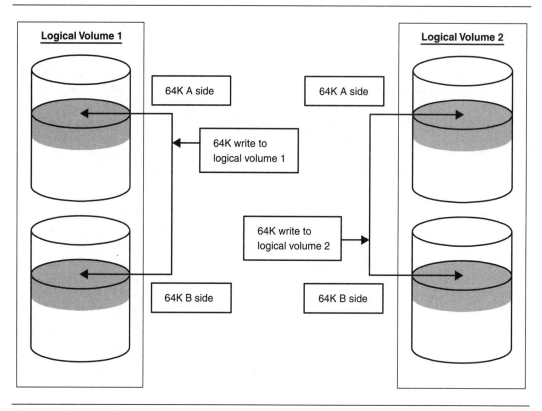

Figure 10-2.   Simple mirrors (RAID 1).

On the plus side, you can lose a single disk and the database keeps running. In fact some boxes allow you to pull out the failed disk and put in a replacement without switching off. When the new disk is in place you can tell the system to "resilver" the copy. Really clever modern boxes accommodate the "hot spare"—a blank disk plugged permanently into the box. When a disk fails, the box spots the problem, starts the blank disk spinning, rebuilds the mirror on it, and phones the hardware engineer to send in a new disk!

There are two or three drawbacks to this approach. In the first place, every write becomes two writes, so you effectively double the probability of write-time contention. Many Oracle systems do much more reading than writing, though, and to balance the write-time problem you do get the benefit that a read request can be satisfied from two different places, and the driving software is usually smart enough to go for the copy that is likely to be acquired in the shorter time.

The problem of double write becomes worse if the mirroring is done at the software level, somewhere close to the operating system, rather than at the hardware level close to the disks. If the mirroring is software mirroring, then for safety reasons you need to enable DIRTY REGION LOGGING—a facility used by the operating system to recover and resilver properly in the event of a crash. Let's step through a scenario that could arise in the absence of dirty region logging:

1. Oracle issues a write to file of block 12345.
2. Block 12345 is written on one side of the mirror.
3. The machine crashes before the other side of the mirror is written.
4. The machine restarts, and Oracle starts crash recovery.
5. During crash recovery Oracle reads block 12345 to determine whether it needs redo applied to bring it up to date. Oracle happens to read the good copy, written before the crash, so does not update it.
6. Crash recovery completes.
7. Some time later Oracle reads block 12345 again, but this time from the side of the mirror that was *not* written prior to the crash. The block appears to be bad, and the process crashes.

Because Oracle does not know that each file is on a mirrored device, it cannot know that one half of the mirror may be out of sync with the other half. Therefore, it is necessary for the mirroring software to maintain some form of log that shows which side of the mirror has been updated most recently and which is out of date, and changes to this log have to be flushed regularly to disk. The log is usually some form of bitmap in which each bit represents 64K or 128K, so the volume of data written is small, but the problem remains that there is still some extra write activity contending for the limited number of disks on your system. As usual, you can reduce the scale of the problem by applying cash, or in this case cache. With a suitably sized, battery-backed write cache in front of the disks, the impact of the extra writes may well be negligible. Of course, you've already doubled the number of disks from the nominal requirement, so you may have trouble persuading the accountants to finance the cache.

Tales (possibly untrue) that I have heard about dirty region logs: One site decided that the dirty region logs were so very small they might as well put them all on one disk, out of the way, and then spent weeks trying to figure out why they had an I/O bottleneck. Then there was the company that won the contract by beating the benchmark with dirty region logging switched off. When the system went live with dirty region logging switched on, the customer never figured out why they couldn't get the same performance. You may judge for yourselves how true these tales may be, but it is definitely a fact that dirty region logging is currently a requirement for systems running software RAID 1 (or any of its variants, and RAID 5) and few people seem to be fully aware of its significance. I believe that Oracle Corporation is actually working on enhancements that will allow them to interrogate the underlying system to find out if they are addressing a mirrored system, so that they can recover both sides of the mirror if they have to.

Another big issue with simple mirrors is Oracle-based load balancing. Unless you take great pains with creating multiple files on different mirrors for each tablespace, you can easily find that all the I/O for a critical object is going to just one pair of disks. Even when they start with a good plan and the best of intentions, systems that depend on DBAs manually spreading objects across multiple files eventually tend to end up with the most recent, hence most heavily used, data all located on just one pair of disks. The effort needed to maintain manual striping is a terrible waste of a good DBA's time. Fortunately, when a new tablespace consists of several files, Oracle automatically tries to allocate the extents for a new object in a round-robin fashion across all the files, but the DBA has to choose a good (which means not too large) extent size for this to be beneficial. The distribution algorithm can start to break down as objects in a tablespace get dropped and rebuilt.

> *RAID 0 gives you load balancing; RAID 1 gives you resilience. If you can afford the disks, go for both at once.*

RAID 0/1 and RAID 1/0

What, you may ask, is the difference between mirroring and striping, and striping and mirroring? The answer is: recovery time, performance during recovery, and risk.

Both 0/1 and 1/0 are very good for resilience and load balancing. As with simple mirrors they suffer from the cost of a single logical write turning into two physical writes, so there is some write contention introduced. Similarly, if the implementation is software RAID rather than hardware RAID, you need to worry about dirty region logging, which introduces another overhead. However, because we have striping we have load balancing, and no single disk, or pair of disks, is likely to be overstressed, so the cost of the second (and intermittent third, dirty log) write is unlikely to become an issue.

Of course, we are now beginning to talk about quite a lot of disks. You have to have four disks at a minimum to be able to have both mirroring and striping, but it is highly likely that you will have rather more than that. Ten or a dozen is really the minimum number needed for effective use of RAID 0/1 or 1/0.

If you have a large number of disks, you introduce an interesting budgetary feature. How do you "grow" the system? If you have carefully arranged your first build in sets of ten disks, say, mirrored and striped five wide, are you going to add a couple more disks in six months? Of course not. You have to go out and buy another ten disks; otherwise, you wouldn't be able to maintain the pattern, and future I/O performance would change dramatically as the data grows into the last couple of disks. If your budget limits you to buying just two new disks, you should rebuild the entire database to spread it evenly across all 12 disks.

> *A good disk layout not only covers the initial build, but accommodates future growth.*

Coming back to the initial point, what is the difference between these two variants of RAID? Figures 10-3 and 10-4 give you a clue.

In Figure 10-3, which is stripe then mirror, we have two mirror sets. Assume that disk A4 breaks and has to be replaced. The entire mirror is dead until further notice. This means that all five disks in the A set have to be resilvered before the system is back in its safe state again. Apart from the extra I/O load (all reads have to take place from the B set for the duration, and the whole B set is being scanned and copied to the A set), it takes just one more failure (in the B set only) and the entire database is down and will need recovery.

In Figure 10-4, mirror then stripe, we have five mirror sets making five logical volumes that happen to have data striped across them. Assume that disk 4A breaks and has to be replaced. The only disk that has to be resilvered is disk 4A. All other disks can continue participating in database activity, so 80% of the system can still take advantage of having two locations from which to read, and only one disk is going to experience I/O contention as the resilvering takes places. Lastly, the probability of a database crash has been

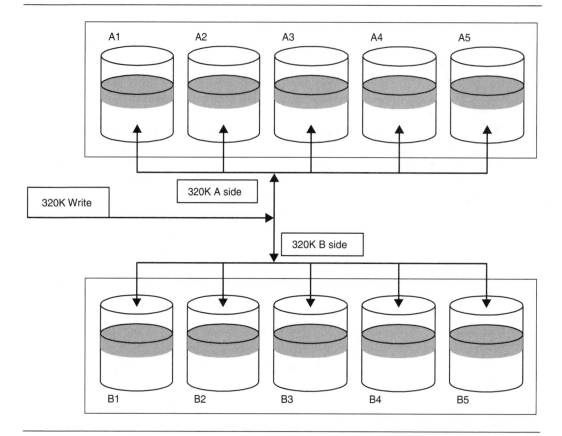

Figure 10-3.   Striped then mirrored (RAID 0/1).

reduced by a factor of five because it will take a failure of disk 4B, to bring down the system.

Having spent some time describing the differences between RAID 1/0 and RAID 0/1, it is worth noting that this difference is of most impact if you are using software RAID. Under software RAID 0/1, you could stripe across 4 × 8GB disks, create another stripe against 8 × 4B disks, and mirror the two resulting 32GB logical volumes. It could be worse. You could pick any pair of equal-size logical volumes, even if they have a partial overlap on the same disks, and mirror them against each other. In real life, though, people tend to take the clean, simple view that I did in Figure10-3, which almost makes RAID 0/1 look like RAID 1/0. In fact, I have observed recently that there is at least one vendor selling black boxes with a hardware implementation labeled as RAID 0/1 (the less desirable option) that is *actually* implemented as RAID 1/0. I suspect that this may be the only time I have seen a computer system

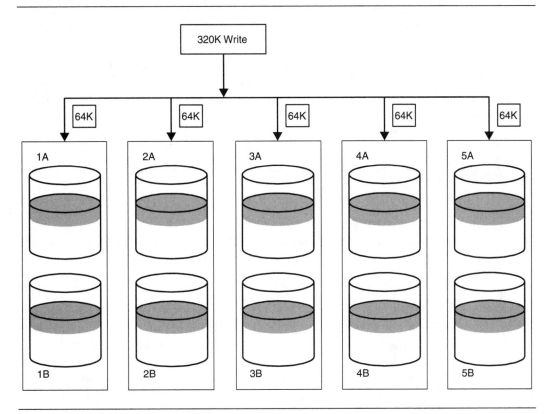

Figure 10-4.   Mirrored then striped (RAID 1/0).

undersold. If you do buy a hardware RAID implementation, check very carefully to determine which of the implementations it uses.

> *A quick-and-dirty method for checking whether you are looking at RAID 1/0 or 0/1 is to ask the salesman to pull a disk out of the cabinet and see how many disks start to thrash when it goes back in. If it is just two, you probably have RAID 1/0.*

RAID 5

RAID 5 has an undeservedly bad reputation as far as Oracle database systems are concerned. The immediate response to the question, Should I use RAID 5 for my Oracle database? seems to be, Never. However, for most small systems, it is almost necessary and perfectly acceptable; and for many large systems it is totally adequate.

Why has RAID 5 got such bad press? The answer lies in the *parity block*. RAID 5 is made up of sets of $N + 1$ disks. Effectively, you use N disks for data storage, and the spare +1 disk for parity information. In fact, with RAID 5 the parity blocks are distributed evenly across all the disks so that you don't get one hot "parity disk."

However, every time you write a data block (usually a device block, but possibly a file-system block or logical-volume block) to a disk, the system has to

- Identify the matching parity disk
- Read the corresponding parity block
- Factor out the previous values for the block being written, which may mean rereading the original version of the block
- Factor in the new values for the block being written
- Write the new image of the data block
- Write the new image of the parity block and, whoops! It just went past after the read, so you have to wait for the extra rotation to rewrite it.

Basically you can expect a single write to a RAID 5 device to take approximately twice as long as a write to a simple disk. And unlike RAID 1 (mirrors) you don't get a payback from being able to read from two different disks, so RAID 5 appears to be all cost and no benefit as far as performance is concerned.

Actually, the no-benefit comment is something of an exaggeration. With RAID 5, your data is striped across several disks (the normal RAID 5 setup tends to be five disks in a set), so you do get a reasonable amount of I/O load balancing (Figure 10-5).

Also, you do get resilience. If one disk in the set blows up, the system continues running. The driver will derive the data that was on that disk by reading all the other disks and calculating backward. For example, if disk 4 in Figure 10-5 fails, we can still read data chunks A1, A2, and A3 directly. To derive the value for data chunk A4, we have to read parity A and factor out the contents of A1, A2, and A3. Thus, one read in four becomes very expensive and has massive side effects on all other reads. (In fact, if disk 4 fails, we can read the data from all four of the Bn chunks, so on average the overhead occurs on one read in five, but that's still pretty disastrous.)

If RAID 5 is implemented through software, it experiences the same dirty region logging problem as RAID 1. After all, a single logical write has to turn

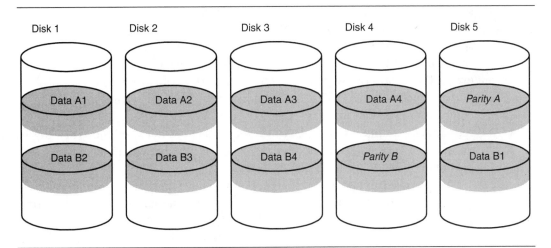

Figure 10-5.   Rotating block parity (RAID 5).

into two physical writes, and the order in which the writes take place is not guaranteed because this would introduce an unacceptable level of contention into the system.

Given the obvious inefficiency of RAID 5, why am I prepared to say that it is perfectly acceptable for most small systems and many large systems?

The first point is that many Oracle systems do far less writing than they do reading, and the writing is usually in the background anyway, so although the write penalty is a notional 100+%, this isn't necessarily all that significant an overhead to the total I/O operation and may not impact the user directly anyway.

Second, although a single, small, random write is likely to sustain a heavy penalty, RAID 5 suppliers are aware of the issues and have taken steps to reduce the problem. Typically a write that fills a whole stripe does not need to reread and recalculate the parity as it writes each disk. It simply discards and re-creates a new parity block. Large writes (for example, from sorting, index builds, CTAS) that use direct multiblock writes need not experience such a large penalty as small writes.

Third, it is becoming common practice to stick a reasonably large battery-backed cache on the front end of a RAID 5 device (particularly). If this is configured purely as a write cache, the effects of the double-write requirement can be pretty insignificant for all but the most write-intensive, high-volume applications.

Finally, many Oracle systems are sufficiently small that five disks (and the minimum disk size these days seems to be 9GB) is more than enough space. You just have to do the best you can with what you have. The security offered by RAID 5 is good, and the load balancing resulting from the even spread over five disks is highly beneficial. For a small office, the benefits of cost-effectiveness and resilience are likely to be far more important than even a theoretical doubling in the I/O overhead. If you are worried about performance with RAID 5 and can't get a write cache, then the single best compromise you can make is to get a couple of extra small disks and put the redo logs on a simple mirror. Because redo logs tend to experience very large numbers of very small writes, they are otherwise likely to generate a disproportionate fraction of the I/O overhead.

If you take this approach though, don't remove disks from your RAID 5 configuration to use as mirror disks. The industry standard for a RAID 5 stripe seems to be five disks, and five is probably the best number. First (not to labor a point), 5 = 4 + 1, and handling four "real-data" disks makes the arithmetic of space distribution nice and easy. Second, if you don't choose 4 + 1 disks, then the next "obvious" choices are 2 + 1 disks and 8 + 1 disks. The problem with three-disk RAID 5 is that it takes only two writes to the logical device to get contention. The problem with nine-disk RAID 5 is that when one disk goes, every attempted read to that disk requires eight I/Os to derive the data value. The I/O performance drops dramatically, and resilvering takes forever.

Generic RAID

In the examples of striping (Figures 10-1, 10-3, and 10-4), I showed stripes that use 64K per disk. Before I go on, I should point out that there is a conflict of terminology here that you should always seek to clarify in discussions about installation. Some people refer to this as a stripe size of 64K; others refer to it as a chunk size of 64K and a stripe size that is 64K multiplied by the number of disks in the stripe set. This gets even more confusing with RAID 5. If you have five-disk RAID 5 with 64K per disk, do you have a stripe size of $5 \times 64K = 320K$, or a stripe size of 256K because you have $4 \times 64K$ of data, and parity doesn't count? To avoid confusion, I tend to talk about "striping at 64K per disk," and avoid using either terminology.

An important decision is how much you should write per disk for the best effect. The most important thing to say is that you can probably mix and match stripe sizes to suit your needs. This does depend on your logical volume manager of course, but the ones I have used have all been very flexible, although I have heard of some that are a bit limited. Going back to Figure 10-5, it would be perfectly feasible to set up these five disks as two volume groups in such a way that the A slices belong to a volume group writing 64K per disk, and the B slices belong to a volume group writing 256K per disk.

There is no such thing as the perfect stripe size. However, when you list the different types of activity that can occur, it is possible to come up with a few reasonable ideas.

- On-line redo log files generally do a large number of relatively small sequential writes on OLTP systems, but may do very large sequential writes on DSS systems during data loading. When they are archived, they are subject to large reads.

- Archived redo log files are subject to large sequential writes. Because archived redo logs have to be created in file systems, it is important for a busy system to give them the best possible chance of being written quickly with minimum interference. Wouldn't it be nice to have enough spare disks to keep them separate from the rest of the I/O too?

- Files containing indexes tend to be subject to very small, highly random I/O in OLTP systems, but in DSS systems you may find that large indexes are being re-created regularly, and the files are subject to large scan reads and big sequential writes.

- Files containing simple tables also tend to be subject to very small, highly random I/Os in OLTP systems but may be subject to parallel scans in DSS systems. And files containing LOBs (see Chapter 17) are likely to be subject to very large sequential I/Os, depending on the LOB chunk size you choose.

- There are then two special classes of "data" files, those containing the rollback segments and those containing the temporary segments. Rollback is often the busiest part of an Oracle system as far as I/O is concerned. Ideally, it is "write once and forget." In practice, it is often reread with a rapid-fire string of random I/Os. Temporary files tend to be low use in OLTP systems, but can take on massive concurrent reads and writes in DSS systems.

Remember that different parts of the Oracle database have different I/O characteristics, and that different applications have different characteristic I/O patterns.

In theory, then, we should simply get hold of vast numbers of disks, dedicate batches of them to different types of operations, and stripe them accordingly. In real life, however, many systems have to survive on just a handful of disks. So you need a strategy for minimizing the side effects of mixing all the incompatible operations in one amorphous stripe-set.

Rule 1—Get a larger number of smaller disks, rather than a smaller number of larger disks. Under any reasonable kind of load, a disk typically handles a maximum of 30 to 50 I/Os per second, whether it is 4GB or 36GB. Having bigger disks just encourages people to put more data on them, and then you can't get it off fast enough. Personally I think that 9GB is currently the maximum useful size of a data disk. However, for archiving I would be quite happy to mirror a pair of the largest possible disks and dedicate them to a continuous stream of archived redo logs.

Rule 2—Don't put too many disks in a single stripe-set. My preferred setup is RAID 1/0, mirrored and striped. For a really big system I wouldn't put together more than 20 disks in a set (that's ten mirrored pairs, not 20 mirrored pairs). The critical number is the number of logical devices, so if you want to use triple mirrors the figure goes up to 30 disks. If I had to use RAID 5, I would stick with the traditional set of five disks to make a logical device. But for really large systems, I would check to see if I could put together four RAID 5 devices and stripe across them to aim for a uniform I/O spread across 20 disks.

Rule 3—Don't use very large stripe sizes or you lose a lot of the benefit of striping. Anything more than 1MB per disk is probably suboptimal.

Rule 4—Don't use very small stripe sizes, or lots of I/O requests will end up having to access multiple disks, which will increase the contention of the system and have a dramatic impact on the I/O response time. For indexes and busy tables in an OLTP system I *may* be persuaded to drop as low as 32K per disk if I was confident that the system did virtually no table scanning and few operations that lead to large sorting requirements.

Rule 5—If you put file systems on top of the logical volume manager, give yourself several file systems, and put different types of objects in different file systems. This makes it much easier to work out what type of activity is happening to which objects.

Guideline 1—Temporary segments and archived redo log files should have larger stripes—256K per disk is probably a good size to choose.

Guideline 2—On a DSS system, 256K per disk is a good bet for tables and indexes that are subject to frequent rebuilds and scans.

Guideline 3—Just about everything else will do reasonably well at 64K per disk.

Disk Cache

A few months ago I was at a site that had some performance issues with its database. But they *knew* it wasn't anything to do with the I/O because they had a massive 4GB disk cache.

It's very easy to be misled by numbers. Although 4GB sounds very big, it was in front of a 1TB disk array, so the cache was less than 0.5% of the total disk storage. Not only that, there were several databases addressing the disk array, and the combined SGAs of all the instances was 5GB—25% larger than the disk cache itself.

The problem was, of course, I/O. There were too many extremely random reads taking place, and the disk cache was totally overwhelmed and a complete waste of space. However, reconfigured as a write-only cache, the disk cache became an extremely effective tool for flushing the redo logs to disks that were otherwise quite slow.

It is necessary to think carefully about disk caches, and how they can be applied most effectively to the way your system works. In extreme cases, a cache could become completely flooded after the first few seconds of activity and offer no benefit at all. However, in more normal cases, a write cache can help redo logging and "checkpointing"; a read cache may be able to help a shortfall in main memory and a small Oracle buffer.

Problems and Quirks

There is little to choose in performance between properly configured file systems and logical raw volumes, but a mismatch between file-system block size and Oracle block size can have a severe impact on performance.

The impact of archiving redo logs can be the most severe performance threat to the system, and it is often overlooked.

Because of the increase in disk size, many small systems need only a basic "black box" RAID device. This tends to leave them with a small number of disks, which reduces the options and the need for fine-tuning at the I/O level.

Software RAID requires a dirty region log to be safe. This is often overlooked when working out disk layouts.

When a mirrored RAID device breaks, at least one disk has to be resilvered. With the wrong RAID strategy, this can have a severely negative impact on overall performance.

Strategy Notes

In an ideal world you would probably have a large number of disks. Archived redo logs would go on a mirrored pair of dedicated disks, or even on a larger number of striped and mirrored disks to assist multiple archive writers. Redo logs would be on mirrored raw logical volumes, perhaps with an A and B pair so that ARCH could be archiving from the A disks while LGWR was writing to the B disks. Data files would be RAID 1/0, with approximately ten mirrors in a striping group, and two or three different configurations of stripe sizes. Everything except the archived redo logs would be on raw devices.

In the real world, most systems have to make do with a small number of disks, and administrators tend to be uncomfortable with the idea of raw devices. If all you have is a small number of disks for the database, then a RAID 5 configuration with 64K per disk is probably a good compromise setup. If you can afford to double the number of disks, RAID 1/0 is better. If you can get a couple of spare disks on the side for redo and/or archived redo that is better still.

If you have battery-backed disk cache that you can configure, it is probably better to bias it toward writing rather than reading.

Apart from disks dedicated to archived redo logs, you should assume that there is no point in having more than 9GB of active data per disk. If you view this as a waste of space, you may be able to use spare capacity for keeping hot backups nearly on-line.

CHAPTER 11

Views

Okay, I will admit it. There is nothing new in views in Oracle 8.1, except perhaps for materialized views (see Chapter 23), and they aren't really views anyway.

However, there are a number of features of views that are not yet in common use and that are worth explaining because they can have a beneficial impact on both performance and clarity of code. This chapter also gives me an opportunity to mourn the passing of partitioned views.

Basics of Views

In essence, a view is a stored *select* statement. If you can run a SQL statement to select data, you can precede it with "create or replace view XXXX as" and have that SQL statement stored permanently in the database. What gets stored in the database is the text of the view (with ∗ expanded to the list of columns available in the table at the time the view was created) and a set of column definitions for that view in the view family xxx_TAB_COLUMNS.

> *If you create a view of the form CREATE OR REPLACE VIEW V1 AS SELECT ∗ FROM T1, then Oracle will base the view on the current set of columns in the table. If you add a column to the table, it does* not *become visible in the view until you replace the view. Do not use ∗ in view definitions.*

Thus we may create the view

```
create or replace view employee_details as
select
        emp1.surname,
        emp1.forename.
        emp2.surname,
        dpt.department
        loc.streetname
from
        emp      emp1,
        emp      emp2,
        dept     dpt,
        address  loc
where
        emp2.id = emp1.mgr_id
and     dpt.id  = emp1.dept_id
and     loc.id  = emp1.address_id
;
```

Any future use of the thing called employee_details will behave in many respects as if the object was a table, with five columns. In terms of ease of use of data, and clarity of presentation, crafting a view like this is clearly a sensible thing to do; however, there are a couple of frequent complaints about views that are worth reviewing.

The first common complaint is that views add a significant performance overhead. This is generally not true, although the misuse of views certainly can add a performance overhead—in just the same way that the misuse of a table in a query can add a performance overhead. It *is* true that it is easier to misuse a view by accident (in particular, views with outer joins in them can still cause big problems), so this complaint does have some basis in fact. It is also true that some of the more effective mechanisms for optimizing SQL that use views exist only in the CBO, so users sticking with the RBO will give themselves extra problems when trying to use views.

The second common complaint is that you cannot update (or insert or delete) a view that incorporates a join. This ceased to be true sometime around version 7.3 as far as updates and deletes were concerned, and inserts became possible in 8.0. However, the ramifications have not yet spread all that widely through the user community.

Views for Performance

In-line Views

Cunning use of views can introduce a dramatic performance benefit. The mechanism of in-line views introduced in Oracle 7.2 is a particularly good case in point.

One of the little tasks I run from time to time to check anomalies in the performance of a system is to look at the X$BH object—an internal structure visible only to SYS that gives information about the blocks in the database buffer. In particular it is sometimes interesting to check how many blocks from each well-used object are in the buffer.

The object number in the buffer is the column X$BH.OBJ, which corresponds to the column DBA_OBJECTS.DATA_OBJECT_ID. So I could list the owner, type, and name of objects with a count of their buffered blocks by issuing the SQL statement:

```
select
        ob.object_name, ob.object_type, ob.owner, count(*)
from
        x$bh            bh,
        dba_objects     ob
where
        ob.data_object_id = bh.obj
group by
        object_name, object_type, owner
having
        count(*) > 100
;
```

The drawback becomes apparent when you think about the increasing number of sites that set up buffer sizes in excess of 100,000 blocks. That's an awful lot of joining and sorting.

In-line views allow you rewrite the query as

```
select
        ob.object_name, ob.object_type, ob.owner, bh.ct
from
        (
            select  /*+ no_merge */
                    obj, count(*) ct
            from    x$bh
```

```
                    group by obj
                    having count(*) > 100
            )                                       bh,
            dba_objects                             ob
    where
            ob.data_object_id = bh.obj
    ;
```

Note the way in which I have replaced a table in the FROM clause with a SQL statement, the in-line view, and then have given that statement an alias to allow me to join the result to the next table in the query.

Running this code, my "sort/group by" is still handling the 100,000 rows from the original query, but they are much smaller rows, and when I get to the join, I am going to be joining only a few dozen intermediate results to the DBA_OBJECTS view. The improvement in performance can be huge. Of course, each release of the optimizer improves its ability to push join conditions down into views, so one day Oracle may undo my cunning trick by being too clever. To be safe, it is best to use the /*+ NO_MERGE */ hint, as shown, or the /*+ NO_PUSH_JOIN_PRED () */ hint to tell Oracle that it should not try to merge the in-line view and the DBA_OBJECTS view.

In-line views aren't restricted just to **select** statements though, but I'll be saying more about that in the section on updatable join views.

If you are running an earlier version of Oracle, then you may find that PL/SQL does not recognize the syntax of in-line views, even though SQL itself does. Should you find one day that you want to include an "order by" in the in-line view, this will be recognized as legal SQL by SQL*Plus (it's a feature that is new with version 8.1, but was also slipped into version 7.3.4), but the construct will be rejected by PL/SQL. In fact, variations of this problem still persist in Oracle 8.1. For example, the new CUBE and ROLLUP facilities (see Chapter 23) are not yet recognized in PL/SQL. The workaround is to use dynamic SQL to "hide" the problematic statements from PL/SQL.

SORT_AREA_SIZE

It is perhaps appropriate to review the init.ora parameters SORT_RETAINED_AREA_SIZE and SORT_AREA_SIZE at this point because of the direct effect that they have, particularly on SQL, which uses in-line views to reduce the workload of "group by" joins.

Ideally, sorting should take place in memory because memory operates so much faster than disk. However, memory is often limited, so we set

SORT_AREA_SIZE to dictate how much memory should be used in a single SORT operation before Oracle starts streaming its work area to disk.

When Oracle has to use a multistep execution path that includes some sorting, the sort step has to complete before the next step starts. For this reason Oracle only allocates one sort area up to size SORT_AREA_SIZE. However, as one sort step finishes, another may begin. The previous SQL query is a good example of this. The "group by" on X$BH requires a sort step, but once that has completed there is an "order by" that has to execute two steps later. The nature of the query is such that this later sorting step may start before all the sorted rows from an the earlier step have been forwarded to the later step. Consequently, Oracle has to hold some memory open from the first sort to feed the second sort. The size of this area is given by the parameter SORT_AREA_RETAINED_SIZE. This means that the demand for sort memory for the previous query could peak at SORT_AREA_RETAINED_SIZE (from the "group by") + SORT_AREA_SIZE (from the "order by").

Rollover Views

In-line views aren't the only way to improve performance. There are cases when end users (or more specifically, end-user tools) cannot cope with some of the little tricks needed to get the best performance from the database. Under these circumstances it is perfectly reasonable for the DBA to institute code that regularly redefines views.

Range-partitioned tables (see Chapter 13) provide a very good example of the need for this approach. Front-end tools are often not very good at producing SQL that allows partition elimination to occur, something which is achieved most easily by specifying literal conditions on partitioning columns. Consider a table of sales data partitioned by day, against which users often run queries for "this week compared with the matching week from last year" or "last week compared with the matching week last year." It is possible to write complex one-off static views for this information, which include things like references to the DUAL table and SYSDATE, but there is a runtime overhead to this type of approach, so why not run a script every morning that uses a PL/SQL package perhaps (see Chapter 19) to generate and execute code like

```
create or replace view this_week_year_on_year as
select {list of columns} from daily_sales
where
    (   sale_date >=    to_date('14-feb-2000','dd-mon-yyyy')
    and sale_date < to_date('16-feb-2000','dd-mon-yyyy')
    )
```

```
or
    (   sale_date >=    to_date('15-feb-1999','dd-mon-yyyy')
    and sale_date < to_date('17-feb-1999','dd-mon-yyyy')
    )
;
```

I apply the term *rollover* to views of this type because they contain constant values that move on from day to day. In the days of partitioned views it used to be a bit of a problem scheduling the code to generate such rollover views because you could end up trying to create views that referenced nonexistent tables. With partitioned tables that problem no longer exists.

Views for Security

In Oracle 8.1, Oracle introduced the concept of *row-level security* (see Chapter 21). This entails defining a function to generate an extra WHERE clause for a table, and then associating that function with that table so that the extra predicate is always applied whenever anyone accesses the table.

There are drawbacks to this approach: The extra predicate is invisible to everyone, the extra predicate *may* include references to other tables, and joining several tables each with its own (reference table) predicate may have a disastrous effect on the optimizer's ability to find a good execution path.

In many cases, then, you may feel that Oracle's implementation of row-level security is overkill, and that your requirements can be met through a much simpler view-based implementation. One such option, which combines a little of the flexibility of Oracle's implemenation and the simplicity of views is to use SYS_CONTEXT() (see Chapter 21) in conjunction with tables and views. Consider the outline

```
create table t1 (
    n1          number          primary key,
    v1          varchar2(20)    null,
    sec_tag     varchar2(10)    default sys_context('security','id')
                                not null
);

create or replace view v1 as
select  n1, v1
from    t1
where   sec_tag = sys_context('security','id')
with check option
;
```

If we use a log-on trigger to assign some form of group security ID to each user as they log on, we then have a system in which groups of people have their access restricted to sets of rows based on a single view definition.

In effect, we have extended to a group level the more commonly used mechanism of adding a "user_column" to a table with a default value of USER and creating the view

```
create or replace view my_data_view as
select  n1, v1
from    t1
where   user_column = user
with check option;
```

(For more details on defining a context and using log-on triggers to set values in the context, see Chapter 21.)

Of course there are pros and cons to this approach. On the plus side it is very simple, it applies even to SYS (Oracle's row-level security does not), and it uses only "column = constant" as the extra predicate so it does not introduce a risk of expensive execution paths.

On the minus side it may be too simple: As soon as you want to deal with the option of a user being able to see (or generate) data for two different groups it isn't sophisticated enough.

There is also the problem of bugs. In version 8.1.5 of Oracle there are problems with SYS_CONTEXT() that result in data being lost when queries using SYS_CONTEXT() are executed in parallel. For example, using the previous code you would always get zero returned as the result of

```
select /*+ parallel(v1,2) */ count(*) from v1;
```

However, we can look forward to this bug being fixed soon, and then being able to take advantage of a very elegant method for handling simple group security.

Views for Functionality

Sometimes a view allows you to do something that you cannot otherwise do. For example, I am still trying to work out how to select attributes from a deref()-ed object ID (see Chapter 15). It doesn't appear to be possible to do something like

```
select  deref(ref_value).attribute_name
from    tableX;
```

So to work around this, I have found it necessary to use in-line views:

```
select tab.id, tab.obj.attribute from (
    select  t.id, deref(t.ref_value) obj
    from    tableX t
) tab
;
```

You will, I am sure, come across other circumstances from time to time when this is the only workaround to some simple limitation of SQL.

Views for Clarity

We have already seen a couple of examples of how views can make complex SQL expressions look like simple tables. Our very first example was an end-user view that combined three different tables in a four-way join so that an end user could produce simple reports without needing to know where to find all the related bits of data. This is really the most important general use for views. Carefully chosen and documented, they can allow users and their front-end tools to access the database with minimal understanding of relational modeling and without needing to work out complex join conditions.

There are other ways, though, in which we can improve productivity by concealing complexity behind views. In particular, we can use views to conceal new features from old tools. Again, we have already seen the example of row-level security using SYS_CONTEXT(), and the potential for rolling views. There are many other odds and ends that we could prepare to get the maximum benefit out of the system without requiring users or their reporting tools to learn about new Oracle features.

Functions Returning Datasets

In Chapter 16 you will learn about the CAST() and TABLE() mechanisms that allow conversion between object tables and relational tables, and how they can be used to allow functions returning object tables appear as relational tables. Very few front-end tools could currently generate the following query:

```
select  col1, col2, col3, col4
from    table(cast(pl_sql_function(sysdate) as analysis_type));
```

But conceal the new features behind a view, and you simply have to deal with something that appears to be a table:

```
create or replace view current_analysis as
select  col1, col2, col3, col4
from    table(cast(pl_sql_function(sysdate) as analysis_type));
```

Partition Access

Some of the commonly used analytical tools are still unable to generate the special syntax Oracle has for accessing the partitions of partitioned tables. Such tools are commonly able to hold their own meta-data dictionaries that tell them things like "if condition X, then access table Y." We have already seen how we can generate rollover views to help front-end tools (and end users) achieve partition elimination; another trick that helps is the following simple strategy for view definitions:

```
create or replace view v_sales_data_199912 as
select {list of columns} from sales_data partition (p199912);
```

Analytic Functions and Others

In Chapter 23 we will come across the CUBE, ROLLUP, and new analytic functions. All of them are likely, at present, to be incomprehensible to front-end tools (and in fact are unknown to Oracle's own PL/SQL parser). You can, however, create views like

```
create or replace view sales_view as
select
        bki.sale_date,
        decode(grouping(reg.region_name),
                    1, 'All Regions',
                    reg.region_name
        )                               region_name,
        decode(grouping(str.store_name),
                  1, 'All Stores',
                  str.store_name
        )                               store_name,
        sum(bki.value_of_sale)          tot_sales
    from
```

```
        regions         reg,
        stores          str,
        basket_items    bki
where
        str.id = bki.store_id
and     reg.id = str.region_id
group by
        rollup(bki.sale_date, reg.region_name, str.store_name)
;
```

You will note that SALE_DATE has not had the grouping() function applied to it, even though it has to appear inside the rollup() function. This is deliberate. With this view definition, it is possible to query the view by SALE_DATE. For example,

```
select  *
from    sales_view
where   sale_date between '12-jan-00' and '13-jan-00'
;
```

```
SALE_DATE   REGION_NAME   STORE_NAME   TOT_SALES
----------  -----------   ----------   ---------

12-JAN-00   Reg1          Str11                3
                          Str12               23
                          All Stores          26
            Reg2          Str21               43
                          Str22               63
                          All Stores         106
            All Regions   All Stores         132

13-JAN-00   Reg1          Str11                7
                          Str12               27
                          All Stores          34
            Reg2          Str21               47
                          Str22               67
                          All Stores         114
            All Regions   All Stores         148

            All Regions   All Stores         280
```

This code correctly pushes the predicate on SALE_DATE down into the view before evaluating the rollup values; but there is a bit of a bug somewhere in the combination of views and the grouping() function. If you try to

add a predicate to a column that has been used with the grouping() function
(for example, where region_name = Reg1), then the query crashes with an
ORA-00600 error. You can work around this by adding a second copy of the
GROUPING() columns to the definition, but this is rather messy, and does
little for the argument that views hide complexity:

```
create or replace view sales_view as
select
        bki.sale_date,
        reg.region_name reg_name_sel,
        str.store_name  store_name_sel,
        decode(grouping(reg.region_name),
                1, 'All Regions',
                reg.region_name
        )                               region_name,
        decode(grouping(str.store_name),
                1, 'All Stores',
                str.store_name
        )                               store_name,
        sum(bki.value_of_sale)          tot_sales
        .   .   .
```

Then you can safely select things like

```
select  *
from    sales_view
where   sale_date = '12-jan-00'
and     reg_name_sel = 'Reg1';
```

You can also get a little benefit from analytic views (see Chapter 23), but again
the room for maneuvering is fairly restricted. Consider the very simple query

```
select
        region, store, count(*),
        rank() over (
                partition by region
                order by count(*) desc
        ) as ranked
from    sales_data
group by
        region, store
;
```

When you start using the analytic functions such as rank(), cume_dist(), ntile(), and the rolling window versions of avg(), max(), and so on, you soon find that SQL starts to look quite complicated, especially when you start to move from single table queries to more complex join queries. However, it is possible to make life easier for yourself by using in-line views along the lines of

```
select
        region, store, ct,
        rank() over (
                partition by region
                order by ct desc
        ) as ranked
from (
    complicated SQL select statement that
    does lots of joining and summing
)
where region = 'SOUTHERN'
;
```

You may even find that Oracle is able to push some predicates down to the in-line view. In the example, the definition of the in-line view allowed the predicate "where region = 'SOUTHERN'" to be pushed down inside the in-line view so that the base query could use an indexed access path. You will not always be this lucky; in fact, if you try to conceal the analytic functions inside a permanent view, along the lines of

```
create or replace view rank_view as
select
    region, store, ct,
    rank() over (
            partition by region
            order by ct desc
        ) as ranked
from (
    complicated SQL select statement that
    does lots of joining and summing
)
;
```

Oracle is not (yet) able to push predicates down inside the view. For example, the query

```
select * from rank_view where region = 'SOUTHERN';
```

was unable to find the indexed access path that was available before I wrapped the query inside the view.

Updatable Join Views

Updatable join views have been around since at least Oracle 7.3, and yet it is still a commonly held belief that a view can be updated if it references a single table only. In fact, Oracle can update or delete from a join view if it can identify completely and unambiguously the base table and row in that table to which an operation is to apply.

The manuals at this point start talking about "key-preserved" tables, and define these by saying: "A table is a key-preserved table if every key of the table can also be a key of the join." After pausing to think carefully, I can explain what this means, but the description itself doesn't give me a gut feeling for what it means to be a key-preserved table. I offer, therefore, my two-part explanation of when a table in a join view can be updated or deleted.

1. A table in a join view can be updated if, and only if, for each row in the table there can only be, at most, one row in the view.
2. Rows can only be deleted from a join view if, and only if, there is precisely one table that can be updated through that join view. (In which case the delete will be applied to that table.)

The update restriction asks the question: If I pick a row in a view and change one column in that row, would that change have to be applied simultaneously to some other rows in the view to keep that view self-consistent? If the answer is yes, I am not allowed to update the table that supplied that column to the view.

Simple Join Views

Let's use the EMP and DEPT tables in the scott/tiger schema to clarify the situation:

```
create or replace view accounting as
select  emp.empno, emp.empname, emp.mgr, dept.deptno, dept.dname
from    emp, dept
where   emp.deptno = dept.deptno
and     dept.dname = 'ACCOUNTING'
;

select * from accounting;
```

Empno	Ename	Mgr	Deptno	Dname
7782	CLARK	7839	10	ACCOUNTING
7839	KING		10	ACCOUNTING
7934	MILLER	7782	10	ACCOUNTING

In this example, the EMP table has the DEPT table joined to it by the primary key of the DEPT table. Therefore, at most, one DEPT can be attached to any one EMP. In other words, Oracle can guarantee that if an EMP row appears in the view at all, it appears just once. Consequently the EMP table is updatable.

Examples of legal updates and deletes are

```
update accounting set ENAME = 'CLARKE' where empno = 7782;
update accounting set Ename = initcap(Ename) where deptno = 10;
delete from accounting where ename = 'MILLER';
```

On the other hand, each row in the DEPT table could (and clearly does) appear more than once in the view because it joins to the EMP table by a nonunique index on the EMP table. Many EMPs are attached to each DEPT, consequently the DEPT table is not updatable, and the following attempted updates would result in error "ORA-01779: cannot modify a column which maps to a non key-preserved table":

```
update accounting set dname = 'ACCOUNTS' where deptno = 10;
update accounting set deptno = 10 where ename = 'CLARK';
```

You may be a little surprised to note that we can't use this specific view to move Clark out of the accounting department; it seems to be a counterintuitive restriction. This highlights an important point about join views in general. In a join view, it *does* matter which table you specify in the "select" list as the owner of a joined column. If you look back at our view definition, you will see that we selected "dept.deptno," so the column in the view comes from the DEPT table, which is the nonupdatable table. If we changed the view definition to select and expose "emp.deptno," our attempt to move Clark out of the accounting department would be updating a column from the updatable EMP table, and would succeed. This tiny, but significant, detail actually explains many of the performance problems relating to using views in simple *select* statements. A user may write a query of the form

```
select (list of columns)
from    table1  t1,
        view1   v1
where   v1.colX = t1.colX
and     t1.colY = 'ABC'
;
```

where view1 is defined as

```
select  t3.colX, t3.colY, t3.colZ, t2.colA, t2.colB
from    T3, T2
where   t3.colX = t2.colX
;
```

The user may "know" that the view joins tables T2 and T3, and that the optimum access path is TABLE1 → T2 → T3, but in our view definition we have exposed colX from table T3 instead of from table T2, so the path is simply not visible to Oracle (in this release of the optimizer). If we changed the view definition to select t2.colX, then the path would change to the optimum.

> When creating views that join tables and expose some of the joining columns, think very carefully about which table the exposed column comes from. It does make a difference.

In-line Updatable Views

It's quite nice to be able to update certain types of join views, but how does this relate to the main topic of using the right features in the right places?

One of the more common situations that arises in large databases (particularly of the warehouse type) is the need to apply a large update to an enormous table. There were two traditional approaches: the PL/SQL loop and the update from subquery.

The PL/SQL loop would step through the table of new information one row at a time, locating the corresponding item from the main table and updating it (perhaps inserting it if the item could not be found). The subquery update would be one of the following:

```
update big_table bt
set bt.total_column = bt.total_column + (
        select  sum(delta)
        from    delta_table dt
        where   dt.key_columns = bt.key_columns
        )
where exists (
        select  null
        from    delta_table dt
        where   dt.key_columns = bt.key_columns
        )
;

update big_table bt
set bt.total_column = bt.total_column + (
        select  sum(delta)
        from    delta_table dt
        where   dt.key_columns = bt.key_columns
        )
where bt.key_columns in (
        select  dt.key_columns
        from    delta_table dt
        )
;
```

The best option to choose depends, as always, on the volume of data as well as the peripheral processing required, but each solution has its own problems.

The PL/SQL loop tends to be inherently inefficient because it handles one row at a time; however, it does deal with the inserts and updates in a single pass, whereas the subquery method requires a separate stage for inserts.

The EXISTS subquery method has to do a table scan on the main table and then visit the delta table (or at least its index) twice, once to see if there is any data, and once to get the value.

The IN subquery, which the optimizer may choose to change into the EXISTS subquery, drives off the delta table, jumps to the appropriate related row in the main table, then comes straight back to the delta table to get the correct value to add to the total.

With updatable views, there is another way, which depends on having a unique index on the main table and delta table:

```
update   (
            select /*+ ordered use_nl(bt) */
            bt.total, dt.delta
```

```
                from
                    delta_table       dt,
                    big_table         bt
                where bt.key_columns = dt.key_columns
            )
    set bt.total = bt.total + dt.delta
    ;
```

We create an updatable join view of the main table and the delta table as an in-line view, then simply perform an update by adding one column to another. The access path scans the delta table and indexes into the main table to do the update. The performance is almost inevitably better than the other three options.

There are limitations to this strategy. As I pointed out, both tables must have a unique index on *key_columns*. The uniqueness on the delta table is to ensure that the big table is updatable; the uniqueness on the big table is to ensure that a delta row is applied to only one row in the big table, so you may have to preprocess the delta table (summing by *key_columns*) to enforce the uniqueness. The next problem is that, unlike the PL/SQL solution, you still have to deal with inserting new rows into the big table when there is no row to update. Finally, we may want to delete rows from the big table that have just summed to zero, and we can't use the same trick to do this.

The reason why you can't delete through this join view is that we need both tables to have a unique key on them, which means that both tables in the join are updatable, and you can only delete from a join view if only one of the tables is updatable.

Although it does wander outside the area slightly, for the sake of completeness I'll just outline a generally sound strategy for the large-scale update. Moving from the point at which we have loaded the delta into a table,

1. Sum the data down to get unique keys matching the main table.

2. Update the delta table with a flag to show which rows don't exist in the main table:

```
update  delta_table
set     update_flag = 'Y'    -- should be created with 'N'
where exists (
    select  null
    from    big_table
    where   big_table.key_columns = delta_table.key_columns
);
```

3. Update the main table through the join view where flag is set:

```
update    (
            select /*+ ordered use_nl(bt) */
            bt.total, dt.delta
            from
                    delta_table    dt,
                    big_table      bt
            where   bt.key_columns = dt.key_columns
            and     dt.update_flag = 'Y'
          )
set bt.total = bt.total + dt.delta
;
```

4. Insert into the main table from the delta table where flag is
    not set:

```
insert  into big_table
select  (list of columns)
from    delta_table
where   update_flag = 'N'
and     delta != 0
;
```

5. Delete from the main table where the delta has just made the sum
    come to zero:

```
delete from big_table bt
where bt.key_columns in (
        select  dt.key_columns
        from    delta_table dt
        where   dt.update_flag = 'Y'
        )
and bt.total_column = 0
;
```

Of course there are other strategies for handling such a large update in
the shortest possible time. Partitioning, for example, would allow parallel
DML to update different parts of the table at the same time (see Chapters 13
and 22). This may reduce the elapsed time to completion of the update even
though it may use more resources.

Object Views

A chapter on views could not be complete without some mention of *object views*. However, if you have already read my chapters on objects (Chapters 15 and 16), you will find that I am not enthused by the OBJECTS option, so you will not be surprised to find that I have little to say about object views.

Nevertheless, Oracle Corporation went to the trouble of supplying features that allow you to impose a veneer of objectivity on top of a relational database by creating views that make relational tables look like objects. The point of this was to allow for a less painful transition from pure relational to object relational development, and they should be applauded for making the effort.

The downside was the creation of complex, inherently nonupdatable views that need to be updated! Consequently, the OBJECTS option includes the "instead of" trigger.

The "instead of" trigger is simply a trigger that can be attached to a view definition in much the same way that a table trigger can be attached to a table. However, there are two important differences between view-based triggers and table-based triggers.

First, the view-based trigger is only a for-each-row trigger. Second, the action of the trigger takes place instead of the action that causes it to fire. With a table-based trigger, the action of the triggers takes place in addition to the action that fired it.

> *Although "instead of" triggers were introduced to accommodate object views,* any view *can have an "instead of" trigger attached to it.*

You do have to be careful when you use view-based triggers. With nontrivial views you may need some very subtle code to avoid damaging the integrity of your data. However, the view-based trigger offers many possibilities for hiding complexity in one place inside the database.

Oracle 8 has, alas, made partitioned views a deprecated feature to be withdrawn in Oracle 9. But in Oracle 7, there were numerous occasions when a view-based trigger could have eliminated lots of complicated code created to deal with the problem of inserting rows into a UNION ALL view. Funnily enough, it is exactly this example that Oracle has chosen to use in the Oracle 8 concepts manual to demonstrate the benefits of the "instead of" trigger:

```
create table t1 (
    id      number,
    class   varchar2(1) not null check (class = 'X'),
    v1      varchar2(20)
);

create table t2 (
    id      number,
    class   varchar2(1) not null check (class = 'Y'),
    v1      varchar2(20)
);

create or replace view v1 as
select * from t1
union all
select * from t2
;
```

Given this view definition, which creates a UNION ALL of two identical but disjointed sets of data, we can now allow any program, or user, to insert into the view and have the data arrive automatically in the correct table by creating the following trigger:

```
create or replace trigger v1_trig
instead of insert on v1
begin
    if :new.class = 'X' then
        insert into t1 values(:new.id, :new.class, :new.v1);
    elsif :new.class = 'Y' then
        insert into t2 values(:new.id, :new.class, :new.v1);
    else
        raise_application_error(-20001,'Invalid Class');
    end if;
exception
    when others then
        raise;
end;
/
```

In a similar vein, we could revisit the problem of the delta update in the previous section, where we were unable to use an in-line join view to delete the main rows that had summed to zero. In fact, we could create a permanent view on the join and create an "instead of delete on join_view" trigger that examined the primary key of the incoming row and deleted the matching row of the main table. Of course, this would simply be a way of concealing a PL/SQL batch job inside the database.

It is important to remember that this feature requires a PL/SQL block to execute once *for each row*. This should immediately warn you that the "instead of" trigger is not a substitute for a carefully coded batch process. It exists to take complex code from an OLTP front end and hide it once inside the database. Used in moderation, and with great care, it could make some sections of the user-facing code much easier to maintain.

A Farewell to Partitioned Views

From Oracle 8.0, Oracle Corporation has been deprecating partitioned views. A partitioned view was simply a UNION ALL view of a number of absolutely identical tables. By including constraints on the tables, or built-in predicates in the view definition, it was possible to tell Oracle something about the data held by each table. For example, a view definition using *where clause partitioning* may look like this:

```
create or replace view weekly_sales as
          select * from week_199952 where week_id = 19952
union all select * from week_199953 where week_id = 19953
union all select * from week_200001 where week_id = 20001
union all select * from week_200002 where week_id = 20002
;
```

When running a query against this view with some predicate applied to "week_id," Oracle would recognize that some of the tables were redundant, and would avoid accessing them in much the same way that partitioned tables now operate.

The main drawback to partitioned views was that the access path to each table had to be evaluated separately by the optimizer, and the path for each table in the view could, in theory, be different. This could take a lot of work if you had a large number of tables in the view and joined the view to three or four reference tables. (For partitioned tables, a single, global access path for the table is evaluated just once, and the same path is applied to each relevant partition in turn.)

However, partitioned views allowed you to do something that partitioned tables cannot do effectively. The partitioning mechanism on partitioned tables is a single dimension of a continuous value; partitioned views can be anything.

In particular you can code multidimensional partitioning and you can code multigrain partitioning into partitioned views.

As an example of the constraint-based mechanism, you could define a two-dimensional partitioning constraint of the form

```
alter table p_199912_france
add constraint c_199912_france
check (country = 'FRANCE' and period_id = 199912)
;
```

If you had a collection of 144 tables covering 12 periods and 12 countries, a query for "all sales for France" would visit exactly the 12 tables with the FRANCE constraint, whereas a query for "all sales for June" would visit exactly the 12 tables with the 199906 constraint. The same option is not available in partitioned tables, although this example can almost be faked using composite partitions (see Chapter 12).

Similarly, if you have data partitioned by date (for example, dd-mmm-yyyy), partition elimination in partitioned tables will not work if your query tool asks for all data for week 6 of year 2000, unless you find some two-stage process that turns this into a query for the date range 14th Feb 2000 to 20th Feb 2000. With partitioned views you could store the redundant week, period, year, and so forth, data on each daily table and create partitions, demonstrating the *where clause* variant this time, of the form

```
. . .
union all select * from p_2000_02_06_17'
where year_id = 2000
and period _id = 200002
and week_id = 200006
and start_date = to_date('17-feb-2000','dd-mon-yyyy')
union all
. . .
```

With this definition in place, optimum partition elimination would take place irrespective of the time granularity that the end user required.

A final feature of partitioned views that simply cannot be emulated by partitioned tables is the ability to spread a single object over several databases. You could use a UNION ALL view to keep recent data in a database with one set of performance characteristics, whereas the rest of the data would be stored in a different database with a completely different setup using the *where clause* partitioning approach:

```
Create or replace view all_my_data as
Select * from recent_data
where   date_stamp >= to_date('01-Mar-1999','dd-mon-yyyy')
Union all
Select * from old_data@data_warehouse
Where   date_stamp < to_date('01-Mar-1999','dd-mon-yyyy')
;
```

As long as your queries included the date stamp, they could pick which database would be used to access the data. (I have to admit that there were a few problems if you crossed the boundary date in a single query, and sometimes joins didn't work too well, but that was partly the version 7 optimizer and the way it couldn't cope terribly well with distributed joins.)

I am hoping that partitioned views won't go away completely, because they can still be very useful. Oracle Corporation is always improving the way in which joins can be pushed down inside views. Perhaps one day we will see two-dimensional partitioning on partitioned tables combined with full predicate pushdown in UNION ALL views.

Problems and Quirks

Views are extremely effective ways of making it easy to restrict, or enhance, data that has to be presented to the end users for simple selections. Unfortunately, it is rather easy to include a view in a join in a way that results in appalling performance. This is not really a defect in the concept of views; it is a problem in documenting what can and can't be done efficiently with a view that you have defined. Views with outer joins are particularly easy to abuse.

The text of views is not stored in the dictionary cache or shared pool, so every time a new statement using a view has to be parsed, Oracle has to read the view definition from the data dictionary. This could add a significant overhead to statements that are supposed to return just a little data, and is another good reason for ensuring that you make maximum use of bind variables to avoid "hard" parsing.

Strategy Notes

Views can be used to help third-party tools make optimal use of new features in Oracle. In particular, partitions can be exposed by views, or literal values can be embedded in views to aid partition elimination. Views can also be used to expose precanned use of the new analytic functions to tools that cannot yet cope with the functions directly. However, the scope for optimization is strictly limited, and you may need to document very strict limits on how the views can be used to avoid sessions crashing.

Look very carefully at what you can do with in-line views. There are likely to be many occasions when the use of an in-line view can improve performance dramatically—in particular, in queries that join and group data.

Look equally carefully at how updatable join views can be used. There are occasions, particularly when the requirement is to "update table A from table B," when the best performance comes from an updatable join view.

When creating permanent join views (particularly join views that are intended to be updatable), pay attention to the table that you use to expose the columns used in the join.

You may get some mileage out of "instead of" triggers. There are times when it may be nice to present views to the user as updatable objects when they really shouldn't be. Be very careful coding the triggers though, and remember: The update becomes a PL/SQL call per row, so don't expect to do bulk updates on these views very quickly.

SYS_CONTEXT() is going to be a very powerful tool for creating static views that nevertheless return results that vary from user to user. There is a bug with parallel queries, but in other circumstances it works well and can be hidden using log-on triggers, default values, and views.

CHAPTER 12

Introducing Partitioning

From a purely administrative perspective, I believe that partitioning is likely to become one of the most commonly used features of Oracle databases within the next couple of years. With a little cunning and compromise, there are numerous ways in which partitioning can make the life of DBAs (and accountants) easier in their never-ending search for getting the best out of the current hardware. In addition to the simple administrative benefits, there is also a massive potential for truly extraordinary performance enhancements to all types of system. Where, then, should a description of partitioning begin?

Before the days of CD-ROM and the multimedia encyclopedia, the *Encyclopaedia Britannica* used to appear in a set of 32 handsomely bound and very weighty volumes. Stamped on each spine, in letters of gold, was a short code indicating which section of the alphabet that volume covered. If you wanted to read an article on the diet of the llama, you would walk over to your creaking bookcase, take down the volume marked LA–LO, and flip through its index to find the relevant entry.

If you've ever done this with any very large reference book you probably understand already one of the performance benefits of range-based partitioning with a local prefixed index—one of the data partitioning options available with Oracle 8.

Take a closer look at how you handled the encyclopedia. From a distance of several feet, you managed to identify the correct volume out of 32 because there is a special marker on it that lets you identify it very quickly, with very little effort. When you picked it up you looked in the index of that volume. You didn't have to search through a massive index for the whole encyclopedia, just the small section that you knew was relevant to that volume.

Before we go on to a discussion of partitioning in Oracle, just pause for a moment to imagine looking up the South American llama in a single book eight feet thick and weighing even more than the complete Oracle manual set! If you imagine moving the reference book from one bookcase to another you will also appreciate why there are significant administrative benefits to be had from partitioning.

Partitioning Options

Oracle 8.1 offers three different forms of partitioning. Range partitioning, which was first introduced in Oracle 8.0; hash partitioning, which appeared in Oracle 8.1; and composite partitioning, which combines the two forms.

Range partitioning is largely designed to offer significant performance benefits, whereas hash partitioning is more of an administrative aid but can have some beneficial side effects on performance. Composite partitioning attempts to merge the performance benefits of range partitioning with the administrative benefits of hash partitioning. For certain types of systems this can actually result in performance degradation, but given a little skill and luck, composite partitioning can be used on other types of systems to produce some extremely beneficial performance gains.

The main feature of partitioning is that it aims to solve a big problem by breaking it down into a number of little problems. A table that is partitioned exists in the database as a number of separate and virtually independent data segments. If you choose the only sensible indexing strategy, any index on that table will also exist as a set of virtually independent index segments.

The larger the number of partitions you specify, the smaller the segments will be. In general, smaller segments can be processed faster in queries, and smaller segments are easier to re-create, move about, and reindex. Hence the performance and administrative benefits of partitioning.

Also, because the definition of the partitioned table describes it as a single logical object, the table appears logically to the outside world as a single very large object, and you don't have to write code that needs to work out which particular segment you should be addressing at any given moment.

There was one detail in Oracle 8.0 that stopped partitioning from being totally transparent to end-user applications: A row could not be updated in such a way that it moved from one partition to another. This restriction has been lifted in Oracle 8.1, as long as you remember to set it explicitly. For example,

```
alter table flexible_partitions enable row movement;
```

This is one of the few cases, though, when an update to a row can cause a rowid to change, so partitioning still isn't perfectly transparent to all applications. It is possible to construct perhaps slightly artificial code that does two consecutive updates by rowid, and goes wrong because the first update has moved the row and changed its rowid. The solution to this problem is to write code that always uses "returning rowid" after every update.

Although I pointed out the benefits that small partitions can be re-created quickly, and queries against small partitions are generally faster, it is important to bear in mind that the use of large numbers of small partitions carries a built-in threat. The more partitions you have, the more partitions Oracle has to search if it cannot determine in advance which partitions are suitable targets for a query. The overhead of querying numerous partitions for "imprecise" queries may outweigh the performance benefits you get from "precise" queries hitting just the right partitions.

How Does Range Partitioning Work?

The *Encyclopaedia Britannica* is an example of range partitioning. You have a table (book) of information that is split into segments (volumes). By picking a column or a set of columns (topic of article), you can determine in which segment (volume) each row should appear. By specifying ranges of values (embossing the spine of the book), it is cheap and easy for Oracle (the reader) to determine which segment (volume) is going to hold items that match the search criteria, as long as the search column (topic of article) is directly involved in the query. (LA–LO won't help if I am looking for information on a well-known South American artiodactyl mammal.) The SQL to create a simplified version of the *Encyclopaedia Britannica* as an Oracle table might look like

```
create table britannica (
    article_title   varchar2(120),
    article         blob
)
partition by range (article_title) (
    partition volume_01 values less than ('AM'),
    partition volume_02 values less than ('BF'),
        . . .
    Partition volume_32 values less than ('ZZ')
);
```

With this definition, the partition named volume_02 would correspond to the volume with AM–BE on the spine. This introduces a minor detail of range partitioning that may cause a little confusion and can make multicolumn partitioning a little awkward to get right the first time.

The set of values that defines a partition is an unreachable upper bound for that partition. In other words, the values in the partitioning column must be strictly less than the bounding value. Hence the value BF, which is used to define volume_02, does not appear in volume_02 itself but in volume_03, the next volume.

The lower bound for a partition is the value of the upper bound of the previous partition, and in this case the value may appear in the partition itself. Hence the value AM appears *in* volume_02 because it *defined* volume_01. In algebraic terms, we would write

```
'AM' <= article_title < 'BF'
```

This arrangement appears to be a little awkward and uncomfortable but is a necessary complication, particularly when dealing with continuously variable numeric data.

On a more realistic note, range partitioning is usually applied to data that has a strong date and possibly time element to it (for example, supermarket sales, telephone calls, or stock market prices). Data for a given date appears on or shortly after that date, is subject to enhancement or correction only for a brief period after that date, is usually queried across a narrow date range, and is discarded in bulk when it has reached a suitable age.

In cases like this it makes sense to use narrow date ranges to partition the data into convenient-size chunks. Then each batch of inserts and updates is likely to affect only a small number of chunks, and old data can be discarded very cheaply by dropping partitions rather than deleting rows. The following code is an example of how to define a date-based range-partitioned table:

```
create table sales(
    product_id     number              not null,
    store_id       number              not null,
    date_part      date                not null,
    sales_value    number(10,2)        not null,
    sales_qty      number(6)           not null
)
partition by range (date_part) (
    partition p01 values less than (to_date('01022000','ddmmyyyy')),
    partition p02 values less than (to_date('01032000','ddmmyyyy')),
    partition p03 values less than (to_date('01042000','ddmmyyyy')),
    partition p04 values less than (to_date('01052000','ddmmyyyy')),
    partition p05 values less than (maxvalue)
);
```

It is important to use four-digit years at all times with date partitioning, although you can choose your favorite format when passing the dates to Oracle (I chose ddmmyyyy to keep the partition definition down to a single line). You may note the special value MAXVALUE as the limit on the last partition. This is an indicator unique to range partitioning that means "anything goes." In the *Britannica* example, the last partition has a limit of 'ZZ', which means that Oracle raises error "ORA-14400: inserted partition key is beyond highest legal partition key" if I insert a row with a topic of 'ZZZ'.

> *MAXVALUE is so special that it is the* only *thing that is deemed "larger" than null. If you want to allow null values in the partitioning keys, you have to use MAXVALUE in the range definitions.*

The performance benefit of range partitioning comes from the fact that the optimizer may be able to recognize at a very early stage of processing that a query applies to a limited subset of the available partitions. This technique of ignoring irrelevant partitions is usually referred to as *partition elimination*. Consider, for example, executing the following query against the table we have just defined:

```
select   date_part, store_id, sum(sales_value)
from     sales
where    date_part between    to_date('07-apr-2000','dd-mon-yyyy')
                      and     to_date('13-apr-2000','dd-mon-yyyy')
group by date_part, store_id
;
```

The optimizer determines that the query applies only to the single partition p04, the statistics for the partition no doubt indicate that the query is likely to acquire approximately one quarter of the data, and Oracle can therefore choose to run a parallel table scan across that partition. Note, by the way, that the date format I used to specify the date in the query does not need to match the date format used in the original partition definition.

> *The most commonly appreciated reason for using range partitioning is the tremendous performance benefit that you can get from partition elimination.*

The idea of applying a table scan to a single partition is not quite as peculiar as it may sound. As far as Oracle is concerned, the individual partitions that make up a partitioned table are virtually independent of each other. This independence is so great that each partition can be stored in a different tablespace with its own storage parameters (PCTFREE, PCTUSED), and even with a different buffer-pool declaration. BUFFER_POOL is a particularly interesting option to adjust (see Appendix D). It might make sense to associate the most recent partitions with the KEEP buffer pool and associate the rest with the RECYCLE buffer pool.

In effect, a partitioned table is simply a convenient "umbrella definition" for a collection of small tables that can be treated either as part of a collective or as quasi tables in their own right. This viewpoint is so sound that you can actually take a collection of similar tables and build them into a single partitioned table if you want. In fact, this is the basic strategy for migrating a partitioned view from Oracle 7 to a partitioned table in Oracle 8. The only similarities that *must* hold across the subentities of the partitioned tables are that the column definitions must be almost the same—types must match but there is a little leeway allowed in sizing, precision, and nullity—and the indexing strategy must be identical.

To keep an eye on what your partitioned tables look like, the data dictionary includes the symetrically named view families xxx_PART_TABLES (the list of partitioned tables) and xxx_TAB_PARTITIONS (the partitions belonging to a partitioned table).

Moving on to indexing, you have three basic options with partitioned tables. You can create a single enormous index segment that covers the whole table (a global index), you can create an index that is partitioned in a way that has nothing to do with the underlying table (a globally partitioned index; for example, our supermarket table is partitioned by date but we could choose to create an index that is partitioned by store code, but then any one index partition would probably point to all the data partitions), and you can create an index that is partitioned in a one-to-one match with the data partitions (a local index).

If you create a global or globally partitioned index on a partitioned table, then there are some maintenance actions that invalidate the index and require you to rebuild the whole index. Not only that, but a globally partitioned index has to be pre-fixed—in other words, you have to start it with the columns that define the partitioning method.

In sharp contrast to this, local indexing allows you to treat every data partition as a totally separate entity, to the extent that you can actually drop or truncate a partition or put its tablespace off-line without having any side effect on any other part of the table or its indexes. The options that this feature offers for near on-line maintenance are so amazing that I find it hard to imagine any good reason for using any strategy other than local indexing for partitioned tables.

Another less significant reason for using local indexes rather than global ones is that global indexes store the full 10-byte extended rowid to specify the partition and location with partition of the row. Local indexes implicitly point to a single related partition and thus need store only the 6-byte restricted rowid to identify the row, which could produce a significantly smaller index.

The simplest syntax for creating a local index on a partitioned table is

```
create index big_new_index on partitioned_table (colX)
local
tablespace scratchpad
;
```

The critical word in this statement is "local." In the absence of this keyword Oracle would build a single global index segment covering the whole table. The statement as shown creates one index segment for each of the table segments, copying the table's partition names to the index's partition names for ease of reference. Unfortunately, this example creates all the index segments in the same tablespace, so you may want to use a much longer, more informative statement to allocate partitions to tablespaces. For example,

```
create unique index sale_pk on
sales(product_id, store_id, date_part)
local (
    partition p01 tablespace p01_idx pctfree 0,
    partition p02 tablespace p02_idx pctfree 0,
    partition p03 tablespace p03_idx pctfree 0,
    partition p04 tablespace p04_idx pctfree 10
            storage(buffer_pool keep),
    partition p05 tablespace scratch_idx
)
;
```

In this example I created a unique index so that I can point out that local unique indexes *must* contain the partitioning columns—in this case, DATE_ PART. This is, of course, an implementation choice on the part of Oracle Corporation rather than a strict logical necessity. It is, however, a very sensible restriction because it means that the software need only visit one partition to check the uniqueness of a new row, thus maximizing the independence of partitions.

This example also demonstrates the syntax for assigning index partitions to different tablespaces with different physical storage arrangements. The rationale for the special treatment of partition p04 is that it is the current, active partition, so I want to leave some space for insertions in the index and I want it kept in the buffer pool as much as possible. Partition p05 is in a scratch pad tablespace because there is no data going into it just yet (in theory), and I will be building a new tablespace of the right size and moving that particular partition into it in a couple of weeks.

If you really wanted to create a globally partitioned index on the table, the syntax you would use would be something like the following:

```
create index sale_fk_store on sales(store_id, product_id)
global partition by range (store_id)
(
    partition p1 values less than (10000),
    partition p2 values less than (20000),
    partition p3 values less than (maxvalue)
)
;
```

Globally partitioned indexes must have a top range of MAXVALUE to ensure that any data that can go into the table can be indexed. Also note that STORE_ID has to appear as the first column of the index because STORE_ID is the column used to partition the index.

The data dictionary views for partitioned indexes are named similar to tables. xxx_PART_INDEXES describes the partitioned indexes, and xxx_IND_PARTITIONS describes the partitions themselves.

> *How is it possible to delete millions of rows in seconds, with virtually no overhead? ALTER TABLE DROP PARTITION.*

By now you may have noticed how I keep coming up with date-related partitioning. This is the most obvious and probably the most beneficial area to apply range partitioning. Not only does range partitioning allow for improved performance as a result of partition elimination, it also helps tremendously with getting aging data out of the database and loading data into the database.

Consider the case of a supermarket that keeps 15 months of daily store data on-line, perhaps 1,000,000 rows of data per day for 450 days, or 65 weeks. As data gets past the 15-month age limit it has to be removed from the database. Imagine the effect of deleting 7,000,000 rows from a single table once per week. Every row would have to be written into rollback, and the instructions for the delete and its rollback would have to be written into the redo log, and then there are the index changes to worry about. On the other hand, if we have partitioned the data by week, we could simply use the command "drop oldest partition" to do the work in two seconds.

> *To find the name of the oldest partition, look in view family xxx_TAB_ PARTITIONS for the entry with partition_position = 1.*

To drop the oldest partition from the SALES table defined previously, we use

```
alter table sales drop partition p01;
```

Of course, hand in hand with dropping an old partition, you will probably want to add a new partition for the latest data. Assume for the moment that I did not include a MAXVALUE partition p05 in the SALES table and simply wanted to add a partition to hold the May data. The statement would be something like

```
alter table sales add partition p05
    values less than (to_date('01-Jun-2000','dd-mon-yyyy'))
tablespace data_p05
pctfree 20 pctused 75
;
```

Unfortunately, however, my example did include a "top" partition using MAXVALUE, so instead of simply adding a new partition at the top, I have to split the top partition into two:

```
alter table sales
split partition p05 at (to_date('01-May-2000','dd-mon-yyyy'))
into (
    partition p05 tablespace data_p05 pctfree 20 pctused 75,
    partition p06
);
```

Personally, I am very fussy about where I put things and what I call them, so with this *split* command I have specified the names of the partitions arising from the split. If you don't do this you'll find that you'll have partitions with names like SYS_Pnnnnn, where the nnnnn is a nonpadded number generated by the sequence SYS.PARTITION_NAME$.

I have also specified the tablespace and special storage clause for the lower of the two partitions because this is the one that I am really going to be using for new data. If you don't specify such details for the new partitions, they are created using the definitions from the partition that is being split and not, as you might expect, the default definitions for the table from the view family xxx_PART_TABLES.

There is an issue when adding or splitting partitions that is affected by indexes. For each local index, a matching index partition is created automatically every time a table partition is added or split. However, you cannot specify where the new partition should go or whether it should have any special physical attributes. If you use the ***add*** command, it takes its physical attributes from the index's defaults (found in view family xxx_PART_INDEXES). If you use the ***split*** command, it takes its physical attributes from the index partition that is being split.

Moreover, when you split the partition, you may find that the index partitions on both halves of the split become unusable. This occurs only if the partition has any data in it to start with (which in our scenario it should not have). If either of the new table partitions ends up with data in them, the corresponding index partitions are unusable.

The issue of unusable indexes is addressed, usually fairly rapidly, with the index ***rebuild*** command, which in the form for partitioned indexes reads something like

```
alter index sales_i
rebuild partition p05
nologging
tablespace indx_p05
online
;
```

> *When you add/split table partitions, you cannot specify the storage requirements for the indexes at the same time. The indexes become unusable if the resulting table partitions contain any data.*

Table partitions can be given the same sort of individual rebuild treatment as indexes, and there are a number of minor strategic details that need to be worked out when planning for individual partition maintenance of this sort. For example, a glitch in the code ensures that the **rebuild** command fails with error "ORA-14185: incorrect physical attribute specified for this index partition" if the SALES table is a hash partition rather than a range partition. (The problem is with the NOLOGGING option.) You also have to remember that queries that attempt to access an unusable index partition will fail. Fortunately, the limited time needed to rebuild relatively small partitions may be sufficiently low that it does not impact end users significantly. Nevertheless, you need to think through the costs, benefits, and side effects of rolling partition maintenance at an early stage of the design.

One of the nice, and quite extraordinary, things about splitting partitions is that an end-user query can be running while you do it. Read consistency actually works (with some limitations) across partition maintenance. If I start a query against partition p199912 just before it's split into p199912a and p199912b, my query carries on running even as the split takes place, and may complete successfully. I have to say *may*. Oracle uses layers of read consistency to allow the query to continue running, but to split the partition it creates two new data segments, copies the data into them, and frees the old data segment. This means that the data I am querying is effectively in an area of free space. If any other process decides to demand some space in the same tablespace at that moment, my data may be overwritten by a new object, at which point my query fails with an error about an invalid rowid. Because of this, if you plan to "roll" your data by dropping and adding partitions, and happen to be using the same tablespace all the time, you may choose to create the new partition before you drop the old one, to reduce the risk of your activity causing an end user's query to fail.

This read consistency is also limited to the single query. If I have issued "set transaction read only" and try to requery the table after it has split, I get Oracle error "ORA-01466: unable to read data—table definition has changed."

You may have spotted by now one important penalty to splitting a partition. There is a period when two copies of the data exist at the same time—the old partition and the two new partitions. If space is at a premium, you may be a little constrained in how you manipulate the size of your partitions.

There is one problem with any operation that adds a new partition, whether it is an add or a split. The statistics at the *table level* go to null as you add the partition. This could have a catastrophic effect on the execution path. Fortunately, if you analyze the partition immediately after adding it, the adjusted statistics are restored to the *table* as well as appearing on the partition.

I haven't yet addressed what happens to a global or globally partitioned index when a table partition is split. Do you recall my comment about the

10-byte rowid used in global indexes? Part of that 10 bytes is the object ID for the object holding the row, and each partition of a partitioned table has a different object ID. When you split a partition, the two resulting partitions are given new object IDs, so *all* the index entries for rows in the original partition are wrong, and Oracle brutally, but necessarily, marks the entire index as unusable. If you have any global indexes on a partitioned table, don't split a partition unless the partition is absolutely, definitely empty or you may end up with a long period of denial of service as you rebuild a massive index (another good reason for using only local indexes on partitioned tables).

The opposite of splitting a partition is to merge partitions. For example,

```
alter table sales
merge partitions p05, p06 into
partition p06
;
```

As with splitting partitions, this creates a new object, so global indexes may be made unusable, and two copies of the data temporarily exist at once. You can include the usual sorts of tablespace allocation and storage details for the resulting partition. If you don't, then the default storage details (in view family xxx_PART_TABLE) are used for the new partition. You can merge only two partitions at a time, and the partitions have to be *adjacent* partitions.

Before we go into too much detail about strategies for avoiding denial of service when rolling partitions forward, let's look at loading bulk data. Imagine a SQL∗Load of 1,000,000 rows per day in an existing table of 450,000,000 rows—a bit expensive on index updates, rollback, and redo. How about accomplishing the task with "direct load" then? SQL∗Load using direct load results in an index copy and merge. Do we really want that on a 450,000,000-row table?

Consider, then, what we can do with partitioning. Let's say we have partitioned by week so that we have to direct load 1,000,000 rows into a single partition that is (by the last day of the week) a maximum of 6,000,000 existing rows. With this strategy, the impact is much less ferocious, but we can do better still. Look at the following example:

```
create table this_week nologging
as
select {this weeks data so far}
from partitioned_table partition (this_week)
union all
select latest_day_date from sql_loaded_table
;
```

```
{create necessary indexes on this_week table}

alter table partitioned_table
exchange partition this_week with table this_week
including indexes
without validation
;
```

With a strategy like this, you may even be able to get away with major data maintenance during the work day, giving end users unimpeded access to yesterday's data (although not update rights) and no problems with inconsistent queries or massive consistent-read overhead. At the last moment, users will experience a brief interruption as the exchange partition takes place.

> *The command to **alter table exchange partition** is one of the single most powerful tools for improving the ease of administration of a large database.*

The **exchange partition** statement allows you to replace a partition in a table with an ordinary table. The actual mechanics are simply that Oracle swaps names (and a few numbers) in the data dictionary. The table that gets swapped into the partition has to be very similar in structure to the basic table definition itself. It has to have columns of the same type and order, although Oracle offers a little flexibility in size and nullity, and the names don't have to match.

I have suggested the need to precreate correctly structured indexes. This is a good idea but not a necessity. If you can guarantee that the table is a perfect match for the partition in terms of both content and indexing, then you can safely use both the INCLUDING INDEXES and WITHOUT VALIDATION clauses to keep the cost of the exchange to the absolute minimum.

In the absence of the WITHOUT VALIDATION clause, Oracle tests every row in the table to see if it matches the partitioning condition, blocking the exchange if any row fails. In the absence of the INCLUDING INDEXES clause, Oracle marks any related index partitions as unusable, and you have to rebuild them after the exchange, leaving the data effectively unavailable while you do so.

In fact, my description of building and indexing a small table and exchanging it with a partition relies on local indexing, as does my comment about dropping partitions. If you did either of these operations with a global (partitioned) index, the entire index would become unusable and would have to be rebuilt.

There is, however, a bit of a problem with exchanging partitions that is common to all types of partitioning. Even with the option of avoiding validation, Oracle performs a validation step that ensures that the key values of any primary or unique constraints in the incoming table do not appear in *any other partition* of the partitioned table. This entails a complicated set-wise operation for each index-based constraint that effectively does a unique sort on the entire index, and makes it hideously expensive, and effectively pointless, to do the exchange. If you do an exchange partition *without validation* with SQL_TRACE on, you will find SQL code of the following form in the trace file:

```
select
    pk1 , pk2 , pk3
from
    jpl1.tab_iot_temp
where not(
        pk1 is null
    and pk2 is null
    and pk3 is null
)
intersect
select pk1 , pk2 , pk3
from
(
    select pk1 , pk2 , pk3
    from jpl1.tab_iot
    minus
    select pk1 , pk2 , pk3
    from jpl1.tab_iot partition (p3)
) b
where not(
    pk1 is null
    and pk2 is null
    and pk3 is null
)
;
```

Funnily enough, when I first found this out, I discovered it was faster to do the exchange *with validation* because this limited the overhead to a full scan of the incoming table using code of the following form:

```
select 1
from "TAB_IOT_TEMP"
where
    TBL$OR$IDX$PART$NUM("TAB_IOT",0,"PK1","PK2","PK3")!= :1
```

Fortunately, there seems to be a way to avoid both of these overheads. If the constraints are set to be enabled but not validated, then the exchange really does take place without validation. Of course, you are then in the odd position that Oracle thinks it hasn't validated the constraint even though it has a unique index, which means the data has to be perfect (unless you happen to have a nonunique index representing the unique constraint). To help the optimizer cope with this anomaly, it is a good idea to use the RELY option on the constraint to tell Oracle to treat the constraint as valid even if it has been told not to bother with doing the validation itself. The syntax is

```
alter table tab_iot modify constraint ti_pk rely novalidate;
```

There are plenty of other areas for discussion in range partitioning, but before going into some of the details of how they should and should not be used, we should look at the other types of partitioning.

How Does Hash Partitioning Work?

If you have to handle 8GB of data, it is more convenient to administer it as eight chunks of 1GB each. A single gigabyte can be moved around and reindexed rather more quickly than an 8GB chunk of data. However, there may not be an intuitively sensible way to partition the data, or it may be that the "obvious" way to partition the data leads to huge imbalances between different partitions. Perhaps you will end up with one partition of 7GB and seven partitions of 140MB each. As we shall see later, unbalanced partitions can produce huge variations in performance.

In the age of massive-volume and high-throughput databases in which pure scale becomes the major issue, hash partitioning offers a technique for breaking up big objects into little objects in a fashion that tends to make all the little objects about the same size. Hash partitioning is based on a randomizing approach.

The syntax for defining a hashed partition is very simple. You select the columns that should be used as the basis for splitting the data, and you select the number of chunks into which you want to break it, and Oracle does the rest. In its simplest form the syntax is

```
create table hash_test(
    id_code        varchar2(10),
    date_part      date,
    other_part     varchar2(32),
    padding        varchar2(200)
)
pctfree 5
pctused 90
partition by hash(id_code)
partitions 4
store in (data_p01, data_p02, data_p03, data_p04)
;
```

This creates a table that uses four separate data segments to hold its data, and applies a hashing algorithm to the ID column to decide which data segment should be used to hold a specific row.

Although you can use a partition list to specify the names, tablespaces, and storage clauses for the partitions you want to create, I have used a lazier syntax here, which simply states that I want four partitions, which should be allocated in round-robin order to a supplied list of tablespaces.

Because hash partitioning is supposed to produce evenly balanced data distribution with no built-in biases, such as recent data ending up in a specific partition, there is little point in trying to be fussy about storage for individual hash partitions. Note that in this case I assigned a default PCTFREE and PCTUSED as the table level. These figures are applied to every single partition unless I override them for a specific partition.

By declaring ID_CODE as the column to be used as the hash key, we have scattered rows with different ID_CODEs randomly across the four partitions, and cannot predict to which partition any particular ID_CODE will go. We can only say that it will go to the same partition every time.

This means that any query for a *range* of ID_CODEs is likely to access all four partitions, which in turn means that it will not, generally, be possible to rebuild a partition without the end users noticing. In this respect, hash partitions offer fewer options for on-line administration and performance benefits. Except for carefully crafted special cases, partition elimination is unlikely to occur. However, the randomizing effect does have a very useful performance payback that some systems can take advantage of.

In fact, despite my comment about being unable to predict to which partition a specific ID_CODE will go, there is some scope for testing in advance (for design purposes, rather than runtime purposes). Oracle has introduced a hash function in the DBMS_UTILITY package that seems to be the hash function applied to single-column character strings:

```
get_hash_value(name varchar2, base number, hash_size number)
return number;
```

If you call this function passing in the string values as "name," set base to zero, and hash_size to the number of partitions, then the return value is the partition number appropriate for that string. For example,

```
begin
    dbms_output.put_line(
            dbms_utility.get_hash_value(
                        name        => 'Scotland',
                        base        => 0,
                        hash_size   => 4
                )
        );
end;
/

2
```

Unfortunately, as with range partitioning, the internal partition number starts counting from zero whereas the external partition number, visible as PARTITION_POSITION in the view family xxx_TAB_PARTITIONS, starts counting from one. Consequently, we can predict that if we partition into four by country name, "Scotland" will appear in the partition with the partition position 3. The hash function is case sensitive by the way. "SCOTLAND" will return a value of one from this function, meaning that it will go into partition position 2.

You may have noticed that I chose four as the number of partitions for the example. Oracle's hash partitioning algorithm revolves around powers of two. Any other value leads to unbalanced partitioning. The reason behind this strategy is to allow you to change (which really means halve or double) the number of partitions in the table without having to rebuild the entire table at once if you decide that your original partition count was inappropriate.

The easiest way to explain this is to look at the way that you can change the number of partitions in a hash partition. There are two options allowed to hash partitions: You can add partitions or coalesce partitions. You do not have any detailed control over what these two commands do to the data though, for reasons that will become clear.

Assume you have a hash-partitioned table with six partitions, the following command adds one more partition by splitting the data of an existing partition into two roughly equal sets and copying the sets into two new data segments:

```
alter table hash_table
add partition p7 tablespace ts7
;
```

The "new" partition goes into the specified tablespace or into the default tablespace for the table. The remnants of the "old" partition stay in the same tablespace. (If the table is defined as NOLOGGING, then this copying generates no redo log.)

But which partition will be split? The answer lies in Oracle's suggestion that a hash-partitioned table should always have a power of two as the number of partitions. If we draw a simple diagram laying out our partitions as "the first $2^{\{largest\ power\ of\ N\ that\ will\ fit\}}$" followed by the rest, the answer jumps from the page in a way that is hard to describe with words (Figure 12-1).

In Figure 12-1 we have six partitions that we split into four plus two, because four is the largest power of two less than six. We then see that we need to split partition 3 to produce partitions 3 and 7 (4 + 3). In the abstract case, any number of partitions can be expressed as $2^N + X$, where X is less than 2^N. Find the value for X, and partition $X + 1$ is split into $X + 1$ and $2^N + X + 1$. The upshot of this is that if the number of partitions is *not* an

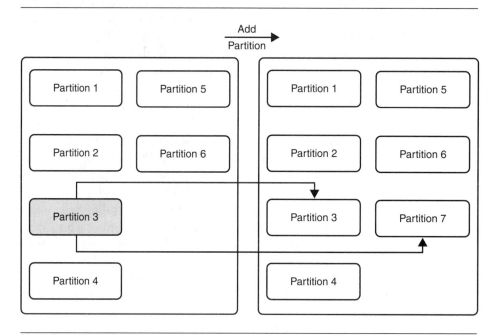

Figure 12-1.   How hash partitions split.

exact power of two, then some partitions are twice the size of other partitions, which decreases the benefit of hashing in the first place.

> *To ensure uniform data distribution across hash partitions you should always specify the number of partitions to be a power of two (2, 4, 8, 16, 32, and so on). If you do not do this, some partitions are twice the size of other partitions.*

You may ask why Oracle has adopted this apparently restrictive strategy for hash partitions. In fact, it is a big benefit to administration. Imagine that the hashing function was a "pure" hashing function, so that a hash table of seven partitions split the data perfectly into seven equal-size partitions. What happens when the data grows or you discover that seven was the wrong number? You have to rebuild the data with a new number of partitions, and because *every single row* will probably move, you have to rebuild the whole table in one go. At least with the Oracle strategy to hash partitions, you can do the job in parts—perhaps splitting or coalescing one partition each night over a week or so.

Having mentioned that it is possible to coalesce partitions, to reduce the number of hash partitions you need to know the command, which is the rather sparse statement

```
alter table hash_table coalesce partition;
```

This takes the top partition and merges it with the corresponding partition in the other half of the list, and copies the results to a new data segment. For example, if we have 23 partitions (23 = 16 + 7), then Oracle would merge partition 23 with partition 7, and would create a new data segment for partition 7. The resulting data and index partitions are built in the tablespaces of the lower numbered partition, and there is no option for changing this.

There are features of range partitioning that are irrelevant to hash partitioning. For example, you cannot drop a partition from a hash table. In most cases it wouldn't really make much sense to do so; however, you can truncate a partition, and if it happens to be the top or equivalent modulo (2^N) partition, you could then coalesce partitions to remove it.

You can exchange a partition from a hash partition with a simple table. However it might be a little hard to prove in general that the table will pass the hash partition's validation requirement on the hash column.

The same conventions apply to indexes on hash partitions as to indexes on range partitions. You can have global, globally partitioned, or locally partitioned indexes. When you add or coalesce partitions, the resulting local index partitions are marked unusable unless the resulting data partition is actually empty, and it is inevitable that any global or globally partitioned indexes will be unusable.

There is a little oddity about the partitioned indexes when adding a partition. It seems that the index is built in the tablespace of the data partition if the default tablespace for the index is not defined. And unlike the partitioned table itself, the default tablespace is not set to the user's default tablespace when the index is created. It is left null, but can be set later with ***alter index partitioned_index modify default attributes tablespace default_ts.***

So far I have pointed out that in general hash partitioning is an administrative aid, not a performance aid, because partition elimination against hash partitions is a little unlikely. However, there are always special cases. Consider, for example, a customer list. Assume I am part of a sales organization in the United States that sells nationally. I could keep a customer list in the following table:

```
create table customer(
    id                  number(14) not null,
    state               varchar2(2) not null, -- with check or fk
    first_sale_date     date,
    total_sales         number(15,2),
    other_data          varchar2(200)
)
partition by hash(state)
partitions 8
;


alter table customer
add constraint cu_pk primary key (id, state)
using index local -- sort out tablespaces later
;
```

Given the number of states in the United States, this is likely to give me an average of six or seven states per partition, so I may get a significant partition elimination benefit on a query of the form

```
select trunc(first_sale_date), sum(total_sales)
from customer
where state = 'CA'
```

```
group by trunc(first_sale_date)
;
```

You may have noticed the oddity. I created the primary key on (ID, STATE). This is because I wanted the primary key index to be a local index, but a unique local index has to include the partitioning columns. More precisely, the index representing the primary key has to contain the partitioning columns, even if the index itself is nonunique. This leaves me with three choices:

1. Make (ID, STATE) the real unique key to the customer.
2. Make ID the proper unique key, and allow the index to be a global index.
3. Code around the problem, but make ID the key, and (ID, STATE) the unique index.

In my discussion of range partitions, I pointed out how undesirable global indexes are because they become invalid and have to be rebuilt in their entirety when you drop a partition. However, I also pointed out that you can't drop hash partitions, and in general you have no need to drop hash partitions. Although sheer size is a good reason for disliking global indexes, I prefer option 2 to option 3, but (depending on the business requirement) I would probably argue in favor of option 1 over option 2 as giving the maximum administrative benefit. The biggest problem with option 3 is that you can no longer use declarative referential integrity between customers and any dependent tables.

There is another (initially invisible) defect to using the previous table as a partitioned table for customers. Hashing algorithms are about random distribution, and randomness depends on large populations. If there were a thousand states, we might find each partition held data on 125 states plus or minus 10 states. But with only a few dozen states, we still might find that the variation comes out to plus or minus 10. In other words, some partitions may be empty and other partitions may cover 12 states. Partition sizes can vary quite dramatically when only a few values exist for the partitioning column. And in this case, different states may have dramatically different customer lists, so even a perfect distribution of states may leave you with a wide range of partition sizes.

The paradox of hash partitioning is that it is most likely to lead to uniform-size partitions only when the number of different values for the hash columns is sufficiently high that the performance benefits resulting from partition elimination have been effectively nullified.

Hash partitioning does not, in general, offer runtime performance benefits. It exists largely as an administrative aid for handling large datasets.

How Does Composite Partitioning Work?

Imagine I operate an extremely popular but highly localized European Web site. Every day of the week I get 500,000 transactions recorded against the site, but on the weekend I get 5,000,000 transactions per day. The data has a very transient use, so I delete it when it is a couple of months old. While the very short on-line transactions are executing, I need to run various analytical reports against relatively new data, preferably without affecting the performance too much. Clearly it would be sensible to partition the data, and conveniently the nature of the application is such that the date of arrival of the data is a good partitioning column.

The simplest partitioning strategy is to partition by day. But this gives me five small partitions followed by two large partitions, so plan B might be to partition by day for the week, and to partition every 3 hours on the weekend to get all my partitions around the same size. This still leaves a problem:

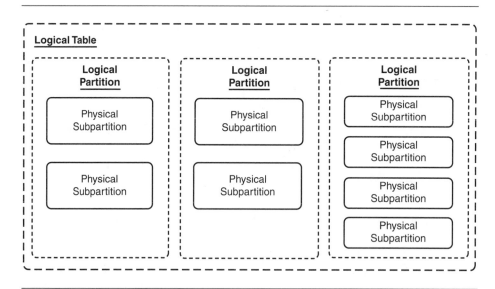

Figure 12-2.   Composite partitioning.

Incoming transactions are given a meaningless sequential ID, which happens to be indexed, and during the heavy load periods on the weekend, this results in serious contention on the leading-edge block of the index as many processes try to insert index entries into that block.

The optimum solution (and one that I referred to in Chapter 7) is to use composite partitioning (Figure 12-2). I first split the table into range partitions, and then split each range partition into a set of hash subpartitions. In much the same way that a partitioned table consists of many physical partitions contained within a logical table definition, when we use composite partitioning we have many physical subpartitions existing within a logical partition, and many logical partitions existing within a logical table. Only the subpartitions have any real existence as data segments in the database.

The syntax (and the struggle to name subpartitions and put them in the right tablespace) gets increasingly complex, but for one week my table may look like this:

```
create table comp_demo(
    id          number(14),
    date_part   date,
    other_part  varchar2(12),
    padding     varchar2(200)
)
partition by range (date_part)
subpartition by hash (id)
subpartitions 1 - default one subpartition per partition
(
    partition p2000_05_24
        values less than (to_date('25-apr-2000','dd-mon-yyyy')),
    partition p2000_05_25
        values less than (to_date('26-apr-2000','dd-mon-yyyy')),
    partition p2000_05_26
        values less than (to_date('27-apr-2000','dd-mon-yyyy')),
    partition p2000_05_27
        values less than (to_date('28-apr-2000','dd-mon-yyyy')),
    partition p2000_05_28
        values less than (to_date('29-apr-2000','dd-mon-yyyy')),
    partition p2000_05_29
        values less than (to_date('30-apr-2000','dd-mon-yyyy'))
        subpartitions 8         -- over-ride the default
        store in (ts1,ts2,ts3,ts4),
    partition p2000_05_30       -- more complex over-ride
        values less than (to_date('01-May-2000','dd-mon-yyyy'))
        (
```

```
            subpartition sp2000_05_30_A tablespace ts1,
            subpartition sp2000_05_30_B tablespace ts2,
            subpartition sp2000_05_30_C tablespace ts3,
            subpartition sp2000_05_30_D tablespace ts4,
            subpartition sp2000_05_30_E tablespace ts1,
            subpartition sp2000_05_30_F tablespace ts2,
            subpartition sp2000_05_30_G tablespace ts3,
            subpartition sp2000_05_30_H tablespace ts4
      )
   )
   ;
```

In this example, I demonstrate three different ways of assigning names and storage to the subpartitions. The weekday subpartitions go into the user's default tablespace because no tablespace has been specified for them at all, and no default tablespace has been specified for the table. The Saturday sub-partitions are given names like SYS_SUBPnnn, and rotate around the four tablespaces TS1 to TS4. The Sunday subpartitions are given explicit names and explicit tablespaces.

By creating hash subpartitions for Saturday and Sunday, I have killed three birds with one stone. I am back to fairly uniformly sized data segments, I still have all the benefits of range partitioning such as getting partition elimination on date-based queries and being able to drop old partitions, and I have also eliminated contention on my ID index blocks. Instead of 128 consecutive inserts, with 128 consecutive sequences numbers all hitting the same trailing index leaf block at pretty much the same time, I have a fair chance that the trailing index leaf block of each of the eight index subpartitions will be hit by approximately 16 inserts, thus reducing the contention (specifically, "buffer busy waits," but also the need for high levels of INITRANS) dramatically. Moreover, unlike other solutions for avoiding contention, each separate index subpartition is populated by monotonically increasing values, so the index is very well packed.

In high-throughput, multiuser systems, hash partitioning can be a very effective way of reducing block contention on the leading edge of sequenced-based indexes while allowing perfect data packing.

The downside to this is that if I want a unique index on the ID, I can't have it because any unique index on a partitioned table has to contain the partitioning columns. One possible solution in this case is to partition and subpartition by

ID. (A little detail that is not immediately apparent from the manuals is that you can actually partition and subpartition a table on the same column.) This is an effective solution for two reasons: First, the application is very artificial, and, second, I know what the application is doing and why I want to partition the data.

There are various other drawbacks to composite partitioning. If you need to split a partition (that's splitting a range partition) you can end up producing loads of new subpartitions in one fell swoop. For example, if I tried to split a Sunday partition I would actually be generating at least 16 new subpartitions (eight for the table, eight for the unique index, and eight for every other local index) and at least 32 new data segments (because each split requires two segments before the old one is dropped). The impact on the dictionary cache and library cache is quite severe. The same effect appears when dropping a partition: All its subpartitions have to go, and the overhead is large.

Even worse, if you want to exchange a partition (taking an old set of Sunday's data out to transport it to a test database, for example, rather than just dropping it) you have to exchange it one subpartition at a time. (Oracle 8.1.6 allows you to exchange a hash partitioned table with a single partition of a composite partitioned table, which makes the job easier, but the impact on the dictionary and library caches is still pretty bad.)

Currently there is also a problem with index rebuilding. If you try to rebuild an index subpartition with the ONLINE or NOLOGGING options (which are highly desirable to minimize denial of service to users) you get error "ORA-14189: this physical attribute may not be specified for an index subpartition." Not only that, the index partitions of a composite partitioned table cannot be compressed (Oracle error "ORA-08113: composite partition index may not be compressed"), so you can't even save resources by reducing the size of the index partition.

Partitioning—General Points

The main, high-visibility improvements in Oracle 8.1 come from the increased range of possibilities in partitioning. Apart from the new types of partitioning, Oracle 8.1 also removes some of the earlier restrictions on partitioning.

Tables with LOB columns can be partitioned, although this leads to three segments or more per partition: one for the data, one for the LOB index, and one for the LOB segment. Tables containing VARRAY and object-type columns can also be partitioned.

IOTs (see Chapter 14) can be partitioned (and IOTs containing LOBs, and . . .) but only by range, not as a hash or composite partition, and there is a restriction on partitioned IOTs in that the partitioning columns must be columns that appear in the primary key. This is just the IOT equivalent of the more general restriction on unique local indexes containing the partitioning columns, thus allowing partition independence. Oracle need only check one partition to ensure that a row is unique if the primary key contains the partitioning key. There is a bug in the code that handles partition maintenance of IOTs, which results in a library cache deadlock (Oracle error ORA-04020): Any DML that accesses a partitioned IOT just after a partition split, exchange, add, or drop waits for the DDL to complete and then fails with this error.

> *Be a little cautious with partitioned IOTs. They may introduce problems that you do not see with heap-organized partitioned tables. Experiment with SQL_TRACE switched on. This may give you clues about some nasty implementation traps.*

You can partition object tables, but there may be little point in doing so because the index on the hidden object ID (see Chapter 15) has to be a unique index, which means it will inevitably be a global index because unique local indexes have to contain the partitioning columns.

You cannot partition a nested table even though you can partition the table in which it is nested. If you create a partitioned table containing a nested table, the nested table will be a single large table, and its creation will implicitly create a hidden (by default global) unique index on the partitioned table. You may be able to drop and re-create the unique index as a partitioned local index if you wish, but only by adding the partitioning columns and mucking about with the foreign key relationship, and who knows what side effects that may have. Even then you lose most of the benefits of partitioning. In particular, you cannot truncate or drop any of the partitions because of the relationship to the object table. To drop a partition from a table with a nested table, you must delete all the rows from a partition (so that the nested table rows are also deleted), then disable the foreign key constraint while you drop the partition. Mechanically, there are a few variations on this theme, but none of them reduce the amount of work done by the database (or by the DBA).

I have mentioned the feature of unusable indexes, and how index partitions may become unusable when you split, merge, add, or coalesce partitions. The impact of this feature on your end users may be fairly slight. There are two points at which an unusable index makes a mark—when querying a table and when changing the contents of a table.

If Oracle decides to use a particular index for a query, and attempts to access a partition of the index that is currently unusable, then the query fails with Oracle error "ORA-01502: index XXX.YYY or partition of such index is in unusable state." There is no option for bypassing this problem. (Remember, Oracle works out the access path for a partitioned table just once for the table as a whole, then every partition is accessed in the same way; the optimizer does not consider every partition separately.)

On the other hand, if a user is inserting data into a partitioned table, and relevant partitions of the associated indexes are marked as unusable, then it is possible to tell Oracle to ignore these partitions and not try to keep them up to date. This is done by setting the parameter SKIP_UNUSABLE_INDEXES to TRUE with the command

```
alter session set skip_unusable_indexes = true;
```

This can be set only at the session level, not at the system level. The effect applies to ordinary tables as well as the partitions of partitioned tables, but is likely to be of most benefit with partitioned tables. This parameter also affects what happens when you analyze an index with unusable partitions. If set to TRUE, Oracle ignores the partitions. If set to FALSE, Oracle gets part of the way through the analysis, updating statistics as it goes, until it hits the unusable partition, at which point the session fails. There is one case, though, when the parameter has no effect. If the unusable partition belongs to a unique index or the index representing a unique (or primary key) constraint, then inserts (and updates that breach the requirement for uniqueness) are blocked.

During this chapter I have commented several times on how undesirable it is to have significant differences in the size of partitions. In part this relates to the way in which Parallel Query works with partitioned tables (see Chapter 22); however, you can observe the effects of unbalanced partitioning even in nonparallel environments.

Obviously if you have partitioned your data to try to reduce the window needed for administrative work, it is a major nuisance if a 50,000,000-row table turns into nine partitions of 1,000,000 rows and one partition of 41,000,000 rows. The reduction in reorganization time is minimal.

More significantly for end-user performance, a query against the 41,000,000-row partition is likely to take much longer than the corresponding query against the smaller partitions. Oracle 8.1 has a PARTITION ITERATION option for execution plans, so the internal steps to produce a summary report could easily be

```
Sort and group the row result from the following iteration
    For each of 5 partitions in turn
        Sort and group all the rows from the partition
```

For the smaller partitions, this SORT GROUP BY operation could complete in memory, but for the large partition the sort would probably result in endless disk thrashing. If we could manage to break up the large partition into 41 smaller partitions, we could perhaps end up doing 40+ quick in-memory sorts rather than a few in-memory sorts, and one very large disk sort.

If we managed to partition the 50,000,000-row table as 10 partitions of 5,000,000 rows, it is quite possible that users would never have to access 40,000,000 rows at a time anyway, and every sort may be limited to a maximum of a couple of blocks of 5,000,000. The biggest trick with partitioning is to find the right thing on which to partition, and the right granularity at which to partition.

There are many views in the data dictionary relating to partitioned objects. Table 12-1 lists them and notes what they contain.

Multicolumn Partitioning

The issue of how multicolumn partitioning works is sufficiently open to confusion that it is worth a little section of its own.

Table 12-1.   Views Related to Partitioned Objects

View	Content
xxx_(sub)PART_TABLES	Identifies tables that have been (sub)partitioned
xxx_TAB_(sub)PARTITIONS	Lists (sub)partitions of tables
xxx_(sub)PART_INDEXES	Identifies indexes that have been (sub)partitioned
xxx_IND_(sub)PARTITIONS	Lists (sub)partitions of indexes
xxx_(sub)PART_KEY_COLUMNS	Lists (sub)partitioning columns of objects
xxx_(sub)PART_COL_STATISTICS	Holds (sub)partition-level statistics on columns
xxx_(sub)PART_HISTOGRAMS	Holds (sub)partition-level histograms on columns
xxx_LOB_(sub)PARTITIONS	List (sub)partitions of LOBs
xxx_(sub)PART_LOBS	Identifies LOBs in (sub)partitioned tables

Hash partitioning is the easy case. Assume we have a table definition of the form

```
create table hash2test(
    id              number(14),
    date_part       date,
    other_part      varchar2(20),
    padding         varchar2(200)
)
partition by hash (date_part, other_part)
partitions 8
;
```

What will Oracle do about the following queries?

```
Select  count(*) from hash2test
where   date_part = to_date('01-jan-2000','dd-mon-yyyy')
;


select  count(*) from hash2test
where   other_part = '7'
;
```

The answer for both cases is that Oracle visits every single partition. The entire composite partitioning key is passed as a single unit to the hash function. So, for example, we see (but only by inserting the data)

- ('01-jan-2000', '7') belongs in partition 3
- ('01-jan-2000', '9') belongs in partition 1
- ('02-jan-2000', '7') belongs in partition 6

For multicolumn hash partitioning, if your query does not include the full partition column set, then Oracle cannot eliminate partitions.

Composite partitioning is an interesting variation. Let's go back to our example of sales to American states. We had a table of customers partitioned by state. Let's now create a table of sales that is partitioned by date (so that we can get rid of old sales) and subpartitioned by state. Of course this isn't really the same as the multicolumn partitioning in the previous hash partition example, but it is interesting:

```
create table us_sales (
    state       varchar2(2)     not null,
    sale_date   date            not null,
```

```
        product_id  varchar2(12)     not null,
        quantity    number(10),
        valuation   number(12,2)
)
partition by range (sale_date)
subpartition by hash (state) subpartitions 4
(
        partition p2000_01
        values less than (to_date('01-feb-2000','dd-mon-yyyy')) (
            subpartition p2000_01_A,
            subpartition p2000_01_B,
            subpartition p2000_01_C,
            subpartition p2000_01_D
        ),
        partition p2000_02
        values less than (to_date('01-mar-2000','dd-mon-yyyy')) (
            subpartition p2000_02_A,
            subpartition p2000_02_B,
            subpartition p2000_02_C,
            subpartition p2000_02_D
        )
)
;
```

Then consider the queries

```
select sum(quantity) from us_sales
where state = 'CA';


select sum(quantity) from us_sales
where sale_date = to_date('15-Feb-2000','dd-mon-yyyy');


select sum(quantity) from us_sales
where sale_date = to_date('15-Feb-2000','dd-mon-yyyy')
and state = 'CA';
```

The first hits subpartitions p2000_01_B and p2000_02_B only (again, a detail I discovered by inserting the data, not something I could deduce in advance); the second hits subpartitions p2000_02_A, p2000_02_B, p2000_02_C, and p2000_02_D only; and the final query hits just one partition, p2000_02_B.

To a limited extent (and with the general proviso I made about hash partitions usually failing to be uniformly sized on low-cardinality columns), composite partitioning can give you a form of two-dimensional partitioning. We come back to the example later (see Chapter 13) when we discuss partition-wise joins.

Finally we come to the option that has caused people the most grief: the two-column range partition. Take the following example, which I have already seen proposed several times to solve problems of two-dimensional date ranging:

```
create table range_2 (
    start_date    date,
    end_date      date,
    padding       varchar2(200)
)
partition by range (start_date, end_date) (
    partition p01 values less than (
            to_date('01-Apr-2000','dd-mon-yyyy'),
            to_date('01-Apr-2000','dd-mon-yyyy')
    ),
    partition p02 values less than (
            to_date('01-Jul-2000','dd-mon-yyyy'),
            to_date('01-Jul-2000','dd-mon-yyyy')
    ),
    partition p03 values less than (
            to_date('01-Oct-2000','dd-mon-yyyy'),
            to_date('01-Oct-2000','dd-mon-yyyy')
    )
)
;
```

What happens with the queries

```
Select  count(*)
from    range_2
where   START_DATE = to_date('15-May-2000','dd-mon-yyyy');

select  count(*)
from    range_2
where   END_DATE = to_date('15-May-2000','dd-mon-yyyy');
```

As you might expect, the first query accesses partition p02 only. The second query, however, tends to take many people by surprise. Although you initially decide that it too will access partition p02 only, it actually accesses *all* the partitions. Why does it have to access all partitions? Consider the following pairs of values:

- ('01-feb-2000', '15-may-2000')
- ('01-may-2000', '15-may-2000')
- ('01-aug-2000', '15-may-2000')

The first row belongs in partition p01 because 01 Feb is less than 01 April, and Oracle doesn't even need to look at the second column to refine its test. Similarly, the second row belongs in partition p02 because 01 May is less than 01 Jul, and again Oracle does not examine the second column. The third row belongs in partition p03 because 01 Aug is less than 01 Oct. Two columns does *not* mean two-dimensional.

In fact, there is another little catch in this example. Consider the rows

- ('01-jul-2000', '15-apr-2000', 'xxx')
- ('01-jul-2000', '02-jul-2000', 'yyy')

Where should these rows go? If we consider the description I gave originally of how boundary values work, the immediate response might be that the boundary value does not appear in the current partition; it appears as the lowest value in the next partition up. But in two-column partitions, you have to consider both columns *at once* when selecting the partition. So when we see the value '01-jul-2000' in the first row, we know it may belong to partition p02 because partition p02 allows '01-jul-200' as long as the end date that goes with it is not too high. At the same time, it may belong in partition p03 because that's where things generally go when the start date is '01-jul-2000' or later. In these examples, the first row goes in partition p02 and the second row goes in partition p03.

Problems and Quirks

A unique index on a partitioned table *must* include the partitioning columns (and for a composite partitioned table, this means the partitioning and subpartitioning columns). If your design for a table does not include the obvious partitioning columns as a natural part of the unique key, you have a problem. This restriction is important for performance reasons, so I'm inclined in most cases to review the application design rather than try to use dirty tricks to work around it.

If you add a primary key or unique constraint to a partitioned table, you can specify that the index should be locally partitioned by taking advantage of the USING INDEX clause in the form USING INDEX LOCAL. However, you cannot use this clause to specify where the different partitions should go. They all go to a single tablespace, and have to be rebuilt later. You may prefer to create the index first, then specify the constraint.

When you make any structural changes to a partitioned table (for example, exchange a partition with a table or drop a partition), the *entire definition of the table* is dropped from the dictionary cache, and all cursors using the table are invalidated. This can result in a massive performance overhead if such operations take place frequently; even every fifteen minutes may be a disaster. It is quite possible that your application will effectively freeze for several seconds, and on a parallel server system the lockout might be much longer.

To avoid massive index scans and sorts when exchanging partitions that have primary or unique constraints, you should ensure that such index-based constraints on both the partitioned and incoming tables are in the NOVALIDATE state.

In general, when you query a hash partition, it seems likely that most of your queries will NOT be of the form "hash column = {constant}." This means that the queries have to visit every single partition. The cost of such a query includes a couple of "current mode block gets" per partition, assuming you access the data via an index. If you have a large number of partitions and the query is supposed to return only a small number of rows, the cost in overhead may rapidly exceed the nominal cost of the query.

When you start to use multicolumn range partitioning, it is very easy to get into the trap of confusing multiple columns with multidimensional partitioning. Multicolumn partitions behave like multicolumn indexes. The first column is the most significant; the second column is checked only if the first column is at the boundary value.

Execution plans for partitioned tables can be very hard to interpret. Sometimes the only good test of the query path that will be used is to do it with SQL_TRACE set, or even event 10046 set at level 8, so that you can see exactly how much work Oracle does and which files it visits to perform a given query. A slightly cheaper, although harder to interpret, option is event 10128 set at level 7, which dumps Oracle's decision on partition pruning to the trace file (see Appendix C).

The manuals suggest that you cannot allow primary key indexes or unique key indexes to have unusable partitions. This is slightly misleading. The indexes may have unusable partitions, but you won't be able to insert data into those partitions until the index partitions are made usable, even if you set the SKIP_UNUSABLE_INDEXES parameter.

Although you can do an on-line index rebuild for a normal table, you cannot rebuild the subpartitions of a composite partitioned index on-line. Also, partitions of a hash partitioned table cannot be rebuilt with the NOLOGGING option. This may be less of a nuisance than it seems: With a good partitioning strategy, the subpartitions that need rebuilding may be subject to very little activity, and therefore offer lots of time for rebuilds.

The size of the subpartitions may be small enough to complete the rebuild quickly before anyone notices.

Object tables can be partitioned, but there seems to be little point in doing so. Actually, from the logical viewpoint, the inside of an object is supposed to be invisible, so it may be considered just a bit naughty to partition an object table on something you are not supposed to see. More important, perhaps, from a mechanical viewpoint, Oracle implements an object table as a table with a hidden, unique meaningless key. But if a unique index on a partitioned table can't contain the partitioning columns, it has to be a global index, which defeats the point of partitioning. Oracle Corporation has to face the problem we saw earlier with the artificial key of (ID, STATE) on our customer list, but made much harder by the fact that the index has to be invisible, and the indexed column may be the target of REF columns in other tables. I guess they are still working to find the best solution to this problem in the backroom at Redwood.

Partitions and imports currently don't mix very well. If you had ideas about exporting a bit of a partitioned table from a production environment to a test environment, you may find that the task is messier than you expect. Although export and import both allow you to specify "table_name:partition_name" to handle a single partition, this works properly only for export. If you create an import parameter file with this syntax, you get a series of ". . . skipping partition partition_name" warnings before the import terminates without errors. You should also bear in mind that if you export a partitioned table, every partition is a separate segment and is exported in a separate transaction. The results are potentially inconsistent with each other. You have to export with the CONSISTENT = Y option to avoid this issue.

Another point to consider about imports: The export file contains a definition of the entire partitioned table, even if you export only a single partition. This means you probably need to precreate a suitable subsection of the partitioned table before importing. Look forward to third-party tools allowing you to extract DDL for partial partition table re-creation in the near future.

Strategy Notes

I believe that partitioning is likely to become the single most useful feature of future Oracle databases. This applies not only to the obvious arena of data warehouses, but also to the high-performance on-line (and automatic) systems. A huge amount of data stored in databases is time dependent, and partitioning allows the DBA to handle reasonable-size chunks of older data very quickly and almost invisibly to the application. Similarly, any option that allows large-scale administration to be reduced to several smaller steps is likely to be of benefit. Even when there is no obvious option for range partitioning, hash partitioning may be beneficial. Whatever the nature of your application, look carefully at what partitioning can do for you.

When deciding on the granularity of range partitions, think about the most common queries that will benefit from high levels of partition elimination. Remember that it is quite awkward to get partition elimination if the partitioning columns are not used with constants in the query WHERE clauses.

In addition to identifying the most appropriate columns for partitioning, remember that you are likely to get the most benefit if the partitions are approximately the same size.

If you have used range partitioning to accommodate dropping old data and loading new data as time passes, you have to go through a regular task of dropping partitions and creating partitions. This maintenance is much easier if you determine a consistent naming strategy that associates partition names with partition range values and tablespace names. You can then write a PL/SQL procedure to find the latest partition from the view family xxx_TAB_PARTITIONS, and generate new partitions automatically. For reasons related to SMON (see Appendix D), it is better to try to recycle old tablespace names for reuse with new partitions.

If you have a rolling window of data that has you dropping old partitions and creating new partitions on a regular basis, and the old and new data goes in the same tablespace, make sure you create the new before you drop the old. If there are queries accessing the old data when you drop and create, this improves the chance of them using advanced read-consistency techniques to complete, even though the partitions have been dropped. If you drop before you create, then the new partitions may overwrite the old partitions and may make any attempt at read consistency fail.

If you can be sure that no premature data will appear in a table in which you are using range partitioning, don't use MAXVALUE; just make sure you have a few partitions predefined and ready, although you may want to trap the error "partition key not in legal range" in your code. If you cannot be confident that incoming data won't overshoot your top range, then you have to use MAXVALUE and keep splitting the top partition. Hopefully, the top partition will be virtually empty most of the time, so that the subsequent *split* command does not take much time.

The process of adding or splitting a partition is not trivial. Make sure you plan it carefully. You need to consider how to get local index partitions into the right place, and allow for rebuilding them, and then analyze the new partitions.

For the purpose of assigning rows to range partitions, Oracle sorts nulls greater than all other values except MAXVALUE. Nulls sort less than

MAXVALUE. This means that if a table is partitioned on a nullable column, and the column is to contain nulls, then you have to make sure that you make use of MAXVALUE as a boundary value in at least some of your partitions, otherwise rows that contain nulls raise error ORA-14400 when you try to insert them. In general I would advise most strongly against allowing nullable columns to appear as the partitioning columns.

Hash partitioning is largely an administrative benefit to split large objects into a number of smaller, evenly sized objects. However, in some rare cases you may achieve partition elimination by partitioning on a low-cardinality column. Note, however, that the column has to be part of any unique index you create on the table, and a side effect of low cardinality is that you may lose some of the benefit of uniform sizing of the partitions.

Hash partitioning on a meaningless indexed sequence number gives you the benefit of spreading contending index inserts across several blocks without the degradation in packing that you get from other strategies such as reverse key indexing.

Composite partitioning can be used to gain the benefits of range partitioning on data that does not partition very uniformly into ranges by letting you split each partition into a different number of subpartitions.

The init.ora parameter ENQUEUE_RESOURCES limits the number of resources that can be allocated for locking objects. There are some operations on partitioned objects that require a large number of locks (creating a new local index, for example) because every partition has to be locked. Make sure that you set this parameter high enough to accommodate the worst maintenance operation you may have to do on your most heavily partitioned objects.

CHAPTER 13

Using Partitioning

As I said in the previous chapter, partitioning simply entails breaking down very large, unwieldy objects into collections of small objects, and there are two reasons for doing so—administration and performance.

From the administrative side, small objects are much easier to handle. You can back them up quickly, and you may be able to find time to move or restructure some of them without disrupting the users. From the performance side, you may find that queries can be restricted to just one or two small objects instead of ranging across enormous objects at great cost. You may also find that breaking up a single large object into multiple small objects gives some scope for processing several of the small objects in parallel. This chapter outlines a few thoughts about how you can take advantage of partitioning in a real system, and describes a few pitfalls of which to beware.

Administration

The most important things that a DBA should do are to keep the database ticking over and ensure that there is always space for properly controlled growth. Anything that makes it easier for the DBA to keep the database alive and running without impacting the proper end-user activity negatively is a good thing, and partitioning has to be one of the most effective ways of hiding the DBA's manipulation of the gross database structure from the end user.

Dropping Partitions

We have already discussed the benefit of partitioning in terms of being able to eliminate old data from the database very quickly. Traditionally, to get rid of the 10,000,000 rows of data from last January that are no longer needed this February, it was necessary to delete these rows (perhaps a few hundred thousand at a time), then consider rebuilding massive indexes to eliminate the performance side effects of all the half-empty index blocks. With suitably partitioned tables we can now issue a command that eliminates all the data and the related bits of index very cleanly, in just a few seconds, with no side effects (except for the problem with partitioned IOTs [see Problems and Quirks]), as long as all the indexes are *locally partitioned indexes*:

```
alter table big_data_table drop partition 199901;
```

There is, however, one nasty little trap in the process. What if you have two partitioned tables with a referential integrity constraint defined between them. Assuming the tables are such that they partition in the same way (the BASKETS and BASKET_ITEMS tables of a supermarket data warehouse, say), you may want to do the following:

```
alter table basket_items truncate partition 199901;
alter table baskets truncate partition 199901;
alter table basket_items drop partition 199901;
alter table baskets drop partition 199901;
```

The two ***truncate*** commands are there so that Oracle can (in principle) detect that while the parent/child relationship holds between the two partitions there are no rows in either partition and therefore it is safe to drop both partitions. Unfortunately, Oracle doesn't quite see it that way. As soon as you try to execute the ***truncate baskets*** command, you get Oracle error "ORA-02266: unique/primary keys in table referenced by enabled foreign keys." If you try this before you have inserted any data into the two partitions, you will find that you can drop them, with or without a preceding truncate, but then a table that never contains any data isn't much use to anyone.

> *Referential integrity introduces an extra level of complexity when you try to drop partitions.*

In real life if you have two partitioned tables with a referential integrity constraint between them, you have to disable the foreign key constraint before dropping the parent partition. Consequently you need to reenable the constraint after the drop. This means that Oracle tries to validate the constraint across an enormous pair of tables! Fortunately, (see Chapter18) you can now enable a constraint without validating it.

You may ask, Why bother to define the constraint at all? In a data warehouse it is usually accepted as reasonable behavior to avoid implementing constraints that would be considered absolutely critical in an OLTP system. The answer comes from materialized views, and query rewrite in particular. There are times when the Oracle optimizer works best if there are constraints in place on which it can rely. To this end you can actually tell Oracle that a constraint exists and that it may not have been validated, but it should be relied on by the optimizer. The following code is an example of creating such a constraint on the child table, and the steps to take to drop matching partitions:

```
alter table basket_items add constraint btm_fk_bsk
foreign key (date_part, store_id, basket_id)
references baskets
on delete cascade
RELY
;

alter table basket_items disable constraint btm_fk_bsk;
alter table basket_items drop partition p03;
alter table baskets drop partition p03;
alter table basket_items enable novalidate constraint btm_fk_bsk;
```

After the two matching partitions have been dropped, and the constraint is reenabled, you will find in the view family xxx_CONSTRAINTS the constraint BTM_FK_BSK described as "enabled, not validated, rely." The significance of the ENABLED, NOT VALIDATED state is that Oracle does not go back to check that all the preexisting data meets the requirements of the constraint, but all future data changes (updates and inserts) are checked as they happen.

Tablespace Management

Once you have sorted out the problems of dropping partitions, you can start worrying about how to make best use of tablespaces. I have already mentioned (see Chapter 8) that for backup purposes I like to deal with "comfortably sized" tablespaces, which tends to mean a small number of gigabytes, perhaps 1 to 4GB. Based on this approach, there are two strategies relevant to range partitioned tables, particularly when the range is date/time based.

For data that in theory is going to grow more or less indefinitely, or is supposed to cycle through a "roll-on/roll-off" after a lengthy time period, choose a time period for a tablespace and create all the partitioned objects within that tablespace. If initial estimates suggest that the tablespace is going to be too large for comfort, then split it into a small number of tablespaces based on the size of partitions and nature of use. For example, for a three-year time scale you may decide to use period-based tablespaces with names like TS_DATA_2000_01, and have just one per period. Some of the partitions in the tablespace could hold an entire period's worth of data, some could hold just a week, and some could hold just a day. The important point is that if there is any partitioned data for period 1 of year 2000 then it will be in this tablespace. Conversely, any data in this tablespace is definitely partitioned data for period 1 of year 2000.

The main drawback to this approach is that it breaks one of my cardinal rules for tablespaces: Reuse old tablespace names if you can because the database never forgets a tablespace name, and SMON wakes up every five minutes to scan the ever-growing list of tablespaces to see if any of them has free space to coalesce.

The alternative data strategy is for the short-term cycle. A site I visited recently supplies a good example. For one aspect of their work they held daily data for a total of seven complete weeks. When I analyzed the work they were doing, it became fairly obvious that the best strategy for performance, load balancing, and administration was to partition the data by day, and define seven different tablespaces to hold it. You may be expecting me to say that each tablespace held an individual week. In fact, I named the tablespaces MONDAY_DATA, TUESDAY_DATA, and so on, through to SUNDAY_DATA. By putting each tablespace onto a separate logical volume, I got a wonderful I/O spread on the queries that kept summing the data for a given week. As for maintenance, each Monday, a PL/SQL procedure works out the dates for the following week, translates them into partition names and tablespace names, and generates the next seven partitions for that one table.

> *There are no hard and fast rules for the "best" way of doing things. Just aim to do something that feels intuitively to be clean and simple, and offers good I/O separation.*

There is an important difference between these two strategies. The second strategy clearly indicates that I have some tablespaces that are going to be reused again and again at extremely regular intervals, whereas the first strategy tends to imply that after a suitable period of time some of the table-spaces will never be updated again.

The most important consequence of the first strategy is that it can help you to reduce your backup requirements significantly. One of the joys of range partitioning is that it can isolate old, stable data into its own set of dedicated tablespaces. If the data in a tablespace is never going to change again, it can be turned into a read-only tablespace using the command

```
Alter tablespace ts_XXX read only;
```

> *Once a tablespace is read-only, you need only back it up one more time to secure it forever. Actually, you should probably take a fresh backup every month or so just to make sure that an old backup tape hasn't gone rusty or otherwise unusable. Range partitioning gives you a tremendous opportunity to reduce the work you have to do in backing up a database.*

The nice thing about read-only tablespaces is that you can build a library of backups of the read-only tablespaces so that the daily hot backup of your database is just the small fraction of recent data (often as little as the last two months of two years of data), turning an impossible 500GB database into a 50GB (one DLT!) backup. Recovering a damaged part of the database is then just a question of picking up the June 1999 tape/Jaz disk, say, from the stack, and copying it back to the system.

Packing Tablespaces

Apart from the simple fact that you can use data partitioning to allow table-spaces to become read-only, you can (with just a little cooperation from your applications) take advantage of partitioning to make those read-only table-spaces as small as possible, and the objects in them as efficient as possible. Assume that during the last month your system has been loading data into the 28 daily partitions for the SALES table. Each day 95% of the incoming data is for the previous day, with a trailing 5% that is anything up to 27 days late. With the passing of time the table becomes a little fragmented (but you included a small PCTFREE to accommodate the updates), and the indexes degrade somewhat and run at 80% efficiency.

Time passes, and a month from now no more data will go into those 28 partitions, and the tablespace becomes read-only. Before it does, you can rebuild every single partition in that tablespace to pack it to 100%. This has two important effects. First, the data is more tightly packed (you could even choose to sort it as you pack it to optimize it for the most important or most commonly used queries), which means the end users will see a performance benefit. Second, the well-packed partitions migrate to the front of the tablespace if you have used locally managed tablespaces with uniform extents (see Chapter 8), so you can probably trim a load of space off the back end of each of the files in the tablespace using the resize command. As an example of this, in a recent restructuring exercise I managed to reclaim 75GB of space on a very expensive, very full disk array by rebuilding partitions in a very cavalier fashion. It took two days, and I interrupted just one end-user query while doing it. Before restructuring, the historic tablespaces were running at an average of 30% wasted space, even though the DBA had tried very hard to calculate space requirements exactly and to specify the "correct" extent size for each object individually. After restructuring the system to use a reasonably small best-fit fixed extent size for each tablespace, the average waste for new tablespaces was running at approximately 6%.

The question is, How can you get away with rebuilding partitions without getting dozens of calls from end users about queries failing? The answer is twofold. If you have managed to pick a good partitioning granularity, the partitions can be rebuilt very quickly, perhaps just a couple minutes per partition, although you may need to set your session's SORT_AREA_SIZE and SORT_AREA_RETAINED_SIZE to something very greedy when doing the indexes. More important, though, if your application and the code it runs are typical of the sorts of databases that need to use range partitioning, most of the queries that hit the table will eliminate all but the most recent partitions, so you can choose to do the rebuild only on those partitions that you expect to be outside the danger area.

> *Partitioning can make it possible for you to rebuild aging data very rapidly, both to improve efficiency and to reduce the total space requirements of the database.*

One word of warning. When you are busy rebuilding partitions in anticipation of going read-only, restrict yourself to one data tablespace (and its index tablespaces) at a time. If things go a little wrong or disaster strikes before you have backed up the tablespace, it is possible to execute TSPITR (see Chapter 8), but this is much more complicated for tablespaces holding a subset of a partitioned object, especially if you have been merging or splitting partitions.

Data Loading

The best way to get bulk data into a partitioned table has to be the ***exchange partition*** command. If a simple table matches the structure of a partitioned table you can issue the command

```
alter table partitioned_table
exchange partition pXXX with table simple_table
;
```

As it stands, Oracle tries to fix the data dictionary so that the data segment that was the simple table is identified as the data segment that was partition pXXX, and vice versa. Before doing so, it checks that all the data in the simple table passes the validation tests required by the partition—in particular, the restrictions on the partitioning key. If the data is perfect, the swap takes place and the local indexes on the partition are marked unusable. Any global or globally partitioned indexes on the table are also marked unusable. If the data is not perfect, then Oracle error "ORA-14099: all rows in table do not qualify for specified partition" is raised and the swap does not take place.

A more useful variant of this command, for data warehousing particularly, is

```
alter table partitioned_table
exchange partition pXXX with table simple_table
including indexes without validation
;
```

This tells Oracle to trust you that the indexes on simple_table are correct and up to date, and that the data would pass all validation tests required for the partitioned table.

Once you can use this command the variations are endless, especially if you can guarantee that no other process is allowed to change the data in the partitioned table while you are manipulating it. For example, you may have a strategy of storing daily partitions for the last four weeks, but weekly partitions for older data. This is a very effective strategy for reducing the overhead on queries that cannot do partition elimination, but how do you effect the changeover? The steps could be as simple as the following:

1. Create a new table using the NOLOGGING option, as select from seven daily partitions, sorted as necessary.
2. Create suitable indexes on the new table.
3. Truncate seven old partitions and drop six of them.
4. Exchange the seventh partition with the new table.

Of course, you may spot a weak point in this schedule of action. There is a significant time period, perhaps a few minutes, as you truncate and drop the partitions, during which user queries can discover that some data has gone missing.

> *Sometimes the only way to get the greatest benefit from partitioning is to deny users access to the data for brief periods. The benefits vastly outweigh the irritation.*

Although there are some manipulative operations that cannot be run while the users are on-line, it is perfectly reasonable to run something like the following to fix up a single, active partition (again, assuming that no other process is allowed to change the data at the same time). In this way, users do not have to experience contention as the data is updated, and they do not run into read-consistency overhead when they start to use the corrected data:

1. Create a new table as select from the target partition.
2. Fix the new table with recent inserts, updates, and deletes.
3. Sort and pack data in the new table into a more efficient arrangement.
4. Create indexes on the new table.
5. Exchange the new table with the target partition.

There are a few circumstances in which an end-user query may crash if you carried out this sequence of steps on-line. But simple queries, even ones that access the target partition, are not affected. (Again, this assumes that the partitioned table is not an IOT [see Problems and Quirks].)

One easy way to deal with the problem of making sure that no other processes can update the data while you are copying and restructuring it is to plan your tablespaces and partitions so that you can make the source tablespaces read-only when you are doing it. You may even consider having a few scratch pad tablespaces available for the first arrival of the data, and only write data into its final tablespace when no more updates are expected.

As usual, though, there are some problems with mixing and matching features. Referential integrity is even more of a problem with exchanging partitions than it is with dropping partitions. Once you have some data in a pair of related partitioned tables, it doesn't seem to be possible to exchange the parent partition again unless you actually *drop* the foreign key constraint from the child table. Even if you disable the constraint on both pairs of tables, Oracle complains about the existence of an enabled constraint. This is probably just a bug waiting to be fixed, but in the meantime it could be a bit of a nuisance. However, the workaround is similar to that for dropping partitions: You can always drop the constraint then re-create the constraint as disabled, not validated, but reliable, then enable it without validating it.

Indexing Existing Tables

In the absence of partitioned tables, what would you do if you needed to create a new index on a massive dataset to address a new user requirement? Can you imagine the time it would take to create an index on a 450,000,000-row table, not to mention the amount of space needed in the temporary segment? It's the sort of job that you schedule for Christmas or Easter, and buy a couple of extra disks to add to the temporary tablespace.

With suitably partitioned tables, and perhaps a suitably friendly application, the scale of the problems isn't really that great because you can build the index on each partition in turn. This trick depends on a little SQL feature that appears to be legal, even though I haven't managed to find it in the SQL reference manual:

```
create index big_new_index on partitioned_table (colX)
local
UNUSABLE
tablespace scratchpad
;
```

The key word is *unusable*. Although the manual states that you can "alter" an index to be unusable, it does not suggest that you can create it as initially unusable. Nevertheless, this statement works. The effect is to put the definition of the index into the data dictionary and allocate all the necessary segments and partitions for the index, but it does not do any of the real work that is normally involved in building an index on 450,000,000 rows. There is a little trap, though. To create an index on a partitioned table, Oracle needs to hold a lock on every partition of the table and every partition of the index. If you have not set the init.ora parameter ENQUEUE_RESOURCES to a large enough value, you will find that you cannot create the index without first modifying this parameter and restarting the database.

> *When handling partitioned objects with large numbers of partitions, you need to set the parameter ENQUEUE_RESOURCES to a suitably large value. Some operations need to take out a lock simultaneously and separately on every single partition of a partitioned object.*

The ***create index*** command takes quite a few seconds to run, and is dependent largely on how many partitions there are in the table. When it completes, the index exists, albeit in an UNUSABLE state. Once the index exists, you need to set its statistics to zero, and this takes two steps:

```
alter session set skip_unusable_indexes=true;
analyze index big_new_index estimate statistics;
```

Setting the session to "skip unusable indexes" means that the ***analyze*** command skips over every single partition in the index (because they are all unusable) and very rapidly comes back with a set of zero figures for the index.

Once the skeleton of the index exists, you can then step through each partition in turn, probably from the most recent to the oldest if your users are most interested in recent data, controlling the load on your system as you wish and rebuilding each index partition in turn. You can also take advantage of the new COMPUTE STATISTICS AS YOU GO option with commands like

```
alter index big_new_index
rebuild partition w199949
tablespace p199912
online
nologging
compute statistics
;
```

Of course there are drawbacks to this method. Any query that tries to use the index and accesses a partition that has not yet been rebuilt fails with Oracle error "ORA-01502: index TABLE_OWNER.BIG_NEW_INDEX or partition of such index is in unusable state." However, if a session has the parameter SKIP_UNUSABLE_INDEXES set to TRUE, then the session is still able to insert, update, and delete rows in the table partitions with index partitions that have not been rebuilt. There is also the usual fiddle about whether ONLINE and NOLOGGING can be used. Both are valid for range partitions. NOLOGGING is not possible with hash partitions, and neither can be used with composite partitions.

I did say that the application had to be suitably friendly. Essentially this means that it conforms to the common behavior of very large databases and tends to focus on the most recent 5% or so of the data. If this is the case, most users will have problems for the relatively short period of time it takes to build the most recent index partitions, after which the unusability of the rest of the index should not be much of a problem.

Performance

From a performance perspective, the most important and commonly occurring benefit comes from range partitioning and Oracle's ability to do partition elimination. So when you start to build partitioning into a system, the first question you have to ask yourself is, Will typical user queries allow Oracle to identify and eliminate partitions?

The most common design error with range partitioning comes from assuming too much about how clever Oracle can be with partition elimination. There are a few special techniques that we will look at in a moment, but generally it is safest to assume that Oracle will not do partition elimination unless the partitioning columns appear in the WHERE clause as a set of constants. In fact, the restriction is slightly looser. In much the same way that indexes can be used if the leading columns appear in the WHERE clause, partition elimination can occur with range partitioning even if only the leading columns of the partitioning set appear in the WHERE clause.

Consider the following incomplete table definition and the two similar queries that follow it. Note that the table is partitioned by date, and each partition represents one month's worth of data:

```
create table sales(
    date_part       date,
    store_id        number(8),
        .   .   .
)
partition by range (date_part) (
    partition p01 values less than (to_date('20000201','YYYYMMDD')),
    partition p02 values less than (to_date('20000301','YYYYMMDD')),
    partition p03 values less than (to_date('20000401','YYYYMMDD')),
```

```
        partition p04 values less than (to_date('20000501','YYYYMMDD')),
        . . .
);

select  sa.date_part, sa.store_id, sum(sa.sales_value)
from
        sales               sa,
where
        sa.date_part between to_date('07-Apr-2000','dd-mon-yyyy')
                        and to_date('13-Apr-2000','dd-mon-yyyy')
group by
        sa.date_part, sa.store_id
;


select  sa.date_part, sa.store_id, sum(sa.sales_value)
from
        sales               sa,
        financial_weeks     wk
where
        wk.financial_week_id = 200002
and     sa.date_part between wk.date_start and wk.date_end
group by
        sa.date_part, sa.store_id
;
```

Although we can look at these two queries and decide that they are "obviously" equivalent to each other, all that Oracle can see, logically, is that the first query specifies a literal date range that it can check against the partition definitions at parse time to discover that all the relevant data is in partition p04, whereas the second query requires access to a set of unknown dates that are derived from another table at runtime. The first query executes very efficiently against just partition p04; the second query has to try to join every relevant row from the FINANCIAL_WEEKS table against every partition in the SALES table.

> *To get partition elimination from range partitioning, the partitioning columns must have a very high degree of visibility (typically as constants) in the WHERE clause.*

Now, if you happen to have created an index on SALES(date_part,store_id), this excessive joining may take advantage of the index and appear to work quite efficiently. This is because of a mechanism that I have seen described as *index probing*—a technical term that means that Oracle simply tries to do the join through the index and, because the index is highly appropriate, discovers very efficiently that there is no relevant data. The critical feature of the index is that it has to start with the partitioning columns (a *prefixed index*) so that when Oracle tries to join a row from FINANCIAL_WEEK to an unsuitable partition, it quickly traverses one of the extreme edges of the index to discover in just two or three logical I/Os that the content of the index is either too low or too high for the incoming data.

In some circumstances, putting the partitioning columns at the leading edge of most of your indexes is sufficient to get reasonable performance. However, it is a solution I particularly dislike because it is inherently sloppy (on the part of the database engine), inefficient, and potentially a huge waste of space. Imagine a 400,000,000-row table partitioned into daily partitions by date. To allow index probing to work, we have to add the date at the front of the indexes on that table, but in any one partition the date value is identical across all the rows. It is a column we would not consider as part of an index if we were dealing with a table rather than a single partition. Nevertheless the manuals advise that we should waste 3.2GB in each index (400,000,000 rows $\times$ 8 bytes, but less if we remember to compress the index) by adding this worthless column to the index so that the runtime engine can decide very quickly that it is trying to select rows from an unsuitable partition. It does seem that there is room for improvement in this aspect of partition elimination.

Of course index probing works only if the optimizer decides to use the index. It might decide to use a hash join, in which case every single row of every single sales partition is scanned and hashed into the FINANCIAL_WEEK table, and discarded only after the hash has taken place.

> *Index probing to eliminate partitions at runtime means simply doing the join and having an index that identifies the absence of relevant data. This isn't necessarily very efficient.*

Even when index probing works well, it doesn't necessarily work *very* well because it really depends on having a relatively small number of partitions and a relatively large number of target rows to fetch. Consider two slightly extreme cases of a query like the one presented earlier that uses seven rows from a date table to join to a partitioned table:

1. Assume the target table has 12 partitions, and the query is supposed to find 5,000 rows in just one of those partitions. This means that Oracle runs through a loop 7 times, accessing 11 partitions very rapidly at a cost of 3 logical I/Os per partition to discover that there is no relevant data. Oracle then accesses the twelfth partition 7 times to find approximately 715 rows, at a cost of 3×715, or 2,145 logical I/Os on each occasion. In total, Oracle wastes $7 \times 11 \times 3$, or 231 logical I/Os on the wrong partitions while performing roughly 15,000 useful logical I/Os on the correct partition. In this example, index probing is a minor overhead.

2. Now take an example at the opposite end of the spectrum. Imagine you have 100 partitions (which is not actually particularly excessive) and your query is supposed to find a total of just 10 rows in one of the partitions. Following the same argument, Oracle wastes $7 \times 99 \times 3$, or 2,079 logical I/Os on the wrong partitions while performing a total of roughly 30 useful logical I/Os on the right partition. The overhead is rather high compared with the useful work accomplished.

There are, of course, several workarounds to the problem of exposing the partitioning column to the optimizer. Primarily, they involve doing the query in two steps to get the start and end dates of the week, but you may be severely hampered by the nature of the front-end tool that you are using. Consequently, it is worth investigating the effect of rewriting the sample join using approaches like

```
select
        sa.date_part, sa.store_id, sum(sa.sales_value)
from
        sales       sa,
        (   select max(wk.date_end)    date_end
            from    financial_weeks
            where financial_week_id = 200002
        )           ed,
        (   select min(wk.date_start) date_start
            from    financial_weeks
            where financial_week_id = 200002
        )           sd
where
        sa.date_part <= ed.date_end
and     sa.date_part >= sd.date_start
group by
        sa.date_part, sa.store_id
;
```

```
select
        sa.date_part, sa.store_id, sum(sa.sales_value)
from
        sales      sa
where
        sa.date_part <= (
                  select wk.date_end
                  from financial_weeks
                  where financial_week_id = 200002
              )
and     sa.date_part >= (
                  select wk.date_start
                  from financial_weeks
                  where financial_week_id = 200002
            )
group by
        sa.date_part, sa.store_id
;
```

These queries allow Oracle to determine at parse time that it will always be possible to generate a fixed date range very early on in the query. In effect, Oracle executes the single-row subqueries as the first step of the two-stage process that we would otherwise have to do manually to find the actual bounding dates, and then restricts the rest of its runtime processing to just the relevant partitions. Interestingly, the two previous examples appear to have dramatically different execution paths and costs according to EXPLAIN PLAN, but with this particular set of test data ended up doing virtually identical amounts of work.

> *Oracle appears to have some ability to perform dynamic optimization when using partitioned tables. Look for ways of rewriting joins into partitioned tables in ways that use single-row subqueries or in-line views guaranteed to contain one row.*

For a few very specific business-related requirements, this type of approach could be wrapped effectively inside a view. For example we could have a CURRENT WEEK view that hides a more complex pair of subqueries of the form

```
select  min(wk.date_start)
from    financial_weeks
```

```
where    financial_week_id = (
            select  financial_week_id
            from    financial_weeks
            where   trunc(sysdate) between date_start and date_end
         )
;
```

Another option for creating views that force partition elimination to take place is to take advantage of the SYS_CONTEXT() feature and "database log-on" triggers (see Chapter 21). SYS_CONTEXT() behaves rather like the USERENV() feature or USER pseudo column in that it can appear as a constant in a view definition, but acts as a runtime variable. The special benefit that SYS_CONTEXT() has over USERENV() is that we can define many different contexts, and use PL/SQL to set values in those contexts.

If we want to introduce the concepts of (current week, previous week) to our application, we can define a context called ***dates_context***, say, to hold variables defining these values, and can set values in that context as the user logs on with a trigger like

```
create or replace trigger logon_trigger
after logon on database

v_start_date    varchar2(11);
v_end_date      varchar2(11);

begin

--  code to get dates from the financial_weeks table

    dbms_session.set_context (
        'dates_context',
        'current_start',
        v_start_date
    );

--      ditto for end date
end;
/
```

We can then create a statically defined view like

```
create or replace view current_week as
select  * from datetest
where   date_part between
```

```
                    to_date(
                        sys_context('dates_context','current_start'),
                        'dd-mon-yyyy'
                    )
                and
                    to_date(
                        sys_context('dates_context','current_end'),
                        'dd-mon-yyyy'
                    )
    ;
```

With this view definition in place, any query to CURRENT_WEEK automatically does partition elimination on the DATETEST table. However, if a user logs on sometime during Friday and stays connected until Monday, then his context will still hold values relevant to the previous week. Don't forget to give your users a profile that logs them off after eight hours of idle time.

I have discovered two drawbacks to SYS_CONTEXT(), and both have to do with parallel queries. First, SYS_CONTEXT() is not passed forward to the parallel query slave, so the volume of messaging sent back to the query coordinator is much higher than it should be. Second, for certain types of queries—specifically GROUP BY queries which exclude the column being tested against SYS_CONTEXT()—the results simply disappear. However, it's worth keeping an eye on this as a useful tool once these two bugs have been fixed.

> *Rolling views can be used to help end users achieve partition elimination.*

Of course, you could decide that complex, although statically defined, views like the ones just presented are too much hard work, and may leave room for optimizer idiosyncrasies that cause performance swings from day to day. What's wrong with creating views that are rebuilt every day?

```
create or replace view week_to_date as
select  * from datetest
where   date_part between to_date('10-Apr-2000') -- Mon
                     and to_date('13-Apr-2000') -- Thu
    ;
```

It is very easy to write a couple of generic PL/SQL packages that use the UTL_FILE package to read templates of views, and then substitute values into placeholders. And in Oracle 8.1 it is extremely easy to execute DDL through the native dynamic SQL mechanism (see Chapter 19). You can then schedule a view creation procedure to run automatically at 12:01 A.M. using the DBMS_JOB package.

You can even make specific partitions visible by explicit reference to their partition name:

```
create or replace view sales_january_2000 as
select * from sales partition (p2000_01);
```

Finally, you can always fall back on the option for accessing your partitioned tables through PL/SQL packages, and using native dynamic SQL (see Chapter 19) to write literal strings. In the case of partitioned tables, the overhead of parsing numerous literal strings may be worth it to gain the absolute maximum amount of partition elimination.

Range Partitions with Dates

It seems almost inevitable that most occurrences of range partitioning will partition by date, allowing old data to go into a READ-ONLY state and very old data to be dropped painlessly off the end of the table. It is worth considering some of the special oddities that creep in to Oracle as soon as you start handling dates. These oddities tend to be caused by one thing: Text looks like text, numbers look like numbers, but dates look like . . . text. Oracle can make a real pig's ear of date handling if you aren't extremely fussy about using the to_date() function to identify text that is meant to be a date.

Do not use dates with only two-digit years when querying tables that are partitioned by date, even when you have the appropriate implicit or explicit conversion defined. Bear in mind that with range partitioning you may know more about your data than Oracle. Although many range partitioning strategies involve dates, it is easy to forget that, to Oracle, a date is a date with a time. Remembering this fact can make a surprising difference in performance.

Assume you have used range partitioning to store data by date, and are *not* storing the time as well. You set up a system in which one partition is one day. Now consider the simple query

```
select count(*) from tablex
where primary_date
            between to_date('14-feb-2000','dd-mon-yyyy')
                and to_date('20-feb-2000','dd-mon-yyyy')
    ;
```

This statement is equivalent to

```
select count(*) from tablex
where   primary_date >= to_date('14-feb-2000','dd-mon-yyyy')
and     primary_date <= to_date('20-feb-2000','dd-mon-yyyy')
;
```

When parsing this statement, Oracle looks at your partition definitions and finds

```
Partition 30 – values less than to_date('14-feb-2000','dd-mon-yyyy')
Partition 31 – values less than to_date('15-feb-2000','dd-mon-yyyy')
       . . .
Partition 36 – values less than to_date('20-feb-2000','dd-mon-yyyy')
Partition 37 – values less than to_date('21-feb-2000','dd-mon-yyyy')
```

The optimizer determines that it has to access data from partition 31 (which nominally holds values from 14-feb-2000 00:00:00 to 14-feb-2000 23:59:59) through partition 37 (which nominally holds values from 20-feb-2000 00:00:00 to 20-feb-2000 23:59:59). Clearly every single row in partitions 31 to 36 is required, but the optimizer has to assume that there are values (such 20-feb-2000 00:00:01) in partition 37 that are going to fail the test. *You* know that any rows in partition 37 will have primary_date = 20-feb-2000 00:00:00. Oracle doesn't. When Oracle executes this query the path will probably be

```
PARTITION  (concatenated)
        TABLE ACCESS tablex (full) Pt Range: NUMBER(31)–NUMBER(37)
```

To eliminate any rows with a time component in partition 37, the SQL code that has to be executed against partition 37 has got to be

```
select  count(*)
from    tablex partition(p37)
where   primary_date <= to_date('20-feb-2000','dd-mon-yyyy')
;
```

However with partitioned tables, the SQL code executed against one partition is executed against all partitions, so exactly the same test is going to be made against every single row in every one of the partitions from 31 to 36, even though it is a redundant test for these partitions. It is unfortunate that, with dates in particular, this adds a significant amount of extra CPU time to the process.

But let's be cunning. Remember that this example is based on the fact that there are no times recorded in the PRIMARY_DATE column. Examine the following query, which gives exactly the same result:

```
select  count(*)
from    tablex
where   primary_date >= to_date('14-feb-2000','dd-mon-yyyy')
and     primary_date < to_date('21-feb-2000','dd-mon-yyyy')
;
```

In this case, Oracle can determine from the query that any row in any of the identified partitions will, by definition, match the query criteria. Consequently, the SQL code executed against each partition will actually be

```
select  count(*)
from    tablex partition({partition id} )
;
```

The absence of any further tests on the date column is a benefit worth having. The moral is clear: If you plan to use partitioning, try to partition the data so that the partitions match the most common elimination requirements, and then try to ensure that the queries are written to match the partition boundaries.

Hash Partitions and Composite Partitions

I have probably said all there is to be said about hash partitioning. It is convenient to be able to split a large object into several smaller ones and store them in several tablespaces that can be backed up individually. But because a query against a hash partition is likely to access all the partitions, it is much harder to find time to rebuild and repack partitions when the end users won't notice.

If you have created local indexes on a hash partitioned table, you can rebuild these with minimal impact on the end users, but you cannot rebuild them with the NOLOGGING option, thus the rebuild takes a little longer than it should. However, queries still run, even though the users won't be able to insert, update, or delete data.

The comments I made earlier while describing index probing on range partitions apply equally well to hash partitions. Because every query is likely to visit every partition, you need to keep the number of partitions relatively small. If typical queries return large datasets, then the number of partitions can be quite large before the partition overhead is significant. If typical queries return small datasets, the number of partitions should be small. The arithmetic is a little different from the index probing example, but I would be inclined to restrict myself to four or eight partitions for systems that tend to execute a lot of small queries.

The most significant use for hash partitioning is to allow multiple concurrent processes to insert rows into a single table with minimal contention, and I described this in the previous chapter. When a high-speed application is inserting rows with meaningless sequential keys into a table, the newest table block is subject to contention unless you have set multiple free lists on the table. Even then, the leading edge of the index is subject to contention. If you attempt to eliminate this index contention by reversing the index, you are likely to degrade the efficiency of the index quite significantly. By turning the table into a partitioned table with a small number of hash partitions (not necessarily hashing on the meaningless sequence number), you effectively make it behave like a number of independent, noncontending tables with highly efficient indexes. Inserts are quicker, but general queries have the overhead described earlier because they have to access multiple partitions.

I haven't said anything in this section yet about composite partitioning. Again, I suspect I said it all in the last chapter. Composite partitioning can help to even out the sizing of data segments in range partitioning and, in special circumstances, composite partitioning can introduce a limited kind of two-dimensional partitioning. The drawback to composite partitioning is that it makes it very easy to allow the number of partitions—and the cost of adding, dropping, or exchanging partitions—to run to preposterous levels. There are also the restrictions that partitioned indexes on composite partitioned tables cannot be compressed and cannot be rebuilt on-line, so they cost a little more in terms of efficiency and convenience than simple range partitioning.

Partition-wise Joins

One of the new features of the implementation of partitioning in Oracle 8.1 is the partition-wise join. Consider the example of the BASKETS and BASKET_ ITEMS tables partitioned by day:

```
create table baskets(
    store_id            number              not null,
    date_part           date                not null,
    basket_id           number(10)          not null,
    basket_value        number(10,2)        not null,
    basket_item_count   number(3)           not null
)
```

```
partition by range (date_part) (
    partition p00 values less than (to_date('01022000','ddmmyyyy')),
    partition p01 values less than (to_date('02022000','ddmmyyyyv')),
    partition p02 values less than (to_date('03022000','ddmmyyyy')),
    partition p03 values less than (to_date('04022000','ddmmyyyy')),
    partition p04 values less than (to_date('05022000','ddmmyyyy')),
)
;


create table basket_items(
    store_id            number              not null,
    date_part           date                not null,
    basket_id           number(10)          not null,
    product_id          number(10)          not null,
    product_count       number(3)           not null,
    product_value       number(10,2)        not null
)
partition by range (date_part) (
    partition p00 values less than (to_date('01022000','ddmmyyyy')),
    partition p01 values less than (to_date('02022000','ddmmyyyy')),
    partition p02 values less than (to_date('03022000','ddmmyyyy')),
    partition p03 values less than (to_date('04022000','ddmmyyyy')),
    partition p04 values less than (to_date('05022000','ddmmyyyy')),
)
;
```

Consider how you would write a query to find the total product count by store for 1 Feb to 3 Feb for all baskets that have a total basket value of more than $20. The SQL code would be something like the following. Note how the date predicates have been crafted to suit the partition boundaries:

```
select
        bsk.store_id,
        sum(btm.product_count)
from
        baskets         bsk,
        basket_items    btm
where
        bsk.basket_value > 20
and     bsk.date_part >= to_date('01-feb-2000','dd-mon-yyyy')
and     bsk.date_part < to_date('04-feb-2000','dd-mon-yyyy')
and     btm.date_part = bsk.date_part
and     btm.store_id = bsk.store_id
and     btm.basket_id = bsk.basket_id
```

```
group by
        bsk.store_id
;
```

This query accesses partitions p01, p02, and p03. Assume that we have approximately 500 stores, and on each day there are roughly 100,000 baskets that meet the basic criterion of a cost of more than $20. Earlier versions of Oracle would be able to use the date ranges to determine the minimum set of partitions that should be accessed from each table, but would then collect all 300,000 rows from the BASKETS table and try to join every single row to each of the three partitions of the BASKET_ITEMS table in turn. Oracle 8.1 is more advanced. It recognizes that a row from partition p01 of BASKETS can join only to a row from partition p01 of BASKET_ITEMS, and so on down the line. Diagrammatically, the difference in the amount of work done by the two different strategies can be seen in Figure 13-1.

Clearly there are likely to be significant performance benefits in partition-wise joins, particularly in a Parallel Query environment. First, there is no

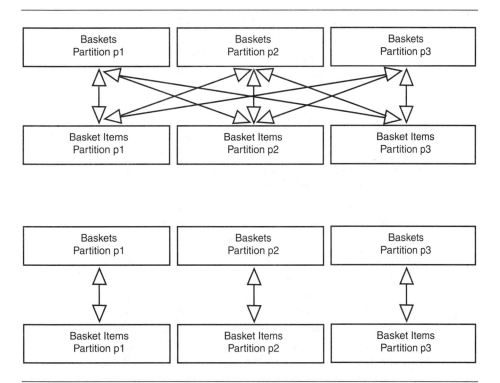

Figure 13-1.   Cross-partition and partition-wise joins.

wasted effort in trying to join a row from one table with rows from all the irrelevant partitions in the other table. Second, if there are parallel query slaves involved, there is no queue contention that would otherwise appear as every lower level slave tried to pass data to every higher level slave.

The problem with partition-wise joins is proving that they are taking place. The first step is to check paths with EXPLAIN PLAN, once with a query that should and once with a query that should *not* be doing partition-wise joins. Sample results are as follows; the partition-wise join appears first, and the join that could not be made partition-wise appears second:

```
SELECT STATEMENT (choose)       Cost (703,1)
  SORT    (aggregate)
    PARTITION RANGE      (iterator) Pt Range: 1 - 3
      HASH JOIN     Cost (703,8989)
        TABLE ACCESS BASKETS (full) Range: 1 - 3 Cost (58,2999)
        TABLE ACCESS BASKET_ITEMS(full) Range: 1 - 3 Cost (171,8989)


SELECT STATMENT (choose)       Cost (1208,1)
  SORT    (aggregate)
    HASH JOIN     Cost (1208,8989)
      PARTITION RANGE    (iterator) Range: 1 - 3
        TABLE ACCESS BASKETS (full) Range: 1 - 3 Cost (58,2999)
      PARTITION RANGE    (iterator) Range: 1 - 3
        TABLE ACCESS BASKET_ITEMS(full) Range: 1 - 3 Cost (171,8989)
```

There is a clear difference between the two plans, and the layout of the first plan seems to indicate quite clearly that partition-wise joining is taking place by the way in which the PARTITION RANGE option appears "outside" or prior to the HASH JOIN option. In the second example, we see that two totally separate ranging exercises take place to cover all the relevant partitions, and that the two resulting sets of data are finally joined. The different degree of efficiency between the two plans is indicated by the different costs. Note that the excess cost of the second query appears *not* in the table scan, but in the cost of the **hash join** step. All that extra work in message passing and so forth has taken its toll.

Despite the significant difference in estimated costs, which was subsequently reflected in elapsed execution times, the datasets and queries used to generate these plans were physically identical. However, I changed the high value on the basket_items partitions by adding a time component throughout to get them out of step with the partitions of the BASKETS table.

There is one minor problem with this plan. You appear to get the "correct" partition-wise join plan from Oracle 8.0, matching the one from Oracle 8.1.5.

Don't be fooled, though, the mechanisms are actually very different, but the difference shows up only when you switch to parallel execution. The first clue is that Oracle 8.1 reports the highly desirable PARALLEL COMBINED WITH PARENT option all over the place, whereas 8.0 shows PARALLEL TO PARALLEL, which is generally a much more expensive option because of the huge amount of messaging that takes place (see Chapter 22).

With Oracle 8.1, with the partition-wise join working, we can see (with a little effort) that a single SQL statement is being executed that joins a partition of the BASKETS table to a partition of the BASKET_ITEMS table:

```
SELECT /*+ PIV_SSF */ SYS_OP_MSR(SUM(A1.C0)) FROM (
SELECT /*+ ORDERED NO_EXPAND USE_HASH(A3) */ A3.C1 C0 FROM(
SELECT /*+ NO_EXPAND FULL(A4) */ A4."N1" C0 FROM
"BASKETS" PARTITION(:B1) A4) A2,
(SELECT /*+ NO_EXPAND FULL(A5) */ A5."N1" C0,A5."N2" C1 FROM
"BASKET_ITEMS" PARTITION(:B1) A5) A3
WHERE A2.C0=A3.C0) A1
```

Moving the high values on the BASKET_ITEMS table to make it impossible to do a partition-wise join, we can see how Oracle 8.1 now produces two separate SQL statements. The second query gets baskets data and passes it to the first query (where it appears as the "table" :Q666000), which hashes it into the basket_items data and sums it:

```
SELECT /*+ PIV_SSF */ SYS_OP_MSR(SUM(A1.C0)) FROM(
SELECT /*+ ORDERED NO_EXPAND USE_HASH(A3) SWAP_JOIN_INPUTS(A3) */
A2.C1 C0 FROM (
SELECT /*+ NO_EXPAND FULL(A4) */ A4."N1" C0,A4."N2" C1 FROM
"BASKET_ITEMS" PARTITION_SET(1) A4) A2,:Q666000 A3
WHERE A3.C0=A2.C0) A1


SELECT /*+ NO_EXPAND ROWID(A1) */ A1."N1" C0 FROM
"BASKETS" PARTITION(:B1) A1 WHERE ROWID BETWEEN :B2 AND :B3
```

For comparative purposes, the following SQL statements show how Oracle 8.0 handles the same problem using a far less efficient strategy for the same query, and shows numerous levels of parallel query slave with millions of messages flying from queue to queue as three separate steps are executed to complete the query. The third query scans the BASKET_ITEMS table and shares the rows, the second query does the same for the BASKETS table, and the first query acquires rows from the other two queues and hashes them together. Note also there is no SUM() visible in the following parallel query code; the massive SORT GROUP BY needed to do that bit at the end takes place serially in the query coordinator:

```
SELECT /*+ ORDERED NO_EXPAND USE_HASH(A2) PIV_SSF */ SUM(A2.C1)
FROM :Q33358000 A1,:Q33358001 A2 WHERE A1.C0=A2.C0

SELECT /*+ ROWID(A1) */ A1."N1" C0 FROM "BASKETS" PARTITION(:B1) A1
WHERE ROWID BETWEEN :B2 AND :B3

SELECT /*+ ROWID(A1) */ A1."N1" C0,A1."N2" C1 FROM "BASKET_ITEMS"
PARTITION(:B1) A1 WHERE ROWID BETWEEN :B2 AND :B3
```

Timing guidelines are fairly meaningless when running demonstration tests of this type, but for this particular sample, the difference between partition-wise joins and cross-partiton joins is approximately 50%, which is actually fairly consistent with the cost. The comparison between the Oracle 8.0 and Oracle 8.1 mechanisms was harder to define because I couldn't run them on the same machine. The two timings were actually very close, despite the fact that the machine running the version 8.0 test had four CPUs running at 500 MHz, whereas the machine running the version 8.1 test had a single CPU running at 266 MHz.

EXPLAIN PLAN

There are a few points to look out for if you use EXPLAIN PLAN to determine how effectively your partition elimination is going to be. The most significant point is the appearance in the plan of lines like

```
1   PARTITION RANGE (iterator) Pt Range: 14 - 17
2   PARTITION RANGE (iterator) Pt Range: KEY - KEY
3   PARTITION RANGE (inlist)   Pt Range: KEY(INLIST) - KEY(INLIST)
4   PARTITION RANGE (all)      Pt Range: 1 - 220
5   PARTITION RANGE (single)   Pt Range: KEY - KEY
6   PARTITION RANGE (empty)    Pt Range: INVALID - INVALID
7   TABLE ACCESS BASKETS (by local index rowid) Pt Range: 2 - 2
```

Example 1 tells you that Oracle has decided at parse time that it knows exactly which partitions it needs (in this case partitions 14 through 17), and all others will be ignored. The iterator is a general-purpose option that shows that the same optimization path will be used for a series of values in turn. Example 2 tells you that Oracle thinks it will be accessing several consecutive partitions, but will not be able to determine which ones until runtime. Example 3 tells you that Oracle thinks it will have to process a number of scattered partitions. Example 4 tells you that Oracle is going to access every single partition in the table. Example 5 tells you that Oracle knows it will have to access a single partition, but won't know which one until runtime. You will often see this appear in a plan when you execute queries that join a reference table to the partitioning column. Example 6 tells you that Oracle has determined at parse time that the supplied values are outside the current boundaries of the existing partitions, and no data can be returned. Example 7 is the perfect example of what appears if Oracle knows at parse time that it has to access a single partition, and can determine at parse time which partition it is. The key word *partition* simply doesn't appear in the plan at all.

If you use AUTOTRACE to get information about execution plans, you won't get the full detail about partition ranges. You need to use one of the EXPLAIN PLAN utility scripts supplied with Oracle 8.1 such as $ORACLE_HOME/rdbms/admin/utlxpls.sql.

At the end of the day, though, if you need to be convinced that Oracle really is eliminating the partitions it is claiming to eliminate, then make sure you build your test tables with partitions spread across several tablespaces. If you do this you can always take off-line the tablespaces holding partitions that Oracle claims to be eliminating. If the query crashes with Oracle error "ORA-00376: file NNN cannot be read at this time," then Oracle is lying about the partition elimination.

Statistics

Partitioned tables are one of the new features of Oracle 8, and as such you have to use the CBO to take advantage of them. This means analyzing the tables to generate statistics. This can be done at the table level or at the partition/subpartiton level with commands like

```
analyze table baskets partition (p03) compute statistics;
```

However, consider the following problem. If there are 100 distinct values of STORE in partition p01, and 100 distinct values of STORE in partition p02, how many distinct values of STORE are there across the two partitions? The answer could, in theory, be anything between 100 and 200.

To deal with this problem, Oracle suggests that you use the DBMS_STATS package (see Chapter 19) to analyze the statistics on partitioned tables, rather than use a simple *analyze* command, because the package is designed to address this issue and to calculate better statistics. Before you do this on a production system, try testing it on a small development system with SQL_TRACE turned on. You will discover that Oracle actually executes code similar to the following:

```
select /*+ */
    count(*) CNT,count(ID),count(distinct ID),
    avg(nvl(ceil(length(ltrim(rtrim(rtrim(
        to_char(
            ID,'9.99999999999999999999999999999999999999EEEE'
        ),'+-0123456789'
    ),'E0.v)))/2+2),1)),
    min(ID),max(ID),
    count(DATE_PART),count(distinct DATE_PART),
    8,min(DATE_PART),max(DATE_PART),
    count(PADDING),count(distinct PADDING),
    avg(nvl(lengthb(PADDING),1)),
    substrb(min(PADDING),1,32),substrb(max(PADDING),1,32)
from
    "JPL1"."DATETEST" partition ("P19") sample(1)
```

It seems to do this for the whole table with a sample size of 1%, then for the partition with a sample size of 1%, then it does it for the *whole partition*. It can be very time-consuming and resource intensive. Funnily enough, if the partitioned table is an IOT, the SAMPLE option is not supported and the package falls back to a simple ***analyze*** command.

> *Don't use DBMS_STATS to analyze the partitions of a partitioned table until the mechansim is more efficient.*

Partitions and Parallel Execution

When using partitioned tables with a parallel query, there are a couple of little extra details to watch out for. Bear in mind that it is possible to use parallel DML to update partitioned tables. This is a little brutal in terms of its effects on other processes, but basically multiple parallel execution slaves can be fired off, one per partition, in the form of "intradatabase" distributed transactions.

On a more common type of use, a parallel query can work in one of two ways against a partitioned table. When the query is known to apply to just one partition, multiple parallel query slaves can access it in much the same way that a parallel table scan works on ordinary tables. (Remember that Oracle 8 also features a parallel fast full scan of indexes and single index partitions.) When the query is expected to access multiple partitions, Oracle fires off one parallel query slave per partition (up to the limit allowed to the session).

Note carefully the comment "When the query is *expected* to . . ." in the previous paragraph. If Oracle thinks a query will access several partitions, then you get a maximum of one slave per partition. If the query actually accesses only one partition, then the query is effectively a serialized query. It is possible that if the optimizer was able to determine that it was supposed to access only one partition, then it would have chosen a different access path that allowed parallel operation on a single partition. This is another good reason for writing your queries carefully.

Bear in mind, by the way, that partitioned tables can be accessed in parallel through an indexed access path, because each index partition can be the target of a separate parallel query slave. Not only that, the indexes are allowed to have a different degree of parallelism from their tables, so the optimizer can, for example, choose between operating a parallel table scan with ten slaves, or an indexed access path with five slaves. Another tiny little trap with writing your SQL code to maximize partition elimination appears with index partitions. If the optimizer can determine at parse time that it is going to access a single partition only, it might find that it can do a SORT BY, NOSORT operation—in other words, use the index to return the data in the correct order without the cost of a sort. If the optimizer thinks it may have to access multiple partitions, then this special execution path is not available.

Problems and Quirks

Partitions make it easy to manipulate large amounts of data for administrative purposes to keep the database as clean and well packed as possible. However, there are some problems when referential integrity constraints exist on the partitioned tables.

If there is an enabled referential integrity constraint between two partitioned tables, it is not possible to drop or truncate partitions in the parent table, even if the tables are equipartitioned and the matching child partition has already been truncated or dropped.

A similar problem occurs with exchange partition. It is possible to exchange data into the parent and child partitioned tables if (1) the partitions have not had any data in them, (2) if the referential integrity constraint has been disabled on the partitioned table, and (3) if there is no matching referential integrity constraint on the simple tables at the other end of the exchange.

Thereafter it seems to be impossible to exchange partitions out of the parent because of Oracle error "ORA-02266: unique/primary keys in table referenced by enabled foreign keys," even when the constraint has been disabled. This looks like a bug, so keep checking your upgrades to see when it is fixed.

If your partitioned tables are IOTs, there is a bug in the code for partition maintenance. Any operation to split, add, exchange, or otherwise perform some sort of DDL on a partitioned IOT takes out an exclusive library cache lock at the wrong moment. The consequence of this is that any subsequent DML or DDL waits for the first DDL to complete, then returns Oracle error "ORA-04020: deadlock detected while trying to lock object."

When it comes to dropping tablespaces containing the oldest partitions, remember that Oracle cannot drop a tablespace including contents if it contains a collection of partitions from a partitioned object. The tablespace has to hold the whole of a partitioned object to use this version of the command, so you have to drop all the individual partitions before you can drop the tablespace. Each drop partition may take several seconds.

Unless the partitioning columns have a high degree of visibility as (pseudo) constants in your query, partition elimination cannot occur. The manuals advise adding the partitioning columns to the start of the indexes to address this issue, but this won't help if you have a large number of partitions and queries that are supposed to access a small number of rows.

If you are using the PARALLEL QUERY option to access partitioned tables, and a query "logically" requires data from several partitions, then Oracle allocates one partition per query slave. If the query *actually* requires data from just one partition, then only one slave does the work. This gives the appearance of extreme variation in performance.

Strategy Notes

Look for opportunities to use date-based range partitioning to make tablespaces read-only.

Always separate partitioned data from nonpartitioned data at the tablespace level.

Before making partitioned tablespaces read-only, consider rebuilding the partitions to pack them into the front end of the tablespace so that you can minimize the size of the tablespace. Locally managed and uniform-size tablespaces make this quite easy.

Partition elimination is a most important aid to performance. Pick the partition granularity to suit the nature of the queries, and then consider adjusting the queries to suit the partition boundaries.

If you are going to partition several tables (hash, range, or composite), then remember the benefits of partition-wise joins and try to partition them in the same way. This helps Oracle to break up a large job into a collection of small jobs, especially if you are using the PARALLEL QUERY option.

The two scripts supplied by Oracle Corporation to display serial and parallel execution paths are much more informative than the output from SET AUTOTRACE ON. The *Oracle 8i Tuning Manual* is also much more informative than it used to be in explaining how EXPLAIN PLAN works. It is worth taking some time to learn how to use it.

When using the PARALLEL QUERY Option with partitioned tables, remember that indexes and tables can have different degrees of parallelism.

If you know that a query need only access one partition, try to write it so that Oracle can determine logically that this is the case (for example, change a join into a MAX() subquery or in-line view) because this could give the optimizer several extra options for handling the query.

When testing any feature of partitioned tables, particularly of partitioned IOTs, make sure that you run with SQL_TRACE set to TRUE so that you can see if Oracle is generating any recursive SQL that is likely to cause problems on a production-size system.

CHAPTER 14

Index-Organized Tables

Imagine you are an analyst in a large financial institution, advising clients on how to spend millions of dollars on buying and selling shares. To support this business you have a database that loads the trading volume and closing prices from all the major stock exchanges around the world at the close of every day. You also have a subtle and sophisticated front end that can take the prices of half a dozen shares during the last two years and can draw complicated charts that help you to decide when to buy and when to sell. (In fact, the analytic functions introduced in Oracle 8.1.6 [see Chapter 23] mean that the software need not be all that sophisticated.) Inevitably you have one of three options: an amazing piece of hardware, a cunning database design, or a performance problem.

Every day the pricing information for some 10,000 different shares is crammed into your database. This is likely to take approximately 1MB per day of storage in a table. But this means that if you pick one specific share, yesterday's price is going to be stored 1MB away from today's price, and the previous price is going to be stored 1MB away from yesterday's price, and so on down the line (Figure 14-1).

So if you execute a query to get two years of prices for a single share, you are going to visit approximately 450 different locations in the table that are so far apart that every single price is likely to require a real physical disk read. Because all but the newest disks rarely allow more than 30 I/Os per second (whatever the notional specification), your request for a single set of share prices is likely to take more than 15 seconds to return results. A chart comparing six sets of share prices could take more than 90 seconds to appear. A response time like that is unlikely to appeal to the typical end user.

Obviously there were tricks and design strategies to address this problem in earlier versions of Oracle—a single-table index cluster was the one most likely to help. In the absence of clustering, this is also a good example of why a

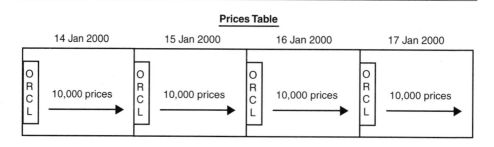

Figure 14-1.   Extreme data scatter.

2KB block size can sometimes be a good idea to optimize the use of memory. However, in Oracle 8, the IOT is the official, efficient, and simplest solution.

Basic IOTs

We have already seen something of ordinary B-trees. Descending through the branches we finally reach the correct leaf, where we find a pointer to the physical location of a row in a table. An IOT in its simplest form does away with the last step completely. There is no separate table; the data for the row is stored in the leaf of the index itself. The code to create our share price table might look like this

```
create table share_history(
        ticker_code      varchar2(32)   references share_codes,
        trade_date       date,
        price_close      number(15,2),
        trade_volume     number(10),
        price_high       number(15,2),
        price_low        number(15,2),
        constraint sh_pk primary key (ticker_code, trade_date)
)
organization index
tablespace INDX
compress 1
;
```

The first point to note is that an IOT *must* have a primary key, and this primary key cannot be disabled, dropped, or deferred. Any attempt to do so results in Oracle error "ORA-25188: cannot drop/disable/defer the primary key constraint for index-organized tables."

If you look in view family xxx_TABLES, you will find a row for the SHARE_HISTORY table, but the row holds some very strange values. For example, there is no tablespace, no value for INITIAL_EXTENT, and so on through all the other storage parameters. What you will find is that the IOT_ TYPE column identifies the table as an IOT.

If you then look in the view family xxx_INDEXES, you will find an index called SH_PK, just as you would expect from the named primary key, but the index type is given as 'IOT – TOP'. If the primary key had not been named, you would have found an index with a name of the form SYS_IOT_TOP_23144, where the numeric section is the object number for the "nonexistent" table. Checking further through the view family xxx_SEGMENTS, you will find that there is no data segment to hold the SHARE_HISTORY table. There is only a segment of type index to hold our primary key index.

The second point to note from the SQL code defining the table is that the location of the index is dictated *not* by a USING INDEX clause, which you would normally associate with the primary key, but by the TABLESPACE clause declared for the table. In fact, you always have to bear in mind that although this object is visibly declared as a table, it is actually an index. Additional consequences of this are that the PCTUSED clause is illegal, and the PCTFREE clause is fairly pointless unless you are doing a rebuild or a CTAS. For the same reason, if you execute ***analyze table XXX validate structure***, you get a set of results in the INDEX_STATS view describing the primary key index.

The third point in the defining SQL code is the COMPRESS clause. This is a new feature of Oracle 8.1 that is designed to save space in indexes in general and in IOTs in particular. When the leading columns of an index are subject to frequent repetition you can tell Oracle to store the leading values once per leaf block rather than once per entry (see Chapter 7 for more details). In the case of the SHARE_HISTORY table, I collected the price for Oracle shares for the last 15 years (some 3,500 entries with a stock code of ORCL). Because the entire row is only approximately 40 bytes long, I should be able to get roughly 100 rows in a 4KB block, but by storing the stock code ORCL (and its overhead) only once per block, I save an additional 500 bytes per block, giving me room for an extra dozen rows in each block.

An added bonus of IOTs is that the typical query automatically accesses the data in the correct order, so Oracle does not need to sort the data after acquiring it:

```
select *
from    share_history
```

```
where    ticker_code = 'ORCL'
and      trade_date between to_date('01-Jan-1998')
                            and to_date('01-Jan-2000')
order by
         trade_date
;
```

My choice for an example of IOTs is very good from one perspective: It is a realistic case for which we need to turn the data around between input and output. However, because I chose to include only a few columns in the table, and then compressed one of them, I concealed one of the penalties of using IOTs. You don't normally get many rows to a block. In a normal index, a *row entry* consists of a primary key plus a rowid. In an IOT, a row entry really is the whole row. If the rows are rather long rows, you do not get very many of them in each leaf block, and this is a bit of a shame because it counters some of the benefits we hope to gain from packing lots of prices for a single stock into a single block. IOTs accommodate this by allowing you to split the nonkey columns into high-use columns and low-use columns. The low-use columns can then be relegated to an "overflow" area.

> *An IOT can be split into* frequent use *and* occasional use *to get maximum benefit from the index-ordered packing.*

Assume that all our analysts are very interested in the closing prices but rarely look at the other prices and volume. We could relegate these columns to an overflow area by adding to our definition the clauses

```
including price_close
overflow tablespace OTHER_BITS
```

This tells Oracle two things. First, that we want to include all the columns up to and including the PRICE_CLOSE column in the index segment, and that the remainder should be stored in the overflow segment. Second, that the overflow segment should be stored in the OTHER_BITS tablespace. If we wanted to we could also add more physical storage details, such as extent sizes, to the OVERFLOW clause.

There is an alternative way to dictate which parts of a row should go to the overflow—the PCTTHRESHOLD clause. The PCTTHRESHOLD defaults to 50, and has to be between 1 and 50. If, as it is inserted or updated, a row exceeds this fraction of the block size (allowing a little for overhead), then the columns causing the excess are pushed into the overflow segment. Conversely, if an update shrinks a row to less than the PCTTHRESHOLD, then the trailing columns migrate back into the "top" section of the IOT. For example, consider the following column definitions in a database with a 4KB block size:

```
create table art_catalog (
        object_id   number  primary key,
        purchased   date,
        description varchar2(500),
        history     varchar2(500)
)
organization index
pctthreshold 10
overflow tablespace other_bits
;
```

With a PCTTHRESHOLD of 10 and a block size of 4KB, Oracle decides that any row larger than approximately 400 bytes has to have its tail end moved to the overflow. If we insert a row with 200 bytes of description and 200 bytes of history, then just the history is pushed to the overflow. If we insert a row with 450 bytes of description, then the description and the history would be pushed to the overflow.

Personally, I would not use the PCTTHRESHOLD method because it implies that I do not really know what my data looks like or how it will be used. It also introduces a degree of uncertainty about where the I/O might take place, and this is always undesirable.

In fact, there is a little trap with PCTTHRESHOLD. As we saw in the very first code sample, it is possible to create an IOT without an overflow. However, if the nominal maximum size of the row definition (including various overhead) exceeds the "free space times PCTTHRESHOLD," then Oracle insists that you create an overflow segment. In the previous example, if you had defined the history and description columns to 1,500 bytes each, totaling 3,000 bytes out of a 4,000-byte free space, then Oracle would insist that you create the table with an overflow segment. If you ever include several large but optional columns in a table knowing that any one row will use only a few of them, you could find that Oracle insists that you create an overflow segment that never gets used. Unofficially, there is a way around this problem. If you set event 28657, which exists to protect Oracle when importing into a database with small blocks an IOT exported from a database with large blocks, you can break the PCTTHRESHOLD rule without raising an error.

If you want to check the storage details of this overflow segment, by the way, you will find it in the USER_TABLES view, with a name like SYS_IOT_OVER_23144. Again, the number corresponds to the object number of the nonexistent table. Unfortunately, it is not yet possible to specify a meaningful name for an overflow segment. If you try to use **alter table rename** you get Oracle error "ORA-25191: cannot reference overflow table of an index-organized table."

Because the overflow segment effectively takes the role of a traditional table, it does make sense to think about using the PCTUSED and PCTFREE parameters on the overflow table. This can result in a slightly odd looking piece of SQL code that appears to have two separate storage clauses:

```
create table share_history(
    ticker_code     varchar2(32),
    trade_date      date,
    price_close     number(15,2),
    price_high      number(15,2),
    price_low       number(15,2),
    trade_volume    number(10),
    constraint sh_pk primary key (ticker_code, trade_date)
)
organization index
tablespace indx
storage (initial 500k next 500k pctincrease 0)
compress 1
including price_close
overflow tablespace other_bits
storage (initial 1m next 1m pctincrease 0)
pctfree 2
pctused 98
;
```

One little trap to watch out for is that the LOGGING attribute of an IOT and its overflow must be the same (unlike an ordinary table and its indexes). If the INDX and OTHER_BITS tablespaces in the previous SQL code happened to have different default LOGGING attributes, then Oracle would raise the error "ORA-28662: IOT index and overflow segments must share the same LOGGING attribute." Having said this, you could use the command

```
alter table share_history move
overflow tablespace somewhere_else
nologging
;
```

Although there is no legal path in the SQL reference manual for this command, it does work. If you use it you could end up with the two segments in different LOGGING states. This does highlight a particularly annoying issue with the current state of the manuals: There are some combinations of command options that appear to be legal and fail; there are others that appear to be illegal but work to one degree or another. The previous example is one that seems reasonable, could be used "by accident," and will get your database into a state that is notionally unsupported. Be very careful if you discover something that appears to work, but is not documented. Check the legality with Oracle Support before you use it in a production system.

Indexes on IOTs

One of the limitations on IOTs in Oracle 8.0 was that you could not create any other indexes on them. B-tree indexes store the rowid of each row, and bitmap indexes use rowid ranges to produce maps. But a rowid is the physical location in the database of a row (expressed as the file, block in file, and row position in block), and the rows in an IOT can move from block to block as new rows are created and blocks get split. IOTs do not have permanent, physical rowids.

In Oracle 8.1, secondary indexes are allowed through the creation of a new data type—the UROWID or universal (logical) rowid. UROWIDs can hold rowids for all types of objects, including non-Oracle data objects. In particular, they may hold data that represents locator information for a row in an IOT.

Secondary indexes can be unique, nonunique, or even function based, but they may not be bitmap indexes because bitmap indexes require an absolutely unmovable physical location for the rows in the map. An odd little detail of secondary indexes is that INDEX_TYPE in the view family xxx_INDEXES is marked as FUNCTION-BASED NORMAL.

For IOTs, one of the items of information that the UROWID holds is the value of the primary key. The strategy for a query on the secondary index is that Oracle should traverse the secondary index to find the related primary keys, and then traverse the IOT to get to the data (Figure 14-2). In effect this means that a query against a secondary index on an IOT does roughly twice as much logical I/O as the identical query against a normal table.

In an attempt to reduce this workload, however, the UROWID also contains a "guess" of the block where the row should be. In fact, this guess is simply the address of the block where the row was located when the index was built or where the row entry was first inserted.

Of course, because rows can move from block to block in IOTs, this guess is likely to go out of date with the passing of time. Because it is *never*

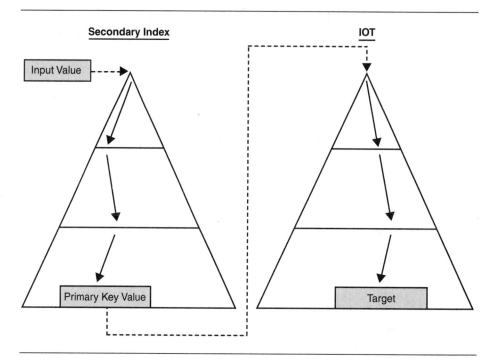

Figure 14-2.   Secondary index use on IOTs.

corrected on the fly, you could end up with a very unpleasant performance overhead as Oracle uses the guess to jump to the wrong block and then goes back to traverse the IOT to find the right block.

The optimizer has some degree of understanding about guesses, and there is a new statistic called PCT_DIRECT_ACCESS in the view family xxx_INDEXES, which is the estimate of the percentage of the guesses that are likely to be correct. This information is probably included in the optimizer's decision to use or ignore the guesses as well as the basic decision of whether to use the secondary index at all. This value is set to 100 when you create the secondary index, and is set back to zero when you rebuild the IOT.

You may think that rebuilding the secondary index (ALTER INDEX REBUILD) would set PCT_DIRECT_ACCESS back to 100. In fact, the *Oracle 8i Concepts* manual does state quite explicitly that "rebuilding a secondary index on an index-organized table involves reading the base table, unlike building an index on an ordinary table." However, this doesn't seem to be entirely true. I have come across cases when Oracle appeared to rebuild the index without reference to the table, and without resetting

PCT_DIRECT_ACCESS. It may be necessary to drop and re-create your secondary indexes to get the guess quality back up to 100%.

Of course, because the secondary index contains the indexed column, the primary key, and a block guess (and a few bytes of extra overhead), it is likely to be significantly larger than the equivalent index on an ordinary table. On the other hand, when you rebuild an IOT the secondary index is *still usable* and does not have to be rebuilt. Because the IOT can be rebuilt on-line, while its secondary indexes stay valid, this offers some interesting possibilities to sites that have to run 24/7. As always, it's a trade-off: some wasted space and a built-in reduction in performance against nonstop operation.

Another side effect of the way in which secondary indexes contain the primary key is that you have a bonus execution path in queries of the form

```
select primary_key_columns
from index_organized_table
where {secondary_indextest is true}
```

At first sight this looks like a simple index access to a table requiring two steps. However, the secondary index contains the primary key columns, so the execution can be just a single-step range scan on the secondary index.

There are a few anomalies about secondary indexes and guesses. First, I'm not sure that Oracle actually uses the guesses, notwithstanding the comments in the manuals. Perhaps it's just a question of data size and statistics, but in all the tests I have done to date, Oracle has always scanned the secondary index then traversed the IOT without jumping to a guess block. (You have to shut down the database and probably reboot the system to be completely sure of this.) Second, it is arguable that the concept of using a guess is a bad idea anyway, as seen in Figure 14-3.

Remember that B-trees actually fan out quite quickly. For clarity and convenience, the diagrams you find in books tend to show each block with perhaps three or four children, but in real Oracle databases it is common for each block to have a hundred or more children. Consequently, it is eminently possible for the branch blocks of an index to be permanently buffered in memory, whereas the leaf layer is so large that it is hardly buffered at all. (I actually read a very interesting postgraduate dissertation recently that came to a fascinating conclusion, but based its entire mathematical argument on the fact that each branch in a B-tree would have roughly four leaf blocks.)

Look at Figure 14-3 and consider what will happen if (1) the leaf layer is not buffered, and (2) we use the guess. We hit two buffered blocks and do one physical read in the secondary index, then read the guess and jump to the

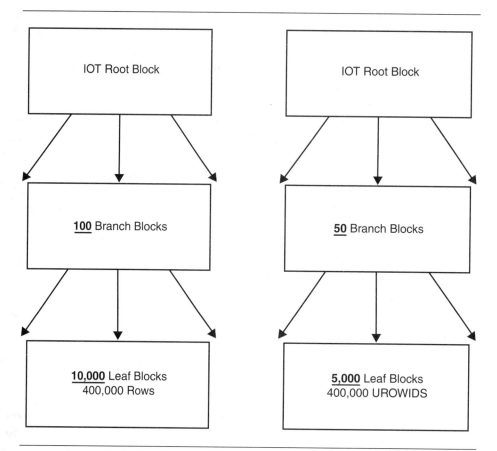

Figure 14-3.   Fanning out of B-trees.

primary. If the guess is right, we do one more physical read. If the guess is wrong, we do two more physical reads.

Now assume we ignore the guess. We hit two buffered blocks and do one physical read in the secondary index. We use the primary key to do two buffered reads in the IOT, and then do one physical read to get the IOT leaf.

In summary, if the guess is good we save two logical I/Os (perhaps one ten thousandth of a CPU second). If the guess is bad we add one physical read (at least one fiftieth of an elapsed second) and all its overhead. Is this a trade even worth considering? In general I suspect not. It seems to me that you really need to guarantee an almost perfect success rate on guesses before the trade is worthwhile.

On-line Moves

One of the important things to remember about IOTs is that they are indexes. So when you do anything to the table, it is worth considering if there are any special side effects that may appear because you are really handling an index.

One of the particular options to consider is rebuilding tables. An ordinary table cannot be rebuilt on-line, but an ordinary index can. So the following command will work, and the table will be built on-line while it is still fully usable:

```
alter table iot_tab move online;
```

Of course it has the same restriction as on-line rebuilds of ordinary indexes. The rebuild cannot start until there are no active transactions on the table, and the rebuild cannot complete until there are no active transactions on the table. Furthermore, if you have an overflow segment, it is not rebuilt at the same time.

However, it is always worth looking a little closer at IOTs. If you execute this command with SQL_TRACE switched on, you will find the following occurring under the covers:

```
create unique index "JPL1"."IOT_TAB_PK" on "IOT_TAB" (OBJECT_ID)
index only toplevel
move
as
select * from "IOT_TAB"
```

And if you examine your session statistics, you may find that to build this index, Oracle does a fast full scan of the existing table and sorts the entire dataset. In all the tests I performed, Oracle did not use a range scan to read the data in sorted order. Be careful about moving a large IOT on-line on a production system; the overhead is high.

There are other catches to using IOTs that revolve around the fact that they are really indexes. You can do a direct SQL*Load into an IOT, but because the IOT is an index, Oracle loads the new data, sorts it, then copies the whole of the old IOT to merge it with the new dataset—a fact that is not obvious if you think of the IOT as a table. In a similar vein, a NOLOGGING table allows you to INSERT /*+_ APPEND */ without generating any redo log. But if the table is actually an IOT, then the logging takes place. Inserts to an index are always logged, even an index created in a NOLOGGING tablespace.

Advanced IOTs

IOTs can be partitioned, can include LOBs and varrays, and can contain nested tables—three restrictions that have been lifted since version 8.0. There is still a little way to go in combining these features, because *partitioned* IOTs cannot include LOBs, varrays, and nested tables.

Because the obvious purpose of IOTs is to rearrange data at load time for subsequent rapid access while avoiding storage overhead, I would think very carefully before including any variant of these large-object types inside an IOT. I don't see the restrictions on partitioned IOTs as a great defect, but I would expect the basic partitioning option to be very useful.

LOBs, Varrays, and Nested Tables

Most of the issues of dealing with "large" objects are addressed in other chapters. However there are a couple of issues specific to IOTs.

If you really want to include LOBs or large varrays in pure IOTs, Oracle rather sensibly stores them out-of-line, irrespective of how small the actual LOB/varray content may be. If you include an overflow segment, then you can **enable storage in row**, as long as the LOB/varray is defined to be part of the overflow.

If you include a nested table in an IOT, then the issues are no different from including a nested table in a normal table. A more interesting situation arises when you consider the fact that any nested table should probably be an IOT anyway. After all, the purpose of a nested table is to associate an open-ended collection of objects with its parent, so that parent and collection can be accessed rapidly. The nested table as an IOT seems ideal. There are a couple of problems though. One problem is that you cannot specify an overflow segment in the NESTED TABLE clause. For example,

```
create type jpl_row as object (
        n1 number(6),
        v1 varchar2(1000),
        v2 varchar2(1000)
);
/

create type jpl_table as table of jpl_row;
/
```

```
create table nest_demo(
        Id              varchar2(32) primary key,
        nest1           jpl_table
)
nested table nest1 store as nested1 (
        (primary key (nested_table_id, n1))
        organization index
        compress 1
);
```

There are two points to notice especially with this ***create table*** statement. First, I have to declare a primary key with an IOT, so I have used the implicit NESTED_TABLE_ID column of the nested table combined with one of the real nested table columns. Second, because all the nested items for a single parent will be very close to each other, and the 16-byte NESTED_ TABLE_ID will be the same for any one parent, I have eliminated repetition of that ID by using the COMPRESS option on the first column of the primary key.

The most important point, though, is one that is not immediately obvious. Because I have a 4KB block size, a full-size row of the jpl_row type (2,000+ bytes) would have exceeded 50% of the block. Because PCTTHRESHOLD has a default value of 50%, I should have got Oracle error "ORA-01429: index-organized table: no data segment to store overflow row-pieces" when I tried to create my nested table as an IOT. This did not happen. Instead, the error message only appears when I try to put in some data that needs to overflow.

I need an overflow segment for the nested IOT, but I can't create it when I create the rest of the table. As with so many of the new, more complex features of tables, you have to create the table and then issue an ***alter table*** command immediately afterward. In this case, to avoid the rather sneaky and unfair runtime error message, you have to add the overflow with the ***alter table*** command, altering the *nested table*:

```
alter table nested1
add overflow
tablespace users;
```

Unfortunately, when I actually tried to do this, I got an error message telling me that I had no privilege on the SYSTEM tablespace. When I gave myself the privilege, the overflow segment duly appeared in the SYSTEM tablespace despite the fact that it was not my default tablespace. Nominally it is possible to move an IOT, including the overflow, with the ***alter table*** command, but when I tried it I got Oracle error ORA-03113. These are known bugs and are likely to be fixed by version 8.1.6.

It has to be said that when you start taking complex and convoluted routes through the descriptions of the ***create table*** and ***alter table*** commands in the SQL reference manual, it is possible to come up with combinations of features that the Oracle code doesn't handle very well.

The other problem with nested tables and IOTs is an internal one that affects performance. When you create a nested table (see Chapter 17), Oracle is supposed to create a unique index on a hidden column of the parent table. Of course, for an IOT this index would be a secondary index rather than an ordinary index. But it does not get created, so there is no efficient access path from the nested table to the parent table, and all queries have to drive through the parent table.

Partitioning

IOTs can be partitioned, but only by range (not hash), and the partitioning columns must be a subset (although not necessarily the leading columns) of the primary key index. There are also some restrictions on the structure of the IOT if it is partitioned. For example, LOBs and varrays are not allowed. Perhaps the most significant restriction is that a partitioned IOT cannot be rebuilt on-line, even one partition at a time. On the plus side, though, if you rebuild a partition of a partitioned IOT, even the global indexes and globally partitioned indexes remain usable (see Chapter 12).

As an example of why we might want to partition an IOT, let us go back to the share pricing system. We decided to create an IOT based on the ticker code and the trade date because most users wanted to query a small number of ticker codes over a range of dates. However some users may, from time to time, want to take a snapshot of a significant fraction of the market on a given date, perhaps to derive some type of in-house market index. Without some alternative access path, this will be a *very* expensive query.

One option is to create a secondary index on the trade date, but this would probably still result in a very large volume of physical I/O because the prices for a given date would be very widely scattered across a very large table. Therefore, we could try partitioning the data by trade date as follows:

```
create table share_history(
        ticker_code     varchar2(32),
        trade_date      date,
        price_close     number(15,2),
        price_high      number(15,2),
```

```
             price_low        number(15,2),
             trade_volume     number(10),
             constraint sh_pk primary key (ticker_code, trade_date)
)
organization index
tablespace indx
compress 1
including price_close
overflow tablespace spare_bits
partition by range (trade_date)(
partition sh_1984_jan values less than
        (to_date('01-feb-1984','dd-mon-yyyy'))
             tablespace users overflow tablespace users,
. . .
partition sh_1999_oct values less than (maxvalue)
)
;
```

This produces a table with approximately 400 partitions (16 years at 12 partitions per year) and 2 segments (1 IOT top and 1 IOT overflow) per partition. Every single segment could be in a separate tablespace if required. The code shows how to put the January 1984 segments into specific tablespaces.

If you took an approach like this, a query for all the prices for 14 January 1999 would have the option to scan just one month's data, which may be much more effective than collecting every ten thousandth row from the table by using a secondary index.

Restrictions on IOT Partitions

As you might expect, it is possible to use the EXCHANGE PARTITION feature with partitioned IOTs. You just have to be a little fussier when doing it. The table with which you are exchanging must be an IOT. If either object has an overflow segment, then both must have an overflow segment. The primary key must have the same columns in the same order. The level of compression of the keys must be the same. Unfortunately, this not checked as the exchange takes place, so if there is a mismatch, subsequent queries can crash with ORA-00600 errors, so be careful. If you discover the error in time you can exchange back without any harm.

The impact of index-based constraints on exchanging partitions (see Chapter 12) applies to IOTs because an IOT is built on its primary key. If you expect to use the EXCHANGE PARTITION feature on a partitioned IOT, don't forget to set the primary key to ENABLED NOVALIDATE. Unlike normal partitioned tables, it is not possible to merge IOT partitions. If you think this is important, you will have to create a procedure to exchange the partitions and drop one, then build a new IOT from the two exchanged partitions before swapping it back in.

Problems and Quirks

There are still quite a few bugs with IOTs in version 8.1.5 (as witness my previous nested table example). A simpler example shows up when trying to use the COMPUTE STATISTICS options of rebuilding an index: For an IOT or its secondary indexes, this results in the process crashing.

Another, perhaps more significant bug, is that referential integrity does not work properly if the parent table is an IOT. It is possible to delete a parent row and leave a collection of orphans, and ON DELETE CASCADE does not work. This may not affect many systems because IOTs are more likely to be child tables than parent tables. The bug has been fixed in version 8.1.6.

One of the bugs that is not fixed in version 8.1.6 shows up as a potentially serious defect in partitioned IOTs. It is very easy to get library cache deadlocks occurring during partition maintenance. For example, if two sessions try to split two different partitions of the same IOT at the same time, the one that starts second waits for the first split to complete, and then fails with error "ORA-04020: deadlock detected while trying to lock object XXXX." (Splitting IOT partitions is also the special case when partitions of secondary indexes become unusable.)

This would probably be bearable, and forgivable, if it occurred only for concurrent DDL, but unfortunately the problem is much worse: Because of an error in the acquisition of KGL (library cache) locks during IOT partition maintenance, even a simple *select* statement that starts while partition maintenance is in progress waits and then fails with a 4020 error.

Added to the problem of functional bugs is the list of errors in the manuals. If you discover that you can't get some feature suggested by the manual to work, it is likely that the manual is wrong. For example, the section in the SQL reference manual on ALTER INDEX suggests that you can rebuild a secondary index of an IOT on-line. But when you try, you get error "ORA-08108: may not build or rebuild this type of index on line."

When you rebuild the table on-line, only the IOT top segment is rebuilt; the overflow and LOB segments cannot be rebuilt on-line. This is not surprising because the IOT top segment holds a pointer to the absolute physical location of data in the other two segments.

Oracle insists that you have an overflow segment if the sum of the declared column sizes (plus some overhead) totals more than 50% of the free space for the block. You cannot override this, officially, even if you know that your data will never use the full space allowed by the column definitions.

Although the table can be rebuilt on-line with the ***alter table move*** command, it has the same problem as a normal index on-line rebuild (***alter index rebuild***). There has to be a couple moments when there are no uncommitted transactions on the table—one so that the rebuild can start and one so that the rebuild can complete. On a high-use, international, 24/7 Web site, this may make it impossible to do an on-line rebuild.

The secondary indexes on an IOT cannot be rebuilt on-line, despite comments to the contrary in the manual. In some cases this may eliminate the benefit of being able to rebuild the IOT itself on-line.

An IOT is an index, so even when you define it to be NOLOGGING, it is not possible for Oracle to add data to it without changing existing blocks. Thus, rollback and redo are always generated for IOTs. The direct-load hint /*+ APPEND */ doesn't do anything. The only exception to this behavior occurs when a complete build (CTAS or ***alter table move***) takes place.

There are some restrictions on using IOTs for materialized views (see Chapter 23). An obvious one is that the materialized view log cannot USE ROWID because IOTs do not have rowids (not that you should be using rowids with materialized views anyway). A less obvious restriction is that certain types of materialized views (for example, aggregate views) simply may not be created as IOTs. Because materialized views provide such enormous performance gains, this restriction is unlikely to be of great significance.

Strategy Notes

IOTs allow data to be packed in a different order from the order in which it naturally arrives. This slows down data entry, but it can enhance data retrieval immensely.

IOTs can be rebuilt on-line using the ***alter table move*** command, provided they are not partitioned and that you do not want to rebuild the overflow segment. Oracle seems to sort the entire table to do this though.

If index organization is relevant, then the table is likely to be of a very simple structure with very short rows. I doubt if there is any significant performance benefit to be found in applying IOT technology to tables that contain frequently used LOBS or varrays.

Nested tables are likely to be very good candidates for IOTs. They are likely to have small rows, and the data for a given parent row is likely to be accessed as a single unit at all times.

If IOTs are likely to be beneficial, then they tend to be suitable for index compression. This is particularly relevant for nested IOTs because there is a 16-byte ID column prepended to the nested rows.

It is sometimes possible to separate a table into FREQUENTLY ACCESSED and RARELY ACCESSED columns. If the table is an IOT you can choose to move the RARELY ACCESSED column to an overflow segment, thus reducing the size of the index and improving the efficiency of accessing the frequently used data.

IOTs can have secondary indexes. These use the primary key as a logical rowid but include a "guess" regarding the physical location of that row in the IOT. Because rows move from block to block in the IOT as the table grows, these guesses become stale and the secondary indexes become less efficient.

Although simple IOTs can be rebuilt on-line, any overflow or LOB segments cannot be rebuilt on-line, which rather reduces the benefit. There is also a restriction in version 8.1.5 that stops the secondary indexes from being rebuilt on-line.

If you have tables that have to be available 24/7, you may consider turning them into IOTs even though they are *not* natural candidates for this treatment, simply so that you can do an on-line rebuild from time to time. Of course, you may have to push all the nonkey columns into the main segment, and the table cannot be partitioned; otherwise the rebuild cannot be on-line. These restrictions should be weighed carefully against the benefit of being able to do the on-line rebuild.

IOTs are a very interesting addition to the tools available when building DSS-type systems in particular, but there are a number of limitations (often apparently minor ones) in how they can be used. I have mentioned only a few of the more significant ones in this chapter, so do make sure that you test every single assumption you make about IOTs before you commit large amounts of data to them.

> *If you think that IOTs may be of use, test everything with SQL_TRACE switched on. There are lots of strange bits of recursive SQL that appear when you start to dig into the features of IOTs.*

CHAPTER 15

Simple Objects

If you have come up through the many historical versions of Oracle, you may still be in the dark about the object features introduced in Oracle 8.0. What is an object in Oracle? Why would you use them? How do they work? What features are there to support them? How efficient are they?

From Oracle's perspective, an object is simply a user-defined data type that can be made up in one of three ways: first as a list of attributes with an optional set of associated functions or procedures (known as *methods*), second as a fixed-size list of items (a *varray*), and third as an open-ended list (confusingly termed a *table*). This chapter examines the first option; Chapter 16 examines the other two options, which fall under the umbrella term *collection types*.

The subtlety, complexity, and capacity for problems of objects lie in the fact that an object can be constructed from any preexisting data type, including other user-defined data types. The convenience of objects is that once a new data type has been declared, both SQL and PL/SQL understand how to use that data type.

Once a user-defined data type has been declared, there are some special ways of handling it. Oracle can store references to object types, it can use a reference to track down an object with the deref() call and convert an object ID into the object itself with the value() call.

Getting Started with Objects

Before you can make use of object types you need the necessary privileges: CREATE TYPE allows you to create types in your own schema; CREATE ANY TYPE allows you to create types in other schemas. If you create a type, you can use it in your own objects, but to use a type defined in another schema you either need the EXECUTE ANY TYPE privilege or you need to have been granted explicit execute rights on that type. You can, if you wish, create a synonym for a type that exists in another schema; but you cannot use this synonym in a *create table* statement. You need to use the fully qualified schema_name.type_name.

The simplest type of object is one that collects a few base data types into a single structural unit:

```
create or replace type occupation as object(
    date_start      date,
    date_end        date,
    description      varchar2(30),
    remuneration     number(7,0)
);
/
```

Apart from the fact that object creation requires a forward slash to execute, there seems at first sight to be little difference between a type definition and a table definition. However, now that we have created a fairly simple new type, we can use it to build more complex types, use it as a column type in a table, create a table containing nothing but objects of this type, or use it to declare PL/SQL variables:

```
create or replace type person as object(
    name                varchar2(30),
    date_of_birth       date,
    current_occupation  occupation
);
/

create table people (
    person_id           varchar2(22),
    current_occupation  occupation
)
;

create table occupations of occupation;

declare
    m_occupation        occupation;
begin
    select  current_occupation
    into    m_occupation
```

```
from      people
where     person_id = 'XX2403D';

dbms_output.put_line(m_occupation.description);
end;
/
```

These examples show in turn

- A type that includes an attribute of our original type
- A relational table that has one column of our simple type
- An OBJECT table that consists purely of objects of our simple type. Don't look in the view family xxx_TABLES for this table though; object tables are listed in the view families xxx_OBJECT_TABLES and xxx_ALL_TABLES.
- A simple PL/SQL block that acquires one row from our table and prints one attribute from our user-defined type. (Note the "dot" notation used to descend through layers of types.)

I mentioned in the introduction that a type definition can include methods. These are functions or procedures (usually PL/SQL, but nominally Java or C as well) that can act on the data "inside" the type to offer added value. For example we could be interested in how long a particular occupation lasted. Traditionally, we would write a piece of code (perhaps several times over) in our application to calculate this from the start and end dates for the occupation. With Oracle's typing mechanism we can build this information into the type itself by adding a ***member function***. Because we have already used the occupation type in another object definition, we have to use the ***alter type*** command to change the type definition. Even then the only changes we can make to the type are changes to the methods, not to the attributes:

```
alter type occupation replace as object (
    date_start          date,
    date_end            date,
    description         varchar2(30),
    remuneration        number(7,0),
    MEMBER FUNCTION     job_duration return number,
    pragma restrict_references (
        job_duration, rnds, wnds, rnps, wnps
    )
);
/
```

```
create or replace type body occupation as
    member function job_duration return number is
    begin
        return self.date_end - self.date_start;
    end;
end;
/
```

Note the key word *self* that appears in the function. Any **member function** for a type implicitly has a first parameter of SELF, which is an IN parameter of the type and (as you probably guessed) holds the value of the "current" item. It is also possible to create **static functions/procedures** instead of **member functions**. The only differences being that a **static function** does not have an implicit first parameter of SELF, so it can be called completely independently of any data of the type to which it is supposed to relate.

Having declared this function, we can now use the pseudo column CURRENT_OCCUPATION.JOB_DURATION() as if it was just another column, remembering to include the parentheses even though there are no parameters:

```
select  p.current_occupation.job_duration()
from    people p
;
```

We can also query the table using the pseudo column as part of the WHERE clause:

```
Select  p.*
from    people p
where   p.current_occupation.job_duration() > 10 * 365
;
```

> *When you use objects in tables, make liberal use of table aliases throughout your SQL statements, and apply them to the columns. Oracle is a little inconsistent, but usually needs an alias on the table to sort out name resolution problems. (In this context, the manuals refer to* correlation variables *rather than table aliases.)*

There are two special examples of **member functions** to consider when you are creating functions for user-defined types. These are the MAP method and the ORDER method. For any given type, only one of these can exist. Its purpose is to allow Oracle to compare and sort user-defined types. In the absence of an ORDER method and a MAP method, simple types can only be compared for equality. Two objects are equal if and only if their individual attributes are all equal.

A MAP method is more efficient if you are likely to sort your data frequently. It is called once per row and must return a simple data type (numeric, date, or character). Oracle uses the resulting set of values to do the sorting.

An ORDER method is called to compare exactly two examples of the type. The two items are passed to the function as parameters, the first as the implicit SELF parameter, and the second as a named parameter. The function must return -1, 0, or 1 depending on whether the SELF parameter is less than, equal to, or greater than the named parameter.

MAP methods can be used in parallel execution for sorts, group by, and so forth, and must be declared if you want Oracle to use a hash join to join objects. ORDER methods enforce serialization and restrict joins to nested loop and merge joins. To identify the MAP or ORDER methods, the relevant key word appears before the word *member* in the type definition:

```
alter type occupation replace as object (
    . . .
    MAP MEMBER FUNCTION sort_by_map return varchar2,
    pragma restrict_references (
        sort_by_map, rnds, wnds, rnps, wnps
    )
);
/


create or replace type body occupation as
    . . .
    MAP MEMBER FUNCTION sort_by_map return varchar2 is
    begin
        return self.description;
    end;
end;
/


select  p.*
from    people p
order by
    p.current_occupation desc
```

Taken out of context, an ORDER method that sorts occupations by start date may look like this:

```
ORDER MEMBER FUNCTION sort_by_order(other in occupation)
return number is
begin
    return sign(self.start_date - other.start_date);
end;
```

Although, as I have said, you can alter a type by adding new methods (or changing the implementation of existing methods), you cannot drop a method from a type. In particular, this means you cannot change your mind about the sorting method because only one of MAP or ORDER can be attached to a type, and once it is in place it cannot be removed.

There are a couple anomalies in the handling of ***member functions***. In the first place it seems slightly bizarre that you should be able to call the MAP or ORDER method explicitly, so that the following (possibly daft) query is valid:

```
select  p.occupation.sort_by_map()
from    people p;
```

You could argue that this is reasonable because you may invent a need to access the internal ordering functions of the type to identify all rows that sort above a fixed value, even though this implies you have too much information about the internal sorting mechanism. For example,

```
select  p.*
from    people p
where   p.occupation.sort_by_map() > 'XYZ'
;
```

or possibly

```
cursor c1 (i_occupation) is
select  p.*
from    people p
where   p.occupation.sort_by_order(i_occupation) = 1
;
```

Second, as with "ordinary" PL/SQL functions and procedures, you can use the AUTHID clause to specify whether the current user's privileges or the owner's privileges should be used to resolve any names and privileges in the type. This could lead to some very peculiar side effects, like different users getting different sorting orders, which may perhaps be useful if different users were supposed to sort data in different linguistic orders.

Finally, I suspect that an object-oriented purist would be very critical of the fact that a ***static function*** is actually usable outside the context of the type in which it is defined. Assume our type and type body contain the following sections respectively:

```
static function rubbish(junk in number) return number,
pragma restrict_references (rubbish, rnds, wnds, rnps, wnps)

static function rubbish(junk in number) return number is
begin
    return (junk * junk);
end;
```

Although this function is completely irrelevant to the object type as such, it is totally legal to declare it inside the object, and use it outside the object with syntax like

```
select occupation.rubbish(3) from dual;
```

So what, you might ask, is the point of having ***static functions*** in a type body? Is there any concrete benefit or is it purely cosmetic? If you do ask yourself this question and come up with a good answer, please let me know.

Objects and Relational Tables

If you have defined an object type you can include it in a table definition:

```
create type simple_object as object(
    n1 number(6),
    v1 varchar2(32)
);
/

create table simple_table as (
    id number(6),
    thing simple_object
)
;
```

A warning: Oracle 8.1 allows you to have as many as 1,000 columns in a single table. If you start using object types in tables, you add numerous hidden columns, and these count toward your total of 1,000. (Personally, I tend to think that anything over a few dozen columns is usually a bad design decision, so I can't take this warning too seriously.)

If you describe the table from SQL∗Plus, you will, by default, see a table with two columns. If you increase the depth of the description ("set describe depth all linenum on"), you see a more complete definition (in some cases even descriptions of the type's methods):

```
        Name                              Null?    Type
        ----------------------------      -------- -----------
1       ID                                         VARCHAR2(22)
2       CURRENT_OCCUPATION                         OCCUPATION
3    2     DATE_START                              DATE
4    2     DATE_END                                DATE
5    2     DESCRIPTION                             VARCHAR2(30)
6    2     REMUNERATION                            NUMBER(7)
```

> *If you want to use SQL∗Plus to describe a table that includes object elements, use the **set** command to "set describe depth N linenum on" where N is a number or ALL.*

In this simple example, you will find (looking at the dictionary SYS.COL$) that the table actual appears to have six columns—two of them named ID and CURRENT_OCCUPATION, and the rest named SYS_NC00003$, SYS_NC00004$, SYS_NC00005$, and SYS_NC00006$, which you can actually select from the table.

> *Whenever experimenting with objects, start with a clean schema, create an object, then look at all the data dictionary views and tables (USER_INDEXES, SYS.COL$, and so on) to find out what else Oracle has created on your behalf to support the object.*

Although you have to remember that the CURRENT_OCCUPATION column is a type column, any SQL code addressing the table behaves very like "standard" SQL. The only change needed is the *type constructor approach* when inserting or updating data, and the *dot notation* needed when selecting data. For example,

```
Insert into people values (
    1,
    occupation(sysdate, null, 'Latest job',75000)
);

delete from people p
where   p.current_occupation.date_end is null
;


create index p_i on people p(p.current_occupation.date_start);
```

Note that the constructor function references the type name whereas the dot notation for identifying data in the table uses the name of the column created in the table. As you can see, the attributes of the embedded type behave very much like ordinary table columns, so much so that you can even build indexes on them. (If you look at the view family xxx_IND_COLUMNS, you will find that the column name for the index p_i defined in the previous example is given as the quoted value "CURRENT_OCCUPATION.DATE_ START.") In fact, if we follow the normal rules of function-based indexes (see Chapter 7), remembering particularly to declare the functions as deterministic, we can even create an index on the method pseudo columns.

If you start nesting types within types, you can still get down to the base-level attributes by applying the dot notation, and can treat these attributes as if they were simple columns in a relational table. Remember the person type created earlier, which included the occupation type as an attribute:

```
create table individual as (
    id   number,
    who person
)
;

select  ind.who.current_occupation.description
from    individual ind
;
```

By and large, then, adding simple object columns to relational tables seems to be little more than a slightly awkward way of adding a few extra columns to the table. What's more, bearing in mind my previous comment that you can't change the attributes of a type once any dependent object exists, objects in relational tables seem to be a liability rather than a benefit.

> *Simple object columns in relational tables seem to add no value and only serve as an opportunity to introduce big maintenance problems.*

Object Tables

Although simple objects can be added as columns to relational tables, a more entertaining possibility comes from creating tables purely of objects. The syntax is simply

```
create table occupations of occupation;
```

Strangely, an object table at first glance looks exactly like a relational table. If you "describe occupations" or "select * from occupations;" you won't be able to see anything to suggest that this isn't just a simple relational table with four columns. It is only when you try "select value(o) from occupations o;" that you get a different display and the nature of the object underlying the table becomes visible:

```
insert into occupations values (
    occupation('24-dec-99','25-dec-99','Father Christmas',100)
);

select * from occupations;

DATE_STAR DATE_END  DESCRIPTION                     REMUNERATION
--------- --------- ------------------------------- ------------
24-DEC-99 25-DEC-99 Father Christmas                         100

select value(o) from occupations o;

VALUE(O)(DATE_START, DATE_END, DESCRIPTION, REMUNERATION)
--------------------------------------------------------------
OCCUPATION('24-DEC-99', '25-DEC-99', 'Father Christmas', 100)
```

If you examine SYS.COL$ after creating an object table you will find two "extra" columns in the table, one named SYS_NC_OID$ with a default of SYS_OP_GUID (globally unique ID) to hold each row's object ID, and the other named SYS_NC_ROWINFO$, which allows you to see the columns of the table presented as an object type when you use the deref() or value() functions.

If you have a look in the view family xxx_INDEXES, you will also find that a strangely named index (SYS_Cnnnnnn) has appeared. The index is named after, and enforces, the unique constraint that is automatically created on the hidden column SYS_NC_OID$. You can specify the name and storage details for this index by using the OIDINDEX clause when you create the table. If you forget, you can always rename the index, although the constraint will still have its original system-generated name:

```
create table occupations of occupation
oidindex occ_id (tablespace oid_ts) -- for the index
tablespace tab_ts                    -- for the table
;

create table occupations of occupation;
alter index sys_c001234 rename to occupations_oid_idx
;
```

The most interesting thing about object tables is the ref() function, which returns a globally unique ID for that object (the SYS_NC_OID$ value for the row). This allows you to define a column type of REF {something} to store the object IDs from another table. In some ways this is rather like creating a parent/child or primary key/foreign key relationship between two tables, but there are some important differences.

If we create a relational table with a column of type "ref occupation," we have two choices with this column: We could allow it to reference any object table of type occupation, or we could restrict it to just the OCCUPATIONS table we created by using the SCOPE feature. We also have the option of appending an extra WITH ROWID clause as part of the column specification to allow Oracle a rapid-access method from the REF column to the target row:

```
create table people (
    id                     number,
    current_occupation     ref occupation   scope is occupations
);
```

To get a value in this REF column, there are a couple of variants of SQL that could be used, all of which make use of the correlation variable (or *table alias* as we traditionally call it). For example,

```
insert into people
select   rownum,ref(o)
from     occupations o
;


insert into people values (
    1,(select ref(o) from occupations o where description='CLERK')
)
;
```

If you have the REFs stored in one table, you can dereference them without naming the target table:

```
select deref(current_occupation) from people;
```

So what are the pros and cons of object tables?

On the plus side, the content of a REF column can refer to a row in any table of the correct type. So, if you habitually design systems where a child table can have many different parents (Figure 15-1), then the benefit of simply dereferencing the column to get to the correct parent data is rather nice. Also, because you don't appear to join the child to its parent, you no longer have to worry about outer joins to cope with "missing parents." A row with a dangling REF (which is what Oracle calls REFs that point to a nonexistent object) or null REF does not disappear from your result set.

On the minus side, the first thing you notice is the double-edge sword of dereferencing. It may be a plus to be able to have dangling REFs and not have to worry about outer joins and multiple parents, but when using REFs you tend not to use declarative referential integrity constraints. This imposes a need for very strict quality control to ensure that some sort of integrity checking is maintained somehow through the code.

There is also the problem of storage. Scoped REFs are 16 bytes that hold the object ID for the row in the SCOPE table. Unscoped REFs are 36 bytes—2 bytes for the length, 2 bytes for structure information, 16 bytes for a row object ID, and 16 bytes for a table object ID. You can only see this by dumping the data block. If you select the column, the output appears to be the same regardless of whether the REF is scoped. If you include the WITH

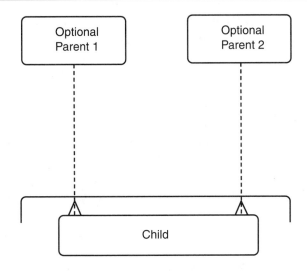

Figure 15-1. A child with two parents.

ROWID clause for REF columns, then the 36 bytes is extended to 42 bytes by the addition of the 6-byte restricted rowid (file.block.row) of the row referenced. Despite the syntax diagrams suggesting otherwise, this option applies only to unscoped REFs—a fact that is mentioned in the concepts manual, but not in the SQL manual.

There is an important performance difference, too, between scoped REFs and unscoped REFs. You cannot index a column containing a REF unless it is a scoped REF. This can be something of a nuisance if you try to build sophisticated cross-referencing mechanisms between object types. It is important to note that if you include a scope on a REF column then you cannot, at a later stage, remove the scope. After all, there may be REFs in the column that would suddenly be too short to point to anything.

The creation of the object table itself includes an overhead of a 16-byte column added to the base definition, and a unique index on that column. All in all, that's a lot of space to waste if you can't find a very positive reason for using an object table.

You are allowed to take a different approach with object tables and specify the "natural" primary key of a table as its object ID with syntax like

```
create table occupations of occupation
(constraint o_pk primary key(date_start,date_end))
object identifier is primary key;
```

The drawback to this is that you can't store REFs to this table in an *unscoped* REF column, which limits the potential benefit of object dereferencing. This is because the referencing table has to be created with (even more) hidden columns to match the primary key.

Actually, there is one very strange, and dangerous, side effect of creating an object table with a primary key object identifier. Oracle creates a clone of your object type with a name like SYS_YOID0000nnnnn on which the table depends. If you accidentally drop this type (which shouldn't be possible, but unfortunately can be done), the table becomes inaccessible and any attempt to drop it will probably crash the database.

Another irritant of using objects with the deref() operator is that you cannot pick a single column from a deref(). There is no syntax of the form "deref(ref_value).attribute." The only way I have found to handle this is to use in-line views:

```
select  p.id, p.occ.date_end
from (
        select
                peo.id,
                deref(peo.current_occupation) occ
        from
                people peo
) p
;
```

Finally, of course, there is always the problem of runtime overhead. In the first case, Oracle executes deref() by applying the stored object ID to the correct unique index unless it is a REF column stored with rowid. However, things get worse if you start to make use of row-level security (see Chapter 21) on the referenced tables as Oracle goes one step further and executes recursive SQL of the following form *for each row* in the main table:

```
select  value(p$)
from    "SCHEMA_NAME"."TAB_NAME" p$
with    snapshot(:2)
where   SYS_NC_OID$ = :1
;
```

Of course, Oracle is always very good at producing unexpected side effects when you start to mix and match new features, and row-level security with object tables is no exception. In this case the quirk shows up in dangling REFs. With a primary key/foreign key constraint in place you cannot delete a parent row without first deleting all the child rows. However, if you implement this relationship using ref()s stored in the child table, then it is possible to delete the parent table without deleting any of the children. (If you choose to use the REFERENCES option for ref types instead of SCOPE IS to restrict the content of the child table, you get referential integrity enforced.

Oracle supplies two new mechanisms for dealing with dangling REFs. The first is a test (similar to the IS NULL test), and the second is an option in the *analyze* command to tidy up dangling REFs. Thus we can issue

```
select * from people where current_occupation is dangling;
```

and

```
analyze table people validate ref update set dangling to null;
```

The little quirk of row-level security and dangling REFs shows up when we apply a security predicate to the OCCUPATIONS table and hide some of its rows. Our first statement reports all rows that reference "hidden" rows as dangling, even though they are not. Fortunately, the second statement does not set these valid, but unresolvable, references to null.

Problems and Quirks

Using persistent objects in the database results in all sorts of hidden items (types, columns, tables, indexes) being created to support object access. The physical overhead may be significant. The side effects can be very unpleasant. One of my drop-everything-for-a-user scripts crashed and permanently damaged one test database I was running because it managed to drop a system-generated type before it dropped the table that depended on it. The dependency was *not* recorded in DBA_DEPENDENCIES.

Your options for changing type definitions are very limited once any other object is dependent on that type. In particular, you cannot change the size of an attribute or add an attribute to a type. This makes the job of a postproduction change much more time-consuming compared with the more traditional fix of *alter table add/modify column* commands.

Object tables have limited value as partitioned tables. Although the table itself can be partitioned, the unique index on the hidden OBJECT-ID column has to be a global index, which more or less defeats the point of partitioning. If you are thinking of using objects in very large databases, this is a pretty good reason for changing your mind (see Chapter 12).

There are some limiting side effects of using objects, and inevitably some bugs when objects are mixed with other features. As an example of the first, if you write a select statement that references an OBJECT column in its GROUP BY clause, the query cannot run as a parallel query. At least, that's what the SQL reference manual says, but the first time I tried it the query seemed to run in parallel. As an example of the second, if you try to create a "before row insert" trigger, which sets the value of an OBJECT column, then any insert statement that does not reference that OBJECT column crashes your session. One possible workaround is to define a default value for the OBJECT column; another is to insert a null value into the OBJECT column.

Strategy Notes

Don't let object enthusiasts get too excited!

The overhead of persistent objects is really rather high, and the added value seems to be nonexistent. Unless you have a huge object-oriented development team with very good development tools, and have an Oracle internals expert on site to tell you what is happening to the database, don't waste effort on it. If you do decide to use objects, make sure you test a real example of every type of critical operation you are going to use, just in case the feature doesn't work properly with objects.

If you create an object table (CREATE TABLE OF {TYPE}), then you can create a REF column in another table that contains references to that type of object—and, in particular, references rows in the object table. The two tables then behave in a fashion similar to the parent/child relationship, with one important difference: Different rows in the child table can hold REFs to different parent tables. There are circumstances when this might be useful.

An interesting detail with row-level security: If you have a parent table with a policy on it, then child rows *joined* to a hidden parent disappear from query results. Child rows that *reference* a hidden parent row do *not* disappear; the parent values simply appear to be blank. Remember, if you have a security policy on the parent, then there is significant overhead in the method Oracle uses to acquire the parent rows.

CHAPTER 16

Collection Objects

In the last chapter I described simple object types. In this chapter I move on to the more complex object types in Oracle—the *collection types*.

There are two collection types in Oracle: the fixed-length list, known as the *varray* (or varying array); and the open-ended list, known, unfortunately, as the *table*.

Although the two collection types can be used in very similar ways in PL/SQL, they have very different storage characteristics in SQL. When a row contains a varray type, the individual elements of a varray are stored in a single structureless clump of data in that row; although, if the varray is large, it can be stored as a blob (see Chapter 17) in a separate data segment. When a row contains a table type, the individual elements of that table type are stored as rows in a separate, notionally nested table, and a parent/child link exists between the two tables in the form of a partly hidden NESTED_TABLE_ID column. This difference in storage methods results in a dramatic difference in the accessibility of the two different types of data.

It is possible to create extremely complex structures using basic object syntax because there are very few limits on how you can nest object definitions within other object definitions. The only clear-cut restriction is that you cannot create a collection of collections. Specifically, you cannot create a varray containing varrays or tables, and you cannot create a table of tables or varrays.

The upshot of this is that (1) by combining several object features into a single structure it is quite easy to break Oracle; (2) it is easy to create structures that require extremely complicated, maintenance-heavy, and inefficient code; and (3) there is no good place to start in a description of how collection objects work.

The rest of this chapter describes the issues of varrays and tables when they are stored in the database as persistent objects. The last section describes some possible benefits you may gain from these collection types when you use them as transient, memory-resident objects.

Varrays

Many applications end up with "repeating columns" defined in the table. Nearly everyone seems to create address tables with columns named ADDRESS_1, ADDRESS_2, ADDRESS_3, and so forth. This strategy is now legal in Oracle 8 with the invention of the varray type, which can be created as a publicly visible type, and then used as a column type. A trivial example is

```
create type address_t as VARRAY(4) of varchar2(32);
/

create table person(name varchar2(30), address address_t);

insert into person values (
    'Tony Blair',
    address_t('11 Downing St', 'London', 'SW1','UK')
)
;        -- example of how to date a book !

select * from person;
```

```
NAME          ADDRESS
----------    --------------------------------------------------
Tony Blair    ADDRESS_T('11 Downing St', 'London', 'SW1', 'UK')
```

We start by declaring an array type that may contain up to four items (this is why a fixed-size list is known as a varying array—the limit is fixed, but the usage may vary between zero and the limit) in which each item is a varchar2(32). Having declared the type, we can immediately use that type as a column type in a relational table.

Note the "function" that has to be used to get data into the table, and that appears in the results of the SELECT from the table. address_t() is the "constructor" function for the address_t data type. Whenever you try to use objects in Oracle, you are almost certain to have to deal with the problem of converting data back and forth from standard data types to object types.

One special point to note is that there is a big difference between the empty object address_t() and the null value. The empty object is an instance of an object with no atomic members; the null value is a complete absence of the object. There is also a third NO DATA option to consider, the object with null members. The following three queries are very different:

```
Select * from person where address is null;
Select * from person where address = address_t();
Select * from person where address = address_t(null,null,null,null);
```

The most important difference perhaps is that the last two queries are illegal and return error "ORA-00932: inconsistent data types" because you are not allowed to compare collection types. Nevertheless it is possible for the PERSON table to have rows that hold empty addresses, or addresses in which every element is null, and the first query cannot find them. For example,

```
insert into person values ('The Flying Dutchman',address_t());
insert into person values ('no-one',address_t(null,null,null,null));
insert into person values ('no-one else', address_t());
```

Note that the constructor for a collection type may be used with no parameters, whereas the constructor for a simple object type must always have a set of parameters supplied. Be careful about setting varray types to empty when you really want them to be null. It is very hard, and very expensive, to find rows with empty varrays. The best legal option I could come up with to solve the problem was the following (the strange syntax of the second half of the union is discussed later):

```
select name from person
minus
(
select name from person where address is null
union
select name
from
    person per ,
    table(per.address) adr
)
;
```

A slightly cheaper piece of code finds the rows in which the address is either the empty address address_t(), or an address that is composed of nothing but null elements:

```
select name from person
minus
select   name
from
    person per ,
    table(per.address) adr
where
    adr.column_value is not null
;
```

Also perverse is the fact that you cannot address the content of the array in the normal array-subscripting fashion (at least from SQL; PL/SQL is a slightly different matter). The following query is *not* valid:

```
select name, address(1) from person
```

This is all part of the basic problem that you cannot handle a single element of an array with SQL. You have to rewrite the entire array if you want to update or add an element. Similarly, it is not possible to create an index on a varray or on an element of a varray.

The consequences of this are threefold. First, you probably have to resort to PL/SQL (or worse) for any processing of tables containing varrays. The cast() and table() operators that I introduce in the next section on table types allow some flexibility in SQL, but are very limited with varrays. Second, a small data change is likely to generate an unnecessarily large volume of rollback and redo, and result in a lot of thrashing about in table data blocks. Third, any attempt to access data based on the values stored in the varray is guaranteed to cause a table scan of the containing table. Clearly, you should not store critical, driving data in varrays.

Given this sledgehammer approach to varray processing, you might ask how severe the impact is going to be when you include varrays in relational tables. Fortunately, Oracle offers an option for damage control.

By default, a "small" varray (which in this context means slightly less than 4K) is stored in-line in the table, apparently as a single column (although there are numerous, extra hidden columns in the SYS.COL$ definition). However, if Oracle calculates that the maximum size of the varray is too large, it insists on the varray being treated as a LOB (see Chapter 17), and creates a LOB segment for it (adding even more hidden columns to the table, and strangely named indexes as it does so).

In fact, even if the varray is not large it is still possible to insist that Oracle treat it as a LOB and store it in a separate data segment with its own index segment with the following syntax:

```
create table person(
    name     varchar2(30),
    address address_t
)
varray address store as lob address_lob
(DISABLE STORAGE IN ROW);
```

The benefit of doing this is that any processing you do on the varray does not cause the rest of the table to become fragmented and produce chained or migrated rows. The downside is that any access to the varray component of the table requires at least two additional I/Os (one to the LOB index and another to the LOB segment). Also, you need to consider the trade-off between the benefits of storing the varray out of line, and the potential for huge amounts of wasted space, because each LOB requires at least a single block (LOBs do not share blocks).

Unfortunately, the nominally legal syntax for specifying a tablespace for the varray is considered to be an invalid option, so the LOB segment and the LOB index segment are put in the same tablespace as the table itself. Thus, you won't be able to get all the separation of activity that you might like. One workaround is to create everything in the tablespace in which you want the LOB to go, then move the table.

Internally, an inline varray consists of a few header bytes, a couple of bytes for the size for the entire varray, a couple more for the usage count, and a couple more for the size of each of the entries. Thus the overhead is quite a handful of bytes. If you choose to store the varray out of line, the pointer to the LOB index is 34 bytes, before you worry about the LOB index space itself (which you cannot coalesce or rebuild) and the LOB space itself.

So where does this leave us? Varrays are lists of fixed maximum length. It is difficult to address items in the array individually from SQL, and you probably have to write PL/SQL to change the contents of a VARRAY column. For space management purposes, varrays can be stored outside the table, but you have very little control over separating varrays from their tables. Frankly, its quite hard to think of any good reason why you should use them. The idea of using a few repeating columns seems so much less expensive and so much more flexible.

Tables

Objects of type table are more flexible than varray objects. The most significant difference is that although a varray is a list with a fixed limit to its size, a table is an unlimited list. The effects of this are that Oracle allows much more of the structure of the table to be visible, and never stores it in line with its "parent." This is best explained with an example.

First let's create a simple object type, then a table type, and finally a relational table with a column of our table type:

```
create type jpl_item as object (n1 number, v1 varchar2(32));
/

create type jpl_tab_type as table of jpl_item;
/

create table demo_nest (
    id      number,
    nest    jpl_tab_type
)
nested table nest store as t_nested
;
```

This last command builds three data segments—all in the same tablespace.

1. The first is the parent table DEMO_NEST, which has a hidden column called SYS_NC0000200003$ that contains a 16-byte globally unique meaningless ID.

2. The second data segment is the nested table itself, named T_NESTED as required. If you describe this table you find that it has two columns named N1 and V1—the attribute names in the underlying type. There are, however, two extra, hidden columns—a column called NESTED_TABLE_ID, which is a 16-byte ID associating nested table rows with their row parent table through the SYS_Ncxxxxxyyyyy$ column, and a column named SYS_NC_ROWINFO$, which displays the data in the table in its object form rather than in a relational/attribute form. This table is listed in the view family xxx_OBJECT_TABLES, not in xxx_TABLES.

3. The third object is an index, which is given a name like SYS_C002528, that represents a unique constraint on the SYS_NCxxxxxyyyyy$ column of the DEMO_NEST table. This index serves two purposes. It ensures that accidents don't happen that allow nested rows to belong to two different parents, and it also allows a rapid-access path from the nested table to the containing table. There is an anomaly here. If you create

the containing table as an IOT (see Chapter 14), then this constraint and the associated index are *not* created; this is probably a bug.

Having taken the first tiny steps in producing a nested table (Figure 16-1), what do you do next? You have a choice. You can either fix up the storage and performance mess you have just created, or you can learn how to get at the data. Let's start by clearing up the problems.

First, all three segments are in the same tablespace, and you can't stop this from happening. The first thing to do is to rebuild the index somewhere more appropriate, and change its name. (You could be really wicked and do this by dropping and re-creating the constraint.) Second, you may want to move the nested table and do something about its storage clause.

Next, nested tables are about open-ended lists of data associated with a parent row. In theory, a query for a parent is likely to want to collect the whole object (in other words, all the nested rows) at the same time. We don't have an index on the nested table that lets us get from a parent row to its nested rows efficiently, so it's time to create an index on the nested table. This is really rather cute because you have to create an index on a column that apparently does not exist. Describing the T_NESTED table mentioned earlier, you can only see columns N1 and V1. The index you need has to be created on, or at

Nominal-Structure

Row A	1	A_A	1_1
		A_B	1_2
Row B	2	B_A	2_1
		B_B	2_2
		B_C	2_3
		B_D	2_4
Row C	3	C_A	3_1
		C_B	3_2
		C_C	3_3

Actual Structure

Row A	1	5F7A3AF01C0711D48111000000000000
Row B	2	5F7A3AF11C0711D48111000000000000
Row C	3	5F7A3AF21C0711D48111000000000000

Parent Table

5F7A3AF01C0711D48111000000000000	A_A	1_1
5F7A3AF01C0711D48111000000000000	A_B	1_2
5F7A3AF11C0711D48111000000000000	B_A	2_1
5F7A3AF11C0711D48111000000000000	B_B	2_2
5F7A3AF11C0711D48111000000000000	B_C	2_3
5F7A3AF11C0711D48111000000000000	B_D	2_4
5F7A3AF21C0711D48111000000000000	C_A	3_1
5F7A3AF21C0711D48111000000000000	C_B	3_2
5F7A3AF21C0711D48111000000000000	C_C	3_3

Nested Table

Figure 16-1. Implementation of nested tables.

least start with, a column called NESTED_TABLE_ID. In fact, we can do better than just creating the index. Part of the reason for using a nested table is that we expect to have reasonably long lists of rows for a single parent, and presumably we always expect to associate the nested rows with their parent. Because we also recall that NESTED_TABLE_ID is 16 bytes long, we can optimize the index by eliminating the repetitions of NESTED_TABLE_ID:

```
create index nt_idx on t_nested(nested_table_id)
compress 1;
```

In fact, we may be able to do even better than this. If we can identify something about the data model that allows us to guarantee that each combination of parent row and nested row is unique, we can declare a primary key on the nested table at creation time, and then build the nested table as an IOT, ensuring that all the nested rows for a given parent are physically clustered at all times. The syntax starts to get messy, so here's an example:

```
create table demo_nest (
    id      number,
    nest    jpl_tab_type
)
nested table nest store as t_nested
(
    (constraint tn_pk primary key (nested_table_id, n1))
    organization index
    compress 1
)
;
```

If you track the resulting bits through the view families xxx_ALL_TABLES and xxx_INDEXES, you will find that you now have two tables and two indexes: a relational table, DEMO_NEST, with normal index SYS_Cnnnnn (representing the unique constraint on the hidden column); and an object table, T_NESTED, of type jpl_item, with unique index TN_PK of type 'IOT-TOP'.

Of course, at this point you have no statistics on any objects, so you should use **_analyze table_** to generate some. Watch out. When you analyze the parent table you don't get any statistics on the nested table; you have to analyze it separately. (This isn't the only trap of a nested table column being an independent table. If you export a table containing a nested table, the two physical segments are exported in two separate transactions, so the subsequent import may import inconsistent data. The correct strategy is to export nested tables using the CONSISTENT=Y option.)

> *Nested tables are not analyzed as part of the parent table. They have to be analyzed separately.*

Using IOTs for nested tables may be the most efficient thing to do, but you should (as always) consider your data access requirements carefully before taking this step. If your only access path is going to be from the parent to the nested table, then it's a good step. If you want to identify data in the nested table and then find the associated parent table, you may want to reconsider.

This brings us to the question of what you can do in SQL to get at nested tables. A simple test (which shows how bulky the SQL code can get with object types) is as follows:

```
Insert into demo_nest values(
    1,
    jpl_tab_type(
        jpl_item(1,'Item One'),
        jpl_item(2,'Item Two')
    )
)
;

select * from demo_nest;
   ID                                                    NEST(N1, V1)
----- -------------------------------------------------------------------
    1 JPL_TAB_TYPE(JPL_ITEM(1, 'Item One'), JPL_ITEM(2, 'Item Two'))
```

The output isn't elegant, but the query works. Is there a way to get a more tabular report in SQL? The answer is yes, but the method is a little surprising. You join, or even "outer join," the nested table to the containing table with a correlation variable (a.k.a. table alias) and the table() function:

```
select
    dem.id, nst.n1, nst.v1
from
    demo_nest          dem,
    table(dem.nest)(+)  nst
```

```
     ID          N1 V1
---------- ---------- ---------------------------------
        1           1 Item One one
        1           2 Item One two
```

The table() function is the most interesting thing here, and is demonstrated in more detail later. It takes a collection object as an input and makes it appear to be a relational table. (In Oracle 8.0, the function was given the rather uncomfortable name of THE()). The most bizarre thing, though, is the way that the FROM clause uses the table alias from the DEMO_TEST table and references a column from that table to convert it into a table. Effectively the SQL code that executes is

```
select
    dem.id, nst.n1, nst.v1
from
    demo_nest           dem,
    t_nested            nst
where
    nst.nested_table_id = dem.sys_nc0000200003$
;
```

Of course, this "notional" SQL won't actually work. In fact, you get an error on the simple statement

```
select * from t_nested;
              *
ERROR at line 1:
ORA-22812: cannot reference nested table column's storage table
```

It seems we can't get at the nested data independently of the parent table, which could be a bit of a performance blow for traditional SQL reporting. In fact, the Oracle engine can, and frequently does, access the nested table directly by using the hint /*+NESTED_TABLE_GET_REFS */. However, it probably wouldn't be safe to assume that this hint will work in future versions of Oracle. It could well be a temporary measure that Oracle Corporation is using until they come up with some faster internal mechanisms.

There is an anomaly here. We have seen that we cannot officially write SQL code that accesses the nested table directly. On the other hand, we are allowed to create indexes, and not just the critical nested_table_id index, on nested tables:

```
create index t_nest_i on t_nested(n1);
```

But if you can't query the data at all, why have an index that is supposed to allow you to query it efficiently? Clearly we may want to select nested data very precisely based on some column in the nested table itself. Performance is going to be disastrous if we have to do a table scan of the parent table to find the associated nested table rows, and then check each nested table row for a given condition. Consider, for example, the following query, written first in its notional form and then in the form that we would actually have to use:

```
select /*+ nested_table_get_refs */
        v1, count(*)
from    t_nested
where   n1 between 20100 and 20200
group by
        v1
;


select
        nst.v1, count(*)
from

        demo_nest       dem,
        table(dem.nest) nst
where   nst.n1 between 20100 and 20200
group by
        nst.v1
;
```

Despite appearances to the contrary, the access path for the correct syntax of the second query is exactly the one you would hope for. In other words, it behaves as if the parent table simply did not exist in the FROM clause. This means that you can effectively treat the nested table just like any other table, using the same indexing strategies and getting the same performance. There is one important distinction relating to indexing, though, when nested tables do not behave in the slightest bit like relational tables. It is not possible to declare a referential integrity constraint on a nested table, even though you can create the index that would allow Oracle to support the constraint efficiently. This does cause people a lot of grief, particularly when they start to create nested tables of REFs. Unfortunately, there is no realistic workaround to the problem.

What about inserts, updates, and deletes on the nested table elements? It should be obvious that adding a new item to a nested table requires you to access the table through the parent. After all, you have to get NESTED_ TABLE_ID from somewhere, and you can't get it from anywhere else (not legally, anyway). This means that an insert to a nested table, which could be viewed as an update to the parent table, can be done to only one parent row at a time—not the most relational or efficient way of doing things.

Of course, we could execute a statement like

```
update demo_nest
set nest = jpl_tab_type (...)
where etc . . .
;
```

This is rather inefficient, though, because Oracle's undercover activity is to delete all the current related rows from the nested table and to insert a new set, using array inserts. This could be serious overkill if you were just trying to add one more item to the current nested list.

The more appropriate approach uses the table() function to turn the nested column into something that appears to be a table. The same method works for updates to items in the nested table, and deletions of specific items from the nested table:

```
insert into table(select nest from demo_nest where id = 1)
values (2,'number 2')
;
```

```
update table(select nest from demo_nest where id = 1)
set v1 = 'No. 2'
where n1 = 2
;
```

```
delete from table(select nest from demo_nest where id = 1)
where n1 = 2
;
```

In effect, Oracle creates dynamically a minitable consisting of the relevant rows from the nested table and performs a simple, efficient DML on this table. The resulting volume of work that Oracle does is then kept to a minimum.

There is one important drawback to this mechanism. You can affect only one parent row at a time. Clearly, objects are for front-end OLTP systems, not for large-scale data-massaging systems. Another point to back this up: Queries that reference nested tables cannot switch to parallel execution. You can't even use this type of object in large-scale reporting systems, despite the trick of the table() function.

There is one point that you should bear in mind if you write code that affects the individual elements of a nested table. As you modify the content of the nested table, the parent row is locked, so two users cannot modify nested items for the same parent, even if they want to modify completely different items. This is perfectly reasonable because all the nested rows are logically part of the parent row. From a practical point of view, it does give you another good reason for ignoring objects and using tables with referential integrity constraints.

One final point about inserts: I mentioned in the section on varrays that there is a big difference between the empty object jpl_tab_type() and the null value—namely, that the empty object is an instance of an object with no atomic members, whereas the null value is a complete absence of the object. This is most significant when you starting using nested tables. If you set a nested table column to null, then you will not be able to use the ATOMIC INSERT method to add items to the list. You first have to set the column to the empty object:

```
update demo_nest
set     nest = null
where   id = 1;

insert into table(  select nest from demo_nest where id = 1)
values (1,'number 1')

ERROR at line 1:
ORA-22908: reference to NULL table value

update demo_nest
set     nest = jpl_tab_type()
where   id = 1;

insert into table(select nest from demo_nest where id = 1)
values (1,'number 1');

1 row created
```

Although inserts, updates, and deletes on nested tables have to be done one parent row at a time, a nested table is an open-ended list, so you may find that PL/SQL (or third-generation language [3GL]) routines particularly operate more efficiently if you can select lots of parent details, then be a little choosy about which sets of nested tables you subsequently query. Oracle allows this to happen through the LOCATOR mechanism. When you define a column as a nested table you have the option of specifying that it should return as a VALUE (the default) or a LOCATOR:

```
create table demo_nest (
    id      number,
    nest    jpl_tab_type
)
nested table nest store as t_nested
return as LOCATOR
;
```

If you return as VALUE, a query that selects the nested column by name returns the actual contents of the nested table, which means all relevant rows and columns. If you return as LOCATOR, the query returns a nested table ID and an SCN, and your program can subsequently choose to use these values to fire off a separate SQL statement to the database, querying the nested table for a much smaller set of data.

Because the program does not know whether the nested table has been defined to return values or locators, Oracle supplies a package (UTL_COLL) to allow the program to check at runtime whether it has values or a locator, and take appropriate action.

For example, we can change the nested table in our DEMO_NEST table to return as LOCATOR. We can run the following PL/SQL procedure that either sends a SQL statement to the server to get one number from the nested table or uses the local in-memory image of the nested table to calculate a running total. The first mechanism is appropriate if the nested table is returning LOCATOR; the other should be used if it is returning VALUE:

```
alter table demo_nest
modify nested table nest
return as locator;

declare
    cursor c1 is
    select id, nest
    from demo_nest;
    m_total     number;

begin
    for p_row in c1 loop
        if (utl_coll.IS_LOCATOR(p_row.nest)) then
            select sum(n1)
            into m_total
            from table(cast(p_row.nest as jpl_tab_type));
        else        -- the VARRAY is already in memory
```

```
                    m_total := 0;
                    for i in 1..p_row.nest.count loop
                        m_total := m_total + p_row.nest(i).n1;
                    end loop;
                end if;
            end loop;
        end;
        /
```

The benefit of this approach is that we may (for suitable types of activity) achieve a huge drop in network traffic when running client/server reporting. The greatest effect appears when the sizes of the nested tables are large, either in terms of row width or number of rows per parent.

There is a temporary problem though. If you also run SQL reports in SQL∘Plus against the nested tables, there is a bug in the code that handles some form of dictionary structure look-up. This results in a very inefficient piece of recursive SQL being run for *every* parent row. The performance impact is catastrophic, so don't use the LOCATOR feature for nested tables until this is fixed (or never use SQL∘Plus against the table).

One thing you may note in the previous sample code is the use of the cast() function. To me, this is probably the most beneficial feature of the entire object implementation, and is largely the topic of the next section.

One final point about nested tables: A nested table cannot be partitioned. You can, however, create a partitioned table that contains a nested table, but if you do so, you probably lose all the benefits of partitioning. The nested table won't be partitioned; it will be a single, monolithic table, and the implicitly created unique index back to the parent table will be a global index until you drop and re-create the constraint. Then you have to do funny things that may be unsupported because unique indexes on partitioned tables have to contain the partitioning columns. Furthermore, you won't be able to drop or truncate any of the partitions of the parent table because you get Oracle error "ORA-02266: unique/primary keys in table referenced by enabled foreign keys."

Transient Collections

So far we have investigated collections when they are to be stored in relational tables. This section deals with table types as pure memory structures. The reason for doing this is that table types can be made more or less indistinguishable from real tables, so code that made use of real tables for scratch pad operations can now save on I/O by using in-memory collection types (possibly by being extravagant with CPU time).

The important functions to look at are multiset(), cast(), and table(). As mentioned earlier, the table() function allows you to tell Oracle to treat a table (or other collection) type as if it was a real table. Conversely, the multiset() and cast() functions allow you to tell Oracle to treat a relational table (or, more specifically, the result set from a SQL statement) as an object of type table.

There are many features to in-memory table types, but the only concept I wish to cover here is that you can use table types in places where historically you would use temporary tables (or repeat SQL time and time again). Let's look at a simple example:

```
create type jpl_item as object (
    owner   varchar2(30),
    type    varchar2(18),
    extents number
);
/
create type jpl_tab_type as table of jpl_item;
/

declare
    m_tab1  jpl_tab_type := jpl_tab_type();
    m_tab2  jpl_tab_type := jpl_tab_type();
begin
    select
        cast(
            multiset(
                select  owner, segment_type, extents
                from    dba_segments
            ) as jpl_tab_type
        )
    into m_tab1
    from dual;
end;
```

In this example we execute a simple SQL statement, but we have predefined a simple object type that matches the structure of a returned row, and a collection type of that object type.

We then use cast(multiset(...)) to tell Oracle to turn a list of rows into a collection of simple objects. Unfortunately, we cannot assign the result directly to a variable, so we have to select it into a variable (from dual).

To reverse the process—in other words, to make a table type look like a relational table so that we can use it in SQL—we use the table() operator. There is one little oddity with this that may disappear in the future. We have to tell Oracle exactly what table type is supposed to come out of the cast() function. The basic syntax, which we saw earlier, is

```
select  *
from    table(cast(m_tab1 as jpl_tab_type));
```

which we could embed in something like

```
select
    cast(
        multiset(
            select  null, type, sum(extents)
            from    table(cast(m_tab1 as jpl_tab_type))
            group by type
        ) as jpl_tab_type
    )
into m_tab2
from dual;
```

Note how in this example we first turn m_tab1 (our PL/SQL variable of type jpl_tab_type) into a relational table, which we then aggregate with our *select* statement, before casting the result back to a table type for further processing.

In effect, by combining these two steps we have created a temporary table, and a summary of that temporary table in memory, without generating any rollback or redo.

It gets more interesting than this example, though, because you can pass variables of type table as parameters to procedures and functions, and expose variables of type table in packages. This means you can actually call a procedure to populate a variable of type table, and then return it to a standard SQL report as the result of a function (see the following example).

Of course, there is a trade-off. We avoid I/O by using memory and CPU time, and it is important to measure the costs and benefits. At a site that I visited recently, the limiting factor of a massive reporting process that had to occur concurrently with a massive, continuous data load was the I/O resulting from the reporting. The design called for "current" data to be copied to "history" while being processed to produce a dozen different summary reports. (In this context, "history" was anything more than 60 minutes old, and the volume was approximately 1,000,000 rows per hour.) The initial design copied batches of 1,000 rows at a time into various temporary tables then ran numerous aggregation reports from those tables before dropping them. With proper temporary tables (see Chapter 9), the cost of the temporary tables wasn't too high, but there was still lots of scope for contention and I/O. By changing to a strategy of using table types, the memory and CPU costs shot up quite dramatically (CPU cost increased by a factor of four), but the contention and I/O cost disappeared.

There are still some problems with this approach. In the first case you should not create very large TABLE variables or you are likely to experience a system crash. The limit seems to be a few megabytes. Another problem is a bug in sorting collection variables. If your query to generate the collection includes an ORDER BY clause, then you will probably find that the entire collection is a duplicate of the last row. I gather this has been fixed in version 8.1.6. You should also remember that these in-memory table types could result in strange access paths under the CBO. They have no statistics, and the CBO has no clue whatsoever about how large they may be. So if you join them to real tables, watch out for some unusual access paths, including the delightfully named COLLECTION ITERATOR (PICKLER FETCH).

Finally, I find it hard to resist my favorite application of this technique—the nonexistent table to generate a sequence of numbers. A frequently asked question is, How do I select the numbers from, say, 1 to 200? This is often answered with 'select rownum from all_objects where rownum <= 200'. Here's an alternative solution that doesn't depend on the preexistence of a large enough table to get enough row numbers.

We start by defining a table type that is simply an array of numbers. We then create a function that returns a table of that type, and takes an integer as its input to specify how many rows the returned table should have. To take advantage of the function in SQL, we simply call the function passing in the number of rows we want to see, then turn the result into a relational table with the table() call, and select the row number:

```
create or replace type int_tab_type as table of integer;
/

create or replace function get_ints (
    how_many    in       number
) return int_tab_type
as
    -- declare a variable, and set it to the empty array
    v_int_tab   int_tab_type := int_tab_type ();
```

```
begin
    -- add the required number of elements to the array.
    v_int_tab.extend(how_many);
    return v_int_tab;
end;
/


select   rownum  id
from     table(cast(get_ints(10) as int_tab_type));
```

Once you have seen this type of table()/cast() trick done a couple of times, you soon discover that there are numerous ways in which you can use it. How often, for instance, have you heard the question, How do I return the result of a query to the user in batches of 20 rows and allow the user to scroll backward and forward between pages? One possible answer, which I go into in more detail in Chapter 19, is to use functions that load queries into TABLE variables, and then call functions to return subsets of those variables.

A Cautionary Tale

It is possible to create all sorts of interesting structures using collection types and different table types. You may even be able to justify using some of them. Before you do, though, remember that it is important to be in control of your database. You need to be able to move data segments around, name them sensibly, restructure them, and so on. If you can't do this easily, you can soon run into silly space management problems.

So try this experiment with Oracle 8.1.5. Create a simple object type that contains a LOB (see Chapter 17), and then create a corresponding table type. We could rationalize this by claiming that each row in the table represents a book, with an ISBN and the book text:

```
create or replace type jpl_lob_row as object(n1 number, c1 clob);
/

create or replace type jpl_lob_table as table of jpl_lob_row;
/
```

Now that we have a collection type, we can create a relational table that has a column of this abstract data type:

```
create table nest_lob (
    id  number,
    jlt jpl_lob_table
)
nested table jlt store as jlt_lob_tab
tablespace users
;
```

This gives us five segments in the database:

1. **NEST_LOB**—The data segment for the base table
2. **SYS_Cnnnnnn**—A unique index on the OBJECT_ID column of table NEST_LOB
3. **JLT_LOB_TAB**—A data segment for the nested table
4. **SYS_LOBnnnnnnnnnnC00004$$**—The LOB data segment
5. **SYS_ILBnnnnnnnnnnC00004$$**—The LOB index segment

After several fruitless attempts to rewrite the code to specify the LOB segment name and tablespace, you give up and write the following SQL code to place the segment where you want with a sensible name:

```
alter table jlt_lob_tab
move lob (c1)
store as jlt_lob
tablespace auto_data
;
```

```
Table altered.
```

You will find that Oracle has indeed moved the LOB segment. The only problem is that it hasn't changed its name, and it hasn't moved it to the requested tablespace. This isn't the only problem I have come across with legal commands not quite managing to work, but it is one of the harmless ones that I am prepared to pass on.

There is a serious point to this example, of course. You may plan and size your tablespaces and data files based on the assumption that you can place objects wherever you want. If you do start building slightly exotic structures you need to test the limits of how easily you can move the separate components of those structures.

Problems and Quirks

The diagrams in the Oracle 8i SQL reference manual for ***create/alter table*** commands form a vast, tangled network in which many of the apparently legal options result in error messages that state you are trying to do something illegal or have the wrong syntax. (For example, the ***alter table*** command suggests that varrays can be returned as LOCATOR rather than VALUE. This is not true.

The options for including persistent objects in tables are vast. For example, you could, in theory, create an IOT that holds the pointer to a large varray (requiring a LOB segment and index) in an overflow segment and a nested table that was also index organized with its own overflow. If you actually try to do this, you may find some features that don't work at all, and a couple of others that may crash the system. (Getting all the different segments into the right tablespaces with the right names and storage clauses is tough.) There are still plenty of fairly serious deficiencies (and bugs) in the OBJECT option.

One perfectly reasonable restriction on varrays and table types is that they cannot contain varrays or table types. A less reasonable restriction is that you cannot create a varray or a table of LOBs.

Varray types and table types cannot have methods associated with them. In particular, you cannot compare varrays or tables; however, you can create a type that contains a varray or table and associate methods with that type. This leads to some strange side effects, so you are probably not really supposed to do it. One of the sillier side effects comes when you try to create a relational table holding a type that contains a table type. If you specify a nested table storage clause you get error "ORA-22912: specified column or attribute is not a nested table type," but if you don't specify a nested table storage clause you get error "ORA-22913: must specify table name for nested table column or attribute."

The code to handle complex object types is fairly unwieldy and nonintuitive. Apart from casting varray types and table types into cursors and back again, the handling of collection types depends on stepping through the data one row at a time. Furthermore, the stored image of a varray type cannot be updated piecewise. The whole array has to be replaced, generating an excessive amount of rollback and redo.

Partitioned tables and nested tables do not mix. If you create a nested table in a partitioned table, most of the benefits of partitioning are eliminated.

Parallel execution and nested tables do not mix. Any query that actually involves joining to a nested table is serialized.

A common favorite with nested tables is to create a table type of REFs. However, because (1) you cannot create indexes on REFs unless they are scoped, (2) you can't create referential constraints on columns of nested tables, and (3) you can't currently get an object's ID value in a trigger, it is very difficult to enforce integrity on such nested tables. Objects are quite hard to work with, and the relational method is often much easier to code and is faster to operate.

Nested tables are often treated by Oracle completely independent of their parent table. In particular, the ***analyze*** command has to be applied separately, and an export including a table with a nested table has to be done with CONSISTENT = Y.

If you are going to use nested tables in standard SQL∘Plus reports, be very cautious about returning the nested table as LOCATOR. This can be effective inside PL/SQL blocks and 3GLs, but there is a bug in the implementation that results in a very slow, recursive SQL query being executed once per containing row when the table is accessed from pure SQL.

Table type collections can use a lot of CPU time and memory. They should be restricted to a few thousand rows, and currently should avoid ORDER BY clauses.

Strategy Notes

I know that I've said this before, but don't let object enthusiasts get too excited. If you do use collection types, make sure that there is an efficient access path for all your important queries.

If you are going to use varrays, make sure you are thoroughly convinced that they will be a good thing. Basically, don't expect high performance; use them only if you have a very good front end that can handle them "transparently," and only store "collateral" data in them (in other words, data that you want to report but don't want to target queries on).

As a rough guideline, if you do use varrays, disable storage in the row unless you can guarantee that the varray values are very small (200 bytes on average for small data blocks). This figure can be increased if you have large block sizes and always expect to use the varray data whenever you fetch the containing rows. However, you do need to trade off this figure against the fact that when stored out of line as a LOB, the smallest unit of storage is one Oracle block per LOB value. (Ideally, Oracle could do with a LOB LIMIT clause on the varray so that you can specify the largest varray that can be stored in-line. The default of 3,960 bytes is really too awkward.)

When using object tables, make sure you plan the build stage carefully. There are many tasks that have to be accomplished to get all the objects in the right place with the correct storage characteristics. Remember also that you need to build at the very least a single column index on NESTED_TABLE_ID.

Perhaps the most important current features of collection types are that the type declaration is visible to SQL and—in conjunction with the cast(), multiset(), and table() operators—allows for some interesting "virtual table" tricks to minimize I/O without resorting to procedural coding through PL/SQL.

Using user-defined table types as PL/SQL variables, especially in conjunction with the cast() function, may be a very convenient way of holding and manipulating reasonably small volumes of temporary data without the need to use physical temporary tables. The saving in physical I/O may outweigh the cost of learning the slightly awkward syntax needed.

You may be able to reduce I/O requirements and contention costs associated with producing several reports of the same dataset by using the table() and cast(multiset()) functions to switch table data back and forth from table type collection variables. Look carefully at the savings to be gained from proper temporary tables (see Chapter 8) and the /*+ APPEND */ hint before pursuing this path.

CHAPTER 17

Handling Large Objects

For most of this book I have described how the newer features of Oracle allow you to get the best out of your system. Most of the advice could be summed up as a directive to recognize which features improve performance by reducing I/O.

Now we come to LOBs—a data type that encourages you to flood huge amounts of formless data in and out of your database with consummate ease, with the potential to make any performance benefits you gain elsewhere appear to be a tiny drop in a massive ocean of endless I/O.

The best thing that can be said about LOBs is that in their binary LOB (BLOB), character LOB (CLOB), and national character LOB (NCLOB) forms they are far more flexible and less damaging than the LONGs that preceded them. In their BFILE form they are much more closely integrated with the database than the "home-grown" mechanisms for storing filenames that were the other alternative in earlier versions of Oracle.

Internal or External

Oracle offers two strategies for handling LOBs. You can leave them outside the database as read-only files (BFILES) or you can copy them into the database (BLOBS, CLOBS, or NCLOBS), in which case you can update them through database calls. Although there are differences in storage overhead and performance to consider, and minor variations in what you can actually do once you have "opened" one of these objects, the programmatic interface is the same irrespective of the type of the object.

There are two extremes of processing that may help you choose whether to store LOBs inside or outside the database. If you have a relatively small number of very large files, then it is probably sensible to keep the files outside the database. The operating system can handle reasonable numbers of files perfectly well, and there is little point in having them in the database. If you are handling very large numbers of relatively small files, then it is probably sensible to keep them inside the database because file systems are generally not very good at handling very large numbers of objects, and Oracle is.

As an example of the latter setup, I was asked some time ago to draft a design document for a database that would, over a period of several years, accumulate the details of an estimated 60,000,000 application forms. Each form would have some highly structured data, but each form would also hold a signature and a small picture, which were to be digitized and stored on the database.

Clearly there was no point in trying to store 120,000,000 image files, each approximately 64KB, on a file system. (Quick arithmetic check: That is a total of roughly 7.5TB. It's easy to make a database sound big when you pad it with pictures.) Fortunately, Oracle 8 was around so we could appeal to BLOBs as the obvious mechanism for holding all these images.

At the time, though, the only available version of Oracle was 8.0.4, which meant that the application had to be more complex than desired, or the administrative overhead would be a pain because version 8.0.4 would not support LOBs in a partitioned table, as version 8.1.5 now does. At 7.5TB, the only sensible option was to partition and do some home-grown fake partitioning for the LOB side of the system. However, because LOBs have to be handled through PL/SQL packages, this wasn't actually too much of a problem.

Why LOBs?

Before going into detail about how LOBs work, it is worth reviewing the enormous differences between LOBs and their predecessor—the LONG:

- You cannot copy LONGs unless you are prepared to write a 3GL program to do so, or take advantage of a hideously inefficient PL/SQL approach to move it 32KB at a time. LOBs can be handled very efficiently by built-in packages.

- LONGs cannot participate in distributed transactions, which is something of a handicap for document replication systems. A LOB can be copied from one database to another with a simple command—"insert into remote table select lob_column from local table"—and can be included in normal replication.

- You can have only one LONG column in a table. For something like a picture-and-signature database, this makes for an awkward implementation.

- Updating a LONG is an all-or-nothing process, generating a huge amount of rollback and redo, creating havoc with read consistency, and (because of the generic space management features of free lists) often wasting a huge amount of space in tables. LOBs can be updated in pages, and there is a level of control over how much rollback and redo are generated. A completely different strategy ensures that read consistency is possible with a fairly predictable and consistent overhead.

- You couldn't actually *do* anything with LONGs, except read them or replace them. With LOBs you can search, compare, append, strip, and generally emulate typical text-processing functions from within the normal SQL environment.

The list goes on. Suffice it to say that LONGs were very limited in use, and had many undesirable limitations and side effects that have been eliminated for LOBs.

There are still some limitations applicable to LOBs, largely to do with the problems of either sheer size or the POINTER/STORAGE mechanism that Oracle uses to handle them, but the remaining limitations are not serious and can often be circumvented reasonably tidily. Note that you still can't do very much with LOBs in basic SQL; most of the functionality requires you to make use of a special PL/SQL package.

Working with LOBs

Let's start with a simple SQL statement to create a table holding some LOBs:

```
create table test_lobs (
    id                  number(5),
    raw_bytes           number(10),
    raw_content         blob,
    text_bytes          number(10),
    text_content        clob,
    file_bytes          number(10),
    file_content        bfile
)
lob (raw_content) store as raw_lob(
    tablespace auto_data
    -- could have a storage clause here: storage ( etc )
    disable storage in row
    index raw_lob_i
);
```

The table is designed to hold as many as three LOBs per row—two internal and one external.

Based on traditional practices of handling LONGs, I have also included a LENGTH column for each LOB. You couldn't find the length of a LONG, so it was best to store it in the table as you created the LONG. (Have a look at the Oracle data dictionary table underlying view family xxx_VIEWS for an example of this technique.) It is easy to find the length of a LOB in Oracle 8, but it wastes resources to do so unnecessarily. The number(10) declared for the BYTE_COUNT columns should be large enough to hold the number 4,294,967,296 (or 4GB), which is the current size limit for LOB types and is twice the size of LONG.

Finally, I elected to use some of the options on one of the two internal LOBs that describe how it should be stored in the database. Specifically, I insisted that the LOB data for the BLOB raw_content never be stored in-line in the table, gave a name to the data segment that should store the BLOB, dictated the tablespace that should be used for the data, and named the index segment that should be used by Oracle to keep track of the chunks that make up the various versions of the BLOB.

At this point you can actually insert, update, and delete rows using SQL, but you won't be able to touch the BFILE column, and you won't be able to select the BLOB, CLOB, or BFILE columns without getting SQL∘Plus error "SP2-0678: column or attribute type can not be displayed by SQL∘Plus." The limitations of SQL also mean that you can insert only very short LOBs into the table:

```
insert into test_lobs (id, text_content)
values (1, 'This is a little LOB');

insert into test_lobs (id,raw_content)
values (2,hextoraw('47656b6b6f'));

update test_lobs set text_content = null where id = 1;

update test_lobs set text_content = empty_clob()
where text_content is null;
```

Looking at the view family xxx_OBJECTS after creating this table, you discover there that you have created three new objects:

1. **test_lob** of type table
2. **raw_lob** of type LOB
3. **text_lob** of type LOB

But looking at the view family xxx_SEGMENTS after creating this table, you discover a total of five new segments with names like

1. **test_lob** of type table
2. **raw_lob** of type LOB segment
3. **raw_lob_I** of type LOB index
4. **SYS_LOB000025812C00005$$** of type LOB segment
5. **SYS_ILOB000025812C00005$$** of type LOB index

The two strangely named segments are the result of failing to specify how the TEXT_LOB column should be stored. The choice of numbers in the system-generated names identifies the fact that the LOB is column five of object 25812.

In the absence of the LOB clause, data for the TEXT_LOB column is stored in the same tablespace as the table itself, and "short" LOBs are stored in-line in the table. In this context, "short" means anything up to approximately 3,960 bytes, so it seems sensible to opt for out-of-line storage. Having said this, the minimum space allocated to a single out-of-line LOB is a whole block. So if your LOB sizes are mostly in the 2 to 8KB size, the most effective storage strategy is not always obvious.

The feature of being able to name the index segment is no longer documented in Oracle 8.1, and the use of the LOBINDEX clause is deprecated. With version 8.0 a LOB segment and its index could be in separate table-spaces, but with version 8.1 they must both be in the same tablespace. I have used this clause to name the index because I dislike having objects in the database with unrecognizable names. Perhaps the limitation means that the LOB index is swallowed up inside the LOB segment in future versions of Oracle. I would view this as a backward step, and because the index and the data have such different I/O characteristics, I would like to be able to keep them isolated.

You may be wondering why a LOB has to have its own index segment. It is all part of the way in which Oracle has implemented read consistency for LOBs in a reasonably cost-effective way. To follow this up, we need to look at some of the special storage clauses that apply to LOBs. The full range of options for the LOB storage clause is

```
lob (raw_content) store as raw_lob(
    tablespace auto_data
    index raw_lob_I              -- deprecated feature
    disable storage in row       -- could be ENABLE
    CHUNK 16K                     -- Can't be changed after creation
    PCTVERSION 25                 -- protect old copies of LOBS
```

```
        NOCACHE NOLOGGING          -- Could be CACHE (implies logging)
                                   -- or NOCACHE LOGGING (the default)
    );
```

The last three parameters control how Oracle handles "out-of-line" LOBs. If you have enabled storage in row, then any LOB smaller than 3,960 bytes is stored as if it was a perfectly normal column (with a bit of internal overhead) in the table. This means that all the usual rules about rollback segments and redo log generation apply to any changes made to that LOB. However, if the LOB is larger than 3,960 bytes, or if the option to disable storage in the row has been set, then a completely different mechanism applies.

When a LOB is stored out-of-line, the row holds a 20-byte descriptor that includes a sequence number that is the ID generated by Oracle for that version of the actual LOB content.

To get at the data itself, Oracle looks up this ID in the LOB index, which is a slightly unusual B-tree index structure that points to the pages in the LOB segment that hold the current version of the LOB. Each entry in the B-tree contains (rather like an IOT) a list of the starting block addresses for as many as four chunks of the LOB. If the LOB is larger than four chunks, then a second entry in the LOB index lists the location of the next four chunks, and so on (Figure 17-1).

The base table and the LOB index obey all the normal rules of rollback and redo, the parameters CHUNK, PCTVERSION, CACHE/NOCACHE, and LOGGING/NOLOGGING apply purely to the actual large chunks of the LOB that are stored in the LOB segment, and allow for some very different methods for dealing with read consistency.

The LOB segment is broken up into pages of "chunk" size. You specify "chunk" in bytes, and can be any value up to a maximum of 32KB; however, it is rounded up to the nearest multiple of the block size. Each chunk is a contiguous set of blocks in the data segment's extents, and chunks cannot spread across extents, so make sure that you set the chunk size to a suitable factor of the extent size.

It seems strange that LOBs up to 4GB can only be stored in chunks up to 32K. However, if Oracle ever allows you to choose much larger chunk sizes, pick the size with care. In all cases compare it with the extent size because LOB chunks cannot cross extent boundaries. You may want to waste a couple blocks in each extent to accommodate the segment header block (and free list group blocks) in the first extent.

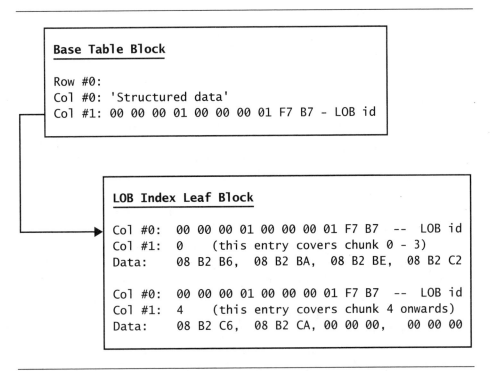

Figure 17-1. Representation of a LOB locator and a LOB index leaf.

A larger chunk size reduces the number of entries needed in the LOB index to describe the location of the LOB, but the potential for wasted space goes up because the smallest single write to a LOB is of the chunk size. Even if you write just 1 byte to an out-of-line LOB defined with a chunk of 32KB, Oracle writes 32KB of data and, if LOGGING, 32KB of redo log. On the other hand, if you are handling lots of larger LOBs, you may want to set a large chunk size to be able to take advantage of large multiblock reads.

It is important to get the chunk size set appropriately for the nature of the work you are doing with LOBs because it is not possible to change it without rebuilding the entire LOB segment and index. This rebuild is a consequence of the strategy used by Oracle to make access to LOBs as efficient as possible. Apart from creating indexes that list the starting locations of four chunks, Oracle also maintains a bitmap in the LOB segment that maps out the chunks in the segment so that a quick scan of the bitmap can be used to locate free space. If you do need to change the chunk size, the command should be something like

```
alter table test_lobs move
lob (raw_content) store as(
    tablespace new_tablespace
    chunk 8K
    nocache nologging
);
```

However, when I tried any variation of this ***move*** command, I found that attempts to select the LOB locator resulted in Oracle error "ORA-22922: nonexistent LOB value," so presumably the LOB locators in the table have become invalid, in much the same way that the rowid values in indexes become invalid when you move the table. I don't know whether this is a bug in the software, or in the manuals, but don't try moving LOB segments until you know you can still see the LOBs afterward.

Caching is the next feature to consider. By default, a LOB segment is defined as NOCACHE. If you insert a new LOB, then it is written a chunk at a time into the LOB segment but does not travel through the block buffer. Similarly, when you read a NOCACHE LOB, Oracle bypasses the block buffer. This means that LOB processing does not have the secondary effect of flushing the buffer and making the rest of the system start demanding real I/O. Reads and writes to LOBs defined as NOCACHE are able to make use of multiblock I/O calls, reducing the total cost of I/O, but the amount of benefit this brings depends on the chunk size actually being larger than one block.

Conversely, LOBs that are marked as CACHE go through the block buffer in a fairly normal fashion, although very clean LOBs are read using a multiblock read that can span multiple chunks. Although the buffer-handling algorithms have changed significantly in Oracle 8.1, and the LOBs are not read into the most recently used (MRU) end of the buffer, they could still manage to flush a fair volume of more useful data from the buffer as they are read. If you cache your LOBs, it is probably wise to include the storage option BUFFER_POOL RECYCLE (see Appendix D) in their definition.

By default, a LOB segment is defined to be LOGGING, so if you insert a 64KB LOB, then you also write (at least) a 64KB redo log entry. You can, if you wish, define a LOB to be NOLOGGING and bypass the overhead of generating redo log. This probably makes sense for a large initial data load (following which you make an immediate backup), but it may be a little risky under normal circumstances. You cannot define a LOB to be NOLOGGING if you have also defined it to be CACHE. You can change the attributes of the LOB segment using the ***alter table*** command:

```
alter table test_lobs
modify lob (raw_content) (nocache nologging);
```

> *By default, inserting a large LOB into the database requires the I/O to be done twice—once for the LOB segment and once for the redo log. Consider defining LOBs as NOLOGGING for handling large data loads.*

To understand how PCTVERSION is used, we need to look in some detail at how Oracle handles updates to LOBs. Assume that we have created a LOB with the default characteristics of NOCACHE and LOGGING.

If you update the LOB, then the new version (or if you have used subtler coding, the new version of the chunks you have changed) is written both to the LOB segment and to the redo log. More important, however, you do not overwrite the original version of the LOB, nor do you generate any rollback for the LOB data (although you will have affected the LOB index, and these changes result in some rollback and redo being generated).

An important side effect of this that is especially relevant for very large LOBs is that when you update a LOB, the LOB segment has to have enough space to hold both the old version and the new version at once. This may result in much more space being required than your initial estimates may have suggested. (A strategy to reduce the space requirement would be to delete the old copy, commit, and then insert the new copy, if you can live with the risk.)

If you delete the LOB, Oracle simply updates the LOB index. Unlike normal data deletions, in which the deleted material is written to the rollback segment and the changes to the rollback segment are written to the redo log, deletion of a LOB causes virtually no extra work. (The updates to the LOB index generate the usual rollback and redo.)

So how does read consistency work in LOBs? This is where the LOB index really comes into its own. Changes to LOBs are made by adding extra chunks to the LOB segment and by updating the LOB index.

If I start a transaction at SCN 999 and don't get to the LOB in which I am interested until it has been changed a couple of times, then the original chunks of the LOB may well still be in the LOB segment. All I have to do to reconstruct the LOB is to build a version of the LOB index as it was at SCN 999. This reverse-engineered index points exactly to the chunks I need to see.

But, I hear you ask, if an update to a LOB results in a new copy of some or all of its pages being created, won't you run out of space pretty quickly? This, finally, is where PCTVERSION comes into play. LOB segment chunks do get reused after a time. PCTVERSION tells Oracle how much of the space below the segment's high water mark may be filled with old versions of LOBs before it starts reclaiming this space by overwriting old copies of LOBs with newer copies.

For example, if you set the PCTVERSION to 25 and then create six LOBs each exactly 1MB in size, then "update" two of them so that the results are still 1MB each, your LOB segment grows to 8MB in total. This consists of six current images of the LOBs and two out-of-date images—in other words, 25% of the current space will be old. If you now update a third LOB, Oracle determines that it has reached its PCTVERSION and frees the space taken by the oldest copy of a LOB based on the commit SCN (Figure 17-2).

Earlier, I indicated that the index appears as a B-tree index based on LOB IDs and holds, in IOT fashion, a list of block addresses. In fact, the LOB index is more subtle than this because it also holds a collection of SCNs with an associated list of block addresses that were "current" at that SCN value. This double action allows Oracle to identify very rapidly those chunks in the LOB segment that are the most out of date, and therefore subject to reclamation (Figure 17-3). As a side effect, though, it does mean that the LOB index in a fluid environment may become much larger than you expect, and very quickly too.

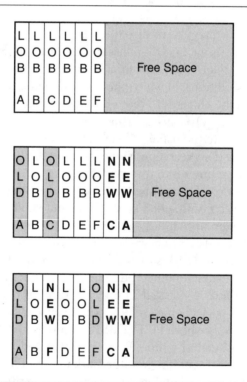

Figure 17-2. Reusing space in LOB segments.

```
LOB Index Leaf Block

-- Entries for current LOBs

Col #0: 00 00 00 01 00 00 00 01 F7 B7    -- LOB id
Col #1: 0             (this entry covers chunk 0 - 3)
Data:   08 B2 B6,   08 B2  BA,   08 B2 BE,   08 B2 C2

Col #0: 00 00 00 01 00 00 00 01 F7 B7    -- LOB id
Col #1: 4             (this entry covers chunk 4 onwards)
Data:   08 B2 C6,   08 B2  CA,   00 00 00,   00  00  00

-- SCN entries for consistent-read LOB blocks

Col #0: 00 01 00 34 F7 9A 00 00 00 00    -- SCN
Col #1: 08 4A 99    (First of up to 5 entries for this SCN)
Data:   08 4A 99,   08 4A 9D,   08 4A A1,   08 4A C1,   08 4A C5

Col #0: 00 01 00 34 F7 9A 00 00 00 00    -- SCN
Col #1: 08 4A C9    (up to 5 more entries)
Data:   08 4A C9,   08 4A CD,   08 4A D1,   08 4A D5,   00 00 00
```

Figure 17-3. Representation of a LOB index leaf with LOB and SCN entries.

There is plenty of room for misunderstanding and misinterpretation in this area, and the consequences can be a bit surprising. The first problem is that the process is an approximate process. Whatever else happens there is plenty of room for departure from the precise PCTVERSION you supply. Be careful when you are using LOBs with large variations in size.

The second problem is forgetting that PCTVERSION applies only to the current high water mark of the segment, *not* to the whole segment. If you declare a segment of 100MB and a PCTVERSION of 25, this does not mean you have an allowance of 25MB for holding older versions of LOBs. If you insert three LOBS at 1MB each, then update one of them, <u>25% of the used space</u> is taken up by the old copy of that LOB, so the very next insert or update to a LOB wipes that version from the system.

Because of the special nature of LOB read consistency, you can actually get two different errors when it is no longer possible to build a read-consistent version of your data. If, for normal read-consistency reasons, the base table holding the LOB locator or the LOB index cannot be made read consistent, you get the standard error "ORA-01555: snapshot too old: rollback segment number. . . ." However, if the table and index can be rebuilt, but the LOB data itself has been overwritten, you get a pair of messages—"ORA-22924: snapshot too old" followed by a now misleading "ORA-01555: snapshot too old: rollback segment number. . . ."

There are a few new features to LOBs in version 8.1: You can include LOBs in IOTs, you can include LOBs in partitioned tables, and you can create temporary LOBs. The ability to include LOBs in a partitioned table is a great convenience to developers and DBAs. In version 8.0 you had the options of either not partitioning, which left the DBA with some very large objects to handle, or of writing code to handle in-house "artificial" partitioning. Despite the convenience of the "official" inclusion of LOBs in partitioned tables, you may find that there are some administrative or performance issues to struggle with, particularly when trying to decide a good partitioning strategy that avoids leaving the base table partitions very small or the LOB segment partitions very large.

Given the general high I/O costs of having to use LOBs, it seems unlikely that there would be any significant gain to be had from making the base table an IOT. The IOT may save you one physical read if you descend the primary key (see Chapter 14), and then go off to read a LOB. Being of a cautious, suspicious, and pessimistic (realistic) nature, I am inclined to assume that the risk of mixing IOTs with LOBs is too high for the possible performance gain.

However, there are a couple of points to bear in mind if you do decide to mix IOTs and LOBs. If you create a LOB in an IOT without specifying an overflow segment for the IOT, then the LOBs are always stored out-of-line in the LOB segment. If you try to use the **enable storage in row** command in these circumstances, you get the slightly misleading Oracle error "ORA-22853: invalid LOB storage option specification." If you create an overflow segment for the IOT then you can end up with LOBs stored inside the index segment, because the default storage reverts to **enable storage in row**, which is likely to have a severe impact on performance. Do be careful of little accidents that could result in DDL like the following:

```
create table test_lobiot (
    id                number(5),
    text_content      clob,
    bytes             number(38),
    lob_type          varchar2(1),
    constraint tl_i primary key(id)
)
```

```
organization index
including bytes
overflow
;
```

In this example, the CLOB column is always stored in the leaf blocks of the IOT, because the INCLUDING clause specifies a column that appears after the CLOB in the table structure.

Working with BFILEs

If you are also going to make use of BFILEs, you need to be able to handle the logical directories in which they are stored. Oracle has introduced the command "CREATE DIRECTORY" to associate an internal logical directory name with a real, physical external directory. For example,

```
create or replace directory HOME as 'c:/users/jpl/lobs/';
```

(Interestingly, the forward slash notation for UNIX directory separators works on NT systems in this command, as it does with the UTL_FILE package.)

Internally you can now refer to "home" in any of your PL/SQL code referencing BFILEs, knowing that this will be interpreted as "c:/users/jpl/lobs/" at the server. If for some reason you need to move all your BFILEs to a different physical location (even to a file system mounted on a remote network), you can simply take advantage of the REPLACE option in the command to change the meaning of the home directory without having to correct and recompile any of your code.

To be able to create directories, you need the system privilege CREATE ANY DIRECTORY. Note that there is no CREATE DIRECTORY privilege, only a CREATE ANY DIRECTORY privilege. A directory is a strange type of object because its name space is global to the database. It is not possible for two different users to have their own versions of a directory (unlike views, tables, and just about any other type of object in the database), and directories cannot be referenced with the usual QUALIFIED NAME mechanism of {username}.{directory}. In fact, if you look in the view DBA_DIRECTORIES (there is no USER_DIRECTORIES view), you will find that SYS owns all directories, even the ones you created under another schema.

To use a directory created by another user, you have to have the READ privilege granted to you. This can be granted through a role, and is an effective method for splitting sensitive data:

```
grant read on directory HOME to public;
revoke read on directory HOME from public;
```

Of course, because most code to read files is likely to be in PL/SQL packages, you probably need only grant READ on the directory to the small number of owners of packages, and then grant EXECUTE on the procedures to the rest of the population.

If you do revoke READ rights on a directory, users may suddenly find that they are getting apparently misleading Oracle errors like "ORA-22285: non-existent directory or file for GETLENGTH operation," so make sure that any procedure you write includes a test for the readability of the BFILE directory and handles the exception in a friendly fashion.

The other thing you have to do is make sure that the operating system ID that owns the Oracle software (which seems to be Oracle on most UNIX systems and Administrator on most NT systems) can actually read the directory, and the files on that directory.

As with LOBs, the range of options you have for using BFILEs within pure SQL is very limited. Basically you can insert a BFILE (or, strictly, the BFILE locator) into a table, update it with a new BFILE locator, or delete it. To generate a BFILE locator, Oracle supplies a built-in function "bfilename":

```
insert into test_lobs(id,original)
values (3,bfilename('HOME','rep_sales_0327.txt'));

update test_lobs
set original= null
where id = 3;
```

At first glance this doesn't seem particularly useful. On the other hand imagine a Web site that uses a reference table to pull reports from the server to the Web client. Every night you can run a simple set of batch files with a framework like

```
--  generate today's date into m_datestamp

spool report_17.&m_datestamp

--  rest of report

spool off
```

```
update   reports_table
set      report_file = bfilename('REP_DIR','report_17.&m_datestamp'),
         last_run_date = to_date('&m_datestamp','yyyy_mm_dd')
where    report_name = 'REPORT 17'

commit;
```

With just a few lines of SQL and a little Web wrapper, you can Web enable your entire report distribution mechanism. The interface to pull the BFILE from the server to the client is highly dependent on the programming tools you prefer to use. It is interesting to note that the Oracle manual devoted to LOBs (the *Application Developer's Guide to Large Objects*) seems to be written from the perspective of doing exactly this sort of thing in all possible types of programming languages.

There is one little trap with BFILEs at present. The size of the data stored in the table column is supposed to be quite small—some locator information (approximately 16 bytes) plus the logical directory name and the actual filename. This is indeed what appears when using the simple SQL method just presented, but when I switched to PL/SQL I found that the BFILE column was padded to 530 bytes with zeros.

Another point to bear in mind is that BFILEs really are files. There is an init.ora parameter that limits the number of files that a session may hold open at once, and you may run foul of this if (1) you want to use lots of files at once or (2) you start writing more sophisticated code that fails to close its files on time. The parameter is SESSION_MAX_OPEN_FILES, it has a default value of ten, and it must be set at database start-up; it cannot be modified on the fly. It is also possible that your operating system will have imposed a limit on the number of files that you can open concurrently and may need reconfiguring.

The LOB Package—DBMS_LOB

There is a PL/SQL package supplied with the database to make handling LOBs easier, and in many simple cases this may be all you need for straightforward purposes such as loading files into the database and making the content available to Web pages. Ultimately, though, if you want to do really clever things, with very fine control, you need to fall back on programming at a low level in C using the Oracle Call Interface (OCI), although I expect the Pro*C and Java interfaces to LOBs will be enhanced over time to make it easier to get at the buffering and precision handling of LOBs.

OCI is outside the scope of this book, but I will mention a few points of the package to give a flavor of what can be done using the basic units supplied. The package name is DBMS_LOB, owned by the user SYS, and you need the EXECUTE privilege before you can use it. The package allows you to operate all types of LOBs in various ways. In particular, it allows you to handle LOBs with some of the more common *string manipulation features.*

The package falls into a small number of classes of functions:

- Temporary LOB handling (temporary LOBs are a new feature of version 8.1)
- String comparison such as instr() and substr()
- String manipulation such as trim(), append(), and erase()
- File handing such as fileopen(), filegetname(), and loadfromfile()
- Reading and writing

In this section I highlight a couple examples of how to use the package, and give a couple warnings about things that can go wrong.

BFILES

There isn't a lot you can do currently with BFILEs in Oracle. They are simply a fairly secure way of identifying to Oracle a file that exists on the database server, but the file is a read-only file. (If you examine the code in the PL/SQL package, note that the command to open a BFILE is nominally allowed to have an "open mode," so perhaps future releases will allow Oracle to have "write" and "append" as legal modes for opening BFILES.)

The SQL bfilename() function can be used to turn a logical directory and a physical filename into a BFILE type, which can be stored in the database. In PL/SQL we can take advantage of a PL/SQL procedure to find out if the file referenced by a BFILE still exists, get its real name if we wish, open it, find out how long it is, read it into memory a bit at a time, check if it is open, and close it. A sample of code to do this is as follows:

```
declare

    m_dirname   varchar2(32);
    m_filename  varchar2(32);
    m_file_size integer;
    m_file      bfile;
    m_buf_size  integer;
    m_buffer    raw(100);
```

```
begin

    select  file_content -- the bfile column
    into    m_file
    from    test_lobs
    where   id = 3;

    if (dbms_lob.fileexists(file_loc => m_file) = 1) then
        dbms_output.put_Line('File exists');
    end if;

    dbms_lob.filegetname(
        file_loc   => m_file,
        dir_alias  => m_dirname,
        filename   => m_filename
    );
    dbms_output.put_line(m_dirname || ' ' || m_filename);

    dbms_output.put_Line(dbms_lob.getlength(m_file));

    dbms_lob.fileopen(
        file_loc   => m_file,
        open_mode  => dbms_lob.file_readonly
    );

    m_buf_size := 64;

    dbms_lob.read(
        file_loc   => m_file,
        amount     => m_buf_size,
        offset     => 1,
        buffer     => m_buffer
    );

    dbms_output.put_line(utl_raw.cast_to_varchar2(m_buffer));

    if (m_buf_size) != 64) then
        dbms_output.put_line('Got past end of file');
    end if;

    if (dbms_lob.fileisopen(file_loc => m_file) = 1) then
        dbms_lob.fileclose(file_loc => m_file);
    end if;
```

```
        dbms_lob.filecloseall;

    end;
    /
```

This code loads a BFILE into a variable from the table and checks that the corresponding file can be read. It then outputs the logical directory name and the real filename of the file. If you want the real directory name, you can look it up in DBA_DIRECTORIES. Note that it is then possible to get the size of the file with the GETLENGTH procedure without actually opening the file.

The code then opens the file, sets the buffer size to read, and reads a chunk of the file (starting from offset 1) into the buffer. The read() call is generic to LOBs and BFILEs; however, if you play by the book and use the highly approved "named parameters" approach as I have, then file_loc has to be turned into lob_loc when reading LOBs.

There are a couple more important points to notice about the READ procedure. First, the buffer *must* be declared as RAW, which is why I have subsequently used UTL_RAW to turn the buffer into character output (in this case, I knew that the file was a text file). Second, M_BUF_SIZE (the variable I passed in as the amount) is set to the amount of data actually copied into the buffer. If there is insufficient data left in the file to meet the demand, then no error is raised, hence my test to see if the output value for M_BUF_SIZE was the same as the input size. However, if I start reading beyond the end of the file (in other words, the offset is larger than the value returned by the getlength() call), then my attempt to read results in Oracle error "ORA-01403: no data found."

Finally, I tested (redundantly in this simple example) to see if the file was open before closing it, and then did the mundane job of closing all open files. It is quite important to close files behind you because you may have a limit set on the number of files that can be open simultaneously. In a more realistic example, you would probably do the test for files being open or the filecloseall call in an exception handler.

There is one funny quirk to the filecloseall call of which to beware: If no files have been opened in the session at all, then it raises Oracle error "ORA-22289: cannot perform FILECLOSEALL operation on an unopened file or LOB," so you ought to wrap the call in its own little exception handler, just in case.

There are several more procedures in the DBMS_LOB package that can be applied to BFILEs. Many of them are generic and apply to any type of LOB; however, there is one very important procedure—the loadfromfile() call, which I cover in the next section.

Permanent LOBs

The first thing to remember about LOBs is that your programs have to handle them through locators. When you select a LOB into a variable, you are in effect creating a pointer to a location. If you want to update the thing being pointed at, you must take exclusive control of the locator by locking it. If you start writing complicated code that passes around LOB locators and overwrites one LOB locator with the value of another LOB locator, you could end up with some very confusing results, where updates seem to disappear.

You can also run into problems with LOBs if you fail to trap exceptions and close LOBs after opening them. Again, the problem is down to the state of LOB locators. We review this after examining a couple of examples of using LOBs.

Perhaps the most significant task you will want to do with LOBs is copy files into them. If you need to do this from a client, you have to write a routine that creates a LOB locator and writes to it. If you are simply loading files into the database at the server, Oracle Corporation has provided a special procedure for you—the LOADFROMFILE procedure. It is very simple to use: Create a LOB locator, open a file, get the length of the file, call the function to copy the file into the LOB, and commit:

```
declare

    m_file  bfile;
    m_bytes integer;
    m_id    integer;
    m_lob   clob;


begin
    m_file := bfilename('HOME','demo.txt');
    m_bytes := dbms_lob.getlength(m_file);
    dbms_lob.fileopen(m_file);

    insert into test_lobs (
        id, lob_type, bytes, text_content
    )
    values(
        4, 'C', m_bytes,empty_clob()
    )
    return text_content into m_lob;
```

```
        dbms_lob.loadfromfile(
            dest_lob    => m_lob,
            source_lob  => m_file,
            amount      => m_bytes
        );

        commit;

        dbms_lob.fileclose(m_file);
    end;
    /
```

In this example, the first interesting statement is the INSERT . . . RETURN line. We need a locked LOB locator to be able to get data into the LOB, so I inserted a row into a table, using the empty_clob() function to create a LOB locator pointing to a null LOB, and I used the RETURN clause (new feature) to assign this locator to the variable M_LOB. I then called the LOADFROMFILE procedure, passing in the LOB locator, BFILE, and the amount of data that I wanted to load. I could also have passed in a source off-set and destination offset if I had wanted to load just a section of the file into some point other than the start of the LOB. Finally, I commit and close the file. In this particular example, I loaded a text file into a character LOB. If I loaded a binary file into a binary LOB, I would simply change the CLOB declarations to BLOB declarations—and the empty_clob() to empty_blob()—without changing any of the other bits of code.

Let's now try to read a bit of the CLOB back from the table, and compare the code with the code for reading a file. The similarity is startling:

```
declare

    m_lob       clob;
    m_buf_size  integer;
    m_buffer    varchar2(100);

begin
    select text_content
    into m_lob
    from test_lobs
    where id = 4;

    dbms_output.put_Line(dbms_lob.getlength(m_lob));
```

```
dbms_output.put_Line(dbms_lob.getchunksize(m_lob));

dbms_lob.open(
    lob_loc      => m_lob,
    open_mode    => dbms_lob.lob_readonly
);

m_buf_size := 64;

dbms_lob.read(
    lob_loc      => m_lob,
    amount       => m_buf_size,
    offset       => 1,
    buffer       => m_buffer
);

if (dbms_lob.isopen(lob_loc => m_lob) = 1) then
    dbms_lob.close(lob_loc => m_lob);
end if;

end;
.
/
```

There is little that needs to be said about this code, given its similarity to the code for reading BFILEs, but there are two important points: The OPEN and CLOSE are not necessary; they were introduced in Oracle 8.1 largely for reasons of consistency, and to address some potential anomalous behavior. However, if OPEN is used, then CLOSE is mandatory. This can lead to odd problems if you fail to include the IS OPEN test in an exception handler. If you open a LOB and fail to close it (for instance, running the previous code but starting at an offset past the end of the LOB, to crash with error 1403), then try to repeat the access, you get Oracle error "ORA-22293: LOB already opened in the same transaction," which is particularly confusing because if you commit and try again, you get exactly the same error.

The second point is the function getchunksize(), which applies only to permanent LOBs and not temporary LOBs or BFILEs. When you define a LOB column in a table, you specify a chunk. The getchunksize() function tells you how much of this chunk is actually used for data (in other words, it allows for the space used for internal Oracle purposes).

Why is used chunk size important? This is when cunning code can become very efficient. If Oracle can determine that a change you made to a LOB replaces one set of bytes with another set of bytes, then it simply takes a copy of a few of the LOB chunks, just enough to capture the before-and-after versions of the LOB, and sets up the LOB index so that one version of the LOB index points to the unchanged pages and the before-image pages, and another version of the LOB index points to the unchanged pages and the after-image pages.

Consequently, if you write code that understands the significance of the getchunksize() call so that, for example, you write reports that can align page boundaries with chunk boundaries, you can update the LOB version of the report by changing a few chunks of the LOB rather than rewriting the entire LOB. The following code, for example, changes the first 17 bytes of a LOB that I had filled with 3MB of data, but Oracle writes only 4KB (plus a little patch of the LOB index) rather than rewriting the whole 3MB because my Oracle block size and LOB chunk size were 4KB.

```
declare

    m_bytes      integer;
    m_id integer;
    m_lob        clob;

begin

    select text_content
    into m_lob
    from test_lobs
    where id = 2
    for update;

    dbms_lob.write(
        lob_loc => m_lob,
        amount  => 17,
        offset  => 1,
        buffer  => 'This is an update'
    );

    commit;

end;
/
```

This, then, is where we come to a use for *temporary LOBs*.

Temporary LOBs

Temporary LOBs are a new feature to Oracle 8.1. In version 8.0, if you
wanted to build a LOB bit by bit, you had to create a row in a table, then
update the LOB a bit at a time, which resulted in a lot of extra work being
done by Oracle. In Oracle 8.1, you can create a temporary LOB, which
appears in your temporary tablespace, and you can manipulate that until you
are ready to copy the whole thing to a permanent LOB. The chunk size of a
temporary LOB is a single block and cannot be set otherwise, so this is reasonably space effective. Also, because a proper temporary tablespace is NOLOG-
GING, the temporary LOB generates no redo log, nor is there any rollback to
consider, so it is much more efficient than a permanent LOB if you are applying large numbers of small updates to it:

```
declare

    m_lob_size  integer;
    m_lob       clob;
    m_buf_size  integer;
    m_buffer    varchar2(100);

    cursor c1 is
    select
        rpad(owner,32) ||
        rpad(object_type,15) ||
        rpad(object_name,32) ||
        chr(10)        report_line
    from
        all_objects
    where
        rownum <= 1000
    ;

begin

    dbms_lob.createtemporary(
        lob_loc => m_lob,
        cache   => false,
        dur     => dbms_lob.call
    );

    for r1 in c1 loop
        dbms_lob.writeappend(
```

```
            lob_loc => m_lob,
            amount => length(r1.report_line),
            buffer => r1.report_line
        );
    end loop;

    update   test_lobs
    set      text_content = m_lob
    where    id = 2
    ;

    commit;

    dbms_lob.freetemporary(m_lob);

end;
/
```

The two important calls here are createtemporary()—which creates a temporary LOB, is defined as NOCACHE, and holds space in the temporary segment only as long as this call to the database lasts (the alternative is to hold the space until the session commits)—and the freetemporary() call, which releases the LOB.

Using a temporary LOB, this code to generate a report of 1,000 lines completed in just a few seconds. Changing the code to use a permanent (NOLOGGING) LOB gave me a runtime of 97 seconds with huge amounts of redo generated.

Of course, there are other ways of doing the same thing. You could dump the report to a file with simple SQL or DBMS_OUTPUT and load the file in one hit, but you can't do this from a client machine because loadfromfile() works only at the server. You could work around this by using UTL_FILE to write the report to a file on the server and loading it from there, but even then I'm always a little uncomfortable about routines that push data out of the database to files and then reload it. I'm always waiting for the chain to break somewhere. You could create the report as a varchar2() in memory, and only transfer it every 32K as the variable reaches its limiting size as a way of reducing the LOB handling overhead, but the code for long reports gets a little complex. Temporary LOBs really do seem to work very well for this sort of thing.

You do have to be a little careful with temporary LOBs because coding errors can leave you grabbing a lot of temporary space that you cannot release until your session ends. In particular, if you overwrite the value of a temporary

LOB with another LOB locator, the LOB to which your locator was pointing cannot be freed because there is no locator pointing at it that can be passed to the freetemporary() call; however, for simple uses (such as building a report to drop into a LOB table for Web access) it is hard to go wrong.

Generic LOBs

I have mentioned several times the general-purpose string-handling functions without giving any examples, so I suppose I really ought at least to mention a couple of them:

- **compare()**—Compares a part of two LOBs and returns zero if they match.
- **instr()**—Returns the position of the Nth occurrence of a pattern in a LOB.
- **substr()**—Returns part of a LOB (as large as 32KB) starting from a given position.

These may be quite useful for handling small LOBs, and in this respect help to make LOBs more useful than LONGs ever were, but I suspect that the general nature of LOBs means they are unlikely to be really useful.

Problems and Quirks

The LOB parameter PCTVERSION is not quite as straightforward as it seems. The space allowed for older versions of LOBs is approximately this percentage of the high water mark of the LOB segment, not of the entire segment.

There are two common points of confusion when using LOB types (as opposed to the BFILE types). The difference between null and empty_blob()/empty_clob()/empty_nclob(), and the significance of the lifetime of the LOB locator. Be very careful with transactions and LOB locators. Adopt a strategy for when you acquire LOB locators and when you commit them. If you copy locators too casually, or mix fetches to locators in a mixture of in-transaction and out-of-transaction states, then it is easily possible for a session to appear to lose its own updates.

The break point at which LOBs switch from in-line to out-of-line is fixed at 3,960 bytes. This is a little brutal, and it would certainly be nice to be able to have a table-based parameter that allows you to set the break size. The probability of in-line LOBs causing row chaining or row migration is so high that it seems to make sense to make DISABLE STORAGE IN ROW the default option. However, if most of your LOBs are relatively small compared with the block size, you will be wasting a lot of space in the LOB segment if you do this, because the minimum unit of storage for a LOB value is a block.

Remember that CLOBs and NCLOBs for varying-width character sets are stored internally as fixed-width 2-byte unicode. This may mean that the internal storage for the LOB is twice as large as you expect.

Don't try to rebuild a LOB column to change its chunk size or other storage parameters. You may lose all access to the data.

Any references to a directory holding BFILEs is always a reference to a directory on the server, not on the client machine. The same is true of the directories specified for the UTL_FILE package. If you want to transfer clientside files to the server, you must develop your own mechanisms for reading them first.

Currently, I keep finding that the locator stored in a table by a simple PL/SQL routine for a BFILE is 530 bytes. This is almost certainly a bug, but it exists in versions 8.1.5 and 8.1.6.

As with many of the high-volume mechanisms, you need to be wary of the multithreaded server. Do not use a multithreaded server and BFILES together, because some necessary session information may not be migrated properly.

When you update a table, triggers may fire. In Oracle 8.1, you can read (but not update) the values of a LOB column as the trigger fires. However, there is a little oddity: When a LOB is updated by dbms_lob() or through OCI, it does not fire the trigger on the table.

Do be careful when passing LOB locators or assigning one locator to another; it is possible to see some very confusing side effects.

Strategy Notes

If you need to store LOBs in or close to the database, then Oracle 8.1 is a great improvement over Oracle 7. If you don't need to store LOBs, don't be in too much of a hurry to do so. Just because it is easy to write code to do it doesn't mean that it's the right thing to do.

As a guideline, consider using BFILES for a small collection of very large objects and using LOBs for a large collection of relatively small objects.

When using LOBs, look for options to partition the data, even artificially. Otherwise, you may end up with some extremely large segments, which means extremely large tablespaces and files, which makes for an administrative headache. Remember that you need a viable backup-and-recovery mechanism, and smaller tablespaces help.

The default setting for a LOB segment is NOCACHE LOGGING, so the cost of an insert is doubled by the logging. When appropriate, set the segment to NOCACHE NOLOGGING, load the database, change the setting, and make a backup of the tablespace.

Choose the chunk size for your LOB segments with care. If the LOB segment is set to be NOCACHE, then the minimum write and redo log write sizes are the chunk size, even when you write only a few bytes. If the chunk size is too small, then the LOB index may get very large because each index entry holds only four chunk addresses.

Temporary LOBs can be very effective for building LOBs piecewise with little I/O overhead. The most obvious use is for building reports in memory that you wish to store in the database as permanent LOBs.

CHAPTER 18

Data Integrity

There are several good reasons for using a relational database for holding your data. One of the more important is probably the ability to make the database protect the quality of its data through the use of declarative integrity constraints that are actively checked at all times by the database engine itself.

Prior to Oracle 7, programmers had to write code that checked the legality of data entering the system; but if users chose to pick any one of numerous end-user tools, this allowed them to bypass all programmed checks and damage the integrity of the data.

Oracle Corporation introduced working declarative constraints in Oracle version 7. In version 8, they gave us deferrable declarative constraints, which introduce a number of nice little touches to simplify database coding.

Sometimes it is impossible to do what you want to do with declarative integrity constraints, at which point you fall back to using triggers. There are some enhancements to trigger technology that may be of use from time to time.

Ultimately, it is always possible to break things if you try hard enough. Oracle has finally given us the official redo log reader to allow us to find out who did what to the database and when. Even if we can't manage to maintain the integrity of our data, we can at least track down the guilty party that broke it.

Types of Constraints

There are currently six types of declarative constraint. They are seen in the view family xxx_CONSTRAINTS, with a single character code defining the constraint type:

1. Primary key, P
2. Unique key, U
3. Foreign key, R
4. Check, C
5. View check option, V
6. View read-only, O

There are a couple of other constraining mechanisms that do not appear as constraints in the view family xxx_CONSTRAINTS—the SCOPE option for object REFs, and the boundary conditions for partitioned tables.

Primary Key

A primary key constraint lists a set of non-null columns in a table that must uniquely identify a row in that table. When you create a primary key on a table, Oracle requires an index on those columns; however, with the advent of deferrable constraints, that index need not be unique and only has to start with the columns of the primary key. You can have only one primary key constraint on a table. A primary key constraint is the default target of a foreign key constraint if the foreign key constraint is defined simply by reference to its parent table.

Unique Key

A unique key constraint is similar to the primary key constraint in that it lists a set of columns that must uniquely identify a row in a table. As with primary keys, Oracle requires an index, although not necessarily unique, on those columns. However, the columns are allowed to be null. Nulls can be a problem in a unique key and can lead to terrible confusion. You are allowed to have more than one row in the table in which every column in the unique key is null. (In part, this is a mechanical implementation issue. Completely null entries do not appear in B-tree indexes, so Oracle cannot check with any efficiency whether a completely null key already exists in the table when you insert a new one.) On the other hand, if *any* of the columns in the key are not null, then only a single row with that combination is allowed. In almost all cases it is a good idea to avoid confusion by explicitly declaring all the columns of a unique key to be NOT NULL columns as well. You can have many unique key constraints on a table. A unique key constraint may also be the target of a foreign key constraint

Foreign Key

A foreign key, also known as a *parent/child relationship* or *referential integrity constraint*, ensures that rows can only exist in one table if an "owning" or parent row exists in another table, and the set of columns used to match the rows form the primary key, or a unique key of the parent table. Again, columns that are allowed to be null can confuse the issue. Consider the following example, which uses a three-column unique key:

```
create table unq_tab (
    n1 number,
    n2 number,
    n3 number,
    v1 varchar2(10)
);
create index un1_i on unq_tab (n1, n2,n3);

alter table unq_tab
add constraint unq_uk unique (n1,n2,n3) deferrable;

create table unq_child (
    n1 number,
    n2 number,
    n3 number,
    n4 number,
    v1 varchar2(10),
    constraint uch_fk_unq
        foreign key (n1,n2,n3)
        references unq_tab(n1,n2,n3)
        on delete cascade
        deferrable initially immediate
        rely
        enable
        validate
)
;

insert into unq_tab values  (1, 1,   1,   'asdf');
insert into unq_child values(2, null, 2,   1,   'asdf');
commit;
```

Both rows are accepted. It appears that Oracle considers (1,1,1) to be a suitable match for (2, null, 2). In fact, if any of the columns at the child end of a foreign key relationship are null, then the child row is accepted.

> *To avoid confusion in referential integrity, define all columns used in unique keys and foreign keys as not null.*

You may note that I have gone over the top in defining the foreign key constraint. I think I've managed to get an example of every possible condition on it. With every addition to Oracle functionality, the need for precision in syntax increases. If you ever get Oracle error "ORA-00907: missing right parenthesis" from SQL code like this, it probably means that you have a couple of words in the wrong order; in this case, for example, RELY has to appear before ENABLE.

Stepping through the definition of the foreign key constraint, we have the list of columns in the child table, the table name to which they refer, and the related list of columns in that table. We then specify the action to be taken by Oracle when a parent row is deleted. Interestingly, this is an example of a definition that affects the performance of one table, but is stored as part of the definition of another table. It is a fairly common problem that people forget that they have a child table, and then wonder why mass deletions from a parent table are taking so much longer than expected. In the example we specified that when a parent is deleted, all its children should be deleted as well (on delete cascade); the other options are to set the child columns to null (on delete set null, ouch!) or to block the delete if there are any child rows (the default behavior, which cannot actually be specified explicitly). There is a special performance feature related to foreign keys: If you do not create an index starting with the foreign key columns, then as a side effect of read consistency and readers not blocking writers, Oracle locks the entire child table when you delete a row from or update a key value in the parent. If you do create the index, there is an added benefit that Oracle can find very efficiently the child rows that should be subject to cascade effects.

The rest of the definition of the foreign key constraint is equally applicable to the primary, unique, and check constraints, although not relevant to view or object constraints:

- **DEFERRABLE**—The constraint may be suspended for the duration of a transaction, so that the data being modified by a user can be temporarily inconsistent. This is of most use when changing a primary key and you do not want to lose the children. (The opposite is NOT DEFERRABLE.)

- **INITIALLY IMMEDIATE**—The constraint is initially active and has to be explicitly set to deferred when a user wants to fudge the data.

(The opposite is INITIALLY DEFERRED—a constraint that is not deferrable cannot be initially deferred.)

■ **RELY**—The CBO assumes that the constraint is valid and the data is consistent at all times, even when the constraint may be disabled or not validated (see Chapter 23). This degree of trust, however, requires the parameter QUERY_REWRITE_INTEGRITY to be set to TRUSTED. (The opposite is NORELY.)

■ **ENABLE**—The constraint should be enabled immediately. (The opposite is DISABLE, which allows you to keep the definition of the constraint in the database without having it checked all the time—a convenience, perhaps, for large data loads.) You have to disable child constraints before parent constraints, and enable them in the reverse order, although there is a facility to disable a parent and cascade the disable command to all the dependent children.

■ **VALIDATE**—If the constraint is currently not validated, then the dataset should be checked to see if it meets the requirement of the constraint before the constraint is enabled. The opposite is NOVALIDATE, which allows you to enable a constraint even when some of the existing data is invalid.

Check

A check constraint is a simple test of a single row, involving only the column values or constants. Pseudo constants/columns like USER and SYSDATE are not allowed. Examples of check constraints are

```
check (sale_date = trunc(sale_date))

check (state in ('NY','TX','CA')

check (
         status = 'X' and pass_date is null
     or  status = 'P' and pass_date is not null
)
```

Sometimes there are gray areas, such as in the second example, which checks against a list of values, when you might argue that the constraint should be turned into a foreign key constraint.

There is a trap to watch for with check constraints. A check constraint is deemed to be TRUE if and only if it is anything other than FALSE. This may sound as if I have been staring at my navel too long, but you have to remember that Oracle uses three-value logic—(TRUE, FALSE, NULL). A check that evaluates to TRUE passes the test; a check that evaluates to NULL also passes the test. It is only a check that evaluates to FALSE that does not pass the test, hence my comment. Look at the second example again. If the state is set to NULL, then the test evaluates to NULL, and the row is accepted.

> *Check constraints pass if they evaluate to TRUE or NULL. Make sure that your tests accommodate NULL columns. Consider changing as many columns as possible to NOT NULL.*

View

A view check constraint is put in place whenever a view is created with the WITH CHECK option, which makes it impossible for users to insert data into a view that could not be subsequently seen by that view. For example,

```
create or replace view my_team_v as
select *
from all_employees
where manager = 'JPL'
with check option
;
```

It is possible to insert rows or update rows in this view, but only if the resulting rows have manager = 'JPL'.

The other type of view constraint stops anyone from inserting, updating, or deleting from a view, even the view's owner. For obvious reasons you cannot apply both these options to a view at the same time:

```
create or replace view my_team_v as
select *
from all_employees
where manager = 'JPL'
with read only
;
```

There is a peculiar little glitch with read-only views: the error messages you get if you try to insert, update, or delete. For inserts and updates you get

Oracle error "ORA-01733: virtual column not allowed here." For deletes you get Oracle error "ORA-01752: cannot delete from view without exactly one key-preserved table."

Scope

I suppose you could say that the SCOPE clause isn't a constraint because Oracle doesn't call it a constraint. On the other hand it, checks and restricts the way in which you may get data into the database, and it is embedded in the object definition, so it appears to conform to the basic behavior of a constraint:

```
create table occupations of occupation;
create table people (
    id                      number,
    current_occupation      ref occupation  scope is occupations
);
```

Unlike the more traditional data constraints that Oracle uses, though, it cannot be turned off and on. Once the scope is set, it cannot be changed, and the table cannot simply be "descoped." A major rebuild operation is required to "relax" the constraint.

Partition Boundaries

When you create a partitioned table, more specifically a range partitioned table (see Chapter 12), you specify boundary conditions for each partition:

```
create table sales(
    product_id      number          not null,
    store_id        number          not null,
    date_part       date            not null,
    sales_value     number(10,2)    not null,
    sales_qty       number(6)       not null
)
partition by range (date_part) (
    partition p01 values less than (to_date('01022000','ddmmyyyy')),
    partition p02 values less than (to_date('01032000','ddmmyyyy')),
    partition p03 values less than (to_date('01042000','ddmmyyyy')),
    partition p04 values less than (to_date('01052000','ddmmyyyy')),
    partition p05 values less than (maxvalue)
);
```

Again, you have a mechanism that checks and restricts the way that data gets into the system, and again the mechanism is part of the static definition of the object. In this example, Oracle enforces the fact that any rows in partition p03 have dates starting at 1 March 2000, but not quite reaching 1 April 2000. You could view this as a check constraint, saying

```
check (
            date_part < to_date('01042000','ddmmyyyy')
        and date_part >= to_date('01032000','ddmmyyyy')
)
```

As with scope definitions, you cannot change the definition of this partition once it is created, although you could go through a REBUILD operation, perhaps splitting or merging partitions. However, you do have an option for bypassing the constraint, thus for bulk data loads you can avoid the cost of Oracle checking the constraint. The *exchange partition* command allows you to replace a partition with a matching table, without checking that the contents of that table meet the requirements of the partition (but see Chapter 12 for a trap with *exchange partition*):

```
alter table main_data
exchange partition pXXX with table load_table
;
```

Using Constraints

Because a constraint is handled very close to the database, it can be checked very efficiently and it can be checked every time, no matter which program fires the data at the database. Clearly it is sensible to define as many data rules as possible inside the database rather than in the code.

There are times, though, when a rigidly locked set of constraints can introduce problems. This is when the newer features of constraints can come in handy. There are four traditional problems to handle:

1. Adding new constraints
2. Truncating a table
3. Loading data
4. Cascading changes to primary keys

Adding Constraints

In earlier versions of Oracle, adding a constraint to a table meant locking that table exclusively so that Oracle could check that all the existing data met the constraint, and be certain that no one slipped in a bad bit of data behind its back while the check was proceeding. For a very large table, that check could take some time; furthermore, if there were two or three constraints to be added they would have to be done one at a time.

Oracle solves this problem in two steps. We can now add the constraint and enable it so that all future data changes are checked to ensure that they meet the constraint. We can then separately validate the constraint to make Oracle go back and check all existing data:

```
alter table unq_tab
add constraint unq_ck_n2 check (n2 > n1)
enable novalidate;

alter table unq_tab
modify constraint unq_ch_n2 validate;
```

If we have to apply several new constraints to a table, we can do so, and then validate them in parallel by running a separate session for each one. There is, however, still a problem. You need a brief moment when there are no active transactions on the table to add the constraint (even in DISABLED, NOVALIDATED mode), and you need another moment to start the validation. (The first seems a bit unreasonable; the second is necessary to deal with problems of active transactions inserting rows that would be in breach of the constraint if they were to be committed.) Consequently, you may have to execute a fast loop (in PL/SQL perhaps), trapping the error "ORA-00054: resource busy and acquire with NOWAIT specified." Recall that the same sort of restriction applies to rebuilding an index on-line, but at least in that case Oracle waits for the exclusive lock.

Truncating Tables

Referential integrity constraints can be a bit of a nuisance when you want to truncate tables. The child table clears quite happily, but you run into problems when you try to truncate the parent:

```
truncate table unq_tab
            *
```

```
ERROR at line 1:
ORA-02266: unique/primary keys in table referenced by enabled
foreign keys
```

This occurs despite the fact that the child table has just been truncated and "obviously" has no data in it. (Of course Oracle is being perfectly sensible here. It is a multiuser system, and one *truncate* command doesn't stop another user from queuing up with a new insert.) The convenient solution is to disable the foreign key constraint:

```
alter table unq_child disable constraint uch_fk_unq;
truncate table unq_tab;
alter table unq_child enable constraint uch_fk_unq;
```

Of course, if someone else slipped in a few rows between your two *truncate* commands, *enable constraint* fails with Oracle error "ORA-02298: cannot validate {table.constraint}—parent keys not found." A slightly better strategy may be to replace the last step with the following code, just in case:

```
alter table unq_child enable novalidate constraint uch_fk_unq;

alter table unq_child modify constraint uch_fk_unq validate
exceptions into EXCEPTIONS;

select * from EXCEPTIONS:
```

ROW_ID	OWNER	TABLE_NAME	CONSTRAINT
AAAFIMAACAAAHZOAAA	JPL1	UNQ_CHILD	UCH_FK_UNQ
AAAFIMAACAAAHZOAAB	JPL1	UNQ_CHILD	UCH_FK_UNQ

By using ENABLE NOVALIDATE, you ensure that all future rows meet the requirements of the constraint. When you then try to validate the constraint, you report the offending rows into an EXCEPTIONS table. If you run the script $ORACLE_HOME/rdbms/admin/utlexcpt.sql, this creates the table called EXCEPTIONS in your schema. You can choose to have a different name for the table. The table lists the offending rows by rowid, and it is the work of moments to run a script that uses this information to delete (or extract and copy) the exceptions to another table with SQL like

```
delete from jpl1.unq_child where rowid = 'AAAFIMAACAAAHZOAAA';
delete from jpl1.unq_child where rowid = 'AAAFIMAACAAAHZOAAB';
```

Then, of course, you can rerun the *validate* command, safe in the knowledge that no more offending data has been created in the interim, because even though the constraint was not validated, it was enabled, so no new problems could be created.

The biggest problem with data cleanouts like this is that they are rarely as simple as a single parent/child relationship. There may be a dozen inter-related children, and several generations of parent tables. Disabling all the necessary constraints is no great problem. In fact, there is a convenient CASCADE option that can make you very lazy:

```
alter table unq_tab disable constraint unq_uk cascade;
```

This option disables the constraint UNQ_UK, and all constraints that depend on it directly or indirectly. The trouble is you won't have a list of the constraints Oracle disabled, so you won't be able to reenable them when needed, and there is no *enable constraint cascade* command.

To address this problem, you have to access the DBA_CONSTRAINTS view, either by writing your own PL/SQL or by using a third-party tool. Basically you need to do a recursive descent through the view, finding the R-type constraints that depend on a supplied unique or primary key constraint, then finding the primary or unique keys of the tables owning those constraints, and then finding their primary or unique keys, alternating between two SQL statements:

```
select
    ch.owner,
    ch.table_name,
    ch.constraint_name
from
    user_constraints ch
where
    ch.r_constraint_name = {supplied constraint}
and ch.r_owner = {supplied table owner}
and ch.constraint_type = 'R'
;

select
    constraint_name
from
    dba_constraints
where
    owner = {next owner}
```

```
and table_name = {next table}
and constraint_type in ('P','U')
;
```

Loading Data

Apart from large-scale elimination of data, you can also benefit from DEFERRABLE constraints when doing large-scale loads of data. To be precise, the trick you use is to disable primary and unique key constraints rather than deferring them. Nevertheless if you want to disable unique or primary key constraints without losing the indexes that enforce them, you have to enable them with nonunique indexes.

This gives you two options, then, create the index before creating the constraint, or simply create the constraint as a DEFERRABLE constraint and the index is automatically created nonunique. So how does disabling the constraints help you with a data load?

Oracle offers various ways of getting a lot of data into the database—in particular, the direct-path mode of SQL*Load, followed by an implicit or explicit CREATE INDEX NOLOGGING. However, the time saved in loading data extremely rapidly can be lost if a dataset that is supposed to contain unique rows actually has a smattering of duplicates. There are few things more irritating than waiting for an index build to complete, then getting the error message "ORA-01452: cannot CREATE UNIQUE INDEX; duplicate keys found." Once the error has occurred, you have a large table full of data and no index to help you find which rows are the duplicates.

If you remember to enable the primary key through a nonunique index, which occurs automatically if you declare it as a DEFERRABLE constraint, you can minimize the problem:

```
create table def_pk_demo (
    n1 number,
    constraint j_pk primary key (n1) deferrable
);

alter table def_pk_demo disable primary key;

--  Some rows to cause problems later on

insert into def_pk_demo values(1);
insert into def_pk_demo values(1);
```

```
--  A PK constraint, enabled to catch future errors
--  but not validated, so won't crash out on the two
--  problem rows above

alter table def_pk_demo enable novalidate primary key;

--  But the next value is in the index,
--  so it gets rejected

insert into def_pk_demo values (1);

--  Now try to validate the PK, and report
--  the exceptions in the EXCEPTIONS table
--  The validation fails with ORA-02437-PK Violated

alter table def_pk_demo
modify primary key validate
exceptions into EXCEPTIONS;

select * from exceptions;

ROW_ID               OWNER       TABLE_NAME    CONSTRAINT
-----------------    ----------  ------------  ---------------
AAAFIfAACAAAC9YAAA   JPL1        PK_DEMO       PK_I
AAAFIfAACAAAC9YAAB   JPL1        PK_DEMO       PK_I

delete from def_pk_demo where rowid = 'AAAFIfAACAAAC9YAAA';
commit;

alter table def_pk_demo
modify primary key validate
;
```

Note that I have used the alternative method for referring to constraints here. Because I am interested in the primary key, I can refer to it throughout as "primary key," rather than "constraint j_pk."

This code demonstrates that if you have a deferrable primary key, then you can disable the constraint, load some invalid data, reenable the constraint without validating it, then use the index to validate the constraint and very efficiently report duplicates that breach the constraint. Of course you would have to do a little intelligent footwork with the EXCEPTIONS table to decide which rows should be deleted, rather than the simple ***delete the first row*** command that I have used. (When using the EXCEPTIONS table with the previous foreign key example, every row it listed had to be fixed or deleted; but with primary key exceptions, one row for each primary key value is allowed to remain.)

Applying this technique to a data-loading strategy, you simply have to write a wrapper that disables the constraint, calls the load, then tries to re-enable and validate the constraint in two steps. Don't forget, though, that when you disable the primary key, you have to worry about any foreign keys that depend on it. You may also want to note that a nonunique index is 1 byte larger per row than the corresponding unique index, because the rowid is stored as part of the key in nonunique indexes and therefore needs a length byte. Don't forget to allow for this growth if you change all your primary keys from unique to nonunique indexes.

Cascading Changes to Primary Key

Although primary keys are not supposed to change, we all know that sometimes they just do. In previous versions of Oracle, you had the problem of how to update the primary key and all the rows in the child tables. Of course, you declared a foreign key constraint, so when you tried to update the parent you were told that the parent key has children and you cannot change it. When you tried to move the children first to a new parent value you were told, the value you are giving that child does not correspond to a parent row. There were various workarounds to the problem, all a little unsavory (delete and reinsert all the rows; clone the parent, move the children, delete the old parent; and so on).

With DEFERRABLE constraints, life is much easier because we can temporarily (for the duration of a transaction) stop Oracle from checking constraints. Only when we try to commit (or if we explicitly demand constraint checking) will Oracle check the constraints. The simplest case would be something like the following:

```
set constraint uch_fk_unq deferred;

update unq_tab
set n1 = 3, n2 = 3, n3 = 3
where
    n1 = 1
and n2 = 1
and n3 = 1
;
```

```
update unq_child
set n1 = 3, n2 = 3, n3 = 3
where
    n1 = 1
and n2 = 1
and n3 = 1
;


-- set constraint uch_fk_unq immediate;


commit;
```

As we update the parent row, the child rows become orphans, but because we have set the foreign key constraint to DEFERRED, Oracle does not check the relationship and does not notice the problem. We then update the child rows and commit. At this point Oracle sets the constraint back to IMMEDIATE and revisits all the data blocks it has changed to see if their current state is consistent with the constraints. If it is, then the commit takes place; if it is not, then *the entire transaction rolls back,* and there is no way of avoiding this rollback. Bear in mind that this strategy is only appropriate to small, quick transactions, because the overhead of revisiting all changed blocks would be very nasty for very large transactions.

Note the line I have commented in the previous SQL code to set the constraint to IMMEDIATE mode. This command also causes Oracle to revisit all changed blocks and check whether they are now in a consistent state. If they are not, then Oracle raises error "ORA-02291: integrity constraint (JPL1.UCH_FK_UNQ) violated—parent key not found." In this case, however, the transaction is not rolled back. Instead the constraint is *not* set to IMMEDIATE, and the data is left unchanged. If you have wrapped the transaction in some PL/SQL, you have the opportunity of writing an exception handler that tries to find out what caused the problem, and can try to fix it.

There are a couple of variants on the *set constraint* command. You can set a list of named constraints with one call, or you can set all the constraints that can be set with just one call:

```
set constraints tb1_fk_xxx, tb2_fk_xxx deferred;
set constraints all deferred;
```

Personally, I like to know that I am doing exactly what I think I am doing, so I wouldn't be inclined to use the ALL option. If someone added a few new constraints to the database, things might work in a way that they shouldn't because the code temporarily disables a constraint in the wrong circumstances.

Data Warehouses and Constraints

We have already mentioned how you can avoid the overhead of data validation when loading partitions of a partitioned table, and how we can disable and reenable constraints without validating them. This leads us to the general question of whether we should implement constraints in data warehouses at all (at least on high-volume data) because data warehouses tend to be read-only and not subject to the risk of large numbers of small, individual processes continually trying to push bad data into places it doesn't fit.

Depending on the circumstances, you could argue either way. Ultimately, it may come down to processing time, code complexity, and the basic way the data gets into the database. Consider the way a typical data load works: Let's load some sales data, checking that the store and product are valid codes:

1. Load 5,000,000 rows into a holding table using SQL*Load in DIRECT mode.
2. Check that the store and product codes are valid by indexed access to the parent tables.
3. Mark any rows that fail the test.
4. Transfer the valid data to the main data tables.

Generally, you don't load the data straight into the main tables because of the effect this may have on existing indexes, and because of the difficulty of identifying and handling bad data efficiently. This means you tend to validate the incoming data completely, in a separate table, before pushing it into the main data tables. Consequently, in this example, a foreign key constraint on the main data table would simply repeat the tests you have already made, adding work without adding value.

In previous versions of Oracle, this argument could be used to make a fairly strong case for not implementing declarative constraints on data warehouses. However, as indicated earlier in this chapter, you can now disable constraints, then reenable them without validation, maximizing the efficiency of throughput on the main data load but protecting the integrity of the data against the fiddling and patching that will no doubt take place from time to time.

Oracle 8.1 also introduces another reason for maintaining integrity constraints in data warehouses, particularly referential integrity constraints.

Constraints can help the optimizer to make decisions about access paths through the data. In particular, the presence or absence of referential integrity constraints may affect the optimizer's decision to use query rewrites (see Chapter 23) to take advantage of materialized views. As far as integrity constraints are concerned, one really important thing to remember in data warehouses is that the guideline about creating indexes to represent foreign keys should be ignored. The guideline exists to reduce contention in OLTP systems. The last thing you want in a data warehouse is to waste space and CPU time by maintaining loads of (probably) single-column foreign key indexes.

Triggers

It would be impossible to discuss database integrity without also mentioning triggers. Until Oracle 8.1, triggers were restricted to code that fired as you changed user data. You could define a piece of PL/SQL code to execute before or after inserts, updates, or deletes on a table, and you could specify whether the trigger should fire just once for the statement or once for every row affected.

There are times when declarative referential integrity simply can't work. An obvious example is when you move into distributed databases and have a child table in one database that depends on a parent table in another database. In fact, for performance reasons, and to reduce risk, you ought to take all sorts of complicated steps to avoid this situation, but sometimes it must be done. You can't add declarative referential integrity across database links, so you just have to fall back to triggers. A very simple example of this, excluding error handling, looks like

```
create or replace trigger uch_bir
before insert on unq_child
for each row
declare
    m_junk  varchar2(1);
begin
    select null
    into m_junk
    from unq_tab@remote_db
    where
        n1 = :new.n1
    and n2 = :new.n2
    and n3 = :new.n3
    ;
```

```
exception
    when no_data_found then
        raise_application_error(
            -20001,
            'No parent found'
        );
    when others then
        raise;
end;
/
```

When a user process inserts a row into the child table for which there is no parent, it gets an Oracle error stack that starts with "ORA-20001: no parent found," and the insert fails.

Of course you need to add lots of effort to this to ensure that (in the event of a network failure, say) the delay between the insert and the error is not too long. Neverthless, the important thing to remember about this approach is that it doesn't really work. The farther you get from the database engine, the higher the risk of integrity code failure. This is why declarative integrity constraints are best, and clientside tests are worst.

Let me explain. When user code, which includes triggers, does integrity checking it has to choose between two evils: One option is to risk allowing illegal data into the database occasionally; the other is to risk imposing significant contention costs on the database. When Oracles does integrity constraints, it avoids the dilemma by cheating. Recall my comments about foreign keys needing indexes if the parent is subject to change? The presence of the index allows the Oracle engine to breach (at least internally) the rules of read consistency by seeing uncommitted index entries and possibly locking index entries that don't exist, to ensure that parent updates won't orphan any data. On the other hand, when user code checks for the existence of a parent row it sees the parent table with all the power of read consistency, which means that if one process deletes a parent row and a second process inserts a child for that parent before the first process commits, the second process sees the parent and commits a row that is about to become an orphan. Conversely, the first process may have checked that no child rows existed, but wouldn't be able to see the uncommitted child from the second process. It is possible to avoid the orphan problem by making the check of the parent row a "select for update." If the first process deletes the parent without committing, then the second process goes into a queue when it does its check and has to wait until the first process commits, then it fails because the parent no longer exists. Conversely, if the second process gets its lock before the first row starts its delete, the first process queues, and by the time it tries to do the delete, the child rows are in place. The problem with locking the parent to insert a child is that *every* other process inserting children for that parent has to queue until your process completes, and this has a dramatic impact on concurrency.

The best you can do with triggers for referential integrity is to minimize the time frame for an error or collision to occur. One way of doing this is to call a procedure that is an autonomous transaction (see Chapter 20) to select the parent for update with NOWAIT specified two or three times in a tight loop then roll back, using an exception to pass the result of the test back to the calling trigger. Because the test is done in an autonomous transaction, it minimizes the time that the lock is held. But having gone for a lock, it gives some protection against seeing a row that has been deleted by another transaction. An outline of the code for the test is

```
create or replace procedure check_parent(
    i_id    in  number
) as

pragma autonomous_transaction;
m_junk          varchar2(1);
resource_locked exception;
pragma exception_init(resource_locked,-54);

begin

    for m_ct in 1..3 loop
        begin
            select  null
            into    m_junk
            from    parent_tab
            where   id = i_id
            for update nowait;
            commit;
            raise dup_val_on_index;   -- this is a funny
        exception

            when no_data_found then
                raise_application_error(
                    -20002,
                    'No parent found'
                );
            when resource_locked then
                if m_ct = 3 then
```

```
                        raise_application_error(
                            -20001,
                            'Parent locked'
                        );
                    else
                        dbms_lock.sleep(0.01);
                    end if;
                when others then
                    raise;
                end;
        end loop;
    end;
    /
```

In this code I raise DUP_VAL_ON_INDEX when I have successfully managed to select and lock the parent row briefly. Of course in a live system I would have done something more sophisticated with a global package so that I could raise a proper user-defined exception. For the purpose of demonstration, this exception could not be raised naturally at this point, so let's keep the example to a minimum. In this code I run a loop three times that tries to lock the parent row. If it succeeds, I raise a spurious error, which is trapped in the calling trigger. If it fails, I go to sleep for 0.01 seconds and try again. After three tries I raise an error for the calling trigger. The calling trigger may look like the following:

```
create or replace trigger chd_bri
before insert
on child_tab
for each row
begin
    check_parent(:new.n1);
exception
    when dup_val_on_index then
        null;
    when others then
        raise;
end;
/
```

This trigger simply calls my autonomous transaction, passing in the incoming foreign key. If the spurious exception DUP_VAL_ON_INDEX is raised, then the trigger ignores it and accepts the row. If any other exception is raised, then the trigger fails and the insert is rolled back.

It is important to note that this complicated bit of coding provides damage control. It tries to reduce the window during which a problem could occur. The very next event to occur should be a commit. If a user inserts a child row successfully and then waits to commit, another user could still delete the parent and leave the first row an orphan when it is finally committed. This, of course, is a good argument for the case that all data updates should be done by calls to procedures that do their own commit. In this way, we could guarantee to execute code that does the parent check and commits as quickly as possible, leaving no room for a user to spoil our best efforts.

Audit Trail

What do you do if, after all your efforts to keep the data clean, something goes wrong and somehow some illegal data gets into the system? It is just possible that some malicious, or perhaps well-intentioned, hacking has taken place.

It is worth mentioning just briefly that Oracle has introduced the *LogMiner*—a tool to read the redo logs, identify who did what and when, write SQL code that represents the changes made, and write SQL code that reverses those changes.

There are some limits to what LogMiner can do. It can't cope with some of the object-type data, or DML on IOTs, for example. And you have to keep refreshing a reference file so that it can still interpret the contents of the log files as new objects are created. Nevertheless, you may get a little entertainment from trying to use it. It is also very instructive to realize how much work Oracle does to execute the SQL code that you issue—something that LogMiner portrays very clearly.

In fact, the biggest drawback to LogMiner is the sheer volume of output. If you execute a single statement to update 5,000 rows, say

```
update cheques set posted = 'T';
```

then LogMiner reports 5,000 pairs of statements like

```
update cheques set posted = 'T' where rowid = 'AAAFIuAACAAAC9YAAB';
update cheques set posted = 'F' where rowid = 'AAAFIuAACAAAC9YAAB';
```

You can restrict LogMiner to time scales and objects, but at the end of the day, trying to find out the change history of a particular row is very time-consuming.

There is one side effect of LogMiner that Oracle introduced to make the output more informative. Prior to version 8.0, the redo log did not record anything about the identity of a person making a change to the data. With the latest release of Oracle, this information is now recorded. Obviously this takes some space (not a lot) in the redo log. If you are really pushed to find the last little bit of I/O performance on the redo log files, you can tell Oracle to stop recording this bit of information by setting the parameter TRANSACTION_ AUDITING to FALSE.

Problems and Quirks

It is now possible to add new constraints to tables without locking the table for a long time, but to do so you still need two very brief moments when there are no active transactions on the table: the first to add the constraint in a NOVALIDATE state and the second to start the validation. Oracle does not wait on the necessary enqueues if there are any active transactions; instead, it immediately returns error "ORA-00054: resource busy and acquire with NOWAIT specified."

Although there is a command to disable a constraint and all constraints that depend on it, there is no matching command to reenable all the constraints. You have to hunt them down and do them one at a time. For this reason it is a good idea to generate an explicit list of constraints rather than depending on the CASCADE option.

Unfortunately, there is no "official" way to find out which index Oracle is using to validate a constraint, but by hunting through the data dictionary it is possible to discover that the ENABLED column of SYS.CDEF$ gives you the object number of the index enabling that constraint. The following SQL code is a sample of how to find the index name for a primary key or unique key constraint owned by a given user:

```
select
    obj.name
from
    sys.user$    usr,
    sys.con$     con,
    sys.cdef$    def,
    sys.obj$     obj
where
    usr.name = 'JPL1'
and con.owner# = usr.user#
and con.name = 'PK_I'
```

```
and def.con# = con.con#
and obj.obj# = def.enabled
;
```

Basically, using triggers for referential integrity constraints doesn't work. If you do use triggers for exotic referential integrity checks, then you may reduce the window for contention and/or error by calling autonomous transactions to check for the existence of parents, especially if you then wrap all data changes in procedures rather than leaving them to the end user to issue the commit.

Strategy Notes

Think very seriously about adding NOT NULL constraints to every column you use in a unique key constraint—in particular, ones that already are the target of foreign key constraints. Define the columns at the child end of such a relationship as NOT NULL as well.

Don't forget to create indexes for foreign key constraints if you expect to delete or update rows in the parent table. The child table locks in the absence of an index starting with the columns of the foreign key constraint.

Consider taking advantage of deferrable referential integrity constraints. Although primary keys are not supposed to change, sometimes you find that they just have to. This can be very painful if there are foreign key constraints in place that are not deferrable.

Defining nonunique indexes to enable primary key and unique key constraints makes it much quicker to find and fix duplicates in data that is supposed to be (very close to) unique.

Do not use the SET CONSTRAINTS ALL option to set constraints DEFERRED or IMMEDIATE. Lack of precision in code leads to nasty side effects and surprises. Always set an explicitly named list of constraints.

If you are using triggers for exotic referential integrity checks, you may reduce the window for contention and/or error by calling autonomous transactions to check for the existence of parents.

Part III

Data Manipulation

CHAPTER 19

PL/SQL

There isn't really a lot to be said about PL/SQL. It is, after all, just a programming language that happens to be quite good at talking to Oracle databases. It was introduced to the world many years ago as the "Procedural Language extension to SQL," which suggests that it is a little add-on rather than a major working environment. This is probably the safest way to view it when you start to develop your applications. Nevertheless, it has to be said that its use seems to have blossomed into something much larger than its name would suggest.

There are a number of useful little jobs that can be done with PL/SQL, but strategically there are only two sensible approaches to using it. Unfortunately, there are three ways in which it is commonly used and the third way often turns into a disaster, so from time to time PL/SQL gets rather bad press.

In my view, the two strategic uses for PL/SQL come at opposite ends of the spectrum. For OLTP systems, a PL/SQL package handles a single (logical) row coming from an end user's input screen and gets it safely to the database. In effect, the package could be viewed as a layer that converts from an object-oriented front end to the relational back end. For data warehouse types of systems, PL/SQL is a useful tool for driving large-scale SQL statements (for example, CTAS), and for trapping the Oracle-based exception when things go wrong.

The one thing that PL/SQL should not be used for, but is frequently, is the movement of large volumes of data to or around the database one row at a time. It can be done, of course, and sometimes it can be done reasonably successfully. However, the overhead can be staggering. I have to say that PL/SQL may, from time to time, be the "least worst" way of getting a complex data load implemented, but it should never be considered the strategic path or first-choice method for data loading.

Of course, no discussion of PL/SQL could be complete without at least a brief mention of the increasingly large number of packages that Oracle

Corporation is supplying with PL/SQL interfaces, so I will make a few comments about some of the more recently added packages.

What Is PL/SQL?

Before talking about the interesting new bits of PL/SQL, it is worth summarizing in just a couple of paragraphs what it is and what it can do. There are two main aspects to PL/SQL. First, it is a simple, elegant programming language. It handles the usual set of control structures such as loops, if . . . then, and so on. It is block structured with strict scoping rules. Each block can have an exception handler to deal with errors. It can construct complex data types from base data types. It can call libraries (known as *packages*). (For traditional programmers, think of languages like Ada, Modula-2, Pascal.)

The second and more important aspect of PL/SQL is that it understands native Oracle SQL, and has a seamless interface between the basic components of the programming language and the facilities of SQL. Consequently, the two following fragments of code are equally naturally expressed in PL/SQL:

```
begin

    -- Simple variable for counted loop
    for i in 1..10 loop

        -- Call a library routine for output
        dbms_output.put_line(i);

    end loop;
end;
/

begin

    -- Record variable for implicit cursor loop
    for r1 in (select table_name from user_tables) loop

        -- Call a library routine for output
        dbms_output.put_line(r1.table_name);

    end loop;
end;
/
```

There are all sorts of additional details about how PL/SQL operates, but these two points are enough to give you a good flavor of how it works.

There were four traditional problems with PL/SQL as a programming language. First, it is interpreted, albeit through a semicompiled "virtual machine code" or PCODE, which makes it slower than a fully compiled language. Second, when it acquired data from the database it used to do so one row at a time, which is very inefficient. Third, it was quite difficult to write programs to handle dynamically generated SQL. The earlier versions of PL/SQL effectively required all your SQL code to be declared when you created the program. Finally, it was too easy, so beginners would write long, rambling programs doing things in very nonrelational ways, because they simply translated their thoughts into PL/SQL as they went.

There isn't much that Oracle Corporation can do about the last problem, other than run training courses. The first problem is a little intractable, although Oracle Corporation is always working to improve the efficiency of the interpreter so that the difference between interpreted PL/SQL and compiled C is not (usually) the most significant CPU cost of a job.

The most significant changes to PL/SQL in recent releases have aimed at making it easy for PL/SQL to handle extremely dynamic SQL (which isn't necessarily a good thing), and allowing data transfers between the program and the database to be much more efficient by using multirow (array) processing.

The Best Bits

There are probably four features in PL/SQL in Oracle 8.1 that would get most votes in a poll:

1. Native dynamic SQL
2. Array processing with PL/SQL variables
3. Passing result sets in to and out of procedures
4. Running procedures with the privilege of the caller

Although there is a lot that could be said about PL/SQL in general, I will restrict this section to a few observations on why these features are likely to be particularly useful.

Native Dynamic SQL

With version 7 of Oracle, it was possible to send text strings to a procedure and have the procedure build them into SQL statements and execute them

dynamically. There were two methods for doing this: the package DBMS_
SQL and the shortcut for DDL statements, the packaged procedure DBMS_
UTILITY.EXEC_DDL_STATEMENT().

For simple DML or DDL statements, these tools were quite straightforward, but when you started to use them for *select* statements, things could
get a little harder. It was possible, but it was not a trivial process. Oracle 8.1
makes life much simpler with native dynamic SQL. As an example of the
change of approach, the following two code samples show the same simple
task being done using the two different methods:

```
create or replace procedure Version7 (
        i_id    in  number,
        i_table in  varchar2
) as

    m_value     varchar2(32);
    m_cursor    pls_integer;
    m_junk      pls_integer;

begin
    m_cursor := dbms_sql.open_cursor;

    dbms_sql.parse(
            m_cursor,
            'select v1 from ' || i_table || ' where id = :b1',
            dbms_sql.native
    );

    dbms_sql.bind_variable(m_cursor, 'b1', i_id);

    dbms_sql.define_column(m_cursor,1,m_value,32);
    m_junk := dbms_sql.execute(m_cursor);
    m_junk := dbms_sql.fetch_rows(m_cursor);

    dbms_sql.column_value(m_cursor,1,m_value);
    dbms_output.put_line(m_value);
    dbms_sql.close_cursor(m_cursor);

end;
:/

create or replace procedure Version8 (
        i_id    in  number,
        i_table in  varchar2
```

```
) as
    m_value      varchar2(32);
begin

    execute immediate
    'select v1 from ' || i_table || ' where id = :b1'
    into m_value using i_id;

    dbms_output.put_line(m_value);

end;
/
```

As you can see, there is a significant difference in the amount of code needed to select a single value from an unspecified table.

You may ask why I have used a bind variable *id = :b1* form of coding in this example. Why didn't I simply concatenate the incoming I_ID to the string in the same way that I concatenated the incoming table name?

```
    execute immediate
    'select v1 from ' || i_table || ' where id = ' || i_id
    into m_value;
```

The answer is that I did it because I could, and it was easy, and it might save computer resources. Even though this SQL is dynamic SQL, it is quite possible that the same function will be called time and time again with the same table name passed in, but with different values for I_ID. I can't use bind variables for the table name (I would if I could), because a bind variable can only be used in places where a quoted string can be substituted. By choosing a bind variable for the incoming I_ID, I have given Oracle the chance of being able to reduce its parse costs by reusing the generated SQL code the next time the function is called with the same table name.

You may have spotted that my initial example comparing DBMS_SQL with native dynamic SQL was just a little unfair, because the example I have given for native SQL is extremely limited and can only fetch a single row from the database. The not-quite-matching example I have shown for version 7 could be modified very simply to execute a loop that fetches all the rows that meet the requirement, as follows:

```
loop
    if (dbms_sql.fetch_rows(m_cursor) != 0) then
        dbms_sql.column_value(m_cursor,1,m_value);
```

```
        dbms_output.put_line(m_value);
    else
        exit;
    end if;
end loop;
```

However, the change needed to give the Oracle 8 code the same feature is relatively small. We have to declare a *ref cursor* type (which for general use I usually declare as a 'weak_cursor_ref' type in a global package) so that we can declare a REF CURSOR variable, then open this cursor for our dynamically created statement. The code after that is fairly straightforward:

```
create or replace procedure version81(
        i_id    in  number,
        i_table in  varchar2
) as
    type weak_cursor_ref is ref cursor;
    m_cursor_ref    weak_cursor_ref;
    m_value         varchar2(32);

begin
    open m_cursor_ref for
    'select v1 from ' || i_table || ' where id = :b1'
    using i_id;

    loop
        fetch m_cursor_ref into m_value;
        exit when m_cursor_ref%notfound;
        dbms_output.put_line(m_value);
    end loop;
end;
/
```

Native dynamic SQL in Oracle 8.1 is much shorter, clearer, and easier to understand than DBMS_SQL. To get selected data into local variables we simply use the INTO clause. To pass the value of local variables into bind variables (the :b1 placeholders), we simply use the USING clause.

There are a couple tips and traps, of course (documented rather well in the manual). The most important one to remember is what to do when your dynamic SQL is actually an anonymous PL/SQL block that calls a procedure and passes it some parameters. The USING clause can actually specify the variables being used as IN, OUT, or IN OUT, and in this case they usually have to be IN OUT. Assume that GET_REFS() is a procedure declared as follows:

```
create or replace procedure get_refs(
    id          in      number,
    ref_code    out     varchar2,
    ref_text    out     varchar2
) as . . .
```

If you use the ***execute immediate*** command to call this procedure, you might do it as follows (and in this case, note how the anonymous PL/SQL block has to end with a semicolon):

```
execute immediate 'begin get_refs(:b1, :b2, :b3); end;'
using IN m_id, OUT m_ref_code, OUT m_ref_text;
```

Be warned, though, that having a clean and easy way of using dynamic SQL is a double-edge sword. A dynamically generated statement is probably a statement that has to be parsed, and parsing is one of the most expensive CPU overhead costs that takes place in Oracle. Do not be too hasty to leap in with dynamic SQL in any sort of OLTP system, or you may find that excessive parsing becomes the primary cause of performance problems.

My favorite type of use for dynamic SQL is in regular DDL jobs— perhaps a daily creation of summary tables, or a periodic generation of new partitions for a set of partitioned tables, or, for example, some code that creates a view for each of the latest partitions in all the partitioned tables owned by a user:

```
create or replace procedure view_gen as

cursor c1 is
    select table_name , partition_name
    from user_tab_partitions      utp1
    where partition_position = (
        select max(partition_position)
        from    user_tab_partitions    utp2
        where   utp2.table_name = utp1.table_name
        )
    ;

begin

    for r1 in c1 loop
        execute immediate
        'create view v_' || r1.table_name || '_' ||
```

```
            r1.partition_name || ' as select {column list} from ' ||
            r1.table_name || ' partition (' || r1.partition_name || ')';
    end loop;

end;
/
```

Apart from the simplicity, ***execute immediate*** has another advantage over DBMS_SQL. It can handle far more data types than DBMS_SQL. Because DBMS_SQL requires you to use a procedure like COLUMN_VALUE to move values from cursors to local variables, it is constrained by whatever options Oracle Corporation happens to have implemented, and currently there are no functions for object types or LOBs.

There is one very important difference between ***execute immediate*** and DBMS_SQL that comes down heavily in favor of the latter. ***Execute immediate*** allows you to process only one row at a time to and from the database. With the DBMS_SQL package, you can get the benefits of array processing (albeit at a cost of making the code even more complex), and array processing is a prize to be sought after. Naturally, Oracle 8.1 offers an alternative.

Array Processing

There are two actions that require array processing: getting data to the database and getting data from the database. However, Oracle 8.1 even manages to introduce an array interface for updates and deletes. There are only two new pieces of syntax required:

1. BULK COLLECT
2. FORALL

The BULK COLLECT syntax allows you to get all the rows for a ***select*** statement from the database into local variables in (nominally) a single call:

```
create or replace type jpl_sel_row as object (n1 number, n2 number);
/
create or replace type jpl_sel_tab as table of jpl_sel_row;
/

declare
    m_selection jpl_sel_tab;
begin
```

```
select jpl_sel_row(n1, n2)
BULK COLLECT into m_selection
from child
where n1 in (1,2,3)
;
for i in 1..m_selection.count loop
    dbms_output.put_line(
    m_selection(i).n1 || ' ' ||
    m_selection(i).n2
    );
end loop;

end;
/
```

The critical point to notice here is the BULK COLLECT that appears just before the INTO clause. This directs Oracle to fetch all rows that meet the test and return them to the relevant PL/SQL variables.

I happen to have used an object table type to hold the return values, which is why I have used the jpl_sel_row() constructor (see Chapter 15) on the base table columns. I could just as well have created variables of ordinary (INDEX BY) PL/SQL tables. In either case, PL/SQL simply extends the table types indefinitely as the data comes flowing in.

This last comment gives you a hint about the problem that BULK COLLECT can introduce. On more than one site I have found that the biggest performance problem on the database occurs when a user accidentally hits the EXECUTE QUERY key before they have filled in any query conditions. This sometimes results in queries like, *Select 20,000 sets of client details sorted by surname.* Imagine this happening through a PL/SQL procedure that does a BULK COLLECT. Not only does the database thrash away for a few seconds with all the selecting and sorting, but the PL/SQL block then starts building a 20,000-row array in memory to hold the result set, and nothing will stop it (short of a kill session).

The drawback to BULK COLLECT is that there is no throttle. Every row is fetched, and the array variable used to collect the results is extended automatically and dynamically to hold the data, irrespective of the volume.

There is a way around this problem, and this is why I started my example using an object type table rather than a PL/SQL type table. If you use a varray instead of an object type table as the target of the select, you have to specify a strict limit on the size of the varray. If you then do a "runaway" BULK COLLECT into a varray, it breaks when the limit is reached, giving Oracle error "ORA-22160: element at index [NNN] does not exist." You can then define an exception to recognize this error number, and get PL/SQL to handle the problem appropriately—perhaps error "ORA – 20001: too much data requested."

Moving to the opposite end of the system. How do we manage array processing when pushing data to the database? Oracle 8.1 has introduced the FORALL syntax. This can be put in front of any type of DML statement and allows Oracle to batch all the values in a contiguous section of a list and send them to the database with the SQL code as a single request. Let's start with the simplest example:

```
declare

    type num_type is table of number index by binary_integer;
    type vc_type is table of varchar2(32) index by binary_integer;

    num_tab num_type;
    vc_tab  vc_type;

begin
    num_tab(1) := 2;
    vc_tab(1) := 'asdf';
    num_tab(2) := 3;
    vc_tab(2) := 'wret';

    forall j in 1..num_tab.count
    insert into test_table values (num_tab(j), vc_tab(j));

end;
```

All we need is a simple list of values, and we can push all of them at the database with a single statement. Although the FORALL looks a little as if it may be a loop construct, it isn't. The syntax looks similar to start with, but there is no *loop . . . end loop*. The *insert* statement is packaged and passed to the database only once, not once per set of values.

We can do better than this, though, because updates and deletes can take the same treatment. Not only that, we can use the RETURNING clause to find out what rows we have updated or deleted, and we can combine the RETURNING clause with the BULK COLLECT clause to do a very efficient two-step dialog with the database. For example,

```
declare

    type num_tab_type is table of number index by binary_integer;
    m_num_list   num_tab_type;
    m_deleted    jpl_del_tab;

    m_n1     num_tab_type;
    m_n2     num_tab_type;

begin
    m_num_list(1) := 3;
    m_num_list(2) := 5;
    m_num_list(3) := 11;

    forall i in 1..m_num_list.count
    delete from child
    where n1 = m_num_list(i)
    returning n1, n2 bulk collect into m_n1, m_n2;

end;
/
```

In this example I've had to fall back to PL/SQL array variables for the information returned by the delete, because I couldn't persuade Oracle to "BULK COLLECT" to an object table type from the RETURNING clause. Note that I have built a little list that identifies parent keys whose children I want to delete. Each parent value deletes a handful of child rows. Because of the FORALL clause, all three target values for the delete were passed in a single call. Because of the BULK COLLECT clause, all 15 compound keys that were deleted were returned in a single call. The efficiency is quite amazing compared with the methods you had to use in earlier versions of Oracle to do this kind of job.

An important aspect of "getting it right" with Oracle is always to be aware of the new options and new possibilities offered by the latest enhancements. FORALL and BULK COLLECT offer an interesting example of how changes in infrastructure may lead to changes in design and coding strategy. Recall in Chapter 11 I outlined a possible method using *join views* to update a large table from a table of changes, and then moved on to the problem of deleting from the large table any rows that had been updated to zero. Array processing in PL/SQL may have changed the relative efficiencies of different types of operations so much that the following may be a viable alternative strategy:

```
select {key_columns, value_column}
bulk collect into {array variables}
from delta_table
;

forall i in 1..array_var1.count
update main_table
set {value_column} = {value_column} + array_value(i)
returning {value_column} bulk collect into {value_array_variable}
;

for i in 1..value_array_variable.count loop
    if value_array_variable(i) = 0 then
        copy {key values} to {key array variable}
    end if;
end loop;

forall i in 1..{key array variable} .count
delete from main_table
where {key_columns} = {key array variable} (I);
```

The steps are simple, and each one should be fairly efficient because of the array processing that is used:

1. Copy the delta table into a set of PL/SQL array variables.

2. For each row in the array, update the matching row in the main table, but return the result to another array variable. I assumed that we already cleaned the delta table so that every row does an update, and updates exactly one row. Thus there will be a one-to-one match between the array driving the updates and the array receiving the results.

3. Check each result row, and copy the key values from the corresponding array into a separate (hopefully much smaller) array if an updated row has summed to zero.

4. For each row in the smaller array, delete the identified row from the main table.

The feature this technique has in its favor is that its cost and time to complete are likely to be very predictable, and depend in a linear fashion on the volume of rows to be processed. The same predictability cannot be guaranteed for the SQL technique described in Chapter 11, in which a sudden change in access paths may result in a dramatic change in performance. The downside to this technique is the amount of memory it could demand. A very large delta table with a four-part key could result in Oracle demanding a lot of memory to hold the array variables.

One warning before you go too far with BULK COLLECT in version 8.1.5. There is a bug in the handling of explicit cursors. You may have problems with embedded code like

```
open c1;
fetch c1 bulk collect into m_num_tab;
close c1;
```

The problem shows up the second time the code is executed. The process goes into a loop during the bind stage of operating the cursor. This bug is fixed in version 8.1.6.

Passing Result Sets Into and Out of Procedures

Oracle has for some time offered ***ref cursor*** as a method for passing sets of results from a procedure to a client. The technique (which we saw earlier) is to open the ref cursor for a SQL statement on the server, and then return it to the client so that the client can select the rows as necessary.

With the advent of the OBJECT option, another method became available, which can be used quite cheaply. Both SQL and PL/SQL procedures (which also means functions) became object aware, which means that they know how to handle object types—in particular, object table types and object varray types (see Chapter 16).

To pass result sets from server to client, you need only declare functions returning a collection type, and you can use SQL at the client side to convert this to a "proper relational table" using the table() operator. The basic syntax is

```
select * from table( {some form of collection type} );
```

It is currently an irritating feature that the {some form of collection type} actually has to include the cast() operator to clarify to SQL exactly what collection type it is, so we get code like

```
select * from table( cast(collection_variable as jpl_tab) );
```

Once we have got this far with SQL, we can note that the COLLECTION variable can actually be a packaged function returning a collection type (in this case, type jpl_tab). This starts to introduce some interesting ideas, because we can do things with collections that we cannot do with relational tables. Consider the following packaged function, which builds an arbitrary collection of results in a nonrelational way, and lets the client ask for the results in batches of rows:

```
create type jpl_tab_row as object(n1 number, v1 varchar2(30));
/
create type jpl_tab as table of jpl_tab_row;
/

create or replace package table_returns as
    function return_tab(
        i_start in number default 1,
        i_size  in number default 20
    ) return jpl_tab;
end;
/

create or replace package body table_returns as

global_table    jpl_tab;

function return_tab(
    i_start in number default 1,
    i_size  in number default 20
) return jpl_tab
is

m_tab    jpl_tab := jpl_tab();

begin

    -- If the call asks for row 0, then a
    -- new set of data should be built.
    -- Anything could be done here to populate
    -- the Object Type table. In this case I have
    -- created 45 rows of meaningless data.

    if i_start = 0 then
        global_table := jpl_tab();
        for i in 1..45 loop
            global_table.extend;
            global_table(i) := jpl_tab_row(i,to_char(i));
        end loop;
    end if;
```

```
        -- Copy part of the table, from the requested
        -- start point, for the number of rows requested
        -- into a temporary variable. If we overshoot
        -- the end of the global table, knock of the extra
        -- row we have added to the temporary table.

        for i in 1..i_size loop
            m_tab.extend;
            begin
                m_tab(i) := global_table(i_start + i-1);
            exception
                when subscript_beyond_count then
                    m_tab.trim;
                    exit;
            end;
        end loop;


        return m_tab;
    end;


    end;
    /


    rem
    rem now a couple of sql calls to the function.
    rem

    select *
    from table(
        cast(table_returns.return_tab(0,20) as jpl_tab)
    );

    select *
    from table(
        cast(table_returns.return_tab(21,20) as jpl_tab)
    );
```

Provided the client stays in contact with the server (in other words, it connects and holds a single session), you can use an approach like this to generate any list of results you like, and then get them returned to the client in any size batch you like, with the added advantage that your application can easily "scroll" backward and forward through the result set. Not only that, the list looks exactly like the result from a simple *select* statement. There were two traditional alternatives to this approach. The first was to generate the list in a temporary table, which would generate rollback and redo, and a need to clean up afterward, although this is not so much of an issue now if you remember to use global temporary tables (see Chapter 9). The second alternative was to reexecute the list generation process for each batch of results, but read 20 rows on the first call, then read 40 rows and discard 20 rows on the second call, then read 60 rows and discard 40 rows on the third call, and so on. This had two problems: It did far too much work, and the data could change between calls, so the returned results could be misleading. Providing your client maintains its session connection with the server, this object type approach could be a good alternative to the temporary table approach.

Passing sets of data to Oracle is equally straightforward. Once a suitable collection type exists (typically you might create a package to hold a few commonly used object type definitions), you can create variables of that type and pass them around just like any other variable. The question often arises, How do I build a list of comma-separated values and pass it to a procedure, or SQL statement, as a single bind variable? For example, I would like a procedure to execute a query like

```
Select country_name
from countries
where country_code in (13, 29, 42)
;
```

but I would like my query to pass the list "13, 29,42" to the procedure as a single bind variable, because bind variables are good and they cut down on the contention and CPU waste caused by large amounts of parsing. The answer is quite simple if we use object types as parameters, although it is somewhat irritating how many different object types we could end up creating just to be able to use this trick. Consider the following type declarations and procedure:

```
create type list_item as object(n1 number);
/
create type list_table as table of list_item;
/
create or replace procedure use_list (i_list in list_table) as

cursor c1 is
    select country_name
```

```
        from countries
        where country_code in (
                select n1
                from table(cast(i_list as list_table))
        );

begin
    for r1 in c1 loop
        -- do something with country names
    end loop;
end;
/
```

We have created an object type to represent a list of numbers. (We could have eliminated one *type creation* statement by creating the table type simply as "create type list_table as table of number," but I prefer to be able to name the attributes of my user-defined types.) We have then used the table type as a parameter to a procedure. The important part of the code, though, appears inside the procedure when we turn the object type into a subquery using the table() and cast() operators. This is the mechanism that allows us to use a single bind variable as a list of values. To use this procedure, we could do something like the following at the client end of the system:

```
declare
    m_list list_table;   -- A variable matching the type above
begin
    m_list :=
        list_table(
            list_item(13),
            list_item(29),
            list_item(42)
        );
    use_list(m_list);
end;
/
```

Of course, one of the reasons for using the table()/cast() operators was to reduce the amount of parsing done by the optimizer when handling lists. So if the anonymous block actually has to be sent to the server for parsing, you have eliminated the benefit. When experimenting with new techniques like this, make sure that your attempts to reduce a problem are not simply moving it.

Invoker Rights

Prior to Oracle 8.1, when one user ran a procedure that had been created by another user, the procedure ran with the privileges that had been granted directly to the owner of the procedure, and not with the privileges of the user. If you want to see the privileges a user has been given and where they come from, you need to check loads of view families: xxx_SYS_PRIVS, xxx_ROLE_PRIVS, xxx_TAB_PRIVS_RECD, xxx_COL_PRIVS_RECD, ROLE_TAB_PRIVS, ROLE_SYS_PRIVS, and ROLE_ROLE_PRIVS.

> *Developers often find that they can write a specific piece of SQL code that works from the SQL*Plus prompt, but is rejected with errors like "object does not exist" when they embed it in a stored procedure. This usually means that they can see the object through a specially granted role, rather than through a directly granted privilege or the PUBLIC role. Try running the SQL code after issuing "set role none" to see what happens.*

In general, this strategy was very convenient and enhanced data security. If DATA_OWNER had created a procedure called INSERT_LOANS, which existed to insert rows into the table DATA_OWNER.LOANS, then any user who was allowed to execute the procedure could get data into the LOANS table, even though they did not actually have the privilege to insert data into that table. This led to a fairly common client/server coding strategy whereby users were allowed to **select** from tables (often through views), but they always did inserts, updates, and deletes by calling procedures.

On the other hand, there were times when this restriction could be a little irritating. If user Joe ran a procedure created by user Fred to create a table T12345, then the table would be created in Fred's schema, not in Joe's. This made it difficult if you wanted a user to be able to create a local table, populate it, and report from it under control of a procedure (a situation that could perhaps be addressed by using global temporary tables).

With Oracle 8.1, a small change to a procedure causes the procedure to run with the privileges (including the currently enabled role privileges) of the user that calls the privilege. Assume that Fred ran the following code to create a procedure, and granted EXECUTE on this code to public.

```
create or replace procedure create_temp
AUTHID CURRENT_USER
```

```
-- the default is AUTHID DEFINER
as
begin
    -- Note the absence of a ';' at the end of the
    -- SQL statement inside the string.
    execute immediate
    'create table temp (n1 number , v1 varchar2(20))'
    ;
end;
/
```

User Joe could then call procedure FRED.CREATE_TEMP and find that the table TEMP was created in Joe's schema.

In this example, I created a stand-alone procedure. You can use the AUTHID clause with the ***create package*** statement as well, in which case all the functions and procedures in the package execute with the given authority.

You do have to be a little cautious with AUTHID CURRENT_USER procedures. Remember that they operate with the *current* privileges of the user, and any objects named in the procedure have their names resolved at runtime. This requires much more work to be done by the parser, and it hits the library cache a little harder. Also, every single user using the procedure may have to reparse it to resolve object names in their own schema and privilege map. So not only is the parse more expensive, it occurs more often.

Supplied Packages

Oracle supplies a very large number of packages with the standard installation. Some of them are loaded automatically as part of the process for creating a database, and some have to be installed manually by running scripts in $ORACLE_HOME/rdbms/admin. Unfortunately, the documentation of and the advertising for these packages was very sparse, so very few people have discovered them. In release 8.1, there is a manual entitled *Supplied Packages Reference,* so there is no longer any excuse for not knowing about them.

For example, one of the very commonly asked questions is, When I have allocated 12,000 blocks to a table, how do I find out how many have actually been used? The two most common answers are, Analyze the table and check the view family xxx_TABLES for the column BLOCKS, which tells you the answer, or run an expensive SQL statement that counts the number of distinct block addresses from the rowids in the table. The first answer may have undesirable effects and may take a long time anyway. The second answer will definitely take a long time. The best answer (probably) is to use a packaged procedure that has been lurking in Oracle for the last seven years: DBMS_SPACE.UNUSED_SPACE, given enough information to identify the object, tells you how many blocks are allocated to the object and how many are not yet in use. Unfortunately this procedure cannot yet deal with LOB segments and LOB index segments, so you have to fall back to dumping data blocks some of the time. Some packages that I think are particularly worth drawing attention to because they answer a number of frequently asked questions are presented in Table 19-1.

Table 19-1. Packages and Their Descriptions

Package	Description
DBMS_APPLICATION_INFO	This has actually been around for some time. It can be used to push module and action names into the dynamic performance view V$SESSION so that standard monitoring tools can get an idea of where in a complex job a process has got to. It can push numeric information into V$SESSION_LONGOPS to indicate how long a job will be and how much of it is already complete. Of course, you could always do this with your own tables, but by using the package you generate no rollback and redo, and you don't have to worry about commits to make the information visible to a monitoring session.
DBMS_JOB	This package has also been around for some time and is the answer to the question, How do I schedule a database process that I want to run every hour? If the process can be wrapped in a PL/SQL procedure, then it can be queued by DBMS_JOB.
DBMS_PROFILER	This is new to Oracle 8.1. To install it you need to run profload.sql as SYS, and proftab.sql in another schema that wants to do profiling. The latter creates a RUN table, UNIT table, and DATA table. Profiling entails Oracle recording in memory the number of calls and time spent in each subroutine as a session executes its normal PL/SQL code. At the end of the profiled run, or intermittently on command, Oracle dumps the results into the profiling tables (using autonomous transactions). You will need to write a little report to

Package	Description
	join these tables to get useful statistics on a PL/SQL run. Be careful. Every single call to a procedure or function gets a row in the DATA table, which could get very big.
DBMS_RANDOM	This package is new with version 8.1 and is enhanced in version 8.1.6. It does not install automatically. In Oracle 8.1.5, the package can only return random integers, but in Oracle 8.1.6 it has been enhanced with such things as the ability to return numbers within a range, random strings, and random numbers from a normal distribution.
DBMS_SPACE	This package has been around for a very long time and is the most cost-effective way of answering the question, How much space is left before a new extent will be allocated? It allows you to find how many blocks are above a segment's high water mark, and how many blocks are in the free lists.
DBMS_STATS	Life with the CBO has always been a little difficult. How do you develop code to run on a 100GB database and test it on a 1GB database when the access path that Oracle takes is dictated in part by the volume of the data? Actually, partitioning helps, because the paths could be the same if the 1GB represents one partition out of 100. To address the general problem, DBMS_STATS allows you to "fake" any statistics you like in object definitions. You can copy statistics from a production system to a development system; you can invent your own. This even extends to the level of inventing column distribution histograms for skewed data.
UTL_SMTP	Introduced in version 8.1.6, this package allows you to send (but not receive) email using the SMTP protocol. The mailer program has to be executing on the server, but is invoked from the client.

Problems and Quirks

If you want to use PL/SQL to handle a bulk data-processing job on a multiple-CPU machine, remember that only one CPU runs the actual PL/SQL bits of code (although the embedded SQL may be able to call on parallel execution to use more CPUs).

SQL tends to advance faster than PL/SQL can keep up, so various features that work with the standard SQL engine are not recognized by PL/SQL. In this release of Oracle, the *cube*, *rollup*, and *sample* keywords are not recognized. Similarly the table() operator is not recognized. The standard workaround for this problem is to use native dynamic SQL with ref cursors so that the PL/SQL engine itself never sees the SQL that it is manipulating.

Any SQL code running under PL/SQL runs with ALL_ROWS optimization, unless the database optimizer goal is "rule," which it shouldn't be in version 8.1.5. This is logically sound, because we can assume that the PL/SQL block cannot return until all the data has been retrieved, but ALL_ROWS optimization often helps Oracle to choose an inefficient path. You might want to be a little fussy about putting hints into critical SQL inside PL/SQL.

Do not be too casual about creating procedures running under AUTHID CURRENT_USER. The parse time costs are much higher than the one-time parse costs of AUTHID DEFINER.

BULK COLLECT allows you to do array fetches from the database into array variables. However, it will fetch *all* rows, which means that a badly constructed query (for example, the user hits Execute Query before putting in any constraints on a query form) could cause a massive memory overload as thousands of rows are hauled into local memory.

There is an unfortunate bug with BULK COLLECT when using an explicit cursor, which requires a parameter. It works fine the first time you open the cursor in a session, but if you run the same bit of code again, even with the same parameter, the session goes into an infinite loop, trying to bind the parameter to the cursor. Try it, and run a 10046 trace to see what I mean.

Strategy Notes

PL/SQL was launched as the "Procedural Language extension to SQL." Even though this seems a little dated as a description of what PL/SQL can do, when creating a job in PL/SQL you should plan it in two stages: Stage 1, what's the best I can do in pure SQL? Stage 2, how do I use PL/SQL to add value?

There are huge numbers of packages defined in $ORACLE_HOME/rdbms/admin/dbms*.sql, and usually described in the *Supplied Packages*

Reference. Make sure you look through them before you start reinventing the wheel.

If you do write large-scale PL/SQL processes, and find that they take a long time to complete (and you can prove that the problem is not the SQL), consider wrapping the process with calls to DBMS_PROFILER. This generates a table of data that gives the time spent in each call to each procedure. (Be warned, though, this could be a very large volume of data.)

Even though native dynamic SQL is very quick and easy to write, don't use it unless you have to, and then make sure that you use bind variables whenever possible rather than taking the extremely simple option of concatenating everything into a string.

You may want to consider using varrays with BULK COLLECT so that a query is limited in the number of rows it can pull from the database, and so that you can trap the exception when the varray hits its limit.

The DBMS_SQL package is not completely redundant, because it is still the only way to do a size-controlled array fetch in batches from the database in PL/SQL variables.

The ability to change the appearance of data from relational table to object table and back again using the table() and cast() operators can make it very easy to deal with various problems of passing the results of queries from one procedure to another or from the server to the client.

CHAPTER 20

Autonomous Transactions

As it enhances its product, Oracle Corporation often slips in little features that hardly make the marketing pages, and yet promise all sorts of potential benefits to developers. The autonomous transaction is such a feature.

How often have you faced the problem of producing some sort of audit trail, including an audit trail of things that go wrong or things that people tried but failed to achieve? Auditing is easy enough when everything goes right, but when an error occurs the audit trail tends to disappear.

How often have you been in a position where you need to use a sequence number but must guarantee not to leave any gaps. Before autonomous transactions, you could use Oracle sequences, with the risk of losing sequence numbers, or set up a mechanism that usually led to a severely choked serialized system.

There are ways to get round both of these problems using Oracle 7 features. The first port of call, although somewhat complicated and error prone, is to use database pipes made available through the DBMS_PIPE package. However, autonomous transactions in Oracle 8.1 make it all much cleaner and easier.

Simple Autonomous Transactions

An autonomous transaction is basically a unit of work that you can execute and commit in the middle of another transaction. The state of the surrounding transaction is *not* affected by the autonomous transaction, and the state of the autonomous transaction is not affected by the subsequent commit or rollback you apply in the surrounding transaction. For example, in a pseudo code form,

```
Insert into tableX values(1);
Begin autonomous transaction
     Insert into tableX values(2);
     Commit;  -- ending the autonomous transaction
Rollback;
```

After this sequence of steps, the value 2 would be found in tableX because of the commit in the autonomous transaction, but this commit would not have affected the insert of the value 1, which is rolled back by the final rollback.

Figure 20-1 presents a more complex example, highlighting the way in which the autonomous transaction should actually be viewed as a totally separate transaction that steps outside the current transaction to do its own thing. A check of the V$TRANSACTION dynamic performance view shows that the single session actually owned two separate transactions, even though (perhaps

```
create table dummy(
    dummy     varchar2(3)
);

savepoint S;

insert into dummy values ('aaa');

select * from dummy;
/* 'aaa'    */

/*
    do the autonomous TX here
*/

select * from dummy;
/* 'aaa'    */
/* 'ccc'    */

rollback to savepoint S;

select * from dummy
/* 'ccc'    */
```

```
declare
    pragma autonomous_transaction;
    v_dummy    varchar2(3);
begin
    savepoint S; -- again !
    insert into dummy values('bbb');

    select dummy
    into v_dummy
    from dummy;
    /*            'bbb'         */

    rollback to savepoint S;

    insert into dummy values('ccc');

    commit
end;
/
```

Figure 20-1. Effects of autonomous transactions.

a little strangely) the second one is not flagged in any special way as an autonomous transaction.

> *If you are going to use autonomous transactions, don't forget to increase the value of the TRANSACTIONS parameter in your init.ora file to allow for the extra concurrent transactions. (You may also need to increase the number of rollback segments.)*

Figure 20-1 shows the autonomous transaction cut out from the normal stream and stepped to one side. In the main transaction we define a "savepoint" called S and then define another savepoint S inside the autonomous transaction. In the normal flow of SQL, this savepoint would supercede the previous savepoint of the same name, but the child transaction has a completely independent context from the parent transaction. Having declared a savepoint in the child transaction as well, we insert another row in the table and check to see that it is there. It is, of course, but what has happened to the 'aaa' row? Nothing. It doesn't appear to exist because it was inserted but not committed by the parent transaction, and the parent and child transactions are independent of each other. Oracle never, ever sees changes made by another transaction until they have been committed. So we get to the rollback in the child and roll back to savepoint S (the child's savepoint S), which eliminates the value 'bbb' from our table. The child transaction then inserts the value 'ccc', commits and ends. Returning to the parent transaction, the **select** statement can see the parent's uncommitted 'aaa' and the child's committed 'ccc'. The rollback to save point S that follows is relevant only to the steps of the parent transaction and cannot affect the child transaction. So in the final select, we see that the 'aaa' has disappeared and only the 'ccc' remains.

It is possible to play all sorts of interesting little games with autonomous transactions as long as you remember just two things: An autonomous transaction occurs completely independently of anything going on around it, and the only restriction is that the transaction *must* commit or rollback before control passes back to the calling process. If you forget this point, Oracle raises error "ORA-06519: active autonomous transaction detected and rolled back" and rolls back *all* the work done in the autonomous transaction.

To declare an autonomous transaction, you can use an anonymous block, as in the previous example, or a (packaged) procedure or function. However, the pragma **autonomous_transaction** must appear in the outermost declare section of the block/function/procedure. You cannot do something like

```
Begin
    Some bits of code
    Declare
        Pragma autonomous_transaction
    Begin
        Code with commit;
    End;
    More bits of code;
End;
```

However, it is perfectly acceptable to do

```
Begin
    Some bits of code
    Call to a packaged autonomous_transaction
    More bits of code;  ·
End;
```

You have to be a little careful calling autonomous transactions, because there is one odd little feature regarding where the autonomy begins, which could easily lead to programming errors that are extremely difficult to pin down. Examine the following function definition and anonymous block, and see if you can explain the surprise:

```
Create table quirk (n1 number);

Create or replace function count_quirk return number as
    m_ct    number;
begin
    select count(*)into m_ct from quirk;
    return m_ct;
end;
/

insert into quirk values (112);

declare
    pragma autonomous_transaction;
    m_junk  number := count_quirk(); -- check current number of rows
begin
    dbms_output.put_line('Row count = ' || m_junk);
    insert into quirk values(112);   -- add one more row
    m_junk  := count_quirk();            -- check the number of rows
```

```
        dbms_output.put_line('Row count = ' || m_junk);
        commit;
    end;
    /
Row count = 1
Row count = 1
PL/SQL procedure successfully completed
```

At the start of the anonymous block, our output says we have a table with just one row in it, then we insert another row and we *still* have only one row in it. The first row reported is clearly from the parent transaction, but I've just explained that uncommitted changes made by the parent transaction cannot be seen by the autonomous child, so how come we can see it? How come it suddenly seems to disappear when we insert a row in the child transaction?

The problem is one of scope. The variables in the *declare* section of the anonymous block are set in the context of the *parent* transaction, so when I set m_junk in the declare section by calling the function count_junk(), the uncommitted row was visible and the value happens to be one. Inside the autonomous block we move into the context of a completely independent child transaction, and suddenly the uncommitted row in the parent transaction cannot be seen. The one row that we count inside the autonomous block is just the one row that we insert in the autonomous block.

The same counterintuitive behavior occurs when the PL/SQL block is called as part of a procedure. Any code that executes in the declare section of the procedure takes place in the context of the parent transaction, not in the context of the autonomous transaction. When the problem is hidden away in a black box like that it becomes much harder to track down.

Autonomous Triggers

Perhaps one of the most obvious uses for autonomous transactions is their use in table triggers. You could write the trigger to call an autonomous procedure, but you can also make the trigger code itself autonomous. The change of syntax in the trigger definition is simply

```
create or replace trigger inv_aru
after update on invoice
for each row
declare
pragma autonoumous_transaction;
--   remember this bit happens in the
```

```
--  context of the update transaction
    .    .    .
begin
--  this bit is the autonomous bit
    .    .    .
    commit;
end;
```

The particular benefit of using autonomous transactions in this circumstance is to trap the situation in which you force an illegal update to fail, but want to record the attempt. Prior to autonomous transactions, if the update failed and rolled back the "write a row to a log table to finger the guilty party" also rolled back. With an autonomous transaction, the audit trail rows are committed even though the failed update has rolled back.

A slightly less obvious use of autonomous triggers is to avoid the dreaded "mutating table" problem. If you try to create a row-level trigger on a table that attempts to examine the current table or, in a cascading update/delete, a parent table, then (except in the special case of a single-row insert of values, combined with a before-row trigger) you get Oracle error "ORA-04091: table is mutating, trigger/function may not see it." The issue that Oracle is circumventing with this error is what to do about a row-level trigger firing for the second row in a multirow update. Should it see the table in its preupdate state, or should it see the table with just the previous row updated? (Or should it perform some curious gymnastics to see the table with all the rows updated, and then with or without the application of the row-level triggers?)

If you make the trigger an autonomous transaction, then the autonomous transaction sees the table as it was at the start of the update—in other words, without being able to see *any* of the uncommitted changes being made by the parent transaction. Essentially this avoids the issue of which snapshot of the database to take when firing the trigger. Consider a table of video rental information in which each new row for a video has to record the date of the previous rental, thus allowing a simple, efficient script to analyze the average time between rentals. The requirement can be specified very easily: On insert, copy the most recent rental date for the same video into the PREVIOUS RENTAL DATE column on the incoming row:

```
create or replace trigger vrh_bri
before insert on video_rental_history
for each row
declare
```

```
      pragma autonomous_transaction;
      --  there is no actual transaction here, so
      --  we don't need a commit or rollback.
  begin
      select nvl(max(date_rented),:new.date_rented)
      into :new.date_last_rented
      from video_rental_history
      where video_id = :new.video_id;
  end;
```

For an insert like "insert into video_rental_history values('X1234', '14-jan-2000',null)," it would not have been necessary to create this trigger as an autonomous transaction because the insert meets the requirements needed to avoid the mutating table error. However, if we decide that we are going to populate VIDEO_RENTAL_HISTORY by inserting the contents of today's VIDEO_RENTAL_DAILY table as follows, we have a problem:

```
insert into video_rental history(video_id, date_rented)
select  video_id, trunc(sysdate)
from    video_rental_daily
;
```

We have to have an autonomous transaction to make our code work. But there is a trap! I was very careful to imply that the VIDEO_RENTAL_DAILY table held only the information about rentals for today. The specification intends to restrict new data to one row for each video in stock. What happens if the requirement is changed so that we hold a recent history of rentals, so that several different rental dates can appear for one video? For example, a video appears on our history as rented on 10 Jan 2000. It appears in the daily rental list on 14 and 18 Jan. We change our insert code to read

```
insert into video_rental history(video_id, date_rented)
select video_id, date_rented
from (
    select *
    from video_rental_daily
    order by video_id, date_rented
);
```

(Note, by the way, the syntax we can use in Oracle 8.1 to insert rows into a table in a presorted order. This can be a very useful trick for packing the data to make a favorite index extremely efficient.)

Clearly, we want the two new rows in our final table to look like those in Table 20-1.

Table 20-1.   What We Want

Video	Date Rented	Date Previously Rented
X1234	14 Jan 2000	10 Jan 2000
X1234	18 Jan 2000	14 Jan 2000

In fact, they look like those in Table 20-2.

Table 20-2.   What We Get

Video	Date Rented	Date Previously Rented
X1234	14 Jan 2000	10 Jan 2000
X1234	18 Jan 2000	10 Jan 2000

Why? Because we have been using autonomous transactions, and autonomous transactions cannot see the uncommitted data from their parent transactions. They see only the data that was committed at the moment the autonomous transaction started. When the trigger fired for the rental of 14 Jan, the row for 10 Jan was already a committed piece of history. When the trigger fired for 18 Jan, the row for 14 Jan had *not* been committed by the parent transaction, so it was invisible to the trigger.

So, autonomous transactions can work around the mutating table problem, but if you don't carefully think through the implications of what it means to be autonomous, and consider the timing of commits, you may be surprised by the actual results.

I have to say that in the special case in this example where the autonomous transaction works (in other words, we guarantee to insert at most one day per video), I rather like the way in which the data enhancement process is packaged into the database, rather than being written as part of the external code of a batch-loading process. It would be easy to see this transfer of data from the daily table to the history table being written as a PL/SQL loop:

```
for r1 in (select * from video_rental_daily) loop

    select  nvl(max(date_rented),r1.date_rented)
    into m_date_last_rented
    from video_rental_history
    where video_id = r1.video_id;

    insert into etc . . .
end loop;
```

Don't forget to consider the performance implications of how you handle such problems though. In fact, there is probably little to choose in performance terms between the two methods. The use of autonomous transactions makes it look as if we are using SQL in a multirow fashion to leverage the proper capability of the database, but actually the trigger merely conceals the fact that we are doing relatively slow, high overhead, row-at-a-time processing.

For this *very specific case,* ask yourselves why, instead of going to PL/SQL, I didn't just write this batch process as a single SQL statement:

```
insert into video_rental history
select
    vrd.video_id,
    vrd.date_rented,
    nvl(max(vrh.date_last_rented),vrd.date_rented)
from
    video_rental_daily      vrd,
    video_rental_history    vrh
where
    vrh.video_id = vrd.video_id
group by
    vrd.video_id,
    vrd.date_rented
;
```

Although for the purposes of demonstration I have chosen to describe a PL/SQL solution to a real problem, remember that you should never be tempted into PL/SQL by features that look cute when there is a simpler (although this may be a matter of opinion), more efficient way of getting the job done through SQL.

Finally, another observation on how you can be caught out by autonomous transactions and may have to think carefully about refining your strategies if you start using them: What happens in the following code fragment?

```
create table dead(
       n1       number       primary key,
       notes    varchar2(20)
);

insert into dead values(999,'parent');
declare
    pragma autonomous_transaction;
begin
    insert into dead values(999,'child');
    commit;
end;
commit;
```

The name of the table is a hint. Because N1 is the primary key of the table, the child transaction cannot insert a row with the same value as the parent transaction until the parent transaction commits or rolls back. But the parent transaction cannot continue until the child transaction terminates. The parent and child are deadlocked, and after three seconds the child will raise "ORA-00060: deadlock detected while waiting for resource" and will rollback, leaving the parent transaction to commit.

If you modify existing code to take advantage of autonomous transactions, you may find that your programs get into "self-deadlock" situations. If you have not changed the code to accommodate this, you may find that some ORA-00060 errors are ignored by your code, and you will suffer from apparently random data loss.

Sequence Numbers

Oracle sequences provide a high-speed, noninterfering mechanism that allows multiple users to produce unique meaningless keys that happen to come out pretty much in order. For many purposes, an Oracle sequence is sufficient to act as a key to a table, but occasionally real life (or at least the auditor) insists that a sequence should either be unbroken or, if it is broken, that there should be a record of the break.

Oracle sequences cannot cope with this scenario. If an instance crashes, sequence numbers are irretrievably lost. If you are running on Oracle Parallel

Server, then an entire batch of sequences will be lost as each instance closes down. Even if you don't cache the sequence generator, there is nothing to stop a user from rolling back a transaction and losing the sequence number.

The alternative to sequences has been to use real tables holding lists of numbers. Several third-party applications can still be found with a SEQUENCES table that has columns SEQUENCE_NAME and CURRENT_VALUE. The drawback to such tables is that they tend to serialize activity. A user wants the next sequence number, selects current_value for update, increments it, and then spends a bit of time doing something else. Until that user commits the transaction, everyone else queues up behind the "select for update."

With autonomous transactions, the queuing factor can be virtually eliminated. You simply enclose the **select for update, increment** steps in an autonomous transaction. (This is effectively how a NO CACHE sequence works. The performance impact is noticeable but not too horrendous, provided you are not running the Oracle Parallel Server.

This leaves the problem of the audit trail. After getting the sequence number, the parent transaction could still throw it away, leaving a gap. To avoid this, you need to include an extra step in the autonomous transaction that records the acquisition of the value—something like

```
insert into invoice_sequence_log (
    id, user_id, acquisition_time
)
values (
    m_id, user, sysdate
)
;
```

If the parent transaction chooses to roll back and throw away the sequence value, then this log will still show that the sequence was acquired, who acquired it, and when. No more missing records as far as the auditor is concerned.

However, on the basis that for every answer there is a new question, this log table will get extremely large, and in most cases the data it contains will be totally redundant because it will be recording sequence numbers that have presumably been used in the invoice table. How can we get rid of the rows we don't need?

Conveniently, the autonomous child transaction has to commit before the parent transaction can continue, so by the time the child passes the sequence value back to the parent, the log row is committed and visible.

Add a postinsert trigger to the table that deletes the log row if the parent commits successfully. A suitable package (stripped to a minimum) might look like the following:

```
create or replace package sequence_pack as
    function next_valuereturn number;
    function curr_valuereturn number;
end;
/

create or replace package body sequence_pack as

seq_last    number(10);

function curr_value return number is
begin
    return seq_last;
end curr_value;

function next_value return number is

    pragma autonomous_transaction;

begin
    select sequence_value
    into seq_last
    from sequence_table
    for update of sequence_value;

    insert into invoice_log values(
        seq_last, uid, sysdate
    );

    update sequence_table
    set sequence_value = sequence_value + 1;

    commit;

    return seq_last;

end next_value;
```

```
end sequence_pack;
/
```

This package would then be used by the two triggers (based on a suitably declared table):

```
create or replace trigger inv_bri
before insert on invoice
for each row
begin
    :new.invoice_id := sequence_pack.next_value();
end;
/


create or replace trigger inv_ari
after insert on invoice
for each row
begin
    --    Better have an index on invoice_log (?)
    delete from invoice_log
    where invoice_id = :new.invoice_no;
end;
/
```

To be completely effective, the package would need at least two other features—a SEQUENCE NAME parameter to make it general purpose, and a loop with a timer (using user_lock.sleep() or dbms_lock.sleep()) to retry the *select for update* in case the sequence row is currently locked.

Who Is Locking My Row?

There are some interesting ramifications that become apparent when you start running code just presented. In particular, there is the peculiarity that the *commit* in the autonomous transaction means that other sessions can see a key value that is about to be used before the session using that key commits the parent row. The chain of events is presented in Table 20-3.

Taking this thought one stage further, a commonly asked question is, How do I see which user is locking a row that I want? Well, if you modify the previous example for updates and deletes so that a pre-row update/delete uses an autonomous transaction to insert a row into a log table, and a post-row

Table 20-3.   Concurrent Sessions

Session 1 (User ID 37)	Session 2 (User ID 43)

Select ∘ from sequence table;
    value (1)
	select ∘ from sequence table
	    value (1)

insert into table invoice . . . .
    Updates sequence table
    inserts row into invoice log
    autonomous commit
    deletes row from invoice log
	select ∘ from sequence table
	    value (2)

select ∘ from invoice;
    one row visible
select ∘ from invoice_log
    no rows visible
	select ∘ from invoice;
	    no rows visible
	select ∘ from invoice log;
	    values (1, 37, '12-Feb-2000')

commit;	

No change from above	select ∘ from invoice;
	    one row visible
	select ∘ from invoice log;
	    no rows visible

update/delete deletes it *in the parent transaction,* then other processes can examine the log table to find out who is doing what to which rows.

Be warned, though, that this adds an enormous overhead to a small job. For each update, say, you are adding the creation of a secondary transaction context, a couple of calls to PL/SQL functions, and an insert and delete on an indexed table with all the attendant rollback and redo log generation. You should also note that the technique still hasn't addressed the issue of identifying rows that are locked because of *select for update* but have not yet been updated.

A Counter Example

One of the common complaints made by DBAs running third-party applications is the need to create new Oracle users when a new user has to be given access to the application. In principle there should be an application administrator who is responsible for creating a new application account, and there ought to be a job that the application administrator executes to create a new Oracle account with the appropriate privileges.

In practice, the DBA often gets a telephone request to create a new Oracle account and a new application account to use it. There may be something of a temptation at this point to create an "after insert" trigger on the APPLICATION_ACCOUNTS table with code to generate an Oracle account automatically. By declaring the code of the trigger to be autonomous, this can be achieved in Oracle 8.1. But should you do it?

What happens if, for some reason, the attempt to insert a new application_accounts row should fail? You end up with an Oracle account for which there is no corresponding application account. Next time you try to create the application account, the autonomous transaction fails (or at least it ought to) because the Oracle account exists. It wouldn't be sensible to assume that a preexisting account with the right name is the account that should exist, so your attempt to create the application account fails again.

Of course you could argue this case several ways, but an attempt to make a job easier by introducing autonomous transactions could actually result in circumstances that lead to obscure complications showing up, particularly when the autonomous transaction succeeds but its parent fails. In the counter example, you might consider using DBMS_JOB to schedule a CREATE USER procedure that sends email to the DBA (Oracle 8.1.6 introduces a PL/SQL call to the SMTP mailing mechanism) if it fails. If DBMS_JOB fails for some reason, you simply have to resubmit the job. You do not have to find a backdoor method for getting the autonomous transaction to run.

Problems and Quirks

There are currently some bugs that crop up when autonomous transactions meet other new features. Do not mix autonomous transactions with database triggers such as the "after logon" trigger. In fact, database-level triggers operate inside their own autonomous transactions with an implicit commit. This is not an excuse for the problem, but may help to explain it. In the worst case, if you execute an autonomous transaction inside an "after logon" trigger, you may find that no one will be able to use the database again. (This bug is actually documented in the readme.doc, which comes with the release, and is fixed in version 8.1.6.)

It is easy to lose track of exactly what is happening when autonomous procedures, triggers, and anonymous blocks start. Do be very careful.

You can nest autonomous transactions within autonomous transactions, but remember that each call starts a new, independent transaction, which counts against the limit defined in your init.ora file. If you are too enthusiastic with autonomous transactions, particularly black box, nested autonomous transactions, you may find that sessions start to fail randomly and spontaneously because you keep hitting the limit on transactions.

Strategy Notes

Before writing a piece of autonomous code, always ask yourself if the task should really be handled by the DBMS_JOB, DBMS_PIPE, or DBMS_AQ mechanisms. In particular, is it all right for the autonomous transaction to commit even if the parent action rolled back? Is it all right for the autonomous transaction to roll back even if the parent action commits?

There are some counterintuitive effects that appear if you start using autonomous transactions. Think very carefully about how a piece of code would behave if it were being operated by two completely different sessions. This may help you to appreciate what the side effects will be.

If you do make use of autonomous transactions, remember to accommodate the number of expected concurrent transactions per session. As a starting point, 2 × sessions may be a better value than the default of 1.1 × sessions.

Most of this book has been devoted to telling you how you can use new features of Oracle 8.1 to reduce the work done by the system because performance is the paramount feature of good design. This chapter went to the opposite extreme and described a couple of ways in which you can play around with the capabilities of autonomous transactions to achieve effects that might otherwise be impossible or difficult—at a massive overhead in data processing and I/O. Be cautious. Using autonomous transactions to store data temporarily in the database, especially when processing one row at a time, is a sure way to chew up resources very rapidly.

CHAPTER 21

Row-level Security

Since Oracle first appeared on the market, designers have argued about the best way to allow different users access to different subsets of the same data. In the age of the Internet, when more and more companies are making parts of their internal databases available to external groups, this type of security is becoming increasingly important.

Imagine you own a supermarket chain. You have a massive data warehouse that lists all your sales by product, store, and date for the last five years. This data warehouse exists to enable your buyers to spot trends, analyze the effectiveness of promotions, and check product profitability.

It would be nice to allow your main suppliers some access to this data. It would be to your advantage if they used your database to discover that they had to supply you, rather than waiting for you to order from them. They might be able to use your data to do some targeted advertising of product that would be sold through your supermarket. The benefits of publishing data like this could be significant, but the risk, overhead, and maintenance requirements in the past have been rather onerous.

Row-level security, also known as the *virtual private database* or *fine-grained access control*, is Oracle's attempt to improve the situation. To use it most effectively you need to deal with database triggers and sys_contexts, as well as the basic functionality of row-level security.

Historic Implementations

Imagine a table that is to be shared by several users, even though each user is supposed to see only her own data. To enforce this rule, we could add a column named OWNER to the table, and ensure that the user ID of the person creating a row is written into this column.

457

We could then enforce our security requirement by creating a simple view and a row-level trigger:

```
create or replace view personal_data as
select {list of columns excluding OWNER}
from complete_data
where owner = user
with check option
;

create or replace trigger cd_bri
before insert on complete_data
for each row
begin
    :new.owner := user;
end;
/
```

In this example, Oracle takes advantage of a pseudo column called USER that is always set to the value of the current user ID to turn this apparently static view into a dynamic view with contents that are different for each user. The trigger then ensures that new rows have the owner column set to the creator of the row, because the users themselves, and their applications, cannot see the column directly.

This is not particularly helpful, however, because most companies will not want data to be totally personal; they want data to be associated with departments. Of course you could make every user in the department log in with the same Oracle user ID, but that leaves the database open to abuse.

To get around this issue and subsequent issues, we start making things increasingly complex, adding cross-reference tables between users and departments. For example,

```
create or replace view department_data as
select {list of columns excluding OWNER}
from complete_data cd
where owner in (
    select  e2.empno
    from
            emp     e1,
            emp     e2
    where   e1.empno = cd.owner
    and     e2.deptno = e1.deptno
```

```
)
with check option
;
```

We could improve the efficiency of this specific example by having a DEPARTMENT column instead of or perhaps as well as an OWNER column, and change the trigger to maintain the DEPARTMENT column. This would simplify the view somewhat, although not eliminate the need for the EMP subquery. You may consider rewriting the following as a JOIN view, but if you did it would cease to be updatable.

```
create or replace view department_data as
select {list of columns excluding owner and deptno}
from
    complete_data cd
where cd.deptno = (
                select  emp.deptno
                from    emp
                where   emp.empid = user
            )
;
create or replace trigger cd_bri
before insert on complete_data
for each row
begin
    select  deptno, user
    into    :new.deptno, :new.empid
    from    emp
    where   empid = user;
end;
/
```

We then start adding views with specific privileges to the database, adding triggers to tables, getting application code to set flags, and so on. Some applications even go to the lengths of embedding SQL generators in a middle tier of code that dynamically generate the entire SQL statement according to coded rules of who is logged in.

It is usually possible to get to the desired level of data visibility, but the complexity, performance overhead, and administrative burden can be quite large. Often, too, the security depends to some degree on application code and can be bypassed by a user entering the database with the "wrong" data access tools.

Security Policies   .

Oracle's solution is to allow you to create security policies on each table. A security policy specifies a PL/SQL function that executes each time a given table is accessed and generates a string that is appended to the WHERE clause of the SQL statement accessing the table. The only user that bypasses security is the SYS, or INTERNAL, account, for which security functions are never executed. The complexity of the function is at the discretion of the designer. A couple of sample functions are

```
create or replace function week_days(
    i_schema    varchar2,
    i_object    varchar2
) return varchar2 is
begin
    if (to_char(sysdate,'Dy') in ('Sat','Sun')) then
        return '1=0';
    else
        return null;
    end if;
end;


create or replace function supplier_check(
    i_schema    in  varchar2,
    i_object    in  varchar2
)
return varchar2 is
m_pred       varchar2(200) := '1=0';;
begin
    if (user in ('DEMO','JPL1')) then
        m_pred:='id in (select id from supps where user_id = user)';
    end if;
    return m_pred;
end;
```

Note that I have given both these functions a pair of input parameters. The code for row-level security passes in the schema name and the object name for the object to which the function applies.

The first function ensures that the data is protected on Saturdays or Sundays simply by supplying the permanently false condition "and 1 = 0" whenever it is called on the weekend.

The second function statement restricts the user's access to the table according to the contents of a cross-reference table that lists the ID values to which each user is allowed access. If the user is not in the reference table, then the default security is to hide all data, again by returning the predicate 1 = 0.

> *Always have a fail-safe predicate such as 1 = 0 returned by your security functions. If something goes wrong, it is probably better to hide all the data than reveal all the data.*

Having created our function, we have to tell Oracle when it is supposed to be used—in other words, to which tables and for what actions it applies. To do this we need to have the EXECUTE privilege on the package DBMS_RLS.

Assume we have created a table called SALES_PRODUCTS. We have been granted EXECUTE rights on the DBMS_RLS package and have created the function WEEK_DAYS in the package LOCAL_SECURITY. To make sure that people can not change the data in that table over the weekend, we can issue a command such as

```
begin
    dbms_rls.add_policy (
        object_schema    => user,
        object_name      => 'sales_products',
        policy_name      => 'weekdays_only',
        function_schema  => user,
        policy_function  => 'local_security.week_days',
        statement_types  => 'insert,update,delete',
        update_check     => TRUE,
        enable           => TRUE
    );
end;
/
```

This creates a policy called WEEKDAYS_ONLY on our table that stops any inserts, updates, or deletes at the weekend, although there is nothing yet in place to stop people from selecting data from the table. Effectively, Oracle replaces the table SALES_PRODUCT with an in-line view defined as "select * from sales_product where 1 = 0" whenever it sees an *insert*, *update*, or *delete* statement involving SALES_PRODUCT.

Other calls exist in the DBMS_RLS package to drop a policy, enable or disable a policy, and refresh a policy, which means forcing a reparse of all the open cursors that currently depend on that policy. The view family xxx_POLICIES tells you all about existing policies.

A few points to note about the ***add policy*** command:

- I have used the ***user*** pseudo constant to identify the schema containing both the object and the function that applies to it. This is convenient for simple schema arrangements, and makes it easy to shift static code from a development schema to a test or production schema. You could, however, use string literals or globally packaged variables if your schema arrangement is more complex.

- The object_name parameter can apply to a table or a view.

- The policy_function used for this policy can be used in as many policies as we want on as many other tables as we want. We do *not* have to write a separate function for each table.

- update_check behaves like the WITH CHECK option for views. You can choose to insist that the data can only be inserted or updated in such a way that it remains visible according to the policy code.

- statement_types is a string listing any combination of the words *select, insert, update,* and *delete.* You can have a single policy to cover all four options, use one policy for each option, or leave some options with no policy at all.

This last point raises an important question: Should you have different policies for the four different operations, and if so, should you impose any restrictions on them? Imagine the confusion and possible threat to data integrity when a user runs through the following steps:

```
SQL>lock table t1 in exclusive mode;
Table(s) locked

SQL>select count(*) from t1 where client_id = 23;
COUNT(*)
--------
      10


SQL>delete from t1 where client_id = 23;
12 rows deleted   -- where did the extra 2 rows come from ?!
```

Pursuing this theme a little further, how do you handle things like primary keys and referential integrity? How is a user going to react to the following apparent contradiction?

```
SQL> insert into t1 values (15,'short name','description');
insert into t1 values (15,'short name','description')
            *
ERROR at line 1:
ORA-00001: unique constraint (DEMO.T1_PK) violated
-- it already exists.

SQL> select * from t1 where id = 15;
no rows selected
-- oh no it doesn't.
```

Adding more subtlety to the possible confusion, row-level security is bypassed when referential integrity constraints are being checked. If you don't make sure that you have designed a perfectly consistent row-level security policy, you could be in a position in which you can insert a child row into a table without being able to see its parent. If you do so and then try to join the two tables, you will find that the row you have inserted "disappears" because there is no visible row to which to join it. For example, T1 and T2 are tables with a referential integrity constraint defined:

```
alter table t2
add constraint t2_fk_p1 foreign key (id) references t1;

insert into t2 values (1,1,'xxx');
1 row inserted

select * from t2 where id = 1;
        ID    LINENO PADDING
---------- ---------- ------------------------------
        1         1 xxx

select t2.* from t1,t2 where t2.id = 1 and t1.id = t2.id
no rows selected
```

This highlights one of the great strengths of row-level security, which unfortunately can also be viewed as a great weakness. It is virtually impossible to detect that a security policy has been active, and there are no indications to the program running a SQL statement that the statement has been subverted in any way.

Even if you scan the V$SQL dynamic performance view (see Appendix B), or generate trace files from sessions, you cannot see the modified text that is actually parsed. There is one tiny clue that row-level security is going on: You may spot several different versions of the same statement in V$SQL with a different PARSING_SCHEMA_ID and strikingly different costs for the statement for different IDs. This could indicate that each of the IDs actually has a different security predicate and is actually parsing a different statement.

> *If a table has a security policy associated with it, then pulling SQL statements from V$SQL does not show the policy, and applying EXPLAIN PLAN to them may not give you the true execution path.*

In fact even the trace files can be very puzzling because the execution paths in the trace files may include tables that don't seem to be part of the SQL statements they are describing. This gets even more confusing, of course, if you use tkprof to analyze the trace files. The row-level security policy for the ID that you use to explain the execution plans may not match the row-level security policy used by the ID that executed the data.

The only cheap way that I currently know to see anything of row-level security being executed is to set event 10730, which dumps a small trace file that shows details of the object, function, and resulting extra predicate the first time a statement is parsed, and even this isn't much help unless SQL_TRACE has also been set so that the statement to which the predicate applies is dumped nearby. The total output of the 10730 dump is as follows:

```
Logon user     : JPL1
Table or View  : JPL1.T2
Policy name    : HIDE_T2
Policy function: JPL1.RESTRICTION
RLS predicate  : mod(id,3) = 0
```

In fact, when I tried to find a way of monitoring the row-level security system, I found that global variables could not be set inside the function when called by row-level security, dbms_output.put_line would not execute, and autonomous transactions caused row-level security to fail with error "ORA-28112: failed to execute policy function." These may be bugs, but it seems that row-level security tries very hard to conceal itself from the end user. In the end, I used **utl_file** commands in the policy function to write to a file every time the function was called. You may prefer to use **dbms_pipe**, which also works as expected.

Of course you may question the complexity of using row-level security for examples as simple as the Saturday/Sunday test. You would be quite right to do so. If you have a nice, clean strategy and it works, why change to a new one? If you want to stop data access on the weekend, what's wrong with a view that embeds the clause WHERE TO_CHAR(SYSDATE,'DY') NOT IN ('SAT','SUN').

There are a couple of arguments in favor of row-level security. What do you do if you want to allow users to be able to see the data on the weekend, but restrict inserts, updates, and deletes to working hours? Do you have two views, or one view and one trigger? Actually, the "right" answer, as far as I am concerned, is that all **select** statements should be through views, and all end-user inserts, updates, and deletes should be through packages. It is very easy for a sophisticated security implementation to acquire lots of little bits of code all over the place. With row-level security it is easier to centralize and minimize the code that controls the policy.

Another point to bear in mind is the potential for efficiency, even on a very simple policy. If you add the predicate 1 = 0 to stop any data access, then the optimizer recognizes that this condition is always FALSE and does not visit the table to look for data. If you supply a more complex condition through a view, you will probably find that the optimizer cannot spot that the predicate is always FALSE and then tests it against every row that would otherwise be returned from that table. (This used to be true for almost any date-based test, such as the "week_days" example, but Oracle 8.1 is much better than its predecessors at spotting opportunities for avoiding work.)

While thinking about efficiency, remember that the security policy is called the first time that a statement is parsed. This generates a significant overhead because the policy function has to be called and has to run. If you have built an OLTP system that doesn't reuse its SQL (by using bind variables instead of building string literals), then the overhead is enormous. OLTP systems should always be designed to use bind variables whenever possible. If you attach row-level security to an OLTP system, then the need for bind variables is absolutely critical, otherwise, the execution of row-level security policy code at parse time becomes the biggest bottleneck on the system.

Refining Row-level Security

As we have seen, row-level security can cause confusion and needs careful planning. It is hard enough for end users that you may put different policies onto a table for select, insert, update, and delete. It gets worse when you realize that even very simple policies can lead to unexpected side effects.

Let us reconsider the function that I defined to ensure that data changes could not happen over the weekend. I attached this function to table SALES_PRODUCT so that any *insert*, *update*, or *delete* statement referencing that table would have the predicate "and 1 = 0" attached to it on the weekend, thus guaranteeing that the statement could not affect any rows.

Imagine, now, that I have a three-tier, Web-serving application that has a limited number of SQL statements built into it. For the sake of efficiency I have set the compiler options to hold cursors as long as possible to reduce the number of hard parses that take place (release_cursor = NO).

I start up the application servers on Saturday morning, and all through the weekend they faithfully protect my data from being modified. Come Monday morning, they carry on protecting my data! Why? Because the cursors are still open and never get reparsed, and the security policy is only executed as the cursor is parsed. Of course, some cursors may get their first-ever parse call on Monday, leaving us with some code that blocks data changes and some code that allows data changes. Isn't that going to have a wonderful effect on data integrity and user sanity? This problem couldn't happen with the alternative view-based approach.

> *Row-level security isn't necessarily the best solution for all aspects of security. Sometimes views and/or triggers are more appropriate or more efficient.*

Based on this particular problem you may be inclined to argue that it is a defect that the security function is evaluated only once for each different SQL statement. On the other hand, imagine the overhead of evaluating the function once for every execution of every statement.

There is also a converse problem. What happens if you do something that changes the predicate returned by the function? You could get into the peculiar circumstance in which the "same" query on a table returns different results, especially if you are using a lot of PL/SQL or a 3GL with the HOLD_CURSOR option set. A fragment of highly artificial PL/SQL shows how this can occur. Imagine I have a predicate function (which I have not shown) that generates a predicate 1 = 0 if the value in RLS_FIX_TABLE is 0, and 1 = 1 otherwise. Consider what happens in the following code fragment, which happens to update RLS_FIX_TABLE as it runs:

```
update rls_fix_table set target_value = 0;
for i in 1..10 loop
    if (mod(i,2) = 1)then
        select count(*) into m_dummy from test_table;
    else
            update rls_fix_table set target_value = 1;
            select count(*) into dummy from test_table;
        end if;
    end if;
    dbms_output.put_line('Row count: ' || m_dummy);
```

The first time you hit the test of mod(i,2) you go through the upper branch of the code where the call to the predicate function sets the predicate to 1 = 0 because target_value is currently zero, so the count in M_DUMMY will be zero.

The second time through the loop the test of mod(i,2) takes you through the lower branch, which changes target_value to one before executing the critical **select** statement.

Because the **select** statement in this section of code is *not* the same statement as the one in the first branch (even though it appears to be identical), it has to be parsed, and so the predicate function is called again, returning 1 = 1, and M_DUMMY is set to the actual number of rows in the table.

The third time through the loop you go through the first branch again. This time the predicate function would return 1 = 1 *if it were called*; however PL/SQL has cached this cursor so it is not reparsed, the predicate function is not called again, and the **select** statement executes with its original predicate attached, so it returns the same zero count as before. As you cycle through the loop, then, count(*) cycles back and forth between zero and the actual number of rows in the table.

Of course, this is a trivial and very artificial example. It is possible, though, to write code that is complex enough that you can get caught in this trap without noticing the error that is so obvious to us now. The best way to avoid this problem is to insist that the text of the predicate generated has to stay constant for the session. This doesn't mean that the *effect* of the predicate has to stay constant, because we could create a predicate that checks the content of a control table as we did in the second example in which the supplier_check function that generates a predicate to test the content of the SUPPS table is based on the user's ID. Even then, we can still get caught in traps like the ('Sat','Sun') problem, so we also have to ensure that our predicates are not generated by code that tests a dynamic

situation to produce the actual equivalent of the boolean values TRUE or
FALSE (for example, 1 = 1 or 1 = 0).

If we do restrict ourselves to predicates that cannot change textually, the
options seem to have a built-in restriction. The only thing that stays constant
for a user during a session is the user's identity. So the only way to write constant predicates is to use the user's name or ID as the basis for a query. But
as soon as you start writing more complex security checks, you start using
increasing numbers of tables in the security predicate. Imagine a system in
which you may only see data in a table if you are in the same department as
the person who created the data. The security predicate would look something like

```
creator in (
        select id from user_depts
        where dept = (
            select dept from user_depts
            where id = user
        )
    )
```

Translated to English, the creator of the row must be in the department that
the current user is in. But to create this simple security test, we have written a
predicate that adds two tables to any query fired at this table. There is a fair
chance that this will add a considerable load at parse time, and especially at
runtime, if the query already uses several tables. To reduce the need for multitable predicates of this type, we can use the new CONTEXT feature (not to
be confused with the text-searching CONTEXT option).

A context is really nothing but a list of (attribute_name, value). The existence of such a list is specified by an entry in a normal Oracle table, but the
actual content is session specific and is held in one of Oracle's dynamic performance views. We can create a context called SALES_ANALYSIS and give it a
couple of attributes called SALES_REGION and DEPARTMENT. As the
user logs on, we can set these two attributes to the sales region and department that the user is allowed to see, which means we can produce a simpler
predicate using the sys_context() function to feed an attribute value back into
a query. For example,

```
creator in (
    select id from user_depts
        where dept = sys_context('sales_analysis','department')
    )
```

> *If you have used userenv( ) in the past (for example, "select userenv ('sessionid') from dual"), then you should note that the preferred mechanism is now the USERENV context: "select sys_context('userenv', 'sessionid') from dual."*

Clearly, then, it makes sense to take advantage of contexts when we start using row-level security. This requires a number of interlocking steps to work effectively. Not only do you want to use a context as a way of carrying user-related values, you also want to ensure that the user can't change the values on the fly to breach your security. Three different features of Oracle cooperate to make this happen.

First, the context may only be modified by a single package, and that package has to be named as the context is created. The full syntax is

```
create or replace context contextname using schemaname.packagename;
```

A fragment of the package may look like

```
create or replace package my_app_context_package as
    procedure set_dept;
end;
/

create or replace package body my_app_context_package as

procedure set_dept is
m_department        varchar2(32);
begin
    if(sys_context('my_app_context','department')is not null) then
        -- It shouldn't be possible to get here but
        -- don't allow the context to change if we do.
        raise_application_error(-20001,'Department already set');
    end if;

    -- some code here to identify the user's department,
    -- and get it into the m_department variable,
    -- then we can set the 'department' attribute.

    Dbms_session.set_context(
            'my_app_context',
```

```
                'department',
                m_department
        );
    end;

    -- rest of package.
```

To take advantage of contexts, you need the privilege CREATE ANY CONTEXT, and so that your context function can set values in the context, you need the EXECUTE privilege on the package DBMS_SESSION.

The context name is public to the database. You cannot have two contexts of the same name in different schemas. The view family xxx_CONTEXT is a little different from the standard families. There is no USER_CONTEXT view, although there are DBA_CONTEXT, ALL_CONTEXT, and SESSION_ CONTEXT views. The first lists all the contexts that have been defined in the database, the second lists all context definitions that are in use in the current session, and the last lists the context name, attribute names, and attribute values that are set in the current session.

> *Do not restrict your use of contexts to row-level security. They can be used anywhere in your application to hold preset values. In particular, you could use them in the views that make up a view-based security system.*

The second feature that allows contexts to be most effective in row-level security is the basic privilege mechanism employed by Oracle. If user A creates a package, then user B cannot use it unless user A explicitly grants to user B the privilege to do so, *or* the package is called by another package that user A is allowed to execute. To protect the context from abuse, we simply ensure that nobody other than the creator of the context has the right to execute the package.

The third feature is the *logon trigger*. The privilege to create logon triggers (and other triggers at the database level) is very powerful, and should not be handed around casually because a logon trigger has to fire for *every* user who logs on. To create a database-level trigger you have to have the privilege ADMINISTER DATABASE TRIGGER. The code for the trigger could be as simple as

```
create or replace trigger rls_logon_demo
after logon on database
```

```
begin
    app_owner.my_app_context_package.set_dept;
end;

/
```

Conveniently for our purposes, the logon trigger fires with the privileges of the creator of the trigger, and that is the final peg on which we can hang our security system.

User A (our application owner probably) creates a context, the package that maintains that context, and a logon trigger that executes to set the necessary values in the context. Because all other users *have* to fire that trigger at logon, their context is automatically set irrespective of the tool they may use to connect to the database. Because the trigger executes the package, users need no direct access to the package and cannot change the context, so we have made it possible to avoid all risks of access anomalies.

Problems and Quirks

Row-level security is very secretive. Users are not supposed to realize that their actions are being restricted. A side effect of this is that Oracle Corporation has made it very hard to find out what SQL actually reached the database. In fact, I hit a couple of extremely nasty bugs when trying to breach security with autonomous transactions. These should be fixed in version 8.1.6.

It is much harder to track down the problem with inefficient SQL when there are performance problems around. Because of a hidden security predicate, the SQL that appears in V$SQL is not necessarily the SQL that executed, and the execution path that you get when running EXPLAIN PLAN on it may be completely different from the live run because your ID may have generated a different security predicate. However, you may be able to spot in V$SQL that the same statement appears under different parsing_schema_ids with dramatically different costs, and this may give you a hint about the presence of row-level security.

End users may see some confusing results if you are not extremely careful about the consistency of your security policy. This is more of a business-related issue than an implementation issue. Nevertheless, the database designer needs to think carefully about the possible anomalies that may appear, particularly when tables are referentially connected, or commonly joined in queries or validation tests.

Most "realistic" security policies are likely to compare base table data with tables listing access rights. This tends to lead to IN subqueries being generated as the security predicates, which in many cases will have a significant effect on performance.

I came across three specific examples of a serious performance impact when combining row-level security with other features of Oracle. First, the PARALLEL QUERY option. Some queries that execute in parallel without a security predicate can be forced to switch to serial execution by some types of predicates. Some predicates using IN subqueries will convert a previously efficient parallel query into a parallel hash join that floods millions of messages between parallel query slaves. Second, summary management. Some predicates, again using IN subqueries, seem to stop the optimizer from spotting the option of a query rewrite. Third, when using the deref() operator to convert a REF column to a row, a trace of the activity that takes place when row-level security and deref()s are mixed suggests that the access mechanism to the referenced object is completely different from the method used when row-level security is not in place. This may be a minor quirk to be ironed out (the very early versions of Oracle 7 used a similar method very briefly to implement primary key/foreign key validation), but in the meantime, applying row-level security to object-style access paths may result in more of an overhead than you would expect.

A security policy is evaluated and the predicate generated only when a cursor is first parsed. This can lead to unexpected behavior if the predicate function is written in a way that is supposed to allow the generated predicate to change during the life of a session. If a cursor stays open (in a Pro*C program or PL/SQL block, say), then the predicate is not regenerated for the next use of that cursor, and the application may not behave as expected.

Another exception to the rule of row-level security being applied is when you export using DIRECT mode. Anyone who can export a table (using the option to name a table as schemaname.tablename) has the ability to bypass row-level security by using a direct export (see Strategy Notes).

If you use **alter table tableX move;** to rebuild a table, and that table has a security policy on it that returns a predicate, even one that lets you see all the rows, then the attempt to rebuild the table results in error "ORA-28113: policy predicate has an error" and stops the move with an ORA-00600 crash behind the scenes. This doesn't occur if the predicate returned is actually a null predicate.

Strategy Notes

If you have a clean, simple, low-maintenance security policy in place already, then you don't need to worry about row-level security. It is unlikely to supply enough benefit to be worth the change, although you may want to take advantage of the benefits of the sys_context() function and logon triggers.

If you are running a high-use OLTP system, then it is absolutely imperative that your code be designed to use bind variables whenever possible; otherwise, the overhead of row-level security policy functions executing for each new SQL statement can become the principal bottleneck on the system.

Row-level security can be a bit of a shock, and can be very confusing to end users. Try to keep the number of tables with security policies to a minimum, and try to keep those policies very simple. It may be best to use the same policy for select, insert, update, and delete. If you have any special rules for inserts, updates, and deletes, it may be best to handle those through triggers. In particular, make sure you don't write policies that allow users to modify more data than they can select.

If you have attached a security policy to a table, it is always applied when any user (other than SYS or INTERNAL) accesses the table. It is very likely that any realistic security policy requires a nontrivial clause to be attached to the WHERE clause on that table. This could make a big difference to the access path used by the optimizer. Be especially careful about having lots of tables with security policies. If every table in a four-table query has a security policy, then that query could become an eight-table query, and the performance impact could be dramatic. (By default, Oracle restricts itself to an exhaustive search of paths for a maximum of five tables—the value given by the init.ora parameter OPTIMIZER_SEARCH_LIMIT).

If you are applying security policies, make sure you write the code so that it always generates a fail-safe predicate. If an exception is raised by this code, you could consider trapping it and hiding all the data by generating 1 = 0 as the default predicate in the exception handler. (It seems more secure to make "see nothing" the default fallback, rather than "see eveything.")

Security policies are always applied unless you are connected as SYS or INTERNAL. This is true even when you export the table using conventional path exports. Fortunately, if a security policy is in place when you do an export, error message EXP-00079 appears, warning you "Data in table 'XXXX' is protected. Conventional path may only be exporting partial table." If you depend on exports as a means of keeping safe copies of your data, you may want to ensure that your security policy manages to produce a null predicate for the ID that you use to do the exports and imports.

On the other hand, if an ID can export a table (which probably means the ID is a DBA ID or has the EXP_FULL_DATABASE privilege), then a *direct* export of the table bypasses the usual SQL-level processing and therefore cannot invoke the security policy. Thus the export contains all the rows, which may not be what you want to happen.

To avoid confusion and the risk of something going wrong, the simplest and safest strategy is to create simple views on tables ("select ∗ from tableX"), and apply the policies to the views rather than the underlying tables themselves.

In many cases you may be able to get away with a simple security policy of the form "security_column = constant," where the constant is actually user specific and is supplied through the sys_context() call. In this case you could hide the SECURITY column from the user by superimposing a view on the table that omits it, and then add a preinsert trigger on the table that uses the same sys_context() call in the form ":new.security_column := sys_context(.....)".

It makes sense to ensure that a security policy is constant for the life of a session, because inconsistent behavior could occur if you do not. A clean way of ensuring that this takes place is to use a logon trigger to set up values in an application-specific context, and define the security policy's function to use this context in a very static fashion.

CHAPTER 22

Parallel Query and Parallel Server

I have put these two topics in a single chapter to make one very important point. They have absolutely *nothing* to do with each other. They are completely independent options of the Oracle database system, and although it is true that anyone implementing Parallel Server may also take advantage of Parallel Query, the converse is *not* true. The only thing that they have in common is that they both require careful planning and design. They are *not* quick fixes for an emergent performance problem.

The PARALLEL QUERY option (recently renamed PARALLEL EXECUTION and included in the standard kernel) is essentially an enhancement to Oracle that allows a single SQL statement to be split "transparently" into several independent but coordinated streams of activity. Although many people tend to think that this implies the need for several CPUs in the box, this is not necessarily the case.

With a little care and planning, the PARALLEL QUERY option can introduce tremendous performance benefits to DSS-style systems. Even in systems that do not normally require large-scale data manipulation, it can be used very effectively to reduce the time needed for restructuring, moving, or re-indexing large objects. There are some traps, of course. The underlying strategy of PARALLEL QUERY option is to be very extravagant with memory and CPU to reduce elapsed time of operations. Sometimes it can be too extravagant, and sometimes its method of operation can conflict with other Oracle features (particularly the newer features) to produce suboptimal side effects.

Oracle Parallel Server is a separately licensed extension to the Oracle database software that cooperates with a suitably enabled operating system to allow several different machines to run their own, apparently independent, Oracle instances, all of which make use of a single set of Oracle data files and control files. Every instance has its own database buffer, its own shared pool, its own log buffer, and its own set of redo log files (on-line and archived) all operating more or less independently, although every instance has to be able to see every other instance's redo log files and archived redo log files so that one instance can clean up the mess when another instance crashes.

Oracle Parallel Server is still a fairly rare beast because it requires some very important design considerations, and then can only run on equipment from a handful of suppliers because it needs a level of operating system support that allows for clustered hardware. The critical operating software that lets it all work goes under several names—*cluster control software, lock manager software*. Whatever the name, its purpose is to allow extremely rapid coordination between actions on a loosely coupled set of otherwise independent machines, and to check that resources that are supposed to be shared are actually visible from every node all the time.

With Oracle Parallel Server it is possible to put together an extremely powerful system relatively cheaply, but the strict design requirements make this possible only for a very narrow group of applications.

Parallel Server

Oracle Parallel Server is a very special configuration of Oracle that allows you to apply the power of several different computers to the same database at the same time. The machines have to be configured as a cluster, so although they can operate in many ways independently, they need a level of operating system software that allows them to operate a common locking and synchronization mechanism. Inevitably, a cluster of machines has to be formed from the same hardware supplier. Almost inevitably, the versions of the machines, their operating systems, and the version of Oracle they use have to be virtually identical. At the physical level, all the machines in the cluster have to be connected by a high-speed link, and all the machines have to be able to see all the disks being used for the Oracle database files (see Figure 22-1).

Each machine (generally referred to as a node of the cluster) runs its own copy of the operating system and its own copy of Oracle, which means that each machine has its own database block buffer and shared pool. This raises two interesting problems:

1. If each machine has its own buffer, how does Oracle cope with the fact that block 999 may end up in two different buffers and may get updated in two different ways at the same time?

2. What happens if one node decides to "lock table ABC in exclusive mode" (which involves setting some flags in various structures in its

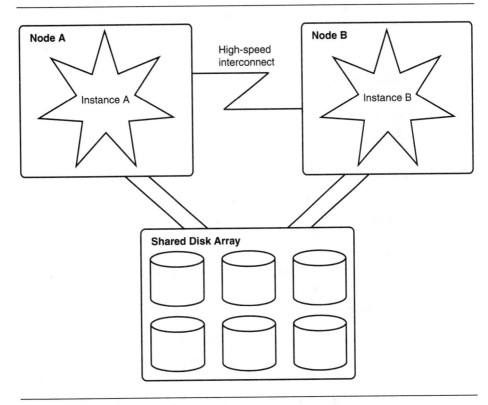

Figure 22-1. Two-node parallel server.

shared pool), whereas another instance already has table ABC locked in a conflicting fashion through flags set in its shared pool?

To handle these problems, Oracle puts its own layer of locking on top of the operating system clustering software: the integrated distributed lock manager, or IDLM. In earlier versions of Oracle, the hardware vendor was required to supply a fairly complex and fine-grained level of software (called the *DLM*) that could be called by Oracle. This layer was actually defined by Oracle Corporation and in some cases was actually written by Oracle Corporation. This has changed with Oracle 8, so that only the vendor's basic internode awareness is needed; the DLM has been integrated into the Oracle kernel.

The two examples I have presented show the need for Oracle to be able to communicate between nodes. The two requirements may be handled differently though because Oracle has two different strategies for internode locking.

One strategy is reserved for database block buffer locks and is referred to as PCM locking (for parallel cache management) and uses static IDLM resources. The other strategy uses dynamic IDLM resources and covers all other types of locks, which are often used in places where single-instance Oracle would normally use latching or pinning. To confuse the issue, Oracle introduced *releasable locks* for data blocks in version 7.3 that are dynamically allocated but statically managed.

The IDLM

Discussing the mechanics of the IDLM is probably a little foolhardy, because it is the sort of low-level detail that is likely to vary from release to release. Nevertheless, it is worth a brief outline to help clarify the potential threats in using Oracle Parallel Server.

The IDLM consists of two major memory components: a list of resources (things that can be locked) and a list of locks (or more correctly, perhaps, lock requests). Each resource may have two chains of locks attached to it—the currently held locks and the pending locks.

At the basic level, an IDLM resource need only be a meaningless identifier. As far as Oracle is concerned, an IDLM resource may correspond to a set of database blocks (roughly equivalent to a PCM lock), an entry in a dictionary cache, an entry in a library cache, or half a dozen other types of objects in need of coordinated protection (in other words, targets for non-PCM locks).

An IDLM lock is associated with an IDLM resource, has a place in the resource's queue, and holds state and node information about the lock request.

The amount of memory that each instance allocates for IDLM resources and IDLM locks is set by the init.ora parameters LM_RESS and LM_LOCKS. However, if these parameters have not been set to suitable values, Oracle can dynamically allocate additional memory from the SGA as needed. This is a relatively expensive operation and is logged in the alert log by messages "dynamic resources allocated" and "dynamic locks allocated." This is something of an improvement over previous releases, in which you had to configure the resources at the operating system level. If Oracle demanded more DLM resources or locks than the cluster software was configured to supply, you could find the database, or the node itself, crashing.

The IDLM operates as a hashed distributed database. It does not clone resource information across all active instances. If node A wants to apply a lock to resource R, then it has to find the appropriate resource record that could, in theory, be in any one of the active instances. To make sure that resources can be found quickly (without interrogating every instance on the

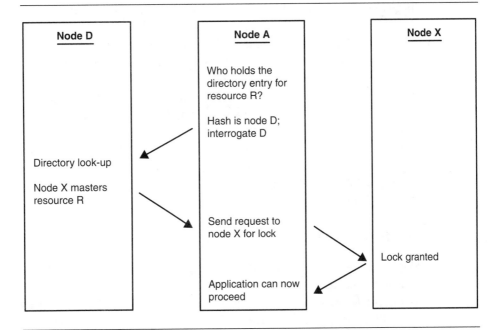

Figure 22-2. Order of actions locking a dynamic DLM resource.

cluster), there is a resource directory that operates through a hashing algorithm. So node A, say, can calculate that the directory entry for resource R is on node D. Node A can then send a request to node D to ask it which node is holding the record for resource R (*mastering* the resource). If the resource is a static resource, it is likely that the instance holding the directory entry is also mastering the resource. If the resource is a dynamic resource, then some other node may be mastering it. Either way, node D tells node A who is mastering the resource, and node A sends a lock request to the master (Figure 22-2).

This has a couple of interesting implications. Because of the way hashing works, the IDLM directory is spread uniformly over all the instances in the cluster, so you have to ask what the cluster is going to do when an instance is added or dropped (possibly by crashing). The hash directory will have to be rebalanced, which may impose a freeze on Oracle processing for a short period. The more IDLM resources that are active, the longer the freeze.

PCM and Non-PCM

I mentioned PCM locks and non-PCM locks at the Oracle level, and I also mentioned static and dynamic IDLM resources. There is a loose association between these terms: All non-PCM locks (such as dictionary cache locks) equate to dynamic resources. PCM locks may be fixed hash locks, which equate to static resources; releasable hash locks, which equate to a pool of static resources with a size that is given by the parameter GC_RELEASABLE_ LOCKS; or releasable fine-grained locks, which equate to pure dynamic resources. The biggest difference between static and dynamic locks is that the resources for static locks have to be allocated at database start-up, and this can take some time. Dynamic locks do not have to be allocated at start-up. Dynamic locks clearly look more desirable from this respect. On the other hand, they consume more CPU and network resources at runtime.

Let's start by looking at non-PCM locks and take as an example the simple SQL statement

```
select count(*) from tableX;
```

As everyone knows, Oracle does not take out "read locks," so the previous statement is clearly not going to involve any locking whatsoever, unless you are using the Oracle Parallel Server. When parsing the statement, Oracle makes use of the library cache and the dictionary cache memory structures, and needs to ensure that the local caches do not become inconsistent with other caches in the cluster. Consequently, there are IDLM resources for items like the dictionary cache entry for tableX, and the local instance of Oracle may have to put out a call for an IDLM lock to ensure that the master node for that resource knows that the local instance has loaded the item into its dictionary cache.

The full life cycle is quite complex, but for a dictionary cache item it looks something like this:

1. Instance A on node A is the first instance to reference tableX. It uses the hash function to work out that node D holds the directory entry for the dynamic IDLM resource QJ 398572.

2. Node A asks node D who is mastering IDLM resource QJ 398572. Node D responds, no one. Thus node A sends a message back to node D saying, I asked for it first; register me as the master. Node A creates the master resource record and then acquires an exclusive lock on it for the duration of the parse, and then drops it back to a null lock.

3. Node B executes a query against the same table, and determines that it needs to ask node D who is the master for QJ 398572. Node B gets pointed to node A. Node B asks node A for an exclusive lock on the resource for the duration of the parse, and then asks node A to drop this lock back to a null lock after the parse is complete.

4. Nodes C, D, E, and F repeat the process. (Note how node A is using up more and more of its IDLM lock ration.)

5. Node B has a shared-pool problem and flushes a bit of its dictionary cache including the entry for tableX, and determines that it needs to ask node D who is the master for QJ 398572. Node B gets pointed to node A. Node B tells node A to release the null lock that node A was holding on the resource to represent node B's interest.

6. Node D has to parse a new statement against the table, but its row-cache is already loaded, and it knows that it is already holding a null lock against the resource on node A, so it does not need to do cross-instance calls.

7. Node G decides to drop tableX, and determines that it needs to ask node D who is the master for QJ 398572. Node G gets pointed to node A. Node G tells node A to invalidate the resource. Node A checks that all the locks on the resource are null locks, sends a message to each locking node that the lock is now invalid so that each node can invalidate the local dictionary cache entry and all dependent objects, and, when all the acknowledgments are in, confirms to node G that it may go ahead, and clears its own rowcache.

Fortunately, dictionary cache locks are quite stable (aided to some degree by the arrival of temporary tablespaces in version 7.3 and global temporary tables in version 8.1), so the expense of IDLM communication for dictionary cache pins doesn't have to take place too often. You can see some of the costs of IDLM activity on the dictionary cache by checking the IDLM-related columns in dynamic performance view V$ROWCACHE.

Other dynamic locks are not so obliging, however, especially library cache locks (type Lx). New ones can be requested and old ones discarded with extreme regularity if too many hard parses take place. This is yet another good reason for trying to use bind variables in SQL as much as possible. Dynamic performance view V$LIBRARY_CACHE also has a number of IDLM-related columns that allow you to see the impact of cross-instance calls.

If cross-instance calls for non-PCM locks are causing a performance problem, you may be able to measure the impact by looking for wait event "DFS lock handle," either in v$system_event or in v$session_event. For an extreme level of detail on these events, you can look at v$session_wait, or run a 10046 trace at level 8 (see Appendix B) to list all wait events for a session. The P1RAW parameter will tell you the type and mode of the lock request (if you know your hex and ASCII codes). For example, 514A0003 is type QJ in mode 3.

For parallel server systems, the GV$ views match the V$ views, but cover all the instances from one node and have an INST_ID number. Oracle needs to use a parallel query slave on remote nodes to get the data.

One important point to note is that the first node to ask for a dynamic resource becomes the master for that resource, which is a sensible strategy because it is quite possible that no other node will ever be interested in the resource. If you start up a parallel server system on just one node for a brief period, there is a risk that it will become the master for a large number of dynamic IDLM resources, and will then need a huge reserve of memory for IDLM locks.

In theory, a perfectly balanced system needs to be configured with two IDLM locks per IDLM resource. In practice, I have had to configure a system with N locks per resource because there were N nodes, and a quirk of library cache locking, partition views, and Oracle 7.3 resulted in almost all the dynamic resources being mastered on a randomly selected node each time the database was restarted. You may find similar, although less dramatic, problems when using partitioned tables that have to undergo regular partition maintenance.

The need to configure excess memory is not the only problem. Performance can be affected too. If a system becomes very unbalanced so that one node masters a large fraction of the dynamic resources, then that one node ends up receiving lots of IDLM requests from all the other nodes, and the excessive IDLM activity makes that node the bottleneck on the system.

Moving on to PCM locks, the mechanism for locking static resources is largely unchanged, although the subsequent Oracle activity is very different. If the resources are static rather than dynamic, the process for finding them is simpler. There is no need to query a directory; the hash function simply identifies the node mastering the lock. Technically there should be a directory, but a couple of the acquisition steps can be eliminated by the rule that the directory node for a resource must be the master node for the resource.

Static resources have a lower runtime overhead than dynamic resources because the node mastering them can be found through hashing, without the need for a separate directory.

This brings us to two topics: how PCM locks work in general, and the difference between dynamic PCM locks (also known as fine-grained releasable locks) and static PCM locks (also known as hashed PCM locks).

PCM Locks and Data Locks

A PCM lock covers one or more blocks from a data file. To be precise, we should say that the IDLM resource covers one or more blocks, and the PCM lock expresses an interest in the resource. Some blocks (for example, rollback blocks, segment header blocks, free list blocks) are treated as special cases, but most blocks are ordinary data blocks (which in this context includes index blocks) and are handled in the same way.

Before an instance can load a data block into its buffer, it must acquire a PCM lock that covers that block to ensure no other instance accidentally acquires it in a conflicting fashion and manages to damage the database by producing two inconsistent images of the same data block. There are numerous scenarios we could consider here, but I will pick just one mixed sequence of events as an indication of the basic problem of PCM locking:

1. Assume that the DLM resource named BL 23,11 covers data blocks 11 to 20 of file 23, and that the resource has a SHARE mode PCM lock placed on it by instance A, which has just read block 15 into its buffer. Instance B wants to read block 12. So, after discovering who is mastering the resource, instance B puts in a PCM lock request in SHARE mode. Because there is no conflict between the requirements of instance A and instance B, the PCM lock request is granted. At the end this step, instances A and B both have a shared PCM lock covering blocks 11 to 20 of file 23, instance A has block 15 in its buffer, and instance B has block 12 in its buffer.

2. Instance B moves to update, without committing, block 12, and puts in a bid to escalate the PCM lock from a shared lock to an exclusive lock. At this point instance A is told to scale down its lock from shared to null, and its image of block 15 changes its state from SHARED CURRENT to CONSISTENT READ ONLY. Instance B gets its exclusive PCM lock and performs its update on block 12.

3. Instance A now moves to update block 15. Because the block is now a consistent-read block, not a current block, instance A has to reread it. But because its PCM lock is a null lock, it must first escalate it to an exclusive lock. However, instance B has an exclusive PCM lock on the same resource, which it must release. Because the PCM lock is

covering a changed block, instance B has to write block 12 to disk before changing its mode to CONSISTENT READ and dropping the PCM lock to a null lock.

4. At this point, instance A has an exclusive PCM lock on the resource covering block 15, and a row lock on a row in block 15. On the other hand, instance B has a row lock on a row in block 12, even though it has a null PCM lock on the resource covering that block. This sequence of events highlights two important points: first that PCM locks and data locks can act completely independently of each other, and second that if you don't design your application carefully you can find that updates in one part of the database by one instance cause other instances to write changed blocks to disk completely unnecessarily.

The process when one instance forces another instance to write to disk is known as *pinging*. In some cases the write takes place because the second instance wants to update the block that has just been written by the first instance. In other cases, the write takes place because the second instance wants to update a different block that is covered by the same resource, which is referred to as *false pinging*.

> *One of the most important design requirements of an Oracle Parallel Server system is to partition the data across the instances, and arrange the PCM lock definitions to minimize pinging.*

It used to be very difficult to avoid pinging. In fact, there was a time when a read request could result in pinging. Remember the work that Oracle does to achieve read consistency? First it finds the current version of a block; then it checks for rollback segment headers and rollback data to reverse the most recent changes until it has built a copy of the block as it was in the past. Imagine instance A has changed a block recently, and instance B wants to see an older version of the block. Before Oracle 8.1, instance A would write the block for instance B to read. Instance B would then need to see the rollback segment header block for the recent change, so instance A would write the rollback segment header block for instance B, which would then want to see the relevant rollback blocks, so instance A would have to write at least one rollback block as well.

Oracle 8.1 has addressed this problem with the *block server process* (named BSP0). Instead of three pings taking place, BSP0 at instance A is notified that instance B would like to see the block as it was at a given SCN, so it uses its local data to build that read-consistent image and passes it through the high-speed interconnect direct to instance B. This can become network and CPU intensive if instance A keeps asking for the same blocks all the time. So after BSP0 has served up the block a few times, it switches strategies and writes it out anyway on the basis that instance A may have more interest in it than instance B. Of course when a block is pinged from one instance to another, the redo log describing the changes to that block has to be written first. The log for a change is *always* written before the block can be written. Although you may think that the appearance of BSP0 would make this log write redundant, it doesn't. Cross-instance demands for read-consistent blocks still result in the log writer process writing prematurely.

> *BPS0 may reduce the amount of pinging that takes place, but it is not a substitute for good Oracle Parallel Server design.*

Defining PCM Locks

Because databases can be millions of blocks in size, you will not be surprised that it is generally not possible to allocate one PCM lock per database block. Thus, each PCM lock has to be able to cover a large number of blocks. There are three ways of doing this:

1. Define some sort of fixed pattern through each file of the database (for example, take 5 blocks, skip 45; take 5, skip 45) and allocate one PCM lock to each occurrence of the pattern at database start-up. This is called *static hash locking* (Figure 22-3). The number of locks per file can be very large so that each lock covers only a small number of blocks.

2. As stated in number 1, but do not allocate any locks at database start-up. Instead, limit the number of locks that may be used for the file, and have Oracle allocate them as needed from a reserved pool of PCM locks defined by the parameter GC_RELEASABLE_LOCKS.

3. Specify that the file should be covered by fine-grained dynamic locks only. These are allocated one lock per block as needed, and are released when the block leaves db_block_buffer.

The three strategies can be mixed as necessary within a single database because Oracle allows each file to use a different strategy. However, any file that does not have a specified strategy uses fine-grained releasable locks in which one PCM lock corresponds at any one time to one database block.

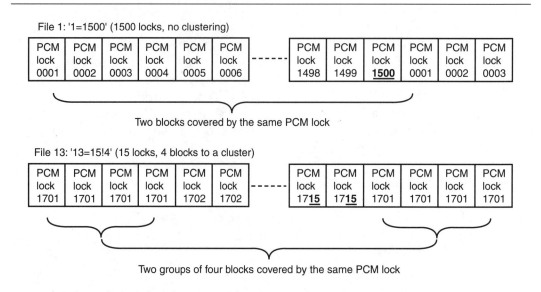

Figure 22-3. PCM hash locking.

You use the parameter GC_FILES_TO_LOCKS to specify PCM strategies, and every instance of the database must have exactly the same string value for this parameter. For example,

```
gc_files_to_locks= '1=1500:6=0!5:23,28=100:13-22=15!4EACH:7=20!10R'
```

This string tells us the following:

1. File 1 should have 1,500 PCM locks allocated, using a round-robin allocation one block at a time, so that blocks 1, 1501, 3001, 4501, and so on, are covered by the first PCM lock; blocks 2, 1502, 3002, 4502, and so on, are covered by the second PCM lock (see Figure 22-3).

2. File 6 is to use completely dynamic fine-grained locking (indicated by the zero), but as each lock is created, it should cover five consecutive blocks in the file.

3. Files 23 and 28 should have a total of 100 PCM locks allocated between them, which implicitly means 50 each, again with a single-block round-robin allocation of blocks to PCM locks.

4. Files 13 to 22 will *each* have 15 IDLM resources allocated, and each resource will cover four consecutive blocks at a time (see Figure 22-3).

5. File 7 is to use 20 PCM locks to cover the file in groups of ten consecutive blocks, but the locks should be taken from the statically declared pool GC_RELEASABLE_LOCKS and released when not in use.

6. Any files not listed, in particular any files above 28, will be subject to fine-grained, releasable PCM locks.

You may immediately spot a flaw in the use of GC_FILES_TO_LOCKS. If you add a file to the database, then its PCM lock policy defaults to fine-grained releasable locking, which may not be what you want. It gets worse, because if you drop a file (by dropping a tablespace) and then add a new file, the new file takes over the file number used by one of the previous files, which may have a totally unsuitable PCM lock policy. If you allow a file to grow, the extra space may have an impact on performance because each lock on that file now covers more blocks.

Every time you change the files in a parallel server system, you may have to stop and restart the entire system to set the new value for GC_FILES_TO_LOCKS.

Avoiding Pinging

Frankly, the only way to avoid serious contention through pinging is to ensure that your application can partition properly. And the only way to make this happen properly is to use partitioned tables (see Chapter 12), even if you have to define some form of artificial partitioning and add extra data columns on which to partition. When you can really partition the data, you then need to assign partitions to instances, so that no two instances modify data in the same partition. Ideally, no two instances will even query data in the same partition. To ensure that this partition ruling then stops instances from colliding on files, you need to ensure that each partition is given its own tablespaces.

If you have to have large cross-partition reports, you may find that BSP0 is sufficient to ensure that you don't have reads generating spurious pinging. If it doesn't, or if the load on BSP0 becomes the bottleneck on the system, you have to start looking for ways to reduce the number of consistent-read demands that hit the system—possibly by restricting the frequency, or scheduling, of long-running reports.

It is unlikely, however, that you will be able to partition your application as cleanly as you would like. There are a couple of features of Oracle that may help you to reduce contention. The first is fine-grained, releasable PCM locking. If you are going to get unavoidable pinging, it is better to have just one block being written rather than an entire group of blocks. For index tablespaces in particular, setting GC_FILE_TO_LOCKS to its default of one releasable PCM lock to one data block is probably the best bet. Because a row has to be inserted into an index in the right place, there is no way you can ensure that the "correct" instance updates an index block, so this is really just a damage-control exercise.

The second damage-control feature is *freelist group*. This applies only to inserts, not to updates and deletes. In a single instance, when we have contention at the end of a table because of multiple processes inserting rows, we can define multiple freelists for the table, and then different processes are able to insert to different blocks. If we have four free lists, we have four blocks being used for new rows. However, in multi-instance Oracle, we still have contention for two reasons: First, all the freelists are in the segment header block, so we get contention on that block. Second, multiple freelists may still list blocks that are covered by the same PCM lock, and any instance can pick up any freelist, so pinging still occurs.

If, however, we define an object with multiple freelist groups—in particular, one freelist group per instance—there will be one extra block allocated within the data segment for each freelist group, and each block will hold a separate set of free lists. Not only that, each instance will associate itself with one freelist group, and only use blocks from the freelists in that group. Finally, Oracle Parallel Server cunningly matches freelist groups with the granularity of the PCM lock to ensure that instances collide as little as possible.

If we go back to our example of file 6—'6 = 0!5'—the granularity of the PCM lock is five, so five consecutive blocks are covered by any single PCM lock. When a freelist becomes empty, Oracle allocates the next five blocks (with some fudge factors that I won't go into) to the freelist so that all the blocks it puts on the freelist are covered by a single PCM lock. Because that freelist may be used only by the one instance that owns the freelist group, those blocks are safe from pinging.

This works nicely for tables with high-volume inserts, but there are two problems. It won't work with updates and deletes because *any* instance could update or delete rows from any block, and any update or delete may be enough to put a block onto a freelist. Thus, any instance may put on one of its freelists a block that started life on another instance's freelist. This introduces a particular drawback to multiple freelists in general, and freelist groups in particular. If a single, very large ***delete*** statement takes place in one instance and frees up a large number of blocks, those blocks are attached to one freelist that belongs to that one instance. Every other instance is unable to access that free space, so you could get into a position in which a table has *lots* of free space that is available only to one instance, and then only to processes that happen to attach themselves to the correct freelist. The upshot of this is that you may find instances busily allocating new extents to tables that actually have loads of free space.

If using multiple freelist groups, avoid very large, single-transaction deletes. You may appear to lose a lot of space as a consequence.

Another defect with the multiple freelist/freelist group strategy is that it just doesn't work with indexes because a sequential set of inserts to a table generally results in a randomly distributed set of inserts to its indexes. However, for meaningless key indexes, you may be able to arrange for the key value to become something like "very large number × instance number + base key value." This would ensure that the inserts from different instances would go to completely different index leaf blocks.

The issue of meaningless keys leads to the misuse of Oracle sequences. If you create a sequence with *default* parameters to use as a meaningless key in Oracle Parallel Server, then you will experience pinging for two different reasons. First, every instance will be inserting rows with very similar key values, so the blocks at the leading edge of the index will be continuously pinging. Second, each instance will have to refresh the cache value after every 20 rows, so the one critical block of the dictionary table SYS.SEQ$ that holds the sequence's definition and state will be pinging all the time. If you do use Oracle sequences, make sure the cache is large. You will lose a lot of values when the instance shuts down, but you will reduce pinging. Also watch out for the trap created by the ORDER option for sequences. A sequence that is ordered is automatically treated as having a zero-size cache. Do not use ordered sequences on Oracle Parallel Server.

If you use sequences for meaningless keys with Oracle Parallel Server, make sure they have a large cache value, and do not use the ORDER option.

Parallel Execution

The PARALLEL QUERY option gets better and better with each version of Oracle, but it is important to remember that its underlying strategy is to be a total resource hog in order to finish a job in the shortest time possible, not in the most efficient fashion. Given the choice between serially accessing a 10,000,000-row table through an index to collect and sum 1,000 rows (elapsed time, 10 seconds; CPU time, 0.2 second) or scanning it in parallel using 20 parallel query slaves (elapsed time, 6 seconds; CPU time, 4 seconds), the optimizer generally chooses the quicker but more CPU-intensive path.

Provided you remember that this is what the PARALLEL QUERY option is supposed to do, you will rarely be disappointed by it. It is not a general-purpose, performance-enhancing, end-user feature. It is a data-crunching, nonscalable, batch processor. Having said this the 8.1 version has become so good at optimizing queries that it often produces very efficient solutions to large problems, instead of just quick but brutally inefficient solutions. It is interesting to note that Oracle Corporation has introduced an option for automatic, dynamic tuning of PARALLEL QUERY option (parallel_automatic_tuning = true), and one of the key features of setting this init.ora parameter is that the optimizer reduces the maximum number of parallel query slaves it allows to a new query if there are already a large number running—a response, perhaps, to the problem of using the PARALLEL QUERY option in an end-user environment.

The name has changed from Parallel Query to Parallel Execution because the code can now handle inserts, updates, and deletes in parallel (with some restrictions). The following statement kicks off four parallel execution slaves that scan and update the table in parallel:

```
update /*+ parallel (t,4) */ pq_test t
set dummy = 45
where mod(dummy,45) = 0;
```

There is a restriction, however. In the general case, the table has to be a partitioned table, and the feature works because each parallel query slave can independently address a different partition. Only in the special case of "insert into tableA select from tableB" can the target table be a simple table, and then the insert follows the strategy used by SQL*Load, in which each parallel slave allocates and fills its own new extents. Parallel DML is blocked if the table contains object or LOB columns.

An added feature of using partitioned tables with parallel execution (both query and DML) is that you can execute in parallel through the index, not just

through a table scan. To force this to happen, you can use the /*+ PARALLEL_
INDEX(TABLE, INDEX, DEGREE, INSTANCES) */ hint.

You can get apparently unbalanced performance from parallel execution
that drives through a partitioned table. Although DML is one slave per partition, queries can run multiple slaves in parallel against a single partition if the
optimizer can determine that only a single partition is required. This means,
for example, that when running a query with degree ten against just two partitions, the result comes no faster than running a similar query against ten parti-
titons. In the former case only two slaves actually do any work, and in the
latter case ten slaves are needed. There is, however, a sudden breaking point.
If you run the query against just one partition, Oracle may find an execution
path that allows all ten slaves to work, and the result appears very quickly.

> *Queries that drive through a partitioned table have a restriction that
> can make performance appear to be inconsistent. Each partition is
> allocated one slave, so the actual degree of parallelism may be lower
> than the requested degree.*

The PARALLEL EXECUTION option introduces yet another reason for
avoiding global indexes on partitioned tables. The maximum degree of parallelism that Oracle uses when applying DML to a partitioned table is restricted
to the smallest value of INITRANS that it can find in any global index that will
be affected by the DML. (This is to avoid a possible internal deadlock.) This is
the sort of tiny detail that takes ages to discover when things aren't working
the way you expect.

The optimizer seems to be much better at picking clever execution methods than it used to be. One of the complaints about earlier versions of parallel
query was that it would do far too much work. A query like the following
would quite happily evaluate "count(distinct store_id)" three times, and
sum(qty), sum(sale_value) twice, generating a huge CPU overhead (particularly on the multiple sorts needed for "count(distinct)":

```
select
    sales_date,
    count(distinct store_id),
    sum(qty),
    sum(sale_value),
    sum(qty)/ count(distinct store_id),
    sum(sale_value)/count(distinct store_id)
from
```

```
    sales
group by
    sales_date
;
```

These types of queries now manage to recognize reuse of column expressions much more regularly, with a tremendous saving in CPU costs. They also tend to push sum() and other aggregate functions lower in the execution stack more regularly, which means far fewer rows being passed between parallel execution slaves. There is still one apparently wasteful feature: When aggregate values are passed from slave to slave, they use the full 22-byte allocation for numbers every time. Fortunately, the other improvements make the impact of this far less significant.

Apart from this, Oracle simply has more options to choose from when "parallelizing" a query. For example, the very simple

```
select count(disintct colX)
from tableY
;
```

Even in version 8.0.5 this would result in a parallel full scan of tableY, with all rows being sent to the query coordinator for sorting and handling the distinctness and uniqueness. To get any useful benefit from parallelism, you had to know that you needed to rewrite the query as

```
select count(*)
from
    (select distinct colX from tableY)
;
```

With this alternative syntax, Oracle would use one set of slaves to scan the table, and would pass rows by range values to the next set of slaves, which would sort these smaller sets of data for uniqueness, and would count the result before passing the nearly complete answer to the query coordinator.

With Oracle 8.1, the rewrite is unnecessary. Oracle 8.1 has a mechanism that allows the lower-level slave to do most of the sorting and uniqueness with a call to a function of the form

```
SYS_OP_MSR(COUNT(DISTINCT A1.C0))
```

This may mean that you will see more SQL statements in the V$SQL dynamic performance views that have had to use multiple sorts, but you can be reasonably confident that the sort area requirements have been reduced significantly.

Unfortunately, the improved optimizer can work against you sometimes. You may have to review some of the performance tricks that you used to use. Consider the following query:

```
select
        group_code,
        decode(sm,0,null,sm)
from    (
        select /*+ no_merge */
            group_code,
            count(distinct product_id) sm
        from
            sales_group
        group by
            group_code
        )
;
```

In the absence of the /*+ NO_MERGE */ hint, Oracle cunningly folds the in-line view into the main *select*, and runs

```
select
    group_code,
    decode(
        count(distinct product_id),
        0,null,
            count(distinct product_id)
        )
from
    sales_group
group by
    group_code
;
```

The consequence of this is that the DISTINCT operation has to be carried out twice, and Oracle does 50% more sorting to get the same result.

When multiple layers of parallel execution slaves are involved in evaluating a query, they have to pass intermediate results from layer to layer using shared memory areas (referred to as *table queues*). In earlier versions of Oracle, the size of this area was set to just more than 2KB, which resulted in a lot of contention as multiple slaves tried to send data to multiple queues (Figure 22-4).

This problem was exacerbated by the twin problems of the 22-byte aggregate value, and the tendency of Oracle to repeat columns in the slaves' SQL

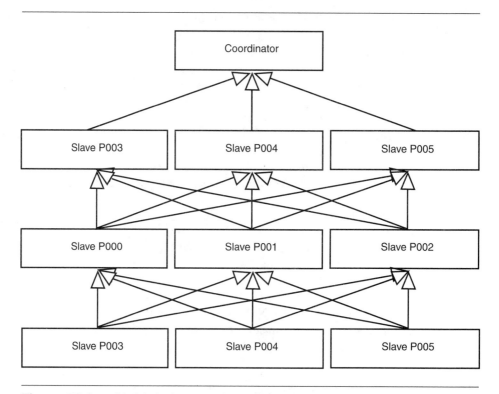

Figure 22-4.   Multiple layers of parallel query.

code. Often, a single row passing from one slave to another would take up most of the 2KB available. In version 8.1.5, the size of the table queues may be increased. In fact, it is changed to 4KB if you set parallel_automatic_tuning to TRUE, and it defaults to 8KB in version 8.1.6.

Following up the problem of slave-to-slave communication, there are some occasions when batch queries are much more time-consuming than expected because the distribution of data between slaves is very uneven. To address this problem Oracle has introduced a new hint, /*+ PQ_DISTRIBUTE() */, which allows you to control to some degree how intermediate datasets are spread between the layers of parallel query slaves. When joining a small table and a large table with a hash join, for example, you may find that most of the rows from the small table arrive at one of half a dozen parallel query slaves, so the execution time is hardly improved by running in parallel. With the hint /*+ PQ_DISTRIBUTE(BIG_TABLE, BROADCAST, NONE) */, all rows from the small table would be sent to all the query slaves, and the big table rows would be distributed randomly, thus improving the load balancing quite dramatically.

Of course, one of the options for avoiding the cost of excessive message passing is to encourage Oracle to use execution paths that localize work to a single layer of parallel query slaves. Consider the following very simple example:

```
select
        grp.id,
        count(*)
from
        group_codes grp,
        raw_data    rwd
where
        grp.rid = rwd.id
and     rwd.selector='X'
;
```

There are two obvious access paths for this query:

1. Scan the GROUP_CODES table and for each row index in the RAW_DATA table, grouping as you go (in other words, nested loops).
2. Scan the GROUP_CODES table and the RAW_DATA table, and hash them together.

Frequently you may find that Oracle chooses the latter path. It is almost inherent in the arithmetic of PARALLEL QUERY option that table scans appear all over the place. But let's take a closer look at the two execution plans:

```
SELECT STATEMENT       -- Nested loop path
  SORT    (group by) PARALLEL_TO_SERIAL
   SORT    (group by) PARALLEL_TO_PARALLEL
    NESTED LOOPS      PARALLEL_COMBINED_WITH_PARENT
     TABLE ACCESS (analyzed) GROUP_CODES (full) PARALLEL_WITH_PARENT
     TABLE ACCESS (analyzed) RAW_DATA (rowid)   PARALLEL_ WITH_PARENT
      INDEX (analyzed) UNIQUE RWD_PK (range) PARALLEL_ WITH_PARENT

SELECT STATEMENT       -- Hash join path
  SORT    (group by) PARALLEL_TO_SERIAL
   SORT    (group by) PARALLEL_TO_PARALLEL
    HASH JOIN      PARALLEL_COMBINED_WITH_PARENT
     TABLE ACCESS (analyzed) GROUP_CODES (full) PARALLEL_TO_PARALLEL
     TABLE ACCESS (analyzed) RAW_DATA    (full) PARALLEL_TO_PARALLEL
```

Both queries use multiple layers of parallel query slaves, but there is an important difference. The key point to note is that the hash join uses the

PARALLEL_TO_PARALLEL mechanism to distribute the GROUP_CODES rows and the RAW_DATA rows from one layer of slaves to another before joining them in the second layer of slaves. Working from the bottom up, the bottom two lines have parallel_to_parallel, so they will be distributing their data to the hash_join line. The hash_join line then has a parallel_combined_with_parent, so we can infer that the hash and the sort above it happen in a single slave. The lower sort line then has parallel_to_parallel, and thus is distributing its intermediate results to another layer of slaves to finish off the sorting and grouping. Finally, the upper sort has parallel_to_serial, showing that all the slaves are piping their results back to the single query coordinator.

The nested loop localizes its join and the first pass of sort (group by) to a single layer of slaves, which we can see through the appearance of the parallel_combined_with_parent mechanism in the last four lines of its plan. As a result, it sends far fewer messages between the layers of slaves.

Although the cost of the hash join path frequently seems to be lower, you may find quite often that the nested loop path is faster because of the reduction in messaging.

> *It is often worth trying to improve performance by hinting parallel queries to change parallel_to_parallel to parallel_combined_with_parent/child. The reduction in messaging can make a significant difference in performance.*

In earlier versions of the optimizer, a query could not execute in parallel if it contained a user-defined function. It is now possible to declare a function as "parallel enabled," so that it can be used in a parallel query. For example,

```
create function pq_sum_value (id number)
return number parallel_enable is
begin
   ...
end;
/
```

Be careful about abusing this privilege: The function should not, for example, depend on global variables defined in other PL/SQL packages, because the actual values of such variables may not be the same across different slave sessions. In fact, this works to the extent that parallel queries involving ordering and grouping work with object types provided that the object's sorting method is the MAP method and not the ORDER method.

Although it isn't exclusively a feature of parallel query, Oracle is now smart enough to manage partition-wise joins (see Chapter 13) between pairs of partitioned tables. In the case of parallel query, this means that one slave can join partition 1 of the parent table with partition 1 of its child as another slave joins partition 2 of the parent to partition 2 of the child, and so on. This execution path is extremely efficient in terms of minimizing messages passed between slaves, and especially for eliminating contention because no two lower level slaves will be passing rows to the same upper level slave. You should always be on the look-out for equipartitioning tables so that the optimizer can find this path.

Problems and Quirks

Parallel Server

Although BSP0 can reduce the impact of cross-instance calls for read-consistent blocks, it is *not* a substitute for a properly designed application. Do not expect an application running on single-instance Oracle to perform well with Oracle Parallel Server.

The manuals discuss PCM locks quite thoroughly and the need for partitioning data access between nodes. However, non-PCM locks can be even more important because their side effects are more subtle but more expensive.

Make sure that you use bind variables and consistent SQL as much as possible to avoid the IDLM overhead of hard parsing and its effect on the library cache.

An application running on Oracle Parallel Server must be perfectly partitioned. A very small amount of work applied to the wrong node can have a dramatic impact on performance.

One of the critical performance parameters is the GC_FILES_TO_ LOCKS parameter, which describes how different files can be covered in different ways by different numbers of PCM locks. You can only change this parameter by stopping the database, because every single instance must be set to use the same value. This can make it very hard to deal with a growing database that has to have files added regularly.

Parallel Query

PARALLEL QUERY option is essentially nonscalable. Its primary strategy is to reduce the total elapsed time for completing a task by using excessive memory and CPU time on an execution path that may be inefficient.

Bear in mind that every single slave participating in a parallel query is allowed to allocate its own SORT_AREA_SIZE for in-memory sorting. If all the slaves then dump this memory down to disk (1) that is a lot of I/O, and (2) all the slaves will do it at once, giving you maximum contention on the temporary tablespace.

Although parallel query has been extended to allow parallel DML (and has been renamed *parallel execution*) parallel DML in general only operates against partitioned tables, and even then it cannot operate if the table contains object or LOB columns.

Aggregate numbers are still passed up the layers of parallel execution slaves at a fixed 22 bytes, and you still see the generated SQL code for parallel execution slaves selecting the same columns twice under some circumstances (although it is vastly improved over previous versions).

Parallel query, when applied to partitioned tables, can appear to give very inconsistent performance. This is because Oracle uses multiple slaves on a query involving a single partition, but only one slave per partition to process a query across multiple partitions.

If you use the PARALLEL QUERY option to rebuild tables and indexes, remember that each slave operates independently to allocate a set of extents. When all the slaves have completed their work, the coordinating session ties the extents together in a single segment. As a result, you will find that, on average, one extent per slave in the completed segment is half empty. Unless you are using uniform-size local tablespaces, or have set the minimum extent size for a dictionary-managed tablespace, Oracle trims these extents, leaving you with a number of odd-size holes in the tablespace, and the risk of future space management problems.

Strategy Notes

Parallel Server

You have several choices for defining PCM locks. If you choose fixed hash locking, the database start-up will be slow. If you choose fine-grained releasable locking, the database start-up will be quick, but the runtime overhead will be high.

If you cannot partition your data perfectly between nodes, make sure you use multiple freelist groups, and look at using grouped, releasable PCM locks on data tablespaces (for example, gc_files_to_locks='15=0!15') and fine-grained releasable PCM locks on index tablespaces.

Look for options for making tablespaces read-only. A read-only tablespace needs no PCM lock, although you may want to give it just one lock to stop it from being included in the fine-grained lock algorithms.

When you use meaningless key indexes, look at the options for creating the key value as "instance number $\times$ 100,000,000 + sequence ID" to force inserts from different instances to go to different index leaf blocks.

When using Oracle sequences, make sure you have a large cache value or you will get a significant amount of contention on the blocks of the SEQ$ table.

Plan ahead for downtime to add files to the database. You cannot change the GC_FILES_TO_LOCKS parameter on the fly, and the default allocation policy is fine-grained releasable locks for files not mentioned in this parameter.

Parallel Query

If you are enabling parallel queries and parallel execution, make sure you accommodate parallel index access on partitioned tables. There is a /*+ PARALLEL_INDEX */ hint, but you can also set the degree of parallelism on indexes to be different from the degree on the underlying tables.

PARALLEL QUERY option can be a memory hog and a CPU hog. When writing SQL that is to execute in parallel, always look for ways in which to limit the possible damage. In particular, execution paths that involve passing large numbers of messages from one slave to another are bad.

If you are running on file systems, remember that a parallel query leaves you with several parallel query slaves that are all likely to start writing to the temporary tablespace at the same time. Make sure you have enough space. Also, make sure that the temporary tablespace is sufficiently spread out and created from several files, to avoid undue contention from all the concurrent processes.

If you expect to use PARALLEL QUERY option and partitioned tables, make sure you try to set up the tables as equipartitioned tables because this leads to a minimal volume of message passing between slaves, and probably optimum performance.

If you are using PARALLEL QUERY option with Oracle Parallel Server, then you can execute parallel queries across multiple instances. You can control how far such queries spread by assigning instances to groups with the PARALLEL_INSTANCE_GROUP parameter.

CHAPTER 23

Number Crunching

In Oracle 8.1.5, Oracle added the CUBE and ROLLUP features to SQL along with the GROUPING() function to make it a lot easier to generate running totals without resorting to procedural programming. With these features in place, it became a viable option to produce more sophisticated reports with simple SQL scripts than has been previously possible.

In Oracle 8.1.6, this is taken a lot further with a whole raft of functions that are aimed at reducing the cost of producing fairly sophisticated reports. The cost savings come from two possible directions depending on the mechanisms you use to produce large-scale analytical reports. The savings will be either in programming (and testing) time that would otherwise have been spent in producing efficient analytical programs, or the database resource usage that would have been "wasted" if you had chosen to make the programs simple by giving the database more expensive SQL to execute.

The final major aid to number crunching is the combination of query rewrites and materialized views. By linking the technology of snapshots with enhancements to the optimizer's ability to rewrite a query for optimization purposes, Oracle Corporation has made it possible for the optimizer to recognize that a query against one table can be met by a more efficient query against another table. There are two benefits to having this facility built into the database. First, response times to end users can be vastly improved. Second, the normally complex infrastructure that third-party tools use to achieve the same effect can be discarded.

Cube and Rollup

Imagine you have a table of BASKET_ITEMS for a supermarket showing sale_date, store_id, basket_id, product_id , number_in_basket, value_of_sale, and a very simple report specification such as "for a given date, list sales_region, store and total sales by store, with subtotals on sales_region."

Without even trying to do anything in the slightest bit complicated, we have introduced a need for two layers of operation. We are summing sales by store, but we are also demanding at the same time a sum of sales by region. SQL, the basic language for addressing the database, cannot handle this extremely simple requirement unaided, and we have to use one of three approaches to tackle it.

First we observe that our fundamental requirement is a SQL statement like

```
select
        reg.region_name,
        str.store_name,
        sum(bki.value_of_sale)  tot_sales
from
        regions         reg,
        stores          str,
        basket_items    bki
where
        bki.sale_date = to_date('13-Jan-2000')
and     str.id = bki.store_id
and     reg.id = str.region_id
group by
        reg.region_name,
        str.store_name
order by
        reg.region_name,
        str.store_name
;
```

This statement does almost all the work that we need done, potentially reducing a huge list of sale items down to perhaps just a few hundred store totals. If you were totally in control of the SQL code, you would have chosen to use an in-line view to sum the basket items by store_id before joining to the STORES and REGIONS tables.

> *GROUP BY does not guarantee order. To ensure that results are in the order you need, make sure you use ORDER BY.*

The question remains, How do you get from the result set of this query to the required output? Specifically, how do you generate the summary by region? There are three basic options: procedural programming, expensive SQL, or temporary tables.

Programming Solutions

We could use a 3GL or a PL/SQL cursor loop (see Chapter 19) to step through the result set and keep a running total by region, and to produce the required output. In essence, this is what SQL∗Plus is doing under the covers when we issue commands like **compute sum of tot_sales on region_name** and **break on region_name skip 1**. It is just a pity that the SQL∗Plus option is not pretty enough for most people's tastes.

For a small result set, the cost of a PL/SQL loop is not terribly significant, nor is the possible network cost of passing rows from a server to a client. For more complex reports though, the PL/SQL or 3GL code that has to be written becomes more convoluted, and requires more development time and more test time.

Of course, we could just license a graphical front-end tool that does this for us, and some of the available tools will actually do it reasonably well, following very closely the cost-effective method that we instruct SQL∗Plus to use, but producing a cosmetically superior result.

Expensive SQL

We could use more complex SQL. In this case, we could take the previous statement and a second statement that summed by region only, include them in a single SQL statement that treated them as in-line views, and join them on region. On the plus side, this would give us the benefit that we could actually present each store's sales as a percentage of the region's sales. On the minus side, Oracle has to do a massive thrash through the BASKET_ITEMS table twice.

Again, there are some front-end tools that take this approach in the code they generate in response to certain classes of queries. In some cases they may make Oracle execute the entire SQL statement; in others they may make Oracle execute the two parts separately, and join them internally:

```
select
    v2.region_name,
    v1.store_name,
```

```
            v1.tot_sales                         store_sales,
            v2.tot_sales                         region_sales,
            v1.tot_sales / v2.tot_sales          store_fraction
     from
         (    -- summed by store, pick up the region id
         select  str.region_id,
                 str.store_name,
                 sum(bki.value_of_sale)      tot_sales
         from    stores           str,
                 basket_items     bki
         where   bki.sale_date = to_date('13-Jan-2000')
         and     str.id = bki.store_id
         group by
                 str.region_id, str.store_name
     )   v1,
     from
         (    -- summed by region, pick up the region id
         select  reg.region_name,
                 reg.id                    region_id,
                 sum(bki.value_of_sale)    tot_sales
         from    regions          reg,
                 stores           str,
                 basket_items     bki
         where   bki.sale_date = to_date('13-Jan-2000')
         and     str.id = bki.store_id
         and     reg.id = str.region_id
         group by
                 reg.region_name,
     )   v2
     where
             v2.region_id = v1.region_id
     order by
         v2.region_name,
         v1.store_name
     ;
```

A variation on this theme was introduced in Oracle 8.1, which can, in the correct circumstances, be more efficient. It is now possible to include a **select** statement as a column in another **select** statement. The previous example starts to become a little unwieldy when rewritten in this form, so I have taken a simplified version of the same query as a demonstration, eliminating the basic three-table join. Note particularly that the in-line select can be a correlated to the tables in the main select:

```
Select
        Region_name,
        Store_name,
        Store_sales,
        Region_sales,
        Store_sales / region_sales
From (
    select
        region_name,
        store_name,
        sum(value_of_sale)                      store_sales,
        (   --  In line view as a COLUMN
            select  sum(value_of_sale)
            from    sales_view          sv_2
            where   sv2.region_id = sv1.region_id
        )                                       region_sales
    from
        sales_view  sv1
)
;
```

The main drawback to this type of query is that Oracle does not report a proper execution plan if you try to use EXPLAIN PLAN or tkprof. It seems to report only the outer select, and denies the existence of the inner query. In this particular example, it turned out to be a bad idea to try this approach because the path seemed to be a nested loop, calculating the regional sum for every store in turn, and therefore doing far more work than the previous version that summed all regions only once.

Temporary Tables

We could create a temporary table to hold the results of our original query, and then fire off SQL code similar to the previous code at these intermediate results. This has the advantage that we only thrash the large dataset once, and we also have the option for generating percentage-of-region figures. The disadvantage is that we have to be prepared for the impact that the use of temporary tables has on the system. Fortunately this impact is not as severe as it used to be thanks to the introduction of global temporary tables (see Chapter 9). Of course we might consider making that temporary table a fairly permanent table, and letting lots of other users take advantage of it, but that is taking us into the territory of materialized views.

Again, there are front-end tools that resolve the problem of the complex query in exactly this way, although currently I don't think any of them have been rewritten to be able to make use of global temporary tables.

> *Many analytical systems need to run two-pass queries. The first pass acquires large volumes of raw data and produces a simple summary. The second pass manipulates a relatively small summary in fairly complex ways. Historically, pure SQL was good only for the first pass. The second pass was either computer intensive or programmer intensive.*

In summary, then, we can appreciate that many information-generating reports actually need to operate through two totally discrete operations. During the first stage we want the database to acquire a large amount of information as rapidly as possible, and crunch it down to the sort of volume that the human mind can manage. During the second stage we want to apply some extra manipulative logic to the summary to present it with as much meaning as possible, and usually in the smallest space possible.

Because the definition of SQL allows aggregation only at one level of detail, we have to fall back to complex strategies to handle relatively "ordinary" levels of analysis. The strategies involve trading off extra computer resources or extra development resources, even when the detail of the solution is hidden behind a user-oriented front end.

Enhancements in Version 8.1.5

Glamorous presentation is *always* an issue, so graphical front-end "data-mining" tools will inevitably be required for some work. But in the age of the World Wide Web it is still reasonably acceptable to produce simple tabular reports, and Oracle has already taken some steps to handle the problem of two-stage data access.

Rollup

If we revisit the example, we can rewrite it using the new rollup() functionality:

```
select
    reg.region_name,
```

```
    str.store_name,
    sum(bki.value_of_sale)  tot_sales
from
    regions         reg,
    stores          str,
    basket_items    bki
where
    bki.sale_date = to_date('13-Jan-2000')
and str.id = bki.store_id
and reg.id = str.region_id
group by
    rollup(reg.region_name, str.store_name)
;
```

Note two details: First, there is no ORDER BY clause. Second, instead of a simple list of columns in the GROUP BY clause, I specified the relevant columns as parameters to a function called rollup(). This cues Oracle to produce a report similar to that shown in Table 23-1.

The lines of interest in Table 23-1 are presented in boldface type. The output is implicitly sorted by region and store within region (even though we did not do an ORDER BY). At the end of each region, an extra row has

Table 23-1. Simple Rollup Output

Region	Store	Sales Value
Region 1	Store1_A	24,263.45
Region 1	Store1_B	28,517.34
Region 1	Store1_C	21,813.93
Region 1	**{blank}**	**74,594.72**
Region 2	Store2_X	31,496.12
Region 2	Store2_Y	33,194.87
Region 2	**{blank}**	**64,690.99**
{blank}	**{blank}**	**139,285.71**

appeared for the region, which has a null value for the store name, and the total sales for that region. At the end of the list we have a row in which both the store and the region are blank, and the sales value for the entire dataset appears. Remember, this is "pure" SQL producing this result, so anything that can open a cursor (and not reject the rollup() function) can execute this statement and acquire the result shown. We are *not* depending on SQL∘Plus to produce running totals for us.

Basically, SQL has postprocessed the returning result set to add value to it in the form of running totals. With just a little refinement from a SQL∘Plus (or PL/SQL) wrapper, this could now lead to a perfectly acceptable although slightly ascetic report.

There is one feature of the output that might cause confusion. We have lines where the STORE column is blank to represent the subtotals by region, but what are we supposed to do if the store name is allowed to be blank? How do we distinguish between an unnamed store and a regional total?

To deal with this type of problem, Oracle has introduced a new function— the grouping({column_name}) function. This function returns one of two possible values, a zero or a one. The rule to decide whether the return value should be a zero or one is simple. If the current value of {column_name} is blank because it represents a special subtotal row, then grouping({column_name}) is one. If {column_name} is blank because that is the actual value returned by a real row, then grouping({column_name}) is zero.

So rather than selecting reg.region_name and str.store_name, we ought to select something like

```
decode(grouping(reg.region_name), 1, 'All Regions',reg.region_name),
decode(grouping(str.store_name), 1, 'All Stores',str.store_name),
```

Then the last two rows of our table would look like those presented in Table 23-2.

Table 23-2. Effects of the grouping() Function

Region	Store	Sales Value
Region 2	All Stores	64,690.99
All Regions	All Stores	139,285.71

Cube

There is a second similar enhancement to SQL in version 8.1.5—the cube() function. In theory, this can be used to generate an N-dimensional hypercube of results, but in practice I doubt if many of us will be able to visualize more than a two-dimensional "cube," more commonly known as a *cross-tab*. For example, we could request a report showing the total sales by department and region (Table 23-3).

Table 23-3.   Simple Cross-Tab Report

Department	Region 1	Region 2	Total
Bakery	16,979.60	20,231.1	37,210.82
Delicatessen	21,384.00	18,294.32	39,678.32
Greengrocer	36,231.12	26,165.57	62,396.57
Total	74,594.72	64,690.99	139,285.71

SQL doesn't quite get to this degree of sophistication; instead it takes the REGION, DEPARTMENT, and SALES columns and lines them up one after the other (Table 23-4).

Table 23-4.   Oracle's Two-dimensional cube() Report

Region	Department	Sales Value
Region 1	Bakery	16,979.60
Region 1	Delicatessen	21,384.00
Region 1	Greengrocer	36,231.12
Region 1	**All Departments**	**74,594.72**
Region 2	Bakery	20,231.1

(continued)

Table 23-4.   (*cont.*)

Region	Department	Sales Value
Region 2	Delicatessen	18,294.32
Region 2	Greengrocer	26,165.57
Region 2	**All Departments**	**64,690.99**
All Regions	**Bakery**	**37,210.82**
All Regions	**Delicatessen**	**39,678.32**
All Regions	**Greengrocer**	**62,396.57**
All Regions	**All Departments**	**139,285.71**

The syntax to do this is virtually identical to that for rollup():

```
select
    decode(grouping(reg.region_name),
        1 , 'All Regions',
            reg.region_name
    ),
    decode(grouping(dpt.department_name),
        1 , 'All Departments',
            dpt.department_name
    ),
    sum(bki.value_of_sale)  tot_sales
from
    .   .   .
where
    .   .   .
group by
    cube(reg.region_name,    dpt.department_name)
;
```

Apart from the necessary limitations on presentation, there is a feature of the cube() function that may reduce the immediate value to many people. Assume you want to change your report so that the notional cross-tab shows the region code *and* the region name on one axis, and department code and the department name on the other (Table 23-5).

Table 23-5.

Region Name and Code Department Name and Code	2712 Yorkshire	2954 Lancashire	Total
2112 Bakery	16,979.60	20,231.1	37,210.82
2371 Delicatessen	21,384.00	18,294.32	39,678.32
2423 Greengrocer	36,231.12	26,165.57	62,396.57
Total	74,594.72	64,690.99	139,285.71

It seems to be a very natural extension to the report, just adding a little extra, related information to each title. However, if you try to add the columns to the SELECT and GROUP BY clauses, you find that the only legal syntax results in a four-dimensional hypercube. To get the result you want, you have to use concatenation, so that the final SQL statement contains exactly three (possibly derived) columns, one for the side heading, one for the top heading, and one for the table body:

```
select
    decode(grouping(reg.region_id || ' ' ||reg.region_name),
        1 , 'All Regions',
            reg.region_id || ' ' || reg.region_name
    ),
    decode(grouping(dpt.dept_id || ' ' || dpt.department_name),
        1 , 'All Departments',
            dpt.dept_id || ' ' || dpt.department_name
    ),
    sum(bki.value_of_sale)  tot_sales
from
    .   .   .
where
    .   .   .
group by
    cube(
            reg.region_id || ' ' ||reg.region_name,
            dpt.dept_id || ' ' || dpt.department_name
    )
;
```

Apart from this relatively minor irritation, there is also a CPU overhead to consider. This statement now concatenates a number and varchar2() for every row accessed, requiring an implicit conversion as it does so. As always, I will just remind you that you will be able to eliminate this cost by using in-line views if you are in complete control of the code. In fact, as a general rule when using new features of this type, it is a good thing to get the complicated bit of the SQL code (joining, grouping, and so on) out of the way in an in-line view so that you appear to be applying the new feature to a simple table.

Analytic Functions

The cube() and rollup() functionality are most welcome, but the pair of them pale in comparison with the enhancements in Oracle 8.1.6—a set of features that have been given the title of *analytic functions*.

One of the frequently asked questions about SQL in Oracle is the one about finding the top ten entries in a list. There have always been various inefficient ways of doing this, but with version 8.1.5 you could finally manage a reasonably efficient approach because it finally became legal to do an ORDER BY inside a view, including an in-line view, allowing you to write code like the following:

```
select  product_id, sales_value
from (
    select  product_id, sum(value_of_sale)sales_value
    from    basket_items
    where   date_of_sale = to_date('13-Jan-2000')
    group by product_id
    order by sum(value_of_sale) desc
)
where rownum <= 10
;
```

Of course, you may ask yourself what you would want to have reported if the ninth and tenth items have the same sales value, or if the tenth and eleventh items have the same value. If you did, you would soon realize that the previous solution is far from complete. More seriously, how do you address queries like the following:

- **For each region,** report the top two departments within the region.
- **For each region,** report total sales for the region as a percentage of total sales.
- Report the **three-day rolling average** sales by department.

These are just a few of the fairly typical questions that sales analysts ask that can only be answered efficiently if you break one of the fundamental rules of relational database systems: The order of data in a table is supposed to be irrelevant.

All these queries need more than just a simple aggregate and sort on the data. To operate efficiently they need some form of procedural processing that requires one row to be compared with earlier or later rows in the output. Most queries of this type can be addressed in a nonprocedural way, if you really want to stick to the rules, but the processing overhead tends to be huge once the data sizes are anything other than small.

Oracle Corporation has devised an extension to the syntax of SQL that allows the aggregate functions to operate over subsections of result sets. As with the rest of SQL, these extensions are very compact in their definition but very wide ranging in the effect that they produce. (The extensions have been passed to the relevant standards committee for possible inclusion in the next SQL standard.) At the same time, Oracle Corporation has introduced a handful of new aggregate functions that can take advantage of the new syntax.

The basis of the new syntax is that any aggregate function (both the old, and the dozen or so new) can be followed by a clause starting with the keyword over(). This keyword prompts Oracle to expect a clause that defines a subset of the data (referred to as a *partition* unfortunately) to which the aggregate function should be applied.

Let's take the first example in my previous list. For each region, report the top two departments. As usual we can start with a simple SQL statement that gets us part of the way to a solution:

```
select region_name, department, sum(sales_value)
from basket_items
group by region_name, department
order by region_name, sum(sales_value) desc;

England  Bakery        364,448
         Delicatessen  353,900
         Fish          350,134
         Greengrocer   343,182
         Meat          322,007

Ireland  Delicatessen  359,910
         Bakery        349,770
         Meat          337,634
         Fish          335,370
         Greengrocer   329,368
```

```
Scotland Greengrocer    373,302
         Bakery         367,524
         Meat           353,012
         Fish           345,388
         Delicatessen   333,038

Wales    Bakery         367,296
         Delicatessen   357,238
         Fish           341,896
         Meat           340,970
         Greengrocer    331,210
```

We have more data than our specification called for. We want only the top two rows for each region. Obviously we could put our ***select*** statement inside a procedural loop, but in Oracle 8.1.6 we can invoke the new rank() function and add an extra column to our report that gives the position of each sales figure within the region. This takes three steps:

1. We recognize that we are going to rank() over (something).
2. We are ranking within region.
3. We specify that the ranking is based on value of sales in descending order.

The line we add to our SQL statement is

```
rank() over (
        partition by region_name
        order by sum(sales_value) desc
) as region_rank
```

For the England region, our output now looks like

```
England  Bakery         364,448    1
         Delicatessen   353,900    2
         Fish           350,134    3
         Greengrocer    343,182    4
         Meat           322,007    5
```

As the report moves on to the lines for Ireland, Oracle restarts the rank at one and counts to five again, and so on down the list of regions. One very important point to note is that the results appear in this order because of the ORDER BY clause on the main statement, *not* because of the ORDER BY in the OVER clause. The order in the OVER clause is there solely to tell Oracle how to calculate the rank of each row within the partition, and it has nothing to do with the final order of output.

We are getting closer to what we want to see. At least we have a highly visible number that tells use how to select the target items. We just need to add the clause REGION_RANK <= 2 somehow, but where can we apply the clause? At this point I like to invoke in-line views (see Chapter 11). You will find that you are probably going to start doing that a lot when you use analytic functions. Just before we write out the complete solution, let's get greedy with analytic functions.

When discussing methods of showing partial totals using expensive SQL, I made a feature of how I could report the sales for a department as a fraction of the sales for a region. I can do this much more cheaply with the analytic function ratio_to_report(), so let's add this to our report. Although the function name is ratio_to_report, it can actually be applied to each partition and not just the full report. We want to show the summed sales_value in each row as a fraction of the total value for the region. The appropriate syntax is

```
Ratio_to_Report(sum(sales_value)) over (
        partition by region_name
) as region_ratio
```

Note how the ratio_to_report() function, unlike the rank() function, takes a parameter that identifies the column that is to be processed. If we wanted to go one step further and show each row as a fraction of the total report, we would simply omit the partitioning information from the OVER clause:

```
Ratio_to_Report(sum(sales_value)) over () as total_ratio
```

So our final SQL selects from an in-line view that applies all these bits of code and eliminates all rows in which region_rank is more than two:

```
select *
from (
    select
        region_name,
        department,
        sum(sales_value)                        as sv,
        rank() over (
                partition by region_name
                order by sum(sales_value) desc
        )                                       as region_rank,
```

```
        ratio_to_report(sum(sales_value)) over (
                partition by region_name
        )                                       as region_ratio,
        ratio_to_report(sum(sales_value)) over () as total_ratio
    from basket_items
    group by region_name, department
)       in_line_view
where   region_rank <= 2
order by region_name, sv desc
;
```

```
England  Bakery        364448      1    .210    .052
         Delicatessen  353900      2    .204    .051

Ireland  Delicatessen  359910      1    .210    .052
         Bakery        349770      2    .204    .050

Scotland Greengrocer   373302      1    .211    .054
         Bakery        367524      2    .207    .053

Wales    Bakery        367296      1    .211    .053
         Delicatessen  357238      2    .205    .051
```

The real beauty of this code, and the reason why the topic appears in a chapter on number crunching, is that the actual cost of execution is little more than the cost of execution of the very basic, original SORT GROUP BY with which we started. The final SQL code is a little more complex than you would normally expect to see, but compared with the 3GL or PL/SQL code that would have to be written to achieve the same result, the pure SQL solution is still extremely simple.

The previous example shows how we can define fixed windows on the data, and do interesting things inside each window separately. In fact, the last example with the report_to_ratio showed that we could actually choose to define a number of different-size windows simultaneously. There is another major variant on using analytic functions, which I will mention briefly. It allows you to use *rolling windows* on the data.

There are two commonly asked questions in Oracle forums. How do I use SQL to generate a rolling average report, and how do I use SQL to produce a report in which column 2 is a running total for column 1? I'll answer both questions in a single SQL example.

Imagine a set of data covering two weeks of trading on the stock market. We are interested in the volumes traded over a couple of weeks for one particular stock, and have a requirement for a three-day rolling average, which means on each date we would like to see the average of the day before, the day after, and the current day, and at the same time we want to see the cumulative trade volume since the start of the time period. The following SQL code gets the base data in order, shows two possible variants for the rolling average, and shows the cumulative sum:

```
select
    trade_date,
    volume,
    avg(volume) OVER (
        order by trade_date
        range between 1 preceding and 1 following
    )                            range_average,
    avg(volume) OVER (
        order by trade_date
        rows between 1 preceding and 1 following
    )                            rows_average,
    sum(volume) OVER (
        order by trade_date
        rows unbounded preceding
    )                            cumulative_sum
from
    stocks
where ticker = 'FAKE'
and trade_date between '01-NOV-1999' and '14-NOV-1999'
order by
    trade_date
;
```

Date	Volume	Range avg	Rows Avg	Cumulative
01-NOV-1999	190	150	150	190
02-NOV-1999	110	150	150	300
03-NOV-1999	150	127	127	450
04-NOV-1999	120	150	150	570
05-NOV-1999	*180*	*150*	*163*	*750*
08-NOV-1999	190	180	180	940
09-NOV-1999	170	157	157	1110
10-NOV-1999	110	143	143	1220
11-NOV-1999	150	150	150	1370
12-NOV-1999	190	170	170	1560

We start with the simple avg(), and sum() functions that have been in Oracle for at least the last 15 years but, as with the earlier examples of analytic functions, we cue Oracle that we are going to do something special by following with the keyword over(). In this case, we have not used the PARTITION clause to break the output result into fixed subsets because we are interested in the full set of data returned by the query. If we had selected several stocks, we could have included a clause PARTITION BY TICKER. Instead, with the **range** or **rows** keywords, we have indicated to Oracle that we are going to move a "window" through the dataset and produce a result for each row that is dependent on the size of the window.

When you use this windowing variant of the analytic function, it is mandatory that you include an ORDER BY clause in each OVER() clause, because Oracle works out a value for the current row by stepping through the partition in the right order to generate the relevant window. All windows need a start point and an end point, which are specified in the BETWEEN clause, but there are several variants that use specific syntax. I have shown one of these special cases for the cumulative sum—the ROWS UNBOUNDED PRECEDING option—which means from the start of the partition to the current row.

For the rolling averages, I show an example of the more general syntax. There is an important difference, however, between the ROWS and RANGE options that show up on the highlighted line of the output. When you specify ROWS, Oracle uses the boundary values supplied (one, in every case of my example) to count backward and forward by physical row position. So my rolling average by rows of 5 November comes from the row before, the current row, and the row after—in other words, 4, 5, and 8 November. When you specify RANGE, Oracle applies the boundary values to the actual value of the ordering column and uses the rows that fall within the test range. So my average by range for 5 November comes from any rows in which trade_date is between 4 and 6 November—strictly speaking, the current row, any preceding rows between 4 and 6 November, and any following rows between 4 and 6 November.

There is obviously a lot more that could be said about analytic functions, and I could produce all sorts of cunning and complicated examples of how you can use them and combine them. The important point is that they exist, and they allow you to do all sorts of complex analysis directly within the SQL engine right next to the database.

The avg(), sum(), and count() functions are perhaps the ones most likely to be of use with rolling windows; the new rank(), dense_rank(), cume_dist(), and ntile(), as in ntile(4) for quartile and ntile(100) for percentile, are perhaps the ones most likely to be of use with fixed partitions.

Miscellaneous

Case Statements

One of the "little surprise" changes in SQL that appears in version 8.1.6 is that Oracle has finally implemented the ***case*** statement as it appears in the SQL 92 standard.

Of course the highly powerful decode() function has been around from time immemorial, but it has always introduced a lot of pain into "banding" data. How, for instance, do you set up a report that reports stores with the number of customers that made purchases between 8:00 A.M. and 12:00 noon, the number between 12:00 noon and 4:00 P.M., and the number between 4:00 P.M. and 8:00 P.M.?

Code to do this sort of banding tends to degenerate into complex nesting of decodes, or (when circumstances allow) cunning mathematical tricks. Taking a simpler example, which tries to count the number of clients in the age band $25 \le age < 30$, we may write something like

```
decode (sign(age - 25),
-1,      0,                  -- under 25 so get a zero
         decode(sign(age-30),  -- otherwise are they under 30
         -1, 1,              -- yes
           0
         )
)
```

The syntax available in Oracle 8.1.6 is shorter, and certainly much more comprehensible:

```
case when (age >= 25 and age < 30) then 1 else 0
```

More generally,

```
case
    when (condition A) then resultA
    when (condition B) then resultB
    when (condition C) then resultC
    else default_result
end
```

For example,

```
select
    case
        when (to_char(sysdate,'hh24') < 6) then 'Early'
        when (to_char(sysdate,'hh24') between 6 and 11) then 'AM'
        when (to_char(sysdate,'hh24') between 12 and 18)then 'PM'
        when (to_char(sysdate,'hh24') > 18 )then 'Late'
    end as time_of_day
from dual;
```

SAMPLE Clause

The SAMPLE clause is another one of those little items that you hardly notice in the publicity, but it can make a huge difference to your application. This clause allows you to query a randomly scattered fraction of a table to get an indicative result, rather than an exact result:

```
select {complicated expression} from tableX sample block (1);
select {complicated expression} from tableX sample (0.01);
```

You can select blocks at random and examine all the rows from those blocks, or you can select rows at random. The parameter to SAMPLE is the percentage of the table you want to sample. Because the best reason for using the SAMPLE clause is to reduce I/O, you should think carefully about the sample size you use for sampling rows. A single block could easily hold 100 rows, so a row sample size of 1% could visit every single block in the table. For this reason, the sample size can be as small as 0.000001 (1 in 100,000,000).

There are a couple of important points to remember about SAMPLE. The first is that the method is extremely random. Each time you reexecute, a statement will usually get different results. Even the simple statement *select count(*) from tableX sample (0.01);* gives you a different result every time.

The second point is that you can only use the SAMPLE clause on a SQL statement involving a single table. There is no easy way to get a sample of rows from one table and join that sample to another table. Actually, if you use native dynamic SQL, object type parameters, and cast(), you can. There is a hidden init.ora parameter to allow multitable sampling, so this may become a legal option in a near-future release. You can't even sample from a view created by joining two tables; the query is accepted without returning an error but the SAMPLE clause is ignored.

There is one restriction on sampling that perhaps gives a clue on how Oracle does it. You cannot sample an IOT, so perhaps sample() uses the random number generator exposed in the package DBMS_RANDOM to generate a number between one and num_rows, then uses the bitmap conversion routines to turn that number into a rowid.

Materialized Views

Databases are getting bigger and more business critical, and end users are getting more sophisticated and demanding in their use of databases. This tends to show itself in the increased demand for facilities to produce high-density management reports with an open-ended facility to drill down to increasing levels of detail.

For example, a "dense" management report may sum sales by month for four regions. A simple graphical representation of the report shows that the northern region had unusually high sales in June, so attention turns to that one item (out of 48), a drill-down report lists sales by 12 product categories and 16 districts in June. This shows that most of the anomaly was the result of two product categories in one district. When we drill deeper, we discover which towns in the district, which products in the categories, and so on.

Of course our starting point (just for one month in one region) could easily be looking at a summary of 100,000,000 rows of data. Each district/product category would still be an aggregate of approximately 500,000 rows. How can you possibly manage to do that much work in time to satisfy a curious user who is just "pecking" his way through the database looking for anomalies?

The obvious answer is to do the work while no one is looking. Just pre-create a load of summary tables the night (or weekend) before, and make sure that the user looks at the right summary at the right moment. Instead of summing 100,000,000 rows of the SALES table to get the figures for a month and region, perhaps the user will actually sum 12 × 16 = 192 rows from the SALES_BY_PROD_CAT_AND_DISTRICT summary table.

Perhaps it would be a SALES_BY_PROD_CAT_AND_TOWN summary for which we need to pick up 5,000 rows—a number of rows that would still be returned in a reasonable amount of time in response to a quick-peek type of query.

This introduces a different kind of problem. How does the end user know which table to address with what level of summing to get the best possible answer in the shortest possible time?

There are several tools on the market that help work around this problem. Such tools tend to have their own internal data dictionary in which you can define relationships between summary tables, give it information about the relative numbers of rows, explain how one summary is aggregated from another, list which columns in one level of summary correspond to which other columns in another level of summary, and so on. Once you have done this, the tool then works out how to use the available summary tables to address a query like

```
select   region, product_category, financial_period, sum(sales)
from
         stores      str,
         products    prd,
         sales       sal
where
         sal.financial_year = 1999
         str.store_id = sal.store_id
and      prd.product_id = sal.product_id
group by
         region, product_category, financial_period
;
```

Most of the tools I have come across tend to be fairly adequate at getting to the right answer in a reasonably effective way once they are set up correctly, but there are usually two problems that need to be handled. First, it often takes a lot of administrative work to set up the tool. Second, the SQL code that ends up firing off at the database is often far from optimal (even Oracle's own Discoverer product is guilty of this from time to time).

In some cases the tools actually start creating scratch pad tables left, right, and center to generate small, intermediate results that can be joined, or unioned, to produce a final answer, and they won't be the superefficient global temporary tables that avoid generating redo. One of the main reasons for this type of behavior is that Oracle is not the only relational database product in the world, so the tool has to be designed to work at the level of the lowest common denominator.

Oracle's resolution of these two issues lies in the built-in functionality of the materialized view and the query rewrite. With these two features, Oracle internalizes the functions of the data query tool. The data dictionary aspect of the problem can collapse down to writing a single SQL statement to define the materialized view, and the query rewrite operations are built into the optimizer, so that Oracle can take full advantage of its knowledge of what it can do to produce the most efficient solution to the problem.

For example, the previous query that addresses the SALES table can be rewritten internally by Oracle to address the SALES_BY_PRD_AND_DST table, extracting referenced data through in-line views as follows:

```
Select
        Region_name,
        product_category,
        financial_period,
        sum(sales)
from
        (
            select distinct
                    region_id,
                    region_name
            from stores
        )                               reg
        (
            select distinct
                    product_category_id,
                    product_category
            from        products
        )                               cat,
        (   select
                region_id,
                product_category_id,
                financial_period,
                sum(sales)
            from
                sales_by_prd_cat_and_dst     sal
            where
                sal.financial_year = 1999
            group by
                region_id,
                product_category_id,
                financial_period
        )                               sal
where
        reg.region_id = sal.region_id
and     cat.product_category_id = sal.product_cateogry_id
group by
        region_name,
        product_category,
        financial_period
    ;
```

If you have read Chapter 11, you will be familiar with in-line views and my comments on how in-line views can dramatically reduce the work done by Oracle in producing summaries. In many ways, the materialized view developments in Oracle are a cunning example of how one piece of technology can piggyback an existing piece of technology. If the QUERY REWRITE mechanism can recognize an opportunity for rewriting a query to do a "group by then join" instead of a "join then group by," then the optimizer will handle it automatically. In addition, the materialized view technology is in fact nothing more than the simple snapshot technology of replication, which has been with us since Oracle 7.0. The rest of this chapter constructs an example of using a materialized view, and highlights some of the issues surrounding their use.

Implementation

Before we can build and use any useful example of a materialized view, we need to have some system privileges set: CREATE MATERIALIZED VIEW, CREATE DIMENSION, and QUERY REWRITE.

We then need a sample data table and a couple of tables to join to it for typical queries. Let's use a SALES DATA table representing daily sales totals for a supermarket chain, with the structure

```
sale_date       date,
product_id      number(6),
store_id        number(4),
qty             number(4),
value           number(8,2).
Primary key (sale_date, store_id, product_id)
```

Each product belongs to a product group, and each product group belongs to a department, so we need a hierarchy of product tables with the obvious primary key/foreign key relationships:

```
products (
        product_id,
        prod_name,
        product_group
)

groups(
        product_group,
        group_name,
```

```
        product_dept
)

departments(
        product_dept,
        dept_name
)
```

For our initial demonstration, let's create a table called SALES_SUM, and tell Oracle that the materialized view is a preexisting table, and that it should always trust the DBA that the table is current and valid. The table will hold the data summed to the product group level, rather than being summed all the way to the department level. Choosing the best level for a summary of this type is an important task. If the summary is too low (hence, too big) it adds little value, and is rarely used. If it is too high, there are not many occasions on which Oracle can choose it. In this particular case I chose a level that would compress the data by a factor of approximately 20, leaving the optimizer the option of using it for product group reports and product department reports. I have shortened the code here somewhat, but the table I used for my first tests was a subpartitioned table, and my summary table was a partitioned table. Oracle coped with both of them perfectly well. (Interestingly, an ordinary snapshot may not be partitioned, even though materialized views and snapshots are convergent technologies.)

```
create table sales_sum
nologging
as
select
    sal.sale_date,
    prd.product_group,
    sum(sal.qty)    qty,
    sum(sal.value)  value,
    store_id
from
    sales           sal,
    products        prd
where
    prd.product_id = sql.product_id
group by
    sal.sale_date,
    prd.product_group,
store_id
;
```

Having set up the data, we need to define a materialized view, pointing out to Oracle that the view has already been instantiated as a table:

```
create materialized view sales_sum
on prebuilt table          -- the table already exists
with reduced precision     -- allow column precision mismatch
never refresh              -- we rebuild it ourselves
enable query rewrite       -- the point of the exercise
as
select
    sal.sale_date,
    grp.product_group,
    sum(sal.qty)     qty,
    sum(sal.value)   value,
    store_id
from
    sales          sal,
    products       prd,
    groups         grp
where
    prd.product_id = sal.product_id
and grp.product_group = prd.product_group
group by
    sal.sale_date,
    grp.product_group,
    store_id
;
```

There are a couple of points to note here. The clause ENABLE QUERY REWRITE means that this particular materialized view can be used for query rewrites. Without the clause, it would simply be considered a snapshot that (for some bizarre reason) is never to be updated according to the NEVER REFRESH clause just above it. The second point is the appearance of the GROUPS table in the definition of the materialized view. It didn't appear in the creation of the summary table, and the column that it introduces into the SELECT clause is the PRODUCT_GROUP column, which could have been exposed from the PRODUCTS table itself. The reason for its presence is that we want to use the same summary table/materialized view to generate summaries to the department level, and (as we are about to see in the dimension declaration) Oracle knows only that departments are related to groups, so we have to expose the PRODUCT_GROUP from the GROUPS table rather than from the PRODUCT table.

The next step is to describe to Oracle the product hierarchy that may be used to query the base table. This isn't an essential step in all cases, but if we do it, it increases the number of opportunities that Oracle has for recognizing the option for rewriting queries to use the materialized view:

```
create dimension product_dim
    level    product    is products.product_id
    level    prd_group  is groups.product_group
    level    department is departments.product_dept
    hierarchy product_roll_up(
        product     child of
        prd_group   child of
        department
        join key products.product_group references prd_group
        join key groups.product_dept references department
    )
    attribute product d        (products.prod_name)
    attribute prd_group      es (groups.group_name)
    attribute department      es (departments.dept_name)
;
```

This statement packs a hug   of information into a very small space. As you can see, it falls into thre   levels, rollup, and attributes. The LEVEL clauses tell us the nam   fferent levels of the hierarchy, and name a column (and table) that   he values that may appear in a level. The HIERARCHY section tells   e relationships between the different levels and the join condition   from one level to another. The join key is a little confusing in the way it switches between table names and level names. The generic syntax is "child_table.foreign_key_column references parent_level." The ATTRIBUTE clauses tell us about column names that can be equated to the unique identifying columns that have been specified for each level. Again, there is a wonderful blend of level names and table names. The generic syntax is "level_name determines (list of table_name.column_name)", where the table name *has* to be the table named in the original level definition. If we had created a flattened (denormalized) hierarchy table from our three base tables, our dimension definition would have been a little simpler:

```
create dimension product_dim
    level    product    is product_hierarchy.product_id
    level    prd_group  is product_hierarchy.product_group
    level    department is product_hierarchy.product_dept
```

```
hierarchy product_roll_up(
    product      child of
    prd_group    child of
    department
)
attribute product determines (prod_name)
attribute prd_group determines (group_name)
attribute department determines (dept_name)
;
```

One odd little quirk, by the way: You cannot use create or replace on dimensions or materialized views. You have to drop them and re-create them. Fortunately, you don't have to worry about granting access privileges on them because they are hidden objects as far as end users are concerned, so this doesn't really cause any serious problems.

Finally, we are ready to test if everything works:

```
alter session set query_rewrite_enabled = true;
alter session set query_rewrite_integrity = trusted;

select
    dep.dept_name,
    grp.group_name,
    sum(sal.value)  value
from
    sales          sal,
    products       prd,
    groups         grp,
    departments    dep
where
    prd.product = sal.product
and grp.product_group = prd.product_group
and dep.product_dept = grp.product_dept
group by
    dep.dept_name,
    grp.group_name
;
```

The first alter session tells Oracle to consider query rewrite as an optimization option. The second alter session is very important in our case because it tells Oracle to assume that a prebuilt materialized view is current and may therefore be considered for query rewrites. Then we hit the system with a query that includes a table (DEPARTMENTS) and two columns

(DEPT_NAME and GROUP_NAME) that haven't appeared in either our summary table or in the definition of the materialized view. Fortunately we have told Oracle in the dimension declaration that group_name equates to product_group, that dept_name equates to product_dept, and that departments can be joined to groups on column product_dept. The execution path for the query doesn't touch the SALES table or the PRODUCTS table. Instead, Oracle does the following:

```
SORT (GROUP BY)
  HASH JOIN
    HASH JOIN
      TABLE ACCESS (FULL) OF 'GROUPS'
      TABLE ACCESS (FULL) OF 'DEPARTMENTS'
    TABLE ACCESS (FULL) OF 'SALES_SUM'
```

Materialized views do work and can produce results extremely rapidly. My preferred strategy is the one just shown, which depends on precreating the summary table and defining the materialized view with the NEVER REFRESH option. Obviously this is most appropriate to data warehouse systems that have already invested in code to generate summary tables on a regular basis. In this case the various hierarchies are probably denormalized so that the simpler dimension definition can be used and joins involve only a small number of tables.

There are other options though, in principle. You could create a materialized view in an OLTP system and have it maintained in close to real time. For example,

```
create table base_data
nologging
as
select distinct object_type, object_name
from all_objects
;

alter table base_data
add constraint bd_pk primary key (object_type, object_name);

analyze table base_data compute statistics;

create materialized view log on base_data
with rowid (object_type)
including new values;
```

```
create materialized view fast_refresh
build immediate
refresh fast on commit
enable query rewrite
as
select
        object_type,
        count(*)    ct
from    base_data
group by object_type
;
```

With this very simple materialized view, we have a few important changes to note. The most significant is that we have a clause REFRESH FAST ON COMMIT. Because of this directive, any update to the base data table is propagated to the summary table when the user commits, and is not just passed to the log for subsequent copying as is normal with snapshots. You should also notice that materialized views have to meet several conditions before they can be subject to a fast refresh. Our example of a simple aggregate of a single table is one such case, but we also have to create a snapshot log, the snapshot log has to include the rowid and *include new values*, and the table has to have a primary key. All these things consume resources to allow us to have a materialized view that is kept current in real time.

Even with the conditions being met perfectly, we still have two problems. First, the overhead that hits the system when you commit is large. In a busy system OLTP system, several users could hit that moment together and cause some fairly severe contention for resources. Second, if we execute a query against the base data when we have updated it, but not yet committed our change, the query rewrite may not take place, and we may actually visit the base table rather than the materialized view:

```
Select count(*) from base_data;
1414                    -- visits fast_refresh

insert into base_date values ('VIEW','abc');

select count(*) from base_data;
1415                    -- visits base_data (slow)

commit;

select count(*) from base_data;
1415                    -- visits fast_refresh
```

Why does this happen? I suspect that it is in part a bug, but the answer is also affected by the session parameter QUERY_REWRITE_INTEGRITY, which may take the values TRUSTED, ENFORCED, or STALE_ TOLERATED. If you use prebuilt tables for materialized views you need to set this value to TRUSTED. If you set the parameter to ENFORCED, then Oracle is required to use the base table unless it knows that the materialized view is exactly in sync with the base table. So if you insert a row into the base table without committing it, you have to be able to see the correct result, which has not yet propagated into the materialized view. Thus, Oracle has to use the base table for the query.

The biggest oddity comes from the STALE_TOLERATED option. This exists to accommodate materialized views with refresh *on demand*—in other words, when the DBA or DBMS_JOB invokes the DBMS_MVIEW package to refresh the materialized view. Basically, if your session is set to tolerate stale materialized views, Oracle will use query rewrite against materialized views that are known to be out of date with respect to the base data. However, if you change some data in that table, and requery it before committing, Oracle will suspend query rewrites for that table until you commit. This can lead to some very uncomfortable dialogs if the materialized view happens to refresh *on demand*. In the previous example, but re-creating the materialized view with ON COMMIT changed to ON DEMAND, the results were as follows:

```
select count(*) from base_data;
1414                          -- visits fast_refresh

insert into base_date values ('VIEW','abc');
select count(*) from base_data;
1415                          -- visits base_data (slow)

commit;
select count(*) from base_data;
1414                          -- fast_refresh, without the new row
```

In fact, it really doesn't matter what combination of settings you have for the materialized view REFRESH mechanism and QUERY_REWRITE_ INTEGRITY. If you can change the base data, then you will find a way of getting wild swings in performance and contradictory results as Oracle jumps back and forth between using the base table and the materialized view to return the results of the same query.

In summary, there are all sorts of variations on a theme when using materialized views and query rewrite. Some aspects are very good. You can, for example, do a direct load into a base table and get the materialized view updated without having to rebuild it. Some aspects are still showing their youth. For example, the number of times I crashed out of SQL*Plus when using AUTOTRACE with query rewrite was extremely irritating. For me, the bottom line is that I would be inclined to risk using materialized views in a data warehouse environment with prebuilt tables, but I wouldn't want to have to worry about the overhead or the anomalies of dynamically refreshed materialized views in any other type of system at present.

Problems and Quirks

In Oracle 8.1.5, the CUBE and ROLLUP options are not recognized in PL/SQL. Because it is now so much easier to use dynamic SQL in PL/SQL than it used to be with earlier versions of Oracle (see Chapter 19), the workaround is simply to execute the statement as dynamic SQL, possibly returning a ref cursor.

Don't expect front-end tools to be able to take advantage of the new capabilities of the analytic functions for some time.

Materialized views with *refresh on commit* have a significant overhead at commit. They also introduce odd performance side effects if the query rewrite integrity is enforced, because a query against uncommitted data has to visit the base table, whereas a query against committed visits the materialized view.

There are a number of funny glitches at present with query rewrite. For example, I found some cases in which applying row-level security to base data tables disabled the ability of the optimizer to redirect a query to a suitable materialized view. Similarly, I found that the creation of apparently irrelevant function-based indexes on the base table would stop query rewrite from happening.

To use user-defined functions in function-based indexes, you need to set QUERY_REWRITE_INTEGRITY to TRUSTED. But if you have materialized views that refresh on demand, you need to set QUERY_REWRITE_INTEGRITY to STALE_TOLERATED. There really ought to be separate parameters to avoid this conflict of interest.

If you use bind variables with materialized views, the query rewrite does not take place. In a data warehouse with a few ad hoc queries this may not be a significant problem. In an OLTP system we are always being advised to write our code to use bind variables.

Strategy Notes

There are likely to be lots of opportunities for using the analytic functions, particularly for Web access to data warehouses.

When using cube(), rollup(), and the analytic functions, you may find that the best first step is to put the driving query into an in-line view, and apply the functions to that. Don't be worried about applying two or three layers of in-line views if that helps you to understand how the functions are working.

The clarity of code you can achieve through the case() operator of version 8.1.6 is a huge improvement over the decode() function. There is also likely to be some performance benefit. Consider rewriting SQL to take advantage of it.

The effects of materialized views with query rewrite are amazing, but the technology is still in its infancy. Take advantage of it when you can in data warehouses to avoid building complicated "meta-data translation processes," but be very cautious about using it for anything other than prebuilt summaries.

CHAPTER 24

Fallback

In this chapter I talk about backup and recovery, but by giving the chapter the title of Fallback, I want to indicate that a sound implementation requires you to take a much wider viewpoint than just basic backup and recovery.

There are several books on the market that deal technically with the issue of backing up and recovering an Oracle database (*Backup and Recovery for Oracle 7/8*, by Rama Velpuri, is perhaps the most thorough and technically complete example that comes to mind). However, there is more to having a fallback position than knowing how to recover an Oracle database. For a start, what types of recovery scenarios do you think you are trying to protect yourself from? How much time are you going to allow yourself to solve a problem before you adopt your fallback position? Once you have adopted your fallback position, what is your strategy for getting your system back to normal?

Without reviewing the entire life cycle from the moment of disaster onward, you are unlikely to come up with a satisfactory fallback and recovery plan.

> *A backup mechanism is pointless if you don't also have a workable recovery strategy.*

Choose Your Disaster

There are two driving statements that seem to appear most frequently in business requirements. The first is the generic "response times will be subsecond" for performance; the second is the equally aimless demand that "time to recovery shall not exceed X," where X is usually a pretty small time interval.

The general form of the two targets is quite reasonable. The problem lies with the failure to outline the circumstances to which they should apply. Quite recently I was on a site where the manager was explaining the importance of the database being down for no more than five minutes per day. When I asked him how his current strategy would cope with an airplane crashing into the building (a reasonable question because the office was approximately 400 yards from the runway of a major international airport), he barely paused for thought before replying, "I think there would be more important things to worry about in that case."

It's all very well to propose a hypothetical limit on downtime (which could be met given enough cash), but you really do need to ensure that there is a realistic set of circumstances for which you are planning. In fact, another site at which I worked had a genuine requirement, both operational and financial, for their database system to survive the hypothetical direct hit from an airplane without loss of data. Their downtime had to be limited to a few minutes, and they proved it was possible by pulling the plug on the primary site, and watching the secondary site take over five miles away.

So what constitutes realistic circumstances? If you answer, simple disk failure, this is easy to address. Just use some form of RAID with hot-swap disks. Don't forget to have a highly proactive warning system so that you spot the error as soon as or even before it happens so that there is a hot-swap disk in place. How many spare disks are you going to leave in place as spares anyway? And what degree of performance hit do you want to take for how long as the new disk is resilvered to catch up with the broken one?

What if a complete controller board fails? Better make all the disks dual ported with completely fault-tolerant hardware. The same had better be true of the main computer components. Have several banks of memory, each of which can fail safely and be hot swapped. Have several CPU boards, each of which can fail safely and be hot swapped.

Once you get past doing your best to make the hardware robust, what can you do about the environment? If power to the office is lost, build in an uninterruptible power supply. How many hours are you going to gamble on? Do you want just 15 minutes' worth of power to be able to shut the system down safely, or six hours' worth to keep the system running until the power (probably) comes back on, or perhaps just enough power to keep the disk cache live for 72 hours.

What happens if an office fire makes the machine room unusable? Not all offices have air-conditioned, halon-protected machine rooms. Even if the machine appears to be in full working order, will the emergency services or insurance company allow you to carry on working in the office? There may be some delay before the room is declared safe for human use.

On a less dramatic note, how are you planning to cope with a digger putting a blade through the telephone cable in the road outside? A rather serious threat if you happen to be using your Oracle database as the back end to a Web site. Not only does your real-time off-site replication fail, but the users can't even get to you.

Pick a Time Scale

Having decided on a range of scenarios from which you would like to recover in a "reasonable" time, you then need to decide what you actually mean by a "reasonable time," and how much you are prepared to pay for it. This section gives you some ideas of a few possible strategies, where the holes are in those strategies, the time scale of recovery, and the effect on the cost of implementation.

The 30-Second 100% Fail-over

The fastest option is probably the Oracle Parallel Server. You need to cluster your machines so that they share common disks and have a high-speed, low-latency link between them. Every single machine runs its own copy of the Oracle software, but they all share a single database. If one machine/instance crashes, another instance detects it very shortly afterward and does crash recovery on its behalf. There is a brief period when the instance doing the recovery locks the cache control mechanism for all the instances, but this is typically just a few seconds.

The pure cost overhead with this approach includes the extra licensing required from Oracle and the extra support for clustering (possibly both hardware and software) required from the hardware vendor.

The biggest implementation problem with this approach is that you need to design your application very carefully; otherwise you can generate massive amounts of contention between the instances and end up with a very expensive, very slow system.

You could, of course, use the Oracle Parallel Server on just two machines, with the understanding that only one of them would ever be addressed, and the other one would be up and running, ready to become "instantly" available if the first machine failed. There are some fiddly bits to set up in network connections to make this work, but essentially you can specify that there are two service providers for the database and that the second service provider should be used only if the first one cannot be contacted for, say, 30 seconds.

Although this is possible in principle, there are two risks—first, that the secondary machine would accidentally be activated from time to time and wreck the performance of the system, and second that it wouldn't be activated quickly enough when the first machine crashed. (At the time of writing, Oracle 8.1.6 promises a new two-node active/passive configuration to accommodate this option.)

Of course, part of the fail-over strategy should cover the steps to take after a fail-over has taken place. How do you fail back? With the parallel server solution, this may be very simple but is hardware dependent. With the right choice of hardware, you can just connect a new machine to the cluster (or fix and restart the old one) and keep on going.

The Five-Minute 100% Fail-over

Again this relies on clustering, but eliminates the need for Oracle Parallel Server. Instead, you rely on the hardware platform to supply a heartbeat between the two machines. One machine runs all the services, and when it fails, the other machine takes on its identity.

This takes longer than the mechanism offered by Oracle Parallel Server because the two machines are effectively substitutes for each other rather than partners. This means that the second machine has to acquire the network identity of the first machine, claim ownership of the disks, and then start up all the packages that the first machine was running (including starting up and recovering the Oracle database).

Given the correct hardware, the post-failover actions are identical to the Oracle Parallel Server option, just replace or fix the failed machine and restart. You could even choose to fail-back straightaway if you elect to have a lower power machine as the normal fail-over machine.

Oracle Corporation even supplies a packaged solution known as Oracle Failsafe for NT systems to ease the administration of this type of clustered fail-over system. Users of UNIX, on the other hand, still have to adapt their vendor's base offering by writing their own fail-over scripts.

Off-site 100% Fail-over

There is an obvious weakness with both of the previous fail-over options. The machines running the databases have to be very close to each other. You may be able to separate them to a degree, but if an external agency causes a major problem (an office fire, say), then it is likely that both machines will be equally affected.

The solution to this is to mirror the disks off-site in real time. Using fiber technology and fairly large disk caches, it is possible for disks to be several miles apart and still act sufficiently rapidly to be mirrors of each other. Of course only the local disks would be used for reading, whereas local and remote disks would be used for writing, so you would be paying all the penalties of mirrored disks without getting the usual performance benefit.

As far as I know, it is not yet possible to have two machines acting as a cluster at that sort of distance. This means that the fail-over mechanism would have to be controlled programmatically or manually at a much higher level than just the machine identity.

Again, you would have to have a secondary machine start up when the primary machine failed, and either take on the network address of the first machine or otherwise ensure that SQL∗Net connections to the first machine are redirected to the second machine by a mechanism such as flushing out the cache of your name server and loading the new details. In principle, this might require just a few minutes; in practice, you are likely to lose as many minutes in administrative overhead as you are in actual technical issues, so your targeted speed of fail-over probably ought to be 10 to 20 minutes.

The postfail-over steps are still notionally simple, but the increased complexity of the setup is such that you may be less enthusiastic to fail-back unless you really have to. You may also find that the time required to fail-over and fail-back is undesirably high, so that you only fail-back if it is really necessary.

The main problem with this approach is likely to be the cost. Not only the cost of all that hardware and the fiber link, but also the cost of the extra space for the secondary systems. Your network must be 100% reliable, and extremely fast 100% of the time because successful mirroring requires synchronous writes (or at least two writes to cache) at two sites before a write request is considered to be complete.

Clones at 99%

The fail-over strategies listed so far are supposed to ensure that we lose absolutely no data in the event of a single machine failing. The fail-over machine does a "simple" crash recovery, bringing the database up to date with its last commit.

Instead of using disk mirroring at the operating system level, you could move up one level from the operating system and use database mirroring by applying Oracle replication techniques to keep two independent databases closely in sync with each other through multimaster replication.

This is not a technique I would be keen on myself because it introduces the risk of a fairly significant performance overhead, the potential to lose temporarily a little data, and the probability of ending up with a major data discrepancy just when you think you've managed to tidy everything up. On the other hand, it allows your two machines to be separated at a reasonable distance for a reasonable cost, with a relatively low impact on activity when the communication link breaks.

There are two minor variations in approach, but both use the multimaster option of Oracle's replication facility. In the first arrangement you would take full advantage of multimaster capabilities, with users connected to both machines and updates flying back and forth down the wire between them. The second arrangement is to have an active/passive setup with only one of the two nodes receiving direct user activity (perhaps using the other database as a read-only reporting database with a slight time lag). The active/passive setup would at least eliminate the problems of potential update conflicts, such as two users operating at opposite ends of the wire doing different things to the same row at the same time.

In the first situation, users would transparently reattach themselves to the remaining node if one node failed. In the second, you would need a mechanism to ensure that users were only ever attached to the database they were supposed to be using, and so would need a mechanism for redirecting end users to the fail-over machine if the active machine failed.

The first obvious drawback to this approach is the performance overhead. Every table would have to have the multimaster replication triggers created for it, so overhead number one is that every insert, update, or delete would fire at least one row-level trigger. As each trigger fires, it populates a DEFERRED PROCEDURE CALL table with a row that describes the change just made, so overhead number two is the cost of an extra and potentially large insert into another table for each row of real data affected. Then, every time the queue was propagated to the remote machine, the row in the DEFERRED PROCEDURE CALL table would have to be deleted, giving you the third local overhead, which includes a surprisingly large volume of redo log writes.

The next performance bottleneck is the network connection from one machine to the other. Bandwidth usually does not make a difference here; the problem is more likely to be turnaround time on the synchronous dialog that goes from one Oracle instance to the other. If possible, you should try to set up multiple Oracle job queues and multiple network devices between the two machines to allow you to make full use of the available bandwidth.

Finally, at the remote machine, Oracle has to handle the incoming procedure to change its data one row at a time. In the case of updates, particularly, the default conflict resolution code is not cheap to execute because for every single column it has to go through a process like

```
if (    my_table.col1 != incoming.old_col1
    or  my_table.col1 is null and incoming.old_col1 is not null
    or  my_table.col1 is not null and incoming.old_col1 is null
)then
    something has gone wrong
```

Oracle 8.1 has improved on the performance of earlier implementations of replication by internalizing most of the code, which used to be pure PL/SQL. Nevertheless, it is pretty CPU intensive on each row.

The next big drawback to this approach is that it is asynchronous (or at least it should be, otherwise the whole system stops when one database goes down). This means that changes at one database appear at the other database only after a time lag. Naturally you will want to make this time lag as short as possible because (1) this keeps the databases very closely up to date, and (2) it keeps the tables of deferred procedure calls as small as possible, which can only help performance. Nevertheless, when one machine fails, the other machine could well be a little short of data. The solution is not as "perfect" as the full-hardware fail-over option.

How do you decide which of the two replication options to choose? The benefit of allowing users to update at both machines until a failure occurs is that the different types of replication overhead are shared evenly between two machines, which may give you slightly better performance. On the other hand, if you allow data entry at both machines, then you may find two users updating the same row in two different ways at opposite ends of the system. This introduces two human workloads.

> *Conflict Resolution: If you implement multimaster or updatable snap-shot replication, you need to define up front how contradictory updates should be handled—for example, newest update takes precedence, head office takes precedence, numeric changes are summed, and so forth. This takes a lot of planning.*

First, at the design/business level you need to decide how to handle conflicts of this kind when they occur so that you can configure automatic conflict resolution as much as possible.

Second, at the day-to-day administrative level, you will probably hit occasions when the replication of changes fails for reasons you had not predicted. In fact, most of the complaints I have had from clients have been about the time it takes to unravel a problem, and the pressure that results from the backlog of updates that can build up while you are working on sorting out why a replication task has failed. This backlog introduces an important line of thought. We have not yet paid any attention to what happens when one of the machines fails. There are two issues.

The first problem to strike when a machine fails is that some of the updates may not have reached the second system. From a business perspective, it may be very hard, or at the very least, time-consuming to determine to which updates this applies. But even if you do identify them, what are you going to do? You might apply them again at the second system, but then again you might not because of the ramifications of the second issue.

The second issue is, What do you do about the replication setup if the first machine breaks down? If you leave replication live on the second database it is going to build up an enormous queue of postponed updates that it will want eventually to push to the first database. If this is allowed to happen it will generate a massive load on the entire infrastructure if you don't manage to restart the first machine very quickly. Moreover, if your users have reentered on the second machine the updates that got "lost" as the first machine went down, you are going to run into conflict resolution problems and broken replication jobs as soon as you restart. It seems, then, that the first thing you have to do when one of your machines goes down is to break the database out of the replication loop completely.

You then have to worry about what you do when the first machine is brought back on-line. Unfortunately, if replication has been switched off at the second machine, you have to throw away the database on the first machine and go through the steps of building your multimaster replication all over again. Fortunately, Oracle introduced mechanisms for off-line bulk replication of a database a long time ago. Nevertheless, this is not a quick job.

It seems, then, that fail-over by multimaster replication is feasible within limits. In particular, it is probably only appropriate for a low-speed manual OLTP system. The overhead of replication is quite high, and the fail-over will probably lose a little data. The fail-over itself can be quite quick and simple, but if it happens, the amount of effort needed to get back to a fully cloned system ready for another failure is pretty high.

Backups

All the mechanisms described so far are relatively expensive, delicate, and in some cases labor intensive. This is the price you have to pay to minimize downtime and loss of data.

Apart from everything else, there is also the stress factor. The success or failure of the fail-over can't really be tested on a regular day-to-day basis (although on a *large* parallel server system I did once instigate a procedure of restarting one instance per day to minimize the effects of a memory problem). Thus, it is hard to be confident that everything is still working correctly when that one-in-a-thousand event occurs and you need the fail-over.

If you can afford a small delay and a relatively small loss of data, there are other cheaper, more reassuring, less technologically threatening options available that you can test and prove every single day of the week. Specifically, these are variations on the theme of backup and recovery.

Cold Backups

Backups fall into two categories—the hot, or on-line, backup in which the database is still up and running, and the cold, or off-line, backup in which the database has been shut down.

If your office hours are 9 to 5, or thereabouts, and you can afford the time to rekey yesterday's data occasionally, then the cleanest, simplest, least technical solution is simply to stop the database (using a clean shutdown) and take a copy of every single data file, on-line redo log file, and control file to another machine (using FTP, say) or to tape.

If your database gets corrupted, you copy back yesterday's image and start rekeying. If your machine fails, you start the second machine. Apart from the labor costs of rekeying, the cost of recovery is limited to the cost of the second machine, which as a temporary fallback could perhaps be a lower power machine than the primary machine.

As with the fail-over solutions, if you switch machines you have to have some mechanism in place to make sure that clients can reach the second machine, either by using something like the Oracle name server or by making the second machine take on the identity of the first machine.

One of the advantages of this system is that you can test it every single day. As soon as you have copied the latest set of files, you can start the backup database to see if it works, then shut it down again.

There are minor variations on a theme, of course. If you have switched some of the tablespaces to read-only status (see Chapter 8), then they only need to be backed up once after the change, reducing the time of backup.

Backing up from disk to disk can be much faster than backing up from disk to tape, so you might consider having plenty of spare disks in the primary machine, backing up from disk to disk as a first stage to secure the backup, then copy the backup to tape. With care you can even arrange to use the disk copy *in place* as the first option for recovery should the database corrupt itself. Again, you can be confident that this will work because you can always start (and stop) this database to check it before you restart the primary copy. There are some steps you have to take to let Oracle know that files have been moved or renamed before you start up, and the best time to do it is immediately after you have the backup copy and before the pressure goes on to do a quick recovery.

Hot Backups

At the beginning of this book, I described how Oracle maintains data files and redo log files. I mentioned at the time that the redo log files contain an ordered list of all the changes made to the database. I also mentioned that redo logs fall into two classes—on-line and archived. The time has come to explain what this is all about.

Because the redo log files contain a list of changes made to the database, you appear to need an endless stream of log files to keep a complete record of the life of the database because you could then, in theory, re-create the current state of the database by "replaying" all the redo logs if you could find a suitable starting point for the playback. In theory, you don't ever need to stop the database to take a backup copy; you only need the log files and a lot of patience, and you can rebuild it from scratch right up to the moment it died.

There are two problems with this theory (plus a handful of minor technical details that I am going to ignore). First, it isn't feasible for a database to be created with an endless supply of log files, and, second, it wouldn't be feasible to play back all the log files ever created into a new, empty database when disaster struck. So Oracle needs a mechanism for (1) keeping the number of log files manageable and (2) finding a sensible starting point for replaying the log files when necessary.

The solution is actually quite straightforward. We start by telling Oracle to run in ARCHIVELOG mode, and to generate copies of each on-line redo log as it is filled. The first part is achieved with the command ***alter database archivelog*** when the database is mounted but not open. We then set various parameters in the init.ora parameter file, telling Oracle to copy the logs automatically, and where to copy them (and how many copies should succeed, and so on). Once we have done this, we can start taking hot backups of the database (in other words, copying the database while it is still running). Once we have a hot backup of the database, we can discard all the archived redo logs that were created before the hot backup began. The new hot backup is the starting point for replaying log files.

I won't go into all the technical details of exactly how to put all the pieces together; there's too much to explain in just one chapter. What I want to discuss is the side effects this strategy has on your system, and the strengths and weaknesses of the strategy.

So, we have Oracle copying a redo log as soon as it is full. This means that the redo log file is being read and being copied to a new file. Archived redo log files are the only files that are being continuously created as new files by Oracle; every other file is initialized in a one-off exercise and then continuously reused. This means that archived redo logs have to be created on file systems and tend to result in more intensive I/O than the rest of the Oracle files. Ideally, they need to be isolated from the rest of the system. Whatever, a database running in ARCHIVELOG mode does significantly more I/O than a database that is not running in ARCHIVELOG mode. If you switch to hot backups as a fallback mechanism you have to bear this in mind.

When you start taking a backup copy of the database, you have to tell Oracle that you are doing so. Oracle will only acknowledge the attempt if it is running in ARCHIVELOG mode. Typically you do this copying one tablespace at a time, and you tell Oracle what is going on with the commands

```
alter tablespace XXX begin backup;
    -- whatever you do to copy a file here
alter tablespace XXX end backup;
```

When a tablespace is in backup mode, Oracle takes special steps to protect a possible future recovery from a "split block" problem. If the database writer is writing an 8K Oracle block just as your copy program is copying the corresponding 4KB operating system blocks, it is possible that the copy will contain half of the older version of the block and half of the newer version—a *split* or *fuzzy block*. The mechanism Oracle uses to circumvent this problem is to write entire data blocks into the redo log file. Although it is not necessary for Oracle to do this every time it writes a data block, the side effect of putting a busy tablespace into BACKUP mode is to increase the volume of redo log generated, thus putting extra pressure on the I/O system.

There are various strategies that can be used to reduce the amount of time that a tablespace is in BACKUP mode. The first obvious one is to keep the tablespaces as small as reasonably possible, and back up one at a time. The second strategy is to make the copy mechanism as quick as possible—perhaps backing up to disk while the tablespace is in BACKUP mode, then copying the backup to tape later.

Some sites use mirrors (even triple mirrors) and switch the tablespace into BACKUP mode just long enough to split off one mirror, then back up the mirror before bringing it back on-line to be resilvered. The drawback to this strategy is that (1) it really does need a triple mirror to leave you protected while doing the backup and (2) the I/O overhead of resilvering could be pretty heavy. Oracle Corporation actually introduces the commands *alter system suspend/alter system resume* to make it as easy as possible to use this approach because some platforms cannot split mirrors while any I/O is going to the mirror. Of course you could find that user activity is impaired while the system is in suspense, so use these commands with care.

The best way to reduce the backup time and I/O is to have read-only tablespaces. If you can partition your data so that data that becomes static and unchangeable is isolated into identifiable tablespaces, you can tell Oracle that those tablespaces are read-only. Once you have taken a final backup, you never need to back them up again, unless you make them read/write again at some point.

> *If you can make part of your database read-only, then the window you need for backup decreases.*

At this point, then, you have a complete hot backup of the database, you take a special backup of the control file (using the Oracle command *alter database backup controlfile to {filename} ;*) and you copy all the archived redo logs from the moment you started the hot backup. You can transfer all these files to another machine, start up a database instance there in a special state, and start replaying the archived redo log files into the hot backup. If you replayed all the archives you had copied, you would eventually get a message from Oracle saying, "Media recovery complete," and you would be able to open up a database that was complete up to a few moments past the point where your backup ended. You can, however, do better than that. Because the production database is still busily generating archived redo log files, you can keep copying these new archived redo log files from the production machine to your backup machine and replay them. This keeps your fallback database nearly up to date with your production machine all the time. When your production system destroys itself, you have the option of starting the fallback database, knowing that you have lost, perhaps, just the work done in the last few minutes. If you are lucky, you may even be able to retrieve the on-line redo logs from the failed production machine and run them into the fallback database, and bring it 100% up to date.

It isn't always necessary to do a fallback. Not every drama turns into a crisis. Sometimes your production system will just have a small accident. In this case, you may be able to recover by copying back a small set of the data files and then replaying some of the archived redo logs into just those data files. Once you have mastered the hot backup and use of archived redo logs, the possibilities are really quite extensive.

In summary, then, by adding the overhead of copying each redo log file as it completes, you have made it possible to take safe copies of the Oracle data-base while it is still running. While you are copying the database files, though, you are adding an extra I/O load on the redo (and archived redo) log files because Oracle may be copying entire Oracle blocks into the log some of the time. (Actually, that's another thought to bear in mind when trying to decide the Oracle block size.) By copying the backup and continually applying archived redo logs to it as they are created, you can keep a fallback database running just a little behind the production box. If the production box fails, you can start that database with only a small loss of data. This brings me, fairly naturally, to the *standby database*.

The Standby Database

The hot backup strategy with an "almost immediate, almost up to date" recovery is something that has been used by DBAs the world over since Oracle version 6, with increasing levels of support coming from Oracle Corporation in version 7.3 onward. However, there were a few version-dependent actions (such as taking a tablespace off-line) that could make the recovery cycle break down and require a new hot backup.

Apart from possible breakdowns, there was the problem of getting the archived redo logs to the fallback machine in as timely a fashion as possible. Typically a UNIX system would use the "cron" or "AT" utilities to check every few minutes for new archived log files, and then would send them via FTP from one machine to another (sometimes breaking because the archived log was incomplete; sometimes succeeding in sending an incomplete file and breaking the recovery).

In Oracle 8.1, the hot standby database is more or less fully automatic. There are a few special setup steps for the standby database itself, along the lines of "create standby controlfile" instead of "create backup controlfile," but in essence there is little difference between the work needed to set up a standby database and the work needed to create an old-style, rolling hot backup.

The biggest difference is the mechanism for getting the archived logs to the fallback machine. Oracle 8.1 uses SQL∗Net to move the files, and has a whole new set of parameters for the init.ora file to handle the archive log destinations. In fact, for backward compatibility, the pre-8.1 method for specifying archive log destinations still works. In Oracle 8.1, instead of specifying log_archive_dest and log_archive_duplex_dest, you can specify up to five different log_archive_dest_n, and enable or disable them using five different log_archive_dest_state_n parameters. You can demand that a minimum number of the archive copies must succeed before the redo log is deemed to be secure and can be overwritten by setting log_archive_min_succeed_dest. If Oracle cannot make the required number of copies, then the next time the log writer process cycles back to that redo log, the database stops. To help you get the archiving done as quickly as possible, Oracle can run multiple archive copying processes, and you can set a limit to this with log_archive_max_processes. There is also a standby_archive_dest that you need to set on the standby destination to tell that instance of Oracle the directory and root name of the incoming archived log files that need to be applied.

The parameter log_archive_dest_n can be used to specify a SQL∗Net service name as the destination for an archive, rather than a filename. The following example shows an example of using multiple destinations:

```
log_archive_dest_1 = (LOCATION=/u01/archive,MANDATORY)
log_archive_dest_2 = (SERVICE=standby.jlcomp.com,MANDATORY)
log_archive_dest_3 = (LOCATION=/u02/archive,OPTIONAL)
log_archive_dest_4 = (SERVICE=stand2.jlcomp.com,OPTIONAL,retry=300)
log_archive_max_processes = 6
log_archive_min_succeed_dest = 3
```

This tells Oracle to try to make four copies of each redo log, using a maximum of six archive processes (to allow for catch-up in times of stress), and requiring at least three copies to succeed. The first copy goes to a local drive and must succeed. The second copy goes to a SQL∗Net service and must succeed. The third copy also goes to a local directory and may fail. The final copy goes to a SQL∗Net service, may fail, and if a problem occurs in the transfer, Oracle waits at least 300 seconds before trying to use that destination again (and also waits for the next redo log switch). Because I have demanded that three copies succeed, and have specified two of the copies as mandatory, at least one of the optional copies must also succeed.

To summarize, then, once you have created the hot backup as a standby, and set the archive destinations, Oracle takes over. The primary database sends archive logs down SQL*Net, and the standby instance can be told to wait for them and apply them automatically as they appear. If your primary machine crashes, you simply issue a command to the standby database to activate itself and open as a normal read/write database with just a little lost data. After you have done this it can no longer go back to being a standby database. Part of your fallback strategy has to accommodate creating a new standby database once you are back to running at full production levels.

Provided you have used the newer LOG_ARCHIVE_DEST_N parameters when setting up your database, it is actually possible to install a managed standby system without stopping the database. All the relevant parameters can be changed while the database is running.

You get an extra, added bonus from the standby database. You can stop it from doing its automatic recovery and can open it as a read-only database. This means you could, for example, use it at the end of each day to run massive reports on the day's data while the production system is busy coping with a batch load for the next day. You could use it to do the daily batch extract for the data warehouse load.

In fact, although the database can only be used for reading and not writing, if you have created a proper temporary tablespace (see Chapter 9) in the production database, you can add tempfiles to it in the standby database to give yourself more space for sorting. But you can't use the temporary tablespace for populating global temporary tables with intermediate results, because they still require data to be written to the rollback. You also have to be careful about not using the primary database for auditing (audit_trail = DB in the init.ora), otherwise you won't be able to open the standby as read-only.

A standby database can be opened as read-only, and its temporary tablespaces can be extended for massive batch reporting.

There are some caveats to consider when using the standby database. You have to be very careful about NOLOGGING options. Any object that is created in the production system with the NOLOGGING option (or is targeted by SQL*Load in DIRECT-LOAD mode, or is subject to parallel DML or an insert /*+ append */) exists on the standby database, but its content is marked as invalid because it is never written into the log file. This won't matter for the odd few indexes (as long as your fallback procedure allows you time to rebuild them), but if you rebuild data using, say, "create table nologging as select," you will need to set up procedures to ensure that the resulting data gets into the standby database by other means. Basically this means you have to identify the tablespaces containing such objects, take a new hot backup of just those tablespaces, stop the standby just long enough to overwrite those tablespaces with the new hot backup, and restart the standby.

You also have to fall back to manual intervention each time you add tablespaces, or data files, to the production database because the files will not exist on the standby when the relevant redo appears. Because you can, in principle, rename files on the standby database, Oracle does not automatically create files just because they come into existence on the production system. You have to use the command *alter database create datafile 'XYZ' as 'XYZ'* then restart the recovery.

You may also have to switch temporarily to manual recovery if a network service fails, or the standby database stops. In fact, if all the archive destinations are mandatory, there are circumstances when the production database will crash repeatedly with an ORA-00600 error, until you restart it with with network destinations set to optional, then use manual recovery to bring the standby up to date.

You may also be concerned that the standby database is only up to date as far as the most recent archived log. If the production system is broken, but the disks are still reachable, you may be able to copy the on-line redo logs and apply them manually, but you should plan for the worst, So what can you do? The least worst option is probably to pick a scale of data loss that you can live with (in minutes), and rig the system to switch and archive a redo log at that interval. To make this happen, you can issue the command *alter system archive log current* on a regular basis, possibly through a stored procedure that can be called by DBMS_JOB. If you want to be really clever about it you could code the procedure to execute the call every 15 minutes during the day, say, but not fire while the overnight batch was running. This would allow you to have very large log files to keep checkpointing to a minimum through the batch, while still forcing small archived logs to appear at the standby database during the day.

Checkpointing is an issue of course. If you want to send a log file every 15 minutes, then Oracle must release a log file for archiving and jump to the next one every 15 minutes. However, when Oracle switches log files, it issues a checkpoint, which tells the database writer to start dumping all recently changed data blocks to disk. On a busy database this could have a severe impact on the I/O subsystem and could slow things down significantly. In extreme circumstances you could find that every physical read takes twice as long as you would expect. So another downside to keeping your standby database as close as possible to the live system is that the live system has to experience an I/O hit. This can be softened slightly by telling Oracle to work at keeping the number of dirty blocks in the buffer down. Two parameters with slightly different purposes and degrees of precision exist for this purpose:

1. DB_BLOCK_MAX_DIRTY_TARGET
2. FAST_START_IO_TARGET

DB_BLOCK_MAX_DIRTY_TARGET limits the number of dirty blocks that Oracle should allow in its buffer. Setting this to, say, 10% of the buffer size (the minimum is 1,000) ensures that Oracle never has a vast number of dirty blocks to write at the moment the checkpoint arrives. Instead of a spiking I/O demand, this flattens the I/O to a continuous, level stream. FAST_START_IO_TARGET has a similar effect by making Oracle write out dirty blocks continuously so that the size of redo that has to be applied at recovery time is limited. Although this is a better parameter for controlling the database recovery time, and has the effect of flattening I/O throughput, it doesn't have the intuitively clear effect of DB_BLOCK_MAX_DIRTY_TARGET, and isn't exactly relevant to what we are trying to achieve.

The final issue to worry about is the network. If you are going to run a busy database and push the archived redo log files down the network through SQL*Net, you will be pushing a lot of small packets down the wire, and writing them to a new file when they arrive at the far end. If you are not careful, this could become the limiting factor on how fast you can archive a redo log file, hence a limit on how much work the database can do. It is a good idea to make sure you have a private network connection between the primary and standby systems, and then set up a dedicated listener on the standby machine purely for the service that handles the incoming archived logs.

In conclusion, then, the standby database is fantastic, but you have to be aware of its limitations—in particular, the necessity to assume that you lose a few minutes of data. In addition, you do need to stress test it to find out how much of an impact the side effects will have on the rest of your system.

Recovery Manager

In my discussion so far I have not mentioned the recovery manager (a.k.a rman). This is a relatively new product from Oracle Corporation that may be described as an intelligent backup tool. Its unique selling point is that it understands how Oracle databases work, so it can do incremental backups of Oracle data files, copying only those blocks that have changed since the last backup. This means that backups created by rman are physically smaller than any other backups you can make.

Other features of rman are as follows:

- It is controlled by very short, concise scripts, so it is easy to configure a backup strategy.

- It communicates with the instance it is backing up, and can bypass the problem of split blocks, so you do not need to put tablespaces into BACKUP mode, which saves on redo log I/O. (You still have to run the database in ARCHIVELOG mode though.)

- It keeps a catalog of all the actions it has taken, the history of your database and where the backups are, so it is fairly easy to recover the database to almost anywhere you want to put it, and to almost any point in time that you want to get it.

You might ask, then, why I haven't made more fuss about it. It's the usual problem of the right tool being in the right place at the right time. I have been told by more than one user that it is actually slower to take an rman incremental backup than it is to take a full operating system backup. This is perfectly believable because rman has to examine each Oracle block in turn to check the block SCN and compare it with the SCN from the last rman backup. Of course, the benefit of smaller backups may be more important than the penalty of slower backups. A feature of backups, though, is that you have to restore them and you usually want to restore them rather quickly. If you have to superimpose a handful of incremental backups on top of each other to restore the host backup, might this not be rather slower than dumping a single, larger backup into place? Finally, of course, there is the issue that Oracle Corporation suggests that rman should be given its own instance on a separate machine to hold the catalog—and that's quite a cost overhead for a product that otherwise looks fairly suitable for the small to medium office site without the expert DBA.

Problems and Quirks

There are plenty of ways of making an Oracle database as safe as you want it. There are many ways of keeping fail-over time as short as you would like it. They all cost money. But what you can't have is extremely robust *and* extremely fast fail-over—yet.

Strategy Notes

Before you worry about the technical features of how to implement the purely mechanical aspects of Oracle backup and recovery, decide on the types of events from which you want to recover, the quality of the fallback position that you need, the time you can allow to get there, the infrastructure changes that have to take place to support the fallback position, and how you expect to get back from the fallback position to production-level running.

Mechanically, it is quite straightforward to back up and recover an Oracle database. However, a working database, even an up-to-the-second working database, does not ensure that your entire environment is going to work.

APPENDIX A

Feature Reference

This appendix is a simple summary of the more interesting features of Oracle 8.1. What makes a feature interesting is, of course, personal opinion. Broadly speaking I have included those features that look as if they are aimed at making the database engine easier to handle or more effective. Most of the features described here are included in the main body of the book, but there are a few that have not been mentioned elsewhere that rate a brief mention here.

Standby Database

The standby database mechanism allows for a fully automated transfer of your archived redo logs to a remote site with a backup copy of your database running in a semipermanent RECOVERY mode. The standby database can be taken out of RECOVERY mode and opened in a READ-ONLY state for reporting purposes, and then returned to RECOVERY mode. Proper temporary tablespaces can be enlarged on the standby database to improve facilities for heavy-duty reporting.

Availability—Automated standby and opening for read are not available to Oracle Standard Edition.

Plus points—Full, fairly low-cost option for relatively rapid fallback. Useful to be able to use the database for heavy-duty reporting, taking the load off the primary machine.

Minus points—The fallback database is only up to date as far as the last fully transmitted archived redo log, and the time to roll forward and restart may be several minutes, which may make it inappropriate as a fallback mechanism for busy OLTP sites. Operations that can use the NOLOGGING options (DIRECT LOAD, CREATE TABLE, CREATE INDEX, REBUILD, and so on) must not be used because the resulting changes would not appear on the standby. The archived log file has to be transmitted through SQL⋅Net before being written to the remote disk. This may have an impact on your network performance, and may be the limiting factor in how fast your database can operate.

Row-level Security

The most common "traditional" method of implementing row-level security was to add a column and create a view on each table that included extra predicates relating to the current user ID. Row-level security is an internalized enhancement of the same concept, with the following improvements: You may not need to have the extra column on the table, you don't need to create the view, the predicates can be a degree simpler and therefore operate more efficiently, and you can use a very complicated test *once* as the user connects to decide on a very simple predicate for the table.

The mechanism works by associating PL/SQL functions with a table, which return the text of a predicate. The function executes whenever a query involving the table is parsed, and the returned predicate is built into the query before parsing. To enhance the flexibility of the function and potential performance of the predicate, both can call the sys_context() function to use values set in the current user's context. The context can be set as the user logs on to the database using a "database logon" trigger.

Availability—Row-level security is not available to Oracle Standard Edition.

Plus points—There is no longer any need to maintain numerous different views, synonyms, and access rights for different users. Security mechanisms that needed to add subquery references to security tables may not need to do so. The performance benefit (particularly when several secured tables are involved) would be significant.

Minus points—The text of the security predicate is never visible. This makes it much harder to determine why a particular query is running slowly because attempts to "debug" the query may be using a different security predicate from the actual runtime predicate. The exp utility applies any security predicate, so you need to ensure that any ID that is supposed to be taking a full export of the data has a security predicate that allows all rows to be seen. There are a couple of bugs associated with parallel queries and materialized views that need to be fixed.

Tablespace Management

Historically, many DBAs have spent a huge amount of time building and rebuilding objects for efficiency, and worrying about the fragmentation of tablespaces that often occurs as a result of this. Also, with the increasing object size and the increasing number of concurrent users, there have been more problems of contention on the space management tables in the data dictionary.

Oracle has addressed both issues with locally managed tablespaces. To create an object in such a tablespace you still insert a segment definition entry into the data dictionary, but the subsequent allocation and deallocation of extents is handled locally through a bitmap at the head of each file. Each bit in the bitmap corresponds to a fixed-size section of the tablespace.

You can choose "system managed" or "uniform size" as the extent sizing policy. The latter is better, assuming you know roughly the scale of the objects to go into the tablespace.

Plus points—Locally managed tablespaces eliminate almost all the wasted administrative effort once spent on space management within tablespaces. At runtime, space management through the bitmaps is also quicker than space management through the data dictionary, and tends to keep objects near the front of the files, thus allowing files to be resized downward if they have been oversized.

Minus points—I haven't thought of any yet.

Transportable Tablespaces

Transportable tablespaces are a boon to anyone distributing large amounts of data from a data warehouse to a data mart. It is now possible to describe the contents of a tablespace in one database, then copy the files that make up that tablespace to a second database, and load the description into the target database's data dictionary to make the contents of the tablespace available. The target database must be on the same platform and use the same block size as the original database.

Availability—Transportable tablespaces are not available to Oracle Standard Edition.

Plus points—You can shift huge amounts of data very quickly, with an overhead that is little more than copying files around.

Minus points—There are some restrictions on the types of data that you can move using this method. Most important, perhaps, is that you cannot move individual partitions from a partitioned table with this method. You need to turn them temporarily into stand-alone tables. When you come to replace the previous version of a transported tablespace with the latest version, you first need to drop the tablespace and its contents, which can be very slow.

Temporary Tablespaces

Everyone referring to the temporary tablespace means the one that Oracle writes to on behalf of a user when a SORT operation is too large for the memory allowed to the session and has to be paged to disk. Usually, a single tablespace is defined in the database as the temporary tablespace for all the users.

Typically this tablespace can be extremely large and can become an area of contention when many users (or many slaves under the PARALLEL QUERY option) are sorting concurrently. The time to build such a tablespace can be considerable, and the waste of space and time in backing it up could be significant.

These issues have been addressed with the introduction of a temporary tablespace made up of tempfiles. These tablespaces are locally managed tablespaces, and thus have reduced contention on the data dictionary when multiple processes are using them. When the files are created, only the bitmap section at the start of the file is initialized, so very large files can be created very quickly. The files are not required in the normal course of the backup and recovery cycle.

Plus points—Quick to build, less contention for multiple users, no need to back up and recover, and can be extended on a read-only standby database.

Minus points—Tempfiles seem to be created as "sparse" files, and some UNIX utilities on some platforms do not report their space allocation correctly, or copy them properly.

Temporary Tables

A common complaint historically has been the awkwardness of storing intermediate or scratch pad results in the database. Either you create tables temporarily, populate them, then drop them, which hits the data dictionary quite hard, or you have a set of precreated tables that users insert to and delete from, which is expensive on rollback and redo at runtime. In either case you have to remember to clean up any mess you have made after you finish (and before you start, in case there is some mess left over from last time!).

In version 8.1, Oracle has introduced the global temporary table. This consists of a permanent definition of the columns, constraints, and indexes on the table, but each user that "uses" the table gets their own space allocated dynamically to them. That space is freed when the user has finished using the table. Because of the known temporary nature of the table, less redo log is generated when inserting data into it.

Plus points—Less impact on the data dictionary, so less contention if there are lots of users creating and releasing scratch pad data. You don't have to clean up the mess afterwards. The scratch pad disappears on commit or end of session (depending on your choice). Your scratch pad is completely isolated from everyone else's scratch pad, even though you appear to be using the same table, so there are more options for NOLOGGING activity, which reduces rollback and redo.

Minus points—The space allocated to the global temporary tables comes from the same tablespace as the user's default sorting tablespace. It would be nice to have some control over this, because it may introduce a conflict of requirements between the need for small scratch pad areas and large sort areas. You cannot collect statistics for global temporary tables, so it is possible to get very inefficient access paths when joining to permanent tables. You cannot add indexes to global temporary tables once there is some data in the table, so this can push up the cost of use because of the extra rollback and redo required for index updates.

PL/SQL

In earlier versions of PL/SQL, it was quite difficult to execute dynamic SQL. Oracle 8.1 introduces a new native dynamic SQL facility that makes it much easier to build strings that can be passed to PL/SQL and executed on the fly.

The main performance issue of PL/SQL was that you could only process one row at a time, unless you used DBMS_SQL to construct array fetches. Using object tables and varrays, Oracle 8.1 allows you to fetch an entire row set with one call, and do array-based DML with one call. The array fetch introduces a bit of a threat because it is all or nothing. There is no mechanism for fetching a large result in reasonable-size batches.

In earlier versions of Oracle, a PL/SQL procedure would run only with the static privileges (not role-based privileges) of the schema that created the procedure. This often led to problems that had to be circumvented by devious or annoying means, often using the DBMS_SQL package to execute dynamic SQL. In Oracle 8.1, you now have the option of defining a procedure to run with the privileges of the current user. This feature should be used with care, because it could lead to undesirable side effects.

Plus points—Includes some features for improving performance of PL/SQL-based operations quite significantly, and some features that make it much easier to handle previously impossible tasks.

Minus points—New features may encourage proliferation of inappropriate PL/SQL solutions to problems. Several new features could lead to dangerous abuse of the database.

Database Triggers

It is now possible to create triggers that fire on DDL and database events, rather than just table-based events. These include logon/logoff, database startup/shutdown, and server errors; and create, alter, and drop object. The DDL triggers can be applied to a schema or to the database as a whole.

Uses for database triggers cover preshutdown actions to warn applications to detach cleanly, and poststart-up actions to tell them it is safe to reconnect. Another good use for the poststart-up trigger is to pin important packages in the shared pool as soon as the database starts.

Availability—"Instead of" triggers are not available to Oracle Standard Edition.

Plus points—Useful functionality enhancing the audit facilities of the database.

Minus points—We could still do with an "on commit" trigger for some of those more troublesome integrity checks. You can get really stuck if you create DDL triggers at the database level and something goes wrong.

Partitioning

Partitioning is possibly the most useful feature for all types of Oracle applications. It allows a very large object to be recognized logically as a single object and allows it to be handled physically as a collection of independent small objects.

With range partitioning it becomes very easy to administer "rolling" data by dropping off very old partitions, adding new empty ones, rebuilding and packing partitions that are no longer subject to change, and putting static partitions into read-only tablespaces to reduce the backup load.

Indexing on partitioned data should almost invariably be local partitioning because global partitions restrict the independence of the partitions and eliminate almost all the original benefits of splitting up your large objects.

Hash partitioning can be used to reduce contention (typically "buffer busy waits") in high-throughput systems by spreading newly arrived data across several separate partitions. Savings in space (hence query performance) also appear because this strategy avoids degrading indexes and reduces the need to allocate multiple transaction slots in each data block.

The downside to partitioning is that queries that don't make some very explicit reference to the partitioning columns do not do partition elimination, and have to access every partition in the object. For low-volume queries, the overhead of visiting many partitions could be much larger than the basic cost of the query itself.

Partitioning can allow parallel DML to be applied very effectively to large systems. In general, a separate slave process can handle each partition, giving almost perfect scalability not only on select statements but also on inserts, updates, and deletes.

Partitions can also allow excellent separation of work on parallel server systems, but the side effects of non-PCM locks may restrict the amount of partition maintenance you may wish to carry out.

Availability—Partitioning is not available to Oracle Standard Edition and is a separate cost option on the Enterprise Edition.

Plus points—Terrific opportunities for vastly improved performance and administration

Minus points—Can easily be implemented counterproductively. Picking the wrong partition size, index, and access strategy can have a disastrous effect on small queries. There may be some unpleasant side effects on parallel server systems. Unique local indexes (necessarily) have to include the partitioning columns. Object tables can be partitioned, but the unique index on the hidden OBJECT_ID column is a global index, which makes the exercise a bit pointless. There are some undocumented restrictions about what you can do with partitioned indexes. For example, on-line rebuilds and compression are not available for partitioned indexes on composite partitioned tables.

Autonomous Transactions

Historically, a single session could not execute independent transactions. All changes made to the database during the course of a single transaction had to be committed or rolled back together. By introducing autonomous transactions, it is possible to suspend a transaction and execute a totally independent transaction while the first transaction is in suspension. The two transactions have no effect on each other (although they could deadlock each other), and each may be committed or rolled back without affecting the outcome of the other.

Plus points—Autonomous transactions allow much more auditing of actions, even actions of the main application that fail and roll back.

Minus points—Autonomous transactions can be abused to do terrible things to the database. The interaction between a transaction and its autonomous children can lead to strange and unanticipated side effects that could easily be missed in application tests.

Three-tier Applications

Oracle has introduced a couple of very useful features if you use OCI to write the middle tier of your own three-tier architecture.

The first is the ability of an application to log on as a "trusted" user that has been given the privilege to "become" another user. This solves the standard problem of losing the identity of the real end user as you go into the database, and being unable to audit their actions and set resource limits for them.

The second is the SHARED MEMORY option. This is of interest if you run several copies of a single application server on a single machine, and are in the habit of avoiding round-trips to the database by holding copies of reference data in the application server. You can now keep just one copy of such data on the machine, and allow all the application servers to address it by registering their interest in a single, shared-memory segment.

Availability—N-tier authentication is not available to Oracle Standard Edition.

Plus points—Many of the usual three-tier problems are solved in two easy steps.

Minus points—Only available through OCI, which needs a high level of programmer skill

Indexes

There are numerous little changes to indexing. The facility to compress the leading columns of an index is likely to have the most significant effect on performance, and the ability to coalesce an index to reclaim free space without rebuilding it is likely to offer administrative benefits as well as performance benefits. Reverse key indexes may not be the boon that they may first appear to be. Function-based indexes require a little caution because they can easily be disabled by accident, but are likely to be a great convenience, particularly for case-insensitive searches.

Availability—Function-based indexes, bitmap indexes, star transformations, index coalesce, and on-line index rebuild are not available to Oracle Standard Edition.

Plus points—New ways for getting better performance

Minus points—Nothing serious, but you do need to take steps to prove that any particular new feature *will* work for you before committing to it

LOBs

Oracle 8 offers vastly improved capabilities for handling large objects, and in version 8.1 the tables that hold them can be partitioned. I do not think that it is a good idea to hold large objects in the database, but if you have to you can now do it in a clean, consistent fashion. Oracle 8.1 also introduces the "proper temporary LOB," which may improve the efficiency or ease of some of the data manipulation of LOBs that once had to be done using a permanent LOB as a scratch pad.

Plus points—There are very few restrictions left on LOBs. They can almost be viewed as just another ordinary database object.

Minus points—LOBs should be avoided in general data processing if possible. They are far from ordinary as a database object. When the LOB is the reason for the database, you should still try to maintain a strong degree of separation between the LOB component and the structured data component.

Analytic Functions (Version 8.1.6)

Like partitioning, analytic functions offer a great opportunity to do things much more effectively at the level of the database engine. Complicated SQL, two-stage processing, or 3GL loops can be replaced by relatively simple SQL code that does secondary processing on a result set as it is generated at the database engine. This looks like a particularly useful feature for exposing complex data warehouse results to Web pages efficiently and with low programmer costs.

Plus points—The work gets done in one step, at the best point, with minimal overhead.

Minus points—Although the concept is, in most cases, quite straightforward, the resulting SQL code can be a little hard to follow. In the short term it may be difficult to reverse engineer the features into existing systems, particularly third-party data-mining tools.

LogMiner

Oracle has finally introduced a tool for interpreting the redo log. By generating a special dictionary file and invoking the LogMiner, you can generate a list of paired SQL statements that show the forward change and the reverse change represented by a log entry. Your statement

```
update tx set tot=100 where pk_id = 123445;
```

appears as the pair of statements

```
redo:   update tx set tot=100 where rowid = 6.315.5;
undo:   update tx set tot=90 where rowid = 6.315.5;
```

Plus points—When data goes missing or appears to have been patched, you can find out who did what to it, and when. This may be particularly useful for changes to the data dictionary.

Minus points—The concept sounds nice, but practical application may be rather unrealistic. Remember that a single statement to update 1,000 rows is stored in the log as 1,000 pairs of separate changes. The output from LogMiner can be much larger than expected when you are trying to track down a small data anomaly.

Replication

The first big change with replication is that the replication code has been taken into the database kernel instead of being generated as PL/SQL triggers and procedures. This should have a fairly significant impact on performance. The second big change is that the scope for "fast refresh" snapshots has increased dramatically. Certain classes of aggregate views and join views can be refreshed using suitably defined snapshot logs; however, to enable complex snapshots to be updated incrementally, the content of the log has to be much bigger. Instead of recording just the rowid of changed rows, the log may also have to record old and new column values. The third big change is that you have to call things materialized views instead of snapshots.

Availability—Advanced replication is not available to Oracle Standard Edition.

Plus points—Replication is faster because kernel code rather than PL/SQL procedures and triggers handle it. The FAST REFRESH option is now available for far more types of materialized views, including aggregates and join views.

Minus points—The materialized view logs for join views and aggregate views with the FAST REFRESH option have to contain much more information from the base tables than the logs for simple, single table views. It is very easy to consume excessive amounts of space and CPU time on materialized views of this type.

Query Rewrite

The optimizer has always been able to rewrite queries to a limited degree to find the best access path (for example, turning EXISTENCE subqueries into joins). With Oracle 8.1, this minor detail has turned into a major feature, which allows Oracle to decide to use a predefined summary table as the cheapest mechanism for answering an expensive (usually aggregate) query.

Query rewrite goes hand in hand with the newer features of replication, using "in-database" materialized views as possible targets for rewriting a query. In conjunction with DIMENSION definitions, which describe relationships between supporting tables, and maximum application of valid (or at least RELY) constraints, query rewrite can manipulate a range of queries much larger than the basic definition of the materialized view would suggest.

Availability—Materialized views and query rewrite are not available to Oracle Standard Edition.

Plus points—In a data warehouse environment with summary tables that can be nominated as prebuilt materialized views, query rewrite can make a dramatic difference to ease of use and ease of implementation and administration.

Minus points—Materialized views that refresh themselves either on commit or on demand can lead to unexpected swings in performance because a user querying for her own uncommitted changes will find that query rewrite suddenly stops working until the changes have been committed or rolled back. Query rewrite is also a little fragile, and may simply not occur if used in conjunction with some uses of other newer Oracle 8 features.

IOTs

IOTs can now have secondary indexes. Prior to Oracle 8.1, this was not possible. Secondary indexes on IOTs are likely to be larger than the equivalent index on an ordinary table, and therefore are not as efficient. However, secondary indexes do not become invalid when the IOT is rebuilt.

IOTs can now be partitioned (although the primary key must contain the partitioning columns), and IOTs can (if you really want) hold LOBs, so the range of functionality of IOTs is coming close to that of ordinary tables.

Although IOTs can be rebuilt on-line, the overflow segment of an IOT cannot be rebuilt on-line (for much the same reason that it is rather hard to rebuild an ordinary table on-line in any efficient fashion). Similarly, secondary indexes cannot be rebuilt on-line, although as pointed out earlier, you do not need to rebuild them when you rebuild the table. Nevertheless, there are times when you will want to rebuild a secondary index.

Plus points—IOTs can now have secondary indexes for alternative access paths, and can be partitioned as long as the partitioning columns are part of the primary key.

Minus points—You cannot rebuild secondary indexes on-line. There are a number of problems that can appear when you start mixing IOTs with other newer features of Oracle, especially partitioning. Test any exotic use of IOTs very carefully.

Integrity Constraints

It is possible to defer integrity constraint checking, so a user may make data pass through an uncommitted, inconsistent state to get to a consistent, committed state. For example, a primary key value and all its foreign key dependents may be modified by deferring the foreign key constraint for the duration of the transaction. The primary key/foreign key relationship will only be checked at commit time.

A particular detail of DEFERRABLE constraints is that primary keys and unique keys may be represented (and, to be deferrable, must be represented) by nonunique indexes. This is a great convenience for large data loads, which can load data, update the nonunique index, and identify very cheaply the rows that breach the unique constraint.

A constraint may be enabled but not validated. This allows Oracle to check that new data meets the requirements of the constraint, but old data is not checked. The constraint can then be validated (in other words, old data is checked) without locking the table.

Plus points—DEFERRABLE constraints have a natural place in some systems. Previous implementations required unpleasant workarounds to be coded to handle them. Data loading with DEFERRABLE or DISABLED constraints can be used to reduce downtime quite significantly.

Minus points—I haven't thought of any yet.

Parallel Execution

The biggest change to parallel execution is indicated by the change of name. Prior to version 8.1 we had the PARALLEL QUERY option. With version 8.1 we moved to parallel execution, meaning that inserts, updates, and deletes can all execute in parallel, and we are no longer restricted to just parallel *select* statements. As with the DIRECT LOAD option of SQL∗Load and parallel CTAS and "insert /∗+ append ∗/," parallel execution can result in suboptimal use of the available space.

As far as the query side goes, parallel execution has had a number of "invisible" changes introduced that basically make it significantly more efficient. Where previously parallel queries would generate slave code that resulted in vast numbers of rows being passed between the two layers of slaves, the optimizer is now able to find far more methods for pushing joins and aggregates down to low-level slaves so that far fewer rows, and much less redundant data, get passed around. One of the more obvious examples of this is the partition-wise join that can be used with partitioned tables. Instead of trying to join "all rows to all rows" across two tables, Oracle recognizes the option for joining only "partition X rows to partition X rows."

Oracle Corporation has introduced an automatic tuning feature into parallel execution that tries to avoid the worst excesses of parallel execution hogging the system. Basically it checks the number of query slaves in use as a new parallel statement starts, and reduces the maximum number of slaves that the statement may use if there are too many already in use.

Availability—Many of the features of parallel execution are not available to Oracle Standard Edition.

Plus points—The optimizer is much more clever with its optimization paths and slave queries. The ability to execute DML in parallel without special coding can be an excellent way to reduce the complexity of large data loads.

Minus points—Parallel execution is still a specialist tool that requires careful planning. It is not just a quick solution to a performance problem. It is possible for "unlucky" statements to become massive resource hogs.

JServer

In the beginning of the book I described Java as "just another programming language," and have avoided mentioning it since. However, as Neil Harvey (one of my early reviewers) pointed out when reviewing this appendix, there are advantages to having a Java Virtual Machine in the database because there are so many Java programmers making "toolkits" available on the Web.

Do you need a column encryption function? Download a cryptographic toolkit from the Web, wrap it with a few classes, and load it into the database. You could do the same with PL/SQL, or C using the extproc library calling facility, but you are much less likely to find what you want in those languages.

Plus points—Easy availability of useful add-ons

Minus points—Like PL/SQL, don't demand terrific performance

Tuning to 90%

I believe that tuning is a highly overrated pastime and that very few systems should need extremes of tuning or cunning design to perform perfectly adequately.

The odd high-throughput system run by a large telecommunications company, or a system with extremely large numbers of users like a real-time credit card system, needs to be designed and tuned rather carefully, but virtually every other system is likely to be seen as a great success if it runs at anything better than 50% of its notional optimum. Oracle systems, like many modern sports events, are about the percentage game. The winner is the team that makes fewer mistakes. If you can avoid the worst mistakes when designing an Oracle system, whatever's left will be more than adequate.

Nearly every system with performance problems that I have been called to review has had a few extremely expensive, extremely obvious design or coding errors. Only one or two systems have needed any of the more sophisticated investigation techniques. In saying this, though, I am begging the question about what constitutes tuning. In fact, I spend a lot of time with sketch pad and pencil working out how a system could perform before I even create a single table—and that's where proper tuning starts. However, the word *tuning* seems most frequently to apply to an exercise that takes place after a system has been built, and sometimes only after it has gone live and the users find that it doesn't work very well. Tuning of the former kind is very important; tuning of the latter kind is too little, too late, and too popular a pastime.

There are enough books already written about cute and esoteric ways of squeezing the odd few percent more out of an Oracle system, so I don't plan to say very much about the latter kind of tuning. However, I would like to present just a few simple tips that are likely to be sufficient for almost all systems.

Apart from the log buffer, data buffer, dictionary cache, and library cache, Oracle maintains a number of other memory-based structures to keep track of what is going on and to make best use of resources. Many of these internal structures have been made visible to privileged users through the X$ and V$ virtual tables. Over the years, Oracle Corporation has exposed more and more of this information. In version 6.0.27 there was no documentation on the V$ views; nowadays the SQL code used to generate the V$ views from the X$ internals is available in the view V$FIXED_VIEW_DEFINITIONS. In fact, articles in magazines and published on the World Wide Web regularly describe how to make direct access to the X$ structures to get at undocumented bits of information.

Of the many available V$ views, there are really only a very few that are sufficient to solve almost all tuning needs. By far the most important one is V$SQL—the list of recently executed SQL, identifying logical and physical costs, number of executions, rows processed, number of concurrent SORT operations, OPTIMIZER mode, and the user parsing the statement.

Next on the list for ease and useful value is V$FILESTAT and its new partner V$TEMPSTAT, which give system relative count of I/O calls and blocks read and written for each Oracle file.

Finally, V$SYSTEM_EVENT (and the more precise V$SESSION_EVENT) can be useful for telling you about where the time goes. Unfortunately, many of the events reported by this view are irrelevant to the typical user, and some are misleading, so the view can cause more concern than it should.

Although I generally advise against getting too stuck in the low-level technical details of Oracle, and warn people from wasting their time on X$ objects, there are two that I think should have been exposed in V$ views, so I have made a couple of comments about them.

V$SQL—Recent SQL with Costs

Some statements are inherently very expensive; some are expensive because of extreme levels of use. Sometimes statements run that should not be running at all. V$SQL is the place to look for obvious problems.

There are many tools on the market that tend to offer top-ten analysis. Basically, they execute a query against V$SQL (or sometimes V$SQLAREA, which is a rather more costly option because it is a summed view of the same internal object X$ object). The query I typically use is of the form

```
select
    first_load_time,
    parsing_user,
```

```
        optmizer_mode,
        sorts,
        executions,
        parse_calls,
        disk_reads,
        buffer_gets,
        row_processed,
        sql_text
    from
        v$sql
    where
        command_type != 47 - exclude PL/SQL blocks
    and (   disk_reads > 1000
        or buffer_gets > 300000
        or executions > 1000
        )
    order by
        disk_reads * 300 + buffer_gets desc;
```

Looking back through various magazines, I discovered that I first published something like this in the *UK Oracle User Group* magazine way back in the winter of 1994. And although I have changed the details over the years, it is still the most effective way to find out what's going wrong with an Oracle database.

My very first version of this query had a very serious defect, though, which is still in common use today. It used V$SQLAREA rather than V$SQL, but it also joined V$SQLAREA to V$SESSION to find out who, if anyone, was executing the query, then joined to V$SQLTEXT to find the full text of the SQL statement because V$SQL(AREA) holds only the first 1,000 characters of the SQL code. On a system with a very large shared pool, the cost of executing such a query could be very large, and could have a severe impact on performance for tens of seconds, especially if the system is in need of tuning.

I vary the values of the constants from site to site, and set them to restrict the output to just a couple of dozen SQL statements. Similarly, the ORDER BY clause is subject to variation. The version here tends to sort the statements by total elapsed execution time (using a broad approximation that many systems running on file systems may do approximately 100 file system reads per second or 30,000 buffer gets per second. Other obvious options are to sort purely on buffer_gets or purely on disk_reads.

An important variation on the WHERE clause is to hunt for possible table-scanning code. This can be identified by checking for SQL code where a very high proportion of buffer_gets results in disk_reads. The following test seems to work quite well, again with a site-based adjustment to keep the number of rows down:

```
where
    disk_reads > 50
and buffer_gets < 2* disk_reads
```

There is, however, a generic problem with the top-ten approach. What do you do to find statements like

```
select * from client_transactions
where client_id = 14325 and date_tx = '23-Jan-2000'
```

with costs like

```
    Executions: 1
    Disk_reads  39
    Buffer_gets 191
```

The numbers are so low that a statement like this won't show up in a top-ten report until line 4,000 or so. The first defect with this statement is that the numbers suggest that there are probably two single-column indexes on this table and no index on (client_id, date_tx) or (date_tx, client), which look as if they may be useful. More significantly, it is not until you reach line 4,001 of the report that you find the code

```
select * from client_transactions
where client_id = 72109 and date_tx = '23-Jan-2000'
```

Then at line 4,002, you find the code

```
select * from client_transactions
where client_id = 393874 and date_tx = '23-Jan-2000'
```

and so on—all with similar costs. And, given the repetition of the same date, all suggesting that the two-column index starting with date_tx may be more appropriate than the one starting with client_id.

Sometimes the top-ten report isn't the important part of the problem. It may be that something relatively cheap but exceedingly common and constantly varying is much more of a threat. Unless you do something rather more drastic with V$SQL, you won't discover that the obvious top-ten are not the actual performance problem. In this case, one option is to dump all the rows of the V$SQL view, perhaps with just the disk_reads and buffer_gets. Another is to try something like

```
select substr(sql_text,1,40), count(*), sum(executions)
from v$sql
group by substr(sql_text,1,40)
having count(*) > 10
order by count(*) desc
```

Again, you may need to adjust the constants to produce a reasonable-size output to work with initially. If substr() is too long, you may hide repetitious strings; if it is too short, you may turn up misleading quantities.

The purpose of the exercise is to identify strings that may be variations of the same string. Typically, the first part will be "select {list of column name} from table." If the number of appearances is large, and each appearance has been executed only once or twice, then the full text could well be a constructed string literal SQL statement coming in from the application.

Once you have a few suspect strings you can start checking V$SQL for rows in which the SQL_TEXT column starts with that value, using code like

```
select   first_load_time etc.
from     v$sql
where    sql_text like 'select col1, col2, col3, from table_x%';
```

Remember, though, that with a large shared pool, the number of cached SQL statements may be very large, so the initial *substr()/sort group by* statement may be a fairly ferocious hit on the system. Don't do it frequently.

Code of this type should generally be modified to use bind variables. Remember that the optimizer cannot use histograms to work out optimum paths for statements with bind variables. So, not only do you have to change the SQL code itself, you may have to ensure that some hints are embedded to force a particular path. You may even have to go to the highly undesirable extreme of coding your front end to allow for special case values, along the lines of

```
if (v_status = 'NEW') then
    select /*+ index(t) */ . . .
else
    select /*+ full*(t) */ . . .
end if
```

If you do, don't forget to include this in your dependency documentation. Because hints are only comments, Oracle has no internal mechanism for highlighting this sort of issue.

V$FILESTAT/V$TEMPSTAT

Because much of this book talks about I/O, you won't be surprised to discover that I do make use of the main dynamic performance views for file I/O. Until Oracle 8.1, there was just one of these views—V$FILESTAT—but with the appearance of temporary tablespaces (see Chapter 9), Oracle added V$TEMPSTAT. Both views have the same structure that (in an order that doesn't match the *describe* command) is presented in Table B-1.

Table B-1.

Column Name	Purpose
FILE#	File ID; matches file_id in dictionary view DBA_DATA_FILES or DBA_TEMP_FILES
PHYRDS	Number of read requests sent to the operating system
PHYBLKRD	Total number of blocks read
READTIM	Total time (in hundredths of a second) waiting for reads to complete
MAXIORTM	Longest completion time for a single read request. Hit a problem once, and this statistic ceases to be useful until the next time you bounce the database; but it is a good warning of a (perhaps historical) problem.
PHYWRTS	Number of file write requests sent to the operating system
PHYBLKWRT	Total number of blocks written
WRITETIM	Total time (in hundredths of a second) spent waiting for writes to complete
MAXIOWTM	Longest completion time for a single write request; see MAXIORTM
AVGIOTIM	Average time for an I/O request (read or write) to complete. Not really useful except as a bearer of bad news. Large numbers of I/O hide any significance.
LSTIOTIM	Time for the last I/O request (read or write) to complete. Not really useful because it tends to change too rapidly to be observed usefully.
MINIOTIM	Shortest I/O time recorded. Not really useful, almost invariably zero.

Note: The time-based columns in this view are always zero unless the parameter TIMED_STATISTICS is set to TRUE in the init.ora file. If necessary, this parameter can be changed on the fly, either at the session or system levels with an ***alter system/session*** command.

You may wonder what the difference is between PHYRDS and PHYBLKRD, and between PHYWRTS and PHYBLKWRT. Remember that Oracle allows multiblock reads, as well as direct reads and writes for sorting purposes. A single read or write request can actually result in many blocks being read or written, and a comparison of these pairs of statistics can give you an indication of how much multiblock I/O your application is performing.

As with all statistics (not just in Oracle), you need to be careful of large-scale averaging hiding the important detail. You also need to be careful that the side effects from some of the new features (and bugs) don't confuse the issue. For these reasons, it is usually best to take snapshots of V$FILESTATS/V$TEMPSTATS and calculate differences. I tend to do this with simple PL/SQL packages.

The problems with V$FILESTAT and V$TEMPSTAT are legion. If you are running with file systems then the read times can be incredibly small because of buffering effects at the operating system. If you are running with a big write cache, then most write times will be reported (truthfully) as very small, hiding intermittent problems. If you are running with multiple I/O slaves, multiple database writers, or asynchronous I/O, you may find both read and write times being reported (probably untruthfully) as very large. On top of this, there are bugs (which can be in Oracle or the operating system) that occasionally throw completely misleading times for no apparent reason.

I remember being called to one site that was worried about a performance problem they could not track down, particularly because their average write time was being reported as 800 milliseconds per write. They had been using a monitoring tool that had not been coded to display the MAXIOWTM. It is a fairly common complaint of third-party tools that they take time to catch up with the new reporting features of the database. The first dump I took from V$FILESTAT showed that their longest write on every file had taken (apparently) 81 days (approximately 7,000,000 seconds), which clearly had to be wrong, and not just because the database had only been up for five weeks. Doing some arithmetic to factor out this one glitch (which we assumed was an error from the big black box of disk drives) the average write time dropped back to a much more acceptable 20 milliseconds.

Assume, then, that you take a 30-second snapshot of V$FILESTAT. What sort of thing should you look out for? The following output is a space-saving sample. I usually dump the filenames with statistics as a quick way of reminding myself of the special cases. As a variant, I may also sum the statistics by tablespace, but this loses some precision of information if a tablespace is split between an overloaded device and a nearly idle device:

```
-----------------------------------
File Stats - 09-May 18:16:06
Interval: 600 seconds
-----------------------------------
```

Fno	Reads	Blocks	Avg Csecs	Writes	Blocks	Avg Csecs
1	4,092	12,140	1.341	191	191	1.175
2	26	26	2.120	51,491	51,491	9.243
3	73	553	0.972	1432	1432	4.856
7	634	634	1.316	132	608	4.015
9	71,845	165,243	1.273	179	179	2.000

Note: The average times are *not* the average times supplied by Oracle in the view. They are (change in readtim / change in phyrds) and (change in writetim / change in phywrts).

File 1—System: a rather high number of reads. This may well be SMON doing its check of a lot of tablespaces for free space. (This dump is just the first few files of a longer listing.) It may be a symptom of a small dictionary cache and frequent rereads of the data dictionary. It may be the job queue process hitting the DBMS_JOB views too frequently.

File 2—This is the RBS file. There is a lot of writing going on here. Should I split the RBS tablespace into a couple of files to reduce file system inode contention? Is there an issue with rollback segments being much too large? There isn't much reading, though, so the volume of I/O resulting from read-consistency requirements is not a big threat, but check this over a much longer period.

File 3—This is the TEMP file (which has *not* been created using the new tempfile/temporary tablespace option, and should be re-created). The reads are multiblock reads, which is expected. The writes are single-block writes. From the latter, I can infer that sorting is done through the buffer and *not* as direct writes. This should be investigated.

File 7—The average write size is 4.6 blocks. There must be a lot of multiblock writes going on. Why? Multiblock writes are for sorting and table/index creation only.

File 9—The average read size is 2.3 blocks. There is a fair amount of table scanning going on, especially given the very large number of reads. This is worth a look. Perhaps there are a couple of objects that should be split into their own tablespace.

Now take a look at times. The read time is generally sound, one to two hundredths of a second; faster times for files with higher I/O and slower times for files with low I/O are fairly typical of a database running on file systems when the system is not overstressed. The write times are suspect though. They are far too high. However, in this case you may note that the average write time correlates roughly with the number of writes—higher I/O gives higher average write times. This is symptomatic of a reporting error when multiple database writers or asynchronous I/O is used.

Finally, take the high-level view. Might there be anything going on that would explain the overall pattern of the statistics? The giveaway is my comment about file 7, and its multiblock writes. In the interval I chose, someone was creating an index on a table in file 9, and writing it to file 7. This has skewed the statistics quite dramatically. This also explains the activity on the TEMP file, and some of the activity on the SYSTEM file, but not all the activity on the rollback segment tablespace.

V$SYSTEM_EVENT/V$SESSION_EVENT

There are two gaps in the V$FILESTAT/V$TEMPSTAT views. First, they don't give any indication about what is happening to log files and control files. Second, there are some things, particularly contention, that can waste time and have nothing to do with I/O. The V$xx_EVENT views are usually enough to complete the picture because they allow you to ask Oracle where it has spent its time kicking its heels (Table B-2).

The problem with these views is that there are many rows that can be ignored and actually tend to conceal the significance of the waits that are of interest. The view also has the usual statistical problem in that an average can easily conceal a problem. It only needs a bad 25 seconds every 15 minutes to make an application virtually unusable. But if that 25-second problem comes on one wait of 10,000, you won't notice it by looking at the average. Luckily, MAX_WAIT is there to give you a clue.

The full list of possible events is quite long—currently, 197 possibilities. The meaning and significance of many of them is in the Oracle 8.1 reference manual, but a few that occur commonly and that are potentially significant are presented in Table B-3.

Table B-2.   Columns in the V$SYSTEM_EVENT/V$SESSION_EVENT View

Column Name	Purpose
SID	Session ID in V$SESSION_EVENT only; matches SID in V$SESSION
EVENT	Name of the event waited for
TOTAL_WAITS	Number of times the event has caused a wait
TOTAL_TIMEOUTS	Number of times a fixed-length wait has timed out
TIME_WAITED	Total time spent (in hundredths of a second) on that type of wait
AVERAGE_WAIT	Average wait time for that event
MAX_WAIT	Single longest wait for that event; in V$SESSION_EVENT only, but see notes in the text

Table B-3.   Significant Wait Events

Name (approx.)	Significance
BFILE (several variations)	General cost of handling operating system files as LOBs
Buffer busy waits	Usually means that processes are colliding on blocks they both want to change; blocks at the new end of a table with lots of inserts; indexes on sequence-based columns; find out what the sessions are doing (see also X$KCBFWAIT)
Control file read and write	Time to access control files; doesn't happen often, but watch out for times more than two hundredths of a second
Db file read and write	Time to access data files through normal buffer I/O; anything more than one or two hundredths of a second is suspect
Direct read and write	Time to access data files bypassing buffers; anything more than one or two hundredths of a second is suspect
Enqueue waits	Enqueues (lock requests) are keeping each other waiting (see also X$KSQST); can mean that different processes frequently

Name (approx.)	Significance
	want to affect the same data items; identify the sessions and the tasks they are performing
Global cache lock related	A measure of time lost to cross-instance calls with Oracle Parallel Server
Library cache related	May indicate that you are using too many different SQL statements or your shared pool is too large
Log file writes	Possibly the most important wait for write-intensive systems; if time is lost here the whole system will be slow; should be (comfortably) less than two hundredths of a second on average
Write complete waits	If this is high then the database writer is having trouble writing dirty blocks; it is being called too frequently or too infrequently

Note that most of the events I picked are to do with file I/O. There are a few others, though, that may be indicative of more subtle forms of contention.

The trouble with these events is deciding how much impact they have. Take just one, the "write complete waits," as an example. In absolute terms this simply means that some processes have been waiting for the database writer to write a block that they want to pin and change. This wait times out after one second, and the waiting process then spins back and starts again. Some waits, such as "log file parallel writes," never time out; they just wait until completion.

So what can you infer from the values in V$SYSTEM_EVENT for "write complete waits" of

- Total waits, 1,001,826
- Total timeouts, 5,180
- Time waited, 521,384 hundredths of a second
- Average wait, 0.511 hundredths of a second

The first thought is that there are a lot of waits. But this should be compared with the total work done by the database, which was several million transactions and a few gigabytes of redo log. Nevertheless, the total lost time on waits is a pretty hefty 90 minutes. At this point you may start looking for reasons why the database is perhaps writing too much, or writing in very large batches that pin blocks for a long time. But pause for thought. Before you go any further, you really need to know whether this is a large number of small waits or a small number of long waits. Unfortunately, V$SYSTEM_EVENT doesn't give you a MAX TIME column, even though V$SESSION_EVENT does, and even though it is available to Oracle 8.1.5 in the underlying X$ object.

There are just a few times when it is worth knowing a little about the X$ objects in the database, and this is one of them. Log in as SYS and create an enhanced version of V$SYSTEM_EVENT with the following SQL code:

```
create or replace view v$max_system_event
as
select
            d.kslednam          event,
            s.ksleswts          waits,
            s.kslestmo          timeouts,
            s.kslestim          tot_csecs,
            s.kslesmxt          max_csecs
from
            x$kslei s,
            x$ksled d
where     s.ksleswts != 0
and       s.indx = d.indx
and       d.inst_id = userenv('instance')
and       s.inst_id = userenv('instance')
;
```

The problem I described was a real database with a real issue. By taking daily snapshots, and even hourly snapshots, it was impossible to find out *why* the database was reporting so many "write complete waits." But once I created this view, I could see that the maximum wait time was 25 seconds. There were only two conclusions to be drawn: either there was an error in the report or there was a hardware problem.

In the most extreme case, we could assume that all the lost time (roughly 5,000 seconds) was the result of 25-second waits, in which case there would have been a total of only 200 serious waits and a lot of very short waits, rather than a very large number of fairly significant waits. With this hope in mind (and some corroborative evidence from other wait events), I started a loop that dumped the statistics for this wait every 60 seconds, and discovered that basically the file system stopped working every 15 minutes for 22 seconds.

The most important point to make, really, is that V$SYSTEM_EVENT can give you some hints, but don't leap to conclusions. Once you get a hint, you need to refine the statistics. Either collect one suspect event for all sessions a few times from V$SESSION_EVENT, or collect an event from V$SYSTEM_EVENT at regular intervals to get a better picture of how often and how expensive the event is over time. You do have to be careful when taking regular snapshots, though. You would be surprised how often I find that the most expensive SQL code being run on a system is the code being run by the performance monitoring tools.

The X$ Files

There is generally little point in going into detail about the X$ objects. They are too prone to change, and at best you are only guessing what they hold by cross-referencing to the V$ views that use them. True, it is very entertaining to try to figure out what obscure function some strangely named column holds, but because the things are subject to dramatic change, it's usually a waste of effort to worry about them too much. (If you doubt this, compare the 68 columns in X$KCBWDS for version 8.1.5 against the 50 columns in the same table in version 8.0.4.)

There are, however, two X$ objects that have never been exposed through a V$ view when it is obvious that they should be. These are X$KCBFWAIT, which sums "buffer busy waits" by file, and X$KSQST, which keeps a running total of enqueues and enqueue waits.

X$KCBFWAIT

Buffer busy waits occur when two processes both want to pin the same buffered data block either to clone it for consistent-read purposes or to update it. The view V$WAITSTAT exists to summarize the waits that have occurred by class of block.

An extract from V$WAITSTAT is presented here, and the basic tuning manuals tell you that waits for "undo header" or "undo block" indicate the need for more rollback segments. The appearance of waits for class "data block" indicate that some of your tables or indexes need to be rebuilt with a larger value of freelists:

CLASS	COUNT	TIME
data block	143	3
sort block	0	0

        . . .

```
undo header              13        1
undo block                1        0
```

There are two important omissions in this advice. The first is that you can often ignore these numbers. This list shows 143 "data block waits" for a total of 0.03 second lost time. If my database had been up for 10 minutes and it showed 143 waits 10 minutes later, I would be worried. On the other hand, if the database had been up for 6 weeks I wouldn't be in the slightest bit worried about losing three hundredths of a second to buffer contention.

The second important omission applies only to "data block waits." It's all very well and good to be told that some objects need to be rebuilt, but which ones? In theory you will know because you understand your application so well, and you know which tables are subject to very heavy concurrent inserts, which is the most common cause of "buffer busy waits."

It can be quite difficult and resource intensive pinning down which blocks are causing the problem, but with X$KCBFWAIT you can get a little closer quite cheaply. The following query (which can be run only by SYS) lists file-names, and the number of "buffer busy waits" that have occurred on each file:

```
select  count, time, name
from    v$datafile df, x$kcbfwait fw
where   fw.indx+1 = df.file#


  COUNT     TIME NAME
--------- ---------- ----------------------------------------
        1        0 C:\ORACLE\ORADATA\O8I\SYSTEM01.DBF
      142        3 C:\ORACLE\ORADATA\O8I\USERS01.DBF
       14        1 C:\ORACLE\ORADATA\O8I\RBS01.DBF
        0        0 C:\ORACLE\ORADATA\O8I\AUTO_01.DBF
```

This may not move you much farther forward, but it could be enough to focus your attention on the correct group of objects. A little tip if your waits are on the SYSTEM tablespace: There is a good chance that "buffer busy waits" on the SYSTEM tablespace are the result of having a number of sequences with low (or perhaps zero) cache sizes in an environment of high concurrent activity. Busy sequences should be created with a reasonably large cache size. If this is not possible, then you might consider dropping the sequences and rebuilding the SEQ$ dictionary table with PCTFREE set to 99 and PCTUSED set to 1 before re-creating the sequences. This results in Oracle storing one sequence definition per data block, which may be enough to reduce the "buffer busy waits." (Don't do this without approval from Oracle Corporation.)

X$KSQST

An interesting measure of how busy your system has been is the amount of locking that has taken place. TX locks tell you about transaction locks on rollback segments; TM locks tell you about locks applied to tables. There are other kinds of locks, but these two constitute the vast majority of all locking that takes place. Global statistics about locks appear in V$SYSSTAT as enqueues:

```
select   name, value
from     v$sysstat
where    name like 'enqueue%';


NAME                                 VALUE
_____  _____

enqueue timeouts                         0
enqueue waits                           55
enqueue deadlocks                        0
enqueue requests                    162345
enqueue conversions                    226
enqueue releases                    162274
```

Apart from general interest in what your application is doing, if you are getting more than a very small percentage of waits and timeouts (the 55 waits out of 162,000 is a little puzzling but not really significant as a percentage), you can get a quick, cheap indicator of the cause by looking at X$KSQST, which lists all enqueue types and the number of gets and waits.

The total of gets and waits should be very close to the enqueue requests and waits in V$SYSSTAT, but probably won't be exactly the same because of the small time delay between the two queries you run.

```
select
         ksqsttyp     eq_type,
         ksqstget     gets,
         ksqstwat     waits
from     x$ksqst
where    ksqstget != 0;


EQ  GETS      WAITS
__  _____  _____
CF        23         0
    . . .
MR         9         0
    . . .
```

```
TM    121170         0
TX     40854        31
UL       178        24
US        18         0
```

This shows that a small number of transactions (31 out of 40,854) have had to queue up, and that the application is doing something with user-defined locks, which doesn't happen often, but often causes queuing when it does. This gives us a hint that perhaps we should start by reviewing code rather than tuning the database.

As a side note, the statistics also show that the "average" transaction seems to involve three tables (120,000 TM locks, 40,000 TX locks). Ask yourself if this seems likely with your application. If it isn't, don't be surprised. It's just another example of large-scale statistics hiding any detailed meaning.

Helping the Developers

I haven't made much mention of V$SYSSTAT, but it does contain some useful information about the state of the system. Again, though, the very large numbers that arrive summed over a long period of time can hide any proper issues. As usual, the best line of attack is to find differences between snapshots. You can also focus on individual sessions with the session-level statistics in V$SESSTAT.

I find that the best point at which to raise awareness of these statistics is at the programmer level. There is a little-used view called V$MYSTAT that lists the statistics for my session. Unfortunately, it doesn't include the name of the statistic, only its number, so I tend to connect as SYS and run the following little script:

```
create or replace view v$my_stats
as
select sn.name, ss.value
from
    v$statname sn,
    v$mystat ss
where
    ss.statistic# = sn.statistic#
;


create public synonym v$my_stats for v$my_stats;
grant select on v$my_stats to public;
```

Similar views, although slightly less efficient, can be created for the other V$ views that are session based. For example, the V$SESSION_EVENTS view can be personalized by SYS with the following statements:

```
create or replace view v$my_events
as
select * from v$session_event
where sid in (
        select sid
        from v$session
        where audsid = sys_context('userenv','sessionid')
);

create public synonym v$my_events for v$my_events;
grant select on v$my_events to public;
```

I then encourage developers to run a quick before-and-after query against these views when testing a new piece of SQL code or new module. Better still, it is possible to code a little PL/SQL package with a before-and-after query to these views that only reports the changes in values. Those of you familiar with the AUTOTRACE feature will appreciate that this is just an extension of the method used by AUTOTRACE to report statistics. Version 8.1.6 has also implemented the idea with a new dynamic performance pack to supplant bstat/estat. When given the right tools, and a little early help, developers tend to become aware very quickly of how to avoid the worst coding excesses that destroy an Oracle system.

Conclusion

It is very easy, and quite entertaining, to get stuck into the internal mechanisms of Oracle and spend time trying to understand all sorts of subtle technical features of the way the software works. In most cases, though, this is not a cost-effective use of your time. There are usually only two things that really hammer a system to death—doing too much work and letting too much of that work get to the disks.

V$SQL tells you the SQL code that is causing the problem, which can be one of three variations: a small number of very expensive statements, a large number of variegated clones of cheap statements that should be using bind variables, and regular table-scanning queries. V$FILESTAT (and V$TEMPSTAT) tells you the files that are getting the worst I/O as a result, perhaps allowing you to balance the load or pin down the most important targets to hit first.

V$SYSTEM_EVENT, and in better detail V$SESSION_EVENT, tells you about the possible side effects that your code is generating. There are, of course, features of Oracle that result in some completely baffling lost time (a parallel server with high rates of partition exchange gives some wonderful side effects), but if you address the SQL code first through just these three views, you are unlikely to need any more subtle tools.

When all is said and done, the best strategy for tuning is to do it before the database is designed, and then keep doing it at every step of development by ensuring that the developers are aware of the importance of efficient SQL code and that they have the tools to help them spot problems before posting them to production.

Testing to Destruction

There are many interesting features of Oracle that can be used to great effect to process staggering amounts of data extremely efficiently, with great resilience, and a high level of security. Unfortunately, the manuals are rarely up to scratch in describing how the features should be used, what side effects and pitfalls exist, and which bits don't work. More significantly, they never mention how some features can collide with each other with serious consequences.

The main purpose of this book has been to tell you about some of this uncharted territory, but my experience is limited to the scenarios I have encountered, and the hypothetical situations I have invented and on which I have experimented. If you want to avoid serious failures whenever you venture into the newer features of Oracle, it is always important to test for yourself that things work the way you expect them to.

In this appendix I outline my approach to testing, and tell you about some of the internal mechanisms of Oracle that I frequently use to convince myself that Oracle is doing what I want it to do.

The Basis of Testing

One simple little hint for getting started is to build the standard Oracle database from the install procedures. Hack it up a little bit—adding and dropping a couple tablespaces and redo logs is a good idea—then shut it down and make a copy. When you test a new feature, you ought to test it from a clean start. It's a real waste of time to have to build a whole new database from scratch.

The second little hint is always create a new user for each significant feature you are trying to test. It's also a good idea to take a note of the init.ora parameters you use. Don't create a user with one of the standard "connect, resource, dba" roles. Oracle has been insisting for the last few years that these roles exist for backward compatibility only and will be withdrawn at some point. Work out the exact details of how a real user would connect to the database and the privileges they would have, and how a real data owner would create the data and expose it to a user, and create precise roles with the minimum privileges to get the job done. It is a very easy trap to create a DBA role to test a theory, hack a couple of init.ora parameters (perhaps at the session level) as you go along, and forget that the ID that creates the data is not necessarily the ID that finally uses the data. When you eventually manage to get things working, you find that you can't work out how to reproduce the schema infrastructure on the production system because you took several shortcuts in the test.

> *Always start with a clean schema whenever you test a new feature.*

Decide what it is you are trying to prove. This is likely to be some concept of how you are going to implement an important physical feature of the database you are about to build. Let's say you want to check that partition-wise joins actually work, and work in parallel. You need to decide on a series of experiments that first prove or disprove the theory. Then, if the feature actually works, you need to determine the effectiveness of the mechanism and whether there are any side effects.

Let's say we are building a supermarket database and have two sets of data—baskets and basket contents—and need to join them on basket ID for some of the analysis we do. We expect to get roughly 200,000 baskets per day across all stores, and the typical basket has 12 items in it. Let's partition by date. We will access the baskets by store code and date, and the basket contents by store, product code, and date. The data will be loaded by polling stores at the end of each day, so we can expect the basket data to be clustered by store code, and the contents data to be clustered by store and meaningless basket ID.

At this point you may appreciate that an important aspect of testing is that you *must* know what your data looks like, how it will be distributed, and how it is going to be handled. In the very early stages of testing, you may be content to prove that a feature works in principle. During the later stages you must be satisfied that it works effectively in practice, and the effectiveness will often be dictated by the actual activity of the system rather than the theoretical method.

The best motto for testing is "start cheap." There are some features of Oracle that might be fiddly and irritating to set up (multimaster replication is an example; there are lots of little bits to do all over the place if you aren't using the wizards), but the actual scale of the operation is rarely very large. The other motto for testing is "how easily can I break it?" The purpose of the exercise is to prove that your idea is sound and can work; the best approach is to try to make it fail as quickly and as cheaply as possible.

> *Don't just test it, try to imagine things that might break it.*

A simple SQL script can usually generate a million rows of data in less than 15 minutes on even fairly small machines, so even if you decide that your initial tests are not quite appropriate, it shouldn't take long to repeat them with a different data pattern. Don't waste time and effort getting real data from the legacy system if you can fake it reasonably with SQL.

Because we want to test partition-wise joins in parallel, we can start with a simple script that creates two tables of five partitions each. We can easily write this SQL script to generate the right model of the data (for each of five dates, many baskets per store, 12 items per basket) but needn't, at this point, generate very much data (keep it cheap, remember).

To test then, we start simply: Select only from the basket table. Do we get partition elimination? Does anything stop us from getting partition elimination? How do we actually *know* that we have partition elimination? How do we know that we are executing in parallel? Do we always execute in parallel? Are there some cases when it might be more efficient to serialize the query? If anything goes wrong, and we discover that we have set up the data incorrectly or defined the table in a way that handicaps what we are trying to achieve, we should go back to the original script and rerun it to re-create the tables from scratch. We may need to do this several times until we get it right, which is why the first stage of testing should try to get by on a fairly small number of rows.

> *A quick test for partition elimination: Put each partition in a different tablespace and try running with some of the tablespaces off-line.*

We ought to repeat the tests on the basket content table to ensure that there isn't some difference between the two tables that may be significant. Did you remember to create the indexes as parallel indexes? And what are your procedures going to be for analyzing the new data as it arrives? The more little tests you do, the more questions you may think of that are worth addressing.

You may find at this early stage that Oracle isn't behaving in the way you expect. The CBO is quite expensive to run, so when you have only a small amount of data Oracle may decide to short-circuit its calculations and simply slam through the data with a brute force serial table scan instead of the partition-eliminating, parallel, index access that you were hoping for.

If this does happen, it's worth trying to put in a couple of hints to see if you can persuade the optimizer to take the path you expect. Keep it cheap, remember. Don't make unnecessary work for yourself too early. If this fails, then try choking the optimizer a bit. Fix some of the session parameters such as DB_FILE_MULTIBLOCK_READ_COUNT, SORT_AREA_SIZE, and OPTIMIZER_MODE to see if you can make the brute force path sufficiently inefficient that the optimizer decides to work out something better.

The next step, if you have the time, may be to investigate the DBMS_STATS package. Write a script that lies to the optimizer, telling it that the table has 1,000,000 rows per partition, and 10,000 distincts stores, and that the index on the store is very large but very tightly clustered, and so on. Only if all low-cost options fail should you scale up the dataset to the real-life size (plus 100% to spare to allow for next year's growth) to see if things still don't work the way you expect.

Of course for the simple tests, Oracle will work. You may discover a few details about how it works that may impact the way you set up your front-end systems or data-loading sessions. You can now move to the real purpose of the test: Does partition-wise joining take place, and does it work in parallel? You need to decide what may reasonably go wrong, and how to prove whether things are actually going right. Perhaps it is wise to start with serial queries, then move to parallel queries.

Perhaps partition-wise joining takes place, but partition elimination stops working. How do you prove it? Perhaps, for some reason, your configuration stops partition-wise joins. How do you show that they are actually happening? Does partition-wise joining still take place if you drop the oldest partitions of the BASKET_CONTENTS table, but keep a longer history for the BASKETS table? (No, it doesn't.) Perhaps partition-wise joins do take place, but are three times as slow as nonpartition-wise joins. Why? What side effect is occurring? Will it still be there if you have 500 partitions instead of five? Maybe it all works perfectly. Can you spot anything about how it works that suggests that it won't scale? If so, can you think of a cheap test for scaling?

Don't just check that the right things are happening. Make sure that there aren't a few wrong things happening on the sidelines.

Once you are satisfied that there is some chance of success, you can start scaling up your model. Increase the volume of data in the partitions to realistic size. Create a few extra tablespaces because in the final model you would probably put each month's data in its own tablespace. Does this have any side effects? Increase the number of partitions. Make some of the tablespaces read-only. Does anything go wrong? How about getting in some of the infrastructure tables (store names, product classes) and seeing if they introduce any new problems?

Finally it's time to get a few days' worth of real-life data. Don't worry about coding bulletproof routines to load the data automatically into the database. If the concept is going to fail, the code is a waste of effort. Push the data in by hand, but use the experience to find out and document some of the data traps with which the final code will have to cope, and get some light-weight bits of the procedure outlined. Does the actual data size match the predictions of the model? Does the data distribution pattern match? Does the model still perform as expected?

It's time to get a real-live user in, model the system into the front-end tool, and see what the user does with the data. Experience dictates that the user will want to do all sorts of things that you hadn't predicted and will be completely uninterested in at least half the things that the system can do well. Do things work as expected? Has the user introduced some new factors that require the model to be rebuilt and retested?

At this stage, you have a few SQL scripts and a few days of data loaded into an Oracle database. What you may have wasted is two or three weeks of effort. What you haven't done is spend nine months building a monster that is unworkable when it goes live, and then gets worse.

Of course by picking a data warehouse example, I happen to have chosen an example of a system that is (1) very easy to get right from the database perspective and (2) very easy to massage if things go wrong. Oracle is very good at crunching large amounts of data, so even a lost cause can be turned into a winner fairly quickly.

The same principles apply to the other end of the scale. If you have worked out the strategy for an OLTP system, there will only be a handful of critical features (either highly complex or extremely frequent) that you must be able to perform. Such things can be approximated in testing to increasing levels of detail and accuracy to determine the breaking point. For example, is it really possible to call a remote procedure passing 74 parameters across a wide area network 1,000 times per second? Is it possible for that procedure to insert 7 rows in 5 different tables doing 23 validations tests on the way, and summing an open-ended list from a sixth table as it does so? And if not, what ideas for revising the mechanism do your tests prompt?

A Cautionary Tale

In the very early days of Oracle 8, I was asked to design a system that needed to hold approximately 2GB of data per day for a year, and meet certain data-loading and query performance criteria. Most of the targets were very straight-forward (big doesn't mean difficult these days; it just means hard to administer) and it didn't take long to decide on issues like partition sizing, strategies, and physical layout. There was one critical query, however, that was likely to be a little tough to handle, so I tested my model very carefully (or so I thought) to see if it would work properly for this query.

I worked out a program for generating realistic data, created a small table (approximately 100MB) with the relevant indexes, and checked the execution path and results of the query. It worked as predicted (bitmap AND), so I scaled up the model to a simple table of 2GB (representing one day). The model still worked as predicted. Finally, I created a partitioned table with 10GB of data, representing 5 days or approximately 1.5% of the total data requirement. The model still worked as predicted (except it was now running as a parallel bitmap AND, as required), so we started loading the full dataset.

When we had about 30 days of real data on the system, we stopped data loading to rerun our tests. The critical query no longer ran as expected, unless the number of days queried was five or fewer. In my testing I had picked an unlucky boundary condition on the data volume. Fortunately, I got lucky. It was a bug in the optimizer that went away in the next release, and could be patched temporarily by injecting a hint from the calling program.

With hindsight it was obvious that I should have predicted the problem if I had looked at my results a little more closely, and followed through with a couple more tests. When querying one partition the optimizer showed a cost of 2,000, at two partitions the cost was 4,000, and at three partitions the cost was 6,000. Spot the pattern. Because there were as many as 32 parallel query slaves that could have been thrown at the query by Oracle to keep the cost flat up to 32 partitions, this should have given me a warning that something was not right.

The problem hit because at six partitions, the query plan changed to a hash join. Forcing the hash join onto smaller datasets using hints, I found that the cost for one partition was 11,000, the cost for two partitions was 11,000, and the cost for three partitions was 11,000. Clearly, the cost for anything more than five partitions was going to be 11,000, and therefore was going to make the hash join more desirable than the bit map star from the sixth partition onward.

So, if I had used the 10053 trace dump and run the test against 1, 2, 3, 4, and 5 partitions in turn, I would have noticed that the cost of one access path was increasing with the number of partitions, and that the cost of the other, initially discarded, access path was absolutely flat.

The moral of the story: You can't just test that things are working right; you have to figure out what might go wrong and what it would take for this to happen. Then find out why that isn't happening in your tests.

Generating Data

A critical feature of good, quick testing is the ability to generate suitable data without having the hassle of chasing after real-world data and waiting for extracts and file transfers from legacy systems. The more easily you can generate fairly reasonable approximations to live data, the more implementation ideas you can test.

This section describes a few of the standard methods I use to generate volumes of data with distributions that match the sorts of real-life scenarios I want to test.

The first problem is simply being able to generate a table with a reasonable number of rows in just a few minutes. The easiest thing to do here is to look at the view ALL_OBJECTS. Depending on the installation, this view holds somewhere between 2,000 and 12,000 rows as the basic installation set (the extra 10,000 come from the Java engine). If this is a sufficiently large number, then I might choose to do something like the following:

```
create table test_xxx
tablespace xyz
nologging
as
select
    rownum id,
    rpad('x',10)     pad1,
    rpad('x',140)    pad2
from
    all_objects
;

create index tx_pk on test_xxx(id)
tablespace abc
    pctfree 25
nologging
;
```

The rpad() function pads a column to a given size with spaces. If I need to set up a model with an average row length (in this case, 160) I set up two padding columns, one long and one short. The long one is simply to waste the space; the short one is so that I have something other than the index column from which to select. Of course if I also need to pad the index to a particular size, I might add another column (INDEX_PAD varchar2(10)) to get a suitable size. Coming to the index, I try to specify this with a realistic PCTFREE. If I believe that the index will tend to be very tightly packed, I would set the PCTFREE to zero or one. In the absence of any good information, I would set it (as here) to 25% free, because this is the notional degree of degradation that you can expect from B-tree indexes. In both cases I create the object NOLOGGING, because there is no point in wasting redo log and slowing things down.

If I need a table with more than a couple of thousand rows, I would build it in two stages: First, create a small "numbers-only" table to produce a reference list that I then join to itself. For example, to create a table with 1,000,000 rows, I could do the following:

```
create table small_rows
    nologging
as
select  rownum id
from    all_objects
where   rownum <= 1000

create table big_table
nologging
as
select  /*+ use_nl (s2) */
        rownum  id,
        rpad('x',10)    small_pad,
        rpad('x',80)    big_pad
from
        small_table s1,
        small_table s2
;
```

The nested loops hint is only necessary if you want to join a larger table to itself and stop after a counted number of rows. If you don't use it you may find that Oracle goes to the efforts of generating N-squared rows and then discards all but the ones you have demanded with a ROWNUM clause.

A third option that I also use when the number of rows I want isn't too extreme and CPU time is plentiful, is the REF CURSOR CAST procedure that I introduced while discussing collection objects. This requires you to create a function, but once created you can easily generate a list of numbers as long as you need:

```
create or replace type int_tab_type as table of integer;
/

create or replace function get_ints (
    how_many    in      number
) return int_tab_type
as
    v_int_tab    int_tab_type := int_tab_type ();
begin
    v_int_tab.extend(how_many);
    return v_int_tab;
end;
/

create table number_table as
select  rownum  id
from    table(cast(get_ints(1024) as int_tab_type));
```

The benefit of the function is that you don't have to work out any careful details of how many rows are going to be generated, or what performance accidents may happen if you accidentally kick off a sort/merge join instead of a nested loop. Nor do you have to depend on any specific intermediate tables. On the downside, however, is the fact that the function does chew up CPU time and memory quite heavily. I wouldn't be inclined to use it to generate more than the odd 100,000 rows.

If you have access to the X$ objects underpinning the dynamic performance V$ views, the quickest option for generating lots of rows is to fall back on "select rownum from {object}." The X$KSMMEM object can usually be relied on to produce a couple million rows.

The tables we have generated aren't very similar to real sets of data, of course. So far, all we have produced is simply a long list of numbers, in order, with some padding added to waste a bit of space. We usually need to introduce some level of scattered access and clustered access to emulate real life.

The easiest way to do this is to use the trunc() and mod() functions on the numbers, optionally converting the results to character form. For example,

```
create table test_xxx
as
select
    rownum id,
    trunc(rownum/10)            clustered,
    mod(rownum,100)             scattered,
    trunc(mod(rownum,100)/4)    mixed
from
    all_objects
where rownum <= 1000
;
```

Using trunc() on its own in the CLUSTERED column, we get clusters of values, but the clusters do not repeat. In the example we would get 10 zeros, followed by 10 ones, and so on until we got to 10 ninety-nines.

Using mod() on its own in the SCATTERED column, we get streams of data that eventually recycle. The example gives us the number 0 to 99 in order, then comes back to zero again to repeat the cycle for a total of ten runs.

By mixing trunc() and mod() in the MIXED column, we can arrange to have small clusters of numbers, with lots of clusters scattered evenly throughout the table. The example gives us 4 zeros, then 4 ones, and so on up to 4 twenty-fours, then cycles back to zeros again and starts to repeat. Consequently, in 1,000 rows we would have 25 clusters of zeros, with 4 zeros to a cluster, scattered throughout the table.

Obviously the data distribution is far too regular to be totally realistic when we do this, but the general effect of scattering or clustering data is often a good enough approximation of real life to meet the statistical requirements of the CBO.

If you need to generate truly random data, you can still handle it within the database through a simple SQL script (at a fairly hefty cost in CPU time, though) because Oracle 8.1 introduced the DBMS_RANDOM package. In version 8.1.5, the package generates only random integers between ± 2 to the power 32, but it has been enhanced in version 8.1.6 with calls to return random strings, random values in a supplied range, get a random 38-digit precision number between 0 and 1, and finally get a random number from a normally distributed set. For example (in Oracle 8.1.6),

```
execute dbms_random.seed(31415926);
create table random_strings
as
select  substr(dbms_random.string('a',12),1,12)    id
```

```
from      all_objects
where     rownum <= 1000
;
```

The example shows how to generate a table of 12 character strings that are allowed to contain all alphanumeric characters. The presence of the substr() call is to overcome the usual problem of PL/SQL functions returning strings as 4,000 characters.

Validating the Results

It's all very well to be able to generate suitable datasets of experiments quickly and easily from SQL scripts, but how do you actually *prove* that the execution path that Oracle takes is the execution path on which you are depending?

All too often I have seen developers set up a reasonable, albeit small, test of what they are trying to do, and then assume that everything worked as expected because the result was returned pretty quickly. Of course it's quite understandable that someone could believe that Oracle must have used an efficient access path when a query against a 10,000-row table returns almost immediately. It's easy to forget that when you've just created a table this small it will probably still be completely buffered and that a 500-MHz CPU can thrash through 10,000 comparisons rather snappily.

You need to know what Oracle has actually done. And having found out what it has done, you need to record the details with the script that generated the dataset so that you can try it again with a different set of database parameters, or the next version of the database.

Generating data through scripts is very convenient. It controls the data quality and distribution, and it makes the test easily repeatable for the next Oracle upgrade. Check especially for changes in default values of init.ora with new releases. For example, pq_min_message_ size changed from 2,148 in version 8.1.5 to 8,292 in version 8.1.6.

Execution Paths

The first step to take is to ensure that you are happy with the execution path that Oracle is taking. Learn how EXPLAIN PLAN works and make sure you put every important piece of SQL through it and record the results.

As a fallback to EXPLAIN PLAN, execute your test statements with AUTOTRACE on. (It may help to set LINESIZE to 120, and LONG to 20000 or more in your SQL*Plus session, and format column PLAN_PLUS_EXP to A80 while doing this.) Check that the execution path and costs given by AUTOTRACE match those given by EXPLAIN PLAN. Decide whether the volume of logical I/O (effectively a measure of CPU cost) and physical I/O reported by AUTOTRACE is reasonable for the volume of data you think should have been processed. If you don't want to execute the statement to get the results and the actual runtime statistics, you have the option of using the setting SET AUTOTRACE TRACEONLY EXPLAIN, which simply produces the execution plan without executing the statement:

```
Execution Plan
-----------------------------------------------------------
   0  SELECT STATEMENT Optimizer=CHOOSE (Cost=44 Card=121
                                    Bytes=. . .)
   1    0  SORT (GROUP BY) (Cost=44 Card=121 Bytes=16456)
   2    1    NESTED LOOPS (Cost=32 Card=121 Bytes=16456)
   3    2      HASH JOIN (Cost=5 Card=1 Bytes=113)
   4    3        HASH JOIN (Cost=3 Card=4 Bytes=348)
   5    4          TABLE ACCESS(FULL)OF 'GRPS' (Cst=1 Crd=21 Bytes=997)
   6    4          TABLE ACCESS(FULL)OF 'DPTS' (Cst=1 Crd=21 Bytes=777)
   7    3        TABLE ACCESS(FULL)OF 'PRDS' (Cst=1 Crd=21 Bytes=546)
   8    2      TABLE ACCESS(FULL)OF 'SALES' (Cst=27 Crd=12138
                                    Bytes=. . .)


Statistics
-----------------------------------------------------------
          0  recursive calls
        688  db block gets
       6963  consistent gets
       6960  physical reads
          0  redo size
       1617  bytes sent via SQL*Net to client
        928  bytes received via SQL*Net from client
          4  SQL*Net roundtrips to/from client
          2  sorts (memory)
          0  sorts (disk)
          8            rows processed
```

Switch AUTOTRACE off and set SQL_TRACE to TRUE for the session. Run the query again, check the trace files directly, and determine the result from applying tkprof to the trace files. Check that these are in agreement with AUTOTRACE and EXPLAIN PLAN. All three should agree, but sometimes they don't. Common problems include reanalyzing statistics between tests, changes in data between tests, row-level security being different between tests, session parameters being modified between tests, and bugs in Oracle.

Before and after the execution of the test statement, take a snapshot of V$MYSTAT (see Appendix B), V$ROLLSTAT, V$FILESTAT, V$TEMPSTAT, and V$SESSION_EVENT to see how much work your statement is making the database do.

If you are expecting to invoke parallel execution, dump the contents of V$PQ_TQSTAT and V$PQ_SESSTAT to see how many messages were passed between the parallel execution slaves, how big the messages were, and whether the volume and size seem to match your expectations.

Events

If things don't seem to be working as effectively as they should, you can start digging deeper to find out what Oracle is doing in detail by setting events. The most common form for the event setting command is

```
alter session set events '10046 trace name context forever,level 8';
```

This particular example makes Oracle dump a description of all its wait events into the trace file. Although V$SESSION_EVENT will summarize these for you, a detailed list of what happened when may help you to determine why there are problems:

```
WAIT #6: nam='db file sequential read' ela= 0 p1=1 p2=3801 p3=1
WAIT #6: nam='db file sequential read' ela= 0 p1=1 p2=3983 p3=1
WAIT #6: nam='db file sequential read' ela= 0 p1=1 p2=3982 p3=1
```

The meaning of the p1, p2, and p3 values is usually in the Oracle reference manual, but as a fallback you can check the view V$EVENT_NAME. The most common wait is for I/O requests. The longest waits are usually for "SQL∗Net message from client," which is usually perfectly reasonable and harmless. It's just Oracle complaining that we don't type fast enough. Although, in the special case of a batch process running across a network, SQL∗Net waits at a session level may indicate a network overload problem or a client CPU overload. There are other useful events that may help you figure out what is going on (Table C-1).

Table C-1.   Events to Trigger Execution Dumps

Event	Level	Effect
10046	4	Dumps the values in bind variables
10032	1	Dumps details of sort runs to disk
10053	1,2	Dumps details of how the CBO came to a decision
10128	1,2,4	Describes decisions about partition elimination
10391	N	Traces activity of parallel query execution

A Sample of Output Following Event at 10046, Level 4

```
select text from view$ where rowid=:1
BINDS #2:
bind 0: dty=11 mxl=16(16) mal=00 scl=00 pre=00 oacflg=18 oacfl2=1
size=16 offset=0
    bfp=09cc8fa4 bln=16 avl=16 flg=05
    value=00000FF7.0000.0001
```

The first bind variable in cursor number 2 is of data type 11 (restricted rowid) and has a value of 00000FF7.0000.0001—an interesting little demonstration that Oracle still makes uses of restricted rowid types internally. Sometimes "value" = is followed by a dump of memory when the code to produce a structured output of the value does not exist (for example, with a user-defined type).

A Sample of Statistics from Event 10032, Level 1

The first thing to check is that the SORT parameters were actually what you were expecting, then check whether you are getting direct reads and writes:

```
---- Sort Parameters ------------------------------
sort_area_size                    65536
sort_area_retained_size           65536
sort_multiblock_read_count        2
max intermediate merge width      7
---- Sort Statistics ------------------------------
Initial runs                         7
Number of merges                     1
```

Input records	12192
Output records	12192
Disk blocks 1st pass	286
Total disk blocks used	288
Total number of comparisons performed	78930
Comparisons performed by in-memory sort	50371
Comparisons performed during merge	28559
Temp segments allocated	1
Extents allocated	1
---- Run Directory Statistics ----	
Run directory block reads (buffer cache)	8
Block pins (for run directory)	1
Block repins (for run directory)	7
---- Direct Write Statistics ----	
Write slot size	2048
Write slots used during in-memory sort	3
Number of direct writes	286
Num blocks written (with direct write)	286
Block pins (for sort records)	286
Cached block repins (for sort records)	11
Waits for async writes	1
---- Direct Read Statistics ----	
Size of read slots for output	4096
Number of read slots for output	16
Number of direct sync reads	57
Number of blocks read synchronously	64
Number of direct async reads	113
Number of blocks read asynchronously	222

If you think you know roughly how many rows should be accessed and sorted in a particular SQL statement, check "Input records" and "Comparisons performed" very carefully. Oracle sometimes does surprising things with sorting, particularly under parallel execution. I once saw a 300,000-row dataset turned into a 7,000,000-row sort because of the way that the query coordinator decomposed the query for the query slaves.

A Sample of a Dump Following Event 10053, Level 1, Showing Optimizer Calculations

Again, the first check should be that the optimizer parameters are as you expect, particularly OPTIMIZER_MODE/GOAL. It is often overlooked that SQL executing inside a PL/SQL block runs at ALL_ROWS optimization even when the init.ora parameter is set to FIRST_ROWS. If you use this event at level 2, the table and index statistics are omitted:

```
QUERY
select min(date_part) from skip_test where product_id = 45
*******************************************
PARAMETERS USED BY THE OPTIMIZER
********************************
OPTIMIZER_PERCENT_PARALLEL = 0
OPTIMIZER_MODE/GOAL = Choose
HASH_AREA_SIZE = 131072
HASH_JOIN_ENABLED = TRUE
HASH_MULTIBLOCK_IO_COUNT = 0
OPTIMIZER_SEARCH_LIMIT = 5
SORT_AREA_SIZE = 131072
PARTITION_VIEW_ENABLED = FALSE
FAST_FULL_SCAN_ENABLED = TRUE
DB_FILE_MULTIBLOCK_READ_COUNT = 8
ALWAYS_STAR_TRANSFORMATION = FALSE
***********************************************
BASE STATISTICAL INFORMATION
*************************
Table stats    Table: SKIP_TEST    Alias: SKIP_TEST
  (Using composite stats)
  TOTAL ::  CDN: 2000  NBLKS: 85   TABLE_SCAN_CST: 14 AVG_ROW_LEN: 66
-- Index stats
  INDEX#: 17847  COL#: 2
    USING COMPOSITE STATS
    TOTAL :: LVLS: 1  #LB: 24  #DK: 257 LB/K: 1 DB/K: 1 CLUF: 1729
*********************************************
SINGLE TABLE ACCESS PATH
Column: PRODUCT_ID  Col#: 2     Table: SKIP_TEST   Alias: SKIP_TEST
  NDV: 390         NULLS: 0        DENS: 2.5641e-003 LO:  0 HI:  256
  TABLE: SKIP_TEST      ORIG CDN: 2000 CMPTD CDN: 6
  Access path: tsc  Resc:  14  Resp: 4
  Access path: index (equal)
    INDEX#: 17847  TABLE: SKIP_TEST
    CST: 11  IXSEL:  0.0000e+000  TBSEL:  2.5641e-003
   Parallel resp:  4  deg:3
  BEST_CST: 11.00  PATH: 4 Degree:  3
*******************************************
OPTIMIZER STATISTICS AND COMPUTATIONS
*********************************************
GENERAL PLANS
*************************
Join order[1]: SKIP_TEST [SKIP_TEST]
```

```
Best so far: TABLE#: 0  CST:     11  CDN:      6 BYTES:     132
Final:
   CST: 11  CDN: 6  RSC: 11  RSP: 4  BYTES: 132
```

A few hints on decoding the dump are included in Table C-2.

Table C-2.   Decoding Optimizer Trace 10053

Code	Meaning
CDN	Cardinality, number of rows
NBLKS	Number of blocks in the table
LVLS	Number of levels in the index
LB	Number of leaf blocks in the index
LB/K	Number of leaf blocks per key value
DB/K	Number of data blocks in the table per key value in the index
CLUF	Index clustering factor
NDV	Number of distinct values found in a column
DENS	A nominal "density" of the column values, 1/NDV if there is no histogram

A Sample Dump Following Event 10128, Tracing Partition Pruning

The example is for a partition-wise join, and is much longer than the dump for a query against a single partitioned table. In this case the most significant line is "Range partition pushed up above join." The iterator can also be useful for identifying that the partitions visited are the ones you expect, and the flags item can tell you whether the partitions are identified at runtime or at parse time, come in as bind variables or literal constants, and so on:

```
flags = {single, bind, set by parser, }
flags = {single, known, }
```

```
partition pruning descriptor:
type = 1, level = 1
flags = {single partition from join key, }
partition mapping descriptor:
    partitioning method = range
    number of partitions = 3
    number of partitioning keys = 1
    partitioning columns = (1)
RANGE partition pushed up above join between BASKET_ITEM (left) and
BASKET (right)
Partition Iterator Information:
    partition level = PARTITION
    call time = RUN
    order = ASCENDING
    Partition iterator for level 1:
        iterator = RANGE [0, 2]
        index = 0
    current partition: part# = 0, subp# = 65535, abs# = 0
    current partition: part# = 1, subp# = 65535, abs# = 1
    current partition: part# = 2, subp# = 65535, abs# = 2
```

A Sample of a Dump Following Event 10391, Level 2114 (2048 + 64 + 2)

This is possibly the most useful combination to dump from the query coordinator because it shows the partition breakdown, the granules allocated, and
the timing for each granule processed. The dump is pretty verbose, and needs
no explanation:

```
so:07442F34 mo:09E80148
    flg:0541( KXFRO_PSC KXFRO_PART KXFRO_MP KXFRO_HINT )
    nbparts:5 nfiles:1 nnodes:0 ninst:0
    ecnt:5 size(blocks):37 mtfl:0
    files for object 1:
      kfil:4 size:37 nnodes:0 nodes:00000000 naff:65535
    partitions of object 5:
      part 0 (abs:0 pnum:0 spnum:65535 objn:-1 objd:17848 tsn:8)
        ecnt:1 size:10 nfiles:1 naff:65535
        Files in partition 0:
          kfil:4 size:10
      part 1 (abs:1 pnum:1 spnum:65535 objn:-1 objd:17866 tsn:8)
        ecnt:1 size:6 nfiles:1 naff:65535
        Files in partition 1:
          kfil:4 size:6
      part 2 (abs:2 pnum:2 spnum:65535 objn:-1 objd:17850 tsn:8)
```

```
                    ecnt:1 size:10 nfiles:1 naff:65535
                    Files in partition 2:
                       kfil:4 size:10
                 part 3 (abs:3 pnum:3 spnum:65535 objn:-1 objd:17851 tsn:8)
                    ecnt:1 size:10 nfiles:1 naff:65535
                    Files in partition 3:
                       kfil:4 size:10
                 part 4 (abs:4 pnum:4 spnum:65535 objn:-1 objd:17852 tsn:8)
                    ecnt:1 size:1 nfiles:1 naff:65535
                    Files in partition 4:
                       kfil:4 size:1
     kxfr: dumping granule generator 09E802B8
       fobj:0 nobj:1 nfiles: 1 ngra:5 ndist:1 nslv:3 sset:0
       flg:0002 ( KXFRGG_PART )
       Distributors associated to that generator:
         dist:0 nbgra:5 nid:65535 nbslv:3 size:37
         filedist:0 filno:0 nbgra:0
         filedist:1 filno:4 nbgra:5
         gnum:0  sz:10 #frag:1 = (pnum:0)
           abs:0 pnum:0 spnum:65535 obji:0
         gnum:1  sz:6 #frag:1 = (pnum:1)
           abs:1 pnum:1 spnum:65535 obji:0
         gnum:2  sz:10 #frag:1 = (pnum:2)
           abs:2 pnum:2 spnum:65535 obji:0
         gnum:3  sz:10 #frag:1 = (pnum:3)
           abs:3 pnum:3 spnum:65535 obji:0
         gnum:4  sz:1 #frag:1 = (pnum:4)
           abs:4 pnum:4 spnum:65535 obji:0
       Slaves associated to that generator:
         slave 0: defdist=0 curdist=0 szsofar:0 dgpos:0 start:0 phase:noaff
         slave 1: defdist=0 curdist=0 szsofar:0 dgpos:0 start:0 phase:noaff
         slave 2: defdist=0 curdist=0 szsofar:0 dgpos:0 start:0 phase:noaff
     kxfr (t=0ms): preparing to get granules from gg 09E802B8
       (t=0ms): gnum=0 fil=4 filgra=0 slv=0 dist=0 sofar=10
       (t=0ms): gnum=1 fil=4 filgra=1 slv=1 dist=0 sofar=6
       (t=0ms): gnum=2 fil=4 filgra=2 slv=2 dist=0 sofar=10
       (t=20ms): granule completed slv=1 filedist=1 dgslvs=2
       (t=20ms): gnum=3 fil=4 filgra=3 slv=1 dist=0 sofar=16
       (t=20ms): granule completed slv=0 filedist=1 dgslvs=2
       (t=20ms): gnum=4 fil=4 filgra=4 slv=0 dist=0 sofar=11
       (t=30ms): granule completed slv=2 filedist=1 dgslvs=2
       (t=30ms): slv=2 DONE
       (t=30ms): granule completed slv=0 filedist=1 dgslvs=1
       (t=30ms): slv=0 DONE
```

```
(t=30ms): granule completed slv=1 filedist=1 dgslvs=0
(t=30ms): slv=1 DONE
```

Database Dumps

If the crunch comes and you can't figure out why Oracle is doing something that seems completely unreasonable, there are a couple of final physical fallbacks. Have a look at the data as it is stored on the database.

The main tools I use here are the data block dump and the index tree dump. The data block dump gives a symbolic dump of the contents of any type of data block in the database given the file number and the block number. DBA_SEGMENTS is a good source of numbers to use, and block_id+1 is a good starting point for the actual data:

```
select header_file, header_block
from dba_segments
where segment_name = 'SPREAD_DATA';

HEADER_FILE HEADER_BLOCK
----------- ------------
          4         2497

alter system dump datafile 4 block 2497;
alter system dump datafile 4 block min 2498 block max 2500;
```

If I think that an index may be giving me a problem, I use a tree dump to dump a summary of how many rows are in each block of the index, and then follow this up by dumping a few suspect leaf or branch blocks. Unfortunately, this doesn't currently work for partitioned indexes. This tree dump for an index block uses object_id and an alternative version of the ***set events*** statement.

```
select
    object_id,
    data_object_id,
    object_name
from
    dba_objects
where
    object_type = 'INDEX'
and owner = 'JPL1'
```

```
OBJECT_ID DATA_OBJECT_ID OBJECT_NAME
---------- --------------- --------------------------------
    17801          17801 PD_I
    17679          17882 RD_PK
    17683          17683 RD_PK1
    17840          17840 RT_I
```

```
alter session set events 'immediate trace name treedump level 17679';
```

```
----- begin tree dump
branch: 0x1001342 16782146 (0: nrow: 16, level: 1)
   leaf: 0x1001343 16782147 (-1: nrow: 66 rrow: 66)
   leaf: 0x1001344 16782148 (0: nrow: 66 rrow: 66)
   leaf: 0x1001345 16782149 (1: nrow: 66 rrow: 66)
   leaf: 0x1001346 16782150 (2: nrow: 66 rrow: 66)
   leaf: 0x1001347 16782151 (3: nrow: 66 rrow: 66)
   leaf: 0x1001348 16782152 (4: nrow: 66 rrow: 66)
   leaf: 0x1001349 16782153 (5: nrow: 66 rrow: 66)
   leaf: 0x100134a 16782154 (6: nrow: 66 rrow: 66)
   leaf: 0x100134b 16782155 (7: nrow: 66 rrow: 66)
   leaf: 0x100134c 16782156 (8: nrow: 66 rrow: 66)
   leaf: 0x100134d 16782157 (9: nrow: 66 rrow: 66)
   leaf: 0x100134e 16782158 (10: nrow: 66 rrow: 66)
   leaf: 0x100134f 16782159 (11: nrow: 66 rrow: 66)
   leaf: 0x1001350 16782160 (12: nrow: 66 rrow: 66)
   leaf: 0x1001351 16782161 (13: nrow: 64 rrow: 64)
   leaf: 0x1001352 16782162 (14: nrow: 12 rrow: 12)
----- end tree dump
```

Conclusion

This chapter covers most of the work I do if I have to put together a design for the critical operational parts of a database. In many cases it doesn't really take very long, if you can manage to think up a good, relevant test of the features.

In most cases Oracle either works exactly as expected, with just a little fiddling about to get the right configuration (usually some init.ora parameters or system privileges to enable features). When things go wrong, they usually go completely wrong very obviously. At least it is very obvious if you look at the execution paths and don't just rely on a stopwatch.

The biggest trap is not taking the tests quite far enough, and not checking completely why things have gone right. And there's always the problem of not knowing how far you have to go to prove a point. At the end of the day, that's the curse of the CBO.

Space Management

Space management ranges across all levels of an Oracle system, from the lowest level (How much free space should I leave in a block for rows to extend?) to the highest level (Should I add another 4 disks or another 20 disks the next time I extend the database?). In an Oracle database, space means time. If your data is wasting space, then Oracle has to do more I/O to get the job done, and more I/O means worse performance. It is important to understand some of the details of how Oracle uses and loses space so that you can keep your database running at optimum efficiency.

On the other hand, disk space is cheap and disks are so large these days that if you pack them with Oracle data they probably won't be able to do enough I/Os per second to support your application. This means that you can, at least temporarily, be very wasteful with space to minimize your administrative effort.

The following discussion moves from small to the large, covering the many, sometimes contradictory, issues revolving around space.

The Block

The smallest unit of the Oracle database is the Oracle block. Typically 2KB, 4KB, 8KB, or 16KB, the Oracle block size is selected when the database is created, and virtually all future data management revolves around how effectively your application uses blocks, and how efficiently Oracle transports those blocks.

There are, of course, a few special cases of block management (blocks in LOBs, bitmap blocks at the head of locally managed tablespaces, and sundry other internal-use blocks), but on the whole most blocks follow the same, broad four-part pattern: an integrity section, a transactional section, a directory section, and a data section.

The integrity section (or block overhead) is typically approximately 90 bytes and holds various odd items of information about the block itself—what type of block it is, where the different sections start, how many entries there are in each section, a checksum, time stamps, and so on. The existence of this fixed overhead is actually sufficient to persuade some people to choose the largest possible block size for their Oracle database. This is a slight overreaction, but the overhead is a point to bear in mind, particularly when you realize that there is also a runtime memory overhead per buffered block of 136 bytes (down from 200+ bytes in earlier versions of Oracle) for buffer management.

The transactional section is a short list (commonly called the *interested transaction list* or ITL) that records the identifier and state of some of the more recent transactions applied to the block. A single transactional entry is approximately 24 bytes. (Platform-specific figures can be found in the dynamic performance view V$TYPE_SIZE as "transaction variable header.")

The directory section is simply a list of pointers to the items in the data section. Depending on the nature of the block there actually may be more than one directory section and data section. For example, in an indexed cluster a block contains a list of tables and a list of rows, hence two directory sections. The directory section takes 2 bytes per pointer.

The bulk of the block is the data section—the collection of rows stored in that block. I use the term *rows* rather loosely here. A row may actually be a row from the table, but it could be a branch or leaf entry of an index, a table reference in a cluster block, a rollback entry in a rollback block, or any of the esoteric lists that Oracle keeps for internal usage. However, from this point onward most of the detail I discuss is based around basic table and index blocks.

Of these four sections, the integrity section is fixed, the transactional section can grow but never shrinks afterward, the directory sections can grow and shrink (although circumstances rarely allow them to shrink), and the data section simply takes up whatever space is left. Schematically, and with a little license to ignore a few details, a data block from an ordinary table looks something like that shown in Figure D-1.

The integrity section starts at the beginning of the block, although there are also 4 bytes at the very end of the block used by Oracle to detect fractured blocks after hot backups. The integrity section is followed by the transactional and row directory sections. If the row directory section needs to grow, it simply extends itself down into the data section. If the transactional section needs to grow, then the row directory section is pushed farther down into the data section.

The actual data is inserted into the data section, starting from the end of the block and working backward. As you can see in Figure D-1, if a row is

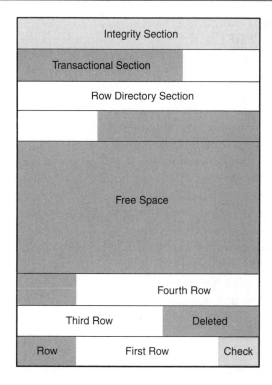

Figure D-1. Typical block structure.

deleted, the space it leaves in the data section is not necessarily squeezed out at once. Oracle maintains three numbers about the data section: where the free space starts (just after the directory section), where the *available* free space ends (in this case, just before the fourth row), and the total amount of free space. Oracle only tidies up the block, pushing all the rows down to the end, when it needs a piece of contiguous space that is larger than the available free space.

> *The optimum packing of a data block comes from setting INITRANS, MAXTRANS, PCTFREE, and PCTUSED to the most appropriate values.*

Oracle has four parameters associated with how space inside table blocks is used, three of these are also relevant to index blocks. These are INITRANS and MAXTRANS, which put limits on the transactional section of the block, and PCTFREE and PCTUSED, which affect how hard Oracle tries to keep the data section as full as possible. PCTUSED is not applicable to indexes, and PCTFREE is only relevant to indexes during creation.

INITRANS and MAXTRANS

INITRANS specifies the initial number of slots in the transaction section of the block. It defaults to one for table blocks and to two for index blocks. Because the transaction list can grow dynamically, the default is usually sufficient. If a block becomes very full, so that there is no space left for the transaction list to grow when it needs to, it is possible, although unusual, for a transaction to have to wait for another transaction to commit and free a slot in the transaction list. If you intend to use serializable transactions on a table, you should increase the default values on both the table and its indexes because a serializable transaction needs to be able to hold one transaction slot for itself while using other transaction slots as starting points for unraveling the recent history of a data block.

MAXTRANS specifies the maximum number of transaction slots that can be created in a block and defaults to 255. If packing data into the available space is very important, and you are prepared to put up with transactions queuing to some degree, then you may have a few tables and indexes in which you could consider dropping MAXTRANS to a small value, no larger than double the number of CPUs in the system, say. However, if you are in a position to predict that certain tables or indexes are likely to be subject to hot spots with large numbers of transactions continually hitting the same small number of blocks, you may want to take other steps to avoid serious contention problems before you worry too much about the impact of adjusting MAXTRANS. In some cases you may actually want to set PCTFREE artificially high to spread rows thinly across blocks because wasting space is less of a problem than block contention.

It is usually very difficult to determine if you have unsuitable values for INITRANS and MAXTRANS. If INITRANS is too low on some tables, you are likely to see large numbers of TX enqueue waits, but these are actually quite hard to spot (see Appendix B for a discussion of X$KSQST). If it is too high, you will simply be wasting space. The only way to judge how wasteful you are being is, currently, to do a block dump of every block in the table/index. Similarly if MAXTRANS is too high, then you may be allowing Oracle to push the transaction table to a size that is unnecessarily large for most of the life of the table/index, when a restriction of MAXTRANS might cause some transaction waits at one brief point in the data life cycle, but would benefit the performance of the system for the rest of the data life cycle by allowing just one or two more rows to be packed into each block.

Fortunately, if you do discover that you have inappropriate values of INITRANS and MAXTRANS, you can change them on the fly with the *alter table / alter index* commands:

```
alter table lots_of_transactions
initrans 4
maxtrans 10
;
```

These changes won't apply retrospectively, of course. A block that has a transaction table with 12 entries in it will never recover any of those entries, and a block that has only one entry in its transaction table will not spontaneously grow to four transaction slots. However, as all future blocks are initialized for data, they will be given four slots in their transaction table, and all blocks (even the ones previously created) will be limited to ten slots in their transaction table if they have not yet reached that limit.

> You may find special cases when restricting MAXTRANS gives you better data packing, but the penalty may be reduced performance in the early stages of the data life cycle.

PCTFREE and PCTUSED

Moving from the transaction section to the data and directory sections, PCTFREE tells Oracle how much of the remainder of the block (excluding the overhead and transaction table) may be used for inserting new data. For indexes, this parameter is relevant only when the index is (re)created. After all, a "row" in an index has to go in the right place, and there is no point in leaving space for rows to change. If they change, they probably have to go into a completely different block. For tables, this parameter has ongoing significance as rows are inserted, updated, and deleted, so the following notes should be considered only in light of handling a table.

Why not use all of the available space? Because you may want to update some of your data later, and if you don't leave a little free space in the block then your row may not fit in the block after you have updated it. If this happens, Oracle moves (or *migrates,* to use the term from the manual) the row into another block. But because there may be an index entry pointing to the row, Oracle leaves the original row entry behind with a forwarding address that points to the new location. From this point onward, any attempt to access the row through an index has to work harder. The index will always point to the old location, so Oracle has to read one table block to discover that the row has moved, and then read another to get the data. To put the icing on the cake, the migrated row takes up an extra 6 bytes, with a rowid pointing back to its original address. All in all, row migration clearly introduces an undesirable performance penalty, so it is important to leave some free space in each block to allow for rows growing.

Of course, it's easy to produce trivial examples (and luckily most data in most systems fits that pattern) such as—"rows are created at roughly 60 bytes, and grow to approximately 120 bytes, so we set PCTFREE to 50% to leave half the space in the block for growth." In real life, though, there are usually a couple of more awkward tables: "Half the rows start at 50 bytes, half start at 80 bytes; 10% of the small rows grow to 90 bytes; and 15% of the large rows grow to 100 bytes. Every week we delete approximately 8% of the rows in the table." Setting a good value of PCTFREE in this sort of situation requires you to know a lot about when the data arrives, when it changes size, and when it is deleted.

It is not a trivial exercise and you can't always take an easy option like, "call it 25% and we should be okay," because you may then end up with a lot of empty space in every single block. The more empty space you leave in each block, the more blocks you may have to read to find the rows you want, and the more blocks you have to read the more blocks you have to push out of the data buffer and reread later. Sometimes you just have to try to work it out in detail. If in doubt be generous, then monitor very closely the average amount of free space and how many migrated rows are reported in the view family xxx_TABLES, column CHAIN_CNT.

One thing you may find about free space, even in a very simple example, is that the average free space is always bigger than you expect. This comes down to the way Oracle uses the limit. Imagine you have left PCTFREE at 10. In a 4KB block this means you expect to leave approximately 390 bytes in each block for rows to grow. The block currently at the top of the freelist (see the later section on Segments for more on freelists) has 510 bytes of free space when the next row, which happens to be 130 bytes long, arrives. Oracle subtracts 130 from 510 and gets 380, which is less than the required free space margin, so the block is rejected as a home for the new row. The block is taken off the freelist, and Oracle moves on down the list to see if the next block has enough free space for the row. In this way, even without doing any deletions, you can end up with blocks that actually have much more free space in them than you originally specified.

There may be nothing useful you can do about this, but you may find, for example, that the default value for PCTFREE of 10% allows an average of something like 11.8 rows in a block, which really means 11 rows with 0.8 of a row of wasted space, whereas a small reduction in PCTFREE to 9% can push this up to 12 rows and a nominal improvement of 8% or 9% in space usage.

> *It is worth checking the typical row size (on very large tables) to see if a small change in PCTFREE results in just one more row being squeezed into each block.*

We have just seen that PCTFREE works to tell Oracle when to stop inserting new data, but what happens when you delete data and leave some empty space available for reuse? Unless you set PCTUSED to a suitable value, the answer is nothing. Until the amount of space still in use in the block drops below the PCTUSED value, Oracle ignores the newly freed space. Unfortunately, the default value of PCTUSED is 40, which means that once a block is "full" it has to drop back to 40% used (or 60% empty) before Oracle starts reclaiming the space. Let's run through the life cycle of a 2KB block with the default parameters to see what this means.

The initial free space for data is 1,958 bytes. This means that Oracle will try to leave 196 bytes of free space, so it will use no more than 1,762 bytes in the block before moving on to the next block.

We insert a series of rows that all happen to use (including the various overhead costs) exactly 200 bytes each. After eight such inserts we are down to 358 bytes of free space. The next insert would reduce this free space to 158 bytes, which is less than the limit specified, so the next insert goes into another block and the current block is removed from the freelist. No more rows will be inserted into it (for the present) even though it has much more free space than we originally demanded.

A little while later, we add 50 bytes to each row. After the first seven updates, we have used 350 of the 358 bytes left in the block and have only 8 bytes left. On the eighth update, Oracle detects the impending overflow problem and migrates the row out to a different block, replacing the row with a 6-byte rowid (plus a bit of overhead, for a total of 11 bytes). The total free space jumps to $8 + 200 - 11 = 197$. On the minus side, we now have a migrated row, which is not nice. On the plus side, we do have some free space for updating other rows in the block.

We now start deleting rows. Although the total space taken by each row was rigged at 250 bytes, the space reclaimed on each deletion is only 248 bytes because 2 bytes were allocated to the row directory entry. After three deletions we have 941 bytes of free space in the block, but Oracle will not make use of the space for new rows. After a fourth deletion we have 1,189 bytes of free space in the block, but 60% (100 − the default PCTUSED) of 1,958 (the total possible free space) is 1,175. We have just fallen below the critical value, and Oracle finally puts this block back on the freelist and starts inserting rows again. Of course, there may still be a bit of a time lag before this block actually gets used for insertions, because there may be several blocks ahead of it in the queue.

Remember the migrated row? It wouldn't fit in its original block when we updated it, so it was copied to another block and a rowid was left behind to point to the new location. The original block now has lots of free space in it, so what happens if you update that row again? Will it migrate back to tidy itself up and use some of the free space? The answer, surprisingly, is no. Despite that pointer back to the previous address, once the row has migrated it tends to stay migrated. It takes some fairly unlikely circumstances (such as if it extends farther so that it won't fit into the current block, but because of other deletions can now fit in the original block) to make it migrate back. Migrated rows are very difficult to clean up.

> *CHAIN_CNT and "continued row fetch" cover both chained rows and migrated rows. Row migration may be avoided by picking a suitable value of PCTFREE. Row chaining may be avoided by rebuilding the database with a larger block size.*

There is a little confusion about migrated rows, caused by the oral history passed from DBA to DBA. There are actually two reasons why a row may start in one block but finish in another. There are the migrated rows discussed earlier, in which a row *can* fit into a single block but is stored with a pointer in one block and the data in another because of an accident of creation and update. Then there are the chained rows in which a row *cannot* fit in a single block for the simple reason that it is too big. Historically (until about version 6 of Oracle), there was little distinction made between the two types of rows, and both were referred to as *chained rows*. Even in version 8.1.5 of Oracle, the system statistics still record fetches of "continued" rows without discriminating between migrated rows and chained rows, and the view family xxx_TABLES refers only to CHAIN_CNT to cover both chained and migrated rows.

Migrated rows are a problem that can often be eliminated, or at least controlled. On the other hand, chained rows can only be addressed by changing the strategy used for the data model, or by increasing the block size. It is best to make sure you understand your data sufficiently well to recognize the potential for this problem before you start building the database.

Choosing a Block Size

There are endless arguments about the best Oracle block size to choose when building a database. I have already been through some of them in Chapter 10. The only important point to remember is that there is no absolutely correct answer. There is an often-quoted rule of thumb that says smaller blocks are good for OLTP systems, and larger blocks are better for DSS systems, and this is actually quite a sound idea. However, when memory is not an issue, there is little point in not using a large block size. When memory is constrained, it is worth considering smaller block sizes.

In OLTP systems, data access is largely through indexes. Indexes tend to be smaller than tables, and important indexes can become fully buffered, whereas the corresponding tables may be too large to benefit from any great degree of buffering. In this case a query for 100 randomly scattered rows may equate to 100 physical reads irrespective of the block size. If the nature of the application is such that a single user is likely to reread her "personal" data with some degree of frequency, then small blocks may still be buffered on the second read. On the other hand, big blocks means fewer buffers, which leads to a higher probability that someone else's query may flush her data from the buffer sooner rather than later.

Remember, though, that the basic block overhead, including transaction slots, is approximately 120 bytes, and buffer management requires an additional 136 byes of memory, so each data block uses a total overhead of 256 bytes. So the overhead on 3,980 bytes (a 4KB block) of data is roughly 6%, but for 8,070 bytes (the 8KB block) the overhead is only 3%. If your critical data tends to be well clustered, or is *not* commonly accessed by indexes, then there is a space benefit in larger block sizes.

Do remember that Oracle now allows you to define three different buffer areas (or pools) in the data block buffer. The KEEP pool, the RECYCLE pool, and the DEFAULT pool. The three pools currently use the same aging algorithm to discard data, but because specific data objects can be assigned to specific buffer pools, you can arrange to limit the interference between different types of object. This may affect your choice of buffer size, because you can choose (for example) to **keep** one critical index, while setting its table to **recycle**, thus ensuring that the index blocks are not flushed from memory by excessive hits on the table. As the names imply, the KEEP pool is for objects of high interest, the RECYCLE pool is for objects that are only ever examined occasionally and that would have a serious impact on the "useful" buffered data if they were allowed into main buffer, and the DEFAULT pool is for everything else.

Of the three buffer pools, it is perhaps the RECYCLE pool that is most beneficial and allows you to survive with a smaller total buffer than you might otherwise expect. Traditionally, any data blocks accessed via indexes would be loaded into the buffer at the MRU end of db_block_buffer. Querying a very large but rarely accessed table in this way could have the effect of flushing lots of useful information out of the buffer. Although this behavior has changed significantly with all sorts of new buffering algorithms in Oracle 8.1, you can still help the system by creating a small RECYLE pool, and allocating such tables to it. With a pool of just a few dozen buffers, you won't waste much memory, and the offending tables will simply cycle themselves through a very small memory space on the odd occasion you access them, without impacting the rest of the working buffer.

The Extent

Although the unit that Oracle uses to manage data in memory is the block, the unit of space allocation that Oracle records in the database is actually the extent, which is a set of adjacent blocks in a single data file. There are two extent allocation mechanisms in Oracle: the dictionary-managed extent management of earlier releases and the bitmapped mapping management used by locally managed tablespaces in Oracle 8.1.

With dictionary management, an arbitrary number of adjacent blocks in a single file can be allocated as a single extent. To allocate this space, Oracle deletes a row from the free extent dictionary table FET$, and inserts it into the used extent table UET$. If a suitable extent did not exist in FET$, Oracle would have to find a row describing a larger free extent, and update it so that it "releases" the required space and describes the remaining free space before inserting an entry into UET$. Because this activity was recorded in normal database tables, it resulted in the normal rollback and redo processing taking place. In very busy systems with very frequent space management it could become a bit of a bottleneck, especially because only one space-management transaction of this type is allowed to take place at any one moment. To free space, the reverse process, with minor differences, takes place.

With bitmap management, each bit in a file's header section corresponds to an extent in the file. Allocating space merely requires a bit to be changed from zero to one. The task of allocating the extent to a segment simply requires adding an entry to that segment's extent map in the segment header block. Oracle still permits only one such space transaction at a time, but the time to complete is shorter, and there is less associated rollback and redo logging.

I like the idea of using locally managed tablespaces (particularly with the UNIFORM option) throughout a new system—not just because the space management is quicker and cheaper, but because the consequences of the mapping technology reduce the time wasted by DBAs in monitoring the space used and the growth of the objects in the database.

There are few rules you have to follow when picking sizes for extents. I follow just four:

1. Don't set any extent size to be smaller than the physical maximum single read size that your operating system can manage, which usually means 64KB but can be as much as 1MB on some systems. I obey this rule on the basis that if the object could at some time be scanned, it would be a waste of runtime resources if Oracle had to issue more than one read request to get its single maximum read.

2. All extents in a tablespace should be the same size. This occurs automatically in locally managed, uniform tablespaces. The purpose of this rule is to ensure that it is possible to drop several objects in a tablespace (for example, several indexes that disappear when a table is dropped) without having to worry about being unable to rebuild them because of unlucky honeycomb effects that may appear in the tablespace as you do so.

3. Don't worry about wasting space at the extent/tablespace level if it makes administration easier. It doesn't affect runtime performance. (This is actually a corollary to the previous rule, rather than a whole new rule.) I prefer to give a dozen tiny tables a single extent of 1MB each, and waste 12MB, rather than add another tablespace to a system or have a few odd-size objects in a tablespace.

4. Don't let any one object have a very large number of extents. This is actually a bit of a holdover from dictionary-managed tablespaces, in which a large number of extents (multiplied by a large number of objects) had a serious impact on the efficiency of SMON and other processes that needed to do space management. Nevertheless, I like the idea of keeping the number of extents in an object to a reasonable size. For example, when an object is continually growing, I like to see it add an extent every two to four weeks, which means there will be between 26 and 52 extents after two years. Numbers in the 20 to 50

range are fine. Objects that grow an extent every couple of days are a
threat and need to be rebuilt with a larger extent size (which means in
a different tablespace).

> *It is too easy to waste a lot of valuable DBA time trying to be fussy
> about extent sizing. Uniform sizing per tablespace is the most sensible
> option. Creating a few dozen extents per object is not a performance
> threat.*

There is one special exception to the rule about being free with the number of extents in an object. If you are expecting to use parallel execution on an
object, it is better to aim for a smaller number of larger extents. I haven't managed to reverse engineer all the strategies used by the query coordinator when
passing out work to parallel slaves, but there seems to be an attempt to generate at least 13 "granules" for each slave. It seems to be possible, when extents
are many and scattered, for these granules to vary quite dramatically in size.
There are two side effects to this. First it may be inefficient to process a job in
too many tiny fractions. Second, if some extents are adjacent and others are
scattered, Oracle may end up giving one slave a contiguous section of 20
extents, whereas all the other slaves get one extent each. Given suitable circumstances you can leverage this behavior to suit your requirements, but in
general you are likely to get more consistent performance if you can aim to
have the number of extents equal the number of parallel query slaves plus or
minus a couple. Having said this, I also have to propose a counterargument to
the "fewer/larger" argument. When you create an object in parallel (CTAS,
"create index on large table"), then each parallel slave works in total independence, building a number of extents. When each slave finishes building its
extents, it passes them to the coordinating process, which links them to a
single segment. On average, each slave is likely to have left approximately
half an extent empty, which will be a large fraction of the total used space if
you are going for fewer/larger. This won't make any difference to performance
on indexed accesses, but it will increase the I/O load on scanning.

> *Parallel query seems to work better with fewer, larger extents, but par-
> allel "create table/index" is less wasteful of intraextent space if you
> choose a smaller extent size.*

The Segment

Any physical object stored in the database is stored as a segment. A segment may be made of many extents, resides within a single tablespace, and can be spread across many files. Some objects, such as partitioned tables, consist of many segments, but each segment is an independent subunit of the object. Most segments are for user data, but some (rollback segments, temporary segments, and the bootstrap segment) are for system use.

Each segment has a header block that contains a map of the extents that make up the segment, a set of freelists, and a few other items of control information. The size of the database block dictates the number of freelists and extent entries that will fit into the segment header block. For a 4K block, this is approximately 80 freelists and 250 extents. It is possible to allow a segment to have unlimited extents, in which case extra blocks will be allocated within the segment as needed when the extent map is full; it is **not** possible to increase the *total* number of freelists.

In fact, for very busy systems that do a large amount of inserting and deleting, the limit on the number of free lists is another factor to consider when deciding on the block size. If a transaction deletes enough data to push a block onto 'the' freelist, it actually puts it onto a **transaction** free list. Entries on a transaction free list are usually only transferred to a **segment** freelist after the process has committed and the segment free list needs more blocks. The number of segment freelists is dictated by the FREELISTS parameter when you first create an object; the remaining freelists are used as transaction freelists.

If a system has a very large number of processes that behave in a way that pushes blocks on and off freelists very frequently (and this would be a fairly exotic system), it would be possible for all the freelists to be in use when a process wanted to delete enough data to put yet another block onto a transaction freelist. In this extreme circumstance, the process would have to wait until a freelist became available from another process committing. This would show up as a wait for a TX enqueue (in V$LOCK or X$KSQST, see Appendix B). One of the standard methods for reducing contention on the leading-edge block of a table is to increase the value of FREELISTS so that multiple segment freelists are created, and concurrent processes insert into different blocks; however, increasing segment freelists reduces the number of process freelists, and thus increases the risk of this unusual problem occurring.

Because it may be desirable to rebuild segments occasionally (to pack table data or to move the object to another tablespace), I prefer to keep a tight limit on the maximum size of a single segment. Personally, I feel that 500MB is a cause for investigation, and anything more than 1GB is a potential problem. When tables are expected to be this large, I tend to look for options to partition them to allow for a small set of more manageable segments. When thinking about this strategy, and doing the arithmetic, remember that partitions of composite partitioned indexes cannot be rebuilt on-line, and partitions of hash partitioned tables cannot be rebuilt on-line nologging. This affects the downtime associated with rebuilding a table segment.

A fairly common question about segments is, How do you determine how much space is actually free in the segment? There are various answers to this, such as using the ***analyze*** command if the segment is a table or an index. However, the cheapest way to find the answer is to look at the DBMS_SPACE package, which has two procedures in it:

1. **UNUSED_SPACE**—To derive the number of blocks above the high water mark

2. **FREE_BLOCKS**—To determine how many blocks are on each free-list in turn

As far as performance is concerned, blocks above the high water mark are not a problem. They have never had data in them and they will never be visited. However, blocks on freelists are somewhere in the middle of the segment, and could be wasting runtime resources. It is worth using the FREE_ BLOCKS procedure from time to time to determine if you have any segments that may need to be rebuilt and repacked. Be warned, though, that the procedure walks the blocks on the freelist, so it can be quite expensive in terms of I/O and should not be used casually.

The Tablespace

I spent an entire chapter talking about tablespaces, so I won't repeat it all here. However, I will highlight a few points.

By splitting a database into multiple tablespaces, you make administration, backup, and recovery much easier because you need only deal with relatively small objects at any one time. Personally, I still tend to stick with 2GB as a good maximum size for a tablespace. When high-speed removable disks appear in larger sizes I may be persuaded to move up to 4GB or 8GB.

If you have split data into multiple tablespaces, you have made the job of monitoring your database for performance and growth much easier. Oracle offers various dynamic performance views that operate at the tablespace (actually in a file within a tablespace) level so that a quick and simple report can isolate I/O costs or buffer contention costs to a subset of the database. There are also views that report the total space, space used, and free space in a tablespace. If you are using uniform-size extents in your tablespaces (even if you are imposing this feature on a dictionary-managed tablespace), a very simple SQL script will allow you to monitor the rate at which space is used up, giving you the change to add space proactively.

By splitting data into "age-based" tablespaces you may be able to arrange for some tablespaces to get into a state in which the data they hold is never due to be updated again. At this point you can make the tablespace read-only, copy it once (onto a CD, for example), and never back it up again.

The typical strategy for doing this is to build tablespaces with dates built into their names, but there is one little detail to be wary of when allowing tablespaces to proliferate. The tablespace definition is kept in a dictionary table called TS$. This is part of a cluster, which is defined to use one Oracle block per tablespace entry. This cluster gets very large if you have a lot of tablespaces. Even if you drop a tablespace, its row is not deleted, so the block is never released for reuse by another tablespace name. Because SMON scans this cluster every five minutes (looking for dictionary-managed tablespaces that have free space to coalesce), you could find that stepping through lots of tablespace names results in a staggering, real physical I/O hit on your SYSTEM tablespace even though you may have dropped the very old tablespaces.

As a sensible strategy for dealing with this problem, and to handle the issue I mentioned earlier regarding parallel creation of objects leaving lots of half-empty extents, you could choose to work with a limited number of fixed-name tablespaces for historic tablespaces. By keeping track of the time period that belongs in each tablespace, you can then empty the oldest data and reuse the tablespace for newer data at the appropriate time. Not only does this limit the number of tablespaces in use, but you can choose to make the extent sizes in the historic tablespaces different from the sizes used in the current working tablespaces to reduce the side effect of parallel object creation.

The Disk Array

When worrying about database design and space management, it is easy to look at the available hardware and produce an absolutely brilliant plan for spreading the I/O load evenly across the available spindles, and forget that in 18 months you will need to add more disks. The problem with adding disks to a system is that you rarely seem to add very many at a time, so the wonderful 20-disk layout you designed this year gets an extra five disks bolted on next year, and you find that there is no easy way to extend your plan into the new disks. You are left with two options: a massive rebuild of the database, perhaps concealed in logical volume rebuilds and file moves; or a high-performance, well-balanced historical database bit of the database, with a massively over-loaded new bit of database.

When planning your database layout, try to allow for future hardware purchases, and build the gross system structure in units that match your antic-ipated scale of growth. If you have 20 disks and think that the next hardware cycle is likely to allow an extra five disks, then lay out the system as four groups of five disks, rather than one group of 20 disks. It is probably better to have a slightly reduced, but level, performance rather than optimal performance now and a big problem in 18 months.

Conclusion

Most Oracle databases can get by with lots of default storage parameters and just a few simple rules of thumb, particularly if they use locally managed, uniform-size tablespaces. If you can identify the few special objects in your database, and can think carefully about the most appropriate parameters for their storage at all levels of granularity, you may gain some useful administra-tive and performance benefits with virtually no effort.

Efficient running is most affected by focusing on how blocks are used. Efficient administration is most affected by focusing on how extents are used.

Don't forget to match your database layout with the expectations of your hardware purchasing plan. Space management for performance and adminis-tration takes place at every level of the system.

About the Author

Jonathan Lewis is a qualified mathematics teacher who, after many years of being an amateur computer user, moved into the computing profession 17 years ago, and became self-employed 15 years ago. His initiation into Oracle was on version 5.1 running on a PC when he designed and built a risk management system for the crude-trading floor of one of the major oil companies. He wrote the first version of the system in dBase III, and the difference was rather like discovering screwdrivers after years of knocking in screws with a hammer: Oracle was a proper relational database management system (RDBMS).

Since that day of revelation he has focused exclusively on the use and abuse of the Oracle RDBMS. Ten years ago he decided to move from the contractor market to the consultant market, and now tends to spend his time on short-term, high-level advisory work.

In some of his spare time he is (at the time of this writing) director for products and services for the UK Oracle User Group (www.ukoug.com), and a regular contributor to their quarterly magazine. He also maintains a Web site (www.jlcomp.demon.co.uk) of articles, updates to this book, and notes on things that you can do with the Oracle RDBMS. During the rest of his spare time (and there was some before starting this book) he used to be interested in music, theater, squash, and swimming.

Index

Scaling Oracle8i™

Building Highly Scalable OLTP System Architectures
James Morle

As open systems continue to replace traditional mainframe systems, system scalability is becoming an increasingly important topic. Although far more flexible than mainframe systems, open systems applications tend to be less reliable and more difficult to scale. There is no cookbook approach to solving this challenge. A thorough understanding of the technologies involved is essential for designing scalable solutions that meet long-term business needs. **Scaling Oracle8i™** offers valuable insights and techniques for designing reliable and scalable online transaction processing (OLTP) applications using Oracle.

0-201-32574-8 • Paperback • 544 pages • © 2000

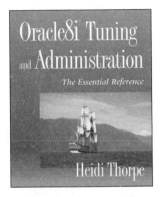

Oracle8i™ Tuning and Administration

The Essential Reference
Heidi Thorpe

For an Oracle DBA, poring over the thirty volumes of official Oracle documentation is a daunting task. **Oracle8i™ Tuning and Administration** crystallizes the essentials of what you need to know to perform your job with intelligence and skill. Rather than delve into obscure technical details, the book answers three essential questions for each topic: what, why, and how. In this way, less experienced DBAs will acquire the framework they need to understand important details in the documentation and grow in sophistication. Advanced DBAs will find this book a practical reference to effective configuration and troubleshooting.

0-201-70436-6 • Paperback • 608 pages • © 2001

SQL Queries for Mere Mortals

A Hands-On Guide to Data Manipulation in SQL
Michael J. Hernandez and John L. Viescas

In the past few years, SQL has gone from a language known only to computer specialists to a widely used international standard of the computer industry. The number of SQL-compatible databases shipping each year now totals in the millions. If you are accessing corporate information from the Internet or from an internal network, you are probably using SQL. **SQL Queries for Mere Mortals** will help new users learn the foundations of SQL queries. An essential reference guide for intermediate and advanced users.

0-201-43336-2 • Paperback • 528 pages • © 2000

Database Design for Mere Mortals

A Hands-On Guide to Relational Database Design
Michael J. Hernandez

Sound design can save you hours of development time before you write a single line of code. Based on the author's years of experience teaching this material, **Database Design for Mere Mortals** is a straightforward, platform-independent tutorial about basic principles of relational database design. Database design expert Michael J. Hernandez introduces the core concepts of design theory and method without the technical jargon. This book will provide any developer with a common sense design methodology for developing databases that work.

0-201-69471-9 • Paperback • 480 pages • © 1997

The Practical SQL Handbook, Third Edition
Using Structured Query Language

Judith S. Bowman, Sandra L. Emerson, and Marcy Darnovsky

The Practical SQL Handbook is the best-selling guide to learning SQL—the standard language for accessing information in relational databases. This book teaches SQL as it has been established by the ANSI standards committee. Step-by-step, you'll learn the basic vocabulary and functions of the language, how it is used to solve real business problems, and the processes and issues involved in developing robust applications. This book provides a thorough grounding in the basics of database design, security, and integrity. You will learn SQL pragmatically, by creating a sample database and working through dozens of examples with it.

0-201-44787-8 • Paperback • 496 pages • © 1996

Practical SQL
The Sequel

Judith S. Bowman

Written by the author of the best-selling ***Practical SQL Handbook, Practical SQL: The Sequel*** takes up where the first book leaves off. It goes beyond basic SQL query structure to explore the complexities of using SQL to meet real-world business needs. It will help you make the transition from classroom to reality—where you must design, fix, and maintain imperfect SQL systems.

0-201-61638-6 • Paperback •320 pages • © 2001

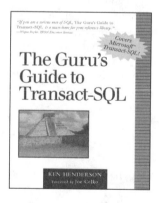

The Guru's Guide to Transact-SQL

Ken Henderson

Since its introduction more than a decade ago, the Microsoft SQL Server query language, Transact-SQL, has become increasingly popular and more powerful. The current version sports advanced features such as OLE Automation support, cross-platform querying facilities, and full-text search management. This book is the consummate guide to Microsoft Transact-SQL. From data type nuances to complex statistical computations to the bevy of undocumented features in the language, ***The Guru's Guide to Transact-SQL*** teaches you to become a virtuoso of the language as quickly as possible. It contains the information, explanations, and advice needed to master Transact-SQL and develop the best possible Transact-SQL code. Over 600 code examples illustrate important concepts and best practices, and provide Transact-SQL code that can be incorporated into real-world DBMS applications.

0-201-61576-2 • Paperback • 592 pages • © 2000

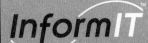
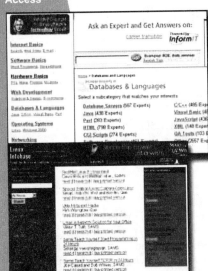

Register
Your Book
at www.aw.com/cseng/register

You may be eligible to receive:

- Advance notice of forthcoming editions of the book
- Related book recommendations
- Chapter excerpts and supplements of forthcoming titles
- Information about special contests and promotions throughout the year
- Notices and reminders about author appearances, tradeshows, and online chats with special guests

Contact us

If you are interested in writing a book or reviewing manuscripts prior to publication, please write to us at:

Editorial Department
Addison-Wesley Professional
75 Arlington Street, Suite 300
Boston, MA 02116 USA
Email: AWPro@aw.com

Addison-Wesley

Visit us on the Web: http://www.aw.com/cseng